The Government of the UK

General Editors:

Max Beloff
*Former Gladstone Professor of Government and
Public Administration in the University of Oxford*

Gillian Peele
*Fellow and Tutor in Politics,
Lady Margaret Hall, Oxford*

Further Titles to Be Announced

The Government of the UK

POLITICAL AUTHORITY IN A CHANGING SOCIETY

Second Edition

MAX BELOFF
*Former Gladstone Professor of Government and
Public Administration in the University of Oxford*

GILLIAN PEELE
Fellow and Tutor in Politics, Lady Margaret Hall, Oxford

W · W · NORTON & COMPANY
NEW YORK · LONDON

First edition published 1980, reprinted 1981
Second edition published 1985

Copyright © 1985, 1980 by Max Beloff and Gillian Peele

ISBN 0–393–95523–0

W. W. Norton & Company, Inc., 500 Fifth Avenue, New York, N. Y. 10110
W. W. Norton & Company Ltd., 37 Great Russell Street, London WC1B 3NU

Printed in Great Britain

1 2 3 4 5 6 7 8 9 0

Contents

Maps and Tables

Abbreviations

ACAS	Arbitration, Conciliation and Advisory Service
ACC	Association of County Councils
ADA	Association of District Authorities
ALB	Association of London Boroughs
AMA	Association of Metropolitan Authorities
AUEW	Amalgamated Union of Engineering Workers
BBC	British Broadcasting Corporation
BMA	British Medical Association
CBI	Confederation of British Industry
CLPD	Campaign for Labour Party Democracy
CLP	Constituency Labour Party
CND	Campaign for Nuclear Disarmament
COI	Central Office of Information
CPRS	Central Policy Review Staff
CSD	Civil Service Department
DES	Department of Education and Science
DHSS	Department of Health and Social Security
EEC	European Economic Community
FCO	Foreign and Commonwealth Office
GCHQ	Government Communications Headquarters
GDP	Gross Domestic Product
GMBATU	General and Municipal Boilermakers and Allied Trades Union
GRE	Grant Related Expenditure
IBA	Independent Broadcasting Authority
MAFF	Ministry of Agriculture, Fisheries and Food
MEP	Member of the European Parliament
MINIS	Management Information for Ministers

MPO	Manpower and Personnel Office
MSC	Manpower Services Commission
NALGO	National and Local Government Officers Association
NATO	North Atlantic Treaty Organisation
NEB	National Enterprise Board
NEC	National Executive Committee
NEDC	National Economic Development Corporation
NHS	National Health Service
NUPE	National Union of Public Employees
PCA	Parliamentary Commissioner for Administration
PCA	Police Complaints Authority
PR	Proportional Representation
SDP	Social Democratic Party
TGWU	Transport and General Workers Union
TUC	Trades Union Congress
UGC	University Grants Committee
USDAW	Union of Shop, Distributive and Allied Workers

Preface to the Second Edition

We should like to thank the large number of colleagues and friends who have helped with the second edition as well as those who helped us with the first. In particular we should like to thank the Baroness Platt of Writtle, Priscilla Baines, Eric Barendt, Michael Barnes Q.C., Mary Brown, Gareth Butler, Andrew Durand, Genie Turton, C. M. Kay, Martin Holmes, Professor George Jones and Philip Norton.

A large number of organizations helped us with particular enquiries. Our special thanks are due to them and to the staff of the House of Lords library and the range of library staff in Oxford who have helped our researches.

We thank Professor R. M. Jackson and the Cambridge University Press for permission to reproduce tables from *The Machinery of Justice in England* and David Butler, Anne Sloman and Gareth Butler and the Macmillan Press Ltd for permission to reproduce tables of election results from successive editions of *British Political Facts*. We also gratefully acknowledge permission from the comptroller of Her Majesty's Stationery Office to reproduce a map.

The preparation of the book has been greatly aided by the help of Mrs Macaulay and the secretarial staff at Lady Margaret Hall. Robert Baldock and Elspeth Henderson were patient and helpful editors. John Bennett produced the index with efficiency and skill.

THE UNITED KINGDOM OF
GREAT BRITAIN AND
NORTHERN IRELAND

0   20   40   60   80   100 MILES

0 20 40 60 80 100 120 KILOMETRES

SCOTLAND

Inverness

Aberdeen

Dundee

Perth

Glasgow

Edinburgh   Berwick

Dumfries   Newcastle upon Tyne
Carlisle   Sunderland
            Hartlepool
Londonderry   Larne
NORTHERN   Darlington
IRELAND   Belfast
            Barrow
            Heysham   Leeds   York
            Preston   Hull
            Blackpool   Bradford
            Liverpool   Manchester   Grimsby
REPUBLIC OF   Doncaster
IRELAND   Holyhead   Sheffield   Retford
            Newark
            Crewe   Stoke   Nottingham   King's
                    Derby   Lynn
            Shrewsbury   Grantham
                    Stafford   Leicester   Peterborough   Norwich
            Wolverhampton   Coventry
            Birmingham   Rugby
            Worcester   Northampton   Cambridge   Ipswich
                        Colchester   Harwich
Fishguard   WALES   Cheltenham
                Gloucester   Oxford
            Swansea   Newport   LONDON
            Cardiff   Bristol   Bath   Swindon   Reading   Margate
                            Salisbury   Ashford   Dover
            Taunton   Southampton   Portsmouth   Brighton   Folkestone
                                                        Hastings
            Exeter   Bournemouth   Worthing   Eastbourne
            Newton Abbot   Weymouth   Newhaven
            Plymouth
Penzance

Introduction to the Second Edition

The aim of this book is to give an outline of the basic elements in the United Kingdom's system of government and to draw attention to the most important changes in the country's recent politics. The British form of representative government has been accorded by students of politics a significance extending well beyond the shores of Britain itself. Many of the basic features of British constitutional practice were taken over by countries once under British rule and retained when they became members of the Commonwealth. There they have been modified to suit the different political conditions of such societies as those of Canada, Australia, New Zealand and India. The 'Westminster model' has therefore been studied as often as a prototype of other political systems as for its implications for the conduct of current British politics. The United Kingdom's governmental structure has also attracted interest because of the way in which it has combined the historical continuity of the state – unbroken since the revolutions of the seventeenth century and epitomized in the institution of monarchy – with radical changes in the basis of political authority. And, in the refined set of programmes that came to be designated by the title of the 'welfare state', the United Kingdom offered an early example of governmental intervention in many fields of social policy.

The first edition of this book was written in 1978–9 and, although it was able to make reference to the general election of 1979, it could not deal with the implications of the Conservative victory in any detail. This second edition includes developments up until early Spring 1985. In the introduction to the first edition it was noted that there had been important changes in Britain's position in the world, and in her people's perceptions of her institutions, which would make the emphasis of such a work different from what might have been found in a study of this kind written a couple of decades earlier. Another five years have served only to underline many of the points then made. The importance of the British contribution towards the political developments of some major Commonwealth countries has been overshadowed by the failure of the Westminster model to take root in much of Asia and Africa and by the increasing involvement of Britain with her associates in the European Communities. From a situation in which Britain's practices were held up as a model for other countries to follow, we have moved into one in which Britain's own political behaviour is being affected by other very different political and administrative traditions. Complacency about the ability of British institutions to adapt to the demands of mass democracies has been undermined by a growing, if inconclusive, scrutiny of many of them, and by the seeming disillusion of the electorate with the capacity of government to handle many of the country's most urgent problems. These doubts have been reflected in the fluctuations in support for Britain's two major parties and in the growth in support for various third parties and minor parties. The welfare state has also been subject to greater criticism as the conflicting criteria at work in the various aspects of social policy have become more apparent and as the constraints on public expenditure began more clearly to bring out the imprecision of values in the welfare system itself.

The major part of this book is concerned with the operations of the formal and informal institutions through which Britain is governed and not with the wider changes in the economic and social environment which help to explain both recent developments and the continuing erosion of consensus about the future courses to be followed. However it is important to note some of the major changes in British society, since it is against that background that the changes in the political and administrative system must be placed.

The first major social change which must be borne in mind has been in the composition of British society itself. The United Kingdom, despite migrations from earliest times, has generally been considered a relatively homogeneous society. The late nineteenth and early twentieth centuries had seen a short-lived but concentrated degree of Jewish immigration from eastern Europe. Although there was a generally restrictive immigration policy during the interwar period, there was a relatively small addition to the number of Jewish immigrants in the period immediately before and after the second world war. The special situation of the Republic of Ireland has meant that there has been freedom of movement from Ireland into Britain even after the Republic became an independent state outside the Commonwealth in 1949. What distinguished the high-employment decades of the 1950s and 1960s was the influx first of West Indian and then of Asian immigrants to the United Kingdom. Political reaction to this immigration – which was heavily concentrated in a number of major cities – brought about a reversal of Britain's traditional policy of allowing freedom of access to the United Kingdom to all members of the Empire and Commonwealth.[1] By the middle of 1977, when immigration other than that of dependents of those already settled had virtually ceased, it was apparent that the United Kingdom had acquired a substantial 'New Commonwealth' population distinguishable from the rest of society by colour and culture and often also by religion and language. Estimates of their number varied, but one reliable body reckoned that there were in mid-1977 some 1,771,000 residents of New Commonwealth or Pakistani origin – a figure which would at the end of that year have represented about 3.2 per cent of the total population of 55,900,000.[2] By the mid-1980s this proportion had almost certainly grown, but since the growth was increasingly the result of children being born to families already settled in Britain, who were – except for colour – largely indistinguishable from other young people, reliable estimates of the numbers involved were difficult to make with confidence. The immigrant communities themselves were reluctant to see statistical inquiries such as those in the census take account of these differences for fear that the figures would be used to their prejudice.

The highly visible transformation of some urban areas in England into multiracial communities had a number of consequences. Race became an issue in political debate and new legislation established machinery to prevent discrimination and to encourage racial harmony. Local authorities and a variety of other public agencies – which frequently discovered it necessary to provide information about their services in Hindi and Urdu – found themselves confronted with novel problems as the concentration of immigrants and their families put pressure on such facilities as schools, health services and housing and made it necessary to take into account particular demands arising from the different cultures.

By the mid-1980s the political parties also found themselves obliged to tailor their strategies to deal with the concentrations of electors from the new communities in particular constituencies and to find ways of associating members of these communities in the routine political life of the country both at the national and the local levels. Occupational differences within the communities had an effect on the immigrants' choice of party. The West Indian community, which was largely employed within heavily unionized industries such as public transport, was seen as a natural pool of potential Labour supporters. The Asian community, especially the East Asians admitted from Africa, were seen as possible Conservative recruits because a large number of them had a background of small business ownership.

However, while there were these differences between the communities both groups encountered substantial difficulties in getting themselves selected for council and parliamentary seats. Many from both communities did succeed in being selected for local council vacancies, but the parliamentary ladder proved a much steeper climb. Neither major party found that constituency parties were anxious to adopt non-white candidates in seats where there appeared a chance of victory. Perhaps in this respect the selection committees were reflecting the assumed prejudices of the constituents as a whole; but in fact, as two authorities put it when commenting on the 1983 election results, such non-white candidates as did stand 'fared worse than their party colleagues'. For the Conservatives Pramila La Hunte suffered a 10.6 per cent drop in Birmingham, Ladywood, while in West Hertfordshire Paul Boateng, in what was assumed to be a marginal seat, lost 23.7 per cent of the Labour vote and finished in third place nearly 15,000 votes behind the Conservative victor.[3] Faced with this experience, Asians in the Conservative Party mounted a campaign to get more candidates adopted, while there was some pressure in the Labour Party for separate black sections – an idea which found no favour with the leadership.

A second change which affected British society and British political debate in the 1970s and early 1980s was the return of unemployment as part of the economic and social scene. Full employment had been the principal goal of Keynesian economic policy in the 1940s and 1950s; indeed in 1951 only 0.2 million Britons were unemployed – a fact which stimulated mass immigration to the country from the parts of the Commonwealth where employment prospects were less good. By the middle of 1971 the number of those unemployed had risen to 0.7 million and by mid–1977 it had risen to 1.5 million. The seemingly inexorable rise in the numbers of those out of work continued and passed the 3 million mark by the beginning of 1983.

The level of unemployment in Britain and the problem of finding policies for dealing with it became a subject of major party controversy. There was some debate about the figures on which the official figures were based, because the number officially out of work was based on those who registered as unemployed and it became clear that many potential workers felt their prospects of employment too poor to make registering worthwhile. On the other hand demographic fluctuations meant that from early in the 1980s there were actually more people in the relevant age groups, so that the numbers in work could be rising while the numbers of the registered unemployed did not fall. Overshadowing those particular considerations were others reflecting the fact that growing unemployment had become the common lot of all the EEC countries.[4] How far, it was asked, was this due to the current technological revolution rather than to the mere ebb and flow of the business cycle? Was it true that the jobs lost could never be replaced since the new and more flourishing industries were less labour-intensive?

Whatever the answers to these questions, high unemployment was seen as in part responsible for the widespread violence which was experienced in many British cities – most notably London, Liverpool and Bristol – in 1981. The fact that many of the rioters were young members of the non-white section of the population gave additional cause for concern, as did the evident animosity between these groups and the police who attempted to contain the disturbances. The riots of 1981 in many ways simply gave dramatic evidence of the underlying tension between the ethnic minorities and the police forces; but the extent of the problem occasioned a major inquiry and proved the catalyst of a number of institutional changes in this respect.[5]

When the first edition of this book was written, inflation was seen as an economic problem which was as difficult to solve as unemployment. Indeed one of the oddities of the 1970s had been that both economic ills had appeared at the same time, since it had hitherto been thought that there was a trade-off between them. Moreover the combination of unemployment and inflation had been a powerful factor in casting doubt not only on the competence of governments since the second world war but also upon the adequacy of the Keynesian economic analysis which had guided those governments. That analysis had emphasized the use of the fiscal mechanism to iron out fluctuations in the trade cycle by putting money into circulation to stimulate employment and withdrawing it to cope with inflation.

The government that took office in 1979 declared its intention of giving priority to curbing inflation and originally placed its faith in the 'monetarist' doctrine of controlling the money supply. Subsequently however it concentrated more on reducing inflation through the control of public expenditure and borrowing, as well as on using its position as a major employer to control rising wages and salaries and thus prevent them from exerting inflationary pressures on the economy. As a result, although inflation reached about 20 per cent in the government's first year it was reduced by 1983 to about 5 per cent – a figure which brought Britain's inflation rate much closer to the rates of its major trading partners.

The government's success in bringing inflation under control was nevertheless held by the Labour Party to have been achieved at the expense of employment, and it was argued that the previous failures of Keynesian policies had been due to the general commitment to free trade and in particular to British membership of the European Economic Community. The alternative canvassed by some sections of the opposition was the infusion of public money into job creation schemes within a highly protectionist economic framework, so as to prevent the new money from going into imports. This divergence of economic policy mirrored an absence of consensus among professional economists and was part of the background to the difficulties of British government in the 1980s as it had been during the previous decade. The twin evils of inflation and unemployment had been thought to explain the growth in trade unionism in the 1960s and 1970s – a growth which brought the membership of the movement from 9.5 million members in 1951 to over 12 million in 1978. Its composition also changed from being overwhelmingly a movement of manual workers to reflect the increasing participation by professional groups, particularly in government employment, in education and in the health service.

The trade union movement also increased in militancy over this period as some workers tried to improve their own standards of living while others reacted against the erosion of traditional differentials which were usually an inherent part of incomes policies, especially when such policies were designed to give special protection to the lowest-paid workers. A particular feature of the 1970s and 1980s was the continued decline of employment in former staple industries, notably coalmining, shipbuilding and steel, as well as the continuation of other technological changes which had an impact upon the docks and inland transport and made road transport more viable financially than rail.

By the 1970s the militancy of the trade unions had become more visible as a political factor: the Heath government was brought down by the miners in 1974 and the effect upon public opinion of the so-called winter of discontent, with its strikes in the public services, was thought to have been an important contributing factor in the defeat of the Callaghan government in 1979. Yet the combination of recession and of a Conservative government with an overall majority had its own impact on the industrial scene. The trade unions lost members as the number of unemployed rose, so that after the steady expansion of the 1960s and early 1970s the number of trade unionists fell to about 10 million in 1984. Fear of unemployment also proved a deterrent to militancy, especially in the private sector, and the number of working days lost as a result of industrial action declined sharply after 1979. On the other hand there were major strikes in the public sector – in the steel industry in 1980, in the Civil Service in 1981, in the health service and in the railways in 1982 and in the water industry in 1983. And in 1984–5 there was a major strike in the coal industry (with accompanying disruption in the docks and on the railways) – a strike which, though unsuccessful, became a central issue of politics and raised a number of questions both about the future of the coal industry and about such issues as relations between the police and trade unionists.

Britain's economic position in the 1980s was particularly disappointing because it had been believed that once Britain was in a position fully to exploit the discovery of oil and natural gas in the North Sea, the state of the economy would be transformed as a result of no longer having to make massive payments for imported fuel. Britain did indeed achieve a position as a net exporter of energy in 1981, but the promised prosperity that was supposed to arise from this development did not materialize. Doubts about future energy resources thus continued to compound more general economic uncertainties and were indeed made worse by the recurring disputes in the coal industry, the increased frequency of objections from environmentalists to the use of nuclear energy (a form of energy which Britain had helped to pioneer) and the knowledge that the energy assets of the North Sea had only a limited life.

On the other hand, the 1980s continued to see a rise in the standard of living of most of those in employment. While Britain was comparatively low down in the EEC table, the dramatic rise in living standards which had been so marked in the 1950s and 1960s was still in evidence. By 1982 the British standard of living was 12.2 per cent higher than in 1976. Of British households, 61 per cent owned a car, 60.5 per cent enjoyed at least partial central heating, 80.7 per cent owned a washing machine, 96.1 per cent owned a refrigerator and 96.6 per cent had access to a television set. The proportion of British households with a telephone was 75.8 per cent – a number which had doubled in the space of a decade.[6] The new electronic devices which became fashionable in the early 1980s – video recorders and home computers – also found a ready market. More importantly the life expectancy for men and women continued to rise.

Educational opportunities were significantly greater at the beginning of the 1980s than they had been in 1951. There had been a major growth in the number of universities and in the overall numbers of those taking up university places. From a figure of just over 100,000 students in 1949–50, the number in 1981–2 had risen to over 330,000. In addition the expansion of other institutions of higher education – mainly polytechnics – meant that the number of students at these institutions had risen from 130,000 in 1951 to 524,000 in 1977. By 1982–3 the figure stood at approximately 724,000. In 1981–2 it had been reckoned that 12.9 per cent of the 18–20 age group were enrolled in higher education. While the growth of higher education, especially of the universities, was restricted as part of the public expenditure cuts of the early 1980s, Britain was clearly a more educated society than it had ever been before, even though it was thought that many of its industrial competitors were still ahead in terms of the techno-logical and scientific education which they offered.

By the late 1970s, as was noted in the first edition, Britain had in many ways become a more tolerant and liberal society than it had been previously. The laws affecting divorce, homosexuality and abortion had all been reformed in a direction more appropriate to a society where there was decreasing religious observance and only a limited moral consensus. And, although there were signs of a reaction against some aspects of these developments – and attempts to revise the law in a more conservative direction on abortion and on capital punishment – it did not appear that moral issues in Britain were playing the same role in the British political arena as they were in the contemporary United States.[7]

Yet the Britain which was by the early 1980s so obviously improved in terms of affluence and tolerance was also a society in which crime seemed more prevalent and violence a more common aspect of the country's life. The number of notifiable offences rose from 479,400 in 1950 to 800,300 in 1960; this figure rose further to 1,588,400 in 1970 and again to 2,520,600 in 1980 when the method of recording was altered. The figure per 100,000 of the population, which had been 1,094 in 1950, stood at 5,459 in 1980 and at 6,577 in 1982.[8]

While no other part of the United Kingdom had to endure Northern Ireland's toll of terrorism, sectarian murder and arson, there were serious terrorist crimes in mainland Britain and a considerable increase in the number of crimes against the person. The long-drawn-out miners' strike of 1984–5 saw an overflow from the picket-line of crimes of violence against non-strikers and against their families and a degree of high-profile policing unusual in recent British history. To all these phenomena the ubiquity of television gave an almost instant coverage which some suggested actually exacerbated the conflicts.

Disquiet about some aspects of British social life added to Britain's economic problems to produce scepticism about the ability of British governments to solve the nation's problems. One typical poll taken at the beginning of 1977 showed that only 6 per cent of adults thought the existing parties capable of solving the economic and political problems facing Britain; 31 per cent said they were 'quite capable' of solving them; 26 per cent thought that the parties were 'not at all capable' and a further 37 per cent thought they were 'not very capable' of doing so.[9] And this disillusion was strongest in the 18–24 age group. A survey in the same year also showed that only 27 per cent of the sample thought that Parliament represented their interests very well or at least quite well, as against 73 per cent who thought that

Parliament represented their interests not very or not at all well.

A rather different impression was however given by another survey taken in the first half of 1983 and asking rather different questions. Although there was no question about the House of Commons as such, other major political institutions including the monarchy and the House of Lords received a strongly positive rating.[10] Not merely did there seem to be an unexpected degree of satisfaction with the country's basic institutions; there also seemed to be a strong attachment to individual political parties, even though the decline in party polarization on class lines appeared to be continuing. On the other hand the survey found a greater willingness, particularly in the younger generation, to contemplate some kind of action to express dissatisfaction with government policies even if such direct action was in defiance of the law. The electors of the 1980s were thus seen as more active than their predecessors of a couple of generations back. And this conclusion seemed to find illustration in the proliferation and prominence of extra-parliamentary forms of protest in relation to matters as varied as disarmament, the environment and animal rights.

As far as the political parties are concerned, actual elections are of course a safer guide than opinion polls. The 1983 general election did in fact show a fall in turnout of 3.5 per cent as against 1979 and the actual turnout (72.7 per cent) was only very slightly above the postwar low recorded in 1970. With the rise of the SDP-Liberal Party Alliance, the voters at least had a larger range of options in all constituencies in 1983, although of course the chances of returning a majority for the Alliance were low. But the combined share of the vote received by the two major parties was 70 per cent in 1983 as opposed to 80.9 per cent in 1979 and 97 per cent in 1951.

In the 1970s there had appeared to be a further political consequence of disenchantment in the rise of nationalist movements in Scotland and in Wales. By the time of the 1979 election the peak of this reaction had passed for the time being. What seemed most to concern analysts of the 1979 and 1983 election results was the division within England itself – a division between a prosperous and Conservative-leaning south and midlands and a less prosperous north which, outside the rural areas, maintained its traditional fidelity to Labour. Such a state of affairs was obviously not a healthy one, since it represented a form of uneven economic development which could have profound social consequences.

It is against this background of uncertainty about the future of British institutions and policies that our discussion of some of the more familiar themes of British government should be set. We realize that at times our interpretation will be a controversial one, but we have tried to ensure that our suggestions for further reading on each chapter will be a guide to the range of opinions on the topics with which it deals. At the very least we hope that the reader will feel at the end of the book that the complexities of British government are a little more comprehensible and that he will be able to identify some of the intriguing questions which confront the British citizen as much as the student of politics about the character of the United Kingdom's government in the 1980s.

1 The Constitution

The 1960s and 1970s saw political developments in the United Kingdom which caused many of the traditional interpretations of the country's system of government to seem in need of revision. The election of Mrs Thatcher's Conservative administration in 1979 and its re-election in 1983 did, it is true, direct attention away from some of these developments and imposed on the political framework an apparent stability at the constitutional level while generating different pressures at other points in the body politic. Yet, even with Mrs Thatcher's pronounced unwillingness to contemplate any of the major changes mooted in the preceding decade it was clear by 1984 that changes of a fundamental character had been occurring within the British system and that, while some of the questions of the Wilson, Heath and Callaghan years had been resolved, others had not been conclusively settled.

The reappearance of constitutional issues on the country's political agenda in the 1960s and 1970s involved questioning some of the most basic features of the state – the traditional electoral and party systems, the role of Parliament generally and the special position of the House of Lords and even – in the long debates over devolution – the unitary character of the constitution. That such central features of British government should have been questioned so radically was itself difficult to reconcile with the idea that in the United Kingdom political change is gradual and evolutionary rather than radical and abrupt. In the period 1979–84 different questions – though no less significant – were raised about the relationships which govern British political life. Thus, for example, Mrs Thatcher's style of leadership and her use of advisers from outside the Civil Service called into question both the balance between the premier and cabinet and the efficacy of the existing instruments for directing government strategy.[1] The priority accorded to the objectives of reducing inflation and arresting the growth in public expenditure (together with Mrs Thatcher's own brand of radical Conservatism) inevitably undermined traditional presumptions about the role of the Civil Service. And the emphasis on curtailing public expenditure produced a new effort to subject local authority spending to central control – an effort which in the view of many observers further weakened the position of local government and created a new constitutional balance between centre and periphery. Thus, although it is important not to exaggerate the impact of constitutional changes in the United Kingdom in the period since 1964, there is evidence for the belief that the country is in something of a transitional period as far as its constitutional arrangements are concerned and that new institutional patterns are continuing to emerge. If it is still too early to assess the precise extent of these changes, it is possible to identify the points of the system which have produced tension and the constitutional relationships which have come under strain. The reader must then judge for himself whether these tensions cumulatively confirm the view that important aspects of the constitutional system are in the process of transformation, or whether in the event the older structure will be able to integrate and accommodate the changes of the last two decades.

The Character of the British Constitution

One of the problems of discussing the British constitution stems from the difficulty of defining what is meant by the concept of a 'constitution' in a country where there is no readily available central constitutional text. Of course, even in countries where there is a constitutional text and perhaps a bill of rights as well as specialized constitutional courts – for example the Supreme Court of the United States or the *Bundesverfassungsgericht* of West Germany – it will sometimes prove difficult to distinguish with perfect precision the constitutional issues from ordinary political questions. In the United Kingdom, however, the absence of any basic political document containing the ground rules of political life and the lack of any constitutional court or council to enforce them have produced a noticeable political vacuum when serious and fundamental disputes arise. These deficiencies have meant that the vocabulary of British political debate is not characterized by concepts and ideas with fairly firm and familiar meanings.

The absence of a distinct constitutional text and a body of constitutional rules with their own institutions to enforce them has often led observers to remark that the British had no constitution. Such a mistake, however, generally confuses the constitution with what is usually only one of its sources. Any constitution can be defined as the sum of those norms or values which prescribe the nature of the relationships between the several institutions of authority in a state – for example between the executive and the legislature or between central and local government – and also between the public authorities and the individual. In other words, a country's constitution is the whole body of rules which govern and shape the distribution of authority within the political system. The rules may be derived from a number of different sources – from a written constitutional text, from a declaration of independence, from statutes, from judicial decisions and from political habit or practice. What will vary from country to country will be the balance between those elements as sources for constitutional values and doctrines.

In the United Kingdom – and this is what makes the country's constitution appear amorphous – the least formal source of constitutional norms, political practice, has, at least until very recently, proved a particularly fertile source of constitutional values. Constitutional rules, values or norms derived from political habit or traditional ways of doing things are known as 'conventions' to distinguish them from constitutional rules derived from statutes or from judicial pronouncements. The courts could and did apply constitutional rules derived from formal legal sources; they would not apply conventions. Hence there was no legal sanction against a politician who deviated from a convention; indeed the occasional deviation in the light of changing circumstances was generally thought to be desirable, and the flexibility which the British constitution displayed was regarded by its supporters as one of its most admirable features. Thus, for example, as government became increasingly dependent upon political support in Parliament rather than upon royal favour, it became conventional for the monarch to choose as prime minister an individual whose ability to elicit that support was clearly demonstrable. In the twentieth century – with the extension of the franchise and the reduction of the powers of the non-elective upper chamber (the House of Lords) – it is by convention that the monarch chooses as prime minister the leader of the majority party in the House of Commons.

The importance of conventions in the British constitution should not however be allowed to obscure the fact that statutes and judicial pronouncements are also important sources of constitutional rules and values, as in other constitutions. A number of the most basic questions of British institutional practice are now in fact governed by statute so that, for example, anyone wishing to know the formal powers of the House of Lords in relation to the House of Commons must start by referring to the Parliament Acts of 1911 and 1949. It will be necessary thereafter to investigate what unwritten rules govern the use of those powers – in what circumstances, for instance, the Lords might challenge a decision of the Commons – but the initial framework is now statutory.

Sometimes doubts about the force or meaning of a convention, or a deliberate political challenge to one, will result in legislation to settle the point. Thus, although it had been assumed for many years prior to the Parliament Act of 1911 that the House of Lords should defer in matters of finance to the House of Commons, the convention was challenged in 1909 when the House of Lords threw out the government's budget. That challenge in turn led to a political crisis and a statutory definition of the powers of the upper House in the Parliament Act of 1911.

In the same way there are occasions on which challenges to conventions may lead to court actions and judicial resolution of disputes. However, it should be borne in mind that in such cases the court will not be applying a convention as such but will perhaps be developing its own common law rules to cover the issue. One such event occurred in 1975 when the convention covering the publication of ministerial memoirs and cabinet documents was breached by the publishers of the diaries of a former cabinet minister, Richard Crossman. There, the High Court claimed that it had the power to control such publications where necessary, although it did not in that case act to prevent publication.[2] Indeed the period after the Crossman Diaries affair saw the appearance of a number of similar accounts, including ones from civil servants.[3]

Judicial pronouncements and the rules of common law are of especial importance in the area of civil liberties. The absence of a comprehensive bill of rights defining the safeguards which the citizen may invoke against the state has meant that civil liberties such as freedom of speech and freedom of political association are dependent on statutes and the judicial interpretations of the scope of those liberties. The role of the courts in this area illustrates the traditional position of the judges in the British political system. In the seventeenth century it seemed possible at one point that common law doctrines would be applied so that the judges could review or restrict parliamentary statutes which did not conform to their interpretation of 'right reason'.[4] Yet by the end of the eighteenth century the supremacy of parliamentary legislation and the absence of any power to review legislation were established; and by the middle of the nineteenth century the doctrine of parliamentary sovereignty had become judicial orthodoxy.[5] Although, as will be seen throughout this book, there are now important reasons why the traditional doctrine of parliamentary supremacy needs to be subjected to scrutiny, the courts have in general been reluctant to articulate broad statements of individual rights which would be protected judicially in all circumstances. They have also shied away from pronouncements which would suggest any ambition on their part to develop a power to review legislation such as, for example, the Supreme Court of the United States developed after 1803.[6]

Even when individual judges have been at their most creative and innovatory in developing legal protections for citizens – as some have been in the past two decades – judicial intervention has usually been carefully justified by reference to the court's wish to give effect to the true purpose of a statute; alternatively the judges have appealed to values which Parliament is assumed to share even if it has not explicitly acknowledged them in an individual piece of legislation. Ultimately, therefore, many of the judicial remedies and protections which the citizen is afforded at law are available only where Parliament has not deliberately limited them and where the attitudes prevailing among the judiciary encourage them to use their powers to defend the interests of the individual. The uncertainty that can exist in relation to the powers of British courts was indeed forcefully underlined when a High Court judge in 1984 suggested that the government's use of its prerogative powers to ban trade unions at the Government Communications Headquarters at Cheltenham had been contrary to natural justice – a suggestion which was not supported by the Court of Appeal or the House of Lords.[7]

The realization that civil liberties could not be fully guaranteed, combined with legal uncertainty surrounding a large number of traditional areas such as freedom of speech and political association, led in the 1970s to a demand in some quarters for the incorporation into the British system of a formal declaration of individual rights.[8] The serious consideration afforded to the suggestion that the circumstances of British politics required the introduction of a bill of rights to protect individuals and minorities against the majority was perhaps the most eloquent evidence that the United Kingdom's traditional constitutional values and assumptions had altered. Formerly it would have been almost universally assumed that British citizens had no need of this sort of formal legal protection, since there was sufficient general agreement about the principles which ought to limit state action. Previously a Parliament which enjoyed the support of the majority of the population and where government and opposition could expect to alternate in power had been regarded as a sufficient safeguard for democracy and liberty; devices such as bills of rights would, it was assumed, only hand power to a non-elected judiciary and impede the ability of Parliament to make laws in the interests of society as a whole.

Scepticism about the traditional assumptions on which the British system of representative government was based stemmed from a number of sources. Many people were critical of the way in which the electoral system distorted voter preferences so that the 'majority' in Parliament might be completely without any foundation at the popular level, even when a government was first constructed. Secondly the changed nature of British society led others to doubt whether its diversity could be channelled into a simple two-party duopoly. Finally, and most significantly, it seemed to many commentators that the consensus of values by which all politicians acknowledge the existence of restraints upon their powers, and on which a large number of the constitutional rules depend, had broken down. The complex web of common attitudes and beliefs which enabled British democracy to work with very few formal statements of powers, rights and obligations no longer appeared to bind either the political elite or the electorate at large.

The erosion of this implicit common understanding was reflected in an increased ideological tension between the two major parties. In part the sharpened doctrinal conflict at the national level of politics can be traced to the leftwards shift within the Labour Party, which quickened noticeably after Labour was forced into opposition in 1970. This movement of opinion within the Labour Party was paralleled by a growth of ideological divisions and factions within the Conservative Party, although the change was much less marked than in the Labour ranks and the trade unions. The development of this heightened partisan and ideological tension was constitutionally significant because it showed how many of the orthodox practices of British political life require an atmosphere of tacit agreement for their successful operation. The stability which had for so long seemed a characteristic of the United Kingdom's political arrangements was in truth based on the fragile understanding between the two major parties that neither of them when in power would alter the country's most important political institutions, and that neither of them would use the power of the state in ways which could not command the support of a cross-section of the population. Although the election of Neil Kinnock as leader of the Labour Party in 1983 was seen by many as a prelude to an attempt to reunite the Labour Party, the internal dynamics of the two major parties in the period after 1970 seems at the very least to have put that understanding in jeopardy; and some would suggest that they have destroyed it altogether.

Britain's political parties are of course central to any account of the constitution for a variety of reasons. In normal times one of the two major political parties can be expected to form a government and to control, by virtue of an overall parliamentary majority, the legislative process. The 1970s were distinguished by the extent to which British voters deserted the two major parties and either did not vote at all or cast their votes for one of the minor political parties. In the course of this 'decade of dealignment' there were two Parliaments – between March 1974 and May 1979 – in which the government either had only a fragile majority or no majority at all.[9] In the situation which endured between 1974 and 1979 a number of assumptions about British parliamentary practice no longer applied. And the experience raised the question of how far the electorate's disenchantment with the major parties was the prelude to a realignment, as well as the question of whether back-bench MPs would abandon their new-found opportunities to influence legislation.

The volatility of the British electorate in the 1970s suggested at the very least that the political homogeneity that had once buttressed the country's social and political institutions had been eroded; and in those circumstances it seemed that the whole constitutional order might lack legitimacy for a part of the population if some of the diverse elements of British society could not find expression through the existing party system.

A new twist was given to these concerns in 1981 when the internal disputes within the Labour Party led to the foundation by a group of senior Labour politicians of a separate party – the Social Democratic Party. This party, which soon formed a working relationship with the Liberal Party, caused speculation about the likelihood of a three-way split in the popular vote producing a Parliament without an overall majority. And that concern in turn gave rise to much discussion of a range of constitutional issues – involving for example the role of the monarch – which had scarcely been considered when majoritarian government was always the most likely outcome of an election.[10] The failure of the SDP-Liberal Party Alliance to maintain its position in the opinion polls and the overwhelming Conservative victory in the general election of May 1983 terminated some of the immediate speculation. Yet underlying the apparent strength of the Conservative position there was the reality that a large number of Tory victories had been won because of the Labour-SDP split and that the Conservative percentage of the total vote had not risen since 1979. Normal constitutional patterns had been made possible by the distortions of the electoral system and it might equally be possible that the electoral system would render those patterns uncertain again. It is against this background of mounting concern about the continued efficient operation of the delicate and integrated mechanism of the constitution that some specific areas of constitutional tension must be analysed. Not all of the areas identified have been of continuing controversy and some – such as the challenge to the unitary state – appear to have subsided markedly. In identifying these individual themes of constitutional tension however it is important to remember that they are not in practice separate or self-contained, since changes in one ostensibly discrete area of the constitution can hardly be expected to occur without an effect on other parts of it.

Parliamentary Sovereignty and the Challenge of Europe

The first and most significant problem which has been created in Britain's constitutional arrangements arises from the success of Britain's application to join the European Communities. From 1972, when the United Kingdom signed the Treaty of Rome and related agreements and Parliament passed the European Communities Act incorporating the provisions of these treaties into British law, Britain has been a full member of the Community of now ten nations pledged to augmenting their own economic and political integration. The implications of British membership of the European Communities have not as yet been fully appreciated, although increasingly the routine work of government and of business have had to adjust to Community membership. Some of the results of British participation in the European Communities are discussed further in chapter 14. But one aspect of British accession to the Communities is clear enough: the doctrine of parliamentary sovereignty, which has traditionally been seen as one of the distinguishing features of the British constitution, now stands in need of substantial modification.

The traditional doctrine of parliamentary sovereignty has normally been expressed in two propositions – first, that under the British constitution Parliament has the 'right to make or unmake any law whatever', as Dicey's definition put it; and, second, that 'no person or body' will be recognized as having a right to override or set aside the legislation of Parliament.[11] The proposition that Parliament may legislate as it pleases has generally been understood by British politicians and by British courts, if not always by British academics, to mean that no Parliament could bind its successors. A bill of rights, for example, while it might prevail against legislation in force at the time it was enacted, and while it might provide a fertile source of values to which judges and politicians alike could appeal in argument, could not offer much protection against subsequent legislation which either deliberately or inadvertently violated its provisions. Nor could it be guaranteed against direct repeal.

The obstacles to entrenching legislation in the British constitutional system – of giving particularly important laws protection against easy repeal or amendment – seem difficult to overcome. Some authorities, it is true, argue that although Parliament cannot bind itself and its successors with regard to the substance of legislation, it can do so with respect to the manner and form of legislation. Thus, for example, Parliament could enact that in future all bills in the United Kingdom affecting freedom of speech should be subject to a special procedure before they could be passed into law. They could for instance be made subject to a referendum, or there could be a requirement that a two-thirds majority of the House of Commons would be needed for passage. Nevertheless while Parliament – or either House – could choose to follow certain conventions in its treatment of important bills, unless there is a radical change of attitude by the judiciary it is equally free to depart from those conventions at any time: the courts will not look beyond the bare facts of an Act's existence on the Parliament roll nor inquire into its legislative history to determine whether certain procedures have been followed.[12]

There have been several attempts to challenge this aspect of the British constitution in the courts, but in general such assaults on the doctrine have proved unsuccessful. Even where a later Act has not explicitly repealed the provisions of an earlier piece of legislation the courts have given effect to the later amendment: an Act of 1919 dealing with the provisions for compensation for property acquired by public authorities included the phrase 'so far as inconsistent with this act [other statutory] provisions shall not have effect', but it was held to have been superseded by an Act of 1925 which did make different provisions.[13] However in two Scottish cases – *MacCormick* v. *The Lord Advocate* (1953) and *Gibson* v. *The Lord Advocate* (1975) the question of whether the Scottish courts would be bound to give effect to legislation which was in breach of the Treaty of Union of 1707 (which united the English and Scottish Parliaments) was left open; indeed in *MacCormick*'s case doubt was expressed by Lord Cooper as to whether the doctrine of parliamentary sovereignty really applied in Scotland: 'The principle of the unlimited sovereignty of Parliament,' he said, 'is a distinctively English principle which has no counter-part in Scottish constitutional law'. Yet neither of the plaintiffs succeeded in their cases, and most legal authorities think it unlikely that Scottish courts would, except perhaps in an extreme case such as an attempt to disestablish the Presbyterian Church or to abolish the Scottish legal system, strike down an Act of Parliament as incompatible with the Treaty of Union.[14]

The second proposition entailed in the doctrine of parliamentary sovereignty – that no body or person can set aside or override parliamentary legislation – does not imply merely that the courts cannot disregard or review legislation when it is not in conformity with their interpretation of the constitution. It also implies that they cannot invalidate an Act of Parliament when it is in conflict either with the general principles of international law or with some treaty to which the United Kingdom is a party.

The change which occurred as a result of British entry into the European Communities was that as a condition of membership British courts must now give effect to legislation emanating from the Communities and, where there is a conflict between European legislation and parliamentary legislation, European legislation has priority. The European Communities Act of 1972 defines the rules of statutory interpretation in such a case of conflict: where there is a dispute about the validity, effect, or interpretation of the European Treaties or of secondary legislation made under them, the matter is to be treated by the British judges as a question of law. Such a conflict cannot therefore be avoided on the grounds that it is politically contentious or involves matters that are not justiciable. If this kind of conflict should reach the House of Lords there must – under Article 177 of the Treaty of Rome – be a reference to the Court of Justice of the European Communities, which has the task of harmonizing laws within the European Communities; such a reference to the Court's opinion may also be made if a lower court in the judicial hierarchy wants guidance in order to be able to resolve a dispute with a European element.

This development has a significance which the former Master of the Rolls, Lord Denning, recognized during a suit designed to prevent British entry into the Communities precisely because it would fetter parliamentary sovereignty. Although his remarks were *obiter dicta* (i.e. not necessary for the decision and therefore not binding on other courts) Lord Denning said he believed that if Britain entered the European Communities the United Kingdom would be taking a step that was 'irreversible'. The sovereignty of these islands, he declared, would 'thenceforth be limited'.[15] Certainly legal theory taught that one Parliament could not bind another; but that was now out of harmony with constitutional and political reality. Despite a later evaluation of the European Treaties as 'equal in force to any statute' rather than superior to them, Lord Denning during his tenure as a senior appellate judge continued to draw attention to the significance of European law in limiting the autonomy of the British legal system.[16]

It would however be a mistake to suppose that the discrepancies between European and British legislation when they arise are likely to produce major constitutional controversies. For one thing most of the points of disagreement occur over British delegated legislation – i.e. rules or orders made under an enabling statute so that the challenge is at one remove from the Act of Parliament itself. Thus even where individuals have based their defence to a criminal charge on the fact that Parliament no longer had the power to legislate on a given subject because of European law, the change has seemed of less than spectacular significance. (This was the point in a case relating to Northern Ireland where a man arrested for transporting pigs in Northern Ireland without a licence successfully argued that Parliament no longer had power to make such regulations.) Equally, the British government may prefer not to pursue its arguments where a point of conflict has arisen. Thus when students from the European Communities argued that they were entitled to be charged the same university fees as British students the government chose to amend its regulations on the topic rather than dispute the issue before the Court.[17] And the courts are likely to try to avoid a conflict by adopting rules of construction which assume the superiority of European legislation.[18]

Perhaps the most forceful indication of the courts' acceptance of the change which had come over the legal system was given in a 1982 case which concerned a case of sex discrimination brought by an employee of British Rail. In that case Lord Diplock commented that 'even if the obligation to observe the provisions of Article 119 were an obligation assumed by the United Kingdom under an ordinary international treaty or convention and there were no question of the treaty obligation being directly applicable as part of the law to be applied by the courts in this country without need for any further enactment', it was a principle of construction of United Kingdom statutes 'now too well established to call for citation of authority' that the words of a statute passed after the treaty had been signed, and dealing with subject matter of the international obligation of the United Kingdom, were to be construed, if they were reasonably capable of bearing such a meaning, as intended to carry out the obligation and not to be inconsistent with it. And Lord Diplock seemed to suggest that nothing short of 'an express positive statement' in an Act of Parliament passed after 1 January 1973 that a particular provision was intended to be made in breach of an obligation made or assumed by the United Kingdom under a Community treaty would justify an English court in construing that provision in a manner inconsistent with a Community treaty obligation of the United Kingdom *however wide a departure from the prima facie meaning of the language of the provision might be needed in order to achieve the consistency*' (our italics).[19]

In other words the courts have taken the basic commitment to the European Communities sufficiently seriously to have changed their understanding of the *grundnorm* of the British legal system and have developed appropriate rules of statutory interpretation to deal with it.

The erosions of British parliamentary sovereignty which are implicit in the European Communities Act and European Treaties to which that Act gives effect are of course only likely to be powerful sources of major constitutional and political change while Britain remains in the Community and the Community continues to operate decisively. Yet even with the threat of stalemate and stagnation posed by the questions of the Common Agricultural Policy and the budgetary arrangements of the Community, it would be a mistake to underestimate the extent to which in such areas as agriculture, transport and the general regulation of trade and industry, membership of the Community has altered the structure of the British state by interlocking it with systems with vastly different traditions and values. To that extent perhaps the simple demolition of Dicey's theory of parliamentary sovereignty may be less significant than the acquisition of new influences on the habits of mind and action of British decision-makers.

The Rule of Law and the Challenge of Violence

A second area where traditional constitutional premises came under attack in the period between 1964 and 1984 was that of the rule of law. This doctrine entails the linked ideas of equality before the law and that of procedural fairness. The desire to improve the mechanisms whereby substantive and procedural fairness can be applied to conflicts between public authorities and individuals has resulted in a new set of institutions – a Parliamentary Commissioner for Administration, Local Commissioners for Administration, a Health Service Commissioner and a Council on Tribunals – as well as a renewed determination by judges to develop and apply the fundamental principles of administrative law. Such improvements have given fuller meaning to the principle that the law, whether in statutory form or not, should apply with equal force to individuals, groups and public authorities. What has given cause for concern however has been the increase in the number of groups which have found the parliamentary process inadequate for their needs, and have resorted instead to direct action. In addition to what might be termed the calculated use of direct action for political purposes, Britain also experienced in the early 1980s social disorder of a more spontaneous kind in the form of riots in the major cities of London, Liverpool and Bristol.[20] In some of these disturbances race was a factor, but by no means in all of them, so that it was difficult to produce easy or simple suggestions to ameliorate the situations in these areas. The poor relationships between police and ethnic minorities were underlined by the Brixton riots in particular and they led to a sustained attempt to improve the machinery of consultation between the police and local communities. But the general lesson of the disturbances was that British society could no longer operate on the assumption of harmony and moderation.[21]

One area where direct action and violence competed with orthodox political activity throughout this period was Northern Ireland. The reappearance of terrorism there after forty years of relative tranquillity was followed by an extension of the campaigns by the Irish Republican Army and other terrorist groups to the mainland of Britain. The tactic of placing bombs in civilian centres resulted in the deaths of twenty-one people in Birmingham in 1974, in a bloody incident when soldiers and sightseers were killed in London in 1982 and in the deaths of three people in the Christmas period of 1983 when a bomb exploded just outside a large London department store. Although the figures of death in the mainland were small by comparison with Ulster itself – where it has been estimated that 2,300 people were killed between 1969 and 1983 and a further 24,000 maimed or injured – they did bring home to the British population the extent to which regular government had broken down in Northern Ireland and the need for more effective security measures to combat terrorism.[22]

The immediate result of the bombings was the Prevention of Terrorism (Temporary Provisions) Act, which Parliament passed in its entirety within a week of the bombings in 1974 and which it renewed in later years. This legislation made it a criminal offence to belong to the IRA or to aid its cause and strengthened the powers of the police in matters such as the length of time suspects could be held for questioning. Later amendments introduced controversial changes such as the possibility of deportation from the mainland.

The terrorism of the IRA in the years after 1971 was complemented by a growing determination on the part of Ulster's Protestant population to resist policies which in its view undermined Protestant hegemony in the province and threatened Ulster's links with the rest of the United Kingdom. The suspension of Northern Ireland's system of devolved government in 1972 and the reintroduction of direct rule from Westminster was effected in the hope that such a move would increase respect for the law; by replacing Stormont, Ulster's regional Parliament, the British government had hoped to remove a sectional Parliament which lacked legitimacy in the eyes of the province's Roman Catholic population. Once the instruments of the Protestant domination of Northern Ireland had been destroyed the government in London assumed that it could build a new constitutional structure which would have the support of both the Roman Catholic and Protestant sections of the Ulster community. Unfortunately it has become increasingly clear that Westminster's legislation lacks legitimacy for sections of both the majority Protestant and the minority Catholic portions of the Ulster population. The complex constitutional solution of 1973 – which attempted to create political institutions in which power was shared between the two religious communities – could command no real support in Northern Ireland when it was brought into operation. That constitutional settlement was destroyed as a result of a fourteen-day strike by the Protestant Ulster Workers' Council, which used its control of the power stations and other essential services to bring to a halt normal life in the province.

The success of the Ulster Workers' Council Strike illustrated Westminster's impotence in the face of powerful organizations which preferred the techniques of direct action and intimidation to the electoral process. It also demonstrated the difficulty of rebuilding support for constitutional values and democratic methods of resolving disputes in a situation where large sections of the population had already accepted resort to direct action as legitimate. Perhaps it is not surprising that no political solution to the Northern Irish problem has emerged since 1974, although increasingly the strategy of the British government has appeared to be to try to place the onus of finding an accommodation on the Ulster parties themselves while concentrating for its own part on the routine administrative and security problems of the province. Although from time to time there has been evidence of an attempt to break the stalemate – for example by improving relations with the Irish Republic – it has to be admitted that the period since 1974 has not been marked by any sustained policy towards the problems of Northern Ireland.

It could be argued that the violence and erosion of respect for the rule of law which became so marked in Ulster over the 1970s and 1980s was the consequence of a special problem and had few implications for British society as a whole. Yet challenges to the rule of law were not confined to groups concerned with Northern Ireland, and at some points in the 1970s even groups such as the Young

Liberals endorsed direct action to prevent juggernaut lorries from entering the United Kingdom and to stop sporting teams from South Africa from touring the country. However it was noticeable that both the Liberal Party and the newly formed Social Democratic Party after 1981 were anxious to distinguish their position on direct action from that of extremists and to assert their respect for the rule of law. And in part their concern reflected the mounting opposition to both the ideas and tactics of the far left in British politics and to some aspects of the conduct of the trade union movement.

The trade unions' position had become increasingly uncertain in the late 1970s and early 1980s. At the beginning of the 1970s the unions had provided a clear example of a challenge to the principle of the rule of law when they determined to resist the implementation of the Industrial Relations Act of 1971. That Act embodied the Heath government's industrial strategy and was an attempt to regulate trade unions' powers in a comprehensive manner. The trade unions' denial of the legitimacy of this piece of legislation appeared at times to amount to a general refusal to acknowledge Parliament's right to legislate in the field of industrial relations without first securing the consent of the unions themselves. Certainly the history of trade unionism in the United Kingdom has always been marked by a suspicion of the judiciary and of the country's legal machinery; an attempt to introduce detailed legal regulation in an area which had hitherto been immune from legal intervention was bound to arouse trade union opposition. What was remarkable, however, was the support which the trade unions' campaign to thwart the operation of the Act received both inside and outside Parliament and the way in which appeals to respect existing parliamentary legislation were overridden by claims that the unions were under no obligation to obey laws that conflicted with their views of their members' interests. Ultimately the trade unions won their battle by persuading the Labour Party to commit itself to the repeal of the legislation; when a minority Labour government replaced the Heath government as a result of the February 1974 general election (which was itself called, as the prime minister saw it, to determine the issue of who had the right to govern Britain) a series of measures tailored to trade union demands were quickly passed, and the legislation of 1971 was repealed.

The Industrial Relations Act of 1971 was not the first attempt by a government to change the framework of industrial relations in the United Kingdom. In 1969 the Labour government headed by Harold Wilson had attempted to introduce legislation to regulate industrial disputes, but such was the reaction to these proposals that a cabinet commitment to legislation had to be withdrawn. The Conservatives' difficulties with the unions between 1970 and 1974 were compounded by the fact that while they were seeking to introduce new machinery to settle industrial disputes they were also trying to secure trade union agreement for their incomes policy. These two issues undoubtedly dominated the relationship between government and the unions over the period 1970–4; but other features of industrial relations, especially at the shop floor level, were also of constitutional significance. Indeed it became increasingly clear after the miners' strike of 1972 that violence and intimidation could arise from an industrial dispute, and that many of the traditional assumptions about picketing, for example, would have to be re-examined.

The increase in the amount of violence occasioned during the strikes of the early 1970s was influenced by two developments which seriously worried many trade union leaders as well as the police. The first was the growing popularity of a technique of mass picketing whereby large numbers of people – many of them unnecessary to the purpose of persuading workers to comply with the strike and sometimes conveyed from areas far away from the dispute itself – would stand outside a factory or industrial site to demonstrate solidarity with the workers, and physically to impede access. Inevitably in such circumstances, as was graphically illustrated during the miners' strike of 1984–5, the notion of peaceful picketing became difficult to distinguish from the practice of intimidation.

The second development was the exploitation of these industrial disputes by extremist organizations and the acceptance of a certain level of violence in industrial confrontations. With these developments it was hardly surprising that a number of confrontations with the police should occur and that arrests and criminal charges arising out of industrial disputes became more frequent in the 1970s. Yet such was the hostility to the apparatus of the law in some sections of the trade union movement that even clear examples of intimidation and violence to fellow workers were not immediately condemned. One such case occurred at Shrewsbury, where the pickets convicted in December 1973 for offences committed in the summer of 1972 were regarded as 'martyrs' because their assaults on fellow workers earned them prison sentences – sentences which were not quashed on appeal and which caused controversy when Labour came to power.

The general confusion about what the role of law should be in the field of industrial relations and the successful resistance to parliamentary legislation by the trade unions undoubtedly contributed to the decline in respect both for the courts and for the authority of the government. The experience of the clashes between trade unionists and the police contributed to the campaign to make operational and policy decisions of the police more susceptible to control by elected authorities as well as to the general atmosphere of suspicion of the police forces which had also been fuelled by the inner city riots. And it also highlighted the failure of British constitutional practice to accommodate the corporate strength of the trade unions. As has been seen, the decision to call a general election in February 1974 posed the question 'who rules the country – the unions or the government?' in stark terms. But the electorate's indecisive response revealed that the question was infinitely easier to ask than to answer. The defeat of Edward Heath and his subsequent replacement as party leader by Mrs Thatcher led to the search for a new strategy for dealing with the trade unions on the part of the Conservative Party, a search made substantially easier by the unpopularity which the trade union movement as a whole encountered during the late 1970s as it refused to follow the pay policies of the fragile Labour governments led by Wilson and Callaghan and engaged in a series of strikes in the run-up to the general election of 1979.

The increasingly close relationship between government and the unions, which had in part been fostered by the perception of a need for some kind of incomes policy agreed with the trade unions, had led many commentators to see the British political system as increasingly adhering to the corporatist model. Mrs Thatcher's election on a platform of a reduced role for government in the economy – as well as the increasingly apparent inability of the groups at the apex of the trade union and business sectors (the TUC and the CBI) to control their members – cast doubt on the relevance of this model after 1979. Yet the fact that it should have been applied at all indicates the degree to which British politics and government have ceased to fit a model in which all authority ultimately depends on parliamentary elections and where decisions are taken by an independent political authority, the cabinet.

The Unitary State and the Challenge of Nationalism

One of the major constitutional challenges of the 1970s had been the result of the growth of electoral support for the Scottish National Party and to a lesser extent of Plaid Cymru in Wales. By-elections in the 1966–70 period had indicated a degree of support for these parties which was unusual given the normal dominance of the two major parties (but especially the Labour Party) in the peripheral areas of the United Kingdom. The establishment of a Royal Commission on the

Constitution in 1969 was in part a response to these developments; it reflected the extent to which dissatisfaction with the operation of British political institutions had increased in the 1960s. Given the amorphous nature of the constitution it was hardly surprising that the Royal Commission did not reach unanimity even about the scope of its inquiry; its report in 1973 was rapidly overtaken by the results of the general elections of 1974 which gave the Scottish National Party and Plaid Cymru enough parliamentary seats to persuade the Labour government that new arrangements had to be devised for the government of Scotland and Wales.

The proposals for devolution contained in the Scotland Act of 1978 and in the Wales Act of 1978 represented a fundamental questioning of the framework of the United Kingdom and a recognition that the country's distinct geographical and national areas needed separate political treatment. Indeed in some respects the Acts, if they had been implemented, would have transformed the United Kingdom into a quasi-federal state: the law-making powers which Westminster had exercised on all subjects for Scotland would have been replaced by a system in which power was shared between an Assembly in Edinburgh and a Parliament at Westminster. Moreover the question of where powers might constitutionally be exercised would have been determined by a politically neutral body – the Judicial Committee of the Privy Council – and not by the superior legislature. Where the proposed system would have differed from a wholly federal one would have been in the absence of any uniform pattern in the division of powers between the component parts of the United Kingdom. Unlike the situation in the United States, for example, where certain powers are exercised by the federal government and others by the states individually, the United Kingdom after devolution would have had a different distribution of powers in Scotland – where the Assembly would have been able to legislate directly – from that in Wales, where the Assembly would have had only the power to make secondary legislation within the broad framework of policies established at Westminster. Northern Ireland would have been different again: the province enjoyed substantial legislative devolution between 1921 and 1972 on the lines envisaged for Scotland in the Scotland Act; but the use of that autonomy in the interests of the Protestant section of Ulster's population resulted in the abrogation of this arrangement. England would presumably have continued to be governed as before from Westminster, as Ulster would have been while direct rule remained, albeit with some variations in the legal system between the two.

The other main difference between the devolution proposals of the late 1970s and a fully federal system was in the suggested financial arrangements between the several parts of the United Kingdom. The devolved units were not to have their own taxing power or to be able to determine the overall expenditure on services within their areas. Together with the inequalities of powers between the several parts of the United Kingdom this failure to devolve financial control could have created a degree of uncertainty in the proposed arrangements which would have meant that a number of British constitutional relationships would have been in flux for many years thereafter.

The Scotland Act and the Wales Act were never implemented. The legislation was made dependent on the confirmation of both Acts in their separate countries by a referendum, and in neither area was the necessary majority obtained. The use of the referendum on the question of devolution confirmed suspicions that its earlier use in 1975 to determine whether Britain should remain a member of the European Communities had not been a once-for-all event. The need for that referendum had arisen because of Labour's internal divisions on the issue of Europe – divisions which could not be resolved by the normal convention of cabinet government whereby minorities simply have to abide by the decision of the majority or resign. The issue of Europe cut too deeply into the Labour Party for such a settlement to be possible and so it was decided to transfer responsibility for the decision directly to the voters. However, the experiment had constitutional implications, for it posed the question of whether or not it could be used on a broader range of issues.

The Referendum and the Challenge to Parliamentary Government

The possibility that the referendum might become a regular feature of British political life became apparent when Mrs Thatcher as leader of the opposition announced her interest in extending the use of this mechanism. The most serious attempt to secure a national referendum in an earlier period of British history was that made by the Conservative opposition during the interlocking crises over the powers of the House of Lords and Ireland in 1910. It had been suggested that a Home Rule bill that had twice been rejected by the House of Lords should be put to the electorate for its verdict. However the proposal found no favour with the Liberal government of the day, which preferred to reach its goal by restricting the powers of the Upper House. Nor did the proposal for a referendum on protection, which was frequently mooted between 1906 and 1931, meet with much approval among parliamentary leaders.

The circumstances of the 1975 referendum were very different. Although an unsuccessful attempt had been made by the previous Labour government to gain admission to the European Communities – following an earlier attempt by Harold Macmillan's government in 1961 – the Treaty of Accession by which Britain joined the Communities was secured by Edward Heath's government in 1972. A bill to incorporate its provisions into British law was passed in 1972, although on its second reading it was approved by only 309 votes to 301, a reduction in the government's normal majority which reflected the divisions in all parties on the question. In the Parliamentary Labour Party, there was by then a majority opposed to British membership, although at its highest levels there were some passionate pro-Europeans.

The divisions over Europe within Labour ranks made it difficult for the party to devise a common policy for the election manifesto of February 1974. Labour eventually fought that election on a policy of renegotiating the terms of entry and of offering the British public a clear choice on the principle of membership. It was not entirely evident from the Labour manifesto whether this choice was to be exercised in the traditional manner – i.e. from the sentiments of the House of Commons – or whether a referendum would be held. Whatever the success of the renegotiation, however, it became plain that any Labour government would be hopelessly torn on the issue, so that the option of a referendum became all the more appealing. Thus the referendum was not merely a device to allow the normal rules of cabinet responsibility to be suspended; it also became an aid in the immediate and increasingly difficult problem of holding the Labour Party together. As James Callaghan is reported to have remarked in the shadow cabinet, the referendum was a 'rubber dinghy' into which all the senior Labour figures could climb to survive the rough seas of Labour's internal politics.[23]

Similar considerations of party unity caused the referendum provisions to be written into the devolution legislation. The government was not entirely in control of the devolution bills as they proceeded through Parliament, because Labour did not have an overall majority in the House of Commons. Backbench amendments accounted for a provision that at least 40 per cent of the electorate of each country – and not just a simple majority of those voting – had to vote 'yes' in order for the provisions of the devolution Acts to become operative. While this provision made the task of the pro-devolutionists more difficult it did not resolve the status of such referendums. Moreover there was no provision for any referendum to be held in England, even though it could be argued that any movement towards federalizing the United Kingdom would have had as much impact on England as on Scotland and Wales.

Although referendums have now been used on significant national issues, no clear rules governing their operation have had time to develop. No referendum is possible without the passage of legislation through Parliament, so it could be said that to that extent the introduction of the national referendum is not detracting from parliamentary government. On the other hand, referendums on major constitutional issues are a way of bypassing Parliament as much as of overcoming internal party difficulties. They could very easily lead therefore to a conflict between the authority of the people as expressed in a referendum and the authority of the people's representatives in Parliament. Indeed it was not without significance that one of the issues for which a referendum was discussed, although not proceeded with in Conservative circles, was that of capital punishment, where it has frequently seemed that there is a real difference of opinion between Parliament and the general population.

The constitutional impact of the referendum on Europe would perhaps have been greater had the vote gone the other way. The government would in theory have been committed to introducing legislation to take the United Kingdom out of the Communities; ministers who deplored such a course could have resigned, but many ministers might have felt bound to follow the referendum verdict rather than their own consciences. The traditional Burkean theory has been that MPs exercise their own judgement on issues and are not delegates either of their electors or their constituency parties. This theory has already worn a little thin in the Labour Party, where the doctrine of the mandate – which binds Labour MPs to proposals contained in the manifesto – plays a much larger role than in other parties. It is unclear how far the theory could survive the frequent use of referendums.

Table 1
The Results of the 1975 European Referendum: Turnout and 'Yes' Vote by Area

	Turnout	Yes Vote
England	64.6%	68.7%
Scotland	61.7%	58.4%
Wales	66.7%	64.8%
Northern Ireland	47.4%	52.1%

The possibility of a clash between individual MPs' preferences and the verdict of their constituents makes the arrangements for counting a referendum a somewhat sensitive subject. In the European referendum it was suggested that because a simple 'yes' or 'no' vote was required the whole country should be treated as a single constituency. Such a course would have met the objection to counting by parliamentary constituencies – that in some cases individual MPs who knew the way their constituents voted might suffer reprisals if they thereafter defied those constituents' wishes on a parliamentary vote. On the other hand, the coincidence of the European issue with the pressure for devolution made Scottish and Welsh nationalists anxious to have a form of voting which would enable differences in sentiment between the component parts of the United Kingdom to emerge. The ultimate decision was a compromise which allowed the votes to be counted on the basis of the units of local administration – the counties – thereby concealing in all but two cases the views of individual parliamentary constituencies while revealing geographic divisions. As it happened there was a noticeable conformity both between the component parts of the United Kingdom and among the English regions, though Scotland, Wales and Northern Ireland were rather less enthusiastic about membership than was England.

One final constitutional implication of the referendum device is that its introduction may have provided the United Kingdom with a way of entrenching future legislation if desired. A government which has induced the electorate to support a measure at a referendum (in addition to persuading Parliament to accept it) may feel that an incoming government of a different political colour would hesitate to repeal an Act without at least putting the issue to the population again. Although the Conservative government elected in 1979 showed no enthusiasm for enacting a bill of rights, it is possible that a future government might well endorse such a move and that it would consider strengthening the position of such an Act by referendum.

The Cabinet and the Challenge of Open Government

The introduction of the referendum into British constitutional practice was one sign of the strains to which the orthodox theory of cabinet government was being submitted over the 1970s. There were, however, other indications during this period that the norms governing the behaviour of the cabinet had altered. Initially this was as a result of the need to accommodate the distinctive features of Labour government which from 1964 to 1970 and again from 1974 to 1979 set its stamp on the constitutional practice of Britain. After 1979 however it became clear that many of the subtle changes which had occurred because of Labour's internal tensions had to be maintained under a Conservative government – albeit in less obvious and marked form. The assumptions of collective responsibility and secrecy could not be maintained in an atmosphere of a divided Conservative Party any more than in a divided Labour Party, and the tradition of 'leaking' information to the press had become too well established to reverse in the climate of the late 1970s and early 1980s.

The classic doctrine of collective responsibility which lies at the heart of British understanding of cabinet government can be interpreted in a variety of ways. In essence, however, it means that once a majority has decided an issue in cabinet those in the minority must accept that decision and defend it, if necessary, as a decision of the cabinet as a whole. In theory, whatever the internal divisions of the cabinet, its members should both be reluctant to reveal disagreements and should contribute to giving Parliament the impression of cabinet unity.

Between 1945 and 1964, however, it became increasingly common to find the supporters of a minority position inside the cabinet identified as such in the press. Sometimes this was the result of a so-called 'unattributable leak' to the press; sometimes it was sheer guesswork on the part of journalists who knew an individual cabinet minister's likely position on a particular issue. But after Labour returned to power in 1964 the number and extent of these leaks increased; the press was able to draw conclusions about disunity within the cabinet from the participation by some cabinet ministers in extra-parliamentary Labour Party activities, even where the tone of those activities was distinctly hostile to the Labour government.

As long as the relationship between the Labour leadership in Parliament and the extra-parliamentary party remained a broadly harmonious one and the instances of disagreement within the cabinet relatively trivial, this trend towards a more open style of cabinet government did not perhaps matter unduly. In the latter years of the Wilson government of 1966–70, harmony was however replaced by acute conflict as the Labour government wrestled with economic problems and attempted to reform the conduct of industrial relations. In the circumstances it was perhaps natural that critics of government policy within the cabinet should publicize their opposition to measures unpopular with the party outside Parliament and use their membership of the National Executive Committee – the controlling organ of the Labour Party in the country between the annual conferences – if they were members, to dissociate themselves from the cabinet position.

Harold Wilson has commented on the difficulty of managing a

cabinet in which some members also held office in the National Executive Committee and consequently had a dual loyalty. Constant reminders were necessary that cabinet ministers should not become too closely identified with NEC policies and in 1969 – a time of heightened tension over the government's *In Place of Strife* proposals for regulating the trade unions – a formal statement about the meaning of collective responsibility was actually read to the cabinet.[24] Again in 1974 when there was disagreement between the NEC and the Labour cabinet over aspects of foreign policy the prime minister had to write to three cabinet ministers who had expressed disagreement with government policy to warn them that they were bound by the doctrine. Finally in 1976 Wilson had to introduce a rule that no minister who was chairman of an NEC subcommittee could undertake press briefings on its behalf, if it meant announcing policies which in any way deviated from those of the government.

The referendum on British membership of the European Communities necessitated the temporary suspension of the rules of collective responsibility so that cabinet members opposed to membership could campaign for a 'no' vote, although the official government position was to recommend the public to vote 'yes'. The justification for this decision was that normal constitutional conventions could not apply in such unusual circumstances. Yet the expectation that life would return to normal once the referendum had been held turned out to be false: the patterns of political behaviour which had been developing throughout the 1960s and 1970s proved hard to break and there were several well publicized incidents of cabinet disharmony both on European issues – such as direct elections to the European Assembly – and on economic policy. The Labour government's decision to adopt a formal pact with the Liberal Party in April 1977 in order to maintain a parliamentary majority was also criticized from within the cabinet; and the resultant divisions were made public.

The need to relax the conventions of collective responsibility to accommodate anti-European sentiment within the cabinet, and the pressures from the left within the Labour Party on economic strategy, arose because of the character of the Labour Party itself. It is a party with strong ideological divisions and factions which must be balanced inside the cabinet; it is also a party with a strong tradition of internal party democracy – a concept which was to become more prominent in Labour activists' thinking over the 1970s. Inevitably, therefore, the management of a Labour cabinet will frequently prove more difficult than the management of a Conservative cabinet, although the first two years of Mrs Thatcher's 1979 government revealed that Conservative cabinets can be deeply divided and less than amenable to prime ministerial dominance. Moreover, members of Labour cabinets have alternative forums for debate and discussion: factions defeated in full cabinet can take advantage of that party's power structure to reopen the battle at other levels of the party. When Labour first became a party of government it was anxious to obtain constitutional respectability, and the norms of cabinet government were therefore an effective brake on party faction. By the 1960s, however, Labour's own internal structure had begun to alter the values and norms of cabinet government so as itself to accommodate Labour's heterogeneity. At one level that change was reflected in the adoption by Labour cabinets of procedural and formal rules such as those governing when matters settled in committee might be reopened in full cabinet; at another level it was reflected in a much greater openness and tolerance of dissent than Conservative cabinets had hitherto permitted.

Mrs Thatcher's early period as prime minister was unusual. Elected as the product of a backbench rebellion, she had as her senior cabinet colleagues politicians who were not her staunchest allies. Initially therefore her position in the cabinet was uncertain, and this fact combined with policy divisions to produce a cabinet where the prime minister was openly seen to be in a minority position on many issues. To some extent she too used cabinet committees to preempt the full cabinet. The removal of many 'wets' in the cabinet reshuffle of 1981 and the additional prestige which the prime minister gained as a result of the successful prosecution of the Falklands war enhanced prime ministerial dominance of the cabinet. However, even the prime minister's strength vis-à-vis the rest of the cabinet after 1981 could not totally restore the position with respect to leaks and collective responsibility. Despite efforts to prevent information about internal discussion and divisions from reaching a wider public, Mrs Thatcher had to accept that her critics might reveal the cabinet's internal disharmonies; and indeed in 1984 it was widely suggested that the cabinet and its committees had become so prone to leak that they could no longer be regarded as responsible forums for the discussion of many sensitive political issues. The once influential 'E' Committee (dealing with economic policy) acquired a public reputation for leaking discussions and was increasingly ignored as decisions were taken by a group of selected ministers and advisers; this trend was not limited to the 'E' committee alone or even to the committees where those most at variance with Mrs Thatcher's policies were thought to be powerful. Although there was a marked unwillingness to recognize the fact, the style and ethos of cabinet government had changed to accommodate greater controversy and openness in the decision-making process. If that accommodation involved the transfer of decision-making away from the cabinet, it was a price many were willing to pay.[25]

The challenge to the secrecy which had surrounded the British administrative system for so long and which was deemed by many to be intrinsic to the efficient operation of cabinet government did not thus arise simply as an inevitable byproduct of ideological and other divisions within the major parties. There was increasingly a general intellectual case put forward for greater openness in government. The Fulton Committee on the Civil Service had condemned the unnecessary secrecy which surrounded the operations of Whitehall in the 1960s. Some faltering steps towards greater openness had been taken in the 1974–9 period, although there was nothing approaching the American Freedom of Information Act. A new phase seemed to begin with the launching of a campaign for open government by Des Wilson in early 1984 – a campaign remarkable for being supported by a number of former civil servants such as Sir Douglas Wass and Sir Patrick Nairne and welcomed by the First Division Association of Civil Servants.[26]

The attitude of the Thatcher administration to these demands was unresponsive. Yet it was a mark of the change which had come over British government that, although Mrs Thatcher would not give a full list of the cabinet committees which existed to the House of Commons, in 1979 she was prepared to acknowledge four of them in answer to parliamentary questions and give their names.[27] And there was little that could be done when in 1984 *The Times* not merely published an allegedly complete list of the cabinet committees thought to exist, but identified those who were believed to be their chairmen.[28] The constitutional fiction which maintained that such committees did not exist could hardly survive the greater iconoclasm of journalists and the publication by former ministers of their memoirs.

The Changing Role of the Civil Service

Attitudes which tended to demystify the workings of government at the highest level over the 1960s and 1970s were complemented by developments elsewhere in the political system which tended to illuminate the understanding of the role and function of the Civil Service. The inquiries instituted by select committees – especially after the reform of the whole select committee system in 1979 – and the work of the parliamentary commissioner for administration (PCA) provide detailed knowledge of how departmental decisions had been taken and how ministers and civil servants interacted. In part such developments reflected Parliament's realization that it could only perform its scrutiny function properly if it had the specialized staff available to investigate complaints of maladministration, and that sporadic and *ad hoc* examinations of policy areas were unsatisfactory. However the other side of this growing desire to penetrate the mysteries of departmental decision-making is a changing role for the Civil Service. As Parliament and public acquire more knowledge about who is really responsible for decisions and as there is more public speculation about the influence of individual civil servants, some – though not of all – of the assumptions about an apolitical Civil Service become eroded. The constitutional theory may still be that civil servants only implement their political masters' wishes; but in practice the more that is known about civil servants' views and contributions to a debate the harder it becomes to assume their neutrality, not so much in partisan terms, as in terms of commitment to intellectual and policy positions.

This development was compounded by the attitudes towards the Civil Service displayed by Mrs Thatcher and her administration when they took office in 1979. The goal of reducing the level of public expenditure and of altering the balance between the public and the private sectors had obvious practical implications for the Civil Service in terms of its size and level of pay. To this almost inevitable targeting of the Civil Service as the institution that was the most vulnerable to radical Conservative policies there was added the administration's determination to apply outside standards of efficiency and effectiveness to government and the prime minister's preference for individual civil servants in whose judgement and capacities she had confidence. As a result the prime minister's formal responsibilities for senior Civil Service appointments were interpreted by Mrs Thatcher as enabling her to promote and appoint as permanent secretaries men whose views she supported or whose style she admired. Moreover the personal interest taken by Mrs Thatcher in many of these senior appointments gained publicity. What is significant about this development is that it is difficult to imagine a senior civil servant who has been publicly identified as someone in whom a Conservative administration has particular faith commanding similar support in a succeeding administration. And since many of the appointments which were controversial were of relatively young men (such as Peter Middleton at the Treasury) it is possible that this will have further implications for the Civil Service career

37

structure. Indeed it is likely that serious thought will have to be given to the problems which will inevitably arise if a system of *pantouflage* consequent upon accelerated promotion is established in the United Kingdom.

A further indication that traditional assumptions about the Civil Service were being eroded was given when in 1985 Clive Ponting, a civil servant in the Ministry of Defence, was prosecuted under the Official Secrets Act for leaking documents about the sinking of the Argentine ship *Belgrano* during the Falklands War. He was acquitted, and claimed that he had sent the documents to an opposition MP because he felt that the government was deliberately deceiving the House of Commons about the matter. The case brought to the surface not merely a range of tensions between the Conservative government and the Civil Service but also a number of questions about Civil Service ethics in a changing constitutional environment.

The Relationship between Central and Local Government

The changing role of the Civil Service and the profound constitutional implications of those changes had, as has been argued, come about in part not because of any explicit desire to alter the basis of the relationship between politicians and civil servants but because a series of developments elsewhere in the governmental system (for example in the select committee system), together with some radical shifts of policy, had combined to change the institution in certain fundamental ways. Much the same was true of the constitutional relationship between central government and local authorities, where although Conservatives had frequently proclaimed their belief in decentralization and local authority independence in the past, under Mrs Thatcher's administrations they adopted a series of policies which taken together pushed British government into a much more centralized mould.

The explanation for this development (which is more fully discussed in chapter 10) is perhaps a threefold one. At one level it reflects the absence in both the Conservative and Labour parties of any coherent theory of what the relationship between the local government structure and central government ought to be, so that policy departures were rarely set against any underlying set of beliefs in the value of local democracy. Secondly, the increasing prominence of measures to control financial expenditure meant that the budgets and policies of local authorities would be subject to more central direction and control, and the process of centralization of local government finance which had already become a marked feature of central-local relationships was simply brought into the open. Finally, many of the changes which the Conservatives wished to see introduced in the most important domestic policy areas such as education, housing and social services necessitated intervention from the centre, and could not be reconciled with a local authority's freedom to resist them. It was therefore likely that the central government would use its powers to force policies on recalcitrant local authorities. If for some people this seemed to be an unwarranted intrusion into matters that were properly the reserve of local government, it was for many others a reflection of the extent to which politics was already nationalized, in the sense that electors looked to central government to determine the broad outlines of policy, and of the extent to which popular demands in a relatively small country were increasingly incompatible with divergent standards of provision. The constitutional significance of the changes however should not be understated. Much of the reorganization of the early 1970s which had been found to have undermined the strength and cost-effectiveness of local government had ostensibly been designed to strengthen a system of local democracy. Now it seemed that these units had been transformed even more surely into units for the administration of central policies rather than being authorities capable of taking an independent political line.

Parliament and the Party System

The role of Parliament in the 1970s and 1980s had come under challenge from several different sources. Doubts and ambiguities about the functions which Parliament was meant to be performing had existed since the 1960s, when a vigorous debate had been opened about the adequacy of the British legislature either as a law-making body or as an instrument for controlling and holding accountable the executive. This scepticism led to a series of experiments with the procedures of the House of Commons, most notably the expansion of select committee activity. This remedy for the alleged weaknesses of Parliament was devised on the assumption that what made Parliament ineffectual and purposeless as a body was that through party discipline the government was able to exert a considerable amount of control over its proceedings. If, it was argued, select committees could become a useful forum of activity in their own right, and if party factors could play a reduced role in their work, the individual backbench MP might again be able to make a substantial contribution to policy and to legislation. As will be seen however (in chapter 5), although the radical reform of the select committee system introduced in 1979 has gone some way towards redressing the balance between legislature and executive in Britain, other developments – such as the growth of party dissent and the experience of a different system of party competition – have contributed to the new environment in which the role of Parliament must be discussed.

The years between the February 1974 general election and that of May 1979 were highly unusual as far as the organization of Parliament was concerned. The steep rise in the Liberal Party vote, the defection of the Ulster Unionists from the Conservative Party with which they had been long associated, and the growth of support for nationalist parties in Scotland and Wales contributed to the rise of minor parties in the House. And even when the 1979 and 1983 general elections returned governments with secure overall majorities, the emergence of the Social Democratic Party and its Alliance with the Liberals ensured that many of the simple understandings appropriate to a legislature dominated by the fight between government and opposition had to be rethought. The rise in the number of small parties represented in the House of Commons – and the seniority of some of the figures who represented the SDP – posed problems for the Speaker when applying Standing Orders and when exercising his discretion about the conduct of a debate.

During the period between 1974 and 1979 it was not the details of parliamentary procedure that posed the major constitutional problem. For much of that time there was no government majority and one of the normal assumptions of British political life no longer held good. (The election of February 1974 produced no overall majority, and although the October general election gave Labour an overall majority of three, that majority was rapidly destroyed by by-election defeats.) The combination of uncertain government majorities and a large number of minor party representatives meant that for the duration of those Parliaments the government was unsure of being able to pass its legislation through the House. The government had to accept the loss of second reading divisions as well as major amendments to many of its measures, including its elaborate scheme for devolution.

In order to try to remedy its parliamentary weakness the Labour government negotiated in 1977 a formal pact with the Liberal Party which, while short-lived, gave the United Kingdom a taste of the style of coalition bargaining which might be expected if ever the electoral system were to be reformed. It also gave many Liberal MPs access to decision-making and generally gave greater prominence to the role of minorities in Parliament. Most important of all, perhaps, the experience complemented the already documented growth of dissent within the major parties and further reduced the willingness of MPs to act as simple 'lobby-fodder'.[29]

While the results of the 1979 and 1983 elections did remove the insecurity of the government about much of its legislative programme, there was evidence in the Parliaments elected in those years that MPs were willing to take the risk of diverging from the line advised by the whips, so that on issues such as the immigration rules, MPs' pay and select committees, the executive had to modify its position. And although its intervention was somewhat unpredictable, the House of Lords also revealed a determination to act as a counterweight to the massive majority held by the government in the House of Commons after 1983.

Dissatisfaction with Parliament's role as a legislative body and as a check on government was supplemented in the period after 1974 with a growth of the movement for electoral reform. All of the elections between 1974 and 1983 gave rise to accusations of unfairness, since from the point of view of the smaller parties and especially the Liberals and the Liberal-SDP Alliance the number of seats yielded by the system was grossly disproportionate to the number of votes which they could claim. A change to some form of proportional representation would, it was argued, both be more just and produce a House of Commons that more accurately reflected public opinion.

The criticisms levelled against the 'rough justice' of the British electoral system were in many respects familiar ones, because electoral reform had been part of the Liberals' platform for many years. What was novel in the situation after 1974 was that the electoral system in the eyes of many commentators came to be seen as the single most important example of a wide range of structural weaknesses in Britain, especially the nature of party competition. From a limited case for improving the mechanics of representation the argument for electoral reform was extended into a comprehensive critique of the British style of politics. This argument linked the first-past-the-post method of electing MPs to what was dubbed 'adversary politics'; it traced the cause of the discontinuities of British policy and what was perceived as electoral apathy to the current nature of the two major parties and especially to the ability of their elites to ignore public – as opposed to party – opinion on a wide range of issues.[30]

According to the adversary politics argument, the Labour and Conservative parties each felt obliged when in opposition to attack the policies of the government whatever the merits of those policies; and in many cases the parties would pledge themselves to reverse measures undertaken by their opponents. In developing alternative policies the party hierarchies would be guided, however, by party activists whose perceptions reflected neither electoral opinion as a whole nor the realities of the problems with which governments were confronted. The policies framed by a party in opposition would be included in its manifesto and, in the event of a general election victory, a party would seek to implement them. Reality and moderation might however intervene at this stage, and the policies might be adjusted to accommodate the experience of government. Indeed frequently the new government would find itself being pushed by events towards the very policies of the former government which it had attacked in opposition. Yet by this stage the former government party, by now in opposition, would have begun its own process of policy reappraisal and would certainly want to distance itself from anything endorsed by its opponents. Consequently its policies in opposition would be likely to produce further disruption if there were a change of a government.

On this analysis the party system, and particularly the proclivity of incoming governments to reverse the work of their predecessors, created a climate of instability in which investors and other citizens could have no faith in the future. Electoral reform, it was argued, by broadening the political contest and making coalitions more likely, would break the pattern of two-party alternation and create the conditions for a political system in which all parties could search for agreed solutions to problems and for policies which would reflect the moderate consensus.

The importance of this argument was not that it found favour inside the two major parties, for it manifestly did not, although it was significant that the Social Democratic Party emphasized many of its themes. The significance of the debate was that it reflected a changing attitude towards British institutions and the erosion of the country's constitutional complacency. A generation ago most commentators would have identified the electoral system and the two-party system as important contributors to an ordered structure of cabinet government, stable representative democracy, and policies which harmonized with the moderate views of the electorate. Now for many critics – though not of course for all – the electoral and party systems are the joint villains in a scenario of increasingly extremist policies, economic decline and political stagnation.

The adversary politics argument may to some extent appear to have been eclipsed by the experience of slightly better economic conditions, a new Labour leader in the form of Mr Kinnock, and a Conservative Party which, by winning two elections, seems able to provide some of the stability demanded by business. Indeed it may even be that Mrs Thatcher's robust combination of free market economic policies and populism reflects a consensus at least as powerful as that predecessor – based on Keynesian economics and support for undifferentiated welfare policies – which is known as Butskellism and has been advocated by so many champions of electoral reform. Yet it would be a mistake to assume that the fundamental questioning represented by the adversary politics debate has subsided; for it forms part of a wider pattern of general dissatisfaction with many of the most entrenched aspects of British life.

2   Functions of Government in the Welfare State

The pattern of a country's political institutions will in large part reflect the functions which that society expects government to perform. Inevitably the range and character of those functions will change from one generation to another as new problems are identified or as existing problems come to be seen as suitable subjects for governmental treatment. The flexible nature of Britain's constitutional and administrative arrangements makes it possible for government to intervene swiftly when an emergency occurs and to respond to new demands in the manner which seems most convenient at the time. In some cases additional governmental responsibilities will be tackled by creating new agencies to deal with them; in others it will seem more appropriate to expand existing institutions. The continual redefinition of the tasks of government means that both the structure of central departments and the allocation of responsibilities between them have proved extremely fluid. In the period from the end of the second world war until the late 1970s there seemed to be a consensus that the functions of government would continue to expand as government adopted more detailed and comprehensive responsibilities for a variety of welfare functions. However towards the end of the 1970s there developed within British politics a trend of thought which was determined to halt, if not to reverse, this movement towards more collectivist policies. The Conservative government of 1979 was elected on a platform of a reduced role for government, and the politics of Thatcherism – the blend of politics and economic policy associated with Margaret Thatcher's two administrations – implied a reassessment of the role of the public sector in a range of policy areas.

In addition to the changes which one might expect from alterations in the intellectual climate and differences over the proper role of government in British society, the organization of British governmental activities has been made more complex by the preoccupation which successive governments have had with redistributing governmental functions within the political system. This perpetual mutation – which has affected local authorities and regional administrative agencies as well as central departments – has been inspired by few clear principles, so that there has frequently been no yardstick against which to measure the success of any of the readjustments and reorganizations that have been made.

Ingrained administrative habits can prove resistant to permanent change. Although both world wars left permanent legacies to the structure of government, the striking thing in many respects was the degree to which after the emergency was over the former administrative patterns reasserted themselves. By the end of 1922 Britain was governed very much as she had been in 1914; by 1950 the differences from the position in 1939 were probably fewer than the similarities. It is therefore more accurate to regard wartime experience as a catalyst for existing trends than as a main source of innovation in governmental practice. It is difficult to believe, for example, that some kind of cabinet secretariat would not have evolved sooner or later as a response to the increased complexity of the government's responsibilities and as the informality of pre-1914 cabinet proceedings became less and less appropriate. Nor could government for long have avoided assuming some responsibility for the development of applied science and technology along the lines indicated by the establishment of the Committee of the Privy Council for Scientific and Industrial Research in 1915 and of the new Department of Scientific and Industrial Research in the following year.

The dismantling of economic controls after both world wars also reminds one that the line of development has never been a straightforward movement from less government to greater intervention, or from an individualistic and laissez-faire approach to some kind of collectivism. Such aspects of modern government as intervention in the economy to control the labour supply and the public provision for the relief of poverty are not innovations of the present century. While it is true that the structure of government today is in many respects very different from that presided over by Gladstone or Disraeli, it still reproduces in some sectors the attitudes of an earlier age.

The truly novel elements in the welfare state are to be found in its methods rather than its objectives. Improvements in communications have made possible a degree of centralization impossible to contemplate in earlier periods; what previously had to be done locally can now be performed by central government. Even those services which are still administered on a local basis are largely – and increasingly – centrally inspired, centrally directed and centrally financed.

Uneven historical development and the preference of politicians for improvisation makes it impossible to set out in any logical order the wide variety of functions performed by British government in the 1980s apart from its classic responsibilities for national defence, law and order and the administration of justice. An additional complication arises in describing the British administrative structure, because while some functions are the responsibility of the central departments, others have been allocated to the Scottish, Welsh and Northern Ireland Offices. Therefore although the present discussion will focus on England's administrative arrangements it must be remembered that in the other three parts of the United Kingdom parallel but slightly different administrative arrangements exist.

In this chapter an account will be given of how the main functions of government were distributed in 1984 between the various departments headed by ministers and some of the multitude of non-departmental agencies; we shall also examine some of the developments of recent decades which help to explain the current patterns of governmental responsibilities. Here the focus is very much on the extent to which the British system of government has responded to the series of disparate demands made upon it. The more general questions about the making and execution of policy will be examined in the next two chapters which deal with the executive and the Civil Service.

The pattern of distribution of functions then reflects no logical approach to the problem of how a modern government should cope with its tasks but rather a series of incremental decisions built up over successive administrations. In the 1960s for example there was particular concern with industrial problems and especially with those brought about by the development of new technologies and by labour questions. In the early 1970s the government of Edward Heath was concerned about the fragmentation of decision-making and the difficulty of taking a synoptic view of the whole field of public policy. As a result it experimented with the creation of very large departments which incorporated work once divided between a number of smaller ones.[1] In this way it was hoped that differences could be reconciled within departments rather than taken to cabinet, and that the size of the cabinet itself could be reduced.

It could be argued that after 1979 there was a qualitative change in government's view of its role and functions. It has been suggested that the government which came to power in that year and which successfully presented itself for re-election in 1983 was committed to a view of the state and its responsibilities that at least in its own mind differed profoundly from that of its predecessors of either party. It believed itself to be entrusted with diminishing the degree of state intervention in the economy and with re-examining the boundaries between public and private enterprise. It wished to give priority to lowering the levels of taxation, both central and local, over the growth of public services. In pursuit of its desire to control and limit the total of public expenditure it was drawn into making a shift in the relations between central and local government. Moreover the government also began to question the rationality of the highly complex system of benefits and their financing that had developed as successive governments had adapted various aspects of the welfare state. And the importance that the Conservatives attached to law and order required a reconsideration of fundamental issues in policing, as well as a review of the penal system and the role of the judiciary and the courts.

The magnitude of the task undertaken by the new Conservative government in 1979 should not be underestimated. Apart from the general difficulty of changing a deeply entrenched system of government and administration, there was the fact that there had been since 1945 steady increases in the role of government, in the numbers of its employees – both local and central – and in the proportion of the GDP it spent. However, even with the new ideological inspiration the government's share of GDP went on rising, and reached 44 per cent in 1981–2, although it had fallen to 43 per cent in 1983–4 and was expected to fall again to 42 per cent in 1984–5.[2] Reductions in the size of the Civil Service proved easier to execute, and considerable cuts were made, so that by 1984 the overall size of the Civil Service had reached its lowest level since the second world war, with further important reductions planned for the immediate future.[3]

One reason for the difficulty in putting a brake on the growth of government is that once government has assumed a particular function it rarely abandons it, even though it may change the agency through which it executes it. For example the Post Office was one of the oldest government departments, originating during the Cromwellian protectorate. In 1969 the Post Office became a public corporation but continued to act as an agency for government departments in matters such as the payment of pensions on behalf of the Department of Health and Social Security. The postmaster-general's position was also abolished in 1969 and a new minister for Posts and Telecommunications was created; but this office was in turn abolished and the ministry was then absorbed into the Department of Trade and Industry. The 1979 government created a separate public corporation – British Telecom – with a view to its subsequent privatization. Now that privatization has taken place, the public interest is safeguarded by a new non-departmental Office of Telecommunications (Oftel), so that there is still some governmental role in the discharge of the telecommunications function, albeit of a rather residual kind.

One way of classifying governmental functions would be to

separate those directly run by central departments and headed by ministers responsible to Parliament from those delegated to the organs of local government that Parliament has created. But quite apart from the interdependence of central and local government there are now regional agencies of various kinds; these are essentially emanations of central government and have no directly elected element. There are in addition a number of *ad hoc* or special purpose authorities – regional health and water authorities, for instance – and these further complicate the picture.

From the point of view of central government or 'Whitehall' as it is popularly styled, there is a spectrum ranging from government departments such as the Home Office, the Department of Health and Social Security and the Department of Employment to regulatory commissions and quangos (quasi-autonomous non-governmental organizations). Government departments, headed by ministers, will be directly answerable to Parliament for their policies. Other bodies may be distanced from political control.

Particularly important from the constitutional point of view are the arrangements made for dealing centrally with certain functions for which organization on the departmental model, and the direct responsibility of ministers, are deemed inappropriate. Thus while the principles of taxation policy have always been a matter for ministers responsible to Parliament, the collection of taxes from individuals has been shielded from direct ministerial intervention through the operation of the quasi-autonomous Boards of Inland Revenue and of Customs and Excise. Some of the more recently created institutions have similar aims: for instance the University Grants Committee created in 1919 was intended to act as an independent buffer between the government as paymaster and the universities as the recipients of funds. Its formation was regarded as a guarantee of the universities' continued 'academic freedom', though its value in this respect diminished after 1964, when responsibility for the UGC was transferred from the Treasury to the Department of Education (which was then renamed the Department of Education and Science, in part because of the universities' important role in scientific research).

The reason for greater government intervention in higher education has not of course been simply the changes in organization but rather the growth in the size of the higher education sector and its importance in the national budget. It has also reflected the desire of governments to shape the university system in ways which in their view would best serve the national interest.

More recently there have been created bodies under independent office-holders such as the Office of Fair Trading and the great variety of non-departmental public bodies which are sometimes called quangos.[4]

In very general terms the institutions of the British state which must be examined here have to administer seven distinct categories of government action. However these categories overlap in practice, and separate functions of government are not necessarily or invariably the responsibility of distinct departments.

The earliest positive functions of government were those of external defence and the maintenance of law and order, including the provision of courts for handling both civil and criminal cases. The machinery of justice and law enforcement will be outlined in a subsequent chapter; together they form part of the overlapping responsibilities of the lord chancellor, the home secretary and the law officers of the Crown – the attorney- and solicitor-general.

The second and perhaps the most ambiguous category of governmental responsibility is that of taxation combined with the overall control of credit. It is ambiguous because taxation is used to further several objectives: there is the basic one of providing revenue for supporting all the other aspects of government, including of course such fundamental responsibilities as defence and law and order; also taxation has increasingly become the instrument through which in accordance with egalitarian or humanitarian principles some resources are shifted from one sector of the population to another; and in addition it is regarded as a means of influencing the general economic climate, as is the control of credit. A national budget is thus an instrument of economic as well as of fiscal policy.

The third area of governmental activity – and it is the increasing scale and sophistication of operations here which has caused the label 'welfare state' to be applied to that form of government enjoyed in the United Kingdom – is that of services provided by the government whether in cash, as with pensions, or in kind, as with education. The basis of this provision has varied; some services are supported out of taxation while others are financed by compulsory insurance.

The fourth area is that of direct state intervention to protect by law certain categories of persons such as those employed in mines, in factories, or at sea; women and children at work; and tenants and consumers. Such a principle was well established by the end of the nineteenth century but it has been expanded during the twentieth century. Recent legislation against discrimination on the basis of race and sex might be regarded as extending the state's powers of this kind; so too could legislation intended to redress the alleged weaknesses in the bargaining process of various groups such as trade unions at one time and employers at another.

The fifth field of activity has been created by government itself as a result of its entry into the economic arena as the owner and manager of particular branches of industry through public corporations.[5] The reasons for this development have been varied: natural monopolies vital to state security and the existence of particular industrial relations problems in certain sectors have encouraged the taking of such sectors into public ownership. Sometimes the objective has been sought through partial public ownership and developments in this direction have figured in recent Labour Party policy.

The sixth area of activity is that of economic controls short of public ownership – in other words government intervention in such matters as prices and incomes or legislation on mergers and monopolies. The government's powers to award contracts in private industry became a matter of controversy under the Callaghan government when used to promote an allegedly voluntary incomes policy. In addition to the controls affecting the entire workforce or particular branches of production there are ways in which the government can intervene – through assigning subsidies or other fiscal privileges – to ensure that the location of particular enterprises suits its economic or even its electoral requirements.

The seventh area is the hardest of all to define. It consists of all those areas of government which relate to long-term ideas about the development of the country's human and physical resources. These functions are difficult to disentangle from the more immediate concerns to which they are likely to be sacrificed. The debate about energy resources has been a conspicuous example: a balance has to be struck between current demands, future needs, natural amenities and – in the case of nuclear energy – questions of safety. Land-use planning, a major function of local government since the Town and Country Planning Act of 1947, has become an even more tangled issue. Should one give priority to people's preferences for low-density housing over the need to preserve agricultural land? How does agriculture fare in the scale of importance by comparison with roads and airports? There is no easy way to answer such questions, which involve balancing issues of amenity against those of economics. Where population is concerned the state has long exercised powers over immigration, and in the past over emigration as well. The unusual scale of immigration in recent decades has highlighted this aspect of policy and the agencies responsible for its implementation. Attempts by fiscal and other means to influence the birth rate are yet another feature of modern government.

The word 'planning' which occurs in so many contexts in modern government is thus an ambiguous one. Effective planning depends upon the ability to forecast successfully developments in a variety of overlapping fields, many of them outside national control; because this has so far proved an impossible task, the planning related to it has lost much of its credibility. Demographic projections have been particularly misleading. The Department of the Environment, created in 1970, which could be thought to have a special responsibility for the country's natural resources, suggests by its title a more ambitious frame of reference than its actual performance has justified. It remains little more than a loosely coordinated collection of functions under a single minister. All of those functions had previously been performed elsewhere in the governmental machine, and indeed the department has, since its creation, shed one of its most important original areas of responsibility, namely transport.

Defence

The organization of the country's defence forces has responded to changes in technology. By the present century, the two professional services – the army and the navy – had become wholly national in their recruitment and deployment. In addition, there were at one time various reserve services intended largely for home defence and reflecting in their locally based organization the traditional duties of citizens to be equipped for an emergency. In the first world war demands for much larger forces led to general conscription. After 1919 the old system of voluntary recruitment was restored, with the significant addition, after much debate, of an independent air force. Conscription reappeared on the eve of the second world war and was maintained as 'national service' for a number of years after the ending of hostilities; by 1962, however, Britain's armed forces were again composed wholly of volunteers.

The proportion of public expenditure going into national defence has obviously varied with different perceptions of the threat to national security. In 1978–9 defence took a little less than education and only just more than health and personal social services.[6] By 1983–4, as a result of the new priority attached to it by the incoming Conservative government of 1979, defence took more than either of those areas. Two particular aspects of the new trend may be noted: there was a revival of interest in reserve forces, with an expansion of the Territorial Army; and importance began to be attached to civil defence, for which arrangements had been allowed to lapse in 1968. But the latter move met with opposition from a number of Labour-controlled local authorities who had sympathy with the campaign against the nuclear element in British and NATO strategy.

Changes at the centre have paralleled the increasing tendency to see the three armed services as part of a single whole and to encourage their use, where possible, of joint facilities. The modern Ministry of Defence is headed by a secretary of state whose office has superseded the three historic offices of first lord of the Admiralty, secretary of state for war and secretary of state for air. Its junior ministers and arrays of boards and committees are organized partly on a functional and partly on a service basis. The ministry's staffing is partly military and partly civilian. The new defence system survived its first real operational test – the Falklands war of 1982. Nevertheless in March 1984 the secretary of state announced further changes in the department's arrangements which would have the effect of strengthening the role of the chief of defence staff, hitherto the chairman of the Chiefs of Staff Committee. He would now be served by a combined defence staff. This staff would help him to discharge his duties as adviser to the secretary of state on 'defence policy, military policy, military priorities and the conduct of operations'. The chiefs of staff of the individual services would retain only their managerial responsibilities in respect of their particular services, although they retained their individual right of access to the prime minister.[7]

It was pointed out that these changes carried forward the moves towards a unified ministry made by Lord Mountbatten in 1964 and that an increased role for the chief of the defence staff had been approved in 1981.[8] On the other hand some experts on defence argued that the use of the armed forces could not be dissociated from their management, and it was clear that there would be a good deal to do if the secretary of state's hopes were to be fulfilled. In one area – that of combating terrorism in Northern Ireland – there is an obvious need for a single service role, especially as a good deal of the army's manpower is currently absorbed there.

As a purchaser of increasingly sophisticated and costly equipment the Ministry of Defence is closely involved with an important aspect of industry and with the promotion of scientific and technological research.

Finally, one might add that the professional character of Britain's armed forces does not mean that their members are as remote from society in general as in earlier times. It is no longer the case that officers have passed through a wholly segregated educational system or have spent most of their professional lives overseas. Nowadays officers have much more often passed through universities, and the opportunity for training in skilled trades has become one of the main incentives for joining the forces.

Taxation, Finance and the Economy

The principal financial department of the British government is the Treasury, which deals both with the provision of funds and with the control of their expenditure. A major function of the Treasury, particularly following the changes in organization after the first world war, involved personnel matters in government, although this must always be a direct concern of the prime minister. In 1968 this aspect of the Treasury's activities was separated from it and a new Civil Service Department was created, with the prime minister as its nominal head but with another senior minister without portfolio – such as the lord privy seal – responsible for day-to-day administration. Its permanent secretary, rather than the permanent secretary to the Treasury, then became head of the Home Civil Service.

These arrangements were altered again during Mrs Thatcher's first term as prime minister. The Civil Service Department ceased to exist at the end of 1981; its responsibilities were divided (as will be detailed later) between the Treasury and a new Management and Personnel Office which was eventually incorporated in the Cabinet Office. The headship of the Civil Service reverted to the secretary of the cabinet. Despite these attempts to separate some of its functions, the Treasury is nevertheless more than a Ministry of Finance especially as many permanent secretaries in the spending departments are likely to have experienced some time in the Treasury and to have imbibed its distinct traditions. (Although perhaps less true now, this has in the past occurred because the Treasury would frequently get the first pick of administrative recruits – the fliers who would then go on to become permanent secretaries in other departments.)

The Chancellor of the Exchequer is the minister responsible for the national system of taxation and for changes both in the nature of the taxes levied and in their level. Historically, changes in either were presented to Parliament in an annual budget in the spring when the fiscal year begins; this was the climax of the parliamentary session. The British budget was thus concerned only with the ways and means for raising money, and not with expenditure. Proposals for expenditure were dealt with earlier in the parliamentary year as 'estimates'. A great deal of secrecy attaches to the budget procedure; even the chancellor's colleagues are only informed of his proposals immediately before their presentation to the House. The ostensible purpose of this secrecy is to avoid the possibility of financial speculation; the disadvantage is that it inhibits full consultation with interests likely to be affected and a proper scrutiny of new provisions.

In recent years, however, there have been some important changes, though these have to some extent had opposite effects. On the one hand most public expenditure is supposed to be planned on a 'rolling' five-year basis; this means that government commitments should in theory be well known in advance, thus limiting the chancellor's freedom of action. On the other hand, the economic vicissitudes that the country has been undergoing and the attempts to correct its undesirable features by fiscal means over and above the regulative powers of the chancellor have meant that there have been a growing number of summer or autumn 'mini-budgets' in addition to the annual spring budgets. The more frequent budgets become, the less is the mystique attached to them and the less perhaps their importance compared with all other means of intervention in the economy that modern governments possess. In addition to taxation, large-scale borrowing to meet current outgoings – in the past mainly a feature of wartime finance – has become normal practice. This may involve winning and retaining the confidence of the international monetary institutions and the governments they represent; an important part of the chancellor's task is therefore now a diplomatic one.

The section of the Treasury that deals with policy is small. The detailed working out of tax proposals and the responsibility for their implementation are in the hands of two other departments, the Board of Inland Revenue and the Board of Customs and Excise which stand in a quasi-autonomous relationship to the chancellor. The organization of the Board of Inland Revenue is perforce largely a localized one; this situation stems from the practice of earlier periods, when it was necessary to rely on groups of local notables to assess and collect taxes due to the Crown.

Although the Treasury decides what proportion of the public outgoings are to be met by borrowing rather than by taxation, the raising of loans and their management are again something entrusted to other bodies. Savings by the population at large and their investment in different forms of government stock are a matter for the Department of National Savings, which in 1969 took over the former functions of the Post Office in this area. The day-to-day management of the national debt and government intervention in matters affecting the international money market are the responsibility of the Bank of England, which has been the principal agent of the state in these fields since its foundation as a private institution in 1694. The Bank of England's nationalization in 1946 did not conspicuously diminish its independence in representing the City's interests to the Treasury, nor detract from its role and standing among foreign and international monetary and financial institutions.

In recent years the Bank of England has been drawn further into the Whitehall network in many ways; the gulf in outlook between the Bank and the Treasury may have diminished as a result of the Bank's increased recruitment of senior personnel with an academic rather than narrowly banking background. Even so the Bank is still largely staffed by men who have made their way in the banking world, by contrast to the directly-recruited university graduates who dominate the Treasury. The governor of the Bank of England occupies a special position. Appointed for a five-year period, his tenure is unaffected by political changes. On the other hand unlike a permanent secretary or other senior civil servants he claims the right to make his views known through speeches to the public as well as to ministers in private. His perspective is rather different from that of ministers or Treasury civil servants and his views may not accord with those of the government's spokesmen. Although the possibility that discord over the conduct of economic policy may become public is thus a real one as a result of the governor of the Bank of England's unusual position – and that possibility has given cause for concern – it is difficult to see how he could fulfil his dual position as spokesman of government to the City and of the City to government if it were otherwise and if his freedom were further curtailed.

Historically the main work of the Treasury itself was the control of public expenditure; a variety of constitutional rules and conventions made its consent necessary for any projected expenditure by departments. This consent was also required for all legislative proposals involving expenditure. More recently under the influence of Keynesian economic thinking this primary function was supplemented – or some would think superseded – by a wider concern. The Treasury came to believe that it could influence the economic climate as a whole by managing demand; this confidence has latterly declined.

The role of the Treasury has been enhanced by the growing importance of government as an employer and spender: its own industrial activities now obviously do much to determine the general state of the economy. The other factor that gives particular importance to central economic management is the extreme significance to Britain of foreign trade and overseas investments. Despite the increased importance of invisible exports – shipping, banking, insurance, consultancy work, higher education and training – Britain still depends upon her exports of manufactured goods to pay for a high proportion of her food and raw materials. The position in this respect has not been static: domestic agricultural production has increased; the share of foodstuffs in the total import bill has been falling; so too has the share of raw materials, with the substitution of synthetic for natural products.

The growth in the production of oil and gas from the North Sea has for the time being limited Britain's dependence upon external sources of energy and added appreciably to her exports, though it is recognized that this self-sufficiency is a temporary phenomenon.

One significant feature of Britain's economic situation has been the tendency for imports of manufactured and semi-manufactured goods to increase with any upturn in the economy. This has helped to inhibit increased public expenditure as a method of dealing with unemployment and to produce pressures in favour of protection for various aspects of home production. The long-term factor of the greatest significance has been the declining share of Britain in the world's export markets – from 18.2 per cent in 1958 to 9 per cent in 1977 and to 8.2 per cent in 1982. The balance of payments and the stability of the currency have thus been preoccupations of all postwar governments.

It is not surprising that it is in the economic field that changes in the machinery of government have been most conspicuous. To some extent these changes reflect differences in the theoretical perception of the economic problems and the divergent philosophies of the two main parties. Administrative arrangements for ordered and detailed forms of government intervention in the economy may turn out to be less important than the ability of senior ministers to respond swiftly to the signs of an economic squall. Rapid improvisations rather than systematic treatment have also been characteristic of attempts to curb the growth in public expenditure. Whether these attempts have taken the form of new machinery for Treasury or parliamentary control, or of formal reviews of significant aspects of public expenditure, notably defence, they have usually been superseded by measures taken rapidly and under pressure to meet a particular financial crisis. It could be argued that the successive innovations which have taken place in the administrative structure were largely ways of escaping from a head-on confrontation with problems that no government felt strong enough to solve; their chief result was to dissipate the energies of senior civil servants and to some extent of ministers on the mere mechanics of organization, when they would perhaps have been better devoted to examining the substantive issues involved.

In the early 1960s there were moves towards a greater degree of intervention in the economy. The National Economic Development Office and Council (NEDC) were set up in 1961, to bring about tripartite discussions between government, the employers and the unions about the handling of problems of the domestic economy. The incoming Labour government in 1964, influenced to some extent perhaps by the French example of indicative planning, divided up ministerial functions in a new way. A Department of Economic Affairs was set up to handle the long-term planning of the economy while short-term responsibilities in the economic sphere remained with the Treasury. A new Ministry of Technology was created to give government assistance in the modernization of British industry. In 1965 a National Board for Prices and Incomes was added to the system in the hope that a non-political and presumably impartial body of this kind would help to restrain inflationary wage settlements and avoidable price increases. As a further complication it was decided to treat as a separate issue the highly varied effects of economic developments on different regions, and in particular the uneven geographical spread of unemployment. Questions of regional policy and the types of government intervention required to make it effective were left to the Board of Trade. In April 1968 the major responsibility for incomes policy – which was of increasing importance in the overall government strategy – was vested in the Ministry of Labour; this was renamed the Department of Employment and Productivity.

The economic difficulties of the latter years of the Labour government of 1966–70 forced ministers to devote more attention to the monetary and fiscal aspects of policy and produced a reaction against the earlier confidence in long-term economic planning. In October 1969 the Department of Economic Affairs, which was already much weakened by its rivalry with the Treasury, was abolished; its general economic responsibilities reverted to the Treasury, and its direct relationships with particular industries were transferred to the Ministry of Technology.

The Conservative government that came into office in 1970 was at least as convinced as its predecessor of the importance of devising a correct administrative framework for making and executing government economic policy. Its initial steps were greatly influenced by an ideological preference for minimal intervention and its consequent hostility to a formal incomes policy. The National Board for Prices and Incomes which had played a reduced role in the last years of the Labour government was abolished. The Department of Employment and Productivity was renamed yet again and became simply the Department of Employment, with the accent on its conciliatory functions in industrial disputes. The Ministry of Technology was merged with the Board of Trade to form one of the new 'super-departments', the Department of Trade and Industry.

The course of economic events and particularly the high rate of inflation forced the government back towards an incomes policy. Ideally it would have looked to cooperation with the unions to bring about a voluntary restraint in wage claims. But relations with the unions had been soured by the Industrial Relations Act of 1971 and by union resistance to the two organs set up under its provisions – the Industrial Relations Commission and the Industrial Relations Court. The government therefore gave itself statutory control over prices and incomes by the Counter-Inflation Act of 1973, setting up two new bodies, a Pay Board and a Price Commission.

The defiance of the incomes policy by the miners and the government's defeat in the general election of February 1974 brought into power a Labour government hostile to the idea of a compulsory incomes policy and pledged to abolish the industrial relations legislation to which the trade unions objected. Repeal was achieved in full only after the election of October 1974 gave the government an overall majority: the machinery set up under the Industrial Relations Act and the Counter-Inflation Act, except for the Prices Commission, was abolished. The formal link between government and labour remained the Department of Employment; however two important aspects of its work were hived off to semi-autonomous bodies – the Manpower Services Commission (MSC), responsible for employment services and industrial training, and the Advisory Conciliation and Arbitration Service (ACAS), which was supposed to advance the cause of trade union recognition and to handle strikes and other forms of industrial strife.

When the Labour administration of 1974–9 in turn embarked upon an incomes policy it hoped that this would prove acceptable if combined with improved welfare benefits – the concept of the 'social wage'. The Labour government did not take compulsory powers to control incomes but relied upon a general agreement with the TUC. The only sanctions available were those which arose from the dependence of individual employers upon various forms of governmental patronage and assistance. Prices, however, remained under statutory control and the Prices Commission was an important weapon in the government armoury.

The Department of Trade and Industry did not long remain as originally created. The Conservative government had already removed all aspects of energy policy from it to the newly established Department of Energy. The Labour government of 1974 now also separated off the Department of Trade, which was to be largely concerned with the international field, and a Department of Prices and Consumer Protection, which in addition took over some of the powers formerly exercised by the Ministry of Agriculture, Fisheries and Food. The latter – along with the Department of Energy – and the Ministry of Transport were the survivors of the old system where ministries had specific aspects of the economy under their care.

The survival of the Ministry of Agriculture, Fisheries and Food must in part be ascribed to the political weight of the agricultural community, which persists despite its relatively small size. At the beginning of the 1980s agriculture accounted for only 2.5 per cent of the employed workforce in Britain as against 2.6 per cent in Belgium, 5.6 per cent in West Germany, 7.8 per cent in France and 12.8 per cent in Italy. The importance of the Common Agricultural Policy of the EEC has also given the ministry a considerable international role.

Much of the work of MAFF is conducted through negotiations with organizations representing the agricultural industry – most notably the National Farmers' Union. Until 1979 this could be regarded as only a particular instance of a general truth about the British system of government – that it has a corporate bias and that there are some interests which work very closely with government departments to get arrangements for their sectors which sometimes seem unduly favourable.

The legislation of 1975 and 1976 and the close political cooperation between the trade union movement and the Labour government for the period of the so-called social contract gave trade unions new opportunities for influence. In the years 1974–9 many basic decisions in the field of public policy were the fruit of government negotiation with organized labour – and to a lesser extent with organized business through the CBI – rather than the result of any independent government strategy.

The fall of the Labour government and its defeat in the general election of 1979 were largely attributed to the strikes of the 'winter of discontent' in 1978–9 and to the belief that this style of government with its dependence on bargains with the unions had been found wanting.

The economic tasks of government had been further complicated by the particularly ambiguous position occupied by the nationalized industries, the most important of the public corporations. The favoured model for their organization had been the 'Morrisonian' one, named after Herbert Morrison, a leading figure in the 1945 Labour government. This means that nationalized industries are not run directly by government departments but organized in a quasi-autonomous fashion under their own boards, whose members are nominated by the minister. It was hoped that this form of organization would combine the principle of public ownership with the

59

flexibility of commercial concerns. In fact the industries concerned have been unable to meet the different demands made upon them – by the public for high-quality services at low prices; by their workers for better wages and conditions; and by government as it pursues its own economic and social objectives. They have been expected to recruit the best managerial talent but have been restrained from paying the high salaries needed to attract it by fear of backbench criticism. Above all the chairmen of the boards have encountered great difficulties in their relations with ministers: their wish to follow policies suggested by economic criteria has conflicted with the wishes of ministers who have had to take party and even constituency considerations into account. The result has been an ever-growing intervention by ministers and civil servants.

The 1979 Conservative government had as one of its top priorities the reduction of public expenditure as part of its general strategy for coping with inflation. That government also wanted to increase the role of the free market in the distribution of resources. The Prices Commission was abolished and the Department of Trade absorbed the Department of Prices and Consumer Protection. In June 1983 the departments of Trade and Industry were once again merged. Inevitably the government's goals had an impact on the nationalized industries. It was hoped on the one hand that greater financial discipline could be exercised over the nationalized industries, and more radically that some of them could be 'privatized' – i.e. returned to private ownership in whole or in part. The new Department of Trade and Industry was expected to be less interventionist than its predecessors, so it was assumed that less time would be spent on propping up or encouraging particular enterprises. 'Corporatism' was to be a thing of the past and the trade unions were to cease to enjoy privileged access to ministers outside the tripartite organization of the NEDC. While the Advisory Conciliation and Arbitration Service was still available to assist in the resolution of industrial conflicts, the Department of Employment itself was largely occupied with drafting new legislative proposals intended to restore a better balance in the machinery of collective bargaining.

Education, Social Services, Science and Information

The governmental provision of social services is carried out mainly by two very large departments – Health and Social Security (DHSS), brought together in 1968, and Education and Science (DES). These have serious problems of internal organization because of the variety of services they provide and there is also some overlap between them. They are confronted with three sets of problems.

First the DHSS to some extent and the DES to a much greater extent deal with matters which are the direct responsibility of local rather than of central government: local authorities, either individually or through their associations, are involved in the making as well as the execution of policy. The problem is complicated by the fact that at any given time many local authorities will not be under the control of the party in power at Westminster, and yet the main political parties may hold radically different views on some issues. In extreme cases a consensus may be unattainable and the government may seek to compel recalcitrant local authorities to fall into line.

Second, both departments are large-scale employers of labour either directly or indirectly through the local authorities. The trade unions into which the workforce is organized are therefore able to use industrial action not merely in pursuit of higher remuneration or better conditions for their members but also to promote their own views of what the departments' general policy should be.

Finally, unlike the nationalized industries, which are expected to follow pricing policies enabling them to 'break even taking one year with another', the DHSS and the DES, which supply mainly free or heavily subsidized services, have no economic criteria for deciding upon the distribution of the resources at their command.

The British system of state education is organized on a dual basis. Primary schools, most secondary schools, teacher training colleges – now mainly affiliated to universities or polytechnics – colleges of further education, adult education and polytechnics are the responsibility of the local authorities; however their expenditure is subsidized out of central funds. Part of the school system and some of the training colleges are connected with religious denominations, although they depend for finance largely upon public funds. The forty-five universities – the two ancient English foundations of Oxford and Cambridge, the ancient Scottish ones, the nineteenth-century largely civic foundations and the more recent plate-glass institutions – as well as the colleges of advanced technology which acquired university status in the 1970s and the Open University are all financed overwhelmingly from public funds and all except the Open University (funded directly by the DES) are financed through the University Grants Committee. The Cranfield Institute of Technology – a postgraduate institution specializing in management and engineering – is also directly funded by the DES. And while Britain's one private university, the University of Buckingham, does not receive public money directly for its expenses, it does receive public money indirectly because some of its students are entitled to grants from public funds for tuition and maintenance.

The division in higher education (known as the binary system) between the locally controlled and financed polytechnics and the universities has been the subject of a good deal of controversy. The spokesmen for the polytechnics claim that they receive a less generous apportionment of funds than the universities and are discriminated against by the Research Councils through which most government money for research is channelled. It is probable that the boundary between the two types of institution is not yet finally settled; some would like to see it disappear. The recent tendency has been for more attention to be paid to higher education seen as a whole, which included the colleges provided by local authorities partly for degree-standard work. The setting up of the National Advisory Board for the non-university sector may be taken as a portent of things to come. Controversy over the disposition of funds has been heightened by the fact that higher education is no longer a rapidly expanding part of the educational system. Between 1961 and 1970 the amount spent on universities went up from 10.8 to 14.2 per cent of the total educational budget while the proportion spent on schools declined from 65.6 to 56.7 per cent. During the 1970s however the priorities changed and there were persistent pressures for economy upon the higher education sector. Considerable cuts were imposed as part of the 1979 government's attempts to limit public expenditure. Nevertheless in comparison with her western European neighbours Britain provides a system of higher education notable for the lavishness of its provision of physical facilities for students, a high ratio of staff to students, and also for its system of grants – subject to a parental means test – for all students who succeed in obtaining a place in higher education. This means that quite apart from the direct financing of the universities by the UGC, students themselves are normally the beneficiaries of public funds in the form of fees and living expenses.

There have been deep controversies over the organization of secondary education within the state system in which legislation, its interpretation by the DES and the wishes of individual local authorities have all been involved. As the system stood after the important 1944 Education Act, British education was characterized by the existence of two major groups of schools whose intake was determined on a selective and hence primarily academic basis – the state-funded grammar schools, which were one of the local authorities' responsibilities, and the direct grant schools, which were partly fee-paying but had some free places directly subsidized by the central government. The direction of change was towards eliminating the grammar schools and basing all local authority schools on the neighbourhood comprehensive school – a pattern similar to the American high school model. The direct grant schools were obliged to choose between entering the state system, which involved abandoning selection by ability, or becoming fully independent. Wherever possible they have opted for the latter course. The existence of an independent sector is itself a matter of political controversy.

In the past, grammar schools had provided the opportunity for children of working-class and lower middle-class parentage to go on to university or professional training. The disappearance of such opportunities – for many comprehensive schools cannot provide them – could combine with the survival and expansion of the private sector to create significant social effects quite contrary to those intended by the proponents of the comprehensive schools, whose motives were both educational and egalitarian. There is a strength of conviction in the argument over the organization of secondary education which explains why it plays so much more of a part in politics in Britain than it does for example in the United States and why a new Education Act was one of the first pieces of legislation introduced by the incoming Conservative government in 1979.

The actual structure of the educational system has not been much altered by the Conservative government. Pressure on local authorities to introduce a fully comprehensive system has been removed but there has been no serious attempt to return to a selective system. The direct grant schools have not been restored, although 'assisted places' at independent schools are funded for academically able pupils who might previously have taken advantage of the existence of direct grant schools. On the other hand there has been a tendency to give the system a greater degree of centralization. This has been evident in the effort to divert resources to the applied sciences as a contribution towards economic recovery and growth. Collaboration between the education authorities and the Manpower Services Commission was in this respect something of an administrative innovation and one which was made at the expense of the DES. The training of teachers is also an area in which central powers can be exercised both in relation to numbers entering the profession and, to a lesser extent, with respect to the quality of the output.

While it would be an exaggeration to say that the highly decentralized character of the British educational system has been changed by the government elected in 1979, it is certainly the case that, contrary to previous Conservative statements about education, the most recent Tory administrations have acknowledged the political and educational benefits to be gained from planning the educational system as a whole and from being able to exercise tighter control over its component parts. Together with the more fundamental changes in the relationship between central and local government, which will be dealt with elsewhere, these developments point to a significant alteration in the pattern of relationships in this sphere.

The organization of the health services suggests both similarities with and differences from education. In the field of health as in education the state originally stepped in to fill the gaps in private provision but has gradually become the major provider. In both the education and the health fields important private sectors remain in being, though there is pressure within the Labour Party to have them abolished. However because of the existence of private beds in the National Health Service hospitals, which were being phased out by the Labour government of 1974–9, and because practitioners within the national system can also engage in private practice, the two sectors are more closely involved with each other in health than is true in education. In conflicts over policy and remuneration the medical profession is better organized than the teaching profession and in a better position to secure its interests – partly because its skills are more readily internationally marketable.

Local authorities which once played a major part in developing health services are now mainly confined to such matters as the enforcement of standards of hygiene and the medical aspects of personal social services. The National Health Service itself, which was established in 1948, comes directly under the authority of the secretary of state. In England his powers are exercised through fourteen regional health authorities; in Wales the NHS comes under the secretary of state for Wales. An intermediate tier, Area Health Authorities, was abolished in 1982; the regions now work directly through the 192 district health authorities. Similar arrangements for Scotland come under the jurisdiction of the Scottish Office. The health districts are run by boards mainly composed of unpaid part-time members, mostly nominees of the secretary of state; the rest are local government representatives. The system is thus both centralized and bureaucratic. Concern about the welfare of individual patients under this system led to the establishment of a Health Service commissioner or ombudsman with powers akin to those of the parliamentary commissioner for administration, although the Health Service commissioner, unlike the PCA, can receive complaints from the public directly without the complaint being forwarded via an MP, as is necessary for the PCA. Both offices – in addition to the theoretically separate appointments for Wales and Scotland – are in fact exercised by the same individual (see chapter 13).

There are some points at which the health and education services overlap. There has for instance to be close cooperation between the National Health Service, which is responsible for the management of the teaching hospitals, and the universities, which provide the teaching given in them and are represented on the relevant health authorities.

To the secretary of state for the Social Services falls the governmental function of paying cash benefits to individuals. The system of social security includes national insurance against sickness, unemployment and widowhood and for retirement; insurance against industrial injuries; family allowances and housing benefits; and the supplementary benefits available to families or persons in need, together with war pensions.

Although administrative convenience now dictates the handling of all these schemes within a single departmental framework, their historical roots and the contemporary policy goals are by no means identical. Part of the system has developed from the assumption by the Tudor state of the responsibility for relieving distress, which followed the religious and social upheaval of the Reformation; part is the outcome of early twentieth-century ideas – largely inspired by German models of social provision – for compensating through insurance for the vicissitudes befalling the individual worker in an industrial society; and part arises from the state's acceptance of particular responsibilities for those who have served it, whether in a civilian or a military capacity.

However the total expenditure on such services and the manner in which it is raised and disbursed remain matters of political controversy. Family allowances, for instance, may be regarded as an instrument of population policy rather than as a palliative for poverty. Benefits awarded subject to a means test have always been criticized as humiliating for the recipient. In the area of pensions the transition from flat-rate to earnings-related benefits after retirement has anti-egalitarian implications. There is also the problem of the conflict between the general provision for old age made by the state and the particular provisions made for government servants, especially now that the latter are calculated to take inflation into account. Some aspects of such provision may affect people's readiness to change their employers or even their occupations. Furthermore there may be a clash between a governmental priority given to economic growth – which calls for a highly mobile population and a fluid social structure – and an existing system of social security which is conducive to the maintenance of a rigid status quo.

Further attention has been called to the financial burden of both the health and social security systems by a growing realization of the fact that demographic trends point to a declining proportion of the population being engaged in the productive process with a higher proportion dependent upon its output to meet the obligations entered into by the state. Further anxieties have been expressed about the administrative complications of the welfare system so that a large number of potential beneficiaries may be handicapped in making their proper calls upon it. Major reviews were initiated by the DHSS in early 1985 to see whether there could be any way of rationalizing the system.

Where services provided by local authorities are concerned there is a further complication in that their main source of funds is the Department of the Environment, which may have a different policy perspective from the DHSS. The Department of the Environment has itself to grapple with a number of policy contradictions and conflicts in the various areas for which it is responsible. The large-scale provision of housing by local authorities at a time of housing shortage has, it is held, tended to make people reluctant to move outside their own locality for fear of losing their place on the council's waiting list for accommodation. Encouragement for the sale of council houses to sitting tenants – which has been a feature of government policy since 1979 – may have the same effect unless the sale and exchange of houses can be simplified.

The Department of the Environment has to grapple with other policy conflicts. The problems inherent in the different approaches to land-use planning – economic and environmental – may be noted. The problem of industrial waste and pollution bring the government into another area where the application of economic criteria may be challenged and where a local community's interest may conflict with that of an individual enterprise or with the national interest. The siting and regulation of nuclear installations provide an example.[9]

The diverse activities of government with more specifically economic functions demand an ever larger apparatus of statistics and an increasing sophistication in their interpretation. The Central Statistical Office is part of the Cabinet Office; the importance of its own interpretation of economic trends as a factor in government policy has been stressed by some observers of the Whitehall scene. If long-term planning is to be successful, future demands for manpower and physical resources will require study in greater depth; for instance attempts to match provision for places in higher and further education with employment opportunities demand calculations about the future shape of the economy, and these have hitherto been extremely unreliable.

From at least the time of the first world war, the need to be internationally competitive has obliged British governments to encourage research in the sciences and to allot an increasing amount of public expenditure for this purpose.[10] Advice on non-departmental research is now given by the five Research Councils, which are composed of specialists in the relevant disciplines – respectively the Science and Engineering, Agricultural, Natural Environment, Medical, and Economic and Social Research Councils. Government-financed research may be undertaken at establishments directly under their authority or by contract at universities and other independent institutions.

The steep rise in the research budget and the claim that the aims of some publicly-funded research were too remote from the nation's requirements led in 1972 to an investigation by Lord Rothschild, the head of the Central Policy Review Staff. Many of his proposals were accepted by the government and implemented: the budgets of three of the Councils – Agricultural, Medical and Natural Environment Research – were cut, and the money made available to government departments so that they could contract directly with outside bodies for research projects tailored to their own needs. There was some criticism of the Rothschild Report on the grounds that it misconceived the nature of the research process and that the customer-contract formula was inappropriate. These criticisms had some foundation, since it is felt that departments are bound to think in a short-term or 'tactical' framework in contrast to the 'strategic' thinking of the Research Councils. Universities have undoubtedly suffered as a result of cuts in the funds that were formerly obtainable from the Research Councils.

One problem that has proved controversial in the United States is the possibility of conflict between government funding of research and academic freedom. Can government control the publication of the results of such research? This question is especially acute where defence matters are involved. In Britain however such research, which is done not only for itself but for its spin-off effects, is undertaken not in universities but in governmental establishments. The most powerful government scientist of recent times, Lord Zuckerman, was both chief scientific adviser to the secretary of state for defence and chief scientific adviser to the government, with offices in both the Ministry of Defence and in the Cabinet Office. After his retirement the two posts were divided.

After 1976 the post of chief scientific adviser to the government was not filled and the main scientific input left to the chief scientific adviser attached to the CPRS. Since the demise of the CPRS, the chief scientific adviser has been in the Cabinet Office with the rank of deputy secretary. In the Ministry of Defence each of the three services has its own scientific adviser in addition to the chief scientific adviser to the secretary of state. But a centralization of scientific advice was part of the new proposals put forward in March 1984.[11]

In the field of the humanities and fine arts, government patronage is both more restricted than in the scientific field and in many respects more recent. The British Academy, a private body, acts in lieu of a research council for the humanities. National museums and libraries and the care of historic buildings and monuments are important governmental responsibilities. A new Historic Buildings and Monuments Commission dealing with much of the work came into being on 1 April 1984. Subsidies to music, theatre and the plastic arts are given, if not very lavishly by some standards, through the medium of the Arts Council established in 1946. Until 1979 and between 1981 and 1983 these activities were coordinated by the Arts Council. Until 1979 and between 1981 and 1983 this responsibility was discharged at ministerial level within the DES by a minister with the title of minister for the arts. Between 1979 and 1981 this responsibility was allotted to the then Chancellor of the Duchy of Lancaster and Leader of the House of Commons Mr Norman St John Stevas. In 1983 the Office of Arts and Libraries became a small independent department under the Minister for the Arts, the Earl of Gowrie, who was himself a minister of state in the Privy Council office, and later became Chancellor of the Duchy of Lancaster.

The predominance of central government in support for the arts is noticeable in comparison with some other countries such as Germany where municipal patronage is more conspicuous. British local authorities, although empowered to spend money to promote the arts, have in many cases done little in this direction. On the other hand the system of public libraries, which is very highly developed, is organized locally, although there is a central mechanism for inter-library loans. Some progress has been made by local authorities in developing libraries as centres for musical and dramatic activities.

Money for sport in Britain is channelled through a Sports Council. This body works with a minister for sport, an under-secretary in the Department of the Environment. Much governmental intervention in recent years has been directed to discouraging sporting links with South Africa, a highly contentious policy arising from the Gleneagles Agreement entered into by James Callaghan along with other Commonwealth heads of state and prime ministers.

An important feature of modern government is the need to make its activities known to the general public and to those sections of it likely to be especially affected by policy decisions. The Stationery Office publishes the mass of formal government documentation as well as the principal series of historical records. The Central Office of Information (COI) brings out the more popular presentations of different aspects of government's work under the direction of the relevant departments.

More subject to question is the use by ministers of press officers to present their policy through the media to the wider public. The press officer attached to the prime minister at No. 10 Downing Street is for the time during which he holds the post a temporary civil servant and it has been argued that it is improper for him to be used to present what is essentially a partisan viewpoint on matters of current controversy. But it is hard to see a prime minister of any party finding it possible to do without an official of this kind.

The two functions of information and the promotion of the arts and sciences are linked in the British Broadcasting Corporation, one of the earliest public corporations. Although its role in television is shared with commercial television – which is under the supervision of the Independent Broadcasting Authority – the peculiar stamp given by the original BBC has not vanished. Television is available to government for presenting information, and its role in presenting party politics depends upon agreements reached between the parties and the television authorities; television's more general function as an opinion-former is always likely to be controversial. Whether the BBC should try to reflect all shades of opinion or try to lead in moral, social and artistic matters will always be a matter for debate, as will the balance to be struck between serious journalism and entertainment. In comparison with France and some other Western democracies where broadcasting is similarly a state function but where it is much more closely controlled, Britain gives greater scope to broadcasting in the political and the general cultural field. And it gives greater weight to maintaining independence from government in the content of programmes, even in the context of such highly unusual circumstances as the Falklands operation. Elected persons play no role in either the BBC or the IBA except in an advisory capacity; as in many other public bodies the senior posts are decided by appointment, although there is a professional career structure for employees. Parliamentarians are however quick to call attention to any perceived departure from neutrality on the part of the BBC or the IBA.

As we shall see in the concluding chapter of this book the handling of the domestic tasks of government has been greatly affected by the growth of international institutions, especially the European Communities. Meanwhile the traditional British apparatus for dealing with foreign states and international institutions remains in being. The fact that traditional diplomacy has had to be supplemented with a good deal of economic or technical expertise has meant that the primacy of the FCO and of the Diplomatic Service has been repeatedly challenged. Much multilateral and conference diplomacy has for a long time required the participation of officials from departments other than the FCO, and often of their ministerial chiefs. Despite financial stringencies which fall particularly heavily on the technical side of broadcasting, the promotion of Britain's image abroad has been quite effectively managed. Some of this work is done by the FCO itself, often employing the Central Office of Information as its agent. Non-political tasks such as English language teaching and cultural exchanges fall to the British Council – a semi-autonomous body maintained mainly from public funds and informally collaborating with the FCO when its work has foreign policy implications. The external services of the BBC are the only agency through which British opinions, official and unofficial, can be made known to peoples whose governments are hostile to their dissemination. Because all such broadcasts, even the simple presentation of news, are politically significant the FCO control is perforce tighter here than it is over the British Council.

Not all areas of government activity fall neatly within the responsibilities of particular departments. An example is the vexed question of immigration controls: here the Home Office is the department responsible for administering the relevant legislation though the impact of its procedures is felt more acutely by the FCO; and the controls have therefore to be administered at overseas posts for which the FCO is responsible. It is in areas of overlapping responsibilities such as immigration that the machinery of co-ordination is especially important.

3 The Executive

The growth in the number of functions discharged by the government would perhaps have been sufficient by itself to create an imbalance of power between the executive and the individual and between the executive and the legislature. In addition, however, the British executive has inherited powers and a degree of autonomy which reflect the fact that the origins of the British state are monarchical rather than republican and that in consequence some of the features of royal absolutism have been retained in the constitutional arrangements of a mass democracy. Thus for example, although the legislative authorizations which ministers and departments require to carry out the routine tasks of government are derived from statutes (which have been passed by Parliament), the executive carries out some of its functions by virtue of powers, known as prerogative powers, which were those of the monarch. These powers enable the government, among other things, to sign treaties without recourse to prior parliamentary approval and to reduce punishments imposed by the courts. The prerogative of mercy, which derives from the theory that the monarch is the fount of all justice, is obviously less significant now that Britain has abolished the death penalty. However, it can still be significant when long-term prison sentences are at issue. The decisions need no legislative endorsement, although the personal responsibility of the home secretary (who exercises the prerogative of mercy on the monarch's behalf) is in part mitigated by the existence of a specialized board to advise on the parole of prisoners.

The fact that foreign affairs, including the making of treaties, was originally the personal preserve of the monarch has meant that a British government, although it might feel constrained to offer Parliament an opportunity to discuss international developments, has considerable freedom of action in this field. The fundamental constitutional change which occurred when the United Kingdom joined the European Communities was achieved by the *executive's* signature of the relevant European treaties. Admittedly parliamentary legislation was required to make the treaties part of British law; but the formal accession to the Communities was achieved by the executive alone.

The form of the executive in modern Britain, as well as its powers, reflects the monarchical origin of the British system of government. By the executive in Britain we generally mean both the cabinet – the senior part of the ministry formed from the majority party in the House of Commons – and the civil servants or other officials acting under its direction. The cabinet has developed from that group of the monarch's most intimate advisers who came to constitute the Privy Council. It was only in the eighteenth century that the outlines of a modern cabinet emerged; but it is important to note that at that time the authority of the executive was still derived from the sovereign, and the continuation of a government more dependent on the sovereign's good will than on being able to command parliamentary support. Only in the nineteenth century did the Crown lose the power to choose who should become prime minister and to veto ministers who were personally objectionable to the sovereign.

The Privy Council has survived as the formal machinery through which the monarch exercises her prerogative powers when necessary. Although nominal membership of the Privy Council is extensive – comprising all past and present cabinet ministers and a number of other public figures to a total of about three hundred in all – its working character is that of a small number of ministers who are called together to witness the signature by the monarch of some formal document such as the declaration of a state of emergency under the provisions of the Emergency Powers Acts of 1920 and 1964. There are also standing and *ad hoc* committees of the Privy Council which the monarch does not attend and which carry out specific functions in various fields. The Privy Council office is under the supervision of the lord president of the Council; but his formal responsibilities are not onerous. His post is therefore available – along with the other ancient offices of lord privy seal, chancellor of the Duchy of Lancaster and paymaster-general – for the prime minister to confer upon ministers to whom he wishes to entrust special non-departmental duties.

The cabinet will include a number of these so-called 'sinecure offices', although most members of the cabinet will be the heads of major departments. The cabinet presided over by the prime minister both makes policy and presides over its implementation. Lesser ministers outside the cabinet and senior civil servants also have this dual function. Even civil servants far removed from the policy-making apparatus may affect policy if their contacts with members of the general public suggest the need for change. The domestic departments will differ greatly among themselves because they have different responsibilities, traditions and clienteles. Their internal organization will also be affected by whether or not their function is one administered directly by the department concerned. Some functions, such as social security and employment, are the direct responsibility of departments of the central government which have their own local offices. Other functions, such as education and housing, are not exercised directly by central government and involve a complex set of relationships with local government and other bodies such as new town corporations. The variety of regional and local structure is in striking contrast to those continental systems of which France is the exemplar. In France the Prefect represents at the local level the general political interests of the government of the day. In the British system, there are simply the separate outposts of the government departments whose work is coordinated only at the summit.

Prime Minister and Cabinet

Although a discussion of British government will frequently start with a description of the prime minister and cabinet as the formal apex of the decision-making procedure, the environment in which they operate must constantly be borne in mind. It would be easy but too simple to see British administration as a machine and to treat the cabinet as the central powerhouse to which one transmission belt carries information and from which another expedites instructions. In reality, however, there are a number of other sources of influence and information which affect the way in which problems are analysed and decisions implemented. The machinery of the governing party, the formal and informal contacts which ministers and officials have with pressure group leaders in the industrial, commercial and professional worlds, the regular experience of ministers in Parliament and even the information obtained from the media – all these will provide alternative sources of information and keep ministers aware of attitudes which exist outside their departments.

It might be thought that with such a range of contacts and sources of information the system would function with great success and would possess inbuilt safeguards against error. Yet even with the increasingly sophisticated data available to it the recent record of British government suggests that there are weaknesses in the system itself which constrain the policy-making process and which limit the achievements of governments. Policy failures are not, of course, unique to contemporary British politics; however, a combination of raised expectations that governments can solve national problems, together with a general decline in the economic sphere, has perhaps

73

made such mistakes less acceptable than in the past.

Broadly speaking two main culprits have been identified in the attempt to explain the mistakes made by governments over the postwar period. One is the modern British party system. Governments, it is argued, may feel tied to the doctrinal views expressed in the party manifesto. Thus they may feel obliged to implement a manifesto despite the later discovery of the factors ignored or underestimated by party zealots when the commitment was initially made. Or, if the commitment is abandoned in the light of changing circumstances such as altered economic conditions, the party may lose their own supporters and present an uncertain and divided picture to the electorate. Both major parties have in their different ways suffered from this characteristic of Britain's system of party competition. And some would go further and say that the tendency of modern governments to reverse the legislation of their predecessors in the light of their own manifesto commitments is itself an important source of uncertainty and weakness.

A second major explanation of policy failures highlights the role of the Civil Service in the decision-making and implementation processes of government. Although the Civil Service will be examined in more detail later (see chapter 4) it is necessary here to outline the part it plays in the construction and implementation of government policies. It is not simply that Labour politicians and commentators may be tempted to blame an 'elitist' Civil Service for impeding socialist policies or that Conservatives may suspect that civil servants have a vested interest in preserving collectivism; it is rather that civil servants can too easily become insulated from the outside world. Thus, if ministers wholly rely on officials for policy advice, they may neglect opinion from other quarters, especially if there is a strong departmental policy which coincides with the sympathies of a particular government.

In addition to these two potential sources of error there are features of the cabinet system itself which may weaken the quality of decision-making. If the cabinet is viewed as the institution with responsibility for major policy decisions, one might expect the questions which come up to the cabinet for resolution to be the most significant ones, and that the cabinet would be the place where those decisions with the greatest implications for the rest of government policy were taken. Yet the reality is by no means as logical or as consistent as that. Apart from parliamentary business, the only issues which seem to be regularly discussed as a matter of course by the cabinet are those related to foreign affairs and defence. In many other fields the cabinet is largely a body which ratifies decisions which will have been taken elsewhere – in cabinet committees, through direct negotiations between Treasury ministers and the spending departments, or in committees which operate at a sub-cabinet level. Sometimes – and much will obviously depend upon the personal style of a prime minister – the decision will have been taken with a small group of colleagues without any kind of formal or institutional status. The management of cabinet decision-making is thus something that varies from administration to administration and can vary also within administrations; but to assume that it is the full cabinet which is the most important decision-making body across the board in functional terms would clearly be a mistake.

The structure of committees at all levels is thus a crucial part of the British system of government. Of especial importance is the structure of committees which underpins the full cabinet.[1] In order to preserve at least the fiction of full cabinet responsibility, it is a convention that the names and members of most cabinet committees are not revealed. Indeed cabinet ministers may not themselves always know the complete structure of cabinet committees in existence during an administration; and of course the prime minister can set up a new cabinet committee to cope with any special problem which emerges, such as the need to draft a white paper on government policy in a given area.

The most familiar cabinet committees are those which are standing committees. The committee dealing with the planning and progress of the government's legislative programme must be regarded as a permanent feature of the committee system. (This committee will normally include *inter alia* the whips on the government side in both the Lords and the Commons as the people most responsible for securing the passage of legislation on time.) The Defence and Foreign Affairs Committee must also be regarded as a permanent and known part of the structure of cabinet committees. Other committees set up to deal with specific issues which have suddenly erupted may be regarded as temporary at first; but they may then acquire permanence if the issue becomes part of the administration's regular concerns.

Conversely *ad hoc* committees – labelled Miscellaneous or Misc. – can be established in response to an emergency which then dies down. Such committees may quickly cease to have any meaning or function, although they will formally remain in existence. Thus the structure of any administration's cabinet committees may well contain ones which are moribund. The real significance of *ad hoc* committees at any one time can probably only be known by the prime minister and his or her closest cabinet colleagues. However, Richard Crossman and others have made the point that the use of miscellaneous committees – as opposed to regular standing committees of the cabinet – tends to enhance prime ministerial power because the prime minister can appoint the members to an *ad hoc* committee and define its terms of reference in a way which is not possible with standing committees. Even with these powers however prime ministers may find that they wish to bypass the formal structure of cabinet and cabinet committees altogether. An example of this occurred in 1981 when the 'E' committee of the cabinet allegedly became so leaky that major discussions of future economic policy were effectively transferred elsewhere.

The need to associate the cabinet as a whole with decisions taken by only some of its members and which may not have been comprehensively discussed in cabinet derives from the nature of cabinet government itself. Collective responsibility in the British system demands that a decision taken by government must be defended by all the members of the cabinet, regardless of whether those members as individuals were initially in favour of it. The divisions inside the Labour Party have in recent years caused this doctrine to be interpreted rather more flexibly; but in essence the doctrine of collective responsibility still requires a minister to resign from the administration if he cannot support the final decision of the cabinet on an issue. Yet it would obviously be a mistake to assume from this formal doctrine that all the cabinet's individual members are equally significant in the decision-making process. The special position of the prime minister is clear and will be discussed in detail later; but on many matters the chancellor of the Exchequer is also at an advantage in relation to his cabinet colleagues. The Treasury remains a law unto itself in the Whitehall hierarchy, and its superior position has in the past occasioned attempts to reduce its influence by redistributing its functions. Yet its role remains crucial to the whole strategy of an administration – although it has long been a curious feature of British government that the budget which embodies the most salient aspects of that strategy is not revealed to the cabinet as a whole until it is much too late for changes to be suggested.

The leadership which the prime minister exercises within the cabinet is of great significance because it enables the system of collective cabinet government – which might otherwise prove so unwieldy – to function smoothly. It is not necessary here to rehearse all the academic arguments about the relative powers of the prime minister and the cabinet, nor to see that relationship in the stark terms employed by some contributors to the debate. The interests of a prime minister and his cabinet are usually the same and in any serious conflict a prime minister could not follow policies he could not persuade a majority of his cabinet colleagues to back. Undoubtedly he has the power to delay matters and to shape the form in which they come to cabinet; and he certainly has superior opportunities to control the debate within the cabinet. But a prime minister is unlikely to want to exploit such advantages unless he feels that there is also a substantial body of opinion in cabinet on his side.

The prime minister's position will normally stem from his or her leadership of the political party which has won a majority of seats at a general election. The fact that the prime minister will be the leader of the largest party in the House of Commons thus confers authority on him or her in Parliament – although the amount of time which modern prime ministers can devote to the House of Commons has declined since Baldwin's day, despite the prominence of Prime Minister's Question Time and the occasional set speeches on the floor of the House. Moreover since 1942 the office of leader of the House of Commons has been separated from the premiership as it was also, albeit temporarily, during the Lloyd George coalition government of 1916–22.

The authority conferred on the prime minister as leader of his party in the country varies between the two major parties. In particular the autonomy of a Conservative leader is generally greater than that of a Labour leader both because of the different traditions which exist in the two parties and because, in tangible terms, the Conservative Party leader has greater control over the making and breaking of political reputations than has his or her Labour opposite number. To become a Conservative minister it is necessary to attract the attention of the leader, and usually an apprenticeship will be served while the party is in opposition. When the Labour Party is in opposition, however, the Parliamentary Labour Party as a whole elects the central core of the shadow cabinet, so that the leader has to work with some colleagues who may not be his personal choice. Moreover there is much more scope in the Labour Party to build up a reputation by cultivating the party's extra-parliamentary elements. Thus although a Labour prime minister – like his Tory counterpart – is constitution-ally free to decide who shall hold what office in his administration, he operates under some additional constraints and cannot necessarily count on personal loyalty to the same extent.

The changes in the Labour Party's arrangements by which the leader (and the deputy leader) are elected not by their parliamentary colleagues but by an electoral college in which MPs play a subordinate role have not yet been tested in relation to the impact which they will have on the relationship between the prime minister and his colleagues either in the party as a whole or in the cabinet. However it would appear likely that the effect would be further to weaken the prime minister's discretion.

As has been seen, an important part of the daily work of the cabinet is carried out through committees. The prime minister not only decides on the membership of the government and the cabinet as a whole but also on what cabinet committees shall be created and on who shall serve on them. The prime minister himself will chair the most important ones. The ability to control the structure of the cabinet committee system can be significant if a prime minister expects policy differences within his cabinet on specific issues or even if he wishes to minimize the general role played by an individual or group within his government. However such manipulation is best done with subtlety if it is not to prove counterproductive. The prime minister also controls the actual agenda of cabinet meetings, and the conclusions of cabinet discussions are recorded under his direction.

The conventions which govern the operation of cabinet government are usually flexible enough to allow every prime minister to adapt his cabinet's practices to the personalities and politics of his particular colleagues. On a trivial level this is reflected in such minor rules as whether or not smoking is allowed; on a more important level it may be reflected in the quite different procedural habits between different administrations. The prime minister decides how to conduct cabinet deliberations and determines whether he can assume consensus or should take a formal vote on a contentious issue. The formal vote – which may have become more frequent under recent Labour administrations – does of course entail the risk of identifying and perhaps alienating the minority; and many prime ministers would prefer to avoid a course which might lead to open splits and resignations. The prime minister can also decide on what terms he will allow matters decided in a cabinet committee to be reopened in full cabinet. Harold Wilson, for example, operated the convention that issues settled in a cabinet committee could only be raised again in full cabinet with the consent of the committee's chairman or the prime minister. Such a rule gives the prime minister substantial power: as he determines the composition of these committees he can thereby isolate opposition and structure the agenda of cabinet debate. Edward Heath, on the other hand, appears not to have needed such a rule – presumably because he had a cabinet that was more homogeneous in outlook than that of Harold Wilson.[12] Margaret Thatcher began her period as prime minister with a cabinet which was not entirely of her ideological persuasion; and although she was able to bring it more in line with her thinking there still seems to be a sense in which the Thatcher style of management is not entirely in harmony with the formal structure of cabinet government.

The desirability of avoiding confrontation in full cabinet acts as a powerful incentive to ministers and to the prime minister to iron out inter-departmental political and personal differences in committee. If a dispute is serious enough of course the most rigid conventions will not contain it; but matters rarely reach that level of conflict.

Whatever machinery is created to facilitate its business – and although in a body of the cabinet's size an informal hierarchy of some kind is bound to develop – the cabinet itself remains the decisive element. The published lists of ministers give the order of precedence among them determined by the prime minister, but whether an inner cabinet of some kind develops in addition is wholly a matter for him to decide. Formal indications of the existence of an inner cabinet, such as Harold Wilson's 1968 announcement of the establishment of a Parliamentary Committee, are unusual and that particular experiment did not survive long. After Harold Wilson resumed office in 1974 a new form of 'inner cabinet' consisting of the head of the social services departments and the prime minister was created with a view to improving the overall coordination of the services offered by government and their administration and expenditure.

The system is also flexible enough to respond to an external emergency. Thus in making the decisions in response to the Argentine invasion of the Falkland Islands in 1982, the prime minister worked with a subcommittee of her colleagues on the defence and foreign affairs committee. Through this small working group the whole conduct of the war was directed, but it proved able to accommodate the chancellor of the Duchy of Lancaster – Mr Cecil Parkinson – who was then chairman of the Conservative Party and thus presumably in close touch with opinion as well as being a close political ally of the prime minister.

One variation in the cabinet system has been in the size of the cabinet, which in recent years has fluctuated between seventeen and twenty-three. Each prime minister has tried to create a cabinet of what he or she regards as the optimum size, but each has been subject to political and personal constraints. There must be enough members to man the principal committees of the cabinet and to provide posts for the leading party figures whom the prime minister wants to include. Most prime ministers have however found it easier to augment than to diminish the size of their cabinets. Mrs Thatcher started her administration in 1979 with a cabinet of twenty-two and reduced it to twenty-one after the 1983 general election by merging the departments of Trade and Industry into a single department; with

79

the appointment in 1984 of a Minister Without Portfolio with special responsibilities for dealing with unemployment, the number went up to twenty-two again.

But cabinet posts are not the only ones in an administration to which the prime minister has the power of appointment. The total number of ministers of all ranks had reached 100 before 1970; the Heath government made some reductions but the upward growth was resumed in the Labour administration that followed that of 1970–4. In July 1978 ministers numbered 113, of whom 97 were in the House of Commons. Mrs Thatcher made reductions again so that in February 1984 the Ministry numbered 101, of whom 79 were in the House of Commons. This still means that a high proportion of members on the government side of the House are subject to collective discipline in addition to the normal loyalty and pressures exerted by the whips. The number is further increased if the unpaid parliamentary private secretaries attached to individual ministers are also taken into account, since they are also expected to toe the line in relation to voting behaviour. Furthermore, although chosen by the ministers they serve, it is to the prime minister that they look for promotion. These formidable powers of patronage must be taken into account when reckoning the weight of the prime minister in the British cabinet system.

The Departments

There are no clear doctrines governing the appropriate scope of a single department or the correct distribution of functions between departments. No attempt at an overall view of this problem has been made since the Haldane Committee reported in 1918.[3] That Committee, like all other efforts at resolving this question, was influenced by contemporary controversies over particular issues. The guiding principle of the Haldane Report was that government work should be organized according to the service rendered rather than the clients served; thus it was felt that all questions of health, whether adults or children were concerned, should be the responsibility of a single ministry. On the whole this principle has been followed in British government, but never with complete consistency. As services have multiplied a needy person or family might require attention from a number of different government agencies. Critics have frequently urged reorganization of departments on the basis of a more family-centred approach, so that all a family's social policy needs would be handled by a single department. Such an approach was supported by the Seebohm Committee on the Social Services (1965–8) and by the Redcliffe-Maud Commission on Local Government (1969). However it has been implemented only to a very limited extent, and voluntary agencies such as the National Council of Voluntary Organizations and the Citizens Advice Bureaus have also tried to meet the problems caused by the continuing dispersal of responsibilities between governmental agencies and departments.

As regards the organization of departments, governments have found three ways of dealing with the accretion of new functions. The first was that adopted by Winston Churchill between 1951 and 1953. The theory was that a number of government departments could each be headed by non-cabinet ministers under the supervision of a non-departmental minister or 'overlord' who would represent them in cabinet. This system may have owed something to Churchill's wartime experience. It could also have been influenced by the ideas of the former minister Leo Amery, who had argued for a small cabinet of ministers largely free from departmental duties and therefore theoretically able to spend more time on considerations of general policy.[4] The experiment did not however last long; its abolition was largely the result of parliamentary difficulties because MPs resented the blurring of the delineation of responsibility.

The second method of accommodating additional governmental functions has been to exclude some departmental heads from membership of the cabinet. They would be summoned to cabinet meetings only if their own department were directly involved in a matter on the agenda. Today this device is rare, because so much business cuts across departments and adequate discussion demands that every interest is represented at cabinet level.

The Ministry of Overseas Development created in 1969 was absorbed into the Foreign and Commonwealth Office in the Heath government of 1970–4. When Labour returned to power in 1974 the department was again made an independent one and its head was included in the cabinet for the first time. Under the Conservatives it has again been absorbed in the FCO.

The final method of avoiding the proliferation of departments has been to amalgamate existing departments into larger ones sometimes known as 'super-departments'. However this notion conceals two different processes of amalgamation. First the new unit could really be thought of as a single department and the ministries of which it is composed can lose their former identities. Such a process was envisaged when the Ministry of Defence was created in 1964: the political heads of the services – army, admiralty and air force – were demoted by stages to the rank of under-secretary. The second, alternative process was illustrated in the creation by the Heath administration of the Department of Trade and Industry and the Department of the Environment. Here the former departments were allowed to retain their identity and each retained a non-cabinet minister at its head. However the super-departments presented difficulties of their own: the Department of Trade and Industry began breaking up into its component parts even before the end of the Heath administration; and the Department of the Environment did not survive intact under the Labour government which took office in 1974.

The title of 'super-department' might be thought more appropriate for departments with more than one cabinet minister each: in 1978 this was the case with the Treasury and the Department of Health and Social Security but not the FCO.[5] The Foreign and Commonwealth Office, which had enjoyed that privilege more than once in the past, had by 1978 only one minister in the cabinet. In 1979 however when a peer – Lord Carrington – was appointed Foreign and Commonwealth Secretary, another cabinet minister, the lord privy seal, was allotted to the Foreign Office to be its spokesman in the Commons.

With few exceptions senior ministers are now styled 'secretaries of state'. Originally there was only one secretary of state: this history means that any secretary of state can if necessary formally act on behalf of any other. The proliferation of secretaries of state has also helped to limit the access of parliamentary committees to government papers, for there has been a convention since the nineteenth century that papers emanating from a department headed by a secretary of state could only be requested if Parliament itself presented a formal address to the sovereign.[6]

Apart from the law officers, who are in a special position, there are now three tiers of junior ministerial posts. The first is that officially styled 'ministers not in the cabinet' or 'other ministers'. In January 1985 there were in this category 28 such ministers as well as the parliamentary secretary to the Treasury – the government chief whip. It is this tier that has grown most in recent years; in the Attlee government of 1945–51 there were only four or five ministers outside the cabinet. The second tier consists of under-secretaries who numbered thirty. The third tier – known as parliamentary secretaries – has been declining in number and there were only four of them in 1978 and only one in 1985.

Ministers of state and other junior ministers may either share in the general work of their department or be allotted specific areas of responsibility. At a time when changes in the machinery of government were less frequent – broadly speaking before the second world war – parliamentary action was required to transfer functions from one ministry to another. However this process was simplified by the Ministers of the Crown (Transfer of Functions) Act of 1946. Since then parliamentary interest in such questions has declined except where burning political issues or political rivalries are involved. This means that reorganizations can proceed relatively easily. The consequent fluctuations are reflected in the figures: there were twenty-five departments in 1965–6; nineteen in 1970; and only fifteen in 1971. By 1976 the number was up again to twenty; in 1984 it was eighteen.

It could be argued that the disadvantages of constant change are offset by the advantages of political and administrative flexibility. For instance, when it was decided to transfer the personnel functions of the Treasury to the newly-created Civil Service Department, the prime minister was made the political head of the new department; it was thus possible to maintain his involvement with major personnel issues. Another cabinet minister with only a sinecure office, such as the lord privy seal or the chancellor of the Duchy of Lancaster, was able to handle the daily business of the department. Similarly when a senior minister was needed to negotiate the details of British entry into the European Communities the chancellor of the Duchy of Lancaster was given a place in the Foreign and Commonwealth Office, and then transferred to the Cabinet Office when the inter-departmental, as opposed to the purely diplomatic, aspect of the negotiations became uppermost. In 1972 with the development of the crisis in Northern Ireland and the reintroduction of direct rule from Westminster, a new department for Northern Ireland was created with its own secretary of state. New ministries can also be established to deal with finite pieces of work, such as the temporary Ministry of Aviation Supply which existed in 1970–1. In 1974 the lord president of the council was given a minister of state and a parliamentary secretary in the Privy Council Office to deal with the plans for devolution.

Pressures for further change are perhaps endemic in the system; and of course no one can predict when a crisis in some hitherto quiescent area of government may require administrative changes. Sometimes however even where there appears to be a good case for reform there are also reasons for not interfering with existing arrangements. The case for a ministry of justice is resisted on the grounds that the responsibilities for manning the courts and for law reform, for prosecutions and for civil suits on behalf of the government and for the police ought to remain divided between the lord chancellor's office, the law officers and the home secretary for the sake of liberty and impartiality. Even with the present threefold division there is some tension between the attorney-general's role as an adviser to government on the legal aspects of its policies and his role as an initiator of legal proceedings in matters where the public interest is involved and where he is supposed to exercise an independent judgement. This was seen in 1985 when the decision to prosecute Clive Ponting, a civil servant who had disclosed documents, proved controversial.

The creation of super-departments added a further complication to the already difficult issues presented by the convention of ministerial responsibility. It remains constitutional doctrine that the collective responsibility of the cabinet for policy does not impair the individual responsibility of ministers for the work of their departments. The burden of steering bills through Parliament and its committees must fall on ministers or their juniors because civil servants, while at hand for consultation, cannot participate in debate. If opposition develops it is the minister who must personally satisfy the critics; and yet the actual text of a bill is often expressed in obscure language on the basis of departmental instructions and may involve technical legal considerations beyond the lay politician's scope. However it is only in the most formal sense that a minister can be held responsible for decisions within his department taken in his name. The size of departments precludes his knowledge of more than a fraction of the routine business transacted by it.

It has often been argued that this situation precludes insisting upon ministerial resignation when a wrongful action has been taken for which he cannot be held directly responsible. It was argued that the Crichel Down case in 1954, when the then minister of agriculture resigned over a piece of maladministration, might prove to be the last such case. In 1983 neither the secretary of state for Northern Ireland nor his minister of state responsible for the prison service resigned after a massive prison breakout by terrorists. It is true that the invasion of the Falkland Islands in 1982 was followed by the resignation of the foreign secretary and of the lord privy seal (then in the FCO) as well as of the minister of state dealing with American affairs. But whether the culpability of their departments for the failure to anticipate this action justified the resignations or whether they succumbed to the House of Commons' feelings of frustration is an arguable point.[7]

The main reason for this relative immunity of ministers from parliamentary control is the solidarity of cabinets and the cohesiveness of parties. Even if it can be demonstrated that a questioned decision is a minister's own, it will be difficult to press home the attack against him. The appointment of a parliamentary commissioner for administration has not made much difference to this aspect of the system; if the commissioner's inquiries reveal a degree of personal responsibility on the minister's part the government may simply reject his findings.

In a super-department the element of fiction in the constitutional doctrine of ministerial responsibility is further increased because ultimate responsibility rests with the head of the department, the secretary of state. Parliament will not therefore readily accept a defence of the department's actions from the junior minister, even where he is the effective head of the relevant section of the super-department where the decision was taken and when the secretary of state is patently remote from the area concerned. This is also a powerful argument against the overlord system or any other device for separating matters of high policy from routine decisions. And it is also one reason for the government's reluctance to publish either the terms of reference or the membership of cabinet committees, as identifiable intermediate groups between the cabinet as a whole and individual ministers. Clearly there are pressures in the other direction, and the reluctance to reveal the mechanics of cabinet government would have to change if the suggestions of the Select Committee on the Parliamentary Commissioner for Administration were to be accepted and the PCA were given regular access to cabinet papers or cabinet documents were regularly made available to select committees.[8]

Non-departmental Governmental Agencies

The traditional picture of British government as a series of departments manned by permanent civil servants and headed by responsible ministers has never altogether corresponded to reality. As has been seen there have always been a number of boards, commissions or councils with nominated membership and with staff who may not necessarily be civil servants. Such bodies may exercise advisory, executive and even policy-making functions; the relationship with the minister most closely connected with their subjects can vary enormously.[9] These bodies have multiplied in recent years, but it is not only the degree of patronage they provide which has focused attention on them; it is also the fact that such bodies are not subject to even the minimal amounts of control which Parliament can exercise over departments.[10] The acronym quango – quasi – autonomous non-governmental organization – has been used to describe them: some of these bodies are regional or local rather than national in operation. In a national budget as vast as the United Kingdom's the expenditure on quangos cannot bulk very large, though the extravagance that had been detected was seen as an argument for tighter control over them.

The attempt after 1979 to curb their numbers, and the question of patronage, will be dealt with in the context of the government service generally. But it is clear that non-departmental agencies play an essential role in implementing government policy. Many of course have purely advisory functions, and it is the necessity for some of these functions that has been most often questioned. Some of these agencies are national; others are regional or local. And the methods of classifying them vary; certainly it is impossible to bring all quangos within a single classification. In 1976 the Civil Service Department listed 285 national and local bodies with full or part-time membership, but this excluded those bodies where, although members were unpaid, expenses might be claimed. The list was compiled at a time when the number of quangos was increasing: it was estimated that between 1974 and 1978 forty-two new quangos were created of which only five had purely advisory functions. Another method of classification is to take bodies whose staffing is subject to ministerial control, which means that at least half their income is derived from public funds. In 1978 such bodies numbered 171. If disqualification from membership of the House of Commons is taken as the criterion there were in 1975, excluding the courts, forty-five bodies whose members were disqualified from sitting in the House of Commons. This number rose to 107 in 1978.

In 1980 an official inquiry found that excluding the nationalized industries, some other public corporations and the National Health Service there were 489 bodies of an executive character employing 217,000 staff and controlling budgets totalling £5,800 million together with 1,561 advisory bodies and 67 sets of tribunals.[11] At the heart of this proliferation lies the vast extension of the varied services provided by the modern state, facing the citizen with the problem of securing these services where questions of conflict arise.

The origins of these agencies vary. Of major importance are the boards of the nationalized industries which were created on terms specified in the individual statutes nationalizing particular industries. Other agencies are created by ministers exercising powers conferred upon them by statute – the health authorities and the water authorities, development corporations, marketing boards and wage councils for example.

When the bill was introduced it was given out as the government's intention that local authority interests in water and sewage would be preserved by allowing them to suggest members for nomination by the minister to the new authorities. But the reduction in 1983 of the membership of the authorities from fifteen to nine members each was regarded as a further step towards removing local authority interest in this area.

A royal charter or warrant has been used in the past to set up royal commissions and the research councils. Advisory councils and similar groups which are normally unsalaried but whose members may receive fees as well as expenses can be established by ministerial fiat, although parliamentary sanction used to be thought necessary if a body was intended to be permanent. Even such bodies as the now defunct Metrication Board, the National Consumer Council and the now defunct Energy Commission had no legislative sanction, though the first two figured in white papers. (The Metrication Board was mentioned in a white paper for the first time a full three years after its creation.) White papers, despite appearances to the contrary, are simply documents expressing a government's intentions and have no legal force.

The variety of organizations spawned by government could also be classified on the basis of their types of activity. There are the familiar regulatory bodies, governing areas of commercial activity – for example the Civil Aviation Authority. Some bodies exist to distribute public money: the University Grants Committee, the research councils, the Arts Council and several sporting bodies are obvious examples. However other spending bodies also finance themselves by levies and fees.

The local quangos sometimes encroach upon the system of local self-government which, as will be seen in a later chapter, has been held to be a noteworthy characteristic of the British polity. In England there are nine regional water authorities which levy water and sewerage rates at their own discretion; eight regional economic planning councils; nine port or harbour authorities; fourteen regional health authorities and 192 district health authorities usually coterminous with the local authority providing personal social services. Some nationalized industries also maintain a regional organization; thus there are twelve area electricity boards. In addition there are attached to each nationalized industry a number of consultative councils and users' bodies designed to represent the consumers of the monopoly services which the nationalized industries provide.

Finally there are quangos which combine the promotion of social goals with quasi-judicial functions – the Commission for Racial Equality and the Equal Opportunities Commission for example.

Such a proliferation of agencies for which ministerial responsibility is at best ambiguous complicates both the operation and the description of the policy-making process. There is a permanent feedback from these bodies to the departments and to some extent they also make policy themselves.

The public corporations which run by far the larger part of the public sector of the economy raise complex questions for government organization. Their structure and their relationship with ministers and Parliament embody the doctrine that bodies which have a commercial role ought not to be organized like government departments or run by civil servants. Their boards, it is thought, ought to behave like the boards of private companies except that their economic target is not to maximize profit but merely to achieve a balance of profit and loss over a period of years. They may have for social reasons to provide some services that are unprofitable – railways in rural areas for example – but this is a matter for which the sponsoring minister rather than the board is supposed to take responsibility. The minister has specific powers relating to capital expenditure and borrowing by the nationalized industry and can issue a formal directive to the board if it is unwilling to take his advice.

It had originally been assumed that ministerial intervention in the affairs of a nationalized industry would be rare and would be confined to matters of general policy. Matters of day-to-day management would be left to the boards and their employees. Parliament was also debarred from asking questions about the detailed running of public corporations on the assumption that political intervention in these matters could and should be avoided. However experience has cast serious doubts on the practicability of this approach: the minister cannot limit himself simply to such matters as capital investment and uneconomic services. The important role played in the economy by the prices of products or services offered by the nationalized industries makes it impossible for governments worried about inflation to refrain from intervening, and the monopolistic position of these industries increases the pressure for such intervention. An even more significant factor is that the employees in these industries make up a large part of the total workforce, so that the success of any form of incomes policy will depend on the wage settlements in the public sector. Not only does this situation produce inter-departmental strife as ministers primarily concerned with industrial peace clash with those primarily concerned with keeping inflation under control; it can also cause ministers to intervene in the policies of the corporations in order to maintain employment even where purely economic criteria would suggest the need to reduce the workforce.

Nearly all the principal public corporations have failed for much of the time to meet the demands that they should be run on ordinary commercial lines and balance their budgets. Huge losses that have to be met from the public purse – either by taxation or by borrowing or by both – have in some cases become normal. The idea that these enterprises could be shielded from political pressures and scrutiny in a way not possible for central-local relationships for example has therefore proved illusory.

In the late 1960s there was a fashionable idea that central government departments could usefully 'hive off' certain functions – usually ones with limited political implications – into distinct units which could be made separately accountable for their activities. Experience with the public corporations may have discouraged this development. The position of ministers in relation to them has been an uneasy one, for it appears that ministers have exercised less authority over the boards of these corporations than the language of the original nationalization statutes might suggest. Ministers have been unwilling to incur the odium associated with issuing formal directives to the industries and have therefore tried to achieve their aims by bargaining with the boards in a manner that blurs the ultimate responsibility for policy. Their only really important sanction – that of refusing money for investment – is a rather blunt weapon. To use that weapon successfully a minister must know the business from the inside; to be in that position the minister and his department would have to duplicate work already done by the boards in amassing the necessary information.

Another difficulty is that ministers cannot easily use their authority to nominate members of boards in order to influence policy. The opportunity to nominate chairmen largely depends upon the accidents of retirement or death, while some other board members will be required to have specialist knowledge of the industry. Thus the area of recruitment is limited. It is difficult to dismiss a board member or a chairman without risking the accusation of political bias or of manipulating the nationalized industries as part of a spoils system. The result is a built-in tension between the chairmen of these boards who are mainly conscious of economic criteria and their sponsoring ministers who are alive to social and political considerations. It is therefore not surprising that in the 1970s a number of chairmen of nationalized industries left them for the private sector, nor that then and later such posts proved difficult to fill.

A further complication was introduced by the commitment of the incoming Conservative government in 1979 to seek to return as much as possible of the publicly-owned sector of the economy to private hands – the policy known as 'privatization'. Some chairmen of nationalized industries were appointed because their sympathy with this policy made it likely that they would devote their energies to making it possible for the corporation to be privatized on the most favourable terms, or to dispose of such parts of the operation as might seem to have a healthier future in the private sector. Given the general opposition of the trade unions to any measures of privatization, such an assignment called for political as well as financial and managerial skills of the highest order. In the case of public monopolies such as gas and electricity – which were capable of making considerable profits – there was also the tension between the Treasury, which wished to see those profits enhanced for the public purse, and the Department of Energy, which like the industries themselves wished to have a pricing policy more attuned to the needs of the consumer and to lowering the costs of industry.

If ministers find themselves frustrated in their dealings with the nationalized industries, Parliament finds itself in an even more ambiguous situation. The former Select Committee on Nationalized Industries which disappeared in the 1979 reforms of the select committee structure complained that too little information was made available to allow it to exercise a proper degree of supervision. Since 1979 two of the new department-related committees – the Select Committee on Energy and the Select Committee on Trade and Industry – have divided the work related to the nationalized industries. But although departments have been more forthcoming with information about the working of the industries, it nevertheless remains true that there is an inherent contradiction between demands for public corporations to behave more like private enterprise and the wish to see the nationalized industries supervised more closely by Parliament. Close supervision by the legislature inevitably involves a burden on management and risks revealing commercial judgements which would not be revealed in the private sector.

Ministers and Civil Servants

It has been seen that one of the reasons for experimenting with the public corporations was that it was not felt desirable to reproduce in commercial enterprises the structural features of a government department. Of especial importance among those features was the relationship between ministers and their civil servants.

Ministers are not normally expected to be specialists in the subject matter of their departments, and the high turnover of ministers would itself preclude familiarity with the policies and problems involved. The political skills which a minister is supposed to contribute are allegedly independent of the subject matter with which he has to deal, so that he relies heavily on his civil servants for advice on policy matters. To be effective he must therefore become acquainted as quickly as possible with the outlines of the department's responsibilities and the principal personalities within it.[12]

The suitability of the present higher Civil Service to the conditions of modern Britain will be examined in a later chapter; however it is undoubtedly the case that the traditional conventions of ministerial responsibility give it great power. It was perhaps inevitable that as this power became more obvious there should be attempts to penetrate the veil of official anonymity, and in fact the questioning of civil servants on matters with a policy content by parliamentary select committees has become much more frequent. Similarly tribunals and other instruments of public inquiry, as well as the parliamentary commissioner for administration, have also become readier to name individual civil servants or to reveal circumstances which make identification possible.

The power of the Civil Service is inevitably reinforced by the frequent reshuffles of departmental ministers: without continuity in a department's political leadership the department can develop its own attitude or tradition, and this may prove difficult for an incoming minister to accommodate or make his own. While this situation has been to some extent alleviated by the introduction of 'special advisers' with the status of temporary civil servants, some people argue that this still leaves the minister dangerously isolated and have pressed the case for a ministerial *cabinet* within each department. Such a system on the continental model would allow a minister to appoint a body of advisers and assistants from outside as well as from inside government service. It would be distinct from the present private office of a minister, which is staffed by a small group of promising younger civil servants selected from within the minister's own department. In fact the French *cabinet* – the prototype for this idea – consists of civil servants from different branches of government; it could be argued that what British ministers need is not so much outsiders but a group of civil servants seconded from other departments who can help them function effectively in cabinet committees, in full cabinet and inside the department itself. This suggestion draws attention to the fact that the Civil Service is not monolithic: each department develops its own perspectives, which may nevertheless have to be transcended if new policy initiatives are to be successful.

The suggestion that British ministers should have *cabinets* on the continental model would entail major changes in administrative practice. Such a development would in particular affect the position of the permanent secretary in each department, who is in many ways the central non-political figure in British administration. For it is the permanent secretary, appointed by the prime minister in consultation with the head of the home civil service when a vacancy arises, who is both the intermediary through whom a department's views are made known to the minister and the individual responsible for ensuring that the minister's policy is carried into effect.

Objections to the introduction of a *cabinet* system are partly attributable to the natural reluctance of civil servants to downgrade the post of permanent secretary, which currently represents the summit of the ambitions of the members of a highly self-conscious professional body. In addition there is the objection that departments are not to be treated as self-sufficient empires, even if they do develop their own distinct characteristics. Much work has to be done through inter-departmental committees, and although their proliferation was one of the reasons for creating super-departments, the increase in the size of departments has not much altered this aspect of government. Responsibility for manning such committees at the official level must rest with the regular departmental machine. Much can be done by informal departmental consultation between private offices but, if chaos is to be avoided, regular procedures and formal record-keeping are essential; there is no safe way in which the departmental hierarchy can be bypassed. This is also true of the departmental consultation with the Treasury on expenditure which all departments undertake on a regular basis.

The relations between ministers and civil servants have rested upon a general assumption that they work in harmony for the achievement of national purposes as defined by the government of the day. Such a relationship depends in large measure on unwritten understandings, including a commitment by ministers to the general welfare of civil servants and a feeling of professional responsibility on the part of the civil servants themselves. To some extent this position was eroded during the period when the Civil Service was undergoing the vast expansion of the postwar years.[13] The growth of unionization among civil servants and the freedom gained in 1946 for such unions to affiliate to the TUC, the actual disruption of public services including security services by some civil servants in 1979 and 1981 and, on the other side, the breakdown of the Whitley Council system (which had fixed Civil Service pay since the first world war) all produced a crisis of morale in Whitehall. Together these developments created a feeling among ministers that civil servants could no longer be relied upon to put the national interest first; and among civil servants there developed a feeling that ministers were unappreciative of their work and responsibilities. Although the Civil Service will be discussed in detail in a later chapter it must be remembered that these developments have not merely affected the morale of civil servants but have had important repercussions on the general relationship between ministers and officials.

The Machinery of Coordination

In the interwar years the prime minister, as first lord of the Treasury, had as his principal advisers the permanent secretary, who was also head of the civil service, and the secretary to the cabinet, who was also at the time secretary to the revived Committee of Imperial Defence; thus coordination of government business was to some extent achieved by these two powerful civil servants. The Foreign Office remained somewhat apart from the general governmental machine and kept its separate procedures for recruitment and promotion. It was the policy consequences of this separation which caused Neville Chamberlain during his premiership to use Sir Horace Wilson, a home civil servant, as his personal adviser on foreign policy.

In the postwar period a number of changes occurred: the Committee of Imperial Defence was not revived; the Cabinet Office took on wider coordinating functions; and the Treasury acquired new responsibilities and hence more contact with other departments as more interventionist and positive economic policies were adopted. For a time the position of permanent secretary of the Treasury was divided into two posts, with one of the holders also acting as secretary to the cabinet and the other as head of the Home Civil Service. When, following the Fulton Committee recommendations on the Home Civil Service in 1968, a separate Civil Service Department was established and its permanent secretary became head of the Home Civil Service, he became the prime minister's adviser on both personnel matters and the machinery of government. The Treasury then had only one permanent secretary combining responsibility for financial and economic matters. However, for a brief period between 1964 and 1966 the short-term and long-term aspects of economic management were divorced from each other and a specialized department (the Department of Economic Affairs) attempted to exercise responsibilities for long-term planning and growth as opposed to short-term financial control.

As already mentioned and as will be further detailed later, the Civil

Service Department itself was abolished in 1981 and its work divided between the Treasury and a new department – the Management and Personnel Office – which was absorbed as a unit into the Cabinet Office after the 1983 general election. The secretary to the cabinet, who thereby also became head of the Home Civil Service, emerged from all these changes with even more influence than he had previously enjoyed on both the substance of policy and the co-ordination of the governmental machine. The personal position of the secretary to the cabinet should however be distinguished from the cabinet secretariat over which he presides. The secretariat is responsible for framing and circulating the minutes of the cabinet and its committees. It can therefore exert (subject to the prime minister's authority) considerable influence by its choice of the wording of cabinet conclusions should they be left unclear by the discussions. When cabinets are divided and verbal compromises are necessary to maintain the appearance of unity, this role can be extremely important. There is also the tendency for the secretary to the cabinet – whose tenure of the post may outlast several administrations – to regard himself as the custodian of the collective cabinet conscience. Such would appear to be the rationale of allowing him to act as arbiter of what it is proper for ministers to publish in their memoirs or of what documents the parliamentary commissioner for administration may see.

The coordinating role of the Cabinet Office was strengthened in October 1970 by the creation of a new unit within it – a body which was originally styled the central capability unit but which came to be known as the Central Policy Review Staff or 'think-tank'.[14] The creation of a Central Policy Review Staff was announced in a white paper about the new Conservative administration's projected measures to improve the management of government business.[15] It was explained that the new instrument was to be at the service of all ministers, to enable them to work out the implications of their basic strategy in terms of policies in specific areas and to establish relative priorities to be given to different sectors of their programme as a whole. It was ostensibly intended to fill the gap created by the alleged inability of ministers to know enough about the policies of other departments to be able to make a valuable contribution to collective decision-making. The think-tank was thus intended to give them that basic source of additional information. It was however clear that the inquiries the CPRS would be asked to undertake would be decided largely by the prime minister; indeed it was in some quarters regarded as the nucleus of a prime minister's department. It was also clear from the recruitment of the original CPRS – mainly from economists and from people with business experience – that the emphasis would be on cost-benefit analysis of long-term programmes and individual projects.

In its early years the CPRS enjoyed considerable advantages. Its initial membership of about sixteen was able to make free use of outside expertise. The first chairman, Lord Rothschild, was eminent both as a scientist and a man of affairs. He understood the need to combine long-term inquiries with, where necessary, a consideration of short-term and medium-term issues so that his team never felt totally detached from the activities of government itself.

Perhaps the CPRS had already lost some of its initial glamour even before the fall of the Heath government of 1970–4. Lord Rothschild himself ran into trouble when he gave his personal views on the state of the nation in a public speech which earned a rebuke from the prime minister – a rebuke which raised the question of the extent to which temporary advisers and units of the CPRS kind were covered by the existing Civil Service conventions of political neutrality and anonymity. Moreover, growing concern with the immediate economic and industrial situation detracted from interest in long-term issues, as perhaps it always will do once the first period of an administration is past.

Under the Labour government of 1974–9 the CPRS became even more firmly embedded in the Cabinet Office system and its head, Sir Kenneth Berrill – whose experience was basically that of a Treasury official – did not have the political standing to play the kind of independent role that Lord Rothschild had done.

Although the CPRS survived the Wilson, Callaghan and the first Thatcher administrations, it was abolished after the 1983 general election. It was however widely felt that although the particular formula might not have worked too well, there ought to be some institution within the governmental machine which could provide long-range thinking and that such a function could not simply be left to the departments themselves or to independent 'think-tanks'. The fact that the post of chief scientific adviser to the government was retained in the Cabinet Office after the demise of the CPRS perhaps underlines the extent to which Whitehall had accepted the case for maintaining a formal link between the central coordinating machinery of government and individuals capable of analysing the policy implications of scientific developments.[16]

4 　 The Civil Service

Critics of the British system of government from the mid-1960s onwards did not exclude the Civil Service from their indictment. Indeed it increasingly became the focus of a wide range of attacks on the character of decision-making in the United Kingdom and on the overall performance of the machinery of government. Nor was it surprising that this should be so. The Civil Service was not only responsible for carrying into effect the vastly increased range of responsibilities which the state had assumed over the twentieth century, but especially since 1945; it also provided the principal and in some cases the exclusive source of advice available to ministers in shaping their policies. The criticisms of the British bureaucracy followed two different though sometimes overlapping paths. Between the return of Labour to office in 1964 and the Conservative victory in 1979 the main emphasis was on the quality and character of the British Civil Service and the extent to which it was an appropriate vehicle for managing a modern welfare state. Did the higher Civil Service – i.e. the grades most responsible for policy advice – represent too narrow a stratum of British society to enable it to be effective? Was sufficient weight given to specialist training and qualifications – such as those of the engineer and of the economist – as opposed to the more general evidence of educational achievement which had previously been held sufficient? And was the Civil Service as an organization inevitably wedded to values which would prove to be in conflict with a government which wished to implement radical policies, whether of the right or the left?

From 1979, however, a different emphasis in the debates about the role of the Civil Service can be detected. Much more attention was paid to improving the internal efficiency of departments in the hope that better results could be obtained from the money spent, and the total numbers of civil servants limited or reduced with consequent savings to the public purse.

In pursuit of these objectives new machinery was devised for dealing with the Civil Service at the centre, although this in turn was subject to more than one remodelling. A clash also developed between the government's demands for economy and the established methods of dealing with Civil Service pay. Reductions in manpower from some

730,000 to some 640,000 were achieved between 1979 and 1983; over half by achieving greater efficiency, about 20 per cent by dropping or materially curtailing the functions of central government; and about 10 per cent by transferring functions to the private sector. A further small cosmetic cut was made by transferring functions to non-departmental public bodies – those which are sometimes referred to as quangos.[1]

The History of the British Civil Service

Although the permanent Civil Service has a long history – some of its contemporary features were indeed visible by the seventeenth century, as the diary of Samuel Pepys abundantly illustrates – the modern history of the British Civil Service starts with the Northcote-Trevelyan Report of November 1853. Thus when the Fulton Committee came to examine the Service in the 1960s it found that it owed its principal features of recruitment, structure and training to recommendations laid down over a century before.

The principles governing the higher reaches of the Civil Service as it existed in the 1960s can be summarized without much difficulty. First, government service was a commitment normally entered into for the whole of a working career and it was remunerated with that fact in mind. Entrance to the Civil Service was on the basis of merit: recruitment was by objective tests designed to provide evidence of suitability and for the highest grades these were open and competitive examinations. Patronage – the necessity for nomination for entry to such a competition – was gradually eliminated. It survived longer in the Diplomatic Service, however, and until the integration of the Diplomatic Service with the Foreign Office in 1919, it was essential for aspiring diplomats to have a private income.

The work of the Civil Service in its upper strata was broadly administrative: it was concerned with organizing and carrying out the business of the various departments and with advising ministers on matters of policy, including the preparation of primary and secondary legislation. The qualities sought in a civil servant – order, method and the ability to work with others – did not include the entrepreneurial or managerial talents. It was assumed that a civil servant's work called for little specialized knowledge or technical expertise and it was believed that particular training could be acquired on the job. The examinations for entry into what was known as the 'administrative class' were thus tailored to those who had recently graduated from a university, without regard to the subjects which they had studied there. The purely written examinations had given way since 1945 to the so-called 'method II' mode of entry which involved a shortened qualifying examination and extended interviews.[2]

Recruitment was central not departmental, and it was the responsibility of the Civil Service Commission – an independent body appointed by the Crown. While this independence was certainly a guarantee against ministerial patronage where individual appointments were concerned, the Commission was aware of general Whitehall policy on such issues as recruitment. It had become increasingly necessary to recruit specialists of various kinds (such as lawyers, scientists, technologists, statisticians and economists) into government service; yet it had not been thought necessary to fit them into the general framework of the service or to open the most senior posts to them. They remained within distinct hierarchies of specialists separate from the general administrators who ultimately controlled their work.

A civil servant's qualifications at entry would usually determine the level at which he would work throughout his career. The 'administrative class' was, as has been seen, drawn from university graduates; entry into the 'executive class' demanded completion of the secondary school curriculum. Earlier school-leavers could join the 'clerical class'. However, by the 1960s there had been many changes in the British educational system so that a higher proportion of those who completed school were going on to universities. Because the entry into the 'administrative class' was still very limited, many of these graduates were competing for places in the executive class. Although promotion between classes was not unusual, the general expectation was that a recruit's future career would be within his class.

By comparison with the pattern of recruitment of future civil servants in continental European countries the most striking difference was the absence of any demand for legal training or economic expertise. Also, because entry into the Civil Service usually followed directly after the three- or four-year undergraduate degree, the age of entry was lower in Britain than in the European administrative *corps*. Because of the general importance of finance and the particular significance attached to economy in public expenditure when the system was created, the Treasury was recognized as the senior Whitehall department, entitled to be consulted in all matters relating to expenditure and staffing. It was thus understandable that the permanent secretary to the Treasury should have been styled in addition 'Head of the Civil Service' by the Treasury circular of 15 September 1919.[3] Senior Civil Service appointments were thereafter made by the prime minister on the advice of the head of the (Home) Civil Service. This system gave the whole Civil Service a common ethos, although the Foreign Office successfully maintained its independence.

The first move towards change was made in 1966 when the government set up a Committee on the Civil Service under Lord Fulton, an academic with first-hand experience of the Civil Service. The Committee itself was dominated by two senior members of the Civil Service and its conclusions, which were not particularly radical, very much reflected the mood of the time, especially the optimistic assumptions about an expansion of governmental activity financed by a rising growth rate.[4] It wanted to expand access to the higher Civil Service and to reduce the advantages which Oxford and Cambridge enjoyed in the entrance competition. The Committee was conscious of the criticism that the Civil Service had failed to develop a proper role for scientists and technologists and that it had also failed to develop post-entry training. Both of these deficiencies, in the Committee's opinion, made the Service incapable of meeting the demands of a society which appeared to need guiding through a 'white-hot technological revolution'. The Committee also believed that there might be benefits in 'hiving off' to public bodies outside the routine control of ministers some of the functions then discharged by the Civil Service.

However, even before the Fulton Report appeared it was clear that the Committee's terms of reference would hardly permit it to deal with one of the central weaknesses of British government – what one of the present writers called at the time 'the appalling speed of the ministerial merry-go-round'.[5] Ministers, like 'transient and embarrassed phantoms', stayed in office for too short a time to learn the business of vast departments and could only function properly if their permanent secretaries were at least chosen from within the department and not, as was then common, from a different one. No change was recommended in this respect by the Report, and the same criticism of the British method of administration was voiced by Lord Crowther-Hunt, himself a member of the Fulton Committee, in a memorandum to the Expenditure Committee in June 1977.[6]

The Fulton Committee did recommend by a majority that preference in the recruitment of civil servants should be given to those with degrees in subjects thought to be relevant to government, especially the social sciences. This recommendation was rejected by the government, which preferred the traditional view that ability could best be tested by measuring achievement in any academic discipline and that special governmental needs should be covered by

in-service training. In other respects the Committee's recommendations found more favour. It recommended the establishment of a
Civil Service Department which would take over that part of the
Treasury's work related to personnel and staffing and hitherto
performed by the Pay and Management Group within the Treasury.
The Civil Service Department would be under the prime minister.
The Committee also recommended that the system of classes –
administrative, executive and clerical – should be abolished and
replaced by a unified grading system which could cover the whole of
the non-industrial part of the Civil Service. Among the new
administrators – the counterparts of the old administrative and
executive classes – there should be specialization between economic
and financial administrators on the one hand and social administrators on the other. Scientists, engineers and other professionals
should be given opportunities to rise to managerial positions; the
importance of training should be recognized by the establishment of a
Civil Service College which would also have research functions; and
while it was assumed that the Civil Service should remain predominantly a career service, there should be greater mobility between
the Civil Service and other forms of employment. Such interchange, it
was thought, could be achieved by greater provision for late entry to
the Civil Service and the selective use of temporary appointments.

Other recommendations of the Fulton Committee related to the
machinery of government aspects of its inquiries rather than to the
intrinsic character of the Civil Service itself. For example, it
recommended – echoing the Haldane Report of 1919 – that all
departments should have planning units and that at the head of each
of these units there should be a senior policy adviser to assist the
minister. Inquiries into a number of other subjects such as 'hiving off'
were also suggested. In addition the Report attacked the great aura of
secrecy which it thought unnecessarily surrounded a great deal of
government.

Over the next decade some of the Committee's recommendations
were implemented but the progress made did not altogether silence
the critics. It was obvious that it would take some time to bring many
of the changes into effect and that, in making changes affecting the
careers of individual civil servants, regard would have to be paid to
the opinions of the Civil Service unions, which could be voiced
through the elaborate negotiating machinery of the Civil Service
Whitley Council.

The first step was the setting up of the Civil Service Department,
whose nucleus was formed from that part of the Treasury group
which was transferred to it. The prime minister was made the formal

head of the department but most day-to-day responsibilities were devolved upon another cabinet minister, a member of the House of Lords. Splitting up the Treasury in this way was not altogether acceptable to some civil servants, and in 1976 a former civil servant who had been a member of the Fulton Committee argued publicly that since the main period of reorganization was over, the headship of the Civil Service should revert to the Treasury.[7]

The Civil Service Commission was brought within the Civil Service Department. At the same time it was argued that since the Commission derived its authority from the latest relevant Order in Council — that of 1956 — and since individual members of the Commission were appointed not simply by ministers but by Orders in Council, the independence was fully preserved in the new system.

The Civil Service College which took over part of the work of the existing Centre for Administrative Studies was opened formally in June 1970.[8] Its role however has not been as important as that envisaged for it by the Fulton Committee. It has been preoccupied largely with providing specialist skills required in the more routine tasks of civil servants (e.g. the use of computers) and it has not made major innovations in training the upper echelons of the service — partly it is true because the more senior a civil servant is, the more difficult it becomes to release him for study or training. Nor has the college been involved to any considerable extent in research.

Some steps were taken to implement the Fulton idea of a unified Civil Service with a uniform grading system and maximum opportunities for promotion irrespective of a recruit's starting point. The reorganization began with what the Fulton Report had styled the Senior Policy and Management Group — the seven hundred or so top posts at under-secretary level or above. This group was henceforth to be treated as a single unit and the posts within it were to be open to those with general or specialist skills, including scientists. When an engineer from the Farnborough Research Station and the old Ministry of Supply became, after a spell in the Cabinet Office, the new permanent secretary at the Department of Education and Science this was hailed as 'the first real fruit of the Fulton reforms in this area'.[9] However the same example was also used by Lord Crowther-Hunt to make the point that the Fulton reforms were intended to give specialists the opportunity of reaching top positions in their own specialist subject areas rather than in other fields where they had little relevant expertise.

The decision to abolish the tripartite division between the administrative, executive and clerical classes was gradually implemented. The most obvious immediate effect was to abolish direct entry for some seventy to eighty graduates a year into the administrative class. Under the new system, the old rank of assistant principal – which had been the first rung of the ladder of the administrative class – was replaced by a larger category of entrants known as administrative trainees. Although under this revised system the number of successful graduate entrants doubled, only a proportion of them – the 'starred' entrants – could expect rapid promotion to the senior levels of the Service, while the remainder were left to strengthen the middle levels of the structure. The British Civil Service thus introduced, perhaps without intending to, something similar to the French distinction among graduates of the École Nationale d'Administration between those chosen for the *grands corps* and the rest.[10]

Despite the observations by the Fulton Committee about the undue predominance of Oxbridge graduates and its suggestions about how this imbalance might be corrected, there was no great alteration in subsequent years. The imbalance in part reflected the unwillingness of graduates from other universities to consider the Civil Service as a desirable and profitable career. Yet the predominance of Oxbridge graduates at the highest levels of the bureaucracy created the impression of a social as well as an educational bias, because these two ancient universities still admit a higher proportion of their students from independent schools than do other universities. The high proportion of Oxbridge graduates in the Civil Service caused a more specific concern because it was believed that the emphasis on general education in those universities as opposed to specialist training was inimical to the demands which a modern Civil Service would have to meet.

It is not surprising that when in 1977 the Expenditure Committee of the House of Commons came to look at developments in the Civil Service since the Fulton Committee's Report it found that some of the evidence presented to it echoed the Fulton themes.[11]

The other change was the return to what could be seen as a form of political patronage within the departmental machinery itself. The Fulton Committee approved the idea of ministers introducing experts who could help them in their own departments. To a minor extent this was taken advantage of both in the first Wilson administration and in the Heath administration of 1970–4. However, the practice was extended especially after Harold Wilson's return to power in 1974 when one began to see the appointment of individuals not because they were expert in some policy area connected with specific departments but rather because they were needed as political advisers. It was assumed that such individuals, who were often quite young and sometimes drawn from the staffs of relevant pressure groups, would help to keep ministers in touch with the party or sections of it. Cabinet ministers were confined to a maximum of two special appointments each; the policy unit established by Wilson in the prime minister's office varied in size from five to seven.[12] The degree of permissible involvement in politics, actually short of campaigning for election, remained somewhat obscure. In 1978, for instance, the list of 'special advisers' was for the first time included in *The Labour Party Directory*.

The original assumption was that such appointments would in any event terminate at the close of the administration under which they were appointed. In 1972 there was an agreement between the government and the Civil Service unions that such appointees could not remain as civil servants for more than five years without facing open competition. When Harold Wilson resigned in March 1976 there were twenty-eight holders of such posts and all resigned. Many were however reappointed under the Callaghan administration. In August 1978, when there were twenty-five such temporary ministerial advisers, it was announced that the five-year rule would no longer apply. Such advisers had not been included in the scope of the 1969 Order in Council whereby all persons proposed for permanent appointment to the Civil Service had to receive a certificate of suitability from the Civil Service Commission. The reason given was that the advisers could not be treated as permanent, since their tenure of office would come to an end with that of the government itself. It is understandable that the Civil Service unions should try to limit access to what might otherwise appear a form of back-door entry to the Service and a departure from the rules of open competition. At the same time there were attempts to extend the rights of permanent civil servants to engage in political activity, but as far as civil servants with responsibilities to ministers are concerned this development has been resisted.

In the 1976–7 session the Expenditure Committee of the House of Commons conducted as has been mentioned a further inquiry into the Civil Service. By this time there had been changes, and the atmosphere was very different, given that by the mid-1970s the growth of public expenditure – and its contribution to inflation – had become a preoccupation of government. Thus the priorities of both parties were very different from those of the expansionist 1960s. There was also a much greater volume of criticism of the whole governmental machine as Britain's economic failings became increasingly apparent.

At least one school of thought – illustrated in the Crossman diaries of the first Wilson administration – placed emphasis on the alleged resistance by the Civil Service to reform. The centralization of the Civil Service made it impossible for ministers on their own initiative to move out of their departments civil servants whose opinions or abilities they mistrusted. The head of the Civil Service, and behind him the prime minister, stood in the way of such action. There is reason to believe that similar feelings were entertained in the Heath government of 1970–4. The Civil Service as a whole felt itself to be on the defensive, and it was revealed in August 1978 that a committee of civil servants had been set up in October 1977 to discuss ways of improving the public image of the Service.

The Expenditure Committee found itself confronted in 1977–8 with arguments that the Fulton reforms had not been fully implemented, and with a number of additional suggestions for change. Like the Fulton Committee it concerned itself with questions of machinery and also with staff and training. The work of inquiry was done by the general subcommittee, but when the Report was presented to the Committee as a whole deep divisions were revealed. An alternative version was proposed and supported by eleven members of the full Committee led by Mr Brian Sedgemore, who had actually served on the subcommittee. The eleven Labour members were defeated by the vote of the Conservative members combined with the rest of the Labour members, a total of fifteen votes. The minority had wished to report that the real problem of the Civil Service was the unresponsiveness of civil servants to democratically chosen ministers whose wishes it was their duty to implement. Civil servants were seen as men who, while of 'superior intellect', nevertheless lacked the training or experience relevant to the tasks they had to perform, and who had therefore taken upon themselves the role of governing the country. According to this view the civil servants acted together across departmental boundaries and took advantage of ministers' difficulties to pursue policies of their own. The amendment continued by saying that it would 'be as wrong to accuse top civil servants of overt party political bias as it would be foolish not to recognize that Labour governments seeking to alter society in a socialist direction have more difficulty with civil servants (who are seeking in conjunction with other establishment figures from the City, the Bank of England, industry, the established Church and the monarchy to maintain the status quo) than do Conservative governments who wish to leave things roughly as they are'. The radical policies of even the Heath government had in this minority's view encountered obstruction from the Civil Service. In the case of the then Labour government the amendment alleged that civil servants at the Department of Industry had frustrated its interventionist policies and its proposals for industrial democracy as embodied in the Bullock Report.[13] It also drew attention to the Home Office, which was allegedly 'stuffed with reactionaries', and to the way some Foreign Office officials interpreted being a good European as being 'synonymous with selling out British interests'.

The recommendations of the minority related in part to the future composition of the higher Civil Service:

Whether through the appointment of powerful ministerial back-up teams or *'cabinets'* chosen by ministers and including Members of Parliament if ministers so desired and to whom civil servants at Deputy Secretary and Under Secretary level would be accountable, or through the developing role of political advisers, or through political appointments of top civil servants at Under Secretary level and above, or through other devices Ministers must inject more party political clout into the upper echelons of the administration.

This minority group also advocated strengthening the House of Commons committee system with the aim of placing 'far more power than at present in the hands of backbench Members of Parliament in general and in the hands of backbench members of the majority party in particular'.[14]

The majority report was far less radical. The Committee was obviously worried by the continued predominance of Oxbridge over other universities in the competition for places at the administrative trainee level and by the success of candidates from independent schools which, it was held in some quarters, were especially favoured in a system based on interviews. However all the Committee specifically asked for was better statistical information so that the possibilities of bias could be monitored. The Civil Service Commission of four civil servants was held to be too inbred and the Committee recommended that they should be balanced by outside part-time commissioners who would form the majority. The membership of the Final Selection Board should also be broadened. The Committee further recommended an examination of the work of the Civil Service College to see whether this could not be done by individual departments or by institutions outside the Civil Service. It was thought that the administrative trainee scheme should be abolished. Holders of good degrees should be allotted directly to jobs and should compete on equal terms with other graduates and nongraduates for entry to a new higher management training course. Completion of this course – to which candidates from the National Health Service, local government and the Diplomatic Service would also be admitted – would be a prerequisite for promotion beyond the rank of assistant secretary or its equivalent. The unified grading structure should be extended downwards through the Service and there should be further restraints on the employment of ex-civil servants by companies in a contractual relationship with government.

Worry about the possibility that civil servants who took up business appointments soon after retirement with firms with whom they had been dealing during their official career went back some time, and had resulted in the creation of a set of rules governing such appointments and obliging ex-civil servants to seek permission before taking them up. The rules drawn up in 1937, and which apply to diplomats and senior serving officers, were revised in 1975 when a committee was set up to advise the prime minister in relation to applications from permanent secretaries and certain other senior officials and military personnel of equivalent rank. In dealing with the applications the government has wanted to hold a balance between possible suggestions of undue influence and the desire to see people with administrative experience move into business and industry. On the whole few applications seem to have been turned down in recent years.[15] In the 1980s concern about a number of top civil servants accepting industrial appointments, especially in the defence industry, together with the possibility that senior civil servants might find themselves seeking outside careers at an earlier stage than before, led to inquiries by an all-party group of MPs and the consideration of sanctions which might be applied in the event of a civil servant breaching the rules.

The Expenditure Committee devoted some attention to the remuneration of civil servants – a topic of much controversy, since civil servants complained of the suspension of the Pay Research Unit which had been designed to establish comparability with jobs in the private sector. A new independent Pay Research Unit was proposed, and it was left that government would take upon itself any refusal to pay the salaries recommended if restraint was necessary in the interests of incomes policy. The 'inflation-proofing' of public service pensions under the Pensions Increase Act of 1971 and the Superannuation Act of 1972 was criticized; however given the existence of inflation-linked pension schemes elsewhere it was not suggested that inflation-proofing should now be abandoned – although review of the whole policy was in the Committee's view desirable.

The Committee accepted the view that ministers should normally be responsible for changes in the management of their departments, that special advisers had become an accepted feature of the system and that a cabinet minister should no longer be limited to two such advisers. A minister should be able to associate himself with a group of advisers – or even of backbench MPs, though without executive authority – if he thought this conducive to efficiency.

Suggestions were made for improving efficiency and for monitoring the effect of changes by a new system of financial accounting to Parliament. It was proposed that the office of comptroller and auditor-general should be strengthened and his department made more directly responsible to the House of Commons. A reconsideration of the relationship between the Civil Service and local government service was also recommended. The prime minister and the leader of the opposition, the committee suggested, should jointly consider a modification in the rules about non-disclosure of the papers of one administration to its successor.

On one main point the Committee's report represented a retreat from the Fulton proposals. It was now felt that separating the function of manning the Civil Service from that of monitoring its efficiency (which was done by the expenditure divisions of the Treasury) had not proved useful. The Committee therefore recommended that questions of manning should be returned to the Treasury. The Civil Service Department would thus be left only with limited personnel functions, including recruitment, training, pay and pensions responsibilities. The government took time to respond to these recommendations, and when it did so its reply was a tentative one. In its white paper of 15 March 1978 it stated that it had accepted wholly or in part thirty-one of the Committee's fifty-four recommendations; but it remained undecided as to whether the division of responsibilities between the Treasury and the Civil Service Department should be changed.[16] For the moment therefore the Fulton formula held good in that respect. The white paper emphasized the traditional doctrine of ministerial responsibility for the policies of departments and therefore insisted that the advice of civil servants to ministers should be 'confidential and objective' and that it was for ministers, not civil servants, to defend government policy before select committees. While accepting that special advisers should become an accepted feature of the Whitehall scene, the government reiterated its adherence to the long-established tradition that the British Civil Service should remain a non-political permanent career service.

The Conservative government elected in 1979 and returned again in 1983 took a number of steps with regard to the civil service – all of which reflected its wish to reduce the role of the state, to cut the size and cost of the Civil Service and to introduce, where possible, the practices and ethos of private business into the public sector.

Ministers abandoned the idea that special advisers from outside the Civil Service were unconstitutional and sought, as their Labour predecessors had done, for political assistants who were ideologically compatible with them as well as equipped with specialist policy knowledge. A large number of such advisers were drawn from those who had had recent experience in the Conservative Research Department; many of the advisers appointed had been parliamentary candidates. Over twenty such appointments were listed in August 1983, although not all of these were full-time.[17]

Another exception to the normal Civil Service appointments had been the Civil Service Regulation 11a by which certain appointments could be filled externally if the Civil Service Commission agreed that there were particular reasons for such a departure, and eight such appointments have been made since 1974. In December 1983 it was made known that the regulation had been successfully invoked to permit the reappointment after his five-year term of Sir Terence Burns, a former academic, as chief economic adviser to the Treasury and head of the Government Economic Service. This appointment was thus made from outside the ranks of civil servants, and the fact that it was not thrown open to competition created concern in the First Division Association which acts as the Civil Service union for senior officials.

Much attention was also devoted during the Thatcher administrations to the prime minister's position with respect to the advice and staff at her disposal. The policy unit attached to the prime minister was strengthened and slightly enlarged. After the Falklands war the prime minister's staff was expanded to include a special adviser on foreign affairs (Sir Anthony Parsons, a retired diplomat) and an adviser on defence (Roger Jackling) seconded from the Ministry of Defence. The unit was distinct from the prime minister's private office, which was entirely composed of seconded civil servants. It was also distinct from her own political secretariat. The precise functions of the policy unit were not altogether clear; its first head came from the world of business, its second was a professional journalist and its third was a merchant banker who had been a parliamentary candidate. The Downing Street press secretary, Bernard Ingham, was perceived as having an important coordinating role in presenting the government's policies and image, although the position is regarded as a Civil Service appointment. It was also noted that when, after the 1983 election, the prime minister's parliamentary private secretary was given a ministerial post, his successor actually gave up a position as minister of state to take over from him.

Another aspect of the prime minister's relations with the Civil

Service which became controversial during the Thatcher administrations related to promotions. It was reported that the prime minister had been unusually active in selecting the new holders of a number of posts at the permanent secretary level which became vacant in 1983, rather than accepting the ordinary routine of promotions. It was claimed by some that the prime minister was looking for individuals attuned to her own views on economic and social policy; but by others it was suggested that she was simply seeking to promote talented individuals regardless of their position in the Civil Service hierarchy at that point. Whether or not the promotions had an ideological or political motivation, it seems clear that they were regarded within the Civil Service as unusual, and perhaps as a signal that more radical approaches to the deployment of senior civil servants could not be ruled out.

The question of overall numbers in the Civil Service was a primary concern of the Conservative administration elected in 1979. The government was concerned not merely about the size of the Civil Service itself but also about the proliferation of quangos and the size of the nationalized industries and of local government. As regards quangos, the first task the incoming government set itself was to quantify the problem. An unfriendly critic had estimated in 1979 that there were over 3,000 non-departmental bodies giving ministers a patronage of approximately 40,000 places.[18] Sir Leo Pliatzky, a retired civil servant, was given the task of reviewing the situation and making recommendations about measures which might be taken to reduce the number of such bodies.[19] Excluding the nationalized industries he found, as already noted, 489 bodies in the executive agency category employing 217,000 staff and controlling budgets of £5,800 million. At that time the nationalized industry boards had about 1,600,000 employees and an annual turnover of £24,000 million, while the National Health Service had some 900,000 employees and spent about £7,500 million per year.

In its first six months of office the government announced its intention to abolish thirty executive agency quangos and 211 advisory boards. In a written parliamentary answer on 26 January 1982 the prime minister gave a total of 441 quangos abolished since 1979 and another 109 scheduled for outright abolition or reduction in size by April 1984. Although this meant that about one fifth of the total number of quangos which existed had been axed by 1984, in some ways the changes were more cosmetic than real. Policy changes and other new departures frequently entailed the establishment of new quangos, so that it seemed that this form of organization would remain a permanent feature of British government.

The government was also concerned that a greater degree of accountability should be introduced into the workings of these bodies, and many were made subject to the scrutiny of the new system of departmental select committees established in 1979. In October there was a further instruction that ministers were answerable to Parliament for the efficient and economical running of their departments and that departments should subject to detailed financial control all such bodies receiving 50 per cent or more of their funding from government.[20] Nevertheless bodies whose members were appointed by ministers were bound to attract the attention of the opposition if their actions were in a controversial field. Thus when in 1983 there were pressures for economy upon the NHS it was freely alleged that appointments to regional and district boards were being made with the aim of selecting Conservatives who could be expected to cooperate with the minister's policy objectives.

The Conservatives came to power in 1979 believing that there was room both for reductions in the overall level of the Civil Service and for securing greater efficiency in running the departments themselves. By 1984 there had been a number of changes to try to effect these objectives although the changes in the central management of the machinery of government suggested that in this area finality had not yet been reached.[21] These initiatives – together with a range of disputes between the government and the Civil Service over the machinery of pay determination – created a climate in which the administration was seen to be in conflict with the spokesmen of its own bureaucracy.

Early in 1984 there was another clash between the government and the Civil Service unions over the decision to bring the installations for monitoring foreign intelligence – Government Communications Headquarters (GCHQ) at Cheltenham – in line with other intelligence bodies by prohibiting trade union membership amongst its employees. The government claimed that the experience of industrial action by some staff members in 1981 as part of a wider Civil Service strike and the potential damage to security of such strikes justified its decision; the Civil Service unions claimed that many of the employees at Cheltenham were not employed on security-sensitive work and that they should have been consulted before taking such action. Whatever the merits of the government's decision the controversy aggravated the image of poor relations between the government and the Civil Service.

Although the Conservative administration attached great importance to controlling the size of the Civil Service, the reductions in numbers had been started under Mr Callaghan's Labour administration. By the time Labour left office in 1979 numbers had been cut from 748,000 to 732,000. Mrs Thatcher's objective was stated to be a further reduction of 100,000, giving a target of 630,000 by April 1984 – a target which was in fact reached. It was anticipated that the figure could be cut to below 600,000 by 1988.[22]

In respect of efficiency the prime minister took the view that the Civil Service Department had not exerted sufficient pressure upon the departments and that an external stimulus was needed. She therefore appointed Sir Derek Rayner (later Lord Rayner) to head a series of investigations into the efficiency of departments and whole classes of government operations. These were conducted by teams of civil servants under Sir Derek's supervision. By 1983 there had been 194 scrutinies in individual departments and five multi-departmental reviews of government forms, statistical services, running costs, personnel work and of support devices in research and development establishments. Potential savings of over £400 million had allegedly been identified and savings of £250 million actually realized.[23] Sir Derek himself left government service at the end of 1982, but the machinery he set up was kept in being and another businessman, Sir Robin Ibbs, a former head of the Central Policy Review Staff, was given a watching brief in the area as a part-time unpaid adviser to the prime minister.[24]

Departments were also encouraged to develop their own internal arrangements for securing greater efficiency. At the Department of the Environment, a management information system – MINIS – was inaugurated by Michael Heseltine when secretary of state, and despite initial objections this example was subsequently followed in other departments, notably in the Ministry of Defence when Mr Heseltine took over that department.[25]

Parliamentary interest in the matter was renewed when the Treasury and Civil Service Committee embarked through a sub-committee on an investigation of the efficiency and effectiveness of the Civil Service. Hearing of evidence began in June 1981 and the Committee published its report in March 1982.[26] The Committee had available to it the government's own thinking in this field, which had been revealed in a white paper, *Efficiency in the Civil Service*, published in July 1981.[27] The House of Commons Committee pointed out that while there was every evidence that departments had carefully controlled their administrative costs, administration itself was responsible for only a small part of the cost of the major spending departments and that too little seemed to have been done to examine and evaluate the programmes themselves. In this respect the MINIS experiment was welcomed as a system which would enable ministers to assess the objectives of the various programmes administered by their departments and facilitate an appraisal of the cost of carrying them out. The Committee noted the lack of any initiative by the Treasury in pursuing the more constructive aspect of efficient administration as opposed to the simple if negative goal of reducing expenditure.

The Committee felt that the central departments would have to be more prescriptive if further progress was to be made in the direction of efficiency. It also advocated a more active role for Parliament by giving its select committees the power to direct the comptroller and auditor-general to carry out efficiency and effectiveness audits.

It was expected that further changes in the central machinery would await the Committee's report, although it was known that consideration was being given to abolishing the Civil Service Department. However on this matter the government acted without waiting for the report. The abolition of the Civil Service Department was announced in Parliament on 12 November 1981 and brought about by Order in Council on 24 November.[28] Control of manpower, pay and superannuation went back to the Treasury as part of its general responsibilities for public expenditure. Recruitment and the efficiency drive were made the concern of a new department, the Office of Management and Personnel. Baroness Young, who as Chancellor of the Duchy of Lancaster had been in day-to-day charge of the Civil Service Department, became head of the Management and Personnel Office. But when she left the cabinet after the 1983 election, her place as head of the office was taken by the Earl of Gowrie, a minister of state in the Privy Council Office (and Minister for the Arts), who was not in the cabinet although later promoted to it. At the same time the office ceased to be an independent department and became part of the Cabinet Office. It was thus apparent that although a clear decision had been taken to abandon the concept of a single department uniting functions relating to the Civil Service, there was no clear idea about how the redistribution of functions should be effected, nor what should be the status of the department handling Civil Service matters.

Many outside observers therefore doubted whether the division of responsibilities for the public service was a sensible one. Few commercial firms would separate questions of remuneration from questions of efficiency. Only the prime minister was really in a position to take an overall view of matters relating to the Civil Service by this new arrangement, and it could be argued that it was impractical to rely on her for this task given her other responsibilities. Critics of the changes were reinforced in their views by public statements made by a former permanent secretary of the Civil Service Department, Lord Bancroft, who commented that 'managing well over half a million people is not a spare-time occupation split between three or four busy ministers, outstandingly able though they are'. He argued for the former system in which one minister (until 1968 the chancellor of the Exchequer and subsequently the leader of the House of Lords) had 'unambiguous day-to-day responsibility for the Civil Service'.[29]

The main concerns of the new Management and Personnel Office (MPO) were indicated by Lady Young in a statement to the Select Committee on the Treasury and Civil Service on 9 December 1981. It would carry forward the work of scrutiny and review in seeking to ensure greater efficiency, and in personnel management would seek evidence of managerial talent and ways of rewarding it.[30]

The government's considered reply to the Select Committee was the September 1982 white paper, *Efficiency and Effectiveness in the Civil Service*.[31] Its main emphasis was on the need for a coordinated drive backed by the Treasury and the MPO to improve financial management in government departments. Individual departments, it was thought, should take full responsibility in this area and where possible should delegate managerial responsibilities to units within the departments. The white paper gave some encouragement to the view of the Select Committee that more information should be made available about departmental programmes and about the success of those programmes. (Such information is available to some extent for example in the Ministry of Defence's annual statement on the defence estimates.)

The origins of these moves towards greater efficiency could in part be traced to the 'financial management initiative' that was announced in May 1982 and given greater definition in the September 1982 white paper.[32] Under the new arrangements its implementation obviously depended upon cooperation between the Treasury and the Management and Personnel Office and in May 1982 a joint Treasury/Cabinet Financial Management Unit was established to advise individual departments on their responses to the financial management initiative. The unit also took on responsibilities for a varied programme of consultations, seminars and training. Although it was originally intended that the Unit should be disbanded at the end of 1983 its operations were later extended to the end of 1984.

It was hoped that by concentrating on the development of new information systems such as MINIS both the Treasury and the MPO could minimize the need for them to intervene directly in departmental decision-making. Finally it was hoped that all these initiatives would contribute to a generally improved presentation of the government's policies and that such an improved overview would be reflected both in the annual white paper on public expenditure and in the supply estimates presented to Parliament. And in turn it was hoped that this improved presentation of governmental information would enhance the debates of the select committees as they came to work on the material.

The Management and Personnel Office commissioned reports on two other themes of relevance to the Civil Service. One examined the role of professional qualifications in the selection and training of individuals for administrative work, and the possibility of making more use of educational and professional bodies outside the public service. But this report (the Nisbet Report) also warned against giving a guarantee that a particular professional qualification would ensure for its holder a particular kind of post, or making professional qualifications a *sine qua non* in respect of such posts.[33]

The other report (the Atkinson Report) took a new look at 'fast-stream' graduate entrants into the Home Civil Service, the Diplomatic Service and the Tax Inspectorate and methods of internal promotion.[34] One reason for the inquiry that produced this report was the recent failure to recruit enough able individuals. In 1982, in a competition remodelled to deal with 'fast-stream' candidates only, there was an actual gap between the number of vacancies to be filled and those seen as qualified to fill them. The inability to find enough in-service candidates for promotion to the higher grades was even more striking.

The facts suggested questions about the standing of the Civil Service in the eyes of the public. It was shown again that the level of success achieved by Oxford and Cambridge graduates could not be dealt with by any alterations in the method of selection but only by calling the attentions of graduates and potential graduates of other institutions to the advantages of a Civil Service career. Similarly the low figure for those with science degrees accepted was the outcome of the small number of candidates from such disciplines. Raising the age limit for entry from twenty-eight to thirty or even thirty-two was suggested as one way of improving the field; such a move would mean that more civil servants would have had experience outside the public service, though the Report did not consider the implications of moving in this direction. While it appeared encouraging that the proportion of women succeeding in recent competitions had gone up, particularly in respect of the Foreign Service, this might only signify that contemporary industrial and commercial opportunities were less attractive to young women than to men who might find the competitive atmosphere of the private sector more congenial than they did.

Parallel to the work on efficiency and management techniques there was a continuing interest in personnel work, especially some of the problems associated with recruitment and promotion. Many of these issues had already been made familiar by the Fulton Report. In July 1983 a detailed report on the subject was published by the retiring secretary of the Management and Personnel Office, Mr J. Cassells.[35] It followed a detailed study of a number of documents and a survey of the personnel practices of some large private businesses as well as submissions from the Civil Service unions themselves. The Report gives some important statistical indications of the composition and deployment of the Civil Service. By its reckoning there were 521,700 non-industrial civil servants on 1 April 1982. (The definition which the report used was clearly a tighter one than that adopted by the government in its calculations of existing manpower and targets for reductions.) About 56 per cent of the staff were at clerical level and below and only 5 per cent were at the level of principal or above, i.e. were in those grades which compose what is known as the higher Civil Service. Although almost half of all civil servants are women, they form a higher proportion of the more junior grades than of the senior ones: thus 79 per cent of the clerical assistant grades are women but a mere 9 per cent of principals are women. (Indeed another report published in December 1982 pointed out how small was the representation of women in the higher Civil Service; at that time there were no female permanent secretaries, while only 3 per cent of deputy secretaries, 5 per cent of under-secretaries, and 4 per cent of assistant secretaries were women. These figures suggest that in the foreseeable future only a tiny handful of top Whitehall posts will be occupied by women.)[36]

The popular identification of the Civil Service with Whitehall is shown to be an illusion by the Cassells Report. Seventy-six per cent of civil servants are employed outside London, and staff in policy divisions even within Whitehall are no more than 4 per cent of the total. Concerning the simplification of the structure of the Civil Service, the Cassells Report suggested that little progress had in fact been made, despite the fact that pay, grading and conditions of service are common across departments. There were in 1982 twelve occupational groups, twenty-eight general service classes, and 2,500 departmental grades. A system as varied as this, and one in which the actual employers are the individual departments, can hardly be recruited centrally. Although permanent appointments are required to be made on merit through open competition, and those at the level of executive officer and above are undertaken for the departments by the Civil Service Commission, from 1 January 1983 responsibility for recruiting lower grades was devolved upon the individual departments. The methods to be used were prescribed by the Commission but the devolution of the task of recruitment was thought to give flexibility and aid local recruitment.

The question of Civil Service pay has also been controversial in recent years, especially given the government's policies on public expenditure and the abandonment of comparability procedures in favour of cash limits. As a result of these developments a more militant leadership inside the Civil Service unions emerged and there was already a major Civil Service strike in prospect in 1981 which may have influenced the decision to abolish the Civil Service Department. Given the assumption that civil servants would not engage in industrial action, especially when their jobs involved national security and defence, this development raised fundamental questions about the status of the Civil Service. A new situation also appeared to have arisen when the First Division Association, which had not hitherto been a militant organization, decided to affiliate to the Trades Union Congress.

Problems associated with the criteria for determining pay led the government to establish a committee under Mr Justice Megaw to devise a new system for handling Civil Service pay. Its Report, which appeared in July 1982, suggested that comparison with scales of pay outside the Civil Service should have a less important role in the future and that greater attention should be paid to market forces.[37] In December 1982 the government announced that it accepted the broad approach of the Report but was postponing its implementation pending discussions with the unions.

The Treasury and the Civil Service Committee did not get their way over enhancing the role of the comptroller and auditor-general. However, as has been seen, a private member's bill which was sponsored by the former leader of the House, Norman St John Stevas, and supported by two former chairmen of the Public Accounts Committee, Edward du Cann and Joel Barnett, did become law as the National Audit Act of 1983. By this act the comptroller and auditor-general became an officer of the House of Commons (although not subject to its direction) and statutory authority was given to his making efficiency and effectiveness audits of government work.

One point which had been stressed in the Atkinson Report was that more civil servants at the higher levels would require in addition to the familiar skills of the past an ability to present their department's policies outside Whitehall. This view largely rested on the fact that with the expansion of the apparatus of parliamentary select committees civil servants could expect to be called to give evidence before them more often than before. From the Civil Service perspective such additional exposure to parliamentary questioning presented some difficulties. It was the view of the leading civil servants that especial care had to be taken over lines of questioning which might encroach on the advice given by civil servants to ministers and on the workings of inter-departmental committees. Because it was thought essential to keep these aspects of the Civil Service's work secret, guidance had been given from the early 1970s on how to handle such matters and an agreement was reached between the head of the Civil Service and the chairman of the Liaison Committee of Select Committee Chairmen regarding the handling of classified material relating to defence and foreign affairs.

In May 1980 a memorandum of guidance was issued by the Civil Service Department which made it clear that ministers had discretion both as to which civil servants should appear before select committees and what information should be given to the committees. The memorandum suggested that it was essential to preserve the confidentiality of advice to ministers and to preserve the neutrality of civil servants by forbidding them to answer questions which touched upon issues of political controversy. It was pointed out for instance that economists in government service would have to be limited in what they could say in case they appeared to be critical of government policy.[38]

The Liaison Committee itself took the view that the memorandum was 'slightly less restrictive than its predecessor' and on the whole there have been only a few occasions when committees have thought that they were unreasonably prevented from hearing the views of civil servants.[39] But it seems possible that the calm may not endure, since there is an obvious conflict between Parliament's desire to monitor the work of departments more actively than in the past and the traditional reticence of the Civil Service. The constitutional fiction that government departments and their staffs have no policies of their own apart from those of the minister in office has become harder to maintain over the years, and if there were to be an increasing injection of outsiders into the machinery of government the position would become even harder to defend. Equally if more civil servants were to voice their personal views on public policy a further dimension would be added to the problem of preventing a wedge from being driven between the policies of a minister and those of his officials. The 1984 Reith Lectures by Sir Douglas Wass and the writings of Sir Leo

Pliatzky and Sir Ian Bancroft (now Lord Bancroft) are, as has been noted, rather novel in this respect.

Concern about the role of select committees is of course exacerbated by the fact that the taking of evidence from civil servants is normally open to the public and the press. In the past the Civil Service has managed to hold the media at arm's length, although it has recently become customary to release more information to journalists. The danger also exists that some journalists will be selected for preferential treatment if it is anticipated that they will cover a story in a way favourable to departmental policies. An example of this occurred in late 1983 when some critics suggested that the DES was attempting to denigrate authors who had cast doubt on the performance of comprehensive schools. Similarly the ability of the different armed services to get their particular viewpoints across in the press has been a well-known feature of British politics for many decades.

Most important of all however is the very fact that the growth of government and the accompanying workload of ministers mean that much decision-making must be delegated to civil servants. A recent chief secretary to the Treasury has called attention to the way in which cabinet committees are shadowed by committees of civil servants who assume that if they can agree amongst themselves ministers will be certain to go along with them. 'Most of the time,' he adds, 'I have in mind the officials' "cabinet" or weekly meeting of permanent secretaries. Plotting is too strong a word but there is no doubt that officials at those meetings plan how to steer cabinet and cabinet committee meetings along paths ministers may not originally have intended.'[40]

The criticism of the Diplomatic Service which continued to be voiced was largely the result of a new conception of Britain's international role and of the demands that role would in future make upon the Service.[41] It was held that, if Britain had ceased to be a world power and depended for such influence as it retained upon its economic capabilities, then it was incumbent upon the Diplomatic Service to regard the promotion of British trade as its primary function. And for this task it was not unreasonable to question whether such functions could not be better performed by individuals especially recruited for their experience of commerce and industry rather than by career diplomats.

The weakness of the thesis was the assumption that a diplomatic service either is or ought to be the prime vehicle for pushing exports. For even if the economic factor is given substantial significance, much economic activity demands a knowledge of local political conditions which diplomats may be presumed able to supply. However it is probably true that in a service where much attention is paid to career development and hence to varying the experience of its members there will be a tendency not merely to undervalue particular skills on entry but to pay too little attention to developing them afterwards. The criticism which could be levelled at the commercial aspects of the Diplomatic Service's work was even more true of such specialized organizations as the Information Service at a time when the projection of Britain abroad and the winning over of foreign public opinion on such topics as Northern Ireland and the Falklands was very important.

Compared with the Home Civil Service, however, the Diplomatic Service found less difficulty in maintaining its ability to recruit high-calibre graduates, despite the changes associated with the erosion of the conventions surrounding diplomatic staff. As the Atkinson Report commented, the political disorder that prevailed in so much of the world meant that diplomats had to have the 'will and ability' to carry on their duties effectively in conditions of civil strife; in short the day of the 'Land Rover' ambassador had arrived. Even so the Diplomatic Service failed to fill all its vacancies in 1982 and tried to broaden its range of recruits by raising the age limit to thirty-two in 1983 and also by advertising for five posts to be filled at the first secretary level and making them open to applicants between the ages of thirty-two and forty-two. It would appear however that this move was not so much one in favour of broadening pre-entry experience as a response to a situation in which vacancies at the first secretary level could not be filled satisfactorily by promotion from below. Nor could the Diplomatic Service be said to have succeeded in throwing off its Oxbridge image: in 1983 59 per cent of the entrants for the fast stream and 18 per cent of the remainder were still Oxford or Cambridge graduates.

Perhaps the real problem for the Diplomatic Service is in the last analysis a different one: the addition of an international dimension to the work of nearly all domestic departments and the enormous growth of multilateral diplomacy.[42]

It can thus be seen that there are a number of factors operating to change the way in which the Civil Service functions in modern Britain. The demands of politicians, the indirect impact of other developments in the constitutional system and, not least, the mood within the Civil Service itself, have combined to initiate changes in an institution traditionally thought to be impervious to such pressures. If the precise effect of recent arguments on the character of the Civil Service is unclear, what is certain is that it will be difficult to restore the style of an earlier period.

5   Parliament

In the 1975 referendum on whether the United Kingdom should remain a member of the European Communities, one argument of the anti-Europeans was that membership involved a diminution of the sovereignty of Parliament, which they regarded as the distinctive element in the British political system. Yet it was clear that Parliament itself was not, except in the most formal sense, fulfilling the role which the opponents of membership assigned to it.

Behind the rhetoric of the debate about the damage which might be done to parliamentary sovereignty by entry into the EEC there stretched a decade of questioning about the extent to which Parliament as an institution could assert itself against the executive. Parliamentary proceedings seemed to some irrelevant to the nation's life. Between 1974 and 1979, despite the drama inherent in a 'hung' Parliament – a Parliament in which the government had no overall majority – there was little evidence of a recovery in the public's respect for its legislature. The reluctant acquiescence of a majority of MPS in an experiment with radio broadcasting of parliamentary proceedings suggested that they were apprehensive about the impact which this would have on their reputation, and available opinion poll data on the electorate's perception of politicians following the experiment did indeed seem to confirm MPS' initial fears. Criticisms of the quality of British politicians and of the 'adversarial' style of British politics were linked with criticisms of the party system and led during the period to demands for electoral reform which would break the rigid hold of the two major parties over parliamentary and political life.

It is also, however, the role of Parliament itself that has been questioned. What is Parliament meant to contribute to the British system of government and how far is it properly equipped for its task?

The changes in the organization of the House of Commons and in its procedures – changes which began in the 1960s and were mainly directed towards improving Parliament's control over the executive – followed criticisms which had been made by academic members of the Study of Parliament Group and by the younger MPS of the 1966 Labour intake. The changes which occurred in response to these criticisms were not universally welcomed at the time, although the philosophy behind them has perhaps become more widely accepted recently. Some MPs such as Enoch Powell were devoted to the view that the House of Commons should be the place where the great issues of policy were hammered out. Nothing should therefore be done which would diminish the role of the chamber itself. The development of a more important committee system was seen as a threat to the cohesion of the House of Commons and a possible step towards the kind of decentralized legislature which exists in the United States. Others – especially in the Labour Party – were primarily concerned to see that a future government should not be hampered in carrying out the legislative programme for which its Parliamentary majority was assumed to give a mandate, even if it represented only a minority of those voting. From this point of view the more opportunities MPs had of playing an active part in the legislative process itself or even to scrutinize the operations of the executive, the less chance there was for sustained radical action by government.[1] Indeed ever since the 1930s there has been a strand in Labour thinking which would favour confining Parliament to enacting enabling legislation and leaving the executive to fill in the details to a greater extent than is now the case.

The importance attached to macro-economic management and the fact that governments are frequently judged by their ability to deal with the bread-and-butter issues of unemployment, inflation and the balance of payments have further weakened the role of Parliament. In such questions Parliament has no meaningful constitutional role other than to sustain a government in office. When governments in addition choose to become locked into policy processes with outside organizations (and indeed other governments and international organizations), significant decisions may be taken before Parliament has a chance to discuss them and its role is seen to be limited. A vivid illustration of the extent to which Parliament may be forced to the sidelines of economic policy was given when the budget was presented in April 1976. Then important changes in taxation were left undecided pending the outcome of negotiations between the government and the Trades Union Congress on the next phase of incomes policy.

The hopes entertained in the 1960s that the annual white paper giving a 'forward look' at the government's thinking on public expenditure would give an opportunity for effective debate proved without foundation. Not only do most MPs lack the economic expertise or information to participate in financial policy making, but they also show by the distribution of their time and energies that they are well aware of their own limitations.

The traditional assumptions about the workings of the British parliamentary system rested upon the belief that the government would normally command a majority in the House of Commons and that party discipline would ensure that the government's preferences would prevail on most issues. Indeed these assumptions held good without exception in respect of government bills introduced between 1945 and 1970, even though in two Parliaments (1950–1 and 1964–6) the size of the government majority was small. Dissent within the parliamentary parties began to manifest itself in the 1970–4 Parliament when on six occasions Conservative dissidents helped to produce a government defeat in the lobbies. Further adjustment to the traditional view was required by the experience of the Labour government which between October 1974 and 1979 had at first only the narrowest of majorities and, after 1976, was dependent on minority parties for the passage of its legislation. In these circumstances it was possible for minority parties (which were stronger than at any time since 1931) to align with the Conservative opposition and the occasional Labour rebel to secure changes in the texts of measures or even the total withdrawal of bills. In standing committee, where bills are considered in detail, the task of the government was yet more difficult since the loss of an overall majority in the House as a whole meant that the government no longer commanded an automatic majority in committee. Even with the support of minor party representatives the government was therefore vulnerable to absenteeism. From a situation in which the executive might expect the passage of its full legislative programme in virtually unaltered form, the government had therefore to adjust to one in which neither the principles nor the details of bills were immune from parliamentary amendment.

A quick glance at the legislative record of the Labour governments of 1974–9 may indicate the extent of the change. In 1975–6 five bills failed to pass through the House of Commons. One bill – for the nationalization of the aircraft and shipbuilding industries – was passed only after very substantial amendment. It was found that this bill could not be treated as an ordinary bill since it affected some private interests differently from others; it was in consequence a 'hybrid' bill – part public and part private – and was therefore subject to a special and time-consuming procedure which could have led to its being lost altogether. The government therefore chose to drop the parts of the bill which had been challenged. In 1976–7 eight bills out of fifty failed to complete their passage.[2] In the 1977–8 session, the government's legislative programme was more limited but the government failed to carry the commencement orders necessary to make operative an act which had been promised to the Transport and

General Workers' Union and which dealt with dock labour. These difficulties extended even to the question of finance. In both 1977 and 1978, the Liberals helped to force through major changes in the government's tax proposals.

With the general election of 1979 and the return of a government with a majority of forty-three it might have been thought that the old situation would return; in fact in the 1979–83 Parliament there was only one occasion when enough Conservative MPs sided with the opposition to defeat the government. But there were up to a dozen other occasions when the threat of defeat caused the Conservative government to abandon its intentions, and at least two bills were withdrawn after the extent of the opposition on the government side of the House was made plain.[3] In the 1983 Parliament, the Conservative majority stood initially at 144 – a figure which should have made it virtually invulnerable to defeat in the House of Commons. Even so the government sustained an early defeat on the topic of MPs' salaries. Some commentators suggested that the very size of the government's majority might actually encourage dissidence within Conservative ranks.

If the proponents of proportional representation were to succeed it could mean that overall majorities would become a rarity just as an effective three-party situation without PR might have the same result.[4] In these circumstances many fundamental aspects of Parliament and its role in the political system would necessarily change. Even without fundamental changes of that sort, however, it seems clear that Parliament is being forced to adapt to a new set of demands. Yet, even as it does seek to adapt to new requirements, it must as an institution try to preserve the roles which ministers and backbenchers alike regard as important – roles conditioned by the almost unbroken development of Parliament over some seven hundred years. In contrast to the parliaments of other European countries, which had to be created afresh after medieval estates had withered away under powerful dynastic absolutisms, the British Parliament is a direct successor of the English Parliament of the Middle Ages. All three of Parliament's earliest functions – judicial, legislative and financial – are still evident in its composition and procedure, though the judicial role of the House of Lords is completely separate in practice from its position as the second chamber of the legislature.

Parliament's legislative activity originated in the need of the medieval monarchs to associate the great feudal lords and other representatives of the propertied classes with the process of law-making. The monarch also required that the representatives of the tax-paying groups should assent to the levying of taxes. The need for taxation arose whenever some emergency – principally war – made it impossible for the monarch to meet his expenses out of the revenues from his own lands. From this function (known as 'supply') came Parliament's demands for the redress of grievances in exchange for voting for taxation. Eventually it became accepted that ministers must be able to command the confidence of the House of Commons, which became exclusively powerful in all matters of finance.

The composition of the two Houses of Parliament also reflects their medieval origins. In the House of Lords the principle of hereditary membership survives from the period when social – and hence political – power lay with the holders of the great estates and titles; the attendance of these men in person at Westminster was seen as one of many public duties. The presence today of representatives of the established Church of England (the two archbishops and twenty four other bishops) and of no other religious denomination reflects the country's earlier religious unity. And the presence of the lord chancellor and the law lords underlines the extent to which there was once a great deal of overlap between the judicial and legislative work of Parliament.

Like the House of Lords, the House of Commons reflects its medieval origins, though again rather remotely because represent- ation in the Middle Ages was felt to be of communities rather than of individuals. The communities were the counties and boroughs which were also for long the principal units of local administration and justice. Representation of the universities began in the seventeenth century and lasted until 1950; this representation was non-territorial since graduates could vote for their university's representatives regardless of where they resided. Today the system of representation is wholly territorial and based on the single-member constituency. In addition, as will be seen in the next chapter, although some effort is still made to ensure a relationship between parliamentary consti- tuencies and local government areas, even this is proving hard to maintain. Except perhaps in remote rural areas, it is natural that there should be some erosion of territorial loyalties: increased mobility in work and leisure makes it likely that the ties of occupation and social class will be greater than those of locality.

Furthermore the role of political parties has generally had the effect of diminishing the importance of local issues and of concentrating attention on national ones – although the Conservative government's treatment of local government has of late had the indirect conse- quence of making its problems more salient. The overriding role of political parties in the electoral system was for a long time not recognized formally. It was not until 1969 that a parliamentary candidate's party allegiance was allowed to appear on the ballot paper. Now that a start has been made with financing parties out of public funds – for their parliamentary functions at least – it may be assumed that the role of party organization will be more frequently acknowledged in law.. Certainly many of the discussions about the existing electoral system now revolve around whether changes will advance the cause of one or other party rather than whether the system is fair to individuals or localities.

Support for the present electoral system comes primarily from those who regard the principal function of the House of Commons as that of sustaining a ministry in office. The historic distinction between the executive and the legislature – which was never complete – came to an end in the eighteenth century with the emergence of the cabinet as the effective executive. Before the middle of the nineteenth century responsible government – the dependence of the cabinet upon a majority of the House of Commons rather than upon the favour of the monarch – was fully established. In the middle of the nineteenth century cabinet government existed in the context of a party system of a fairly fluid kind in the House of Commons. Groups of politicians had to come together if a government were to be formed with sufficient backing; but because these groups were looser than parties, it was possible to regard the House of Commons as actually choosing the government. After the broadening of the franchise in 1868, the advent of modern mass parties and the discipline which their existence imposed upon their supporters in Parliament meant that the result of an election itself usually determined the complexion of the ensuing government without further parliamentary negotiations. Since the Second Reform Act of 1867 it has been normal for a government defeated at the polls to resign without waiting for Parliament to meet. However, this practice is only unquestioned when the new House of Commons has a clear majority for another party. Stanley Baldwin met Parliament in 1924 because, although he had no overall majority, he was still the leader of the largest single party in the House of Commons; and Edward Heath hesitated before resigning after the election of February 1974, in order to explore the possibilities of remaining in office as prime minister in a coalition government. A single Parliament would not be expected to sustain successive governments of different parties: if, as happened in 1931, there were an internal shift leading to a new government, an election would be expected to follow.

Experience between 1976 and 1979 showed that increasingly the government itself decides when its majority must be considered as lost. So long as the Callaghan government could rely on the Liberal Party's support in any vote of confidence, it was prepared to accept a number of defeats which might have prompted another government to dissolve Parliament and which some commentators thought warranted resignation. In other words, the vital votes, other than formal motions of no confidence, are those the government chooses to regard as such; the possibility of calling a second vote after defeat on an issue normally allows any intra-party rebellions to be contained by permitting the rebels to return to the party fold on the crucial question of confidence after voting against the leadership on the substantive issue.

The basic framework of parliamentary debate takes the form of a dialogue not between the executive and the legislature but between the government and the major opposition party. Where government and opposition differ so greatly that continuity of policy is difficult, the dialogue has been seen as part of the syndrome of 'adversary politics'.[5] In spite of the fact that standing orders of the House of Commons make no mention of party, the distinction between government and opposition is pervasive in the practical organization of parliamentary proceedings in both Houses. In respect of the allocation of time – which is in many ways the key issue – the government has recognized powers of control, subject to a conventional allocation to the opposition of opportunities to raise matters for debate. This convention has recently been formalized, since those days which used to be called 'supply days' and were used by the opposition for debates on subjects of their choosing are now called 'opposition days'.

When parties other than the two major parties have substantial representation in Parliament the conventions governing the day-to-day organization of business are placed under strain, and further complications have arisen from the formation of the Alliance between the Liberals and the Social Democrats. In general the conventions of Parliament assume a two-party system, so that for example the leaders of the opposition in both Houses, their chief whips and deputy chief whips are paid a salary from public funds. No other parties are assisted in this way, although minor parties may choose to use some of the money made available to them from public funds for parliamentary purposes to supplement the income and facilities of their leaders.

The level of salaries and other allowances payable to MPs has been regarded as a matter for MPs themselves, although government has naturally sought to guide those decisions. In July 1983 a severe disagreement between the government and Parliament occurred. The Review Body on Top Salaries – a permanent government-appointed body which deals with salaries for those in government employment other than civil servants – had produced a report on MPs' pay in May 1983.[6] The investigations made by or on behalf of the Review Body included an examination of the remuneration of MPs and the earnings from other occupations reported by 69% of non-ministerial members. It concluded that while MPs in the United Kingdom are paid substantially less than the average for other comparable countries, the discrepancy was much reduced when the generally lower level of earnings was taken into account. It suggested, however, that a substantial increase to a figure of £19,000 was necessary to make up for

the fall in the purchasing power of salaries since 1979, when the last settlement had been made. Such a recommendation if implemented would have meant an increase of 31 per cent at a time when the government was pursuing a limit of 4 per cent in public sector pay increases. The government was therefore initially minded to reject the recommendations of the Review Body; but a revolt among the government's own supporters produced a series of votes in which the Review Body's basic recommendations were accepted, albeit they were to be implemented by annual stages. (An added provision was made for taking into account changes in Civil Service salaries.)[7]

In normal times the domination of the executive rests upon the ability of the cabinet always to command the votes of its nominal supporters. The most significant – though not necessarily the most fundamental – areas of controversy may therefore be within the ruling party itself rather than between government and opposition. The Labour Party, although hitherto less prone to change electorally unsuccessful leaders, has generally exhibited rather more divisions than has the Conservative Party. Moreover these divisions have been more likely to have some durability and organizational basis than have Conservative ones. However, as has been documented since the 1970s, the Conservative Party has developed a willingness to defy the whips in the division lobbies and this greater dissidence has produced a more concrete factionalism, especially since the Conservative victory of 1979.

The fact that modern British Parliaments are dominated by party means that Parliament is a rather weak forum for ventilating grievances of a general kind. Since the executive usually controls the House of Commons, the government no longer has any need to offer to redress grievances in return for the voting of funds, as in the classic model of parliamentary government. At most, Parliament remains a forum in which individual grievances can be redressed if other means have failed. Questions to ministers on the floor of the House, and the work of the parliamentary commissioner for administration, are a part of the modern grievance procedure; and both still rely greatly on the local MP who filters much of this kind of work through his local constituency office and who will sometimes find himself dealing directly with the agency or department which occasioned the complaint. MPs clearly believe they derive a variety of benefits and satisfactions from these activities, although not all MPs pay an equal amount of attention to them. Certainly the expansion of the welfare state has brought individual citizens into additional contact with government and has multiplied the demand for help in securing redress and compensation. In some respects the British MP is very poorly equipped to cope with these demands: even with the improved secretarial facilities of recent years, it is rare to find an MP able to employ more than one secretary on constituency matters alone, and many MPs still deal with a good deal of their own correspondence.[8] However, in some respects the situation of the MP who wishes to pursue an inquiry against a department or agency has improved as a result of the technical aid available from the parliamentary commissioner – even if some MPs are still somewhat jealous of any intrusion on a function they see as peculiarly their own.

The House of Lords

The hereditary basis of membership of the House of Lords was modified in 1958 when the Life Peerages Act was passed. Previously, the prime minister could nominate hereditary peers only (except for the Law Lords), but the increasingly egalitarian character of British society made it undesirable to make too many such elevations to the peerage. The 1958 Act made it possible to create peers without the title passing to their heirs, and thus widened the choice of the prime minister in appointing peers. (In theory the sovereign, who is the 'fount of all honours', creates peers; in practice they are recommended by the prime minister of the day, sometimes in consultation with the leaders of other parties.) Since 1963 it has been possible for someone inheriting a peerage to disclaim it for his lifetime, and from 1964 to 1983 no new hereditary peerages were created. In 1983 Mrs Thatcher decided to depart from this principle and anounced the creation of two hereditary peerages for two former politicians who in fact had no heirs, and then announced an earldom for the former prime minister Harold Macmillan.

The creation of life peerages was intended to broaden the party composition of the House of Lords, which had been overwhelmingly Conservative since the secession of the Liberal Unionists from the

Liberal Party in 1886. Life peerages are therefore created with a view to seeing that all major parties have some representation in the upper chamber and to keeping the numbers relatively constant.

The present composition is a varied one. In May 1983 there were 769 peers by succession (including five women) and thirty peers whose hereditary titles had been created for them and who are known as peers of first creation. There were twenty-six bishops and archbishops and twenty-one law lords. Life peers numbered 335, of whom fifty-nine were women. The nominal total was thus, 1,181, but of these 143 had not received the writ of summons to the House of Lords because they were either still minors (under eighteen), or aliens or bankrupts. A further 143 had applied for and received writs of absence, which permits peers to be absent from the House of Lords and which is in effect a useful device for discouraging the occasional appearance by backwoodsmen in the legislature. Since 1958 peers have been encouraged to attend the House of Lords by the payment of an attendance allowance. While in the mid-1950s the daily attendance of the House of Lords averaged below 100, it had risen to 321 in the 1983–4 session.

The 1958 Life Peerages Act and the 1963 Peerage Act permitted minor reforms in the role and operation of the upper chamber. The Labour government of 1966–70 attempted in 1968 to take the process of reform a step further by turning the House of Lords into a wholly nominated body which would reflect the balance of party strength in each successive House of Commons. This attempt failed – not because of any affection for the prevailing situation but because of the fear that the more popular the composition of the House of Lords, the easier it would be for it to exercise its surviving powers.[9] Labour Party support for unicameralism became stronger during the late 1970s, especially as the Lords' powers were used rather more frequently in the special political circumstances of 1976–8 when constitutional issues such as devolution were being discussed and when there was no overall majority in the House of Commons. By the end of 1978 abolition of the House of Lords had become official Labour Party policy, although this commitment was watered down in the Labour manifesto for the 1979 general election. The 1983 manifesto included a pledge to 'abolish the undemocratic House of Lords as quickly as possible'. Even if it took time to effect abolition, the manifesto promised to remove the legislative powers of the upper chamber – with the exception of those that related to the prolongation of the life of a Parliament – within the first session of Parliament. As Labour moved towards outright abolition of the House of Lords, the Conservatives by contrast became increasingly attracted by the idea of reform which would involve a strong elective element in the upper chamber. However, although there was much discussion of reform measures, nothing has so far been done to effect changes in this direction.

Although the weight of government representation will be in the House of Commons, the administration must keep some representatives in the House of Lords to answer oral questions and to supervise the passage of legislation through that chamber. The current practice is that, besides the lord chancellor, two or three other members of the cabinet should sit in the House of Lords and one of these will act as leader of the House. In January 1985 these ministers were the lord president of the Council, the leader of the House, the chancellor of the duchy of Lancaster (minister for the arts) and a minister without portfolio with special responsibilities for dealing with unemployment. In January 1985 the lord advocate (the principal law officer for Scotland), four ministers of state and five under-secretaries were peers; other departments were answered for by one of the seven government whips.

The organization of political parties in the House of Lords is somewhat less rigid than in the Commons. Whipping does exist but the numbers supporting each party are somewhat fluid. In June 1983 there were about 420 peers taking the Conservative whip, about 130 peers taking the Labour whip, forty peers taking the Liberal whip and forty-one who had taken the new Social Democratic Party whip. About 220 peers belonged to the looser group of crossbenchers, which has its own convenor to give information about business but is not whipped for divisions. The impression of Conservative ascendancy is however largely illusory, because many Conservative peers rarely attend the House of Lords. In divisions on amendments to Conservative government bills, some crossbench support or abstention is usually necessary to avoid defeat. On occasion the numbers participating can rise dramatically: thus in the major divisions on the European Communities bill over 500 peers voted. Such figures are, however, rarely seen and only on four or five occasions in recent years have the numbers voting in the House of Lords exceeded 250. The average figures for daily attendance account of course both for regular attenders and for those who happen to be present on any particular day. The number of regular attenders can be gauged from the fact that during the ninety-four days of the 1982–3 session (which was curtailed by a dissolution) 105 peers attended on at least eighty occasions. Although the sittings in the House of Lords are less numerous and shorter than those in the House of Commons (the peers sit for about six and a half hours each sitting day), the pressure of work in the upper chamber is very unevenly spread. The fact that most major bills begin their life in the House of Commons means that they tend to arrive in the Lords towards the end of a session; this cycle produces a fairly tight timetable for the Lords if the bills are to be passed by both Houses of Parliament by the end of the session. In order to alleviate this pressure governments will try to introduce much of their uncontroversial legislation in the House of Lords.

The special contribution of the House of Lords is derived from the variety of experience and expertise which can be found in the upper chamber and from the fact that its general debates do not normally lead to a division. These features of the upper chamber mean that it is not as rigidly partisan as the Commons and can contribute more freely to informing public debate. When the detailed consideration of legislation occurs, the fact that the membership of the House of Lords is quite different from that of the Commons means that different resources are deployed in the process. Much of the Lords' legislative work will, of course, involve detailed scrutiny of government bills; in the last resort the efficiency and the effectiveness of this procedure will depend upon the government of the day taking the Lords' contribution seriously and not automatically using its majority in the Commons to vote down amendments made in the upper house. In addition to government-sponsored bills, some measures of an important, though non-partisan kind, begin their lives as private members' bills in the House of Lords. Between 1970 and 1981 twenty-five such bills actually became law.[10]

The superior political position of the House of Commons was established in the nineteenth century by convention, but it now rests upon two statutes – the Parliament Acts of 1911 and 1949. While the House of Lords has no powers over finance, it can delay other legislation by up to thirteen months. A bill rejected by the House of Lords can be carried by the House of Commons alone if it is reintroduced in a new session. The effect of this provision is obviously greater if a non-Conservative government is in power, since such a government might find it difficult to carry through a controversial measure introduced in the last session of a Parliament. At other times the House of Commons may find itself forced to spend time debating amendments from the House of Lords even though ultimately the power to override them lies with the majority in the Commons.

How far the House of Lords will use its powers depends upon the tactical sense of the Conservative leadership. Conservative leaders are generally anxious to avoid a direct confrontation between the House of Lords and the House of Commons, especially when this could be exploited electorally. On occasion, however, the House of

Lords will make its point firmly. Thus for example in 1969 it drastically amended a bill to redistribute a limited number of constituencies because it believed that the government ought to have implemented the recommendations of the Boundary Commissioners in full. The government had to withdraw its bill and, although the comprehensive recommendations were not introduced at that time, the House of Lords had succeeded in giving publicity to an issue which was widely seen as a piece of government gerrymandering. (The fact that this particular question related to the composition of the House of Commons made the Lords' intervention all the more remarkable.) In 1974–5 the Government failed to secure the passage of a Trade Unions and Labour Relations Amendment Bill after the House of Lords had inserted a form of words guaranteeing newspaper editors against some of the bill's closed shop provisions. The bill was, however, reintroduced during the 1976–7 session, when an amendment to deal with the position of editors was inserted in the House of Lords but rejected by the House of Commons. The House of Lords did not insist on its amendment thereafter, and the bill received the Royal Assent without recourse to the Parliament Act of 1949 which would have secured its passage by the Commons alone.[11]

In constitutional matters and questions affecting the basic liberties of the citizen, the House of Lords claims a special right to make its voice heard, because it sees itself as less susceptible than the Commons to the immediate pressure of party politics. This sense that it has special responsibilities to give constitutional matters dispassionate consideration was reflected in the handling of the bills to establish devolved assemblies for Scotland and for Wales in the 1977–8 session. In the end the number of points which the opponents of devolution were willing to pursue in the Lords was very small, and the bills reached the statute book by the end of the session. When a Conservative government is in power there are fewer inhibitions about amending government measures, and Mrs Thatcher's Conservative administrations have suffered a number of defeats at the hands of the upper house – sixteen in 1979–80, eighteen in 1980–1, five in 1982–3, and twenty in 1983–4.

The main business of the House of Lords is, as has been said, legislative, and much of the upper chamber's time is consumed by the detailed consideration of bills. While it is a convention in the Lords that there is no division on second reading, amendments are possible at the committee stage, at report and even at the third reading stage. The point of moving amendments is to secure concessions between one stage of a bill and another; because the government will frequently grant these concessions rather than risk its timetable, the impact made by the House of Lords on a piece of legislation cannot be reckoned simply in terms of amendments carried against the government.

While the House of Lords has no standing legislative committees, a number of select committees, whether of a permanent or temporary kind, play an important part in the work of the House. Private members' bills, for example, may be referred to a select committee. The rationalization of the select committee system in the House of Commons which occurred in 1979 had the effect in some subject areas of abolishing a committee with a specialized jurisdiction, and occasionally this has been compensated for by the work of a select committee in the Lords. Thus the Select Committee on Science and Technology was set up when the Commons select committee in this field was abolished and is now the only parliamentary forum for discussing these issues in depth. The House of Lords Select Committee on the European Communities, with its seven sub-committees, is the only machinery available to Parliament for investigation through the examination of witnesses and for discussing in detail the various ways in which membership of the Communities affects the United Kingdom; because of the somewhat lighter workload of the House of Lords by comparison with the Commons, time is found to debate its reports on the floor.

The Legislative Process

Legislation is divided into two broad kinds – public and private. Public legislation, which is far more important in terms of volume and character, is sponsored by government in the case of major measures but may also be sponsored by backbench MPs through what are called private members' bills. Private legislation is a very different thing: it deals with matters affecting the interests of named individuals or bodies. In the nineteenth century, such private Acts of Parliament were very common as a method of dealing with matters for which general statutes did not provide, such as divorce. Today, most of these things can be dealt with under the provisions of general statutes. However, private legislation is still employed when a local authority wishes to acquire some new function which is not covered by existing powers granted to local authorities, or when some local authority or other public body needs to acquire land by compulsory purchase.

The procedure which private bills must follow is more akin to that of judicial proceedings than to the adversarial method of passing public legislation. A private bill must clear a number of preliminary hurdles, which give ample opportunities for local objectors to a measure to be heard and which may involve public inquiries, a town poll, or a town meeting. Only after the completion of this expensive and time-consuming process can the first reading be taken. If the bill is unopposed, progress will be rapid; but an opposed bill after second reading has to go to a Private Bill Committee of MPs, which operates rather more like a court than an ordinary standing committee in that the promoters and opponents of the bill are represented by counsel and call witnesses to give evidence on their behalf. The committee can deal both with the desirability of the bill itself and with its details. If it rejects the measure the rejection is taken as final; if approval is given, subsequent procedure is like that for a public bill. Private bills must go through both Houses of Parliament according to the same procedures.

In questions of public legislation, the pre-eminence of the government has long been accepted. All important bills are presented by the appropriate minister after being drafted on the basis of departmental instructions to one or more parliamentary draftsmen. The draftsmen are the thirty-five or so barristers who make up the office of Parliamentary Counsel. The minister, aided by his civil servants and the draftsmen, will pilot the bill through the various stages of parliamentary scrutiny, aiming to secure the passage either of the original bill or at least of one that has been amended only in accordance with governmental wishes. The government will normally have a majority in the House of Commons, and that majority will be reflected in the composition of standing committees; this means that the executive can control both the principles and the details of a bill.

In recent years there has been criticism of the way bills are drafted and amended because, it is argued, the statutes which emerge from the legislative process lack simplicity and clarity. A committee established to look at the legislative process in 1973 found that little could be done to improve the situation as long as MPs insisted on examining bills in considerable detail. The committee suggested an increase in the number of parliamentary draftsmen, because many bills are thought to be ill-considered and the office of Parliamentary Counsel is generally overworked; otherwise the committee made few substantial recommendations.[12] Thus the problem of the quality of legislation remains a perplexing one. Incoherent or ambiguous legislation can be tidied up by the judiciary when they come to apply a statute; but of course the judges' interpretation of the law may be a quite different one from that originally intended. This may be especially true when the legislation is of a novel kind, as with the Race

Relations Acts or the Sex Discrimination Act.

Apart from financial legislation, government bills are the result either of a commitment in the ruling party's programme or of a departmental initiative. Such an initiative may arise from the practical experience of working an existing law or it may be the result of pressure upon the department from some outside body or group. It is sometimes also the case that a new problem will be identified and that legislation will be held to be an appropriate solution. Some measures simply tidy up or consolidate existing statutes; the Law Commission has been the source of many recommendations of this kind, and its work on consolidation is continuous.

Private members' bills are of different kinds. Priority is given to the twenty MPS successful in the ballot held at the beginning of each session. Those MPS who come near the top of this ballot may stand a reasonably serious chance of promoting their bill into law. The content of the bills promoted by backbench MPS frequently owes much to pressure group activity or it may involve issues of morality or religion where the government may be fearful of taking the initiative itself. In the case of a controversial bill there are delaying tactics which a bill's opponents may use to stop its passage. However, if there is majority support for the bill and the government is sympathetic, the government may be prepared to help it by providing parliamentary time for its later stages. Conversely, a government faced with parliamentary support for a bill which is not altogether to its liking may be prepared to introduce one of its own on the subject in preference to the private member's bill. In these cases there would have to be consultation and collaboration between the bill's sponsor, and relevant pressure groups, and the department which would have the responsibility for administering the new measure.

The introduction of a private member's bill may be a device to obtain publicity for a cause. Thus if the government undertakes to institute an inquiry into the matter or itself to legislate on the topic, the bill may have served its purpose and will be withdrawn.

Any MP may also introduce a bill under the Ten Minute Rule or Standing Order Number 39. However such bills are most unlikely to reach the statute book, and even more than in the case of private members' bills their introduction is simply a way of giving publicity to an issue. Private members' bills originating in the House of Lords are still less likely than those originating in the House of Commons to become law, unless they are taken up in the House of Commons by an MP who has secured a high place on the private members' ballot. But here again the motive of securing publicity for a cause continues to encourage peers to use the device.

When the Parliament which had been elected in 1979 was dissolved in May 1983, it had passed into law forty-four private members' bills. These constituted 13.13 per cent of the 379 private members' bills introduced – a slightly higher proportion than in the previous Parliament. Of the government bills introduced in the 1979–83 Parliament, 95.98 per cent became law.

The difference made to bills by the legislative process is usually not very great. However on occasion important amendments and changes may be made. As has been pointed out, the main negotiations with any interest concerned will have taken place *before* a bill is introduced into the House of Commons, and ministers can therefore always argue that any amendments to the text of a bill would upset accommodations already made. The formal stages of the legislative process are thus of less political significance than those which occur before the bill is introduced.

The parliamentary stages of the legislative process are known as readings. The first reading is a purely formal process in which the title of the bill is put down on the order paper. The second reading however provides an opportunity for the general principles of a proposed measure to be debated. Since the ultimate vote of the House of Commons will usually reflect party strength, the outcome can be predicted; the second reading debate is therefore likely to take the form of an appeal by government and opposition to the electorate on the basis of their rival philosophies. It is at this stage that the adversarial style of British politics is most obvious, and it is also this dramatic ritual which is highly prized by many traditional defenders of parliamentary procedure. The result of the second reading debate will determine whether the bill is to proceed. If the vote is positive the bill will go on to its committee stage, which involves a clause-by-clause and perhaps a line-by-line discussion; this will normally take place in a standing committee of the House of Commons. (Non-controversial bills may also have their second reading in committee, but this is relatively rare.) Only bills of unusual importance or of a constitutional nature and some requiring quick passage (and the government decides which bills fall into these categories) and the main provisions of finance bills are dealt with at the committee stage by the whole House of Commons – 'in committee of the whole House' or 'on the floor' as this procedure is known.

It is significant that 'standing committees' in the House of Commons are no longer what is usually meant by this designation in many other legislatures. They are not committees already in existence with a defined membership so that business can be allotted to them as need arises: the membership of a standing committee depends upon the particular bill under discussion. While the whips on both sides of the House of Commons may well choose members of standing committees from MPs who have a special interest in the subject matter of a given bill, the essential requirement is that the balance of votes on the committee should reflect party strength in the House. Thus except where there is no overall majority in the House – as was the case between 1976 and 1979 – government can nearly always rely on being able to defeat any amendment to which it takes exception. The minister responsible for a bill also has an important advantage over its critics: he has his civil servants available to brief him on the implications of each proposed amendment. Sometimes the occasional amendment will be produced which will raise new issues – perhaps from a backbencher rather than from the opposition; however in theory committee amendments must be in harmony with the overall purpose of the bill.

After the committee stage comes the report stage when a bill, as amended in committee, is reported back to the House. This stage gives a government a further opportunity to put forward its own amendments to a bill, to reverse amendments made in committee or to endorse the treatment accorded to a bill by the standing committee or committee of the whole House. As at the committee stage, the introduction of government amendments here may reflect party or interest group representations made between the formal introduction of the bill and the detailed consideration of it; alternatively they may reflect changed circumstances which make such an alteration desirable.

The final stage in the House of Commons' consideration of a bill is the third reading, which involves the discussion of the principles of a bill again, though now in its amended version. The outcome, like that of a second reading, will usually be determined by a government's majority; however, of course, it is possible that a revolt within the governing party may have grown by this stage and thus on some occasions there may be a setback. The total impact of the House of Commons on the details of legislation is very slight in proportion to the amount of time devoted by members to legislative matters. A detailed study of the fate of government bills over the three parliamentary sessions of 1967–8, 1968–9 and 1970–1 revealed that only thirty-nine amendments were successfully pressed home by opposition members or by government backbenchers, despite the fact that thousands of such amendments were moved. Of the thirty-nine in question not more than nine were substantial.[13]

More recently, however, there was the case of the Local Government (Finance) Bill in the 1981–2 session when the original bill met with so much backbench opposition on the government side that it was withdrawn and a new Local Government (Finance) No. 2 Bill introduced in its stead.

Once a bill has passed through all its stages in one House it must be considered by the other. The House of Lords may thus make changes to a bill already passed by the House of Commons, which in turn has the power to reject these amendments and will often do so. If it does not the reason may be that the government has itself changed its mind or that it is unwilling to incur a degree of popular odium if the issue evokes strong feelings. Thus the provision for making seatbelts compulsory in the Transport Act of 1981 was introduced as an amendment in the House of Lords and accepted by the House of Commons on a free vote. Although the secretary of state for transport was hostile to the amendment, the government did not put on a whip in this instance because it judged that opinion was divided on the issue.

The foregone conclusion of most standing committee deliberations and the technical level of such serious argument as takes place mean that their proceedings attract little publicity and are hence relatively unattractive to MPs. It is because the influence of the House of Commons is thus essentially an indirect one, depending primarily on the relationship between governments and their own backbench supporters, that would-be reformers of the role of Parliament have not on the whole devoted much attention to the legislative functions of Parliament.[14] However, the long-drawn-out nature of the legislative process did attract the attention of some reformers who thought that Parliament could be made more efficient; in the 1977–8 session the procedure committee devoted time to the subject and the issue was taken up again in the 1983–4 session. A limited experiment was also made during the 1979–83 Parliament by which government bills of a technical or non-controversial nature (for example bills on deep sea mining and the law of criminal attempts) could be submitted to a new type of standing committee which would have the power to call for evidence and to examine witnesses. However this move still left procedure in the House of Commons a long way from that of the United States Congress, where it is normal to submit legislative proposals to extensive committee hearings. And it seemed that the limited experiment with these so-called 'special standing committees' found less favour with the leader of the House in the 1983 Parliament than it had in the previous Parliament so that even this attempt to improve the detailed consideration of bills may have been abandoned, although such a committee was used for the Matrimonial Proceedings Bill.

Lack of parliamentary time is always one of the most serious of problems for governments with a heavy legislative commitment. The total output of public legislation rose steeply after 1945, fell again during the 1950s and has shown a substantial rise since then. In 1957, 1,103 pages were added to the statute book; in 1973, 2,248 pages; in 1981, 2,276 pages were added. But recently some legislation has been in the form of consolidation acts which have the effect of actually reducing the number of statutes in force at any given moment. Thus there was a reduction of over 500 between 1964 and 1981 and the process continues. Furthermore the United Kingdom is one of the world's largest unitary states, and much parliamentary legislation is of a kind that elsewhere would be left to subordinate authorities.[15]

To avoid filibustering, either a closure motion – which closes debate – or a guillotine motion – which fixes a timetable for the discussion of each group of clauses in committee and of each remaining stage of a bill – is often required. Guillotine motions have become much more common in recent years. But the opposition will usually contest the guillotine motion and thus further time will be lost. Frequently the opposition will claim that it needs more time to discuss the details of a bill; but what it will really want to do is to proclaim again its opposition to the bill on principle. In the case of the Industrial Relations Bill of 1971, 111 of its 150 clauses were not discussed either in committee or at the report stage. The failure of the House of Commons to debate many of the clauses of the devolution bills in 1978 was one reason for the freedom with which the House of Lords sought to amend them.

Parliament also finds it difficult to deal with the growing output of delegated legislation – i.e. legislation made by the executive by virtue of powers conferred by statute on the Crown, departments or individual ministers. The principal form used is that of the statutory instrument. Statutory instruments are published serially by the year and can be used for instance to vary the amount paid in social benefits, as in number 475 of 1978 – 'mobility allowance uprating order, 1978'. Other subordinate legislation includes the rules made by local authorities and other public bodies. The figures concerning delegated legislation are once again revealing of a general trend. After reaching a peak in the 1940s, the number of statutory instruments declined in the 1950s but started to rise again in the mid-1960s; they now average between 1,000 and 1,300 a year. Their length also increased markedly at one time, but there has recently been something of a reversal of this trend. In 1955, new statutory instruments filled 3,240 pages; in 1965 they filled 6,435 pages; in 1974 they filled 8,667 pages; but in 1981 they filled only 6,557 pages.

Formal parliamentary control over delegated legislation is maintained by a variety of procedures. Acts may require that instruments made under their provisions should be laid before Parliament; the usual procedure in these cases means that an instrument will become effective after a given time – usually forty days – unless a negative resolution has in the meantime been passed by either House. In the case of some instruments an affirmative resolution is required. This requirement applies to all statutory instruments of constitutional significance concerned with the implementation of major aspects of the parent legislation. Even so, Parliament's powers are limited with respect to delegated legislation since statutory instruments cannot be amended by either House but only rejected; on the other hand the affirmative procedure does mean that the minister may have to defend before Parliament the substance of an instrument.

Negative resolutions are only a limited protection against arbitrary or unwise government action: the sheer volume of delegated legislation and the usual limitations upon time make it difficult for Parliament to supervise it effectively. Of course in both the affirmative and the negative procedures a government will use its majority to secure the delegated legislation.

The role of committees is a significant indication of the actions of Parliament in this sphere. The House of Commons Select Committee on Statutory Instruments which existed until 1972 was limited in its terms of reference to dealing with the technical aspects of the delegated legislation examined; it was chiefly important for making departments pay attention to clarity and consistency in their drafting and for preventing them from straying beyond the bounds of the parent Act. The corresponding House of Lords Special Orders Committee had wider powers when it considered statutory instruments that required an affirmative resolution. The Lords' one rejection of a statutory instrument – the instrument renewing sanctions against the Smith regime in Rhodesia – was an important factor in the events leading to the abortive Parliament Bill of 1968–9 which attempted radically to reform the House of Lords. Since February 1973 the consideration of statutory instruments from the technical point of view has been the responsibility of a joint committee of both Houses of Parliament. This device is in itself rather rare in the British system, though a joint committee also exists to consider consolidation bills (bills which bring together in a simple Act provisions in respect of a particular topic previously dealt with in different statutes).

The House of Commons also has a standing committee on statutory instruments which is entitled to consider the merits of the proposed instruments and which may actually debate them, especially if they are of the type which will be ratified by the affirmative procedure. The instruments then go to the House of Commons for formal approval. The opposition can (and sometimes does) object to a statutory instrument being dealt with in committee, and can insist upon its being debated on the floor, though this is not often done.

A new source of delegated legislation is the European Economic Community, some of whose legislation, especially when it takes the form of directives (which are technically primary legislation), does necessitate the passage of delegated legislation in the United Kingdom. The responsibility in the House of Commons for dealing with European legislation in general rests with the Select Committee on European Legislation.

Financial Procedure

Equally important is Parliament's role in finance.[16] Traditionally Parliament has operated on the theory that it will first consider what government needs to spend in the ensuing financial year and then make provision for such expenditure through taxation. Parliament's instrument of control – the Public Accounts Committee, which is backed by the comptroller and auditor general and his staff, is designed to check in detail that money has been spent only on the purposes for which it has been voted by Parliament as well as to guard against corruption. It is thus assumed that Parliament's main interest lies in checking executive extravagance. However, although these elements of parliamentary control have their uses, they have become relatively minor in relation to the role of government in an advanced industrial society.

From the point of view of civil servants, the traditional annual estimates and revenue decisions are artificial divisions in programmes which either make permanent demands on the Exchequer (as in the case of the main government services) or, where capital expenditure is concerned, are based on a five-year or ten-year 'forward look'. Basic decisions about expenditure are taken long before the estimates or the finance bill come up for parliamentary discussion. By that stage usually only minor adjustments are possible. Decisions about raising money in particular ways, whether by taxation or by loan, will be affected not only by government requirements but also by calculations about the effect of such steps upon the general level of economic activity. Taxation and borrowing now perform the dual function of providing for services and controlling demand and the level of investment; however the historic procedures of Parliament for dealing with finance pre-date recognition of this general economic responsibility.

From the Whitehall perspective the important aspect of public expenditure – including local government expenditure and expenditure by the public sector of the economy – is its effect in the long term. Whitehall now takes for granted the necessity of economic forecasting, and of allowing for changes in technology and in the external economic environment. From another perspective however – that of the individual departmental ministers – the vital decisions are those which cause the expansion or contraction of particular branches of government, again not so much in the immediate future but in the medium or long term. For Parliament, as the supreme arbiter of the nation's fortunes, the essential question is whether it can participate effectively in this process; and much of the unease about Parliament's role is influenced by the general suspicion that it cannot.

In recent years governments have become rather more willing to reveal in white papers and through other channels the basic presuppositions of their economic thinking and their consequent projections of the future demands likely to be made upon total resources by public expenditure. The Treasury remains reluctant about extending this experiment in open government further, although more progress could probably be made if there were sufficient public demand for it. Discussions of changes in taxation are difficult to initiate because the economy is extremely sensitive to speculations about such amendments; however even here there is room for more openness. In May 1971 one step was taken when a select committee was established to consider government proposals for the reform of the corporation tax; the detailed consideration of the proposed wealth tax announced in 1974 was also submitted to a select committee. The difficulty perhaps does not lie so much in the recalcitrance of the administration as in the indifference of parliamentarians; there seems to be no direct relationship between the importance of an issue and the interest which MPs are likely to show in it. Debates upon such general questions as the long-term pattern of public expenditure – which must to some extent affect all parties, since decisions taken may become operative only in the next Parliament or even in the one after that – will neither attract MPs nor receive much public attention. They do not provide the occasion for the gladiatorial clashes which can occur when Parliament is at its liveliest. Mere discussion upon which no immediate decisions hang does not attract party politicians, and Parliament is not well equipped as a forum for discussing complex economic ideas.

However, some commentators have argued that Parliament could play an effective part in the control of public expenditure if the parliamentary timetable were changed. The way the annual estimates are put through the House of Commons is complicated by the fact that the financial year, which runs from 5 April, is not the same as the parliamentary session, which runs in most years from November to October (and in that period the last three months or so cover the summer recess). As a result the House of Commons may at various times be confronted with estimates covering the previous year, the current year and the forthcoming year. Similarly, the three consolidated fund bills which form the authorization part of the financial process, and which have been taken traditionally in February, March and just before the recess, are not in a form which enables the House to give consideration to the content of government finance, still less to imposing changes upon it.

The disjunction which exists between the House's constitutional position and practice has long been clear to those responsible for bringing procedure into line with realities. Moreover the trend of development in the present century has been to use the time formally allotted to the estimates – supply days – for general debates upon policy. In those debates the opposition had a share of the initiation of the subjects for debate. Similarly the consolidated fund bills provided occasions on which private members chosen by ballot could initiate debate on subjects of their choice.

This reality was recognized in further changes which were decided by the House of Commons in July 1982. Three full sittings a year were to be devoted to particular estimates which would be chosen for discussion by the Liaison Committee – the body which coordinates the work of the new post-1979 departmental select committees. Supply days have thus disappeared, and in their stead there are now nineteen days in each session reserved for opposition business. The proceedings on the consolidated fund bill are now formal; but after the formal proceedings, time will be given for the initiation of short debates.

A different approach to greater parliamentary control of finance was to seek to strengthen the Public Accounts Committee in relation to the comptroller and auditor general and to widen the scope of his jurisdiction. A bill, the Parliamentary Control of Expenditure (Reform) Bill, was introduced in the 1982–3 session by Norman St John Stevas, a former leader of the House. The bill was in principle accepted by the government, which did however secure a great many changes during its passage through standing committee. As originally drafted the bill would have submitted the accounts of the nationalized industries to the scrutiny of the comptroller and auditor general. This suggestion was strongly opposed, not least by the industries concerned. As a compromise the government tabled a new clause which would have provided for commercial auditors to deal with their accounts in consultation with the industry's sponsoring department, the Public Accounts Committee and the select committee with jurisdiction over the sponsoring department. But the new clause was defeated in standing committee and all provisions related to the nationalized industries were dropped.[17]

It was provided under the National Audit Act, as the bill became, that the comptroller and auditor general should be an officer of the House of Commons and that his department should be known as the National Audit Office. In recommending a person for appointment to the post, the prime minister would need the agreement of the chairman of the Public Accounts Committee. A new body – the Public Accounts Commission (PAC) – was to be established to oversee the expenses and accounts of the National Audit Office; it would consist of the chairman of the PAC, the leader of the House of Commons and seven other non-ministerial members of the House. Most significantly, the comptroller and auditor general would no longer be tied to the technicalities of accounting and the testing of the legality of expenditure but would also carry out 'examinations into the economy, efficiency and effectiveness' with which the departments and other public authorities which came under his purview made use of their resources in discharging their functions. In fact the comptroller and auditor general had been conducting such investigations for a number of years; the new Act gave him statutory authority for the practice.

Although the latest changes take account of the executive's predominance in financial matters they do allow for greater publicity and discussion in relation to these issues. It has however been suggested that something more should be done to give Parliament a role in relating taxation to expenditure. The Treasury and Civil Service Select Committee looked at this subject in the 1981–2 session and the Select Committee on Procedure (Finance) looked at it in the following session. The Select Committee on Procedure's Report recommended that the House should 'take a view' on the need to integrate taxation and expenditure.[18] But so far no action on these lines has been taken by the House of Commons.

The difficulty of dealing with financial and economic matters would exist even if the parties were as little divided in their economic philosophies today as they were in the second half of the nineteenth century. However, the problem of promoting useful economic debate is exacerbated by the deep ideological divisions in Parliament. Parliamentary reformers sometimes ignore the dynamics of party and faction which together with ambition for office constitute the motor forces of the parliamentary system. It may be desirable to try to reform parliamentary procedures on the assumption that an accepted set of national priorities shared by all parties is in theory attainable; in practice neither history nor observation suggest that any such unanimity is likely to be reached.

Select Committees and the Limits of Reform

Many of the obstacles to reforming Parliament's financial procedures also prevent Parliament from establishing greater control over the general processes of administration.[19] Specialist select committees for Agriculture and for Science and Technology were set up as an experiment in 1966 by Richard Crossman when he was leader of the House of Commons. It was hoped that members of such committees would be able to stand back from the party struggle and examine impartially the implementation of policies and the efficiency with which policies were being administered. The so-called 'Crossman committees' had been preceded by the Select Committee on Nationalized Industries (set up in 1956–7) and they were followed by other new select committees. Thus select committees were established to examine race relations and immigration, to examine overseas development and – with the introduction of a parliamentary commissioner for administration or ombudsman – to receive his reports and to provide a mechanism for bringing pressure to bear on the government if it should try to ignore his recommendations.

An attempt to bring together financial scrutiny and the pursuit of efficiency was made in 1971 by replacing the old Estimates Committee with a new Expenditure Committee. This operated through its general or steering committee and five subject subcommittees.

Even those most enthusiastic for an extension of the select committee system had to admit that the essential link between the work of the select committees and the wider public would be debates on the floor of the House. But these, of course, would come up against the familiar pressures on the parliamentary timetable. Between 1970 and 1977, the select committees made 316 reports, of which 115 were from the House of Commons 'domestic committees' which deal with the work and amenities of the House itself. Time was found to debate only forty-four of the total number of select committee reports; and half of those reports debated were from the 'domestic committees'.

Equally disappointing from the point of view of select committee enthusiasts was the sparse attendance at such debates.

It was against this background that the important suggestions for changing the organization of parliamentary business were made in the 1977–8 session. These suggestions were contained in the First Report from the Select Committee on Procedure, which was published in August 1978. In many respects this report was negative: the options it rejected included changes in Parliament's hours of work; the general use of pre-legislative standing committees except in areas remote from party controversy; a return to specialized standing committees; and the device of outline or enabling bills, i.e. bills which deal with their subject matter in very broad terms, leaving the detail to be filled in by the minister under powers granted to him in the enabling legislation. Indeed rather than encourage greater powers for the executive over the detail of legislation, the Report devoted a good deal of attention to suggestions for strengthening the House of Commons' control over delegated legislation. Finally the Report rejected the suggestion that there should be a more comprehensive method of timetabling for bills and upheld the existing system for imposing the guillotine on debates.

The Report made positive suggestions about two topics. One was the idea that a limited experiment in relation to standing committee procedure could take place in order to allow the taking of evidence when bills were of a technical or non-controversial character. The other much more important (and as it turns out enduring) change was the recasting of the whole existing system of select committees in order to give systematic coverage of all the major executive departments and to make the system of select committees more permanent and independent of the government it was meant to be monitoring. It thus endorsed the series of reforms which had been attempted over the previous years, which were based on the belief that backbenchers could best participate in the scrutiny aspects of Parliament's role rather than in its direct legislative processes.

The then Labour government was unenthusiastic about the Report; however its principal proposals formed the basis for the reforms introduced between June and October 1979 under the auspices of the new Conservative government and its Leader of the House, Norman St John Stevas.

The Expenditure Committee and its subcommittees disappeared, as did the Select Committee on Nationalized Industries, the Select Committee on Race Relations and the Select Committee on Science and Technology. In their place were fourteen committees – twelve of them were directly concerned with specific government departments, and one each with Scottish and Welsh affairs. Three of these committees were given limited powers to establish one subcommittee each. The criteria used by the Committee of Selection for choosing the members of the new committees excluded ministers, their parliamentary private secretaries and regular front-bench opposition spokesmen. The chairmen of select committees have been drawn from the members of the individual committees and have included some opposition members – a fact which may be of consequence when a committee decides to investigate a highly sensitive political question. A Liaison Committee was set up to co-ordinate the work of the committees as a whole. It was agreed moreover that the oversight of the executive could be extended to include public bodies exercising authority on their own, even if those bodies were not under the direct authority of ministers. Thus for the first time bodies such as ACAS and the Manpower Services Commission came under the supervision of select committees.

The staffing of the committees remained with the clerk's department of the House of Commons, though the committees made increased use of the power to recruit specialist advisers who could be appointed either for the duration of a Parliament or for the duration of specific inquiries. Where necessary the committees could also appoint full-time researchers. On the other hand, suggestions by the Procedure Committee that the select committees should have powers to order the attendance of ministers and the production of documents were rejected in favour of a general pledge of cooperation.

In the 1979–83 Parliament the new committees were very active. Their membership totalled 149 at any one time. Although it was intended that the new select committees should have a more durable membership than the previous select committees had enjoyed, there was still a certain amount of turnover in the membership as individuals received promotion on both sides of the House of Commons. Attendance at the select committee meetings was variable, ranging from 64 per cent for the Energy Committee to 89 per cent for the Home Affairs Committee's subcommittee on Race Relations and Immigration. In the last full session of that Parliament – in 1981–2 – the number of meetings varied even more sharply, from ten in the case of the Foreign Affairs Committee dealing with overseas development and thirteen in the case of the Race Relations and Immigration subcommittee, to thirty in the case of the Committee on Education, Science and the Arts. The select committees' use of specialist advisers (who were paid at different *per diem* rates) was also very uneven. The Foreign Affairs Committee called on twenty-nine such persons and the Treasury and Civil Service Committee on twenty-eight, while the Education, Science and Arts Committee called on twenty. At the other extreme the Select Committee on Industry and Trade required only six such advisers and the Home Affairs Committee only three. In all 171 persons were employed in an advisory capacity to select committees during the lifetime of the Parliament.

Witnesses included cabinet and non-cabinet ministers, civil servants of all ranks from permanent secretary to principal and – in the case of the Defence Committee – officers of the armed services. Several of the committees made visits abroad – an activity which had been contested in the Crossman period when the Select Committee on Agriculture had wished to travel to Brussels to examine aspects of European agricultural policy. The new select committees published a flow of reports which usually included transcripts of the evidence taken. But, as with their predecessors, there was difficulty in finding time for these reports to be debated: only 3 per cent of those published during the lifetime of the Parliament were the subject of specific debates, and only another 7 per cent were mentioned on the order paper as relevant to other debates. In so far as the reports normally drew attention to a need for a government department to take action, they called for replies, and these were forthcoming from the individual departments. But the lapse of time between the public-ation of a select committee report and the receipt of the government's reply varied between sixty and 150 days. All in all, it was reckoned that the work involved in answering the select committees' enquiries and reports involved about 12,000 man-days per year.[21]

In the Parliament elected in June 1983 it proved impossible to set up the system of select committees before the summer recess, since the Labour Party wished to elect its new front bench before nominating its representatives to the select committees, and these shadow cabinet elections had been postponed to await the leadership election at the party conference in September. But when Parliament met again in November, the full complement of select committees was established. A number of important matters were dealt with and reports of some consequence published during the remainder of the session.

It would appear that committee work is not only taking up more of the time of more members – over 180 MPs have participated in the work of the subject committees in the present Parliament – but that the membership of them is increasingly sought by MPs. Many MPs have found serving on them not merely rewarding in its own right, but a means to political advancement. This was perhaps most true in relation to the Scottish Affairs Committee in the 1979–83 Parliament. And there have been some cases of opposition MPs preferring work on a select committee to being a front-bench spokesman. Thus for example John Golding preferred to be chairman of the Select Committee on Employment rather than seek a Labour opposition front-bench portfolio.

The question of participation in select committees is, of course, connected to the wider one of turning parliamentary activity into a full-time career commitment. Members who retain outside occupations and professional commitments (and there are many MPs who do, especially on the Conservative side) increasingly seem to regard those commitments as subsidiary to their political work. Yet there are vestiges of the older attitude that it should be possible to combine being an MP with another occupation. Thus for example Richard Crossman's experiment with morning sessions was a failure, and it is still difficult to ensure attendance at committees during the morning. Much of Parliament's most important business is therefore still conducted in the evening, a fact which many MPs find disruptive of normal family life.

Although the House of Commons permits its members to continue with occupations and outside commitments which may have been gained as a result of the MP's political connections, members must indicate when they speak in the House of Commons if they have a personal interest in the topic before Parliament. The danger of potential corruption has been further acknowledged by the introduction of a register of interests, although this register is voluntary and has been objected to by some MPs as an invasion of privacy. At the beginning of 1985 it appeared that 388 directorships were shared between 179 MPs and that, although this form of outside interest was still very evident, a new role was also developing for MPs as political consultants.[22] The income which outside commitments generate – whether from directorships, consultancies or journalism – is obviously attractive to MPs given that their salaries are poor by European standards; and there is also the fact that in some cases an association with a commercial firm will provide an MP with a better standard of office and secretarial facilities than he would otherwise enjoy. Whether more generous pay and allowances would reduce the desire of MPs to maintain additional occupations or lead to a greater movement towards committee work in the House of Commons is difficult to say; what can be said with certainty is that it is becoming increasingly difficult for an MP to play a full part in the House of Commons, keep links with his constituency and pursue substantial outside work.

Opinions differ on the extent to which the new select committee system has affected the character of Britain's parliamentary institutions. Certainly much evidence on governmental activity has been made public that might otherwise have remained unexplored; and the views of important pressure groups – especially the CBI and the TUC – can also be better understood from the evidence given to select committees. Naturally ministers are somewhat wary of those committees which take up sensitive aspects of policy, and this will be especially true if the representation from their own party on a select committee is not entirely in harmony with ministerial thinking. (This occurred with the Treasury and Civil Service Select Committee, where the economic philosophy of the government was not entirely shared by all Conservative members, let alone the Labour ones.) Ministers may also be concerned that a select committee report could contain material useful to the opposition. The topics which committees take up have varying degrees of party political content, so that some may represent a narrow line of administrative inquiry while others go to the heart of inter-party debate or reflect the concerns of a particular chairman.

On the other hand ministers and civil servants have found it possible to reconcile the inquiries of select committees with the maintenance of a degree of confidentiality in relation to the advice given by civil servants to ministers. The conventions of ministerial responsibility – as was noted in chapter 1 – have been changing, and the select committees are part of a larger process of accommodation to demands for more information about public policy and less secrecy about decision-making. And indeed some committees have differed over the extent to which civil servants have proved useful witnesses as opposed to ministers.

Parliament and the Road to Office

In addition to Parliament's function as a legislative body and as an institution concerned with the scrutiny of executive activity, it has two other distinct roles. First, it is the source from which ministers are chosen. The possibility of obtaining governmental office is one of the factors which compensates many backbenchers for the routine and often mundane duties which they have to perform – such as marching through the division lobbies when the outcome of a vote is predictable. To impress the party leadership in Parliament an MP must demonstrate to the House of Commons that he or she can shine in the peculiar arts demanded there: exchanges at Question Time or perhaps in standing committee matter more in this respect than technical expertise or intellectual ability. Members of Parliament must thus, if they wish to advance their careers, call attention to themselves; and this obviously puts a premium on those procedural changes which allow backbenchers to discuss topical issues at short notice.

To discuss topical issues has become easier since the debates on the adjournment of the House of Commons at or after 10 pm – when government business is usually completed – can now be used for raising matters of immediate interest with fewer restrictions than in the past. Also with increased committee activity – often focussed on topical issues – MPs may be able to enhance their reputations away from the floor of the House. An impact in a select committee will be reported via the whips to the party leadership; and although there will be occasions on which the government may be irritated at one of its own backbenchers who gives aid and comfort to the opposition either through select committee work or by intervention in standing committee, the overall atmosphere of the House of Commons is generally such that the able and assiduous will be rewarded.

Parliament and the Public

The second remaining role for Parliament – the educative function – is in many ways the one it fulfils best, although of course it does not exercise this function directly but rather as a by-product of its other functions of debate and scrutiny. The great set-piece debates over legislation, the endless reports which rarely get noticed by the general public or receive only a cursory reply from the government, the variety of mechanisms for overseeing administrative activity – all these have their ultimate justification in the extent to which they make available to the public information about the workings and the quality of the British governmental process.

The importance of this educative function perhaps in itself justifies the survival of many of the traditional and ceremonial aspects of Parliament. The formal occasions such as the state opening of Parliament by the monarch emphasize the legislature's link with the whole of the country's history. The constitutional responsibility of the executive to the legislature is highlighted by the twice-weekly appearance of the prime minister at the despatch box; and the formal presentation of the budget to the House of Commons underlines the connection between taxation and representation. Above all there is the role of the opposition, which provides the chairmen of key committees such as the Public Accounts Committee, the Statutory Instruments Committee and some of the newer departmental select committees. The opposition also has, as has been seen, the right to choose the subjects for debate on certain days. For all the control which government now has over the House of Commons, the operation of the system is shown to depend upon compromise and accommodation, upon members sharing – regardless of party or ideology – some common values, and upon the importance of the somewhat stylized conventions of behaviour.

The most important example of the operation of these conventions and informal understandings – apart from the role of the official opposition – is the position of the Speaker. The Speaker was originally the voice of the House of Commons, declaring its wishes to the monarch or to ministers. When ministers began themselves to figure prominently in the House of Commons, the Speaker might have become a party leader operating from the vantage point of the chair, as in the American House of Representatives. Instead in the nineteenth century there developed the idea of a wholly neutral chairman who would hold the balance between factions and parties in the House and ensure that the debates recorded all shades of opinion. The Speaker must thus see himself as a referee and as the natural protector of minorities. What is remarkable is the way in which this role can be successfully assumed by the Speaker and his deputies despite the fact that these individuals have previously been immersed in party politics, frequently at a ministerial level. Thus the impartiality of the Speaker and his deputies is almost always taken for granted by MPs. The definition of parliamentary privilege – the rules which protect MPs against outside interference with their freedom of action and bind them to certain codes of conduct – is determined by a committee and applied by it to particular cases. However, the Committee on Privileges acts upon references to it from the Speaker; and it is at his command that any action upon a report from that committee is taken.[23]

The broadcasting of Parliament – especially during the Speakership of George Thomas (now Viscount Tonypandy) – made the role of the Speaker a vivid one to many who had never witnessed the House of Commons in session. It also brought home to many people how rowdy MPs can be, especially during Question Time. While there have been complaints over the years that Parliament was becoming too unruly, different views may be taken of this behaviour. On the one hand it is possible to criticize the style of those MPs who repeatedly ignore or reject the normal conventions of the House of Commons, sometimes to the extent of getting themselves 'named' by the Speaker; on the other there is a sense in which this behaviour reflects an extreme style of politics which cannot be sanitized by procedural niceties and conventions.

It is perhaps of some interest that the House of Lords (which itself began in January 1985 an experiment in the televising of its proceedings) does not have a Speaker to keep debate orderly and to control the members of the House. The lord chancellor and his deputies in the upper chamber have no disciplinary powers which, while they exist in the House of Lords, can only be exercised by the House as a whole and not by its presiding officer. The interpretation of the wishes of the House of Lords is left to the leader of the House, one of the three or four cabinet ministers who sit in the upper chamber.

Staffing the House of Commons and the House of Lords there are teams of clerks whose role parallels that of the Civil Service in many ways. The clerk of the House of Commons and his team in particular ensure that MPs frame their questions in accordance with the rules of the House and assist MPs in acquiring material for their speeches. In committee work also the capacity of the clerks to regard themselves as servants of all MPs and not just of the majority party is extremely important.

Yet it would be absurd to ignore the fact that while some facilities of the House of Commons are available on non-partisan lines, much of the work of the House assumes the existence of party and indeed is organized through the two-party system. The main form which this party element takes is the office of the whip. The whips of every party perform two distinct roles which, although apparently contradictory, in fact complement each other. The whips are first and foremost the principal assistants of the party leader in organizing debates and ensuring the necessary turnout of votes in each division lobby. But they are also the channel through which backbenchers' views are conveyed to the leadership and the leadership's views are conveyed to backbenchers. It is for this reason that the chief whip of the majority party normally attends cabinet meetings by invitation when he is not himself a member of the cabinet. The whips are thus at the very heart of the power struggle between the parties, although by convention they are silent in parliamentary debates. Without effective communications between the parties they could not do their job. The timetable of Parliament is normally arranged between the whips – although a government with a majority could impose its will unilaterally if it wished. And it is the whips who arrange the 'pairs' through which MPs can miss divisions for personal reasons or to meet external commitments – that is to say agreements between members on opposite sides by which they can both absent themselves, since their votes if cast would cancel each other out. If what are called the 'usual channels' become blocked – if whip cannot talk to whip – Parliament cannot function smoothly. The payment out of public funds of salaries to the principal opposition whips in both Houses is a recognition of the importance of the whips for the orderly working of the parliamentary system.

The operation of Parliament is thus at once facilitated and constrained by the party divisions and party organization. Yet despite the ambiguous role which Parliament performs in the political system and the diversity of views about how it might be reformed there is no shortage of men and women who seek to become MPs. Indeed, it could be argued that the effectiveness of the system depends less on its internal procedures than on the quality of its members. Attention should now be directed away from the House of Commons and towards those factors which determine its composition – the electoral system and the political parties themselves.

6   The Electoral System

The body of rules governing the British electoral process has often been seen as one of the keys to understanding the causes of the country's political stability. The gradual evolution towards universal adult suffrage, and the elimination of various forms of electoral corruption, occurred as ruling elites were forced to acknowledge the need for the political system to accommodate concrete social changes. Abstract discussions of electoral equality and democratic theory were much less important in reforming this aspect of the British constitution than the shrewd realism of practising politicians. The United Kingdom's electoral arrangements are thus suffused with the spirit of pragmatism and with an awareness that imperfections are bound to exist in machinery so intricately involved in the struggle for power between the parties.

The fact that the British have a long tradition of tolerating anomalies in their electoral system should not, however, be allowed to obscure the fact that the electoral system has recently been the subject of criticism. Particular controversy has surrounded the British method for translating votes into seats – the so-called 'first-past-the-post' or simple plurality method. The experience of 1974–9 and the result of the general election of 1983 as well as the publicity given to methods employed by other European countries did much to heighten that controversy. Although most arguments about the merits of the British electoral system now focus on this aspect, it is important to remember that what principally concerned nineteenth and early twentieth-century politicians was the actual extent of the franchise. Indeed every successive change in the franchise was a matter of party controversy as well as a stimulus to debate about the foundations of the constitution itself (though Bagehot was moved to describe the coming of the Second Reform Act as 'the most silent of revolutions'.[1]

Th primary feature of the extension of the electorate in the nineteenth century was its slowness. Compromise and tolerance of anomalies ensured that even when the principle of universal adult male suffrage was implemented in 1918 vestiges of older theories of representation lingered on. Corporate or group representation in the House of Commons survived in the form of university constituencies until the Representation of the People Act of 1948 abolished them along with the provisions for additional voting on the basis of occupation of business premises.[2]

Women achieved the vote only in 1918, and even then the fear that they would be a numerical majority in the electorate induced Parliament to differentiate between the sexes in relation to the age at which the vote was acquired: men could vote at twenty-one, but initially women had to wait until they were thirty for the chance to participate in the electoral process. The Representation of the People Act of 1928 abolished this anomaly, but it was a deeply divisive issue, and many Conservative politicians thought that this so-called 'flapper vote' had lost them the general election of 1929.

The most recent alteration in the franchise occurred in 1969 when the Representation of the People Act of that year increased the size of the electorate by lowering the voting age to eighteen, following the report of the Latey Committee on the Age of Majority.[3] (A Speaker's Conference which had examined the question had suggested that the age should be lowered to twenty, but its advice was ignored.)[4] It is tempting to speculate about the extent to which this extension of the franchise contributed to the electoral volatility of the 1970s; but certainly the change, coming as it did at the end of a decade in which images of student unrest and direct action had received much exposure in the media, was a symbolic one. Youth, like women half a century earlier, had been incorporated into the political system, and the country's politicians had to reconcile themselves to constituencies made marginal by large university populations and to the task of canvassing schools.

Apart from age the right to vote in Britain is dependent upon inclusion in the electoral register and the existence of few formal legal disqualifications from voting. Since 1918 compiling the electoral register has been the responsibility of local authorities whose electoral registration officers supervise all aspects of the process of recording those who are entitled to vote; this process includes the annual house-to-house canvass on which the register is based. The fact that this responsibility now rests with the officials of local authorities reduces the likelihood in Britain of many of the defects which occur when registration is the personal responsiblity of the citizen. Voluntary registration discourages the poorest and least educated sections of society from voting; in the United States until very recently it has also had the effect of reducing the registration of ethnic minorities. (Even in Britain, with its system of semi-automatic registration, it is probable that a significant proportion of the immigrant community is unregistered; one study of Nottingham immigrants found as many as 27 per cent unregistered and commented that it was the 'poorly educated, unskilled and recently arrived amongst them who were least likely to have been registered'.)[5]

The weakness of the system is that registration officers, being anxious not to exclude any qualified voters from the list, often do not remove from it names not returned by householders on the annual questionnaire but leave them on if they have been returned in a previous year. The accuracy of the register may be too dependent on collaboration by householders who have the task of filling in and returning forms on which the register is based. Moreover the period of time which elapses between collecting the names of eligible voters and compiling the register means that it is inevitably out of date before publication and clearly gets even less accurate with the passing of time after publication as voters die or move their residence.[6]

The fact that the registration function is undertaken by the local authority is an enormous advantage to the political parties, who would otherwise have to devote their own energies and finances to the task of encouraging registration through costly advertising campaigns. As the cost of compiling and maintaining the electoral register – outside Northern Ieland – was £6,025,000 in 1973–4 according to the
Houghton Committee on Financial Aid to Political Parties, this is a particular advantage to small parties who have neither the financial nor the membership resources to undertake sustained organizational activity.[7] The disparities of wealth and membership which mark British political parties do matter at later stages of the electoral process – for example when it comes to organizing the postal vote: here Conservatives are generally thought to be superior to other parties in their ability to mobilize absentee voters.

The exclusions among adult citizens include peers who are excluded by common law from voting at parliamentary elections although they appear on the register for the purposes of local government and European Parliament elections.[8] Disfranchisement also occurs when a person is serving a prison sentence. It also applied until recently to all persons in a mental hospital, but disquiet arose when it became plain that some 50,000 voluntary patients in mental hospitals and psychiatric clinics were disfranchised because they would otherwise be homeless.[9] The position was altered in 1982 when the Mental Health (Amendment) Act provided a mechanism by which voluntary patients were entitled to vote.[10]

Eligibility to vote in British elections reflects Britain's imperial past in that it is exercised by 'British subjects' who are deemed to include not only British citizens as now defined but citizens of other

Commonwealth countries resident in Britain. The British Nationality Act of 1981 which now defines British citizenship was specifically declared not to affect the question of voting rights.[11]

Politically the most important legacy of the past is the right of citizens of the Republic of Ireland to vote in Britain. This right is based on s. 32 (1) of the British Nationality Act of 1948 which states that Irish citizens are not aliens.[12] (In June 1984 the Irish government secured through a referendum the authority to amend the law to enable this privilege to be reciprocated by giving the vote to British citizens domiciled in the Republic. It was expected that the necessary legislation would be passed in the Session of the Dail beginning in autumn 1984.) While the question of the Irish vote has been controversial from time to time, the idea of removing it comes up against the practical considerations inherent in the freedom of movement between the two countries as well as the political opposition of some Labour MPs with a substantial Irish vote in their constituencies (most of the Irish voters are manual workers and assumed to be pro-Labour both because of their class ties and because of the strong links between the Conservative party and the Ulster Protestants). It would also be likely to be seen as a provocative action in the context of London-Dublin relationships and, given the reciprocity now proposed in the Republic, the prospects of change are remote.

Persons who are convicted of 'corrupt or illegal electoral practices' in the United Kingdom are disfranchised for a period of five years, although in the case of illegal practices – which are in effect technical breaches of electoral law – the disfranchisement relates only to the constituency in which an offence occurred. Since 1883 there have been stringent limits placed on the amount of money which candidates may spend in the course of an election campaign, and these legal restrictions, together with the strictly enforced procedures for reporting election expenses, have meant that Britain has been relatively free from this form of corruption. Indeed it has been convincingly argued that the British electoral system had eliminated all forms of corrupt practices by the eve of the first world war.[13] However as will be seen later the strict regulation of expenditure really covers only money spent during the limited period of a campaign. Moreover there is also plenty of opportunity for governments as opposed to individual candidates to indulge in activities which could well be interpreted as electoral bribery. The most obvious examples of a government's ability to affect the voters' choice on a large scale is its alleged power to manipulate the economy to make an atmosphere of financial prosperity coincide with a general election or to produce an 'election budget'. The problem is clearly more intractable than the simple one of how best to ensure that electoral machinery itself does not permit corruption; it is perhaps salutary to bear in mind, as the third Marquess of Salisbury suggested in the 1860s, that the elimination of old problems of political morality does not preclude the emergence of novel ones.[14]

Voting in British elections is by ballots individually cast at polling stations on a designated date. Proxy or postal votes have been permitted for voters in the armed services and their spouses and for limited categories including persons whose occupation involves constant absence from their place of residence. Following a report from the Home Affairs Committee of the House of Commons in 1983, the government announced its intention of giving legislative effect in due course to some though not all of the changes the committee proposed, without recourse to the customary all-party 'Speaker's Conference'.[15]

Under the government's proposals the right to be registered as an absent voter for all elections would be restricted to service voters and those who are physically incapacitated. However the right to an absentee ballot would extend to British citizens resident abroad for the first seven years of their residence, provided that such citizens were on the register at the time of going abroad (this right was restricted during the passage of the bill). They would have to exercise the vote in the constituency where they were registered and the right would not apply to local elections. On the other hand the right to register as an absentee voter would be available for a particular election to all those who had reasons for not being able to vote in person on the given date, whether for reasons of employment, the need to care for a housebound relative or simply being away on holiday. The last provision would in the case of elections held in the summer months make a substantial difference to turnout. It would also place a premium on effective party organization in the constituencies. These proposals eventually became law.

Voting at parliamentary elections in the United Kingdom is now done entirely through single-member constituencies. Many defenders of the existing electoral system see the unique link between a single well-defined constituency and its MP as one of the great merits of the British electoral machinery. Most forms of proportional representation would require larger constituencies returning at least three MPs. One form of proportional representation discussed as a feasible experiment for the United Kingdom – the West German additional member system – does not however destroy the bond between an individual representative and his constituency. (The West German system retains the single-member constituency for half of its MPs, and the distortions are corrected when the remaining half are allocated between the parties on a straight party list system.) The United Kingdom's attachment to the single-member constituency is however of relatively recent origin. Until 1885 double-member constituencies were the norm; the last double-member constituencies disappeared only in time for the general election of 1950. In part double-member constituencies survived because of the reluctance of some cities to see their separate identities disappear, even when population growth justified the creation of additional seats. But what this mystique of the constituency with a distinct identity underlines is the tenacious belief that representation in the United Kingdom should in some way be connected with a coherent territorial unit and not simply based on the mathematical allocation of individual voters.

The British electoral system's remoteness from the idea of representing population *per se* may be traced back to the form taken by the earliest Parliaments. These Parliaments were summonses from the monarch to representatives of the counties and the boroughs as well as to the peers of the realm to attend at Westminster; thus the idea of representing a town or shire goes back to the Middle Ages. However, it is not this tradition alone that has shaped the British approach to such questions as constituency boundaries; it has to be admitted that, in addition, factors of party self-interest have played a prominent role in precluding the consideration of reforms which might remove some of the anomalies associated with the existing system. British politicians are not merely untroubled on the whole by the lack of representation which the system affords to minorities; they also display little of that concern for minimizing discrepancies in constituency size which has so strongly characterized the United States districting process since 1962. Individual electoral equality is not in the United Kingdom the holy grail that it has become across the Atlantic; as with the arguments surrounding the simple plurality system, the problem of boundary revisions has been discussed in a spirit which seeks a rough-and-ready fairness rather than absolute equality imposed by a slide-rule.

Until quite recently no machinery existed for securing a regular review of constituency boundaries. In the nineteenth century it was common to revise them following an extension of the franchise; but the upheaval was often so great that the procedure was not institutionalized until the end of the second world war, when steps were taken to provide for regular attempts to relate constituencies to population. (The criticism of the pre-1832 system had largely centred on the fact that many of the ancient boroughs which enjoyed parliamentary representation had by that stage been depopulated, while the new centres of population created by the Industrial Revolution were completely without political representation at Westminster.) The House of Commons (Redistribution of Seats) Act of 1944 established four Boundary Commissions for the four component parts of the United Kingdomn, whose duty it was to review their respective areas to ensure that within them constituencies did not vary from an electoral quota by more than 25 per cent. This electoral quota, obtained by dividing the number of seats available to the area into the electorate for that area, appeared somewhat meaningless as a norm if deviations as large as 25 per cent were to be allowed. Yet even this formula appeared too mechanical, so that when a new Act was passed in 1958 to accommodate objections to the procedure, the obligation to observe the 25 per cent variation was abandoned altogether.

The commissions themselves are nominally chaired by the Speaker of the House of Commons but are now effectively composed of a High Court judge who sits as deputy chairman together with two other members who must not be members of Parliament. For the English Boundary Commission, the Registrar-general and the director-general of the Ordnance Survey sit as assessors, while for the other commissions their equivalents perform the same task. In addition to the power to make general recommendations and revisions every five to seven years, each commission was given authority to make interim recommendations about specific problems. The Act of 1944 also introduced a procedure whereby local objections to proposed boundary changes could be heard. Once local objections have been taken into account the commissioners make their reports, which must be laid before Parliament with a draft Order in Council to give effect to their recommendations; Parliament may then decide whether to approve them by affirmative resolution or to reject them.

It has already been seen how, despite the Boundary Commission's theoretical task of producing equal constituencies, there has been an unwillingness to translate this requirement into an imperative with precise numerical implications. Since 1954 the Boundary Commissions have been urged to produce constituencies with electorates as close to their quota as is practicable, bearing in mind the need to respect such factors as local government boundaries and any special geographical features of the constituency. Needless to say, this still permits the existence of substantial variations in size between constituencies. Thus at the first general election after the redistribution of 1970, constituencies in England ranged from Meriden, which had 96,380 electors, to Newcastle Central – an inner city area –

with only 25,007 electors. While the average constituency had 64,077 electors there were five constituencies with over 90,000 electors, forty-nine with over 80,000, seventy-nine with 50,000 and seven with under 40,000. (In the general election of 1979 the disparities between English constituencies were even greater: Bromsgrove and Redditch had 104,375 voters while Newcastle Central had only 23,678.)

Yet marked though the disparities were after redistribution, they were far worse at the general election before it, as there had been no revision of boundaries to take account of population movements between 1954 and 1970. This failure to redistribute seats was largely the result of the Labour government's refusal to implement boundary changes prior to the 1970 election. Since 1958 the maximum interval between reviews has been increased to fifteen years – a delay which means that gross discrepancies in constituency size are likely to recur unless movements of population slow down or systematic arrangements are made for interim adjustments to boundaries.

A major redistribution took place just before the general election of 1983. The total number of seats was raised from 635 to 650, and only sixty-six constituencies were left unchanged, with another forty-three subjected to minor changes which affected less than 5 per cent of their electorates. The result was a new political geography which put party organization at the grass roots to a considerable test, since constituency associations had to be remodelled. The dynamics of redistribution threatened Labour because the movement of population from the inner cities meant that many safe but small Labour seats were abolished in the redistribution process. It was therefore perhaps inevitable that Labour would seek to delay the implementation of the Boundary Commissioners' proposals.

Table 2
Ratio of Electors to an MP at the General Elections of October 1974 and June 1983

	October 1974	June 1983
England	64,634 : 1	68,011
Scotland	51,927 : 1	54,642
Wales	55,798 : 1	56,273
Northern Ireland	86,377 : 1	62,423

Source: Figures compiled from *Report of the Hansard Society Commission on Electoral Reforms* (1976) and information from the Office of Population & Census.

One important facet of the redistribution which occurred immediately before the 1983 election was that it reduced the impact of the over-representation of Scotland and Wales within the United

Kingdom. Provision for seventy-one seats for Scotland had been made in the 1918 Representation of the People Act and was perpetuated in subsequent legislation. The number was now increased to seventy-two seats, but this was of course a smaller proportion of a larger House of Commons. The 1944 legislation had provided a minimum of thirty-five seats for Wales, but the figure had stood at thirty-six since 1950. It was now raised to thirty-eight. Nevertheless both Scotland and Wales remain over-represented in proportion to population. Northern Ireland had had only twelve MPs – a figure which left it under-represented by comparison with other parts of the United Kingdom. This discrepancy was however in part seen as justified by the existence of a separate domestic Parliament at Stormont. As direct rule had lasted for over a decade this reasoning ceased to be compelling and Northern Ireland was allotted seventeen seats in the new redistribution.

The redistribution in respect of individual constituencies in Britain did not embody the principle of equal representation which would have meant an electorate of just under 65,000 in each constituency. Fifty seats had over 75,000 electors and fifty seats had under 55,000 electors. The largest constituency, the Isle of Wight, had 94,226 electors and the smallest, the Western Isles, had 22,822 electors. The commissioners had clearly paid much attention to local government boundaries and to difficulties of internal communication. What had been achieved was the elimination of very small inner city constituencies. The smallest urban constituency in 1983 was Glasgow Provan, with an electorate of 47,706 electors. Indeed Glasgow remained the great beneficiary of the small urban seat, with nine of its eleven seats falling under the 55,000 level. London, which had had its number of seats reduced from ninety-two to eighty-four, had only eight seats with electorates of under 55,000.

Other parts of the country's electoral machinery are perhaps less controversial than the redistribution machinery. Although there are occasional independent candidates and a range of candidates for small parties, the contest at a general election is essentially between the standard-bearers of the major political parties. They will have chosen their candidates far in advance of the election in most cases and will usually have a well oiled machine ready to swing into action as soon as the date of the poll is announced. (The selection of candidates is further discussed in chapters 7 & 8.) In contrast to the position in the United States and France, specifically local issues play only a limited part in British general election campaigns. Campaigns do, it is true, assume a slightly different character in Scotland; and of course Northern Irish politics have become increasingly isolated from those of the mainland. On the whole, however, national issues predominate in the candidates' election addresses and in England at least the geographic origins of a candidate are fairly unimportant. Candidates do not for example have to fulfil any formal residence requirements, although frequently they will have to comply with informal pressures and expectations generated by activists in their constituencies on such matters as where candidates should live. Equally, if the constituency is one which has special characteristics – if mining, fishing, or farming play a significant role in it – or if it is one of the twenty or so constituencies where the student vote exceeds 5 per cent – then of course a candidate will be well advised to familiarize himself with these aspects of the area. But often the constituency for which a candidate stands will be determined by sheer chance rather than as the result of any objective assessment of his or her suitability for the area, or possession of local roots. Scotland is to some extent an exception to this rule, and after the loss of the February 1974 general election and the threat from the SNP there was a determined effort by Scottish Conservative associations to choose candidates with explicitly Scottish rather than English backgrounds. The hostility to what is seen as 'carpet-bagging' in Scotland was further underlined in 1982 when Roy Jenkins was selected to fight a Glasgow seat for the newly formed Social Democratic Party; although he was ultimately successful there was speculation about whether the size of his majority would not have been greater had he been of Scottish origin.

Once the candidates have been chosen they must be formally nominated by ten electors and pay a deposit of £150 which is returned if the candidate secures at least 12½ per cent of the votes cast. The obligation to furnish a deposit, and its amount, were fixed in 1918, with the intention of deterring frivolous candidates. Since the real value of the deposit has been eroded by inflation, its deterrent effect has been diminished, though the requirement remains a burden for minor parties and for third parties such as the Liberals and the SDP who will seek to cover every constituency. Recent years have seen a large crop of frivolous candidates at by-elections and general elections. Sometimes such candidates are merely using the free publicity afforded to them to further their non-political interests. Under the government's proposals put forward in January 1984 the figure for the deposit was to be increased to £1,000 (rather than the £2,000 which would be needed to make it equivalent in real terms to £150 in 1918 when the level of deposit was set); this figure was changed to £500 during the passage of the bill. At the same time, to try to avoid discouraging serious independent candidacies and minor parties, the vote required to save a deposit would be lowered to 5 per cent.

Certain categories of persons cannot sit in the House of Commons – peers who have not renounced their peerages, clergymen of the Church of England, ministers of the established Church of Scotland, Roman Catholic priests, persons serving prison sentences or in detention under the Mental Health Act of 1959. The holders of certain offices of profit under the Crown are also debarred from sitting there. The House of Commons (Disqualification) Act of 1975 lists those offices which are deemed incompatible with membership of the House. Judges, members of the armed forces, persons on the boards of nationalized industries and civil servants are thus all precluded from sitting, although members of these professions who resign are entitled to stand for Parliament. The aim of the restriction was initially to secure the independence from party politics of the profession concerned and to ensure that the House of Commons was not a body dominated by persons in the pay of the Crown.

During the election campaign itself – which lasts for legal purposes from the announcement of a dissolution of Parliament until the close of the polls on election day – there are strict rules governing the amount of expenditure that may be incurred on behalf of an individual candidate in his constituency. The rules used to be of great concern to the political parties, but the increasing impact of national party propaganda and the growing doubt about whether expenditure at constituency level affects votes to any great extent have perhaps rendered these elaborate restrictions somewhat artificial. Nevertheless these rules form an important part of the ritual election campaigns, since each candidate must appoint an agent – an institution unique to the United Kingdom – who is responsible for recording all expenditure on behalf of the candidate. The maximum level of expenditure is determined in accordance with a formula which may be amended from time to time to allow for the impact of inflation on the value of the sums concerned. At the 1983 general election the maximum expenditure per constituency was £2,700 plus 3.1p per registered voter in a county constituency or 2.3p per registered voter in a borough. In addition to these sums there are certain indirect grants in kind to candidates which the Houghton Committee viewed as indirect state support to the political parties. Candidates are each allowed to send one piece of literature through the post to each constituent free of charge, and are entitled to use, free of charge, any publicly owned meeting hall or school in their constituency during the campaign.

This legal framework was perhaps more appropriate to an age when there were distinct campaigns in individual constituencies and when the formal election period, which is regulated by law, was not preceded by a period of intense pre-election speculation and campaigning. If a Parliament runs to almost its full term – as the 1959–64 Parliament did – there will inevitably be a period in which the major parties are campaigning furiously at the national level. Yet this spate of expenditure, which almost certainly has more electoral impact than expenditure during the formal election campaign, is completely unregulated. Mrs Thatcher's decision to launch a full-scale publicity campaign in the summer of 1978 when there was much speculation – erroneous as it happened – about an autumn election highlighted the contradictions of an approach to political campaigning in which strictly regulated expenditure is but a footnote to a much longer essay in the techniques of influence and conversion. On the one hand, as the Conservative Party leader's opponents argued, the campaign broke the spirit if not the letter of the election laws because the posters used were inevitably sited within constituencies and would therefore have fallen within the regulated expenses after an announcement of an election. Mrs Thatcher's campaign – which was managed by a professional public relations firm and was alleged to have cost over two million pounds – fell outside any regulations because the posters were distributed outside a formal election campaign, although as was thought at the time, immediately prior to one. On the other hand, it could be argued that governments themselves have superior opportunities for the publication of their arguments and do not hesitate to use them even during an election campaign. One of the few legal cases in this complex area decided that a prime-ministerial broadcast could not count as an item of illegal expenditure even though the prime minister was then fighting a by-election at Kinross and West Perthshire in order to enter the House of Commons.[16]

One peculiarity of British election law in relation to illegal expenditure should be noted. The agent of a candidate is the only person who may legally spend money on his behalf. In law this means not only that a sympathizer of a candidate may not spend additional money on a candidate's behalf but also that any organization or group which seeks to persuade the electorate of the uniform unacceptability of all the candidates will be liable to prosecution. This rule affects organizations such as the National Front, which sometimes intervenes at elections without itself putting up a candidate. In August 1978, the Director of the Society for the Protection of the Unborn Child (SPUC) was charged with an offence under the Representation of the People Act 1949 for issuing leaflets during a by-election in which the abortion issue had been raised.[17]

One aspect of national election campaigns which excites special controversy is the allocation of broadcasting time between the parties. Television first became an important force in general election campaigns in the 1959 general election, because between 1945 and 1955 the so-called 'fourteen-day rule' had prevented the media from commenting on election issues during the final fortnight of a campaign. The sensitive question of how to allocate broadcasting time is decided by an *ad hoc* semi-formal committee, the Party Political Broadcast Committee, on which are represented the major parties and the broadcasting authorities. The distribution of time has generally been made on the basis of the parties' respective share of the votes at the previous general election, except that the government and the official opposition are usually accorded exactly equal amounts of broadcasting time. The rise in the Liberals and nationalist parties' electoral support in 1974 complicated the situation and underlined the often-ventilated grievance of minor parties with respect to this system. Since then a minor party representative has been admitted to the Committee, the Liberal and later Liberal/SDP Alliance share of broadcasting time has been increased, and special arrangements have been made to take account of the fact that nationalist parties have a more significant position in their own regions than their share of the total United Kingdom vote reveals. Also, both the National Front and the Workers' Revolutionary Party have been allowed short pre-election broadcasts in recognition of the number of candidates they were fielding. What distinguishes the British approach to election broadcasting however is that access to broadcasting time is seen as a special problem to be resolved on entirely non-commercial criteria: radio election broadcasts are free, and only minimal charges are made for television broadcasts. It may be that the influence attributed to television in this area is exaggerated, especially given the discovery during the October 1974 election that there had been an increase in the number of viewers who thought that the amount of television coverage of the election had been excessive; it may be that the whole approach to party broadcasts is in need of re-examination. Yet as long as it is thought that television and radio have an impact on political attitudes and electoral choice, it is desirable that efforts continue to maintain some degree of all-party agreement in the area.[18]

The need to hold elections to return the British representatives to the European Assembly in June 1979 presented the British electoral system with a novel set of difficulties. First, the number of Euro-MPs or MEPs – Members of the European Parliament – meant that the constituencies in which these eighty-one MEPs were elected would be very large: a typical European constituency covered the territorial area of eight Westminster constituencies. (There were however discrepancies in the population size of European constituencies: two seats – Glasgow and Kent West – had electorates of over 550,000, while Highlands and Islands had only 279,521 electors.)[19] Second, the additional size and cost of a European election campaign raised the question of whether the regulations governing such matters as the candidate's deposit or the necessary number of nomination signatories should be changed from those in force for Westminster elections. In the end it was decided that candidates for the European Parliament should be required to deposit £600 with the returning officer and that thirty signatures in support of a nomination would be necessary for it to be valid. The limits on the amount of money that might be spent in the campaign were initially fixed at £5,000 plus 2 p for each elector in the constituency.[20] In the 1984 election these figures became £8,600 plus 3.5 p. In these matters as with such related questions as the payment of Euro-MPs the government was reluctant to move too far away from existing British practice, although it was eventually recognized that all British political parties could and would seek aid from the European Communities for their expenses incurred while publicizing the elections.

Conformity to specifically British electoral practice was of course most marked in relation to the electoral system itself. The countries of the EEC are committed to using the same electoral system for choosing their MEPs, but were free to select their own system for the first elections in June 1979. There was no majority in the British Parliament for any form of proportional representation and the United Kingdom, alone among the nine, used the first-past-the-post method for European as for Westminster elections. The only exception to the retention of the simple plurality system concerned the three seats allocated to Northern Ireland, where in order to ensure representation for the minority Roman Catholic community proportional representation was used.

Despite the apparent commitment to changing the method of representation it was made clear by 1982 that the next elections due in June 1984 would be fought on the same British system. The boundary commission produced a revised set of constituencies and constituency boundaries earlier that year. These took account of population changes to bring about a closer approximation of each constituency to the average vote. The elections produced the familiar discrepancy between votes cast and seats won. The Conservatives, with 50.6 per cent of the votes, secured sixty seats; Labour, with 33.3 per cent of the votes, secured seventeen seats; and the Liberals, with 13.1 per cent of the vote, won no seats, although the Scottish Nationalists retained one seat and Northern

Ireland again returned a member of the SDLP and two Unionists.

The Impact of the System

Between 1918 and 1983 the British electoral system has on most occasions delivered a government with an overall majority in the House of Commons, although many governments had to operate with very small majorities. Only in 1924, 1929 and February 1974 has there been no single party with an overall majority of seats at the start of a new Parliament. (After the election of October 1974 the government had a majority of three, but its majority was rapidly eroded by defections and by-election defeats, so that by 1976 it was in a minority.) Yet beneath the apparent clarity of the results there are concealed a number of distortions in the system. The first such distortion is that the majoritarian government which the system ostensibly produces so smoothly is in reality a minority government in terms of the votes cast. Indeed only the National Government of 1931 and its more Conservative-dominated successor of 1935 have achieved more than 50 per cent of the total vote at any general election since 1918. The overwhelming control of the House of Commons enjoyed by the Labour governments elected in 1945 and 1966 and the Conservative governments elected in 1959 and 1983 was acquired on the basis of the support of less than half of those voting.

The minority position of most British governments might perhaps be easier to reconcile with democratic theory if it were not for the rise of the doctrine of the mandate in British politics. By this doctrine a political party which secures the right to form a government thanks to the electoral system also claims the right when in power to put through any legislation it thinks fit so long as it is based on some policy statement contained in the party's election manifesto. So deeply embedded in the major parties' consciousness is the assumption that the electorate has somehow endorsed not merely a government but all its programme that it survives even if a government has only a tiny majority of seats, or even no majority at all. For example, the Labour governments of 1974–9 took office with the support of 37.1 per cent and 39.2 per cent of the voters at each election; but the rhetoric of the mandate persisted when the government's legislative proposals were discussed in Parliament and the country.

The fact that the system is not truly majoritarian is evident also at the constituency level, where the increasing number of Liberal, Social Democrat and minor party candidacies have made it more likely that those elected will not have an overall majority of the votes cast in their constituencies.

Apart from the inequity of conferring such a concentration of power on parties even when they have minority support, the electoral system generates other anomalies. For example it is possible for the party which achieves the largest number of votes to end up with a smaller number of seats than its rival. This occurred in 1951, when Labour obtained 295 seats for its 13,948,605 votes while the Conservatives got 321 seats for their 13,717,538 votes. This distortion arises largely because under the simple plurality system it takes an advantage of only one vote to capture a seat, and any additional votes are in one sense wasted. The tendency has been for Labour to pile up huge majorities in safe seats while the Conservative vote has been somewhat more evenly spread. In February 1974 the system worked to Labour's advantage: Labour won fewer votes than the Conservatives (11,639,243 to 11,868,906), but more seats (301 to 297). Possibly if it had not been for the multi-party character of that election and the severance of the tie between the Ulster Unionists and the Conservatives the Tory electoral advantage would have been paralleled by an advantage in seats.

The major parties have continued to support the system, feeling that whatever they lose on one occasion they will gain in another. Both assume they will have an opportunity to benefit from the system and to participate in government. But for the minor parties the system is a barrier to effective parliamentary representation. The Liberal Party has suffered most patently from the electoral system's effects, since although it has frequently been successful in attracting votes, its support has been distributed across the country rather than being regionally concentrated as is the SNP or Plaid Cymru vote. Liberal representation in Parliament did not rise above fourteen after 1945, despite the regular achievement by the party of a share of the total vote which would justify many more seats under a proportional system.

The February 1974 general election results indicated the extent of the disadvantage which the Liberal Party had to overcome. The achievement of over half the votes cast for either candidate of the two major parties brought the Liberals less than one twentieth of the seats gained by either of the major parties: for 19.3 per cent of the votes, fourteen Liberal MPs were returned. And, although at that election regionally based parties such as the SNP were able to make a breakthrough, that party still won only seven seats in return for 21.9 per cent of the Scottish vote. (The Welsh nationalist party, Plaid Cymru, won only two seats in February 1974 on the basis of 10.7 per cent of the Welsh vote.)

The distortions of the system and its unfairness to minorities were given great publicity after the February 1974 election because even against the odds an unusually high number of MPs who did not adhere to the two major parties were returned to Parliament. There were thirty-seven such MPs in the Parliament of February to October 1974 and the number rose to thirty-nine in the following Parliament and to forty-four after the election of 1983. Attention was also drawn to the advantages of other electoral systems by the need to decide what method to employ for direct elections to the European Assembly and for the proposed assemblies in Scotland and Wales. Even the continuing tragedy in Northern Ireland highlighted the arguments against the simple plurality method and the link between a country's electoral system and its style of politics, since the abolition of proportional representation in Ulster in 1929 was clearly a factor in alienating the minority Roman Catholic community from the province's devolved institutions.

The general election of 1979 ended in the classical fashion. The Conservatives with 43.9 per cent of the vote secured 339 seats; the Labour Party with 36.9 per cent won 268 seats. The 13.8 per cent of the votes cast for the Liberals brought them a mere eleven seats. However, the creation of the Liberal-Social Democratic Party Alliance produced a major change in the election of 1983. The Conservatives actually lost a proportion of their vote, the figure falling to 42.4 per cent. Nevertheless they secured no fewer than 397 seats. Labour with only 27.6 per cent of the vote still held 209 seats. But the Alliance with 25.4 per cent of the votes got a mere twenty-three seats – seventeen of which were Liberal seats, despite the fact that the two partners in the Alliance had divided the candidacies between them. The overwhelming Conservative majority in the House of Commons thus represented only a minority of voters. The Alliance's claim that it had been frustrated by the electoral system and that electoral reform was overdue was fortified later by the fact that in the five by-elections held during the first year of the 1983 Parliament, Alliance candidates received in aggregate more votes than any other party although it did not win a single seat: Alliance 75,580 votes (0 seats); Conservatives 68,257 votes (3 seats); Labour 62,482 votes (2 seats).

The relationship between the electoral system and the character of British government and politics had been elaborated, as has been seen in chapter 1, in a range of academic writings in the post-1974 period.[21] The defenders of the existing system could only reiterate what they saw as its virtues. Those virtues – comprehensibility, familiarity and clarity – enabled the voter to cast his vote for the preferred candidate and to see immediately the basis on which a seat had been awarded. By comparison with the intricacies of even the additional member system or the alternative vote the method is intellectually undemanding, and the fact that it has survived has given it a legitimacy which can be balanced against its evident anomalies. It is however interesting that opinion polls taken during the 1974–9 Parliament revealed a majority of public opinion in each age group in favour of a proportional representation system rather than the existing one.

Debates about the merits of existing systems will doubtless continue, and the requirements of uniformity in European elections will fuel the debate. However abstract arguments are not likely to prove decisive in this particular case, for while it is easy to point to anomalies in the system, the procedure for changing it is exclusively in the grip of the two major parties. Certainly there have been occasions in the twentieth century when the electoral system seemed on the verge of substantial amendment (a Royal Commission recommended its replacement in 1910, a unanimous Speaker's Conference condemned it in 1917 and another Speaker's Conference urged electoral reform in 1929), but it has always proved possible to resist the logic of the case for change with more pragmatic arguments. The results of the last general election confirmed the Conservative Party's belief that the system still served both major parties well, and while that belief persists – and it is even more passionately held in the Labour Party – the structure will not be changed and wider arguments about its effects on the quality of British democracy will be ignored.

The customary method of altering electoral arrangements, it should be noted, is the device of a Speaker's Conference, which is constructed to reflect existing party strength in the House of Commons and existing attitudes towards parliamentary life and electoral reform. The only recent test of parliamentary opinion was the free vote on the electoral system to be used for the European Parliament, which the Labour government of the time allowed under the terms of the Liberal-Labour pact. The proposal to use a system of proportional representation was rejected by a majority of ninety-seven, with Conservative and Labour MPs combining to vote it down. While some Conservatives overtly, and perhaps more covertly, feel some qualms about a system that might install a left-wing Labour government on a minority vote and would see in proportional representation a safeguard against such an eventuality, it will remain

23abu .

difficult to convince the majority of MPs to amend a system of which they are the principal beneficiaries.

7   The Political Parties (I): Policy Divisions and the Party System

The British system of government is essentially one of party government. The major British parties determine many of the specific policies which emanate from government and they also exert a profound influence on the general style of British public life. The party system's success or failure as a mirror of the social and ideological divisions in British life will affect the extent to which the institutions of government can command general public support and how far the changing demands of the various sections of society are translated into public policy. British political parties are thus vital to the democratic process as a whole and to the legitimacy and stability of the constitutional structure. Moreover the British party system provides almost the only source of recruitment to political office; in contrast to the situation in France or the United States, where members of the executive are frequently appointed despite a lack of political experience, the elevation to government office of business-men, of academics, of former civil servants or of trade unionists in the United Kingdom has been rare and generally unsuccessful. Thus it is likely that the individuals primarily responsible for policy-making on a number of different levels of the political system will have been immersed in an environment of party politics. Partisan consider-ations will therefore influence the treatment of issues and institutional relationships in the British system of government to a far greater extent than in many other polities. And inevitably developments in the internal affairs of the major parties may have repercussions on the organization of government itself and on the constitutional values underpinning it.

In this chapter it will be necessary to examine briefly the range of parties which compete for the voter's attention, the specific policies and philosophies which they espouse, and their role in the structure of party competition. In the next chapter the internal politics of the parties will be examined, as well as their structure, organization and finance. Finally it will be necessary to examine some of the criticisms which have been made of the role of parties in the contemporary British system.

The Conservative Party

The Conservative Party – officially titled the Conservative and Unionist Party but colloquially referred to as the 'Tory' party – is the oldest of the political parties of modern Britain. The intellectual origins of the modern party can be traced to the debates occasioned by the French Revolution, or even to the Restoration period when 'Tory' was first used; most historians, however, prefer to locate the formation of the Conservative Party in the period of Sir Robert Peel's ascendancy between 1834 and 1846.[1] It was in that period that there emerged an identifiable body of Conservative supporters united behind a single leader and broadly attached to common policies. The policy of the Conservative Party in this early part of the nineteeenth century was to support the agricultural interest, the Church and the established constitutional order. Its electoral strength was firmly rooted in the counties and the smaller boroughs rather than in the larger cities; it was also firmly based in the southern part of England. The significance of Peel's leadership was that he acknowledged the need for the Conservative Party to make a broad and general appeal to the electorate, and indeed the Tamworth Manifesto of 1834 perhaps marks the beginning of the modern system of party competition. Peel's dilemma was how to reconcile the party's need for a national electoral appeal with its vested sectional interests, especially the farming interest. His commitment to the repeal of the Corn Laws in 1846, against the evident interests of his agricultural supporters, split the parliamentary party so that the cohesion which he had introduced was short-lived. Under Disraeli's leadership however the Conservative Party was gradually rebuilt; and the extension of the franchise in 1867 reinforced party unity in the House of Commons and stimulated the formation of an extra-parliamentary machine to mobilize the new voters. By the time of the third great reform of the franchise in 1884 the skeleton of the modern Conservative Party was clearly visible. There was a distinct and increasingly cohesive group of MPs in the House of Commons, a National Union linking the local constituency associations, and a professional party bureaucracy at Conservative Central office to deal with electoral arrangements.

The major opponent of the Conservative Party in the period after 1867 until the end of the first world war was the Liberal Party. However at the general election of 1918 the Labour Party obtained the status of principal opposition party and gradually thereafter party conflict in Britain became dominated by the contest between the Conservative and Labour parties. Yet it is important to remember

175

that minor party representation in the House of Commons has persisted throughout the twentieth century.

The fact that the 1918 Representation of the People Act introduced full adult male suffrage for the first time in Britain accelerated the displacement of the Liberals by Labour and forced the Conservatives to appeal to a wider spectrum of society than previously. The extension of the franchise also forced the Conservative Party to develop modern techniques of electioneering. By and large the party's electoral record has been extremely successful. For over three quarters of the period since 1918 the Conservative Party has been in government either alone or in coalition with other parties, as during the 1918–22 period and the years between 1931 and 1945.[2] Indeed one of the features of the Conservative Party, at least until the post-1964 experience of Labour government, was that it was accustomed to think of itself as the natural party of government; and this feeling was to some extent revived when the Labour Party became so internally divided after 1979.

The Conservative Party's success in surviving the challenge of socialism and the advent of a mass electorate has been attributed to a number of factors. Most important perhaps is the point that it has never become the captive of any single section of British society despite its early identification with some of the country's most established groups and causes. It has thus retained enough flexibility to be able to add to its supporters new groups and classes made powerful by social and political changes. In the nineteenth century, as has been seen, its major concerns included the protection of the agricultural interest (which Peel tried unsuccessfully to defy), the defence of the Anglican Church and the maintenance of the traditional constitutional structure. Yet the party quickly realized the importance of gaining the backing of the country's financial and commercial interests as well as of soliciting support from newly enfranchised (but weakly politicized) groups such as women after 1918. Conservative leaders had thus tended to deny the sectional aspects of their policies and have emphasized their concern for the national interest. They have also stressed the virtues of common sense and pragmatism over ideology and have always applauded patriotism. In the nineteenth and early twentieth centuries it was the Conservative Party which strongly supported Britain's imperial role, and the party retains a strong strand of opinion which seeks to expand or at least retain Britain's influence overseas.

Discussion of what the Conservative Party represents in contemporary British politics must take into account two factors which make its policy orientation rather more difficult to characterize than that of its main opponent. First, the rise of the Labour Party has meant that for much of the twentieth century the political agenda of the United Kingdom has been set up by Labour while the Conservative position has generally been a defensive one. One reason for this aspect of the Conservative Party's political stance is that Labour has normally been an opposition party attacking the government's record. Another reason, however, is that Labour for much of the twentieth century was the initiator of policy challenges, and brought to politics a critical and relatively comprehensive theory about the existing balance of power in British society. The onus of justifying the social and economic structure was thus placed on the Conservative Party, which typically responded by advocating modest measures of reform.

Something of a change in this situation occurred when Mrs Thatcher was elected to the Conservative leadership in 1975. The Conservative Party then became much more interested in exploring the ideological bases of its own policies. An increasingly dominant and vocal section of it took up the cause of reversing what was seen as the tide of collectivism and of reducing the role of the state both in economic management and in social provision. By the time of the general election of 1979 it was in many ways the Labour Party led by James Callaghan which seemed to be defending the intellectual and political status quo against a radical challenge from Mrs Thatcher's version of Conservatism. During the first Thatcher administration (1979–83), the ideas of the prime minister and her immediate political supporters gained ground against a different faction within the Conservative Party – the so-called 'wets', who wished to preserve what they saw as a post-1945 consensus over the mixed economy and the welfare state.[3]

The move of the Conservative Party towards a more free-market orientation and away from the 'Butskellism' which had been its guiding philosophy for a good deal of the post-second world war period should not however be interpreted as a move towards pure libertarianism. Indeed alongside the exploration of a more vigorous free-market philosophy there went a stronger stand on issues with a populist appeal – for example law and order. Although the Labour Party itself moved away from the centre position that Callaghan had tried to occupy in 1979, so that Michael Foot fought the 1983 election on one of Labour's most left-wing manifestos to date, it could be said that the Conservative Party had succeeded in changing the ground of debate in Britain to some extent and in making *its* ideas rather than those of its opponents the staple of public controversy at both the intellectual and the electoral level.

The second point to notice about Conservative policy is that a Conservative manifesto will very much reflect the personal style of the party leader rather than, as in the Labour Party, being the product of a complex process of accommodation and collective decision-making. The Conservative leader enjoys a great deal of autonomy and authority throughout the Conservative Party. Thus although specific commitments such as support for British membership of the European Communities or for strengthening the forces of law and order may be found in a series of manifestos, the emphasis on them will vary from leader to leader. Policy-making in the Conservative Party will be aided by the leader's closest colleagues; but ultimately the tone and the priorities of party policy are as much personal as reflective of party opinion generally.

The machinery for policy-making in the Conservative Party will also reflect the preferences of the leadership. Thus the working out of the ideas for the next manifesto was entrusted in part in the winter of 1982–3 to a series of policy groups. However, these were quite outside the regular machinery of the party itself and its various permanent advisory bodies. The chairmen of these policy groups were appointed under the authority of the chancellor of the Exchequer, since it was to him that the prime minister had delegated responsibility for co-ordinating this aspect of the party's pre-election policy process. The ideas generated by these groups, together with contributions from other sources, were available to the drafters of the 1983 manifesto, which was drawn up under the direct authority of the prime minister and was couched – as is customary with Tory manifestos – in very general terms.

Several recurrent themes can be discovered in recent Conservative manifestos, policy statements and actions by the Conservative Party when in power. The Conservative Party in the twentieth century became the party commited to the maintenance of free enterprise and private property, although initially the nineteenth-century Liberal Party was more identified with laissez-faire capitalism than were the Conservatives. Although their preference had always been for a free-market economy, the Conservatives had until 1979 displayed no consistent interest in reversing the nationalization measures initiated by Labour. Thus the Conservative Party, although in power from 1951 to 1964 and again from 1970 to 1974, did not denationalize many of the industries taken into public ownership by Labour between 1945 and 1951. Indeed, despite its theoretical hostility to nationalization, the Conservative government of 1970–4 actually nationalized both Rolls Royce and Upper Clyde Shipbuilders on the grounds that the former had an international reputation while the latter, which provided numerous jobs in an area already scarred by heavy unemployment, would otherwise have been closed.

The Conservative government which took office in 1979 did not share this pragmatic attitude towards the nationalized industries. It developed a dual policy which involved continuing public ownership in some areas but seeking to denationalize in others. In those industries where for historical reasons, or because of the natural monopoly involved, public ownership had to continue, the government had to be content with securing tighter financial control. But in other areas a policy of denationalization or 'privatization' was adopted, and although only modest steps were taken during the first Thatcher administration of 1979–83, it was clear that the second term would see greater experiments in this direction.

Another main theme of Conservative thought and policy as it developed after 1975 was what has come to be inaccurately termed 'monetarism'. Strictly speaking monetarism is an economic doctrine which links the causes of inflation to the rate of growth in the money supply. However in recent political debate it has come to signify a range of ideas and policies which are sometimes only loosely associated and by no means necessarily derived from the theories of the monetarist economists. Thus 'vulgar monetarism' has come to imply *inter alia* a belief that inflation is the most socially dangerous of all economic ills; that inflation is best controlled by reducing public expenditure so as to diminish the need for governments to compete with the private sector for loans; and that the expansion of public expenditure in all its forms is not only unsound economically but also likely to undermine the fabric of political freedom.

In this sense the direction which Conservative philosophy seemed to take in the second half of the 1970s was in many ways akin to Gladstone Liberalism, which taught that money was best left to 'fructify in the pockets of the people'. By contrast those who resisted this movement within the Conservative Party sought to strike a balance between the free market and the public sector and suggested that there was a substantial role in the modern state both for planning and for state-provided welfare services. They argued that while inflation was a serious ill, to cure it at the expense of high levels of unemployment was no achievement, especially if it led to major social disruption. It can thus be seen that the defence of free enterprise which the Conservative Party has made one of its major ideals was given a sharper focus once Mrs Thatcher took over the leadership and subsequently entered Downing Street. Hand in hand with a defence of free enterprise goes a defence of private property, which has a number of implications for Conservative policy and for the sources of Conservative support. Thus the Conservative Party has always preferred to subsidize home ownership through mortgages rather than to subsidize the construction of houses for local authorities to lease at low rents. Indeed the idea that the creation of a property-owning democracy should be encouraged by extending home ownership was given a new prominence after the Conservatives took office in 1979. Between 1979 and 1984 legislation and accompanying administrative pressures ensured a large number of sales of council houses to their tenants.

Defence of free enterprise is also linked with a desire to keep taxation as low as possible. Although the reduction of direct taxation did not become as central a plank in the Conservative creed in the 1970s as it did in the American Republican platform after 1976, the Conservative manifesto of 1979 did emphasize the importance of reducing direct taxation, and the first budget of the Thatcher administration reduced the basic rate of income tax from 33 to 30 per cent. However, although tax reductions remained a major goal of Conservative policy thereafter, the burden of public expenditure – even with the efforts made to bring it under control – was such that taxation was heavier overall by 1984 than when the Tories took office in 1979.

The desire to keep taxation as low as possible inevitably makes Conservatives suspicious of high levels of public expenditure. As far as the social services are concerned, the Conservatives have come to advocate a selective approach to the distribution of welfare benefits which, from their perspective, means restricting them to those in real need rather than distributing them to all citizens without regard to their financial circumstances. In the last decade the Conservatives have moved away from the 'Beveridge principles' which inspired the modern welfare state. This has not been simply because they, unlike Labour, do not wish to use welfare programmes to advance the substantive goal of equality. They have come to argue that Britain's welfare state could be more efficiently administered if, for example, there was partial 'privatization' and a greater reliance on commercial contractors and volunteer effort. Similarly, the growth of one version of libertarianism within the party has produced an increasing determination to defend the private sector in health provision and in education.

Another argument which Conservatives have also regularly deployed against high levels of public expenditure is that they necessarily create additional power for the bureaucracy. Moreover many in the party doubt whether governments can contribute greatly to certain sorts of social problem such as the elimination of racial or sexual prejudice. Thus the state's resources in the opinion of many Conservatives should be concentrated on what have for long been seen as the basic functions of government: defence against external attack and the maintenance of law and order. The theme of law and order came to be emphasized very heavily in Conservative manifestos and one of Mrs Thatcher's earliest decisions on taking office in May 1979 was to bring forward pay rises for the police and to improve the pay of the armed services – symbolic decisions which reflected the priorities of her administration. An early opportunity was also created for Parliament to debate the issue of the death penalty in the 1983 Parliament, but in fact on a 'free vote' there was an overwhelming majority against capital punishment.

The importance attached to defence expenditure in the Conservative Party is closely linked with the Conservative perception of Britain's role in the world. The opportunities for global influence offered by the Commonwealth have largely been replaced by an emphasis on the potential of the European Communities as a forum for British diplomacy. Certainly the tone and character of Conservative statements on foreign policy are both more realistic and more pragmatic than Labour's approach.

The Falklands war in 1982 seemed to encapsulate both Conservative determination to defend Britain's interests and its willingness to contemplate the use of force in the international arena. Moreover, the successful prosecution of the war evoked a favourable response in the electorate which suggested that, although foreign policy issues used not to be thought of as highly salient to voters, they could at times become so. There was of course general agreement between the parties on the Falklands issue, but on other foreign policy and defence questions – especially the preservation of Britain's nuclear deterrent – the two major parties became increasingly polarized. It seems that in 1983 this divergence on foreign policy and defence issues had become apparent to electors and mattered to them more than might have been expected. Certainly the Conservative Party has been able to defend British membership of NATO and support for the Western Alliance unequivocally in a way which has not been possible for the Labour Party where 'unilateralism' has gained the upper hand. Yet it must be admitted that much of the Conservative Party's policy on defence is constrained by the need to limit public expenditure, so that even the commitment to the Falklands cannot be regarded as permanent.

The Conservative Party's attitude towards the non-English parts of the United Kingdom is complicated. Until the first world war the maintenance of the union with Ireland was a central tenet in the party's creed. (The Conservative Party was popularly known by the name 'Unionists' – originally a breakaway faction of the Liberal Party – until the Irish settlement of 1921 removed the issue from the mainstream of British politics.) The Conservative Party's support for Ulster forged a link betweent the Protestant Ulster Unionists and the Conservatives between 1921 and 1974; but the recurrence of violence in Northern Ireland led to Westminster's adoption of a bipartisan policy towards the province which divided the Ulster Unionists from their former Conservative allies. Although Labour has had some difficulty maintaining that bipartisanship when in opposition, the Conservatives for their part have not wanted to renew the pre-1974 ties.

The resurgence in the 1970s of nationalism within Britain itself also created difficulties for the Tory Party. The Conservatives were by no means entirely hostile to Scottish aspirations for greater decentralization. However, after an initial flirtation with the idea of a directly elected assembly, the sentiments of English backbench MPs and Mrs Thatcher herself brought a large section of the party down against the Labour government's devolution proposals. The organizationally separate Scottish Conservative and Unionist Association (a name which replaced that of the Scottish Unionist Association only in 1965) was deeply divided by the problem of devolution, and the then Conservative shadow spokesmen on Scotland (Alick Buchanan-Smith and Malcolm Rifkind) resigned from the opposition front bench rather than accept the change made by Mrs Thatcher in Conservative policy on the issue. In the administration formed in 1979 both Buchanan-Smith and Rifkind were given posts, and these appointments, together with the poor performances by the Scottish National Party in the 1979 and 1983 elections, may enable the Conservatives to sidestep divisions on the question for some time. However it is unlikely that the question will entirely disappear, and the potential for disunity remains.

Mounting Tory suspicion of devolution reflected in part an affection for the traditional unity of the kingdom and the desire to preserve the essential character of Great Britain. Concern about the preservation of this unity may also explain the continued pre-occupation in some Conservative quarters with immigration from the New Commonwealth, even though primary immigration has now in effect been stopped. Proposals for a total ban on immigration and for financial assistance for 'repatriation' were decisively defeated at the party conference in 1983, although it is worth noting that the issue was one which the leadership did not wish to have discussed.

Conservative philosophy is thus difficult to characterize definitively. At some points ideas such as individual freedom will be clearly articulated and may even produce concrete policy proposals designed to promote such values. At other times no distinctive doctrinal features can be detected. It would generally be agreed that doctrine has in recent years played a larger role than usual in the Conservative Party and that some of that doctrine reflects currents of thought with an appeal beyond the United Kingdom. This in itself is somewhat unusual: it would for example be difficult to think of Friedrich von Hayek or Milton Friedman having much of an impact on a Stanley Baldwin or even a Harold Macmillan. What is interesting is that there has as yet been no really coherent adverse response to the neo-liberalism fashionable inside the Conservative Party, although there have been one or two eloquent personal statements. It is likely that the debate over ideology within the party will continue to rage for some time to come, especially if, as so often happens in Conservative politics, considerations of doctrine and policy become intermingled with those of electoral success.

The Labour Party

The birth of the modern Labour Party dates from the formation in 1900 of the Labour Representation Committee, which was designed to bring together a number of disparate elements in British political and industrial life so that manual labour could be directly represented in Parliament. Twenty-nine Labour MPs were elected in 1906, when Keir Hardie became chairman of the Parliamentary Labour Party, the PLP. The fact that the Labour Party had its roots in organizations external to Parliament has shaped its subsequent constitutional and political history: there is no parallel to the Conservative Party's assumption that the balance of power will be tilted towards the parliamentary representatives. It is extremely important also to bear in mind that from the beginning the Labour Party has been a coalition or confederation of distinct groups and interests, and this diversity – combined with Labour's traditions of internal democracy – has produced an alliance incorporating a variety of political tensions.

The most important element in the amalgam of forces which came together in 1900 was the trade union movement. Indeed it was as a direct result of a resolution passed at the congress of the Trades Union Council in 1899 that the efforts to establish a Labour Representation Committee were made. This element in the Labour Party has been the dominant influence in its structure, although it is not an influence that has been exerted consistently throughout the party's history. The British trade union movement has always been heterogeneous. It only became closely identified with the cause of a single party with the legal threats to union organization which occurred in the latter years of the nineteenth and the early part of the twentieth centuries. Even after the establishment of the Labour Representation Committee the miners' union maintained its distinct representation in Parliament for another decade. And there have always been large unions not affiliated to the Labour Party.

The second element in the alliance forged in 1900 was the band of small socialist societies each of which had evolved its own interpretation of the creed of socialism. Especially significant here was the Independent Labour Party, which had also played an active role in bringing the new alliance into being. The ILP realized that these small socialist societies needed the financial and membership strength of the trade unions in order to be able to compete with the Conservative and Liberal parties. Yet this pragmatic compromise between groups inspired by varieties of socialist theory and the essentially defensive trade union movement created a fertile source of controversy and conflict. In addition to the ILP, which came to be seen as a 'party within a party', two other socialist societies represented at the initial conference to form a Labour Representation Committee deserve special mention. The Fabian Society, although it claimed only 861 members in 1900, was to have an immense impact on the future of the Labour Party, and Fabian intellectuals – especially Sidney and Beatrice Webb – were to leave their marks on the whole constitution and ethos of the party. Second, there was the Marxist Social Democratic Federation, which in 1900 claimed nine thousand members compared with the thirteen thousand claimed by the Independent Labour Party.[4]

The original advance of the Labour Party in terms of parliamentary seats was the result of a secret electoral pact with Herbert Gladstone, the Liberal chief whip. But once the entire male working class was enfranchised in 1918, the Labour Party soon displaced the Liberals as the Conservatives' main challenger. It was in 1918 also that the Webbs, together with Arthur Henderson, succeeded in persuading the Labour Party to pass a new constitution for itself. It provides a convenient starting point for the analysis of Labour's contemporary position, since it was then that Labour committed itself to socialism as its objective. Moreover the end of the first world war saw the resolution of a number of political issues which had troubled pre-1914 Britain, and thus marks something of a fresh agenda for all the parties.

The commitment to socialism is enshrined in Clause IV of the Labour Party's constitution which, as revised in 1929, declares one of the party's objects to be 'to secure for the workers by hand or by brain the full fruits of their industry, and the most equitable distribution thereof that may be possible, upon the basis of the common ownership of the means of production, distribution, and exchange, and the best obtainable system of popular administration and control of each industry or service'.[5] The commitments to socialism and to public ownership of the means of production have thus been linked in Labour politics, though not all members of the Labour Party would now think that public ownership itself constitutes a sufficient basis for a fully socialist society.

Labour's 1945 manifesto, *Let Us Face the Future*, committed the party to taking several basic industries – coal, gas, electricity, inland transport and steel – into public ownership. To those industries already on the party list for nationalization were added by 1950 the sugar-refining industry and the cement industry. By then however it was clear not merely that nationalization was an issue of controversy between the parties but also that it was unpopular with the electorate at large. This hostility to nationalization has increased with time. In 1974 a public opinion survey found that over 66 per cent of the population was opposed to further nationalization of any kind, while only 10 per cent favoured it.[6]

The unpopularity of nationalization was identified by Hugh Gaitskell as a major factor in Labour's run of election defeats in 1951, 1955 and 1959; he duly attempted to persuade the party to modify Clause IV of its constitution. The failure of this attempt to steer Labour away from its more unpopular commitments persuaded Gaitskell's successor in the leadership, Harold Wilson, that while it was necessary to reduce the party's emphasis on nationalization this should be done pragmatically and not by attempts to persuade the party activists to expunge the doctrine from their creed. Very little further nationalization in fact occurred during the Labour administration of 1964 to 1970. Instead the party tentatively initiated an experiment with new forms of intervention and public ownership by which the state acquired controlling interests in the shares of leading firms in the private sector. It was hoped that such 'back-door nationalization' would allow the Labour Party to prove that the state could contribute to the profitability of industry as long as it was not confined to the already declining sectors of industry which had provided the traditional candidates for nationalization. It was also hoped that this new style of intervention would enable government to influence policies in the private sector, especially pricing and investment.

The machinery by which this intervention was secured initially was a body called the Industrial Reorganization Corporation; this was abolished in 1970, and during Labour's 1970–4 period of opposition the idea of a state holding company was elaborated and defined under pressure from the left wing of the party. Accordingly when the Labour Party again took office in March 1974 it established the National Enterprise Board, which was designed to oversee the process of extending state interests in the private sector of industry. By the middle of 1978 the NEB had holdings in fourteen large companies including Ferranti Ltd, International Computer (Holdings) Ltd and Rolls Royce, the last of which had been nationalized by the Conservatives. Thus although there is internal party pressure for the extension of traditional nationalization, this is not popular with the general electorate and it seems possible that the main thrust of any future Labour government's involvement in this area will come in the form of NEB-type activities which do not necessarily entail the nationalization of a whole industry.

During the period of increased leftwing ascendancy that followed Labour's return to opposition in 1979, nationalization – in whatever form – gathered new support. The manifesto for the 1983 general election included not merely a pledge to return to public ownership what had been denationalized or privatized by the Conservatives; it also pledged 'the establishment of a significant public stake in electronics, pharmaceuticals, health equipment and building materials' as well as in 'other important sectors as required in the national interest'.[7] While no reference was made to the nationalization of the clearing banks which had been much discussed previously, especially on the left of the Labour Party, it was intended to create a 'public bank' which would operate through the network of post offices. A commitment to public ownership whether through outright nationalization, partial holdings of the NEB kind or through the encouragement of cooperative enterprises is thus an area of policy where the Labour Party's policy remains distinctive.

Commitment to public ownership is only one policy consequence of Labour's adherence to socialism. Labour is also committed to the redistribution of wealth through a progressive system of direct taxation. The February 1974 Labour manifesto defined Labour's aim as being to 'bring about a fundamental and irreversible shift in the balance of power and wealth in favour of ordinary working people and their families'; the October 1974 manifesto reaffirmed Labour's belief that 'taxation must be used to achieve a major redistribution of wealth and income'.[8]

The idea of enhancing the progressive taxation of income (which after all had a long history) was supplemented in Labour thinking by the additional desire to achieve a direct redistribution of property through what had earlier been called a 'capital levy'. This became known as a 'wealth tax'. Such an innovation was not possible for the Labour administrations of 1974–9 because their parliamentary position was so weak; nevertheless the ground was laid by the Royal Commission which Labour established to look into the distribution of income and wealth in the United Kingdom. Although this body was abolished by the 1979 Conservative government and its chairman Lord Diamond switched parties to join the Social Democrats, it seemed clear by 1980 that Labour's philosophy on tax matters had become more radically egalitarian than hitherto.

There was a good deal of evidence that policies which entailed higher levels of taxation across the board had during the 1970s become increasing unpopular among all sections of society, including Labour's traditional supporters. Nevertheless – as with nationaliz-ation, which was equally unpopular – such policies retained their appeal on the left of the Labour Party. It was, however, appreciated that the additional money which would be required to finance improvements in social services could not easily be met by additional taxation at a time of economic recession. The 1983 manifesto therefore declared that these needs would have to be met by borrowing and that the tax increases which were to constitute 'a shift in the balance to those who can best afford to pay' might have to be postponed.

The commitment to a high level of direct taxation has been complemented by a commitment to a high level of public expenditure, especially in the fields of social welfare and education. Moreover the experience of the interwar period has made the Labour Party hostile to attempts to relate the provision of benefits to financial needs and to most forms of means testing. Thus not only did the Labour Party criticize the Conservative Party's increasing sympathy towards directing benefits only to those who most needed them; it also strongly opposed any suggestion that the provision of services could be expanded by encouraging provision outside the state system and by cooperation between the state and the private sector. As the Labour manifesto put it in 1983: 'We shall remove private practice from the NHS and take into the NHS those parts of the profit-making sector which can be put to good use. We shall also stop public subsidies to the private sector and prevent it expanding further'. Such a commitment did not entirely remove the possibility of retaining a private medical sector in Britain, but it certainly went a long way towards making private health provision more difficult. And in education there was a similarly explicit desire to control private provision, although the 1983 manifesto did not in fact pledge the party to make private education illegal.

The Labour Party would thus like to see state provision dominate the provision of welfare and educational services – although not, it should be noted, housing. For some such an attitude would seem to be a denial of certain basic freedoms, though the arguments of the left in favour of such a position would doubtless be that the very exercise of the freedom to purchase better services in the private sector is both a denial of equality and a contributing factor to a weak public sector.

Some other facets of Labour's domestic policy orientations should be mentioned. The Labour Party displays a strong concern for civil liberties and minority rights and was the party most responsible for securing a number of changes in the law concerning abortion, divorce, female equality, homosexual practices and censorship. However the Labour Party is by no means overwhelmingly secularist – the well-known remark that it owes more to Methodism than to Marx underlines Labour's intellectual debt to religious Non-conformity – and concern about offending religious sensibilities has generally to be balanced against the claims of libertarian or secularist causes. And account must also be taken of the number of Labour MPs whose Roman Catholic affiliations affect their views on several moral issues.

The close connection between the Labour Party and the trade union movement has caused both sides of the partnership some difficulties in the recent past. The Labour Party, as has been seen, came into being partly as a result of a TUC resolution, and political protection of the trade union movement remains part of Labour's *raison d'être*. In 1969 the Labour government attempted to legislate on the basis of a white paper, *In Place of Strife*, which suggested the introduction of greater legal control of industrial relations. This proposal violated the unwritten rule that no Labour cabinet should interfere with trade union immunities or Britain's informal system of industrial relations. The result was a humiliating defeat for senior cabinet ministers, with the exception of James Callaghan, who led the opposition to the proposals in cabinet. It also produced a new mood of hostility between the Labour cabinet and the trade union movement which lasted through the general election of 1970. The two sides drew together again after the Conservatives passed their own Industrial Relations Act in 1971, and in 1972 there emerged a strengthened mechanism for consultation between the TUC and the Labour Party – the Liaison Committee – and a much closer involvement for the unions in Labour's policy-making processes.

The TUC-Labour Party Liaison Committee which one authority has gone so far as to call 'the vital decision-making body in the Labour movement' was established as a result of a TUC initiative.[9] Given the circumstances in which the Liaison Committee began its life it was not perhaps surprising that its first priority was to coordinate industrial relations policy and to elaborate alternatives to the approaches embodied in the wide-ranging Industrial Relations Act of 1971. The series of legislative measures passed after Labour returned to power in 1974 and the establishment of the ACAS machinery to deal with industrial disputes reflected agreements worked out in large part in the monthly Liaison Committee meetings. The area of Liaison Committee discussions was not however confined to industrial relations. As the scope of the TUC's interests broadened into the whole field of economic and social policy, so the Liaison Committee came to seem a suitable forum for pressing its views on the Labour shadow cabinet. The 'social contract' – by which the unions agreed to moderate pay claims in return for policies directed towards improved welfare provision – was the result of these discussions, and the Liaison Committee remained important even following the Labour government's movement back towards a more rigid control of pay increases.

The tension between the TUC's concern to foster a close relationship with the Labour Party based on common opposition to Conservative policy, and accompanied by opportunities to influence Labour policy, and its reluctance to get caught in a situation where it could no longer advocate to government the policies its members really wanted, was but one paradox of the new relationship between the party and the pressure group which had been so significant a factor in its founding. Another was the fact that the TUC as a body was being drawn into an even more intimate relationship with the Labour Party at precisely the time when its own clientele was changing. The TUC in 1976 had 113 unions affiliated to it; but only fifty-nine of those were also affiliated to the Labour Party. Joint policy statements with a political party in these circumstances seemed anomalous, even if the newly unionized white collar workers could hardly expect the TUC to shed its emotional links to the Labour movement overnight. Perhaps the final paradox was that the events of the 1970s had pushed the theme of the defence of trade unions back to the centre of the public's image of the Labour Party just as the party itself was trying to establish its credibility as a national rather than a sectional force.

The results of the 1979 general election, which suggested that groups traditionally loyal to Labour had swung heavily to the Conservatives in the south and midlands, again emphasized the cross-pressures on the Labour Party. It could either look to the electorate first and risk unpopularity with party activists and its trade union financial supporters and allies; or it could exploit its special relationship with the unions to promote an industrial and economic strategy which, if successful, could prove electorally popular but which might also, as in 1978–9, collapse to the enormous electoral disadvantage of the party.

The legislation by the Conservative government on subjects of direct concern to the unions and the Thatcher administration's unwillingness to become involved in direct consultations with the unions on matters of general policy cemented the alliance between the Labour Party and the union movement. Indeed it could be argued that relations between the party and the trade unions were closer during Michael Foot's period of leadership (November 1980– October 1983) than at any previous time. However, the massive electoral defeat of Labour in 1983 once again raised the issue of the role of the unions in the Labour Party. In the past there had been many left-wing socialists who regarded the link with the unions as a block to radical policies because the leadership of the union movement had been frequently cautious and supportive of the Labour leadership. By 1983 it was clear that many on the left of the party now regarded the unions as potential allies in the battle for the soul of the Labour movement. However, even as the Labour Party was experiencing constitutional reform as a result of a determined campaign to 'democratize' the party, the unions were themselves beginning to question their own support for the developments within Labour ranks. It was not so much that the unions and the Labour Party had espoused different policies but rather that they had different policy priorities. The trade unions basically wanted to see a Labour government in office because they saw this as the best method of safeguarding their members' interests; doctrines and policies which might alienate voters were therefore to be avoided if the pursuit of such views made electoral success remote. Thus although the link between Labour and the union movement is an intense and emotional one, it is also a connection which gives rise to policy difficulties and internal complications.

The Labour Party's views on foreign policy have long been ambivalent. Many supporters of the Independent Labour Party were pacifists during the first world war. Thus there was a pacifist strand in the Labour Party almost from its inception. This Labour tradition was also fortified by the pacifism and commitment to international-ism of some of its recruits from the Liberal Party during and after the first world war.[10] The second world war was however a unifying factor, since the struggle against nazism and fascism could be justified both in the name of socialism and in the name of national self-defence and collective security.

However, the so-called 'cold war' renewed divisions over foreign policy within Labour ranks because many Labour MPs and activists were reluctant to support an alliance directed against the Soviet Union, to which there was, especially on the left of the party, a considerable sentimental attachment. During the period 1945–63 foreign policy issues were frequently the cause of dissent within the party and helped to separate the right-wing from the left-wing elements. The issue of British membership of the EEC further divided the Labour Party and led to the 1975 referendum as a method of allowing party leaders to adopt either side of the argument without necessarily splitting the party. Following British entry into the EEC, Labour Party opinion moved more decisively against membership and many Labour members of the European Parliament at Strasbourg used their position to campaign against British membership. One result of this attitude was that there occurred something of a breach between the Labour Party and the Socialist International because all of the latter's other EEC members supported their respective countries' participation in the institutions of the Community and believed that socialist objectives could be pursued within a European framework. Labour included a commitment to withdrawal in its 1983 manifesto, but after the election there appeared to be a shift towards cooperation with the other socialist parties of the EEC in an attempt to secure sufficiently radical reforms to make withdrawal unnecessary. It thus appeared that while hostility towards Europe might be retained in the Labour Party's rhetoric and formal policy statements, in practice the likelihood of withdrawal had perhaps diminished.

An even more divisive factor within Labour's ranks has been the question of defence policy. Outright pacifism, although strong in the party's heritage, remained a minority creed, as was shown during the Falklands war when Labour supported the Conservative government's resort to force. The real issue however has increasingly become the extent to which Labour is prepared to support the possession of Britain's independent nuclear deterrent and to accede to NATO policies which rely on the use of nuclear arms. The revival of the Campaign for Nuclear Disarmament, after the 1979 'two-track NATO decision' had pointed the way to the installation of American medium-range missiles in Britain and other western European countries in response to the Soviet deployment, had a significant impact on the Labour Party. (The NATO decision was to seek an arms control agreement while arranging for the deployment of the missiles if it were not reached). Not merely did CND find a number of new recruits among the Labour rank and file; it also had many adherents among the Labour leadership, including Michael Foot and his successor Neil Kinnock. However, although there was a considerable growth in the party's opposition to siting American missiles in Europe, many senior Labour figures did not want to jeopardize Britain's position in NATO or to abandon Britain's own deterrent except as a part of a general arms control agreement. The 1983 Labour manifesto remained ambiguous about the party's defence policy, but these uncertainties and the differences among the party's leading figures were seen by many observers as contributing factors in Labour's electoral defeat.

The Liberal Party

The Liberal Party is now a minor party in terms of its parliamentary representation and its share of the popular vote. For much of the nineteenth century however it was a party of government, and until 1922 it was the major challenger to the Conservatives.

As in the case of the Conservative Party, the point at which the Liberal Party was formed is difficult to date with precision, but certainly by the general election of 1868 there was a distinct party with a coherent set of policies and a leader – Gladstone – who was in many ways the personification of nineteenth-century Liberalism.[11] Yet the Liberal Party, although it appeared unified in doctrine, was always composed of at least two conflicting elements – the traditional whig and the radical – and, while it could cover up its differences when some fundamental tenet of the party such as free trade was attacked, the potential for disunity was always present.[12]

Free trade – the dogma that allegedly kept the people's food cheap – was the central issue at the general election of 1906. The result was the last spectacular Liberal victory at the polls, and after that landslide Liberal fortunes declined. Between 1906 and the outbreak of the first world war the Liberal Party in office effected a significant shift in the balance of power in the British constitutional system. It laid the foundations of the welfare state, provided trade unions with new legal immunities, disestablished the Church of Wales, limited the powers of the House of Lords and finally achieved the passage of the legislation granting Ireland Home Rule. Unfortunately from the Liberal Party's point of view the expansion of the electorate in 1918 meant that it would be Labour and not the Liberals who inherited the benefits of these measures. By the time of the 1935 general election few commentators would categorize the Liberals as anything but a third party in a system increasingly polarized between the Conservatives and the Labour Party.

The decline of the Liberal Party between 1918 and 1979 was not completely steady. The number of seats won by the Liberals in the post-1945 elections fluctuated a little: they reached a low of six in the general elections of 1951, 1955 and 1959, and a high peak of fourteen in the general election of February 1974. The Liberal share of the popular vote was, however, rather more varied (see table 3).

Table 3
The Fluctuations in the Vote of the Liberal Party and its Allies 1906–83

General Election		% Popular Vote	Seats
1906		49.0	400
1910	(February)	43.2	275
1910	(December)	43.9	272
1918		25.6*	161*
1922		29.1**	116**
1923		29.6	159
1924		17.6	40
1929		23 4	59
1931		10.7***	72***
1935		6.4	21
1945		9.0	12
1950		9.1	9
1951		2.5	6
1955		2.7	6
1959		5.9	6
1964		11.2	9
1966		8.5	12
1970		7.5	6
1974	(March)	19.3	14
1974	(October)	18.3	13
1979		13.8	11
1983		25.4****	23****

Notes:
   * Coalition Liberals and Asquithian Liberals added together.
  ** Lloyd George and Asquithian Liberals added together.
 *** Simonite Liberals, Samuel Liberals and Lloyd George Liberals added together.
**** Total Alliance Vote. The seats won were 17 for the Liberal Party and 6 for the Social Democratic Party.

By-elections frequently offered the Liberals opportunities to make gains at the expense of the major parties and sometimes created hopes of an incipient Liberal revival. However the Liberal Party experienced difficulty in retaining its converts, so that such upsurges in

Liberal support as occurred have generally proved short-lived. The two general elections of 1974 represented a marked advance from the 1970 position, but analysis of the Liberal vote suggested that it was relatively volatile and largely unrelated to Liberal party policies.[13] By 1979 Liberal support had again ebbed away – largely it seemed to the advantage of the Conservatives.

In the period between 1979 and 1983, the position changed, owing to the birth of a new party – the Social Democratic Party. This development occurred with the encouragement of the Liberal leader, David Steel. The subsequent formation of a Liberal–Social Democratic Alliance to fight the election of 1983 jointly was heralded by many commentators as a significant development in the British party system. For this reason neither the seventeen seats obtained by the Liberals in 1983 – their best performance since 1935 – nor the 25.4 per cent of the vote secured by Alliance candidates together is strictly comparable to the earlier figures. Nevertheless since the Liberal Party brought to the Alliance a considerably greater grass-roots organiz-ation than the Social Democrats possessed, and since the Liberals may be expected to have a major role in shaping the policies of the Alliance, it is reasonable to see a good deal of continuity between Liberal Party fortunes prior to 1981 and those of the Alliance thereafter.

Despite the fact that much Liberal support is only weakly linked to Liberal programmes, the ideas and strategies of the Liberal Party have been important both as an indication of what appears to be wrong with the two major parties and as a source of ideas for other groups in the political system. Three themes seem to have dominated Liberal politics in the post-1945 period. First, Liberals have attacked corporatism and the concentration of power in the British state. Liberals have advocated policies which extend the opportunities for individuals to control their own lives, and this concern with individualism, which is nourished by a strong intellectual tradition within the party, has led to such specific proposals as worker co-partnership in industry, a bill of rights and the decentralization of government leading ultimately to the organization of Britain on a federal basis.

The second theme which runs through many contemporary Liberal arguments is a rejection of the existing system of adversary politics and partisan confrontation. The Liberal Party wishes to see the existing electoral system replaced by proportional representation and the present style of politics give way to a new partnership between the different groups in British society. Quite clearly the transform-ation of British political debate in the twentieth century into a dialogue between two class-based parties was not to the Liberals' advantage; they have therefore sought ways of diminishing the connection between class and politics.

A third theme of Liberal politics is internationalism. Liberals in 1970 declared that while the party's position was to stand up for the individual against the 'big battalions' at home, abroad the Liberal Party's goal was world cooperation. Thus its manifestos urged the strongest support for the United Nations, the entry of Britain into the European Communities and the democratization of European institutions. The Liberals are also committed to the greatest possible freedom in international trade.

The Liberal tradition has always placed great emphasis on the need for a moral dimension to foreign policy – witness Gladstone's Midlothian campaigns and the issue of Chinese labour in the South African mines – and its contemporary approach to international affairs maintains that tradition by manifesting concern with such issues of conscience as apartheid and human rights. These issues may well have contributed towards the Liberals' image as a classless party, but its primary problems – how to retain the support it has from time to time acquired, and what strategy it should adopt in relation to other parties – remained questions of debate within Liberal ranks. In the normal parliamentary situation of the postwar period, one of the two major political parties was able to dominate the House of Commons by virtue of its overall majority. In the period 1974–9 the Commons' arithmetic was, however, such that the Liberal Party's parliamentary votes could influence legislative policy and the character of government itself.

In essence the Liberals had to choose between three strategies when defining their relationship with other parties, and the post-1918 period saw them experiment with all three at various times.[14] First there was the option of formal coalition. Senior Liberals might participate in government and legislative policy would then be worked out jointly between the Liberals and their coalition partners. The problem was that such experience of this option as there was suggested that formal coalition tended to divide Liberals and to obscure the party's identity. Thus the coalition effected with the Conservatives in 1915, and still more the Lloyd George coalition of 1916–22, split the Liberal Party internally when the threat from Labour was already severe. The 1931 coalition was short-lived as far as the wing of the party led by Sir Herbert Samuel was concerned, although some Liberals remained in the National government under the leadership of Sir John Simon. The coalition of the second world war was followed by a general election in which the Liberals' parliamentary seats were reduced in number from twenty-one to twelve. Thus when Edward Heath offered the Liberals a formal coalition in March 1974 the Liberal party generally was hostile to the idea, although it seems that the then Liberal leader Jeremy Thorpe might have favoured it.

The second option for Liberals in a confused parliamentary situation was a selective support of those measures with which it agreed. This strategy was employed during Harold Wilson's first administration from 1964 to 1966. The tactic provided the Liberal Party with the equivalent of a veto but put the onus on the governing party to arrange its legislative programme so as to maximize its chances of parliamentary survival. From the Liberal perspective, opportunities for influencing legislation could be combined with retaining independence. The disadvantage of such a strategy was that it was difficult to sell to the electorate and too negative to make much impact at the hustings.

The third tactic was the kind of formal pact to which David Steel committed the Liberals in 1977 after the Labour Party lost its parliamentary majority in 1976.[15] The two parties, Liberal and Labour, agreed to establish a consultative committee so that the Liberal leadership and the relevant ministers could discuss measures prior to their introduction into the House of Commons. The consultative committee which was chaired by Michael Foot as leader of the House of Commons was also intended to examine Liberal legislative proposals. In addition it was agreed that there should be regular meetings between Steel and Callaghan on a personal basis and between the chancellor of the Exchequer and the Liberal economics spokesman John Pardoe.

The arrangement thus appeared to place Liberals in a privileged position regarding the business of the House of Commons and to offer Liberal MPs opportunities for access to government which enabled them to exert influence on a wide range of policy matters. The agreement also made a number of concessions to Liberal opinions, including a pledge that the government would speedily bring forward bills to establish direct elections to the European Assembly and to create assemblies in Scotland and Wales. Moreover the Liberals were able to secure a free vote on the electoral method to be used for the European Parliament, and to gain additional time for a private member's bill on homelessness which the Liberals wished to see enacted. Finally the Liberals were able to persuade the government to modify a bill designed to extend local authority powers to undertake construction work by employing direct labour.

Doubts about the wisdom of such a close alliance with the Labour

Party – an alliance which was twice renewed but allowed to lapse in 1978 – were expressed within the party, especially as the Liberal vote at by-elections seemed poor and the concessions to Liberal opinion ultimately amounted to very little. Certainly the unpopularity of the pact was suggested as a factor in explaining the loss of Emlyn Hooson's seat at Montgomery and John Pardoe's in Cornwall North in the May 1979 general election.

From the Liberal Party's point of view the pact was therefore something of a mixed blessing. David Steel, the Liberal leader, had to defend it by staking his leadership on it before the Liberal Assembly. On the other hand the Liberals were in a weak financial and political state to fight an election in the period 1976–8 and so had an additional motive for propping up the Callaghan government. The Liberal leaders received additional publicity and arguably came closer to the centre of decision-making than they had been for many years. Above all the arrangements introduced into British political life, if only for a short period, the atmosphere of open political bargaining which is customarily associated with countries in which formal coalitions are the norm. The Liberal decision to vote against its erstwhile Labour ally in the March 1979 vote of confidence was however strong evidence that the pressures of the system tended to permit coalition-style behaviour for limited periods only, and that Liberal tactics were difficult to sustain or accommodate within an adversarial system.

With this experience behind them it is not surprising that those who wished to attain a share of power rather than merely bear witness to Liberal values should have hoped that discontent within one or both of the two main parties would enable a new grouping to be formed in which the Liberals would be the leading element, just as the Peelite split in the Conservative Party in the nineteenth century had made possible the birth of the Liberal Party itself. Ideas of this kind had been given expression by Jo Grimond, the leader of the Liberal party between 1956 and 1967.[16] They also explain why David Steel welcomed the impact upon certain factions in the Labour Party of Labour's leftwards shift after the defeat of 1979 and the creation of a new party to which that development led. It might have been possible to argue for the simple recruitment of Labour dissidents of the right and centre into the Liberal Party; but Steel seems to have preferred to see the creation of a wholly new party as a method of changing the structure of party competition in Britain.

The Social Democratic Party

The advent of the Social Democratic Party was brought about, not by new social groupings demanding representation on the political scene, but by changes within one of the major parties (Labour) which caused it to lose the allegiance of a section of its supporters.[17] The leftwards movement of the Labour Party both gave rise to and was strengthened by changes in the party's internal organization which seemed to some members inimical to its claims to be a national party rather than a socialist sect. Many of these changes (which will be dealt with in detail in the next chapter) were broadly intended to shift the balance within the party towards the trade unions and the constituency activists under a more left-leaning leadership. They were thus designed to transfer power away from the parliamentary party, which had successfully maintained its position vis-à-vis the other groups in the party until this time.

The importance of formal voting at the Labour Party conference and within other party institutions had promoted the mobilization of right and moderate factions within the Labour Party no less than on the left; and it was for some time the belief of most of those who opposed the increasingly visible shift to the left in Labour policy that they could counter these developments by increasing the efficiency of their own organization. Many of those on the right of the party who were increasingly worried by the trend of Labour's internal politics were admirers of Hugh Gaitskell's earlier principled stand against left-wing policies. One of the earliest signs that it would be difficult to keep the party united had come in 1973, when Dick Taverne won a by-election in his own constituency of Lincoln after he had been dropped by the local constituency party because of his adherence to the cause of British entry into Europe. Taverne had labelled himself a Democratic Labour candidate and went on in October 1973 to launch a wider movement, the Campaign for Social Democracy. But although Taverne himself held on to his seat in the general election of February 1974 other candidates associated with him lost; and he himself lost Lincoln in the general election of October 1974.

The collapse of the Taverne initiative redirected attention towards activity within the Labour Party itself; in December 1974 came the formation of the Manifesto Group of Labour MPs; in June 1975 a Social Democratic Alliance which was largely concerned to stem the leftward move in Labour's local government representation was formed; and in February 1977 there appeared an umbrella group, the Campaign for Labour Victory. In the general election of 1979, the future leaders of the Social Democratic Party were still fighting on Labour's platform but it was the defeat of Labour at that election – foreshadowing as it did another move leftwards in opposition – that precipitated the move of some sections of the Labour right to make a clean break with the party. (It was indicative of the right's weakened position in the Labour Party that no new recruits to the Manifesto Group were made as a result of the 1979 election.) Yet in many ways the leaders of the right remained constant to an earlier faith. William Rodgers' declaration of political principle, *The Politics of Change*, was conceived in 1978, started in 1979 and published in 1982 with little need to alter the analysis or prescription. Even more socialist in approach was Shirley Williams's *Politics is for People*, which was published in 1981.

In assessing the role and policies of the Social Democrats it must be kept in mind that the issue which did most to separate them from their original home in the Labour Party was not one of domestic politics but Britain's adherence to the EEC. In 1971 sixty-nine Labour MPs defied their whips to vote for entry, and in 1972 the party's decision to hold a referendum on continued membership when Labour returned to office led to the resignation from the front bench of one of their senior figures – Roy Jenkins – who was then the Labour Party's deputy leader. George Thomson similarly resigned from the shadow cabinet and both David Owen and Dick Taverne resigned as front-bench spokesmen. The agreement that in the referendum campaign in 1975 Labour participants could express their views freely enabled the gulf to be bridged temporarily, but the issue of Europe remained a divisive one. The defeat of Roy Jenkins by James Callaghan for the leadership of the party after the unexpected resignation of Harold Wilson in April 1976 was followed by the nomination of Jenkins for the chairmanship of the EEC Commission from January 1977. This appointment entailed his removal from British politics for the next four years, although he kept in touch indirectly. Other Labour dissidents on the right also found themselves drawn away from Labour's internal debates by immersion in European affairs: Jenkins had been preceded as a member of the European Commission by George Thomson, who had been appointed to that body in 1973. David Marquand, another pro-European MP, resigned his West-minster seat and followed Roy Jenkins to Brussels as a political adviser, although he only stayed in Brussels for one year.

An article on the decline of the Labour Party and the need for a new political grouping was written by David Marquand and appeared in July 1979.[18] This was in many ways the prelude to a similar call by Roy Jenkins made in his Dimbleby Lecture, delivered in November 1979, which was interpreted as an anticipation of Jenkins' return to the political arena in a new capacity. The organization of Roy Jenkins' supporters, discussions between Jenkins and David Steel as to the best strategy to be followed in developing a new political force in British public life and another public lecture by Roy Jenkins himself in June 1980 together constituted a part of a movement for change in the British party system. Although the outcome of the movement could not be predicted at that stage, it seemed clear that it represented a coming together of a number of disparate forces in the centre of British politics in a way which was different from traditional Liberalism, although it shared with the Liberal Party the wish to transform British politics – or, as the phrase had it, to break the mould in which existing party alignments were set.

In the Labour Party itself at that time some senior figures had become conspicuously involved in the battle between its different factions. Shirley Williams (who had lost her seat in 1979) and David Owen became increasingly seen as the leaders of a movement to protect the strand in Labour Party politics with which they were associated. Many saw their loyalties as still inherently owing to the Labour Party as an institution and assumed that if they ever left the party it would not be to create some new centre force in British politics but rather to try to rebuild a second Labour Party in what they regarded as its original image.

However on 7 June 1980 the so-called 'gang of three' (Bill Rodgers, Shirley Williams and David Owen) announced that they would leave the Labour Party if it committed itself to a policy of withdrawal from the EEC. Two weeks later the Labour Commission of Inquiry came out in favour of removing the election of the Labour Party leader from the PLP and endorsed the 'mandatory reselection of MPs'. These constitutional changes (which are further discussed in the next chapter) were part of a concerted campaign which was generally seen as strengthening left-wing elements in the party and limiting the autonomy of its parliamentarians. On 24 July the Social Democratic Alliance – from which the gang of three had held aloof – declared that it would run candidates against left-wing Labour MPs. In December the National Executive Committee of the Labour Party declared the Social Democratic Alliance to be a proscribed organization.

On 1 August the gap between the factions in the Labour Party was broadened further when the 'gang of three' wrote an open letter to their fellow members of the Labour Party setting out the causes for their disquiet about developments within the Labour Party. At the same time a certain degree of initiative was being taken by the Liberals, who were anxious for sympathizers with a new political movement to make a definite decision. The Labour Party conference which received James Callaghan's resignation as leader also voted in favour of a new method of electing his successor, although the details of the electoral procedure were postponed for a special conference to be held in the following January. Equally significantly, the conference voted to make it official party policy that Labour should withdraw from the EEC and adopt a policy of unilateral nuclear disarmament. It was significant that both Shirley Williams and Tom Bradley, another right-of-centre member of the NEC, refused to speak from the platform on behalf of these policies.

The division between right and left became more apparent after Michael Foot was elected leader of the Labour Party under the old system, thereby preempting the change in the rules foreshadowed by the autumn conference decision. And Denis Healey, by accepting the deputy leadership, effectively marked off the distance between those whose inclination was to fight for their preferred policies within the Labour Party and those who felt that their cause was hopeless and that they would have to leave the party altogether. David Owen announced that he would not seek re-election to the shadow cabinet, and Shirley Williams declared from outside Parliament that she could not at that stage seek election to Parliament on the Labour platform.

It was however the early months of 1981 which were crucial to the formation of a new party. Roy Jenkins finally returned from Brussels and entered into close discussions with the gang of three, who threw in their lot with Jenkins, thereby forming a 'gang of four'. The group took a major step towards forming a separate party when they issued on 25 January a statement of their views in the so-called 'Limehouse Declaration' and announced the formation of the Council for Social Democracy. This was joined almost at once by nine more Labour MPs and there followed on 5 February the publication in the *Guardian* of a statement of principles by a hundred individuals who supported the aims of the newly formed Council.[19] These names included a number of well-known ones and included many who had long been associated with the Labour Party. One Conservative MP (Christopher Brockle-bank-Fowler) crossed the floor of the House to join the Social Democratic Party on 17 March and on 26 March the Social Democratic Party was formally launched. By the end of 1981 it was joined by many other Labour MPs, so that when there was a dissolution in June 1983 the new party had twenty-nine MPs in the House of Commons.

In part the pace of events had been forced not by Labour MPs but by David Steel, who was anxious that the new grouping should be a separate party rather than, as some of the dissident Labour MPs might have preferred, a Council for Social Democracy. (Equally, some Liberals thought that the dissidents had no need of a new party and could be accommodated in the existing Liberal ranks.) But the new party was also fuelled by press speculation and the favourable reception given to the idea by the general public. The opinion polls registered substantial support for the new party – a figure which went as high as 31 per cent in the first two months of its existence and rose to 48 per cent when the idea of an alliance with the Liberals was mooted. In a sense therefore once the progenitors of the idea of a new Social Democratic Party had appealed to public opinion they had little option but to be carried along by the new mood of enthusiasm for it, even though some aspects of the party's organization and policies had to be improvised in a rather hasty manner.

It remained unclear to many observers just what kind of political party had been formed so quickly, and it remained an open question what its particular contribution to the national debate would be.

It was clear from the beginning that much of the activist support for the Social Democratic Party – i.e. the people who actually took out membership – was middle-class; it was moreover a party membership with a substantial section which had never been politically active before at all. Of those who had been members of other parties, it seemed that the new party was drawing equally on disaffected Conservatives and on disaffected Labour supporters. This phenomenon created some difficulty for the newly formed party, since the leadership of the Social Democratic Party and its original appeal in Parliament had been, with one exception, almost entirely within the Labour tradition. And if those MPs who had crossed the floor were to keep their seats many would depend on retaining a sizeable segment of the working-class vote. Yet it was also argued that such had been the changes in the structure of British society that there existed many voters who might in the past have been expected to vote Labour but who were increasingly tempted to vote Conservative as they had in 1979.

There was thus a question-mark over the class image and orientation of the Social Democrats. Certainly although their ratings in the opinion polls were high it seemed clear that a mass following would take time to establish, and that this would prove especially difficult in traditional industrial areas.

In addition to the difficulties of reconciling the class divisions within the party there emerged a division in the Social Democratic leadership. The election by the general membership of Roy Jenkins as leader in July 1982 suggested that the more centrist element in the 'gang of four' had prevailed, although this was balanced by Shirley Williams' election as president of the new party later in 1982. Electorally the Social Democrats found themselves doing less well than the opinion polls had initially suggested. The local elections of

1982 were disappointing, and in the general election of 1983 only six Social Democrats survived. Roy Jenkins resigned the leadership after the 1983 election and it then passed to David Owen.

With two of the original 'gang of four' (Shirley Williams and Bill Rodgers) out of Parliament and the prospects of favourable by-elections of the 1981–2 kind unlikely – despite a victory at Portsmouth South in 1984 – it seemed likely that the Social Democrats' previous MPS and candidates would be forced to seek alternative career opportunities. Thus even apart from the financial difficulties which small parties encounter it may be difficult for the Social Democrats to maintain their early momentum. A further obstacle to their development may have been that those areas where they offered distinctive policies, such as those on human rights and constitutional reform (stands which in part reflected the number of lawyers recruited to the SDP banner), were not necessarily ones which the electorate as a whole saw as of immediate consequence. On other matters such as trade union reform and defence policy, their positions seemed to differ from those of the Conservative Party only by nuance. Furthermore the acceptance of some kind of incomes policy as inevitable (together with the explicit commitment to trade union reform) made it difficult to see how the SDP could be reconciled with even the more right-of-centre union leadership, despite efforts by leading SDP figures to open a dialogue with the trade unions.

The Alliance

The creation of the SDP owed much to the Liberal leader, David Steel. It was well understood once the new party was founded that it would have to reach some kind of understanding with the Liberals if it were to have a strong chance of making a major electoral impact. On the SDP side even those who found it hardest to shake off their socialist and collectivist inclinations admitted the necessity for such an arrangement. Yet reaching and maintaining agreements over policy and tactics, while at first sight the rational and obvious thing to do, would prove harder than imagined because of the different ethos of the Social Democrats and of the Liberal Party. The Social Democratic Party was in many ways oriented to a centralized leadership both on electoral decisions and on policy questions. The Liberals by contrast were highly decentralized and at times even seemed anarchic. The Limehouse Declaration had done little to spell out the policy stand of the new party but was merely a justification for engineering a break with Labour. Clearly there would have to be a long period of detailed policy consideration and research before the SDP would be ready to fulfil its union with the Liberals. However it was possible to publish a joint statement of principles on 16 June 1981 which showed a clear convergence of policy, despite the fact that both the SDP and the Liberals thought it necessary to emphasize their different philosophical origins. In working out the details of policy thereafter each side of the Alliance frequently found the divisions between the more collectivist social democratic strand and the more liberal-individualist strand of thought reflected not merely between the partners but also within their own policy discussions. This was especially true in the two areas where policy groups were most active on the SDP side – the questions of constitutional reform and of industrial policy and employment.

The early testing of the Alliance as an electoral organization occurred in by-elections in the course of the 1979–83 Parliament. Roy Jenkins' creditable near-miss at Warrington in July 1981 helped David Steel to secure a majority for the whole idea of the Alliance at the Liberal Assembly. The Liberal victory at Croydon North-West, where the Social Democrats supported the Liberal candidate after local Liberals refused to have Shirley Williams as their candidate, and Shirley Williams' own success at Crosby in November proved that candidates could be selected for Alliance support even if there were disagreements about which party should provide the candidate in a particular constituency. It also proved that such candidates in certain circumstances could actually win seats. However if, as was rapidly decided, the Alliance was to fight all the seats in mainland Britain the question inevitably arose as to how the constituencies should be allocated between the parties. The Liberals with their superior organization on the ground and larger general membership could claim the right to fight all the seats where they came second in 1979; but these were nearly all Conservative seats, and such an allocation would clearly exclude the Social Democrats from territory in which their own image was appealing. It could also be claimed that although the Liberals had superior organization, the formation of the Social Democrats had given the central forces of British politics a new momentum and political visibility and that in terms of leadership experience their contribution nationally was superior to that of the Liberals.

It was agreed in October 1981 that each party would fight half of the available constituencies and that there should be negotiations both centrally and regionally to ensure that the allocation of seats was fair to both parts of the Alliance and took account of the interest of long-established candidates. In spite of the long negotiations and a number of well publicized crises, agreement on over 500 constituencies was reached by the original deadline of March 1982. By the time of the June 1983 election only three recalcitrant Liberal associations were left insisting that their candidates should not be displaced by Social Democrats. The process had been made more difficult by the fact that most constituency boundaries were being redrawn, so that the likely political complexion of a constituency was sometimes unclear.

The Alliance manifesto emphasized the themes which both parties had stressed individually. Given that what both partners to the Alliance wanted was to transform the structure of party politics in Britain it was not perhaps surprising that proportional representation was made a central theme of the Alliance's manifesto and its election campaign. There was also an attack on unemployment and a promise to tackle Britain's economic problems with a complicated package of measures including a counter-inflation tax and direct public investment. In addition there was emphasis on the need to review the whole welfare system. Constitutional themes also figured prominently. The Alliance promised decentralization and devolution for Scotland. And in foreign policy it presented itself as both Atlanticist and European. While stressing the need for various forms of multilateral disarmament and greater reliance on non-nuclear weapons, the strong tendency in the Liberal Party towards unilateral disarmament had to give way to the SDP's appreciation of the importance of NATO retaining its nuclear arsenal. Thus in foreign policy terms it was the SDP rather than the Liberals which appeared to have had more of a role in shaping the policies of the Alliance.

The Communist Party

The British Communist Party was formed in 1921 from the amalgamation of a number of small and fragmented Marxist groups. Its membership has always been small and its parliamentary representation has been similarly minimal.[20] At the third congress of the Comintern in 1921 the Communist Party of Great Britain claimed ten thousand members and its total membership as reported to the annual congress of the British Communist Party in 1977 was 25,293. No Communist MP has been elected to Parliament since 1945, when P. P. Piratin was elected for the Mile End division of Stepney.

In the general election of 1983 thirty-five candidates stood, compared with thirty-eight in 1979; all lost their deposits and the average vote per candidate was 0.8 per cent. Communist strength has been falling in numerical terms as well; in 1964 it was above 34,000; in 1977, as has been noted, it was just over 25,000; and in 1982 it was 18,458. By 1983 it had fallen to 15,961.

The British Communist Party had traditionally been distinctly subservient to Moscow, and this fact caused it to lose some seven thousand members at the time of the Russian invasion of Hungary in 1956. Its attitude towards the Russian invasion of Czechoslovakia in 1968 was more critical of the Soviet Union but its long association with a blind pro-Moscow stance continued to be damaging and membership at all levels continued to decline. In 1977, inspired perhaps by the examples of Communist parties in other parts of western Europe, the British Communist Party decided to revise and modernize its doctrine, and its congress, after a long debate, endorsed *The British Road to Socialism*. This suggested that the party should abandon the doctrine of the dictatorship of the proletariat and guaranteed that a Communist government would maintain the freedom of all political parties to contend for office, including those hostile to socialism. The Communist Party also expressed its willingness to work with other groups to create a socialist society in Great Britain. This caused dismay to the hard-line Stalinists within the party, who broke away to form a New Communist Party to maintain the old dogmas.

The secession of the New Communist Party did not end the intra-party feuding. Those who wished for a broader strategy making use of various minority groupings and causes and who came to be styled 'Euro-communists' with their own journal *Marxism Today* were opposed by the hard-liners who preferred to continue to base the party on industrial activity. The latter group was in turn allied with the editorial board of the *Morning Star*, formerly the *Daily Worker*. Although the *Morning Star* was traditionally the mouthpiece of the Party it has been independently organized and funded. Yet another faction represented the supporters of the pro-Soviet line who had not taken part in the New Communist Party secession. At the annual conference in November 1983 the 'Euro-communists' appeared to be in control of the party, but there was no resolution of the struggle with the *Morning Star*, some of whose main figures were expelled from the Party in 1984.

The sorry state of the Communist Party's orthodox political activity in the nation's formal representative institutions is not however the only indicator of its strength. For the party enjoys some support in industry, since many of the large unions have at one time or another been influenced by members of the Communist Party. At the 1977 TUC Congress there were 337 Communist delegates representing a number of major trade unions, and one commentator suggested that some 10 per cent of all trade union officials in Britain are in fact Communists.[21] There were then however only two Communist Party members of the TUC's General Council – a figure which had not changed by 1983; and it is true to say that at the higher reaches of the trade union movement there are probably as many strongly anti-Communist officials as there are party members.

The strength of the Communist Party is not necessarily concentrated in individual unions, although the AUEW has frequently had a particularly heavy concentration of Communists on its executive – perhaps as much as a quarter – and about a thousand of its thirty thousand shop stewards are Communists. There is also a strong Communist presence in the National Union of Mineworkers, where in 1977 six of the twenty-seven member Executive Committee were Communists. The leftwards movement of many unions in the 1970s did not diminish the strong suspicion often felt about the Communists and their tactics. This suspicion lingered on from the 1950s experience of ballot-rigging and fraud in the Electrical Trades Union. Nevertheless their minority position within the trade union movement as a whole does not preclude Communists from having a say in the affairs of the Labour Party, where they may be in a position to influence the block votes of the larger unions, although they are themselves excluded as individuals from party membership. Furthermore there are pressure groups which they can seek to influence. In December 1983 three Communists (and two Trotskyists) were elected to the Executive Committee of the Campaign for Nuclear Disarmament.

The Trotskyists

Beyond the left wing of the Communist Party are a number of smaller groups that claim to be broadly Trotskyist in inspiration.[22] The most important of these is the Socialist Workers' Party, which, although it sometimes contests parliamentary elections, places its main emphasis on direct action whether in the industrial sphere or through joint bodies such as the Anti-Nazi League which was founded to enlist those disturbed by the propaganda of the National Front and other rightwing organizations.

An even more fundamentalist Trotskyist organization is the Workers' Revolutionary Party, whose proclaimed aim is the establishment of a totally socialist state as the result of the civil war for which they believe the capitalist state is preparing. Another Marxist group which deserves mention is the Socialist League, which was known until early 1983 as the International Marxist Group. Finally the Revolutionary Communist Party concentrates on issues of race and on support for the Irish Republican Army, which has itself become more Marxist in the period since 1981.

The National Front

The National Front was founded in 1967 as a result of the amalgamation of several small rightwing groups including the League of Empire Loyalists and the British National Labour Party. Its roots are thus very much in what one writer has called the 'British fascist tradition', and it is often overtly antisemitic.[23] In 1967 it seemed unlikely that membership of the National Front could be more than two thousand overall. However the emergence of race as an issue in British politics and the vacuum created by the apparent unwillingness of either major party to take strong action to prevent further immigration caused the National Front's membership to increase.[24] Yet there is an imbalance between the claims made for the National Front's influence – and its coverage in the press – and the electoral success it has achieved.

Certainly the performance of the National Front in three by-elections between March 1977 and April 1978 when it beat the Liberals into fourth place, and its achievement of an average vote of 4.4 per cent in the eighteen by-elections it fought between 1975 and 1978 appeared ominous. But by-elections are not general elections, and at the October general election of 1974 the National Front had only secured an average of 3.1 per cent of the vote in the seats it contested.[25] The level of electoral support had remained relatively stable over the decade since the Front's formation, so that it may well be that despite the publicity the potential appeal of the National Front is limited, especially when other parties are available to capitalize on the protest vote. Certainly the Front's poor showing at the general election of 1979 (when it gained 0.6 per cent of the total vote) suggested that earlier fears of a 'fascist' advance were unfounded.

What the Front's activities did over the period 1967–9 was to call into question traditional practices with regard to political demonstrations. Street marches formed an important element in the Front's propaganda campaign; but the staging of marches in areas of heavy immigrant concentration – especially in the east and south-east of

London – provoked counter-demonstrations and violence such as that at Lewisham in August 1977 and at Southall in the 1979 general election. Moreover the widespread doubt which has been expressed about the ethics of the Front's policies in a plural society committed to the idea of racial harmony has led some to wonder whether the National Front should be allowed access to television and radio at election times.

The ignominious defeat of the National Front in 1979 produced a three-way split within the party and much of the energies of the extreme right were subsequently spent on strife between the National Front itself, the British National Party and the Constitutional Movement. In 1983 it was believed that as against the 20,000 or so members the National Front could boast in 1977 it then numbered only 5,000. In the general election of 1983 the National Front fielded sixty candidates compared to 303 in 1979; and their average vote in those constituencies where they stood fell to 1 per cent against the 1.3 per cent of 1979. A further fifty-three candidates did however stand for the British National Party, and as with the far left there were allegations that the real influence of the far right was not entirely to be measured by its parliamentary performance since, as some people suggested, some individuals with far right views had managed to infiltrate the Conservative Party. At Stockton South, a Conservative candidate, revealed to have been a former member of the National Front, failed against the trend to dislodge a sitting SDP member.

The Ecology Party

The Ecology Party was established in 1973 and fought in subsequent elections at the national and local levels. In 1979 the fifty-three Ecology candidates secured an average of 1.5 per cent of the vote where they stood; in 1983 108 candidates achieved only 1.1 per cent on average. In March 1983 the party produced a manifesto, *Politics for Life*, which stressed the need for economic self-sufficiency, the decentralization of power, a non-nuclear energy policy and nuclear disarmament. Abroad it has close links with the Greens in the Federal Republic of Germany; at home it enjoys close links with the Campaign for Nuclear Disarmament and similar organizations, and there was in 1984 some discussion of an attempt to build links with the British Liberal Party.

The Scottish National Party

The Scottish National Party was founded in 1934 as a result of the merger of John MacCormick's National Party of Scotland and the rather more conservative Scottish Party which had been formed in 1932. The Scottish National Party could draw on a tradition of nationalism and agitation for Home Rule which went back at least to the beginning of the nineteenth century. It has however been deeply divided over tactics, with some of its leaders favouring alliances with other parties deemed sympathetic to Scottish aspirations and some in favour of independent political action for an independent Scotland. The second world war brought many of these divisions to a head, and in 1942 the Scottish National Party split into two groups – a moderate Scottish Convention designed to build all-party support for devolution and the Scottish National Party, which became a separatist party.

The SNP's electoral record during the 1950s was one of slow growth, but during the 1960s the party made rapid advances to become at the election of October 1974 the second largest party in Scotland in terms of its share of the popular vote. The overriding goal of the SNP remained independence but the circumstances of the 1974–9 Parliament induced the party to support the government's devolution plans as a step towards that goal. The SNP experienced internal divisions once it had to construct policies across the whole range of social and economic questions, since it is undecided whether it should be oriented towards a left-of-centre or a right-of-centre programme. The initial successes of the SNP were in Conservative-held seats, but to proceed further it had to appeal to Labour voters, especially in the heavily populated Strathclyde region around Glasgow. Yet it appeared that the leadership was not entirely committed to socialist-style policies; and indeed the SNP did not always vote together in the House of Commons, although it was united in voting against the Labour government in March 1979 in protest at the government's refusal to implement the devolution proposals contained in the Scotland Act.

The SNP was perhaps the major casualty of the May 1979 election when its representation in Parliament was cut to two seats and its share of the total Scottish votes slumped to 17.3 per cent, putting it way behind both Labour and the Conservatives again.

The divisions within the SNP were not allayed by the election defeat; and one section of the so-called '79 group' (which held that the struggle for independence should be combined with a strong leftwing slant on other issues) was expelled from the party. The SNP was thus in a weak position to face the 1983 election, when it again managed to return two MPs but saw its share of the Scottish vote fall from 17.3 to 11.8 per cent.

Plaid Cymru

Plaid Cymru was founded in 1925 but it did not develop a political platform of Welsh independence until 1932. Its programme has always been heavily cultural and oriented towards the preservation and promotion of the distinctive Welsh tradition and the Welsh language. Its goals have therefore tended to be divisive, since Welsh nationalism has until recently been perceived as the preserve of the minority of the Welsh population which can actually speak Welsh. Since the 1960s however Plaid Cymru has tried to broaden its appeal from rural and middle-class Welsh-speaking parts of the electorate to the non-Welsh-speaking and younger groups in the industrialized south of Wales. Its parliamentary representation at Westminster has been small – three seats in the Parliament elected in October 1974 – and the party has conveyed the impression of greater sympathy for the Labour Party than has the SNP. At the general election of 1979 it lost its leader's seat to Labour, although the party's decline in terms of the total Welsh vote – from 10.9 to 8.1 per cent – was less dramatic than the SNP reversal. Plaid Cymru's surviving two MPs tended on non-Welsh issues to align themselves with the Labour Party, especially with the Labour left. Like the two Scottish Nationalists they retained their seats at the 1983 general election, although Plaid Cymru's share of the total Welsh vote fell once again, from 8.1 to 7.9 per cent.

The Political Parties of Northern Ireland

Northern Irish party politics differ radically from politics elsewhere in Britain. In Northern Ireland the sectarian divisions between Protestant and Roman Catholic – which interlock with the divisions over the constitutional status of Ulster – are the most important factors shaping electoral choice. Because the community is so polarized the scope for genuine competition between the parties is small; parties are typically confined to their own religious constituency for electoral support, and any attempt to broaden the appeal beyond a 'natural' religious base risks alienating the core of party sympathizers. Northern Irish politics thus tend to be isolated from those in the rest of the country. This isolation has become marked since 1974, when the fragile bonds which linked the majority (Protestant) Ulster Unionist Party to the Conservatives snapped almost completely in the wake of the suspension of Stormont and the experiment with power-sharing.

Until the Northern Ireland Civil Rights Association campaign in the late 1960s and the changes occasioned by the return of violence to the province, Ulster's party politics were frozen into a mould of competition between a solid Ulster Unionist Party, the symbol and vehicle of the Protestant majority, and a group of fragmented and somewhat stagnant opposition parties. These parties drew their support mainly from the alienated Catholic minority in the province but there were also occasional attempts to erode the solidity of the Protestant support for the Unionist Party. In general however such attempts were unsuccessful. The distinction between opposition to Unionists and opposition to the constitutional settlement was at best imperfect, and this automatically restricted the room for manoeuvre of such parties as the Northern Irish Labour Party. Protestants feared to join it lest by weakening the Unionist Party they should weaken the instruments of Protestant ascendancy; the Roman Catholics would not join it because it appeared to be committed to the existing constitutional framework. Also the Northern Irish Labour Party's concern with social and economic issues made its relevance to Northern Ireland dubious in a situation where religious questions dominated the political agenda.

The political party which most Roman Catholics supported until the end of the 1960s was the Nationalist Party. This party was the survivor of the pre-1918 Irish Parliamentary Party, but with partition in 1920 its position in Ulster became increasingly difficult. Clearly the goals of the Nationalist Party were anathema to a majority in the new political unit of Northern Ireland, while to participate in the politics of the province in a constitutional manner would entail the Nationalist Party's acknowledging the legitimacy of Ulster's political institutions and of partition. Moreover the border between the Republic and Northern Ireland severed the organization of the Nationalist movement as surely as it created two polities, and although bonds of sympathy remained it was difficult to support a coherent party in the very different circumstances of the north and south. This disorientation of the Nationalist Party in Ulster meant that the party to which, *faute de mieux* perhaps, most Roman Catholics gave their natural support until 1970 was not an effective vehicle of political action. Indeed its primary characteristics were, as one authority noted, its tendency to abstain from the formal politics of the province, a lack of efficient organization, and above all a tendency to concentrate on the single issue of the border even when – as in the late 1960s – new issues of importance for the Catholic population had appeared on the agenda of Ulster politics.

Competing with the Nationalist Party for the Catholic votes were two much smaller anti-partition parties – the National Democratic Party, which originated in 1965 and had its roots in a group called National Unity, and the Republican Labour Party. The Republican Labour Party had been formed when the Northern Ireland Labour Party split in 1949 over the issue of the link with the United Kingdom. The Northern Irish Labour Party remained in favour of the union and thereafter its appeal was limited to Protestants; the Republican Labour party was formed and was able to blend opposition to partition with socialism.

The changed situation in Northern Irish politics in the 1970s stimulated a realignment of forces in Ulster and the formation of new political parties. Although the situation is still extremely fluid there are now at least three groups of importance competing for the Catholic vote as well as one non-sectarian party.

Those parties which had assumed their present shape before the election of 1979 on the 'loyalist' or Protestant side were the Ulster Unionist Party or Official Unionists and the more radical and populist Democratic Unionist Party led by Ian Paisley. Competing for the Roman Catholic vote, the main party since 1971 has been the Social Democratic and Labour Party;[26] however it found it had an increasingly powerful rival in Sinn Fein, the political wing of the Irish Republican Army. The Alliance Party formed in 1970 to try to bridge the gap between Roman Catholics and Protestants in the province is the other main grouping but its appeal has been limited and largely confined to middle-class voters. In addition various splinter groups on both sides have appeared from time to time and occasionally independent-minded politicians such as James Kilfedder have made an impact.[27]

In the election of 1979 Sinn Fein did not participate; the other main parties received the following percentages of the total vote: Ulster Unionist 36.6; DUP 10.2; SDLP 19.7; Alliance 11.9. In terms of seats this produced five seats for the Ulster Unionists, three for the DUP and one for the SDLP, with three others. In the absence of a Parliament of its own, Northern Ireland's Westminster representation was increased from twelve to seventeen in time for the 1983 election. The chance of the Republican minority adding to its representation was however hampered by the participation of Sinn Fein in elections, so that the nationalist vote was divided. In the end in 1983 the SDLP and Sinn Fein won one seat each and five other constituencies with a Catholic majority fell to the Unionists. The Official Unionists with 34 per cent of the vote won eleven seats while the DUP with 20 per cent won three seats. One independent Unionist was also successful.

Minor Parties and Independents

In addition to the political parties which base their appeal on issues specific to the peripheral areas of the United Kingdom, a history of British parties would reveal a range of tiny parties and organizations which have fielded candidates at parliamentary elections. Usually these candidates have no chance of success unless they have already acquired the support of the local organizations of one of the major parties or there is a pact between the parties not to contest an election – a rarity except in wartime. The return of minor party and independent candidates is of course more likely at a by-election than at a general election because then the government of the country is not at stake and maverick candidates acquire more publicity if the contest is an isolated one. However the general election of February 1974 saw the election of two independents – E. Milne and Dick Taverne – who were both denied the support of their former party organizations, so that, though rare, such an achievement is not totally impossible. Equally the candidacy of independents and minor party represent-atives may be significant in a constituency not so much because there is a chance of the candidate actually gaining the seat but because it threatens to split the vote of one of the major parties, thereby letting in the other party.

The Party System

The United Kingdom was for long regarded as the classical example of a two-party system with each of the two main parties fighting all or nearly all of the seats and with the likelihood that one or other of them would secure a majority that would enable it to form a government by itself. This generalization was challenged in the 1960s and 1970s both by the revival of the Liberals and by the growing divergence between England's electoral behaviour and that of the rest of the United Kingdom. The electoral system itself failed to mirror these changes to the full, so that in many ways the composition of the House of Commons concealed changes in voting allegiance and behaviour.

However the fact that both the general elections of 1979 and of 1983 returned a government with a substantial working majority should not be interpreted as a signal that electoral behaviour had reverted to its earlier pattern. Beneath the surface there appeared to be powerful forces for changes in the way electors related to the political parties of Britain, even if it was difficult to predict what the final outcome of such changes would be.[28]

8 The Political Parties (II): Internal Structure

The internal relationships of each of the major British parties can best be understood in terms of tensions between the leader of the party, the members of the parliamentary party and the party organization in the country. The relationships are of course fluid and will change as different personalities occupy key offices and as different political issues grip the attention. The analysis of the relationship between the different elements in the Labour Party is in addition markedly more difficult than in the case of the Conservative Party, because Labour is a federal party comprising several distinct sectors. Thus tensions between for example the trade unions and the constituency parties may cut across simple antagonisms between the shadow cabinet and the NEC.

The style of politics also varies enormously within Britain's parties because each individual party has been shaped by its peculiar traditions and history. The standard interpretation of modern British parties in the 1960s was Robert McKenzie's *British Political Parties*. It emphasized the similarity of the distribution of power in the Labour and in the Conservative parties despite the fact that they appear to have very different constitutions and very different assumptions about the degree of internal democracy to be encouraged in their ranks.[1] That analysis has since been subjected to extensive criticism, although it should be remembered that it was so convincing when it was first written precisely because it reflected aspects of the party system of that time. Its weaknesses in relation to current party politics stem from the changes in the character of the major parties and other developments which occurred after McKenzie's work was published.[2]

The contemporary need to revise the account of British parties which was popularly accepted in the 1960s should not be allowed to conceal the merits of McKenzie's thesis or to produce analyses which veer too far in the opposite direction. Political parties in Britain do still share a number of common features and assumptions which affect such questions as the autonomy of the parliamentary party from external control and limit the extreme interpretation of internal democracy within the Labour party. At the same time however the British constitution may be adapting itself to new pressures, especially those that have been generated within the Labour Party. It could well be argued that the referendum device and the more flexible interpretations of collective responsibility have been instances of this trend. One of the striking features of party politics in the 1970s and early 1980s has been the extent to which problems such as limited finance and the loss of membership have been common to all parties, although the enthusiasm generated by the newly formed Social Democratic Party for a while suggested that there might still be a pool of voters willing to become party activists.

Thus when looking at the internal politics of Britain's parties one is both examining institutions which respond to and shape a common political environment and at the same time attempting to appreciate norms and values which are complex and subtle and do not fit into any simple intellectual or conceptual framework.

The Conservative Party

The most conspicuous aspect of the pattern of relationships within the Conservative Party is the prominent part played by the leader. The Conservative Party's leader has a dominant role in the policy-making process and has virtually unlimited powers to appoint cabinet colleagues when the Party is in power and shadow cabinet colleagues when in opposition. This is not to imply that Conservative leaders enjoy security of tenure in their office; for their considerable autonomy entails a corresponding responsibility for whatever electoral successes and failures the party experiences. There have been several instances in the twentieth century of Conservative leaders who have been forced to resign; however the process is rather different from that in the Labour Party, because until very recently the mechanism for ousting a leader who had lost the party's confidence was an informal one rather than the public machinery of annual re-election which exists in the Labour Party.

The relationship between the Conservative leader and his parliamentary colleagues was radically altered in 1965 when formal election machinery was created so that thereafter leaders would be chosen by vote of the whole of the Conservative Party in the House of Commons. The Conservative Party leadership's attitude towards an elective procedure had until then been hostile; because it had been in government for so much of the twentieth century it had usually proved possible to avoid the issue of leadership selection by accepting automatically as leader of the party the person invited by the monarch to form the administration. That person would in turn have been recommended to the monarch on the advice of a small group of senior Conservatives who would have taken soundings to ascertain which eligible individual would be likely to command the most support and create a consensus behind him. However this situation arose only if a Conservative prime minister died or resigned in the middle of a Parliament so that a new prime minister had to be found. If the party had a leader and a new administration had to be formed as a result of a general election victory then the monarch's choice was limited: since 1923 it has generally been assumed that the monarch must send for the leader of the Conservative Party in the House of Commons rather than the Tory leader in the House of Lords.

A vacancy in the leadership of the Conservative Party occurred when the party was in opposition in 1911. Then Andrew Bonar Law was elected leader at a time when the Conservatives were deeply divided over tariff reform. During the party's shorter spells of opposition prior to 1964 the Conservatives always had a former prime minister who could automatically become the leader of the opposition.

The decision to change to an elective procedure stemmed from the events and controversy surrounding the selection of the Earl of Home – Sir Alec Douglas-Home as he became – as prime minister in 1963. Home's selection as successor to Harold Macmillan was unusual, since at the time of his selection he was a peer and there was a much more attractive candidate from the point of view of many Conservative MPs in the person of R. A. Butler. After the Conservatives lost the general election of 1964 a new and more open procedure was devised and the successor to Sir Alec Douglas-Home was chosen by this method in 1965.

The procedure now involves a ballot of all Conservative MPs; to be elected on the first ballot, a candidate must win an overall majority plus an additional 15 per cent of those eligible to vote. If no candidate achieves this on the first ballot, there is a second ballot in which new candidates may stand and in which only an overall majority is necessary for victory. If there is still no winner on this ballot, a final ballot is held; only the candidates with the three highest votes may stand. Electors rank candidates in order of preference and the winner is determined by adding the number of first preferences to the redistributed second preferences on the papers of the third candidate.

Initially the system was intended only for use when the leadership was actually vacant – in other words when a leader had already indicated his intention of resigning. However after the Conservative Party had lost two elections in 1974 there was increased backbench dissatisfaction with Edward Heath's leadership and a demand for a revision of the rules to allow for annual elections in which the incumbent could be challenged. This change was made in 1975, and in that year Edward Heath was beaten for the leadership by Margaret Thatcher.

The change in the basis of the Conservative leader's authority – the fact that his or her position is no longer determined by the arcane process of nomination but by an open election – has perhaps yet to be fully appreciated by the Conservative Party. Edward Heath's style of leadership and the unexpected election victory of 1970 made his period of office as Conservative leader very similar to the pattern of that of earlier leaders. He showed little interest in cultivating the backbenchers by whose votes he had been elected; indeed one of the reasons for his defeat in 1975 was that he was thought to have been authoritarian and aloof in his handling of backbenchers.[3] Margaret Thatcher's leadership on the other hand has revealed an awareness of the mechanism by which she attained her position, and in oppositon she took care to involve the backbenchers more in policy discussions. Although her style of premiership appears to have become more dominant with time, it remains the case that in terms of relationship with the party as a whole she has taken care to keep in touch with developments in backbench opinion. It is not so much that the Conservative Party has suddenly discovered the power to depose leaders but rather that the machinery of annual elections makes the possibility of displacement more evident to leaders and followers alike. It is inevitably more likely that the kind of leader selected by this machinery will be a clearer reflection of backbench sentiments than in the past, and perhaps even of the outlook of constituency activists; previously the advice given to the monarch could take into account not merely a candidate's acceptability within the party but also his potential vote-winning capacity among the electorate at large, although the judgements on both these issues were necessarily subjective. Now the decision is simply a direct reflection of MPs' preferences.

When the Conservative Party is in opposition the leader will appoint a number of front-bench spokesmen to assist him in his parliamentary duties; the most senior of those appointments will form a shadow cabinet. These spokesmen are the personal choices of the leader; if they appear successful in their tasks they are likely to form the core of any future Conservative administration. The leader also appoints the key officers in the party's central bureacracy. The Conservative Central Office was founded by Disraeli in 1870 in order to help organize the party's electoral efforts in the circumstances of an expanded electorate. It is normally regarded as the personal preserve of the leader. Its chairman is appointed by the leader and may if the party is in power be a cabinet minister, a senior figure outside the cabinet, or a junior minister, depending on political circumstances. If the party is in office the chairman will frequently be required to attend cabinet meetings even if he is not himself a member of the cabinet. The leader also chooses the deputy chairman, the treasurer or treasurers and the four or five vice-chairmen who look after special aspects of the party's organization – for example local government or women's interests. The various sections of Central Office are under directors appointed by the chairman and they report to him at weekly meetings of the top functionaries of the party. These meetings include the whips, so as to maintain liaison with the party's work in Parliament as well as in the country.

Central Office also provides a home for the International Office, which has increasing responsibilities for assisting British members of the European Parliament (MEPs) to maintain relations with like-minded parties in Europe – for example the German Christian Democrats. Central Office is also the location for the Conservative Political Centre, which maintains a network of groups in the country for discussion meetings and which publishes pamphlets on aspects of party policy.

The Conservative Research Department, founded in 1930, was formerly independent of the Central Office machinery, as was evidenced by the fact that it was housed in a separate building. The Research Department played an especially important part in re-shaping Conservative thinking after the defeat of 1945. Despite its name, however, it is not strictly speaking a research institution, since its primary function is to provide background material for the parliamentary party and its backbench committees. It is thus more of a secretariat than a research body. It is responsible also for producing regular documentation in a variety of formats for the party in the country, and at election times it produces the 'campaign guide', with a regular output of notes for candidates and other speakers during the campaign itself. Many appointees in the Research Department – the desk officers – are relatively young and go on to become parliamentary candidates or special advisers to ministers. In 1979 the decision was taken amidst much controversy to bring the Research Department under the direct control of Central Office, and under its roof.[4]

The second element of importance within the Conservative Party is the whole body of Conservative MPs. The character and composition of the parliamentary representation of any political party is significant for at least two reasons. First, the image and appeal of a party is the product not merely of the specific policies and issues with which it is identified but also of the kind of men and women who are seen to represent that party. The electorate's perceptions of the party are thus shaped by such factors as the range of occupations represented among its candidates and MPs. The second reason for attaching significance to the composition of the parliamentary party is that divisions of opinion and ideology may well be compounded by social heterogeneity and thus make the task of leadership more difficult.[5] It is therefore important to ask of a party not simply what range of ideas are reflected within its ranks and how cohesive a group it is but also how diverse are the people it selects to carry its banner.

An examination of the background of Conservative MPs reveals that they are a relatively homogeneous group. Indeed there can be little doubt that the image that the modern Conservative party indirectly projects is still that of an upper-middle-class or 'patrician' party.[6] One index of the upper-middle-class character of the parliamentary party is the high proportion of members who attended a public (i.e. fee-paying) school. Many also attended Oxford and Cambridge, although their access to these ancient universities has in many cases been through the state system of secondary education. Thus for example both Edward Heath and Margaret Thatcher are Oxford graduates who had previously attended state grammar schools.

The occupational background of Conservative MPs has also not changed greatly during the recent past. The vast majority are drawn from the ranks of business, commerce and farming, as well as from such professions as the law and accountancy. However some slight shifts in the occupational groups most prominent in the Tory Party may be discerned. There has for example been a decline over the postwar period in the number of Conservative MPs with a landowning or farming background and an increase in the number of business-men, who form the largest single occupational group. (However, as will be seen in chapter 9, the Conservative Party's identification with the interests of the business community is by no means perfect, and often the policies advocated by the party are out of step with those advocated by financial and business interests outside Parliament.) The proportion of barristers in the parliamentary Conservative Party has also declined slightly, although the Bar still constitutes one of the most numerous professions within the Tory ranks.

The typical Conservative MP is also likely to be a man. As in the other parties women are under-represented both as candidates and in Parliament. In 1983 thirteen Conservative women candidates were elected. The prejudice of selection committees against women candidates means that those women who are adopted tend to be selected for hopeless or marginal seats. In a bad election for the Tories – October 1974 – only seven women were returned as Conservative MPs. The Conservative leadership has tried to encourage constituencies to select a wider social range of candidates – especially more women and members of ethnic minorities – but it has largely been unsuccessful.

Constituency associations are notoriously jealous of their right to select a candidate of their choice and it appears that these committees still find the attributes associated with a public school or an Oxbridge education combined with a career in business or the law impressive. Certainly individuals with these characteristics are likely to find their search for a Conservative seat easier than will applicants from less orthodox backgrounds. The Conservative Party's parliamentary representatives are thus very different both from its electoral supporters and from the activists who man the constituency associations.

The fact that certain educational and professional backgrounds are common to a large number of Conservative MPs has been seen by some commentators as an explanation of the cohesion of the parliamentary party. Social homogeneity, it was thought, reduced the likelihood of party division and faction. Certainly the internal divisions of the Conservative Party are different in kind from those in the Labour Party. For whereas the Labour Party has within its ranks a number of well organized groups who regularly meet and vote together, usually on the basis of some shared ideological approach to policy issues, divisions of opinion within the Conservative Party have been altogether more fluid and less durable. Broad similarities of outlook and the absence of sharp disagreements of principle have generally meant that when intra-party conflict has arisen it has been of a kind which can be transcended. This distinction between the form which differences of opinion and attitude take in the two major parties has been described in terms of a distinction between factions and tendencies – Labour's backbench groups being tangible enough to warrant the use of the term 'faction' while the Conservative Party's overlapping and inchoate divisions have had to be analysed in terms of 'tendencies.'[7] Yet although it is true that such divisions as exist within the Tory party are less clear-cut than those which mark Labour politics, the cohesion of the Conservative Party should not be exaggerated. Some clear divisions of opinion do exist within its ranks and there has been evidence since 1970 that Conservatives are becoming more willing than hitherto to express their dissent from the official line by defying the whips and voting against the leadership in the lobbies.[8]

Political attitudes within the Conservative Party are difficult to place on a simple right-left spectrum. It is necessary instead to consider opinions within the Conservative Party in terms of at least two divisions. The first division, which reflects a long-standing polarization in the party, is that between the traditionalists and the progressives. On such issues as social and penal reform, as earlier on colonial matters, the party is thus divided between those who see Conservatism as a means of defending the existing social order and those who regard it as a method of promoting gradual and non-dogmatic change. The second distinction cuts across this one, since it reflects the increasing significance of economic policy in recent British political debate. At one end of the spectrum of economic policy stand those who have, they believe, a coherent explanation of how inflation should be fought and what the state's role in the economy should be. At the other end of the spectrum are what might be called the pragmatists, who do not feel convinced of the truth of any single economic doctrine and who assert the need for various forms of state intervention in industry and the economy as circumstances demand.

The Conservative Party, although traditionally suspicious of organized groups within its ranks, does contain some pressure groups which can claim adherents at the parliamentary level. The Bow Group, for example, which was founded in 1951, used to be seen as an organization on the far left of the Conservative Party because of its attitude towards decolonization (which it favoured) and because of its problem-solving approach to social policy. Later it developed a strong monetarist element; and its diffuse research activities mean that it rarely seeks to exert any pressure as a group or to speak with a single voice. The large number of MPs and ministers who are members of the Group is thus not an accurate guide to its influence.

The Monday Club was founded in 1961 to combat the influence of 'liberals' and progressives in the Conservative Party, especially on foreign policy and on colonial questions. However it is now almost as divided as the Bow Group on economic policy: it combines a dislike of high taxation and government intervention in the economy with an authoritarian and paternalistic conception of the role of the state. The replacement of issues connected with colonization by such questions as immigration on the agenda of the right wing of the party in the constituencies (where the Monday Club has been strongest) made membership of the Club something of an embarrassment for Conservative MPs, and by the late 1970s its parliamentary adherents were few in number. Two other organizations deserve mention as examples of the style of Conservative pressure groups. One is the

Selsdon Group, founded in order to promote the free-market doctrines enshrined in the Conservatives' 1970 election manifesto – policies which were rapidly jettisoned in the light of the experience of office; the second is the Tory Reform Group, which aims to promote the progressive strand of Conservatism that used to be associated with the Bow Group. It is doubtful whether either of these groups has a great deal of influence, although their research activities are sometimes important. The Tory Reform Group provides one of the reference points for former Conservative ministers who find themselves at odds with Mrs Thatcher on economic and social policy – the so-called 'wets' – and for like-minded backbenchers.[9]

These divisions of opinion have not normally produced regular defiance of the party whips. Although there have been spectacular examples of intra-party dissent in the past – for example over the Government of India Act of 1935, which extended self-government for India against the wishes of a large section of the Conservative Party including Winston Churchill – the norm in the Conservative Party is internal cohesion. Indeed it was the Conservative Party which in many ways was responsible for the extension of party discipline in the House of Commons at the end of the nineteenth century. The degree of cohesion in both major parties can be gauged from the figures of cross-voting.[10] Between 1945 and 1970 cross-voting – defined as an occasion when a member of one party defies the whips' instructions and votes in the opposite lobby – occurred in no more than 12 per cent of all divisions. However between 1970 and 1974 – a single Parliament – there was some cross-voting in at least 20 per cent of the divisions. This increase was especially marked in the Conservative Party, and the increase challenged many of the orthodox assumptions about the party's ideological cohesion. For there was evidence not merely of a greater degree of dissent within the party, measured by the willingness of Conservative MPs to take their disagreement with the leadership to the level of voting against the party line; there was also evidence of a much greater degree of congruence between dissidents on different issues. In other words dissent within the Conservative Party seemed to have been hardening, and although Tory dissenters took no steps to build a formal organization on the basis of their emerging common intellectual and emotional outlook the development was a significant one. It revealed at the very least the existence of a group of MPs whose shared opinions could provide the basis within the Conservative Party for a factional grouping akin to those with which Labour has to contend.

Backbench opinion in the Conservative Party is formally organized through a body known as the 1922 Committee.[11] This is the channel of communication between backbenchers and the leadership, and although it does not use formal votes and resolutions as the Labour Party's committees do, the character of its discussions conveys to the leader the impact which his policies are having in the parliamentary party. The 1922 Committee meets weekly, and when the Conservatives are in opposition the leader and the front-bench spokesmen attend its meetings. If the Conservative Party is in power, however, the members of the administration do not attend and the 1922 Committee becomes the forum solely of backbench opinion. The 1922 Committee's influence is veiled and discreet but nevertheless extensive. It can be assessed from the experience of the leadership crisis of 1974–5, when it was the 1922 Committee which initiated the changes in the rules for election to the leadership to enable an incumbent leader's position to be challenged. And of course the Committee's name commemorates what was probably the most important exercise of backbench power in twentieth-century peacetime history – the decision by Conservative MPs not to support the continuation of the Lloyd George coalition. The 1922 Committee was formed out of the Conservative members returned at the subsequent election.

In addition to the 1922 Committee there are a range of subject committees for the various policy areas of the party. Their operations also provide a mechanism for the expression of backbench opinion; although there is no formal role for them in the policy-making process there is usually a good deal of interaction between the specialized study groups which a leader may establish in opposition and these committees, which obviously serve also to inform MPs on the details of a subject area. Mrs Thatcher's general desire to keep her backbenchers in touch with the progress of her policy ideas led between 1975 and 1979 to some institutionalization of these contacts between backbench committees and the special study groups.

The third element in the Conservative party organization is the National Union of Conservative and Unionist Associations of England and Wales, which comprises the Conservative Associations of each parliamentary constituency. The Scottish Party is a distinct organization, though it sends six representatives to the National Union's Executive Committee. Although the Northern Ireland Unionists are now politically separate from the British Conservatives, the Ulster Unionist Council retains the right to nominate its chairman and four other representatives to the National Union's Executive Committee. The National Union was founded in 1867 as part of the drive to mobilize Conservative sympathizers in the country at large – especially in the boroughs – behind the party leadership in the wake of electoral reform. The primary feature of the constituency associations is their freedom from central control and their self-sufficiency. They largely raise their own funds through a variety of social activities based on the subordinate units of each association – the branches. (These branches are organized on the smallest electoral divisions – called wards – and it is through these wards that much of the routine grass-roots political work of the constituency association is effected.) The constituency associations also employ their own agents and select their own candidates for local and parliamentary elections; and in conjunction with other constituency associations combined for the purpose they select their own Tory candidates for the European Parliament.

This relative degree of independence and autonomy is accompanied by acceptance of the dominant role of the parliamentary leadership in policy-making. The National Union does hold an annual conference to which all constituencies are entitled to send representatives; but its debates on policy are frequently anodyne and its resolutions are advisory and not binding on the leadership. When in 1983 the leadership found itself embarrassed yet again by the tone of the debate on immigration – the topic chosen by the constituency parties in a ballot, unlike the other debates, which are set by the National Union's Executive Committee – moves were made to amend the rules to try to prevent a small minority organizing to get its motion onto the agenda. The Conservative Party tradition with respect to the relationship between the Party's parliamentary leadership and the voluntary wing of the party has thus been to emphasize the autonomy of the MPs and the supportive but subordinate role of the party activists. Recently some commentators have noticed a certain change in style in the relationship, and certainly the annual conferences have become more obviously political occasions as opposed to semi-ritualistic and social ones. The change has been indicated by the increased frequency of votes, the greater willingness of speakers to disagree with the platform and the additional fringe group activity. Yet if the atmosphere at Conservative conferences has become more controversial of late, the role of the conference in the party is quite distinct from that enjoyed by the Labour Party conference: in Labour's constitutional theory, conference is the sovereign policy-making body of the party but for Conservatives the major functions conferences fulfil relate to propaganda, publicity and the general integration of the various groups within the party into a corporate whole.

Although there has been a historical division between the National Union and Central Office the extent to which this division causes difficulties in practice should not be exaggerated. The National Union shares premises with Central Office. The large Executive Committee of the National Union is itself an attempt to represent the various sections of the party in microcosm. Thus it includes representatives from Central Office and from the parliamentary party alongside representatives of geographical areas and of the specialized sections such as women, Young Conservatives, trade unionists and students. The Advisory Committee on Policy (which is chaired by a senior party figure who will be a minister or member of the shadow cabinet) also brings together some personnel from Central Office and representatives of the National Union.[12]

Drafting the election manifesto has always been seen as being ultimately a responsibility of the leader, though, as has been seen, there may be different mechanisms established to prepare the material which will in the end be included.

The leadership has from time to time attempted to use Conservative Central Office to exert control over the constituency associations. The question of candidate selection has been an especially delicate issue, because every candidate before he can be officially adopted must be endorsed centrally. Theoretically this means that constituency parties must select their candidates from a list maintained by the Standing Advisory Committee on Candidates and the party vice-chairman responsible for candidates, although it is always possible for a constituency to consider the name of an individual prior to his inclusion in the central list. The point of the central list is to exercise some influence over the individuals who will represent the party at a parliamentary election, since as one commentator has put it, 'whether he wins or loses the candidate's bearing will affect the reputation of the Conservative Party in the constituency' and could affect the result in a marginal seat.[13] However in practice such sanctions as are available centrally are not very great: the list is large and local associations have proved so determined to maintain their freedom of action concerning candidate selection that such attempts as Edward Heath's efforts to ensure a greater social mix by tightening the vetting procedure have been unsuccessful. (Indeed the Heath initiative caused such ill-feeling that Margaret Thatcher suspended the review of the central list of candidates as soon as she became leader, and any names which had been dropped from the list were replaced.)[14]

The central organization has on occasion attempted to erode the autonomy of constituency parties with respect to the employment of agents. From the central party perspective it is inefficient to have so little control over the deployment of agents, for these individuals are in many ways the key to sound electoral organization. Indeed it would be beneficial for the party as a whole if the best agents could be sent where they were most needed at a general election – that is to the marginal seats on which the overall result will depend. From the constituency point of view, however, local employment of an agent is important both because the funding is raised locally and because the agent could otherwise become – in circumstances of dispute between a constituency and its MP or between a local MP and the leadership – an instrument through whom central pressure could be applied. Indeed agents were used to communicate the leader's displeasure with those MPs who rebelled over the Common Market issue during the 1970–4 Parliament, and some dissident MPs greatly resented these intrusions via the agent into their relations with their constituency parties. The agent is inevitably in a delicate position in any dispute between the local MP and his constituency or between the MP and the leadership; constituency parties have not unnaturally preferred to make quite clear what they view as the agent's primary loyalty by employing him themselves. Thus although attempts were made to start a central agency scheme whereby a certain number of agents would be employed by the party at the national level the idea was both unpopular in the constituencies and costly. It was therefore abandoned.

The Labour Party

The internal relationships of the Labour Party are very different from those of the Conservative Party. The fact that the Labour Party originated outside Parliament and that at times in its history its parliamentary representation has been very small has meant that the Parliamentary Labour Party (PLP) has never enjoyed that autonomy in policy-making which Tory MPs have been accorded. The greater attention which the Labour Party has given to the values of participation and internal democracy has also contributed to the style of Labour politics. Together with the fact that ideology and doctrine have frequently caused divisions these features of the British Labour Party make the tasks of party management more complicated than among the Conservatives, and present different problems for the leadership.

These problems have been accentuated in the period since the 1979 general election by major changes in the Labour Party's rules and procedure. Many of these changes had for some time been advocated by the left of the party, which was disappointed by the lack of radicalism displayed by Labour governments during the premierships of Harold Wilson and James Callaghan. As a result there appears to have been a major shift in the balance between the Parliamentary Labour Party on the one hand and the party outside Parliament (including both the trade unions and the constituency parties) on the other.[15] The magnitude of Labour's defeat in 1983 and its growing financial problems, together with the possibility of changes in the attitudes of individual unions, could mean that some of these issues of organization will be raised again.

Although the Labour Party, unlike its rivals, originated outside Parliament its parliamentary representation fairly rapidly achieved a position of influence. The PLP elected its own leader, who came to be recognized as the leader of the party as a whole, and it was significant that when Labour was invited to form a government it was to Ramsay MacDonald, the leader of the parliamentary party, that the summons to do so went. Until the 1970s it was accepted that it was for Labour MPs alone to choose the leader and more recently the deputy leader as well.

The members of the PLP elect the committee of fifteen (twelve until 1981–2) who as a parliamentary committee aid the leader in carrying out the party's parliamentary duties when in opposition.[16] The fifteen members thus form the core of the shadow cabinet, and although the Labour leader may add to their numbers the fact that careers within the parliamentary party can be built on the basis of popularity and esteem in the PLP as a whole is a significant difference from the situation in the Conservative Party. Initially at least it is sufficient in the Conservative Party for an aspiring front-bencher to gain the support of the leader, and any front-bencher who loses that support will be in danger of losing his position; a Labour leader may have to keep as a front-bench spokesman someone in whom he has lost confidence.

The fact that Labour elected its front-bench spokesmen could have suggested the use of a similar arrangement for the cabinet as a whole when Labour first took office in 1924. However Ramsay MacDonald had no hesitation in following the normal constitutional convention and appointed his own cabinet without further reference to the PLP. Indeed one of the peculiarities of Labour Party history has been the alternation between periods of opposition in which the norms of intra-party democracy have bound the leadership to a greater or lesser extent and periods of office in which the leadership has appealed to the conventions of the constitution against the practices and expectations of the Labour Party.

The composition of the Parliamentary Labour Party is of special interest because one of the explicit purposes of founding the new party was to secure the representation of the working classes in Parliament. In the opinion of Labour's founding fathers the defence of labour interests would be best promoted by sending into Parliament individuals with experience of manual occupations. However the Labour Party in Parliament has become an overwhelmingly middle-class party, and the working-class element in its ranks has been steadily depleted as this century has worn on. The trend to replace MPS from working-class occupations and who have had very little formal education with university lecturers, schoolteachers, broad-casters and journalists can easily be followed.[17] It should be noted that the mix of occupations in the Labour Party is of course different from that in the Conservative Party in that the traditional professions and business are much less evident in the PLP than in the Conserva-tive Party. However it can hardly be said that Labour at parlia-mentary level remains in any sense reflective of the party's electoral base.

The leftward move of the party after 1979, although its supporters often used the language of working-class solidarity and the class war, actually accentuated this tendency as candidates of working-class backgrounds were replaced by more ideologically sophisticated representatives of the middle-class professions. An analysis made shortly before the general election of 1983 showed that of members who had been selected to fight again, forty-five were blue-collar workers and 139 came from other occupations, together with seventeen trade union officials and three cooperative or party workers. Of the new candidates a mere thirty-five were blue-collar workers, with 302 drawn from other professions. Six were housewives, eight were unemployed, twenty-one were trade union officials, and three were MEPS. The two largest groups among the new candidates were lecturers and school-teachers. Labour, unlike the Conserva-tives, had some representatives of the ethnic minorities fighting seats, though none were nominated for winnable ones; and fifty of its new candidates were women. In the end Labour saw seventy-seven female candidates, but a mere ten were elected – only one more than in 1929.

An analysis of Labour's results made after the 1983 election helps further to illustrate the changes in the party's representation and the limits of such change. Over half Labour's candidates were university graduates and thirty of their MPs in the new Parliament had been educated in the 'public schools' which the party was pledged to abolish. Forty-seven per cent of Labour's successful candidates and fifty-two per cent of their unsuccessful candidates were professional people; other white-collar occupations accounted for sixteen per cent of successful candidates and twenty-four per cent of unsuccessful ones. About a tenth in each category had a business background.

On the other hand, a third of Labour's candidates but only fourteen per cent of unsuccessful ones were classified as manual workers, which indicates that working-class candidates stand a better chance of adoption where the seat is likely to be won. Twenty Labour candidates were described as miners – all were elected. The National Union of Mineworkers, with almost a tenth of Labour's parliamentary representation, was thus more strongly placed in the PLP than in the wider party or the TUC.[18]

Labour's complicated constitution reflects the federal nature of the Labour alliance and the fact that the varied interests in the Labour coalition respond to different pressures. The ultimate and sovereign policy-making organ of the party has always been recognized as the Labour Party conference.[19] It debates and determines the policies of the Party and elects the Labour Party officers and the members of the National Executive Committee (NEC) which looks after the party's affairs between conferences. The two principal officers of the Labour Party (other than the leader and deputy leader) are the secretary – who is not an MP but a salaried chief executive – and the treasurer, who is frequently an MP.

It is normal for conference to meet annually, although it may not meet if there is an election in the offing; additional conferences may be called if – as occurred in relation to British membership of the EEC or the constitutional changes proposed for the party in 1981 – Labour wishes to devote a substantial amount of time to a particular issue. The different elements in the party – the trade unions, the Constituency Labour Parties (CLPs) and socialist societies – may send resolutions to conference, and if passed by a two-thirds majority they become official party policy.

Because the resolutions sent to conference are too numerous for the time available for debate, resolutions on similar subjects are grouped together in an obscure process known as compositing. This process is performed on the eve of the conference, although all the original resolutions are printed in full for delegates to read. The mere fact that a resolution has been passed with the requisite majority does not mean that it will be implemented by the parliamentary leadership. Conference endorsement can only make a proposal official party policy. The Labour Party's election manifesto is however drafted by the National Executive Committee in conjunction with the Labour cabinet or shadow cabinet, and until 1979 it was tacitly accepted that the leader had a veto over any item he considered objectionable – a privilege strongly resented by the left.

Equally of course an item which does succeed in being adopted as

Labour Party policy and is included in the manifesto will not automatically be enacted if Labour is returned to office. The legislative timetable is solely dependent on the discretion of the cabinet, and the party as a whole can exercise no control over it. The fact that official party policy is not the preserve of the party's parliamentary wing does create conflicts within the party, because the leadership will generally be concerned with the electoral popularity or practical wisdom of a programme while conference delegates may be motivated by different considerations. They may for example be more impressed by the ideological justifications for a proposal, or they may be responding to pressures at the grass roots of their own union or CLP. The adoption of extreme or impractical programmes by conference clearly offers Labour's electoral opponents ammunition with which to attempt to frighten the electorate and so, even if Labour leaders believe they need never implement the proposals, there is always an incentive to try to influence conference decisions.

Conference is composed of the representatives of different sections of the party: trade unions, CLPs and the small socialist societies. In addition to the attendance of delegates to conference some provision is made for *ex officio* attendance which does not carry voting rights. Labour MPs and selected candidates who are not present as delegates attend in this capacity, as do members of the party's National Executive Committee.

The trade union movement is the dominant force at Labour Party conferences in terms of electoral strength. The number of votes cast by delegates reflects the affiliation fees which they pay to the central party organization. What this means in the trade union movement is that each individual trade union can cast at conference a number of votes equivalent to the number of members the union affiliates to the Labour Party. In trade unions which affiliate to the Labour Party each trade unionist pays a political levy which is a sum added to trade union dues for the union to spend as it likes on political purposes. (Historically the levy has been controversial, because Conservative governments have in the past sought to make it effectively optional by legislating to require trade union members to opt *into* the scheme; Labour governments on the other hand have put the onus on the individual to opt *out* of the levy if he prefers not to pay it. Needless to say, inertia means that the trade unions have a much larger sum of money available to them when members have to opt out than would be the case if opting in were the rule, as was again proposed by the government in 1983.) The trade unions do not need to affiliate on the basis of their total membership and in some cases trade union membership is larger than the number of affiliated members reported to the Labour Party. However the important point is that by counting as a member of the Labour Party every trade unionist who pays the levy, the paper membership of the Labour Party is made very much higher than that of any other British political party, although of course this means very little in terms of active participation in the party's affairs. And it is the distribution of membership between the trade unions and the individual CLPs which gives the trade unions the overwhelming influence over conference and its decisions.

In 1977 the trade unions had a membership of 5,913,159, as compared with a total individual membership of 659,737 in the constituency parties. Together with the 43,375 members of the socialist and cooperative societies this gave the Labour Party in 1977 a total membership of 6,616,271. In 1979 those members belonging to the party by virtue of trade union affiliation or in a small minority of cases through membership of socialist or cooperative societies numbered 6,569,507 and individual members of constituency parties numbered 666,091. There was a sharp drop in the latter figure in 1980 when constituencies were credited with a more realistic figure instead of assuming, as previously, that each had at least 1,000 members. Rises in the annual subscription and recession further reduced their numbers in the following years. In terms of the ability of small groups of left-wing activists to manipulate constituency parties this trend in membership figures is clearly significant. By the time the Labour Party conference met in October 1983 the Report showed that the membership had slumped in 1982 to 273,803 individual members with 57,131 from the socialist societies compared with 6,185,063 from the affiliated trade unions. Nevertheless a further increase in the individual subscription rate was imposed to help the party's dire financial situation.

Because the votes at the Labour Party conference are allocated on the basis of one vote per thousand members or part thereof, and because votes have to be cast as a block – in other words there is no question of a union with a large membership dividing them in proportion to the opinions of its delegates or members – the decisions of one or two big unions can be vital in any policy dispute at conference. In 1983 the voting strength of the biggest unions was: TGWU, 1,250,000; AUEW, 850,000; GMBATU, 650,000; NUPE, 600,000; USDAW, 405,000. It is significant that with the changing composition of the workforce the giants of the past – especially the railway workers and the miners – are now much less significant in numerical terms.

The trade unions do not only dominate the policy-making aspects of the Labour Party conference; they also have a significant impact on the composition of the National Executive Committee. The extent of the trade unions' influence in these elections is a product both of their superior numbers and of the particular constitution of the party. The National Executive Committee is itself constructed to reflect the different sections of the Labour Party, and for some sections election to the NEC is confined to the votes of the particular element in the party which has to be represented. For some sections however the election is by the conference as a whole, and this inevitably means that the trade unions will be able to control the result.

The National Executive Committee currently has twenty-nine members. As might be expected given the unions' importance within the Labour Party, the trade unions are the largest single group represented on the NEC, with twelve of these seats. Positions on the NEC are usually used to satisfy trade union officials of the second rank of the union hierarchy, as most professional trade union organizers will see a seat on the TUC General Council as the summit of their ambitions. Labour Party Standing Orders prevent the holding of office on the NEC and the TUC at the same time, so that one frequently finds a union putting its general secretary on the TUC and some less important figure on the NEC.

The Constituency Labour Parties elect seven members in their section, and these are chosen by delegates representing the CLPs alone. (Until 1937 the representatives in this category were chosen by Conference as a whole, but the anomaly of having trade unions dominating the CLPs even in this respect was too marked and the constitution was amended to provide for separate voting.) The smaller affiliated societies can elect one member to their section. A final division is that of women members, who have five seats on the NEC, although these are elected by vote of the conference as a whole, and thus by a process in which union strength is decisive.

In spite of their guaranteed membership of the NEC, women fare almost as badly in the general running of the Labour Party as in its parliamentary wing. At the 1983 conference 91.5 per cent of the trade union delegates were men; 73.9 per cent of the delegates from CLPs were men, as were 73.7 per cent of the delegates from socialist societies. An attempt by women activists to secure a greater say in the party's affairs – by changing the election to the women's section of the NEC so that only members of the Labour Women's conference would be able to vote – was defeated by the trade union block vote. The members of the NEC women's section are therefore still elected by conference as a whole – i.e. by a body dominated by male trade unionists.

In addition to the twenty-three elected members of the NEC the Labour Party Young Socialists are entitled to one seat on the NEC and the leader and deputy leader of the party sit *ex officio*. There is also the party treasurer, who is elected by the whole conference and whose position is thus regarded as a virtual trade union appointment. Thus the trade unions, although they do not necessarily act in concert, could decide the result of the elections to eighteen of the twenty-nine seats on the NEC.

Initially the influence of the trade unions was seen for good or ill as a moderating force within the movement, since until the 1960s trade unions appeared to have limited political objectives and to be content to follow the policies of the parliamentary leadership. In addition they displayed a marked suspicion of the more ideological style of politics which often marked the CLPs. The explicit opposition by union leaders of the 1945–55 period to left-wing sentiment and the strategic use of their block votes to support the platform and the leadership whenever it was challenged at conference did indeed earn the unions a lot of criticism. The left-wing CLPs greatly resented the fact that a group of union leaders such as Arthur Deakin of the Transport and General Workers' Union and William Carron of the Engineering Union could prevent the operation of internal democracy within the party. However the pattern of politics in the 1950s, in which moderate unions could be counted on for numerical muscle in any internal party crisis, has been succeeded by one in which a more complex pattern of Labour politics has emerged. Some of the movement has been created by a simple shift in the politics of individual unions to a left-of-centre disposition; but in addition there have been a number of other factors within the very heterogeneous trade union movement which have contributed to a new policy environment which has in turn had an effect on the politics of the Labour Party.

Among the factors which contributed towards a change in the role of the unions within the Labour Party, the most visible perhaps was the replacement of a number of key union leaders whose politics had been of the centre with figures whose orientation was more left-wing. Although there have been some recent elections of centrist general secretaries, the trend to the left among union leaders may perhaps be dated from 1956, when Frank Cousins became general secretary of the Transport and General Workers' Union following the retirement of the right-wing Arthur Deakin and the premature death of the latter's successor, Jock Tiffin. Because it was the largest union this change in the character of the TGWU's political leadership was bound to be significant, and the tradition of left-of-centre leadership was maintained by Jack Jones, who became general secretary in 1969, and by Moss Evans, who took over in 1978. During the late 1960s other unions acquired a left-of-centre leadership: in 1967 Hugh Scanlon was elected president of the traditionally left-wing Amalgamated Union of Engineering Workers with Communist support, and Alan Fisher became general secretary of the militant National Union of Public Employees. The latter union was to a large extent responsible for the industrial unrest in the United Kingdom in the winter of 1978–9, which damaged the electoral prospects of the then Labour government and was a direct challenge to its policy of wage constraint.

Changes in the character of union leadership in recent years should not be seen as the only factor affecting the role of the unions inside the Labour Party, however. Of more direct importance has been the changing agenda of British politics and the fact that for much of the period since 1964 it has been a Labour government with which the trade unions have had to deal. The ambiguity of the trade unions' position within the Labour Party is to some extent concealed while the party is in opposition; but when Labour is in power there are inevitable conflicts of loyalty when the priorities of the Labour government appear to be different from those of the trade union movement. The fact that incomes policy played such an important part in the Labour government's economic strategies after 1964 was the primary cause of tension within the Labour Party. The unions were forced to work out their own defensive positions and policies, and sometimes the passions engendered by the resultant arguments prevented general cooperation with the leadership on other issues, or at least made it unsafe for the leadership to count on the unions' support in a crisis.

The decline of voluntarism in industrial relations policy and the 1966–70 Labour government's flirtation with the idea of legal regulation, as well as the 1970–4 Conservative government's actual implementation of industrial relations legislation, meant that another issue touching the fundamental interests of trade unionists was moved to the heart of British political debate. In the 1950s the Labour Party's most bitter internal divisions were over foreign rather than domestic policy, and this meant that on the whole the leadership could assume that the unions would not have an independent line of their own to pursue in any confrontation between left and right. By the late 1960s however the touchstone of the party's ideological divisions was the whole range of economic policies, and here the unions were bound to be active participants in any debate. Indeed one of the first responses of the TUC to Mrs Thatcher's 1979 election victory and her subsequent budget was to outline an alternative economic strategy which it was felt would be able to command support.

The final aspect of the changing relationship between the Labour Party and the trade unions is related to this change in the party's agenda. The trade unions were induced to cooperate with the Labour government of the 1964–79 period on the issue of incomes control; but in return they claimed a greater voice in determining a wide range of social policies. The experience of opposition to the Conservative Industrial Relations Act of 1971 generated new machinery for consultation between the unions and the Labour Party. This was the so-called TUC-Labour Party Liaison Committee, and after 1971 much of the trade union influence in the Labour Party's policy-making processes was exerted through this committee. The initial development of a united front against the Industrial Relations Act of 1971 was broadened into a more comprehensive agreement on economic and social policy in the general election of February 1974. This commitment – the so-called 'social contract' – was unusual in that its implications for Labour policy were worked out in the Liaison Committee rather than in the formal policy-making apparatus of the party – the NEC and its various subcommittees. The Liaison Committee continued to meet regularly and the NEC's 1978 Report to Conference recorded joint discussions between the TUC and the Labour Party on such matters as priorities in the use of North Sea Oil revenue, the wealth tax proposal, child benefits, the common agricultural policy of the EEC, overseas investment, trade and investment in South Africa, and manpower and employment policies. A new agreed joint statement of policies – *Into the Eighties* – was presented to the 1978 conference in addition to the detailed investigation of specialized policy areas.

It should be noted that the Liaison Committee brings together representatives of the TUC, the NEC and the PLP. In other words the Committee offers a forum for influence on party policy for the trade union membership as a whole and not just for those unions who are politically affiliated to the Labour Party. (The number of unions formally affiliated to the Labour Party is of course only a small proportion of all unions, even though some of the affiliated unions are the largest in terms of membership.) Thus the rapidly expanding white-collar unions, including those which are politically neutral, such as the Civil Service unions and NALGO, can exert some influence through the Liaison Committee. The creation of the Liaison Committee therefore means that in addition to the influence which the unions can have in the Labour Party conference there is another point of access into Labour policy and one where the whole range of trade union movement interests could in theory be promoted. Together with the fact that the subject matter of political debate more directly concerns the major unions than in the 1950s it seems likely that this further institutionalization of the trade union perspective will persist. On a number of topics however the unions are themselves divided; and the likelihood of this potential influence on party policy being consistently mobilized is perhaps not very great.

The period of Conservative government after 1979 affected the trade union-Labour Party relationship in two contradictory ways. The government's economic policies and in particular its legislation restricting the immunities of trade unions were clearly matters on which the trade unions and the Labour Party could easily unite in opposition. On international issues many trade unions, like the CLPs, moved towards support for unilateral nuclear disarmament. On the other hand, some trade union leaders took the view that their own interests would be best safeguarded by the advent of a Labour government which would bring them back to the central position in policy-making they had enjoyed in the Wilson-Callaghan era. They were therefore prepared to make some sacrifices in terms of ideological purity if electorally popular policies could be found. When the considerable effort exerted in the 1983 election campaign proved unrewarding and it was clear that there would be another term of Conservative government, the trade unions were pulled in three different directions. One group looked towards a long-term victory for Labour; others held that a new phase of direct action might be called for; and a third group seemed to hold that, since the Conservative government was a fact, it would be better for the trade union movement if less hostile relations could be worked out with its ministers, and discussions entered into, at least on those issues of most direct relevance to union interests. These uncertainties contributed to the doubts about the future direction of the Labour Party itself.

It has already been suggested that Labour's concern with ideological issues and its heterogeneity have both contributed to the proliferation of factions within its ranks. While the issues which have occasioned such factional groupings have varied with the passage of time there has usually existed at least one group which has organized itself to push Labour policy to the left. Sometimes its activity has provoked a reaction by right-of-centre Labour members, as for example when controversy stimulated the formation of the Manifesto Group in the 1974–9 Parliament. Increasingly however it has been the left both inside and outside of Parliament which has set the issues for debate within the Labour Party. Left-wing groups have thus taken on the role of the party's intellectual driving force and conscience, so that counter-groups find themselves having to fight a rearguard action to keep the party on the moderate lines which they think will maximize the appeal of Labour to the electorate.

The post-1945 period saw a number of identifiable left-wing factions emerge in the Labour Party. The Keep Left Group of 1946 elaborated distinct positions on a number of foreign policy and domestic issues and those positions were, for much of the 1950s, associated with the personal supporters of Aneurin Bevan. The revisionist debates within the Labour Party in the period 1955–63 – in which the leader, Hugh Gaitskell, tried to persuade the party to amend many of its fundamental tenets and to modernize its version of socialism in order to enhance Labour's electoral appeal – stimulated Gaitskell's supporters to found their own organization. That faction – the Campaign for Democratic Socialism – was able to mobilize many of the Labour Party's leading intellectuals, such as Anthony Crosland, as well as members outside the parliamentary party who were sympathetic to the cause of moderate socialism. In that sense the CDS was an unusual example of an aggressive faction on the right of the party which was able to seize the initiative from Gaitskell's left-of-centre critics.

In the period after Harold Wilson became leader of the Labour Party groups on the left became more significant than those on the right. The first deserving mention was the Tribune Group, which was founded in 1964 and could claim a membership of sixty-seven Labour MPs by 1967. It became itself split between a hard left and a soft left and by the time of the 1979 general election Tribune membership was by no means the sign of militant socialism that it had once been. The second faction which should be mentioned is the Campaign for Labour Party Democracy. This group was founded in 1973 with the explicit objective of transferring power from the Parliamentary Labour Party to the party as a whole – a movement which would mean greater influence for conference in policy-making, and greater control by constituency activists over their MPs.

Because the goal of the Campaign for Labour Party Democracy involved a reduction in the autonomy of Labour MPs it is not perhaps surprising that it was supported more enthusiastically outside the parliamentary party than within it. The CLPD tried to implement its philosophy by promoting two changes in the party's organization. The first cause to absorb its energies was the attempt to change the procedure governing the selection of parliamentary candidates. The CLPD wanted constituencies to be able, if they found themselves with MPs whose views did not coincide with those of constituency activists, to displace sitting MPs and replace them with people whose views were more in accord with their own. The second crusade which the CLPD conducted was for changing the rules governing election to the

239

party leadership. Instead of having the leader elected by all Labour MPs it was suggested by CLPD and others that election should be either by conference as a whole or, preferably, by a specially constructed electoral college which would not be dominated, as is conference, by the trade unions with their block votes. Such a move would obviously increase the chances of a left-of-centre candidate's winning the ballot, since the PLP was inclined towards the centre-right of the spectrum as well as cautious about the electoral consequences of its decisions. The constituency delegates by contrast might be expected to prefer a candidate whose views were nearer to their own than to those of the electorate as a whole.

The Campaign for Labour Party Democracy launched its operations at a particularly embarrassing time for the PLP. Although many Labour supporters accepted the argument for extending the participation of the Labour rank and file in key political decisions many others were also aware of the ease with which the extra-parliamentary party could be infiltrated by far left factions whose aim was to colonize it for their own purposes – purposes which many suspected were basically not supportive of parliamentary democracy. The process of infiltration by the far left (Communists, Trotskyists and others) had long troubled the Labour Party, and from 1930 it kept a list of proscribed organizations, membership of which was incompatible with belonging to the Labour Party. The practice was abolished in 1973; but in the period 1975–6 the Labour Party again became concerned that some increasingly moribund constituency Labour parties were being taken over by well organized groups who did not fully subscribe to the traditions of the Labour Party. An investigation of such allegations was eventually ordered by the Labour Party's National Executive Committee in January 1977, and although the authors of its report on 'entryism' – the process of infiltration of the party – were anxious to play down the extent of the phenomenon, they did call for renewed membership and political education campaigns to alert the solid Labour Party supporters to the dangers of groups such as the Militant Tendency in the party.

The Militant Tendency presented a particularly difficult problem, since its spokesmen consistently denied that it was a separate organization with its own policy-forming apparatus and argued that it was composed only of loyal party members who found their views represented by *Militant* newspaper.

The implications of according the constituency parties greater control over their MPs had been discussed in the early 1970s when a number of celebrated disputes between MPs and their local parties occurred. In a number of cases, the readoption of a sitting MP was refused for non-ideological or personal reasons; and in some cases the dislodged MP's only defence was to accuse his attackers of an ideologically inspired conspiracy. In other cases however the motive was simply that the constituency party felt itself unable to continue supporting MPs such as Dick Taverne and Reg Prentice when the MPs' views on divisive issues, for example British entry into Europe, differed so markedly from their own.

The cases of Reg Prentice in Newham and to a lesser extent of Frank Tomney in Hammersmith and Neville Sandelson in Hayes and Harlington confirmed the determination of many constituency parties to regard their MPs as delegates rather than trustees. The Newham case was unusual not merely because Prentice was at the time a member of a Labour cabinet but also because the constituency became the subject of litigation as the warring factions tried to test in the courts the credentials of delegates to the constituency party's annual general meeting. In the aftermath of these cases the NEC decided to review the rules of local constituency parties to ensure that members who belonged to a constituency party by virtue of member-ship of an affiliated organization – usually a trade union – were also resident in the constituency, and to try to iron out ambiguities surrounding the appeals procedure.

The broader question of the automatic reselection of MPs came before the Labour conference in 1978 and a compromise NEC motion was narrowly passed as an alternative to the rank-and-file demand – spearheaded by the CLPD – that a fresh selection procedure should automatically be held during each Parliament. Instead a sitting MP had to go through a reselection procedure only if he first lost a vote of no confidence moved against him in the constituency.

The question of broadening the electoral college for the party leader aroused as much passion as the ability of selection comittees to oust a sitting MP. It has already been seen that by comparison with his Conservative opposite number a Labour leader is more constrained by the need to balance the various elements of the party in his cabinet and by the fact that in opposition his senior colleagues are elected by the PLP as a whole. A Labour leader's success thus rests on his ability to unite very different opinions and personalities in a collective body which is electorally credible; the basis of the leader's position would, however, it was said, be transformed if it were to rest not on the support of the PLP but on an electoral college reflecting the values of constituency activists and the trade unions. For then a leader elected on a left-wing platform by the votes of the extra-parliamentary elements of the party could easily prove unable to command the support of his parliamentary colleagues and the Labour Party might find itself, *mutatis mutandis*, in the same difficulty as the backbench Tories in 1963 when their new leader, the Earl of Home (who disclaimed his peerage and became Sir Alec Douglas-Home), was chosen by an inner circle of Conservative leaders without reference to Tory backbenchers.

A working party of the NEC which had been examining the suggestion of broadening the electorate in leadership contests reported to conference in 1978. The suggestion that conference itself should elect the leader of the party attracted hardly any support, largely because the unions themselves did not appear to want such a responsibility. The alternative – a specially composed electoral college – was also defeated.

Nevertheless neither question was laid to rest by these adverse decisions, and after the election of 1979 and the Labour defeat the whole problem of the future organization and leadership of the party was once more in the melting pot. In dealing with subsequent events it should be remembered that the steps towards fulfilling the organizational aspirations of the left went in counterpoint with the departure from the party of elements on its right wing and the creation of the Social Democratic Party. These events both weakened the position of those on the right of the party who for a variety of reasons wished to remain inside it, and gave the left an argument against them, in that they could point to those who had left the Labour Party as proof that it was only the left that was genuinely and fully committed to the socialist ideal.

In the 1979 Parliament both the Tribune Group and the Manifesto Group put up slates of candidates for election to the shadow cabinet, and although the right swept the board the situation was peculiar for two reasons. First, two leading left-wingers, Tony Benn and Eric Heffer, declined to serve in the shadow cabinet in order to be able to pursue an independent strategy. This was taken to mean not merely a redefinition of socialist policies but also the advocacy of fundamental constitutional reform in the party, including a proposition even more radical than those advanced in 1978, namely that members of a Labour cabinet should be elected by the PLP as a whole on the Australian model and not simply selected by the prime minister. Second, the fact that it was the first time that both sides were looking to a future leadership contest gave the exercise of portfolio distribution as well as PLP voting a significance which in normal years they would not have had.

The apparent consolidation of the position of the right and centre was not long to remain unchallenged. It was agreed to set up a Commission of Inquiry into the party's organization, finance and political work. This inquiry started its meetings in February 1980 and the parliamentary party in deciding upon its evidence voted by two to one to keep the choice of leader in the hands of its members. The Commission's Report, which was published in July 1980, dealt primarily with finance and omitted the main constitutional issues on which there was a strong division of opinion. Nevertheless the party conference did take these up in October 1980 when it reversed the decision over mandatory reselection of candidates by providing that it should be automatic not less than three years after an MP's election. It also narrowly reversed the 1979 decision on election to the leadership by providing that the leader should be elected on a wider basis than that of the parliamentary party alone. The matter of which method to use to elect the leader was left to a special conference because the October conference could not agree on this issue. However on the issue of control of the manifesto the conference reversed the 1979 decision to give the NEC the final say over the manifesto – a decision which had already led a confident NEC to publish a document entitled 'Draft Labour Manifesto 1980', despite James Callaghan's protest that neither he nor the shadow cabinet had been consulted.

The 1980 conference came at a time of mounting tension within the party. On the right the question of the Militant Tendency had again been raised when Lord Underhill published a report in March 1980 in which he argued that membership of the group was incompatible with membership of the Labour Party. The Labour Party itself had declined to publish the report when it was orignally drawn up by Lord Underhill in his then capacity as National Agent. On the left there was considerable activity from a variety of groupings and a determined effort to coordinate their activities in a new institution called the Rank and File Mobilizing Committee.

The leadership issue became an immediate one when at the 1980 conference James Callaghan announced his resignation; an election for his successor therefore followed under the old rules, i.e. by the PLP alone. Although Denis Healey had been ahead on the first ballot, Michael Foot (the former deputy leader and acting leader) won on the second ballot. Healey was immediately made deputy without a contest. However at the special conference to decide the issue of new constitutional procedures, held on 24 January 1981, it was decided that conference itself should become the electing body, with the voting weight being 40 per cent to the trade unions, 30 per cent to the constituency parties and 30 per cent to the parliamentary party. The bias against the parliamentary element of the party that was so evident in this decision quickened the departure of the future Social Democrats, who issued their Limehouse declaration the day after the special conference. The new procedure was also soon given its first test when Tony Benn announced that he would challenge the right-of-centre Denis Healey for the deputy leadership. Benn's attempt to symbolize the left-wing spirit of the constituency activists had been underlined when he had voted against the shadow cabinet's defence policy recommendations despite being a front-bench opposition spokesman and therefore bound by the norms of collective responsibility which opposition shadow cabinets as much as cabinets find useful. In the end Healey won in a tight three-way race between Benn, who got the overwhelming support of the constituency parties, and John Silkin.

The special conference called in 1981 also discussed other issues. It decided by a large majority to endorse withdrawal from the EEC, and it very narrowly endorsed the proposal that the manifesto should be the responsibility of the NEC. However because the conference failed to rescind the three-year rule against the reconsideration of constitutional issues the decision had no practical effect at that time.

For the rest of the 1979–83 Parliament the friction between hard left followers of Tony Benn and the right continued. Michael Foot and the adherents of the 'soft' left and the centre had to hold the balance. The issue of entryism became a major concern as the NEC adopted in June 1982 the idea of drawing up a register of authorized groups designed in such a way that the Militant Tendency could hardly qualify. Nevertheless the Militant Tendency – some of whose members were in the process of being adopted as candidates – duly applied. The fate of its application to be registered and the question of the balance of ideological factions within the Labour Party were still in the balance when the election was called.

The defeat of Labour produced an immediate declaration from Michael Foot that he would not seek re-election as leader when the party conference met in October. Thus the new election procedures were given an immediate test and four candidates were able to campaign in the months between the election in June and the October Conference. Neil Kinnock, who had been a relative newcomer to the shadow cabinet, won with a convincing majority in all three sections of the electoral college. The runner-up was Roy Hattersley, who had succeeded Healey as the standard-bearer of the right. He became the deputy leader.

The Kinnock vote was interpreted by many as evidence that the soft left held the key to party reconciliation, which now seemed the urgent task for the Labour Party. Because of the awareness of Labour's image of internal division the much talked of purge of Militant Tendency was given less emphasis and reduced to the expulsion from the party of five members of *Militant*'s editorial board. In the new NEC the right – which had made some gains at the 1982 conference – did not do so well. The right and right-centre could after 1983 claim only six NEC members, as opposed to the nine who were roughly aligned with Neil Kinnock and the nine who were aligned with Tony Benn. The new shadow cabinet elected by the PLP in the 1983 Parliament also represented a balance between these three recognizable trends in the Labour Party. It became clear that Kinnock's wish was to defuse the tensions between the NEC and the shadow cabinet in policy matters and to create some new machinery for resolving the kinds of policy divisions which had so clearly contributed to Labour's disarray.

Yet the leadership's entirely understandable wish to inaugurate a new period of political harmony was not entirely shared by the hard left, which still had an unfinished agenda of constitutional reform for the Labour Party. At the 1983 conference there had been a conclusive defeat for the proposal that the standing orders of the PLP should be included in the Labour Party constitution and a defeat for the suggestion that the PLP should automatically be held committed to policies adopted by conference. There was also a defeat for the idea – which would have had severe and obvious repercussions in the light of mandatory reselection – that the decisions of the PLP should be taken at weekly meetings in which each MP's vote would be recorded and made public. The question of 'entryism' had not been dealt with conclusively, as it was not clear what pressure could be brought upon the constituencies which declined to accept the NEC rulings on the eligibility of persons for membership. There was also the very real possibility of the left making the running if a trade union or a group of trade unions decided to defy the existing law on such issues as secondary picketing and the closed shop. And on policy questions there remained the problem of how defence policy would develop, since Neil Kinnock, like his predecessor, was a supporter of CND despite the fact that CND had adopted a position of withdrawal from NATO while membership of NATO remained official Labour policy.

It can thus be seen that divisions within the Labour Party can occasion a variety of alliances involving the PLP, the trade union movement and the constituency parties in different combinations at different times. The tension between Labour's theoretical commit-ment to internal democracy and the practical problems of party management is a tension which Labour leaders have to accommodate but which has implications not just for the Labour Party but for the political system as a whole.

The Liberal Party

The relationship between the parliamentary element in the Liberal Party and the extra-parliamentary party is conditioned by the fact that the Liberal Party's parliamentary representation has been so small in recent decades. Profound disagreements about electoral strategy have marked Liberal Party politics as a result of the different approaches to policy questions adopted by the Young Liberals and those sections of the party which espoused 'community politics'. Community politics theorists urged the party to concentrate on the local level of politics and to give low priority to Westminster, where an 'unfair' electoral system made it unlikely that a third party such as the Liberals could have much impact. The strength of the extra-parliamentary wing of the Liberal Party by comparison with its tiny band of MPs was reflected in the introduction of new rules for election to the leadership of the party. These new rules were introduced immediately after Jeremy Thorpe's resignation from the leadership in 1976, and they were unique among British parties in making formal provision for rank-and-file participation in the leadership election process as well as giving the major voice in the appointment to the extra-parliamentary party.

Candidates for the Liberal leadership must be MPs. Each constituency association affiliated to the Liberal Party is entitled to exercise ten votes, plus a further ten if it was affiliated for the previous year, plus one further vote for every five hundred votes or part thereof cast for a Liberal candidate in that constituency at the previous general election. (A constituency may opt to count a more recent by-election vote or an aggregate local election vote if that is higher.) By this complicated procedure – which produced David Steel as leader in 1976 – the choice of leader of the parliamentary party is given to the constituencies and weighted towards areas of Liberal strength.

The Liberal Party is strictly speaking a federation of four distinct and semi-autonomous parties for each of the four units of the United Kingdom. Its major institutions are the National Executive Committee, the National Council and the Finance and Administration Board. There is an annual assembly of the Liberal Party which has the function of electing Liberal officers and members of the Council. It also hears progress reports from the various administrative committees of the party and considers resolutions on public policy. The general style of Liberal politics has become increasingly 'open' and the emphasis on participation by all sections of the party in policy-making has made it difficult to assess the balance between the party organization in the country and the parliamentary leadership.

David Steel had to defend his strategy of supporting the Labour government to the Liberal Council and the Liberal assembly in 1977, and he had virtually to stake his leadership on the decision to take the Liberals into the Alliance with the Social Democrats. The gains made in local elections by the Liberals during the 1979–83 Parliament strengthened the advocates of community politics; and the disappointment of Liberal hopes in the 1983 general election together with the setback to Social Democratic fortunes provided these sections of the party with further arguments against Westminster-oriented politics. Given the fluidity of the relationship between the parliamentary and extra-parliamentary wings of the party it is difficult to predict how the debate will develop, but it was notable that the chief opponents of the Alliance within the Liberal Party came from within the Association of Liberal Councillors, who obviously see the future of Liberal politics as depending on the party's strength at the grass roots of Britain's political life.

The Social Democrats

The Social Democratic Party is in respect of organization at the opposite pole from the Liberals. As a party which owes its origin to a conscious decision of like-minded parliamentarians and which had to create a party from the top down it is clearly biased towards centralization. For this reason it is difficult to be certain how far some of its innovations were the result of a desire to take a fresh look at the role of a political party in modern Britain and to take account of new developments in such fields as marketing (where the Conservatives have also recently been active, setting up a separate division at Central Office) and how far they simply reflected the need to improvise in the light of the circumstances surrounding the party's creation. Some of the innovations and experiments appear not to have lasted. Thus collective leadership and a conference which moved from place to place were quickly abandoned for more orthodox forms of organization. However other experiments have been more enduring. The party has maintained the central nature of its membership rather than organize on the constituency or ward-based membership rolls of its rivals – a decision which clearly makes sense if the Social Democrats are to take full advantage of the modern technology of computerized direct mail and the facility of credit cards. The party leader and chairman are chosen directly by a vote of the whole membership from candidates put foward by the parliamentary party. The SDP's main authority – which corresponds to the Liberal annual assembly – is the consultative assembly which must meet at least once a year. There is a Council which meets more frequently, as in the Liberal Party.

Instead of constituency parties – which would in any case have been small initially – the SDP set up area parties, each responsible for a number of constituencies. While this meant that in distributing constituencies to be fought between themselves and the Liberals the Social Democrats did not have to worry about disgruntled constituency parties, it is not clear how long the absence of orthodox political organization at the lowest levels can remain effective, especially when local elections have to be fought. Certainly the construction of the Social Democrats would probably function well within an electoral system based on proportional representation; but as the prospects of electoral reform are still somewhat remote it may be that the initial structure may have to be adapted to cope with the demands of grassroots electoral organization. Of course if a complete merger with the Liberals were ever to occur the Liberals' own highly developed local organization could be used to complement the Social Democrats' intermediate level groupings, but again such a possibility seems to have been ruled out, at least in the short term.

The Alliance

Previous electoral alliances between parties in Britain – the Liberal Unionists and the Conservatives after the split on the issue of Home Rule for Ireland in 1886, and the alliance between the National or Simonite Liberals and the Conservatives after 1933 – have ended in the smaller party being swallowed up by the larger. There is little in the way of precedent for two parties which are allied electorally but determined to maintain their distinct identities. The difficulties which arise – even apart from preventing the breaches over fundamental policy questions – are tactical and strategic. How should the decision be taken as to which party is to fight which seat, given the need to avoid splitting the joint vote of the two parties? And what voice should be given, in selecting a candidate, to the party which has not been allotted the seat? Such questions did not merely arise in relation to the Alliance's bid for seats at Westminster; they were also posed in relation to the elections to the European Parliament in June 1984. Although agreements and compromises have for the most part been worked out, the need to make them inevitably creates some friction between the partners and can risk a highly public and weakening quarrel at precisely the time when the Alliance wishes to seem most united – as for example when by-elections occur.

The structure of the Alliance also presents some constitutional, if at present theoretical, problems. If the Alliance were to win an election, who would the monarch summon to form an administration? In the 1983 election it was agreed that while David Steel, the Liberal leader, would lead the campaign, Roy Jenkins with his long government experience would be the 'prime minister designate'. But Jenkins' sudden resignation after the election left the question an open one as between Steel and the new SDP leader, David Owen.

Party Finance: a Catalyst of Change?

What the organization of all British political parties had in common by the early 1980s was a sense of financial stringency – a difficulty in finding enough money to pay for their activities both at the centre and in the constituencies.[20] While electoral law places limits, as has been seen, on the spending of individual candidates, the central activities of the parties are not limited and although they do not, as in the United States, have to pay for television and radio time, professional assistance with television broadcasts as well as the more traditional forms of publicity and public opinion polling are increasingly expensive.

The pressures had been felt by Labour and the Liberals, especially in the 1970s, and had led to the establishment of a committee (the Houghton Committee) in 1975 to examine the whole basis of party funding in the United Kingdom. Its report and the evidence submitted by the parties gave a detailed picture of how matters then stood.[21]

At a national level the Conservative Party's money comes from a number of sources, and there will be fluctuations in the amount raised from year to year. It can however be roughly estimated that a third of its income will come from constituency payments, including the quotas levied on the constituency parties on the basis of Conservative voting strength; about two thirds will come from donations from individuals and business; and a minute proportion will come from investment income. In 1976 the Conservative Party's central income was £1,739,000, of which £1,137,000 came from donations (65.4 per cent), £574,000 from the constituencies (33 per cent), and £28,000 from investment income (1.6 per cent).

A major source of Conservative Party income is thus the money which it derives from individual or corporate donations. The donations which public companies give directly for political purposes have to be declared in the company accounts, so that it is possible to monitor the amounts given by individual companies to the Conservative cause. In 1977 the largest donation was £25,000; but many companies do not give merely to the Conservative Party. They also channel money into other promotional organizations which conduct campaigns thought to be beneficial to the company's interest. Thus in 1977 one of the most regular donors – Rank Hovis MacDougall – gave £41,000 in donations to anti-Labour campaigns, but only £20,000 of that went directly into the Conservative Party's coffers.

The Conservative Party estimated that in 1975–6 its net expenditure at the central level was £1,724,000, of which the largest element was spent on headquarters and regional administration. About 71 per cent of expenditure went on salaries and wages and only 12 per cent went on research. The amount spent on publicity clearly varied from year to year, with expenditure on advertising and propaganda reaching a peak in an election year.

By contrast the Labour Party in 1976 estimated that its annual income was £1,211,000, of which £1,150,000 came from subscriptions – primarily from the affiliation fees paid by the trade unions; £51,000 of Labour's central income came from donations and appeals and a mere £10,000 from investment income. It can thus be seen that the trade unions provide the major source of the Labour Party's annual income. This, it has been suggested, constitutes another important weapon in the unions' hands if they wish to exert their influence over Labour Party policy. Indeed the financial dependence of the Labour Party upon the trade union movement is greater even than the annual income figures suggest; for in addition to the affiliation fees – which in 1978 were 24p per affiliated member – the unions, like major companies, are likely to give out of their own political funds additional money in an election year or for special purposes such as the construction of a new party headquarters. The unions also sponsor candidates for Parliament, in which case they may contribute up to 80 per cent of the maximum legal election expenses of that candidate, may contribute to the constituency party's funds, and may contribute between 60 and 65 per cent of the salary of an agent in that constituency. (There were 148 sponsored MPs elected in May 1979 and 123 in June 1983).

Labour's expenditure at the central level was similar to the Conservatives' in magnitude – £1,280,000 – but over 90 per cent of it was spent on regional, area and headquarters services. It estimated that some £64,000 would be spent on publicity in 1976 and some £82,000 on research and policy formation.

The income and expenditure of the smaller parties, including the

Liberals, is much less than that of the two major parties and is largely derived from individual subscriptions and small donations. The Liberal Party, according to the Houghton Committee Report, had an income of £96,000 in 1975, while the Communist Party appeared to have an average annual income of £88,000. The Scottish National Party in 1976 had an estimated central income of £61,000, while Plaid Cymru expected to have an income for that year of £85,000.

At the constituency level the situation of all parties is complex; but the Houghton Committee's survey found that Conservative Constituency Associations had approximately twice as large a financial turnover as constituency Labour parties and they in turn had double the financial turnover of constituency Liberal associations. Money at the constituency level was raised by a variety of methods and from a variety of sources – social events, bazaars and lotteries, as well as from individual membership subscriptions.

The level of party membership in Britain and the general state of party activity were not only extremely low but had been declining steadily over the past decade. A major survey of electoral attitudes in the period 1963–70 confirmed the impression that the only form of political activity for the majority of British citizens was the simple act of voting at parliamentary elections. The degree of participation in other forms of political work such as canvassing was minimal, as was the level of party membership. The survey also found that low though the level of political activity was in 1964, it had fallen still further by 1970. For whereas the sample who were conscious of belonging to a political party had stood at 14 per cent in 1964, it had fallen to 10 per cent by 1970.[22]

The Houghton Committee discovered a similar pattern of decline: only 11 per cent of the 100 constituencies sampled in a specially designed questionnaire thought that their membership figures were satisfactory, while 89 per cent thought that the level of membership was either unsatisfactory or very unsatisfactory.

The Houghton Committee's survey found an average constituency membership in 1974 of 2,400 for each Conservative constituency party, 500 for each CLP and 300 for each constituency Liberal association. If uniform across the whole of England, Scotland and Wales, these findings suggested an individual membership in 1974 for the three largest parties as follows:

Conservative Party	1,495,200
Labour Party	311,000
Liberal Party	186,900

The problem of ascertaining the accuracy of party membership figures such as these is exacerbated by the fact that as far as the Conservative Party is concerned no national membership totals are collected. And, although Labour does keep membership figures, it is generally agreed that the official numbers used to be inflated because of the rule which until 1980 required a local constituency party to affiliate to the central Labour Party on the basis of a minimum of a thousand members – a figure which most constituency Labour parties in practice do not attain. Thus although the annual report of the Labour Party gives numbers for the individual and trade union affiliated members these figures must be read against the background of a tradition of flexible interpretation of membership. But even if one took the inflated figures given by the Labour Party itself there is still clear evidence of a decline (see table 4), though with a slight upturn in 1983.

Table 4
Individual Membership of the Labour Party 1928–83

Year	No. of Members
1928	214,970
1935	419,311
1945	487,047
1950	908,161
1955	843,356
1960	790,192
1965	816,765
1970	690,191
1975	674,905
1979	666,091
1980	348,156
1981	276,692
1982	273,803
1983	295,344

Source: *Labour Party Annual Conference Report*, 1984.

Indeed the Labour Party launched a membership campaign in June 1977 to try to arrest this decline and commented that 537 of 623 constituency parties had affiliated at the minimum level of one thousand members, so that only eighty-six constituency parties could be presumed to have a membership of one thousand and above.[23]

The Liberal Party in its evidence to the Houghton Committee acknowledged that its membership had declined from the 1964–5 peak of 250,000 but pointed out that the number of Liberal organizations in the constituencies had increased since that date, even if their membership remained small.

The problems which the three major British parties have faced in maintaining a stable level of party membership over the past few years had made it difficult for them to keep in existence efficient machinery for fighting elections. Thus the most basic task of any political party was becoming more difficult to perform as membership levels fluctuated and constituency parties became moribund. Equally, party officials had become concerned that the routine tasks of party organization at the grass roots had to be performed by a dwindling number of people. Parties perform a number of functions, not the least of which is the selection of a parliamentary candidate who may ultimately become a member of the House of Commons. In addition the political parties have a role to play as channels of communication between the institutions of government and the governed. The efficiency and legitimacy of that role will, however, be determined to a very large extent by the degree to which the party organizations themselves are representative of the wider community. Declining membership suggested that not merely were these organizations becoming smaller and more exclusive but that the major British parties were also in danger of becoming isolated from the mainstream of opinion in the country as a whole.

The loss of vitality in British political parties implied by declining membership was aggravated by the problem of finance. Maintaining even a rudimentary organization at the constituency level requires both members and money. A loss of membership impedes a party's ability to raise money by undertaking fund-raising activities as well as reducing the amount which can be raised directly from subscriptions. The Houghton Committee thought that party organization at the local level was on a 'pitifully inadequate' scale in terms of accommodation, equipment, trained staff and resources. The Committee also found that a large number of constituency associations could not afford to employ a full-time paid agent, although Conservative associations were generally better off than Labour and Liberals in this respect: whereas only one quarter of Conservative associations were without either a full-time or part-time agent, three-quarters of the CLPs and 90 per cent of the Liberal associations were without the services of an agent on either a full- or part-time basis. The fact that so many constituency associations could not afford the salaries of paid professional agents was obviously serious for the parties, and both the Labour and the Conservative parties experimented with schemes whereby the salary of the agent could be met in part out of central funds. However in both parties the scheme has been something of a failure, because in the 1970s they both found themselves in financial difficulties at the central level as well as locally. Moreover, as has been mentioned, there was in the Conservative Party a great deal of resistance to the central employment of agents, since this was thought to undermine the jealously guarded autonomy of the constituency associations. Thus by 1976 only one-third of all Labour agents – twenty-six out of eighty-six – were being paid from central funds while the Conservative Party was phasing out its central employment scheme.

The reasons why political parties increasingly found themselves in financial difficulties over the 1970s are not hard to identify. The high level of inflation had eroded the values of their reserves while it had also pushed up the salaries of the staff employed by the parties. The general economic climate meant that individual and corporate donors had less money to spare for political purposes and many public companies became increasingly sensitive about their share-holders' attitudes towards direct gifts to the Conservative Party. The Labour Government's Companies Act of 1967 which forced dis-closure in company accounts of donations for political purposes undoubtedly made many boards prefer to make donations to pressure groups such as Aims of Industry rather than to the Conservative Party. And the trade union movement, the traditional source of much Labour Party income, was increasingly keeping the money in its own coffers. The financial strains which these developments imposed upon the political parties were exacerbated by the fact that the parties had in 1974 to fight two general elections within a short space of time.

The first step in the direction of a subsidy from the state to arrest the spiral of decline in British parties was taken when in 1975 the House of Commons authorized a grant to opposition parties to enable them to fulfil their parliamentary functions more effectively; but the idea of a more general subsidy to all political parties to finance the whole range of organizational and propaganda activities constituted a radical change in thinking about the role which parties play in the political system.

The Houghton Committee's Report of 1976 thus confirmed a general impression of weakness in British party organization and underlined the extent to which economies had been made at the expense of the parties' research and educational activities as well as of their organizational functions. The majority report recommended an injection of public funds as a means of reviving the parties' sagging morale and enabling them to fulfil the tasks required of parties in an advanced democracy. Unfortunately from the point of view of the Labour and Liberal parties who had most to gain from them, there was no unanimous welcome for the Houghton proposals that grants should be made to parties at both the national level (for general purposes) and the local level (for election expenses). The Conservative Party was confident of its ability to survive financially and took the strong ideological line that the taxpayer should not be burdened with the cost of such a subsidy, although the professional staff of the Conservative Party – the agents – whose salaries seemed most at risk in the harsh economic climate seemed somewhat less sure of the enormity of the Houghton proposals. The nationalist parties were spirited in their rejection of the idea of propping up declining parties no longer able to inspire enthusiasm among the general public. And the Communist Party, while willing to accept a small extension of state aid in kind, rejected the idea of cash grants to the parties.

The Conservative objections to state aid for political parties meant that the question of public subsidies was not on the agenda of either the 1979 or the 1983 Parliaments. Supporters of the idea, however, continued to try to promote it, though not necessarily in the form recommended by Houghton but in a way more closely related to actual party membership. And they were prepared to accept that state financial control could be a method whereby greater legal control of the parties and greater accountability were secured. Indeed the prospect of greater public regulation of the parties was one of the features of state aid which some of its advocates in the 1970s found most attractive. Subsidies were thus seen as providing the lever whereby, it was argued, the insulated structures of the parties could be prised open to force a greater amount of internal democracy and electoral participation. That this argument should be used at all was itself revealing of the extent to which the internal processes of the parties – especially the selection and repudiation of candidates and MPs – had created an image of party activists as extremists remote from the values of the general public. Whether the acceptance of state grants would really do very much to make parties more responsive to the electorate at large is questionable, and for some critics the more radical remedy of electoral reform remains the only way of reasserting public control over the party system. But some people did feel that state financial aid would serve at the very least to remind the parties that they are institutions of vital significance to the functioning of government and that the values they espouse are a proper subject for public scrutiny.

The fact that the Houghton proposals were not implemented did not of course mean that the financial problems of Britain's political parties had disappeared. The general elections of 1979 and 1983 were heavy drains on the funds of all parties. One main reason for the increasing expenses of elections was that the practice of using professional public relations firms to advise parties on taking advantage of opportunities in the media on the presentation of policy had become firmly entrenched; and these firms employed increasingly sophisticated techniques. Thus of the central expenses incurred by the Conservative Party in the election of 1983, amounting to £3.6m, £2.8m were accounted for by advertising costs. Labour's central expenses were £2.2m. Both parties spent more centrally than the total spent by their constituency candidates. The bulk of their candidates did not spend anything like the new permitted maximum, which would have been on average £4,200 in boroughs and £4,700 in county seats. The Liberals spent £250,000 centrally during the 1983 campaign and made grants totalling £150,000 to constituency parties in need. The SDP spent £1,000,000, of which about £400,000 went to help local campaigns.[24]

The Conservative advantage over Labour had actually been declining since the 1960s, but it was the Labour Party that seemed to be most in trouble financially.[25] In part this reflected the decline in trade union membership as a result of the recession and unemployment. Nor were unions willing to increase their subscriptions in line with inflation. Indeed one trade union leader, David Basnett, argued at the 1983 TUC that subscriptions were in real terms only one fifth of what they had been in 1939 and that this meant there was less money for party purposes, although the Congress did agree on an increase from £6 to £7 in the subscription paid to the Labour Party for each affiliated member.[26]

The position of the trade unions vis-à-vis the Labour Party was of course especially serious, since it was reckoned by 1982 that 78 per cent of the party's income came from union sources. But the party was also concerned about its continuing fall in individual members, since by 1982–3 the 273,803 individual members were less than half the total of ten years previously and compared unfavourably with the 1.5 million members claimed by the Conservatives. At the end of 1982 the Labour Party had a bank overdraft of £500,000, and although the trade unions gave a large sum in 1983 to the general election fund the position at the end of that year showed no improvement.[27]

The two parties which formed the Alliance were in financial straits also, although in the case of the Liberals this was to some extent compensated for by local strength.[28] By October 1983 it was reckoned that membership of the Social Democratic Party, which had reached a peak of 65,000 early in 1982, was below 60,000 – about a third of the Liberals' membership. The Social Democrats' income of about £650,000 per year was almost all from subscriptions, which at a minimum of £4 per annum and a recommended level of £13.50 were rather higher than in most other parties. The Social Democrats were obliged after the 1983 election to close down every regional office in England and to reduce their complement of staff at headquarters. The failure of attempts to swing over support from some of the more right-wing trade unions had proved a failure and appeared to put the SDP at a permanent disadvantage compared with the Labour Party.

In the new Parliament there were two developments of direct relevance to party finance. One was the government's announced intention to transform the relationship between trade union member-ship and financial support for the Labour Party by going back to contracting-in from contracting-out – i.e. to the situation which had prevailed from 1927 to 1946. Thus trade unionists would have to take positive steps to see that a political levy was added to their subscriptions rather than have it automatically added unless steps were taken to prevent it. However, it looked unlikely that this would result – as the SDP in particular would have wished – in individual trade unionists opting to make a contribution to another political party. Experience suggested that 'contracting-in' would result in a fall in the Labour Party's income, and a good deal of protest was generated particularly in the absence of any proposal that company shareholders should be able to do the same in respect of their company's contribution to political funds.[29] Much was also made of the alleged connection between such financial donations and the various honours lists of the Thatcher governments. The government did not proceed with the proposal, the unions having agreed to make their members more aware of the right to opt out of the levy. The other developments which had implications for the parties' organization was the proposal – as part of the wider package of electoral reform discussed earlier – to extend postal voting to cover those away on holiday and to raise the deposits for parliamentary candidates from £150 to £1,000 (subsequently reduced to £500).[30] The first move would obviously put greater strain on the organizational resources of the parties, as they would have a larger postal vote to mobilize than hitherto. The second proposal had some serious financial impli-cations for Labour as well as the smaller parties. In 1983 – admittedly a bad year for Labour – the number of lost deposits was 119, which if translated into the financial terms proposed by the reforms would mean a loss of £119,000. Even if, as was suggested, the percentage needed to reclaim the deposit was lowered from 12½ to 5 per cent, the reform would mean that the amount of money recovered from Britain's political parties in lost deposits would amount to some £650,000.

In February 1984 the minister of employment agreed to allow the unions themselves to try to impose a code of conduct which would facilitate contracting out rather than contracting in, but legislation was introduced to make unions ballot every ten years on whether they should have a political fund at all.

Thus it can be seen that while political parties remain in Britain a central part of the democratic process, their organization, internal structure and financing have continued to produce problems, and some of the debates about their internal processes have intensified over the 1970s and early 1980s. The very partisan nature of British government makes it likely of course that even those problems which might be amenable to rational or consensual solutions will be neglected and that where citizens are disaffected or disillusioned with the existing parties they will look for other methods for expressing their opinions.

9   Pressure Groups in Britain: Innovation or Immobilism?

In any developed society there will be a range of organizations, groups and movements which exist to promote the common interests of the group's members, to express common concerns and to influence the way in which public policy is formulated and implemented. The range of such groups and movements in existence at any one time is vast and new ones will constantly be emerging to replace those whose purpose or effectiveness has declined. Trade unions will exist to defend their perception of their members' economic interests; business groups and industrial organizations will act to promote what they see as the best policies for their supporters. Groups pursuing a limited and precise cause such as the reform of the abortion laws may launch a campaign to change public opinion on the issue; broad social movements such as the women's liberation movement may pursue a more eclectic and wide-ranging set of goals. And a host of charitable and voluntary organizations may exist to pursue objectives which rarely touch the political process until some threat to this pursuit necessitates political mobilization. By so doing, these groups do not merely articulate interests and communicate the policy needs of British society to government; they also serve as a focus for civic participation, provide selective benefits for their members and relay information to government in respect of particular policy areas.[1]

It was argued in earlier chapters that Britain has become a more heterogeneous society in the last twenty years than ever before, and that there has also developed a new constitutional climate in which, for example, the government will be expected to behave in a way which is at once more open and more conducive to public participation than in the past. Thus planning procedures, for example, have become more reflective of demands for wider consultation. Furthermore, as has been seen, the existing two-party system has for many people seemed increasingly incapable of articulating the range of interests and preferences present in modern British society. Many of these changes are reflected in the operations and interaction of Britain's many pressure groups and in the ways in which some of the more important ones interact with the formal institutions of government. An indication of the increasing importance of pressure groups in the British political system can in fact be gleaned not merely from the sheer number of organizations formed to influence public policy but also from the relative youth of many of these groups. An extensive reference work on British pressure groups found that of the 184 groups listed in the directory exactly half had been founded since 1960.[2]

There are, of course, many explanations for the recent growth of pressure group activity in Britain. A changing society will generate new issues and causes, as has been witnessed by the growth of groups concerned with various minorities, be they immigrants, homosexuals or the disabled. Equally, although the tendency in recent years has been for trade unions to merge and thereby to reduce the total number of individual unions, some pressure groups have found it more efficient to specialize and form separate organizations for separate causes. And there have been external stimuli leading to the formation of new groups so that, for example, the Local Government Act of 1972, which made provisions for optional expenditure, encouraged the development of a variety of local amenity and other pressure groups.

Before further examining the range of pressure groups which operate in the United Kingdom, as well as their various styles and strategies, it may be as well to offer some definitions: even if somewhat arbitrary, these may clarify further discussion. By a pressure group is meant an organized subsection of society which has been mobilized to defend an interest, cause or idea without itself wishing to govern the country. The interest, cause or idea may be primarily economic and self-defensive, as when a trade association seeks to promote its product or a trade union to defend the standard of living of its members. On the other hand, the interest may be highly altruistic or charitable, as when the Royal Society for the Prevention of Cruelty to Animals (which was founded in 1824) seeks to promote policies for animal welfare or when the Howard League for Penal Reform seeks to improve conditions in British prisons and to change penal policy.[3] These kinds of groups may be described as 'ideological', although that definition in many ways suggests too systematic and coherent a source for ideas and activities which are often sporadic and unsustained by any political beliefs or doctrine.[4]

Such definitions are inevitably imperfect. Some pressure groups – for example trade unions – have a general set of objectives which can combine highly specific goals such as the defence of an individual industry with altogether more altruistic causes such as the promotion of racial or sexual equality.

The belief that pressure group activity is an inherent part of a free society has been used by some theorists to associate such activity with democracy itself. But while it is true that totalitarian societies are unlikely to tolerate untrammelled pressure group activity, the relationship between pressure groups and the wider system of representative government is by no means unproblematic. The conflict between sectional interests and the wider public interest may become severe, especially if, as sometimes happens, a sectional group claims the right to veto legislation which it finds unpalatable or proves adept at promoting its interests through public legislation. It is also the case that although pressure group activity is seen as a reflection of the free political life of a democracy, membership of some pressure groups is not really voluntary. For some professions, membership is dependent upon acceptance by a professional society, and there is also the restriction placed on many workers by closed shop agreements.

Other aspects of the role of pressure groups in a democratic society may be similarly perplexing. The common assumption that pressure groups do not want to govern the country but merely to put pressure on the government for a limited set of objectives may be difficult to reconcile with the strategy of some groups such as the ecologists, nuclear disarmers and even ethnic groups who put up candidates for Parliament and who might, if strong enough, participate in a government. (The development of the British trade union movement itself provides a case history of how pressure groups can be transformed from organizations with few political goals into ones where they have substantial political aims.) And while the definition of pressure groups as organizations *outside* government seeking to influence public policy is generally helpful, the conditions of modern political life in Britain, as in other countries, mean that to some extent this simple model must be qualified.

First there is a sense in which government itself is not monolithic and sometimes forces *within* government act as pressure groups might do. Thus one can see major spending departments acting on behalf of their own subject areas such as defence or education and battling for their clients rather than taking a collective perspective. The now defunct Civil Service Department incurred hostility from the Conservative government elected in 1979 because it was thought to act as a pressure group might do, to defend the special interests of civil servants, especially on pay, rather than to put into effect any generalized governmental policy. Similarly the individual armed services have long exerted pressure on policy which has made them the object of some political suspicion when they have offered advice. Where there is a distinct interest being promoted within the central government by a department this is usually concealed as far as

261

possible from public view. However, different levels of government can act as open pressure groups and the various local authority associations have proved highly visible and sometimes effective advocates of their particular concerns.

Local authority associations are of interest for a number of reasons. They do not speak with a single voice, and although reconstituted in the wake of local government reorganization in the early 1970s the causes of local government are promoted through the Association of Country Councils (ACC), the Association of District Authorities (ADA) and the Association of Metropolitan Authorities (AMA), as well as the National Association of Local Councils (NALC). These organizations together with bodies representing professional cadres within local government – for example the Society of Local Authority Chief Executives (SOLACE) and the Society of Chief Personnel Officers (SOCPO) – have enjoyed privileged access to government. Yet although their interests have extended beyond the simple protection of local authority employees to matters of substantive policy, such as the organization of water supply, they have proved incapable of defending local government effectively. And when there was much need for a powerful pressure group to speak for local authorities, as in relation to the Local Government Planning and Land Bill of 1979–80, the divisions between the various groups severely weakened them.[5]

A second reason why it is not altogether accurate to see pressure groups as outside forces attempting to mould the decisions and actions of government stems from the fact that many pressure groups enjoy highly privileged positions with one or other government department and agency, so that frequently the group, the minister and his civil servants develop a shared perspective. The most obvious example of this phenomenon is perhaps the very close relationship which the Ministry of Agriculture, Fisheries and Food has with British farmers and especially the NFU, which represents over 90 per cent of British farmers.[6] Although the clienteles of the various British departments are not equally united or powerful, it would be a mistake to neglect this aspect of the role of pressure groups, especially when considering the dynamics of the policy-making process itself.[7]

A third point to consider – which has caused many commentators to wonder how best to characterize the British system of government – is the extent to which pressure groups have been formally coopted into the policy-making, advisory, and even the executive aspects of government.

The establishment of the National Economic Development Council in the early 1960s provided a statutory role for six trade unionists and six members chosen by the CBI in the development of economic policy; but these so-called 'gold-plated six' trade unionists and their equivalents from the opposite side of industry are but the tip of the iceberg in a system which relies on Royal Commissions, advisory committees and other consultative bodies to help frame policy.[8]

The establishment of the NEDC is usually seen as something of a watershed in the process whereby the government has sought to control the levels of prices and incomes in the United Kingdom, but in fact the whole of the twentieth century has seen a growing involvement between the state and the organizations formed to represent sectional interests – an involvement which although accelerated by two world wars has been seen by some commentators as reflecting a bias towards corporatism in the British political culture. Although Mrs Thatcher's administrations have moved away from the kind of formal incomes policies which require regular and institutionalized consultations with the representatives of both sides of industry, earlier governments of both parties had explicitly sought to involve the CBI and the TUC in the evolution of economic policy and its administration. Whether one calls the upshot 'tripartism' or corporatism, such systematic links between government and pressure groups were difficult to reconcile with a definition of pressure groups which either assumed a certain degree of equality and competitiveness between groups in British society or portrayed them as forces operating outside the formal machinery of government.[9] And even in the post-1979 period much of the machinery established under earlier governments, such as the Advisory Conciliation and Arbitration Service (ACAS), the Manpower Services Commission, the Health and Safety Commission, the Commission on Racial Equality and the Equal Opportunities Commission frame and implement policies with a substantial degree of independence from government departments. Indeed the 1983 Annual Report of the CBI listed these bodies and sixty-six others on which the CBI had representation. These bodies included such very different committees as the DES Further Education Unit, the National Dock Labour Board, and the Genetic Manipulation Advisory Group. Included in the range of committees were ones with significant European responsibilities – for example the EEC Advisory Committee on Social Security for Migrant Workers.[10]

Pressure groups in the United Kingdom as in any society reflect the country's constitutional structure as well as the political environment which may be expected to change as public attitudes and governmental policies develop. Certainly the tactics and strategies of a pressure group must be flexible enough to respond quickly to changes in the political universe if it is not to risk losing influence and being challenged by some newer and perhaps more militant organization. Similarly the way a pressure group operates will also reflect the resources available to it at any given time.

Strategy

It is generally assumed that the most successful pressure groups are those that have regular meetings with government and which are consulted by officials in a routine manner without the pressure group having to demand a meeting. The tone of such meetings will be deliberately low-key and will frequently apply to those relationships where the government agency needs the pressure group as much as the group needs the agency. Such a strategy will frequently be pursued by occupational groups such as doctors, whose professional participation is needed to ensure the effective operation of the National Health Service. (However as has frequently been pointed out the very establishment of the National Health Service in 1946 was done in the face of opposition from the BMA, which threatened to withdraw its members' services but which eventually recognized the overriding will and legitimacy of a government with a parliamentary majority.)[11] Discreet but regular consultation is also the strategy most favoured by groups who know that they have a significant position in the economy – for example building societies, business organizations and that loose collection of powerful financial interests known as the City. The peculiarly close relationship between farmers and the Ministry of Agriculture, Fisheries and Food has already been mentioned. In that case the requirement to consult farmers' representatives before each annual price review in February was given statutory form in the Agriculture Act of 1947.

The routine low-key consultations which mark the relationships between many pressure groups and government do not necessarily have to have statutory recognition. While much of the attempt to incorporate the peak organizations of business and labour into the highest levels of decision-making and policy implementation in the 1970s was backed by statute, the general mood of the times and the so-called 'corporate bias' of British government ensured that even without the highly publicized attempts to get agreements on economic policy there would be a substantial amount of routine consultation between the government and the major spokesmen of both sides of industry.[12] However, even in an atmosphere which was quite radically altered after 1979 there was routine consultation on much more mundane matters between the officials of a department and the representatives of a single firm or a small sector of an industry. And where the issue is not so much the framing of legislation as its implementation, it is frequently the pressure group which will help to monitor new policy initiatives or legislation and report to the department on their effectiveness.[13]

Although some groups can adopt strategies which enable them to articulate their interests in a routine and low-key manner, others may not be so well placed or may not be able to do so consistently. Sometimes the strategy adopted will be a massive publicity campaign, although it may be that a group will wish to avoid this either because it wishes to preserve good relations with a government department or because it fears that such a campaign will simply underline its inability to obtain concessions by other means. However in some cases such a campaign will be the only weapon left to a group – as when the famous 'Mr Cube' campaign was launched to try to protect the sugar refiners Tate and Lyle from nationalization.

More threatening and direct tactics than a simple publicity campaign may also be used not simply as a last resort but also as a method of gaining additional publicity for a minority cause, as for example when the women of Greenham Common set up encampments to protest about the siting of nuclear missiles in Britain and attempted physically to impede military exercises. Non-cooperation by a major occupational group is in itself a formidable threat, in the face of which it is sometimes difficult to introduce new policies. Thus teachers refused to cooperate with an attempt by the then secretary of state to ascertain the content of courses taught in schools, and the views of staff of the Inland Revenue were decisive in the debate about whether child benefits should be paid to the father or to the mother directly. Changes in law and order policy are unlikely to be introduced if the police are adamantly opposed to them, although the issue of capital punishment proved something of an exception to this rule.[14]

A distinction should perhaps be drawn between groups whose position enables them to affect policy in a given subject area and the more familiar sanction used by trade unions who normally use their power to achieve an increase in their pay or an improvement in their working conditions. The strike weapon is obviously important to trade unions, although in Britain as elsewhere they prefer to use the ordinary tactics of interest groups before resorting to the ultimate weapon of the strike. The preference for negotiation and the reluctance to use industrial force may have been strengthened also as signs have emerged that too frequent a use of direct action can be counter-productive, especially when the trade union movement is not united or when damage to an employer is in fact a threat to jobs, as during a recession. Equally the legislation enacted after 1979 which made certain sorts of industrial action illegal has had the effect of endangering union funds if they enter such illegal disputes.

It is not, however, only trade unions who use direct action to promote their ends, and the strike is not the only weapon at the disposal of pressure groups. Some organizations with ideologically inspired goals will use other forms of direct action to make their case known. Thus for example the Campaign for Nuclear Disarmament (CND) has made frequent use of marches and sit-ins to publicize its views, although its highly decentralized organization after 1979 meant that such tactics were rarely coordinated.[15] In some cases, although the pressure group may not appear to have had any impact on policy, its achievement may have been substantial in that it has succeeded in bringing an issue to the public's attention. Indeed on the criterion of placing issues on the public agenda the revived and reorganized anti-nuclear movement has been extremely effective; and although it has not prevented the siting of cruise missiles in the United Kingdom still less achieved its goal of unilateral nuclear disarmament, CND has successfully persuaded Labour Party activists, so that unilateral disarmament is now official Labour policy.[16]

Resources

Pressure groups may possess a wealth of resources which are conducive to success in the political arena. They may, for example be able to call upon extensive funds, as many business groups and trade unions can. They may have the benefit of a large membership, although the sheer weight of numbers is not by itself a guarantee of success. The quality and commitment of a group's membership is important, as is the 'saturation' or 'density' of the membership pool – i.e. the extent to which a group can claim that it really represents a large proportion of a given class or category of employment. From the point of view of a government dealing with a pressure group and the general public, the higher the density the more the group can claim legitimacy. Such legitimacy simplifies the government's task of dealing with affected interests. Equally, the higher the membership of a group, the easier it will be for the group to affect not merely the shaping of policy in the first place but also the way that policy is implemented.

Access is another important resource which may vary between groups and between administrations. Thus for example there is no doubt that trade unions have better access to government when Labour is in power than when there is a Conservative administration. However even as between Conservative administrations there have been profound variations. The Macmillan government of 1957–63 and the Heath government for part of its life were much more amenable to consulting the unions than the Thatcher government has been. It has also been suggested that some groups may gain advantages from sharing the same sociological background as decision-makers – as when company directors and parliamentarians come from the same school or share the same London club. What is closer to the truth however is that a pressure group director will be more successful to the extent that he understands the world of the decision-makers he is seeking to influence. The organizer of a pressure group for the homeless (such as Shelter or the Child Poverty Action Group) who has been a personal adviser to a minister is better placed than one who has spent all his time working for charities and voluntary organizations.[17] Similarly a group such as the Consumers Association which can call upon a range of political expertise is more likely to be successful in a legislative campaign than one which cannot.

However it is also the case that some pressure groups because of their leadership and strategies or their general record will enjoy closer relationships with policy-makers. For example the long-established Howard League for Penal Reform enjoys greater access to Home Office officials than do the more recent and more radical pressure groups in the same field – for example Preservation of the Rights of Prisoners (PROP) and Radical Alternatives to Prison (RAP).[18]

Money is another important factor influencing a pressure group's ability to provide services for its members and also to finance the research and organizational facilities necessary for it to function effectively. The CBI has a fairly large budget: in 1983 it had an income of £7,992,666, of which by far the largest part (£6,167,230) came from members' subscriptions. After expenditure which was largely devoted to staff and offices it had an annual surplus of £42,186. The TUC has functioned on a rather smaller budget which tends to be reduced in periods of recession. Sometimes money will be used to employ professional consultants to make a good case for an industry or interest in Whitehall and Westminster, although this is still much less prevalent an activity than in Washington and is really only a possibility for the more wealthy groups. The promotional or ideological groups tend to have much smaller budgets and sometimes will be financially stretched to provide even minimal central organizational facilities.

It has been mentioned that a country's constitutional structure will affect pressure group activity. This is largely because a pressure group's organization will be so arranged as to make its impact at the point where major political decisions are taken, and groups will therefore seek access to and concentrate resources on some parts of the political system rather than others. In a federal system such as the United States some groups – such as the ACLU or the Moral Majority – will try to maintain a presence at both the federal and at the state level.[19] Similarly in the United States the continued influence of Congress ensures that pressure groups look towards Capitol Hill as much as towards the executive branch for their political access. In Britain the party system leaves little room for independent groups to lobby Parliament, and those pressure groups with a case to put will normally concentrate on the executive branch, which includes the Civil Service as well as the political members of the administration. Parliament may it is true be lobbied extensively if a group wishes to publicize its cause; but in those circumstances the aim tends to be a general effort at altering elite opinion rather than a campaign inspired by the notion that the legislature will take a greatly different line from the executive. Where lobbying can make a difference is at the committee stage of bills, when a group can feed its own technical information into the legislative process or may be able to build up support for a change which although minor in terms of the government's overall policy is nevertheless important from the point of view of the affected interests.

The general assumption that Parliament is not conducive to pressure group activity should be modified in two further ways. Private members' bills in the Commons may be drafted by outside groups and, even if rarely successful, have an outside chance of reaching the statute book if the government of the day is broadly sympathetic to the aims of the bill. And the House of Lords, with its looser party discipline and greater hospitality to subjects slightly removed from the mainstream of political debate, may take up an issue which would be crowded out of the lower House. It is also of importance that many peers have a direct involvement in pressure group activity as a result of holding important posts in voluntary organizations. Sometimes such involvement reflects a long-standing commitment to the group; sometimes it results from the group's search for influential spokesmen in the legislature.

The constitutional weakness of local government in contemporary Britain has meant that the politically more important pressure groups concentrate their attention on the central governmental institutions, although this does not mean that one cannot find a flourishing set of local interest groups dealing with those matters which remain within the province of local authorities.[20] Indeed one could argue that it has been the very success of some of these groups in exploiting the opportunities available to them at the local level – for example various radical groups in the Greater London area such as 'Babes against the Bomb' and the 'Gay Police Monitoring Group' – that has led national government to try to control local expenditure more precisely than in the past. Equally British entry into Europe has had an effect on the operations of some pressure groups both by providing them with an additional arena in which they must operate and by putting a further premium on the effective transmission of information about very specialized subjects to national governments and international agencies. In the case of agricultural interests, which are so powerfully affected by decisions of the EEC, it has been suggested that entry into Europe has had the consequence of welding the farmers more closely to the ministry in the fight to protect and provide resources for British farmers.[21]

Finance and Industry

Although it is customary for many commentators to speak in terms of a simple division between the interests of capital and labour, this conceptualization is not very helpful for understanding concrete political behaviour in modern Britain. Neither business nor labour in fact act as monolithic or homogeneous interests when they deal with each other or with government, so that although this division is arguably the most important one in British politics, its practical and policy consequences are not easily predictable.

A variety of groups and organizations represent the various sectors of business and industry, just as a variety of trade unions represent the different sections of the British labour force. And sometimes the interests of one section of these groups will be very much in conflict with one, if not all, of the others. As far as business is concerned there are major differences in outlook and orientation between the City and financial institutions on the one hand and manufacturing industry on the other. Thus for example it has been frequently noted that the policies pursued by the Conservative government after 1979 in the economic sphere were much more readily accepted by the City than by the CBI which found the high interest rates of the period damaging to manufacturing industry. Indeed Sir Terence Beckett, the director-general of the CBI, went so far as publicly to attack the Conservative government's economic strategy as inimical to the health of British industry.[22] Tensions however exist between the policy priorities of large manufacturing industries and small and medium-size firms, and there is an alternative representative organization for small businesses – the Small Businesses Group. The CBI is heavily oriented towards large private manufacturing companies and does not for example operate to protect the interests of retailers, who use a body called the Retail Consortium to protect them. Other divisions which surface from time to time include the division between public sector industries and private sector ones and the regional divisions which can arise between industries located in Scotland or Northern Ireland and those located in the rest of the United Kingdom.

The peak organization which represents the interests of manufacturing industry in Britain, the CBI, is an amalgamation of three much older organizations all of which represented slightly different sections of the industrial world: the Federation of British Industry (FBI), the British Employers' Confederation (BEC) and the National Association of British Manufacturers (NABM).[23] In the nineteenth and early twentieth centuries industries had tended to be represented on an industry by industry basis rather than in any broad organization, although the Association of British Chambers of Commerce which was founded in 1860 had represented the interests of smaller firms. The late nineteenth century had seen a general growth in employers' organizations, partly in response to the perceived threat from the trade union movement. Thus, although nineteenth-century Britain had seen the formation and operation of industrial organizations and groups protective of business interests, concerted pressure by business and commercial interests manifested itself slowly. The Employers' Parliamentary Council was not formed until 1898, although the Trades Union Congress had been formed some thirty years earlier in 1869.

With the first world war – and the range of new controls and forms of government intervention in industry which it saw – business began to organize on a national level, and during the war and the years immediately thereafter three major institutions emerged: the Federation of British Industry itself (which was formed in 1916); the National Union of Manufacturers (which was also formed in 1916); and the National Confederation of Employers' Associations (which was formed in 1919). Although the period immediately after the first world war saw a loosening of the links between government and industry the trend to greater collectivism was apparent; and of course it was sharply accelerated by the experience of the second world war and the Labour governments which immediately followed it.

One feature of the pattern of industrial representation in Britain that deserves mention is the extent to which government has itself intervened to encourage the formation of representative organiz-ations: the emergence of the FBI in 1916 and the merger much later of a number of smaller organizations into the CBI were partially prompted by government initiatives. Certainly the formation of the CBI in 1965 was a result of a government initiative encouraged by George Brown, the ministerial chief at the Department of Economic Affairs, presumably as an aid to constructive economic planning.[24]

The formation of the CBI brought about a change in the size of its membership, and the scope of its activities began to expand. The amalgamation also spurred the CBI into a more overtly political role than any of its three component parts had hitherto played. The three organizations which had merged to form the larger peak organization had each had rather different constituencies – the FBI had been oriented towards the larger industries, the NABM towards the smaller manufacturing industries and the BEC towards trade associations and employer organizations. Although the newly formed CBI adopted much of the structure of the old FBI rather than that of the other groups, one important and controversial innovation in 1965 was that the nationalized industries were allowed to join, although as a proportion of its membership the public sector is responsible for only a small percentage. In 1981 the CBI's membership was distributed as follows between the various sectors of business and industry:

Employer and trade associations	4.4%
Consumer associations	1.3%
Commercial firms	22.3%
Public sector	0.4%
Industrial	71.6%

Source: *CBI Annual Report*, 1981.

Although the overwhelming dominance of industrial members has been long established, not all the industrial firms represented among the CBI's members are of the same size. The 1979 Annual Report revealed the following breakdown of members:

Employer and trade associations	4.7%
Industrial (1–50 employees)	27.3%
Industrial (51–200 employees)	24.1%
Industrial (201–1,000 employees)	13.6%
Industrial (1,000 and above employees)	11.5%
Public sector	0.3%
Construction	1.1%
Commercial firms	17.4%

Source: *CBI Annual Report*, 1979.

While the primary concern of the CBI remains in many ways the interests of manufacturing industry its membership ensures that it remains representative also of stockbroking, merchant banking and the nationalized industries. It should however be noted that not all firms use the CBI to an equal extent. Some firms such as Rolls Royce and ICI are so important to the market or have such well developed contacts that they can bypass the CBI and negotiate directly with the relevant government department. Others are perhaps too small to have any hopes of putting independent pressure on the government and value their membership of the CBI for the selective benefits which it brings rather than any access which it offers to the firm as a unit. Clearly the decision as to whether to press the case of a firm directly when legislation is being drafted will depend on the nature of the problem, but as far as large firms are concerned it seems that there has been a trend towards establishing specialized units for dealing with government.

It has been suggested that the CBI has a number of weaknesses as a pressure group in addition to its weaknesses in certain sectors. The most important weakness is that while trade unions employ the strike weapon as a sanction against the employer directly, or indirectly against the government, the members of the CBI have few actual sanctions which they can impose. Of course in a period when government is dependent on both sides of industry for the legitimization of an industrial policy or a pay agreement then clearly informal and explicit pressures can both be brought to bear. The efforts of the Labour government of 1974–9 to make its non-statutory pay policy hold by threatening *inter alia* to refuse to contract with firms which did not abide by incomes guidelines produced a concerted response from business. But usually most individual firms will prefer to follow their own discretion and judgement rather than join generalized political campaigns. And in a period such as that which existed after 1979, when government has sought to let the market mechanisms work without government intervention, the need to cajole industry has not been as great. Clearly there are many instances in which government would like to articulate an investment strategy for example, but its capacity to implement one is limited; and the other side of that coin is that there are few direct sanctions a firm or a group like the CBI can exert against a government which is set on a given policy course.

Nevertheless there are ways in which the CBI, simply by being the most visible spokesman of British industry, can have an impact on government, and not merely on Conservative governments. No government wants its economic and industrial strategies to be roundly condemned by those who are presumed to have expertise in the area, and there is therefore a strong incentive to accommodate and listen to the views of the CBI. Similarly governments anxious to pursue policies which need the support of the CBI will recognize that even their most cherished ideological policies may have to be trimmed in the light of industrial objections. The need of a government for an optimistic industrial climate is especially pronounced of course if there is an election in the offing. Thus although Labour may not expect to be the natural ally of the CBI it will frequently adjust its policies if the CBI's arguments are sharply focused. This seems to have been the case in relation to the proposals of the Bullock Committee on industrial democracy, where the CBI representatives were adamantly opposed to being compelled to have worker directors on the boards of companies.[25]

Although the Conservative Party has a closer link with industry than have the other parties, and receives money from it (see chapter 8), this fact alone does not guarantee either Tory subservience to CBI policies or harmony over industrial policy. The experience of the Industrial Relations Act of 1971 showed how the CBI could criticize a Conservative government in a way which was thought to be electorally damaging and, as has been seen, the CBI was not entirely happy with the early monetarist orientation of Mrs Thatcher's government.[26] (This unhappiness with the trend of Conservative economic policy caused conflict within the CBI and some firms such as Babcock International actually resigned from the CBI because of Sir Terence Beckett's public criticism of the government.)

The fact that the Conservative Party cannot automatically rely on the unquestioning support of business was further evidenced in the period immediately after the two general elections of 1974. Then the swing to the left in the Labour Party and the apparent inability of the Conservative Party to obtain a working parliamentary majority made some businessmen consider electoral reform as a means of giving Britain political stability. Accordingly there were donations to the pressure groups established to promote the cause of electoral reform and some concern that the Conservative Party's own receipts from industry would decline if it did not take this suggestion seriously.

The somewhat corporatist style of the CBI means that it may be challenged by groups anxious for policy towards industry to be more radical. Private business in the 1970s and 1980s found a more right-wing voice than the CBI's in the Institute of Directors. Among the campaigns which the Institute espoused was one to try to persuade the government to legislate against the alleged abuse by trade unions of their powers over their members and to limit the closed shop. This campaign to reform the internal procedures of the unions met with some sympathy from the government, and the links between the Institute and the Thatcher administration were strengthened in 1984 when Sir John Hoskyns, the former head of Mrs Thatcher's policy unit and a frequent critic of Whitehall's alleged economic immobilism, was appointed as the director-general of the Institute of Directors.

The City of London – the loose amalgam of merchant bankers, stockbrokers, insurance firms and other financial interests concentrated within the small area of the City – is frequently spoken of as a corporate entity, and indeed its institutions do wield considerable power over the conduct of economic policy. It has been noted that whereas major studies of the role of the CBI and of individual firms in the policy-making process have been undertaken, there has been little sustained analysis of how the City of London influences policy.[27] But that it can act in a concerted manner seems clear enough. The banks for example have a very real and direct influence, in part because of the financial specialization and concentration of power in the world of banking which has meant that from a situation in which there were many British banks, today the scene is dominated by the big four clearing banks. Even more important from the point of view of governments attempting to frame economic and financial policy is that such policy cannot be made simply in the light of domestic considerations. The fact that London remains a major financial centre means that international influences shape the policies and priorities of those who work there. And it is also the case that, even if there is no obvious single organization which will speak for the City, this role is to some extent performed by the Bank of England and its director.

Trade Unions

The trade union movement in Britain – the third partner in the attempts to introduce a more concerted approach to the planning of the economy during the 1960s and 1970s – is in many ways a highly controversial subject. Although it started as a movement designed to protect the exploited and downtrodden there has developed a feeling among the general public that the influence wielded by the unions in modern Britain is both substantial and harmful to the national interest. Thus a report on British social attitudes found that two-thirds of its sample thought that unions had 'a great deal' or 'quite a bit' of influence while hardly anyone thought they had not much influence on the lives of people.[28] Moreover these assessments seemed to be drawn equally from all sections of the British population, with manual as well as non-manual respondents expressing the same views. And when it came to the question of whether unions had too much influence, about the right amount or too little, a full 59 per cent answered 'too much', with 34 per cent saying 'about the right amount' and a mere 5 per cent saying 'too little'.[29]

Yet this seeming public hostility to the role of trade unions in British politics and society conceals a number of problems. Some would say, as Edward Heath and other leading politicians have done, that so far from being too strong the British trade union movement is very weak – at least in its ability to control its members. And indeed the movement does in many respects present a picture of a highly diverse and decentralized body. Individual unions differ greatly in their constitutional arrangements so that some, such as the massive Transport and General Workers' Union (TGWU), are highly centralized and allow general secretaries who wish to do so to make use of a range of powers and introduce major initiatives. By contrast power in other unions such as the Amalgamated Union of Engineering Workers (Engineering) (AUEW (E)) is fragmented. In addition there is the general problem of securing agreement across a whole range of unions whose cooperation has to be secured by the subtlest of strategies.[30]

The overall membership of the trade union movement has fluctuated considerably in recent years. It grew steadily during the early 1970s but underwent a decline with the onset of recession (as well as the growth in self-employment and the so-called sunrise industries where unionization was low) in the late 1970s and early 1980s. Yet the pattern of membership growth itself revealed major changes within British trade unionism and illuminated the extent to which the TUC has to speak for a variety of different and sometimes conflicting interests.

One major division within the trade union movement has been that between the newer white-collar unions and the older unions organized in the railway, transport, mining and heavy engineering sectors. Although the traditional industrial unions have given British unionism its peculiar character and style, it has increasingly been the white-collar unions which have produced numerical growth and expansion. There are also divisions between those unions which are affiliated to the Labour Party and those which are not. And there are divisions between those unions which operate wholly or mainly in the public sector and those which are chiefly concerned with the private sector. When one adds to these divisions the further complication that each individual union will be the guardian of a highly specific political

275

and industrial tradition and a constitution which will display its own peculiarities, it is easy to see why efforts to get British unions to march in step have frequently been frustrated. British unions have frequently been criticized for being reactionary and negative, and to a large extent it is understandable that such charges should be levied; on the other hand the world of the trade unions has been experiencing a good deal of change of late which it would be a mistake to neglect.[31]

As at 31 December 1982 the TUC (which dates from 1869) had a total membership of 10,510,157 members who were organized in 102 affiliated unions. Despite a general tendency to encourage mergers between unions, some of these unions were very small, so that for example the Sheffield Wool Shear Workers' Union recorded a mere twenty-eight, and the Spring Trapmakers' Union a mere ninety members. By contrast the huge Transport and General Workers' Union claimed 1,632,957 members while the Amalgamated Union of Engineering Workers (Engineering Section) claimed 1,001,000 members.[32] Over the period 1961–81 the largest unions have been the TGWU, the AUEW, the General and Municipal Workers (GMWU), the National and Local Government Officers' Association (NALGO), the National Union of Public Employees (NUPE), the Association of Scientific, Technical and Managerial Staffs (ASTMS), the Union of Shop, Distributive and Allied Workers (USDAW), the Electrical, Electronic, Telecommunication and Plumbing Union (EETPU), the Union of Construction Allied Trades and Technicians (UCATT) and the National Union of Mineworkers (NUM).[33]

One of the most important and difficult aspects of the British trade union movement has been the relationship with the Labour Party.[34] It has already been seen that the initiative to create the Labour Party was taken by the TUC conference (in fact through a resolution moved by the railway workers); and a large number of Labour MPs are in fact sponsored by trade unions. This practice of sponsorship – which is not found in any other British political party – means that the relatively wealthy trade unions fund a number of expenses which would otherwise fall on the increasingly impoverished constituency Labour parties. Thus a union may meet a proportion of the salary of a regular party agent. Sponsorship began before the Labour Party became a major party in its own right, and was initially a way of ensuring that the interests of working people were defended in Parliament. It is retained in part because of inertia and perhaps because it gives a union a very tangible piece of evidence of political muscle. (Of course other pressure groups maintain formal contacts with MPs to keep them alerted to developments affecting their interests, but there is no precise equivalent to this kind of long-term sponsorship.) The general question of an MP's relationship with outside interests and the extent to which it is proper for an outside group to try to influence his judgement has frequently arisen in the twentieth century. It has been posed in particularly acute form in relation to sponsored MPs, but the Committee of Privileges and CLPs have generally managed to find formulae to cover the problem.[35]

It is not simply by the mechanism of sponsorship that the unions exert influence in the Labour Party. Britain's Labour Party is also heavily reliant on those unions which are affiliated to it for much of its central financing. However the TUC has broadened its constituency to include unions which cannot affiliate with the Labour Party either because of the nature of the employment (such as NALGO) or because of the varied views of their membership (such as the AUT).

Yet although in one sense the trade union leaders are integrated into the country's political elite, especially through the long-established connection with the Labour Party, they are in another sense for the most part still separated from it by background, education and life-style.[36] And indeed although one of the most significant features of the British trade union movement has been its long association with the Labour Party, even this presents a further paradox, since as the unions grew stronger throughout the twentieth century there developed an unwillingness to allow leading trade unionists to seek political careers for themselves. Except in wartime (when some of the most able trade union leaders such as Ernest Bevin became cabinet ministers) they were not encouraged to seek parliamentary seats. The quota of Labour MPs with a trade union or working-class background has been diminishing, and this is as true of trade union-sponsored MPs as of the whole body of Labour MPs.

The growth of the trade union movement in the 1970s – even if it has been stemmed by the recession – was largely the result of growth in the white-collar sector of trade unions. Their leaders naturally have a different outlook from those of the more traditional manual unions. So far, although the unions do employ some graduates for research, they remain dominated by elected officials and there may be very little internal democracy within an individual union, although generalizations on this front are difficult to make, since each union will have its own constitutional arrangements and *mores*. Certainly, although the TUC has been seen as a representative body which in previous administrations could be looked to for aid and advice in the framing and implementation of aspects of industrial and economic policy, the TUC and its general secretary have in fact very little power over individual unions. It can muster support when it thinks an issue important enough, but its general stance is hortative rather than authoritative, and despite frequent attempts by governments to use the TUC and the CBI to enforce general economic policies on their members there is little evidence of any ability to make such policies stick.

The ruling inner committee of the TUC is the Finance and General Purposes Committee. Seats on this committee are usually reflective of the political and industrial muscle of individual unions, although sometimes too – as in the case of the electricians' Frank Chapple, who was removed from it for comments believed by some to be too critical of other trade unions – it can be used as a forum for ensuring harmony in the movement.[37]

In one way the trade union movement's general perspectives have been broadened by the very experience of having to cope with a variety of political situations. Its policy pronouncements now deal not merely with the traditional themes of wages, conditions of employment and trade union issues but range across the whole spectrum of social and economic policy. The experience of the 'social contract' in 1974, in which trade unions and the Labour leadership reached a concordat on what policies would be implemented in exchange for wage restraint, seemed at the time to be a turning point in the role of the unions in the modern state. In fact the growth of union influence has increased and it could be argued that the turning point came *not* under the Labour government of 1974–9 but under the Heath government of 1970–4, when there was a comprehensive attempt to bargain with the trade unions over incomes policy. It was also significant that the idea of trade unions nominating their own representatives to such bodies as the Manpower Services Commission was explicitly acknowledged by Conservative ministers as a way of giving such groups both an opportunity for influence and a responsibility in helping to run a section of public policy.

The determination of the Conservative government elected in 1979 to legislate on those aspects of trade union affairs which it found most in need of reform was balanced by the recognition that public opinion had to be taken along with any new measures and that it would be a mistake to do anything which would seem calculated to provoke the trade union movement. Instead of comprehensive legislation of the kind introduced in 1971 the Conservatives therefore adopted a pragmatic and step-by-step approach to industrial relations reform. The first important measure was the Employment Act of 1980, which restricted immunities for secondary picketing and certain other types of secondary action and increased the protection available to individuals who were threatened by the operation of a closed shop. In addition the legislation provided that any new closed shop had to be approved by a vote of four-fifths of those affected. Public funds were made available to those unions who wished to hold postal ballots on these matters.

In 1982 another Employment Act increased the compensation payable to those dismissed owing to the operation of a closed shop and enabled the government to pay compensation to some of those dismissed under the legislation of the previous Labour government. The Employment Act of 1982 also outlawed 'union labour only' contracts and revised the law relating to the legal immunities of trade unions so that their legal status was brought into line with that of their officials, thus enabling both to be sued for *unlawful* industrial action. Lawful trade disputes were defined as those between an employer and his own employees in relation to pay and conditions of work. Thus immunity from legal action was removed from action taken by the employees of another employer where no dispute existed to bring pressure on an employer who was in dispute with his own employees. The 1982 Act also made it easier for employers to terminate contracts of employment by those on strike and repealed the section in the 1974 Trade Union and Labour Relations Act which had been interpreted by the courts as permitting sit-ins and occupations of workplaces by strikers.

In 1984 further legislation was passed to provide that strikes would only be covered by the legal immunities of trade unions if they had been preceded by a secret ballot.[38] This move was part of a more general attempt to expand the internal democracy of trade unions, and the legislation also provided that officers and executive committees of unions should only be elected either by a postal ballot or by a secret workplace ballot with a presumption in favour of the former method. Open branch elections were thus to be outlawed, because they were seen as giving rise to intimidation. In order to facilitate ballots, trade unions would be obliged to draw up and maintain a register of their members. Moreover unions which wanted to maintain political funds from which to make donations to political parties would have to ballot their members on the acceptability of this arrangement and to consult them at regular intervals thereafter on whether the arrangement should continue.

Other Pressure Groups

Although the rivalry between the forces of business and capital on the one hand and of labour on the other frequently seems to dominate the discussion of pressure group activity in the United Kingdom, enough ought to have been said already to indicate that the world of pressure group activity is much wider than that of the TUC and the CBI. There are in fact a myriad of groups competing for public attention and while many of them will be highly organized others will be loosely defined and spasmodic in their activities. Without going further into the characteristics of the whole range of British pressure groups it may be helpful to draw attention to two relatively recent developments on this front.

The first development has been the rise of pressure groups which perhaps seem more akin to what would be called public interest groups in the United States than to sectional pressure groups of the more orthodox kind. The characteristic of an American public interest group such as Common Cause was that it typically espoused a wide range of goals which allegedly benefited a large section of the society rather than a specific subsection of it. The pursuit of such goals made the public interest group's activity similar to that of a political party rather than a narrow interest group. In Britain the organizations which perhaps have something of this style have been the consumer movement and the variety of organizations which might loosely be grouped together as environmental protection organizations. The success of late of the environmentalist movement has indeed been startling. It has been noted that the membership of the movement in 1980 had doubled from 1970 and that by the early 1980s environmentalist groups could claim more members than any political party or trade union.[39] Of course much of this claim presupposes the validity of lumping a number of often disparate groups into one movement but nevertheless a case can be made for arguing that the environmentalists have not merely provided an important vehicle for harnessing a number of criticisms of the culture of modern industrial capitalism but have also been adept at exploiting the opportunities for participation in the planning process offered by the British system of government.[40]

Objectors to the values inherent in the environmental movement are of course quick to point to its predominantly middle-class membership. Yet as has been found by a number of sociologial and political studies, the vast majority of members of voluntary organizations and pressure groups – with the exception of trade unions – are drawn from the middle classes. In the degree of active involvement – of civic participation – there is a pyramid which becomes increasingly unrepresentative of society as a whole.[41]

The second development which is noteworthy in the realm of pressure group activity is the way in which ethnic minorities have formed pressure groups to defend their interests. The Jewish immigrants who came to Britain at the end of the nineteenth century and in the early years of the twentieth had also formed protective organizations such as the influential Board of Deputies of British Jews.[42] But what is significant about many of the newer groups formed by immigrant communities is the extent to which these groups have been consulted and coopted by official agencies. The heightened consciousness of racial politics has thus meant that a few pressure groups have come to play an increasingly important role as the spokesmen of communities which, while they have the vote, do not as yet seem to have penetrated the processes of party competition and parliamentary representation very extensively. It is difficult to tell how far these organizations really do represent the beliefs of Pakistanis and West Indians, for example.[43] But if they persist, it seems likely that a new dimension of pressure group activity will have come to stay and that the United Kingdom's version of pluralism will come to look much more like that of the United States.

Conclusions

The whole role of pressure groups in British politics poses problems both analytic and practical. At the most obvious level the question must be asked whether the groups which claim to speak for a specific subsection of society really do transmit the values and preferences of their members to government. The dilemma of how far the spokesmen of the ethnic minorities reflect their communities' attitudes is also found in relation to the trade unions, where increasingly it is suggested that individual union members share neither the attitudes nor the political preferences of their leaders. In such a situation, is it the case that an extension of group participation benefits a majority, or simply the minority who enjoy leadership positions in the group?

A second problem which relates much more directly to the economy and the possibility for creative change is whether the nature of the compromises struck between different pressure groups and government does not itself create a climate of immobilism. Large pressure groups as favoured by government tend to develop characteristics common to bureaucracies and they therefore produce a consensus which, while valuable in some respects, may inhibit radical change and innovation. In such circumstances the will of political parties and of governments may be frustrated in a way which not merely militates against the collective good but which also creates cynicism and alienation from the formal institutions of representative government.[44]

A final question relates to the balance of power between pressure groups. Clearly not all groups have equal access to the decision-making process and not all groups have the capacity even to raise the issues that concern them for public debate. Does this inequality mean that British politics syphons out some ideas and attitudes and gives undue advantage to others? Such questions are difficult to answer with precision, but probably it is fair to say that in the United Kingdom pressure group activity is more generally seen as a useful supplement to orthodox party politics than as a means of frustrating party competition and that the strong traditions of the British Civil Service are a partial guarantee that private pressure will be balanced by considerations of the public interest. The high degree of centralization and the lack of openness which has been seen by many critics as a defect in the system can thus be seen as a defence against the domination of policy-making by special interests. Ultimately however it is difficult to imagine any way in which British government could function without its curious hotchpotch of pressure groups, and recent developments suggest that the tendency will be for such groups to play an enhanced role in the political system.

10 Government on the Ground (I): Local Government

A large number of the services which citizens of the United Kingdom have come to expect are provided, as has been seen, not by central government directly but by local authorities. Such major responsibilities as education, which is local government's most expensive service, roads, housing, planning, libraries, museums and galleries, social services, and refuse collection and disposal fall to the network of elected authorities which are distinct from the central government. They maintain a substantial degree of autonomy despite the inroads made upon local independence by the Treasury's efforts to exert more control over local government expenditure in the interests of overall economic management.

The importance of local government can be illustrated by a few key figures. In March 1983, even after a period of enforced contraction from 1975, local authorities still employed 1,653,000 persons full-time and 917,000 part-time – about one-tenth of the nation's total workforce. The local authorities' current and capital expenditure in 1982–3 was about one quarter of total public expenditure and about 14 per cent of GDP. In 1981–2, the total debt of local authorities amounted to £741 per head of the population. It is therefore not surprising that the decisions of local authorities should be the subject of particular scrutiny from Whitehall, especially at a time when the government's priorities emphasize the control of public expenditure.[1]

It is not only the level of local government spending that makes local authorities important, however, nor even the fact that their policies can significantly affect the standard and style of provision in certain key areas of welfare and regulatory activity. They are also important because they offer additional opportunities for individual and group activity of a political kind and together form a distinct arena of politics and decision-making. Local politics are not wholly divorced from national politics. Indeed as will be seen the two are interlocked at several different levels and the degree of interaction between them has increased over the twentieth century. Nevertheless there remains a sense in which the system of local government in Britain retains distinctive characteristics which are not shared by the country's central governmental institutions.

The period since 1979 has been difficult for local authorities in the

**LOCAL-AUTHORITY AREAS
IN GREAT BRITAIN IN 1985**

England and Wales

County

Metropolitan county

Scotland (as from 16 May 1975)

Region

Island authority

0   20   40   60   80   100 MILES

0 20 40 60 80 100 120 KILOMETRES

Source: *Britain: an official handbook* (H.M.S.O., 1978), by permission of the comptroller of H.M. Stationery Office.

United Kingdom. The election of a Conservative government determined to give priority to reducing inflation and controlling public expenditure meant that local authorities inevitably found their spending subject to greater central pressure. In addition a number of substantive Conservative policies – for example the requirement that council houses should be made available for sale to their sitting tenants – contributed to a further erosion of local government's discretion. Yet it would be a mistake to think that the criticisms of these trends always reflected a genuine concern with the constitutional balance between central and local government in the United Kingdom. Much of the defence of local government in Britain has been a reflection of support for the particular policies being pursued locally and an indication of opposition to the government of the day, rather than of any consideration of the merits of maintaining a strong local government system. Although the British system of government has recognized the importance of local values in the past, neither the electorate nor Britain's decision-makers seem convinced of the role which local authorities should play. Certainly, if electoral turnout is anything to go by, local issues arouse less interest than national ones. Thus the turnout for the Greater London Council elections in 1981 was only 44.8 per cent; in the London boroughs in 1982 it was 43.8 per cent and in the districts – both metropolitan and non-metropolitan – in 1983 it was 41.9 per cent. (Such figures compare with turnout figures for the 1983 general election of 72.5 per cent in England and 76.1 per cent in Wales). And, if local authority powers decline further, even this degree of participation could be reduced.

The modern structure of local government in England and Wales dates from the Local Government Act of 1972, except that London as it stood in 1984 had different arrangements because its local government was recast in 1963. In Scotland, local government was reformed by the Local Government (Scotland) Act of 1973 and follows a different pattern: the Wheatley Commission recommended a structure based on large regional councils and at the lower level district councils. In Northern Ireland there is an anomalous gap in the system of local authorities because a new structure that was due to come into operation following the Macrory Report of 1970 did not in fact do so because of the suspension of Stormont. Many local government functions in Northern Ireland are therefore administered not by elected local authorities but by the Northern Ireland Office and by appointed boards. (Scotland and Northern Ireland are dealt with in greater detail in the next chapter, so that the description here relates principally to England and Wales.)

Since 1972 England and Wales have been divided into forty-five county authorities outside London, and these counties are in turn subdivided into smaller units known as districts. The county authorities exercise all major functions except housing; the district councils deal with housing, refuse collection, traffic control and lesser matters.

There was a major variation in this distribution of powers and responsibilities in the six metropolitan authorities. Because the areas of Merseyside, Greater Manchester, the West Midlands, West Yorkshire, South Yorkshire and the north-eastern conurbation of Tyne and Wear are heavily populated and present different problems from those encountered by the majority of counties it was decided that a different pattern should apply there. In these areas the principle that major functions such as education ought to be exercised by the county was not applied and the lower-level authorities – metropolitan district councils – were considered sufficiently populous to administer education and some other functions reserved to the counties elsewhere. In 1974 when the system was brought into operation the metropolitan authorities were subdivided into thirty-six district councils while the remaining thirty-nine counties were divided into 296 districts.

In London, the old London County Council had been replaced in 1965 by a Greater London Council covering the area of the old LCC and the surrounding London suburbs.[2] The GLC was given a wide range of functions relating to planning, highways and traffic. The staple functions of local government – housing, education, social services etc. – were given to thirty-two London boroughs, except that in the area covered by the old LCC a joint education authority – the Inner London Education Authority (ILEA) – was made responsible for education.

It might have been thought that after a period of disruptive and costly reorganization both major parties would have seen the advantages of a period in which no further structural changes were proposed for local government. However neither the Labour nor the Conservative parties were entirely happy with the system created over the period 1972–4. The Labour Party had initially backed single-tier and multi-purpose authorities and were opposed to the new system based on the counties which was the result of the election of a Conservative government in 1970. The Conservative Party on the other hand became increasingly hostile to the initiatives taken by the metropolitan counties and the GLC over the 1970s, since in their view spending by these authorities constituted a major threat to the government's direction of the economy. The intense politicization of the GLC in particular and its determination to act as a left-wing focus of opposition to the Conservative government elected in 1979 increased the Conservative perception that the metropolitan counties needed to be reformed. The Conservative election manifesto of 1983 accordingly included a pledge to abolish both the Greater London Council and the metropolitan counties.

Although the Conservatives won the 1983 general election, their proposals for the metropolitan counties and the GLC – which were set out fully in a white paper published in October 1983 – proved highly controversial and ushered in a period of intense debate about the role of local government in the United Kingdom.[3] The government's target date for abolition was April 1986, following legislation brought forward in November 1984. However, before the legislation could be passed there would occur (in May 1985) another round of elections to the GLC. The government was determined to prevent these elections being held, since they believed that they would be turned into a referendum on the government's proposals and that the local authorities would have a full eleven months to campaign at the ratepayers' expense against their abolition. It was therefore decided to introduce in 1984 a measure (which came to be known as the 'paving bill') to cancel the 1985 elections and provide for interim authorities nominated by the London boroughs and the metropolitan districts outside London. These proposals would have meant that after abolition of the top tier of local government, the lower tiers would be exercising indirectly (through joint boards) many of the powers previously enjoyed by the GLC and the metropolitan counties.

The 'paving bill' was the subject of much criticism not only from the opponents of abolition *per se* but also from those who thought it premature and unconstitutional to provide for interim authorities before Parliament had agreed to the abolition measure itself. It was also thought highly improper that the effect in London would be to shift the balance of political control from a Labour-dominated GLC to the Conservative-dominated London boroughs without any elections taking place. The main provision of the 'paving bill' – the cancellation of the 1985 local government elections – was lost in the House of Lords on 28 June 1984 in an unusual assertion of power by the upper chamber. As a result the government revised its plans. It was decided to continue with the proposed cancellation of the elections, but instead of transferring powers to interim authorities the life of the existing GLC and metropolitan counties was to be extended by some eleven months. However, since there was a fear that these councils would pursue their declared policies of non-cooperation with the government in the process of handing responsibilities over to their successors, the revised government bill also included provisions requiring ministerial consent before the GLC or the metropolitan counties could dispose of assets, enter into long-term contracts or initiate other financial commitments which might impose unwelcome burdens on the boroughs and districts when they succeeded the GLC and the metropolitan counties.

The revised bill – the Local Government (Interim Provisions) Bill – became law in July 1984. Yet there remained a number of unsolved issues about the disposition of functions between authorities after abolition, and such questions became the subject of vigorous controversy, especially in London. For example although the government had originally proposed an education authority made up of representatives from the London boroughs, it modified its plans and agreed that a new directly elected authority should be established to administer London's education. In general it can be said that these debates about the structure of local government contributed to a souring of the relationship between central and local government and compounded hostilities that already existed as a result of financial pressures which were being exerted from Whitehall.

Many of the difficulties of central-local relations in recent years, including the problems of organization and finance, originate in part from the ambiguity of the British tradition of local democracy. That ambiguity permeates central-local conflicts and makes it difficult to assess the role which the system of local government is supposed to play in the constitutional structure. It has been said for example that one of the most important features of British local government is the *ultra vires* rule, which means that local authorities have no independent legal competence as they do in France and many other continental European countries. Instead British local authorities derive all their powers from Parliament; if the local authorities should step outside the realm of authorized activities the courts could intervene and constrain them.[4] This doctrine has been criticized as being unduly restrictive on local authority enterprise and innovation. Yet it is by no means clear that all local authorities have been hamstrung by it. The eighteenth and nineteenth centuries were periods when local authorities were extremely active as promoters of private Acts of Parliament which enabled them to engage in new activities; and in the twentieth century – especially under the stimulus of Fabian socialist views about the role of local authorities and the activities of local councillors – local authorities produced a number of experiments in municipal reform. The prominence of the *ultra vires* doctrine has been combined with a fierce concern for local values in some quarters and a belief in local self-government as an ideal at least as important as either efficiency in administration or equality in the provision of services. If that concern has seemed on the wane of late, the explanation may be sought in a combination of wider cultural changes which have reduced the importance of local characteristics and in the fact that the central government itself has done much to undermine the structures which support local values.[5]

The contradictions inherent in the British political system's treatment of local affairs partly reflect the absence of a comprehensive written constitution prescribing the relationship between the different levels of political authority. They are also a product of the haphazard growth of local government functions and of the arrangements for administering services. The norms which came to govern the provision of educational facilities were thus not necessarily the same as those which guided the administration of the police or the social services.[6] Moreover although there have been spasmodic revivals of interest in regionalism and devolution, the fact that until very recently Britain was assumed to be a highly homogeneous political entity has meant that claims for local autonomy have found few echoes of a consistent or unambiguous kind within the major political parties. While a party in opposition may take up a local cause from time to time, the considerations likely to prevail when that party is in government are those of administrative convenience, equality of treatment and broad national policy.

It is therefore hardly surprising that the pattern of local government's structure, functions and powers displays no more logic today than it did twenty or even fifty years ago. In the absence of a clear consensus about the role of local authorities, the local dimension of British politics is inevitably subject to two pressures. First, as the Layfield Committee pointed out in its report on local government finance in 1976, it has been subject to creeping centralization, since simply maintaining the *status quo ante* in local government's relationship with central departments has entailed endorsing a partnership in which central government has had an increasingly strong hand.[7] Second, the position of local authorities is bound to appear unstable as the temptation to adjust the structure to suit the current policies of central government is strong regardless of party. In addition to the major adjustments already mentioned, the history of local government is one of changing responsibilities and powers. Indeed there could be no better monument to the tides of administrative fashion than the catalogue of functions which local government has acquired and lost in the twentieth century alone.[8]

Although the basic structure of the United Kingdom's system of local government was completely revised by the reforms of 1972–4, it is necessary to set these against the background of the earlier system, since some of the traditions of local government in these islands can be explained only by reference to the pre-1972 pattern of authorities.

The Modern History of Local Government

The Municipal Corporations Act of 1835 applied only to the larger boroughs; the rural parts of England were still at that time administered as they had been since Tudor days by the justices of the peace assembled in the county Quarter Sessions. It was not until Lord Salisbury's unenthusiastic acceptance of the need to introduce the elective principle into the system of county government in 1888 that the whole country was covered with authorities elected by ratepayers; the franchise continued to be that of ratepayers (and later their wives) until 1945.

The reorganization of local government which took place between 1888 and 1894 laid the foundations of the system of local government which was to endure until the 1972 Local Government Act. Yet the structure was deeply flawed even after the reforms of 1888; for, although the 1888 Act made the county the major unit of local administration, it excluded from the county's jurisdiction the larger towns, which were accorded a degree of autonomy similar to that enjoyed by the county. These towns were given what was known as 'county borough status'; although the 1888 Bill had originally limited the number of county boroughs, the legislation was amended to enable additional towns to become county boroughs immediately, and other towns could apply for this status in the future. Moreover, towns which already had county borough status were allowed under this legislation to seek an extension of their area. Thus the division between town and country, which was to play such a prominent part in the Redcliffe-Maud Commission's analysis of the deficiencies of local government in the 1960s, was established as a relationship of jurisdictional competition: the counties' and boroughs' relationship thereafter was characterized by suspicion that any increase in the area of the boroughs would mean a loss of jurisdiction and income for the counties. The system established in 1888–94 may have appeared stable, but the search by the larger towns for county borough status was a continuing cause of instability.[9] The tension between counties and county boroughs was also heightened by the different styles of politics which prevailed in the two kinds of authorities: in the boroughs, organization of the council and of its committees was increasingly on party lines; in the counties, apolitical organization and uncontested elections were much more frequent except in such counties as Glamorgan and Durham.[10]

The level beneath the county council was organized by the legislation of 1894 into a structure of district councils so that the minor functions of local government could be administered at a level that was closer to the urban or rural community.

Because reform of the local government system was delayed for so long in the nineteenth century there were, in addition to authorities organized as part of the general local government structure, a series of *ad hoc* authorities for special purposes which had been created as the need arose. Localism was not greatly admired by the utilitarian reformers of the mid-nineteenth century, who were inspired by Benthamism and saw in the existing structure of local administration only an irrational set of authorities inimical to the efficient provision of services. The special needs of the poor were taken into account in 1834 when the Poor Law Amendment Act grouped parishes together on principles which took little notice of historical boundaries. The poor law union later became the administrative unit for a number of other purposes, including the registration of births, marriages and deaths. When public health authorities were instituted following deep public concern over the incidence of cholera, the pattern imposed upon them was that of the earlier poor law unit. The advantages of such functional authorities over the traditional units of local government were that they facilitated uniform administration and could be constructed to accommodate the special features of the particular problems which had to be tackled. An obvious example here is that of the sanitary area which needed to be constructed to cover the whole drainage area of a town regardless of local authority boundaries. Above all, the functional authority promoted a greater use of expertise and allowed a greater element of central supervision than did local government proper. The weaknesses of traditional local authorities in this respect have been pointed out by S. E. Finer, the biographer of Edwin Chadwick, the public health reformer who was a great admirer of the highly centralized administrative system which Napoleon had established in France:

> To a middle-class Radical, this new administration contrasted favourably in every respect with the historic patchwork of local franchises and parishes that served in England for the exercise of local government, and with the chaotic efforts of unprofessional officials and self-elected local bodies who, from fear or self-interest and complete independence of the centre, mal-administered the vital social services of justice, Poor Law, public health, police and highways throughout the countryside.[11]

With the simplification of local government structure in 1888 and the introduction of elections into county government, it might have been expected that many of the tasks performed by specially constituted authorities could now be transferred to local authorities. There was some move in this direction when education was transferred to the county and county borough councils in 1902, and when the poor law guardians were abolished and their functions transferred to the local authorities in 1929. However, the trend towards giving the new local government system more responsibilities was by no means uniform, and it was also the case that from the beginning of the twentieth century more intervention in local authority matters was exercised by central government. Sometimes this intervention was on the grounds of efficiency and economy; sometimes it was intervention to affect the way a service was provided, although the relevant legislation rarely prescribed standards of provision. But the overall effect was clear. By the interwar period the defenders of locally based administration had become concerned that central government control was debilitating the structure of British local government.

The current literature which analyses local government's weaknesses and urges reform has its origins in the interwar period immediately after local government had acquired massive new responsibilities in the form of poor law duties. Such writers as W. A. Robson identified, among other weaknesses in the existing structure of local government, the continuing removal of functions from local control either to central government directly or to updated versions of the specially constituted authorities of Chadwick's day.[12] Such a transfer of power and loss of functions were like a slow process of blood-letting which weakened a debilitated patient and proclaimed his unsuitability for arduous tasks.

Between the publication of Robson's early work on local government in 1931 and the transfer of powers to newly created authorities in 1974, local government had lost the responsibility for trunk roads, for hospitals, for public assistance and for many public utilities including water, which was made a responsibility of a network of new water authorities in 1973. The argument for these transfers was that local authorities were unable to perform the tasks efficiently because of their limited financial resources and their unsuitability in size and competence. However, it seemed significant of the inbuilt trend to greater centralization that water and ancillary health services were transferred from local authority control by legislation which followed closely on the heels of legislation designed to remedy some of the defects in the system.

The transfer of local government functions to specially created *ad hoc* authorities in the twentieth century differed from the nineteenth-century establishment of authorities for special purposes because in many of the former cases popular control was lost. The twentieth-century authorities – unlike the boards of guardians, the highways boards, the sanitary boards, the burial boards and the school boards – were not elected and were not accountable to democratically elected bodies for their day-to-day transactions. Indeed, even in policy, their accountability left much to be desired. The inevitable result of this process of transfer was not only that important services were being removed from popular control altogether; it was also that those services which were left under local administration were affected by a consequent lack of confidence and deterioration in morale. It was suggested that the less local authorities retained major social and regulatory functions, the more difficult it became to recruit good professional administrators and talented councillors. Equally, the less the direct impact of local matters on the lives of the electorate, the less likely it was that enough interest in local affairs would be generated even to ensure the casting of votes at local elections. In the late 1950s it therefore seemed that many of the elements which had given British local government its distinct style and vigour were rapidly disappearing and that British democracy at the grass-roots level was very frail. Thus the idea of major reform was generated in part as a way of arresting this spiral of decline and preventing the local arena of politics in the United Kingdom from being transformed into an outpost of central administration.

The election of a Labour government in 1964 meant that some reform of the structure of local government was likely to be initiated. Socialist policies were bound to draw attention to the weaknesses of the existing structure, since measures aimed at improving the quality of welfare services would largely depend for their success on the administrative efficiency of local bodies. The Labour Party had come to power with a programme which highlighted the need for institutional reforms of a comprehensive kind in a number of areas of British life; and there was within the Labour Party a distinct impatience with the improvised remedies which had marked the Conservative government's approach to local government matters between 1951 and 1963. There was also an awareness that – as the reform of London government in 1963 had underlined – there was a distinct party advantage to be gained from being the initiator and controller of such changes.[13] If local government were to be reformed at some point in the future, better from Labour party's viewpoint that it be done under Labour guidance than to wait until another general election allowed the Conservatives to decide the principles upon which reform was to be executed.

The desire to tackle the anomalies in the structure of local government in a systematic and comprehensive fashion was translated into political action largely as a result of the personality of Richard Crossman, the Minister of Housing and Local Government in Wilson's 1964–6 administration. Local government reform was something to which he claimed to have a strong personal commitment, despite knowing little about it, and it seems that Crossman managed to commit the Labour government to major reform before the matter had been discussed in Cabinet.[14] Yet the likelihood that any reforms which might emerge from this initiative would contribute substantially to revitalizing local government or indeed do anything to redress the balance between central and local power was greatly reduced by the decision to exclude the problem of finance from the terms of reference of the two Royal Commissions established in 1966 to investigate the problems of local government in England and in Scotland.[15] Thus the financial relationship which was in many ways the major determinant of the extent to which local autonomy could survive in the second half of the twentieth century, and which reflected the weaknesses of the British local government structure, was separated from the reform of that structure in a way which, as the Layfield Committee later remarked, made it unlikely that reforms in either the organizational or the financial sphere would prove satisfactory.

The exclusion of finance from the ambit of the Royal Commissions' inquiry underlined one of the major difficulties which confronts any government seeking to reform local government – the enormous interest which existing authorities and personnel have in maintaining the *status quo ante*. Indeed the very membership of the Royal Commission on Local Government in England under the chairmanship of Lord Redcliffe-Maud highlighted this difficulty; for it was necessary for the secretary of state to include on the Commission representatives of the existing authorities and to ensure that the perspective of the county boroughs was balanced by representatives of county council opinion. The Commission when it reported in 1969 recommended the complete abolition of the old structure of local government and the establishment of a very different pattern of authorities. Its majority report had followed on from its analysis of the weaknesses of local government; but when legislation was introduced by the Heath Conservative Government to amend the system it was done in a way which ignored the force behind the Commission's reasoning.

The Commission was convinced that the most important fault in the system of local government at that time was structural and that the jungle of areas and jurisdictions was both too complicated and no longer reflective of the habits of life of contemporary British society. It attacked the fragmentation of England into forty-five counties and seventy-nine county borough authorities which, it said, had made 'the proper planning of development and transportation' impossible. Moreover, the Commission attacked the division of responsibility within the county areas between the county councils, which discharged such major functions as education, and the district councils, which performed both major functions such as housing and minor ones such as refuse collection. In effect this division meant that services which should have been administered in the framework of a consistent policy were in the hands of several different authorities. A strong supportive relationship ought, it held, to exist between services such as housing, education and the personal social services, but this relationship was impossible while responsibility was thus divided. The structural divisions which precluded a coordinated approach to social welfare centred on the family were also an impediment to a rational and integrated approach to policy in housing, traffic and planning. The analysis by the Redcliffe-Maud Commission of the problems of local government in England was therefore characterized by the belief that the functions of local authorities were interdependent and ought to be exercised in as close a conjunction as possible. The logical extension of this approach was that, outside the large city areas where different principles might be applied, local authorities ought to be unitary and all-purpose and not, as they were outside the county boroughs, subdivided into distinct tiers.

The principle that the ideal authority would exercise all local government functions had the obvious implication that such local authorities would have to be large enough to be able to handle the number of functions involved and to provide the range of services previously provided by the counties. Indeed the Commission saw the determination of the correct size for a local authority in terms of area and population as one of the most significant of its tasks. Yet here the conflict of values within the system as a whole became most apparent. For, in as far as the survey data commissioned for the Redcliffe-Maud inquiry yielded any information about the unit of administration with which people most readily identified (a criterion which could be used to establish the optimum size of an authority for facilitating civic interest and participation), the results suggested that the majority of the electorate identified with their community in terms of smaller rather than larger units of administration. The implications of this information ran counter to much of the argument made elsewhere in the Commission's report, which suggested that increased mobility in twentieth-century Britain justified a corresponding expansion of scale in local authorities without any danger of impairing the sense of local community. The search for an ideal size of authority also placed in sharp relief the incompatibility of a reorganization based on the assumption that high priority ought to be given to the managerial aspects of local administration with one designed to heighten the sense of local control and self-government of a given neighbourhood or area.

The search for the answer to the problem of what size of authority might best combine the requirements of managerial efficiency and economies of scale with a sense of local control was not easy, nor perhaps was it helped by the research done for the Commission or by its own interpretation of that research. The need to provide a large number of services, in the Commission's view, pointed to a minimum population of 250,000, although representation from officials concerned primarily with education suggested that for education 500,000 was the minimum figure for the provision of a full range of services. At the other end of the scale, the commission felt that it would become difficult to organize services efficiently and to maintain proper liaison between a councillor and his constituents if an authority comprised a population of more than one million, although in fact the research done for the Commission showed no correlation between size and efficiency. The Commission concluded by urging that the existing two-tier system of authorities should be replaced by fifty-eight unitary authorities which would cover most of the country. In three metropolitan areas, however, responsibilities would be divided between the metropolitan county, which would plan overall development, and large district authorities which would exercise responsibilities in education, the personal social services, environmental health and housing.

The Royal Commission's report was published in 1969 and the Labour government, although it made one or two amendments to the scheme, broadly accepted the majority proposals and the analysis on which they were based. But those proposals did not command universal support and, as shown by the research volumes, there was much criticism of the assumption that small authorities could not be efficient. When the time to introduce legislation came, a Conservative government (elected in 1970) was in power and its legislation was based not on the relatively coherent arguments of the Redcliffe-Maud Commission but on the basis of a compromise which made small adjustments to the system of county authorities but retained a division of responsibilities between two tiers of local government.

The Conservative government's decision to maintain a division of responsibility between county and lower-level authorities was in large part political. But it was also influenced by the argument that the size of authority envisaged by the Redcliffe-Maud Commission would be too large to foster a sense of association with the decision-making process. Fear of remote authorities thus significantly influenced the rejection of the Commission's principles. It should, however, be noted that the Royal Commission on Local Government in Scotland – the Wheatley Commission – had favoured a two-tier rather than a unitary system and that Derek Senior's memorandum of dissent to the Royal Commission on Local Government in England had also favoured a two-tier system, although one based on the concept of the city region. But in opposition to the natural political instincts of the Conservative government to strengthen existing county and local government loyalties, it was argued that the cost of reorganization – both financially and in terms of the disruption caused to existing staff and voluntary associations whose activities were focused on local government – could really be justified only if the opportunity were taken to remedy major flaws in the system in a radical and comprehensive manner. (The impact of piecemeal reform and reorganization inevitably was to affect the quality of service provided, and at the very least to limit the ability of an agency to plan or coordinate efficiently. One indicator of this effect of the administrative fashion for reorganization was that an investigation into the operations of statutory social services and their response to New Commonwealth immigration found that no less than seven of the eight types of agency approached were to some extent distracted from their primary duties by the prospect of an impending reorganization.)[16]

A structure was thus created in which functions were divided between two levels of decision-making; and it created one in which the second level – the district – exhibited many of the weaknesses identified in the old system by the Commission, which had thought that areas of that size were incapable of sustaining important services such as housing. The integration of the personal social services with education and housing functions, which the Seebohm Committee had recommended and the Redcliffe-Maud Commission had advocated, thus became impossible.[17] The functions of planning and housing – which had both acquired additional significance since 1945 – remained divided, although the Conservative government acknowledged the need to draw the exercise of these functions together. Indeed it introduced a special device – the structure plan – to coordinate district and county authorities in the process of planning an area as a whole. Thus 'reform' when it came was very much a patched-up affair and the new system, while it has settled some problems, had not stifled criticism of local government.

The New System

The great majority of the county areas created under the 1972 Act were based on the old shires, in order to retain the links with the past which the Conservative Party and many of the county authorities themselves thought important. (Indeed it was largely because of the county authorities' successful lobbying that the 1972 Act created metropolitan areas far less extensive in scope than those envisaged by Redcliffe-Maud, though this saving of areas for the county effectively undermined the principle which had run through the Royal Commission's thinking – that the dichotomy between town and country ought to be obliterated.) In three areas, however – Avon, Cleveland and Humberside – new county authorities were established which represented the subordination of historic loyalties to administrative convenience, as did the abolition of the smaller counties of Herefordshire, Rutland and Westmoreland in order to produce county areas which conformed to the new population norm. (Another small county, Middlesex, had been abolished in the wake of London government organization in 1963.)

In addition to these basic changes there were many minor boundary alterations in order to ensure that as far as possible local government boundaries did not cut across natural social and economic areas and reflected the pattern of life of their inhabitants. This goal is always difficult to achieve, for the pattern of life can alter substantially over a short time in response to such factors as the decline of local industry, the siting of new roads or an airport or even changes in preferences as between inner city or suburban dwelling.

The Royal Commission on Local Government in England had recommended that in addition to the proposed all-purpose authorities which constituted the core of its ideal system there should be two additional levels of authority. In order to meet the criticism that its new pattern of unitary authorities would be too large for real democratic participation and responsiveness the Royal Commission had proposed a system of elected parish councils which could function as the organs of local communities below the unitary authority. These parish councils would have an advisory role and could develop into vehicles for the expression of community feeling on such issues as recreational amenities and planning applications. The Royal Commission had also envisaged a tier of councils above the unitary authorities; it thought that these regionally based councils could exercise responsibility for the range of planning functions which demanded larger areas than the unitary authorities would have covered.

It has been suggested that separating the reform of the structure of local government from the reform of regional administration – like separating the reform of local government structure from that of local government finance – reduced the chances of success in either sphere and meant that a comprehensive and integrated approach to the problems of decentralization was impossible. In Wales and Scotland the reforms were rapidly overtaken by the demands for more radical devolution. The question of parish councils, on the other hand, has to some extent remained a live issue in the politics of local government because, although the 1972 Local Government Act did not adopt the Royal Commission's proposed unitary authorities, it did make provision for the creation of parish councils as well as for the secondary tier of councils, the metropolitan and non-metropolitan districts.

The need for parishes was twofold in the view of the government; they would have the role of transmitting community feeling to higher authorities and play a significant part in the practical functioning of small-scale administration. Rural areas were automatically divided into parishes, but the provision of small-scale units of representation was not confined to rural or semi-rural areas: the district councils of urban areas were allowed to seek 'successor parish status' and some have done so. The problem in an urban area was to identify the community upon which the parish could be based; whereas it was envisaged that parishes would normally have a population of between ten and twenty thousand, the Department of the Environment recognized that in some cases it might be appropriate to grant parish status to a community with slighty more inhabitants than these guidelines would suggest. In urban areas neighbourhood councils – which unlike parishes are non-statutory bodies – are an alternative form of community organization. These neighbourhood councils are extremely diverse in scope and constitution and by no means all are elected. However they have apparently proved useful in conveying local sentiment to housing authorities and in facilitating the participation of residents in planning. Both parish councils, of which there are well over ten thousand, and neighbourhood councils provide arenas in which the various local residents' and amenity groups, as well as the more general pressure groups such as those concerned with the problem of homelessness, can promote their activities on a very small scale.[18]

The review of parish boundaries and the consideration of applications for successor parish status are functions of the Local Boundary Commission. The establishment of permanent Local Boundary Commissions as a result of the reforms of 1972 eased the task of reconciling the discrepancy between local government boundaries and population patterns. The English Commission was responsible for the initial delineation of district boundaries; county boundaries, which were much more contentious, had originally to be settled by the Department of the Environment; but henceforward revision of county boundaries will be the responsibility of these Boundary Commissions, as will all other local government boundaries. In 1978, the English Local Government Boundary Commission announced that its programme over the period 1978–83 would involve a consideration of the reports from district councils on their parish reviews and over 1984–9 the general review of all county, metropolitan and London borough districts as required by the Local Government Act of 1972.[19] (This Act provides that the Boundary Commissions should undertake a comprehensive review of boundaries every ten to fifteen years, although the Commissions could also undertake priority reviews in exceptional circumstances.)

Internal Structure

It was not only the nature of local government areas and the allocation of functions which had been subjected to scrutiny in the 1960s and 1970s. The internal organization of local authorities had also given rise to criticisms, which had in turn led to experiments with the apparatus of local decision-making.

The traditional manner of organizing local government work was through committees of the councils. Some were mandatory: education and police matters are examples of subject areas where local government Acts have ensured that the relevant local authority establishes some forum for dealing with specific business. In a committee organized on party lines, the chairmanship used invariably to be taken by members of the majority group on the council; indeed Labour's model rules explicitly forbid members of a council Labour group from entering into any pact or arrangement which breaks this understanding. A committee was staffed by the local authority's full-time officials, who were recruited for their professional specialisms and organized on a departmental basis – in marked contrast to the way central government recruits its officials.

At the apex of the professional local government under the old system stood the town clerk. His training was almost invariably a legal one – he was usually a solicitor – and his preeminence in the local bureaucracy symbolized how much the *mores* of local government service differed from those of the Civil Service at the national level. Whereas recruitment to the Civil Service has been dominated by the Oxbridge graduates in general disciplines, because the recruitment to local government was on professional lines this feature was never marked there; the development of a general administrative group in the local government service was very late in coming, and is still embryonic. In part the difference reflects the constitutional distinction between the two strata of government. The Civil Service at the highest levels has always been oriented towards advising ministers, and a great deal of its decision-making has involved the exercise of discretion. In local government on the other hand, the *ultra vires* rule and the concept of illegal expenditure made it important to ascertain that any decisions were taken in conformity with statutory authority. Also it has to deliver all its services directly to the public.

That the traditional local authorities were organized on committee lines meant not merely that power was diffused but that it was often difficult to foster a sense of local authority identity and responsibility for the whole range of functions within an authority's jurisdiction. The Maud and the Mallaby Committees of the 1960s recommended a number of reforms in the internal structure of councils; both suggested that the town clerk should be regarded as having a general administrative role, and that his training should emphasize the managerial rather than the legal aspects of local authority affairs. When local government's structural reforms had been decided, a further committee – the Bains Committee – was set up in 1971 to determine what opportunities the imminent reorganization offered for general reform in the internal structure of the new authorities.[20]

The Report of the Bains Committee placed a great deal of emphasis on the need for corporate management as opposed to the compartmentalization of administration by committee subject. The Report also advocated a change in the general administrative hierarchy. Instead of a town clerk the local authority should have as its senior official a chief executive, and each authority, it was suggested, should have a central policy and resources committee as some authorities already did. This committee could set priorities, assess resources and monitor the effectiveness of policy in a way which would give some unity to the diverse activities of the local authority. The concept of a chief executive had been popularized in Newcastle in the 1960s; the theory was that he would have no formal department or indeed any departmental responsibilities of his own but would be responsible for coordinating the work of other departments. He would be advised and supported by a management team of the other professional officers. This recommendation reflected the Bains Committee's concern to change the style of local administration by giving greater attention to personnel and policy matters as opposed to legal and financial ones, although it is doubtful whether such concern has survived the financial stringencies of the late 1970s and 1980s.

The idea of a general strategy committee has become common among the new local authorities. The Local Government Act of 1972 reflected the view, inherent in the Bains Report, that local authorities should be made freer of central controls on their internal organization. Thus there are now fewer committees which are mandatory, although a local authority must still appoint an education committee, a police committee and a social services committee if it is the authority administering those services. (In most cases this will be the county authority.) As well as these statutory committees there is likely to be a range of subject-oriented committees, and in addition some joint committees with other authorities for such purposes as planning. There are also arrangements for councillors to be proposed for nomination to water and health authorities so that these committees have a link with local government.

One of the functions of local government in the wider political system is to offer an opportunity for participation in the country's public life below the level of national affairs. Writers such as John Stuart Mill considered this role to be extremely important, for it was at once educative and an insurance against even benevolent despotism. One of the most marked features of local politics in recent years has been the growth of pressure group activity centred on the local level of administration and concerned specifically with the quality of services provided locally. Thus the activities of groups such as Shelter, the Child Poverty Action Group (CPAG) and Age Concern as well as a host of environmental groups have given a new dimension to local participation which complements the role of more orthodox party activity in providing a channel for civil and political activity. In addition the recent attempts by both parties to cut public expenditure have caused the formation of special groups within the parties to fight local government cuts, so that bodies such as the National Steering Committee Against the Cuts (established in 1976 by a number of public sector unions) operate as pressure groups within Labour ranks.[21]

The Local Government Act of 1972 made four years the period of office for both county and district councillors, although there is no uniformity in respect of electoral districts. Thus while county councillors are re-elected *en bloc* every four years in single-member constituencies, district authorities can choose whether to elect their councillors in staggered elections or as a whole. They can also choose whether to elect them through multi-member or single-member constituencies. The provisions for the metropolitan districts were different again: these now elect one third of their councillors in single-member constituencies in each of the three years in which there is no election for the metropolitan county council.

Since reorganization in England and Wales the vast majority of elections have been organized on party political lines, although in some areas there remains a reluctance to extend the concerns of national politics to the local electoral level. Indeed, even where politics at the local level are apparently organized on party lines, the party label may conceal the fact that the political orientations and beliefs of councillors are much more local than national; the interpretation of a party's values may be modified considerably by the specific problems of a particular area, and the political parties themselves are not monolithic about local government policy nor able to impose policies on their local councillors. Thus, although the growth in party control of local government has led to a marked degree of interaction between the local and national level of political life and a homogenization of political debate, the effect of this trend is not total uniformity.

The growth of party politics in local government was speeded up by local government reorganization. The amalgamation of the style of county politics with that of the boroughs meant that the distinct ethos of the rural areas, where independent councillors are most commonly found, was submerged in the new units. The survival of independent politics can be partly explained by isolation from the issues and the personnel of national parties; but that isolation could no longer persist when town and country were integrated for administrative purposes. Equally important, the process of reorganization created new prizes for the parties, and the wish to control the new structure promoted an extension of party activity and party contests. Also, because under the new system the county was given such important functions as education and social services, there was now a very real reason for local Labour parties to contest county elections, whereas previously they might have concentrated their resources on the county boroughs. The decline of independent local politics is greatest where urbanization is highest; thus over half the district councils which were controlled by independents in 1976 in England and Wales were in the seven western counties of Cornwall, Devon, Shropshire, Hereford and Worcester, Powys, Gwynedd, and Dyfed.[22]

Local government can therefore increasingly be regarded not

merely as a means of extending civic participation but as a new field of partisan activity. Indeed service on the local council provides a training and recruiting ground for national politics. In the United Kingdom it is rare for local politics to be used as a power base from which an individual may enter politics, and only the highly unusual careers of Joseph Chamberlain, Neville Chamberlain and Herbert Morrison spring to mind as ones in which long service on a local authority has been followed by major cabinet office. (Lady Young's local government career was followed by office in the 1979 and 1983 administrations, but her spell in the cabinet itself was short; and it may be that Ken Livingstone's period as Labour leader of the GLC will bring him to similar prominence in a Labour cabinet, but at the time of writing he has yet to enter Parliament.) One term of office as a local councillor as a means of developing credit with the party is a much more common background for an aspiring MP than a decade or two spent administering local government functions. Moreover there seems to be a substantial difference between the parties: the tradition of municipal politics as a background for Westminster is much more common in the Labour Party than in the Conservative Party. As one authority has shown, of all the Conservatives elected during the period 1945–October 1975 the percentage with experience of local government was 25.8, whereas the Labour figure for the same period was 45.3 per cent. The number of Conservatives who see local government as a suitable preparation for parliamentary politics has increased recently, but the influence of such work on the choices made by Conservative selection committees is not entirely clear.[23]

Yet whatever the value of local government in the process of civic education and political training, it has long been recognized that the system of local government is heavily dependent on its personnel both elective and permanent. The structural reforms of 1972–4 were intended partly to make local authority service a more attractive career for officials and partly to ensure that the staff recruited in the future had the appropriate level of managerial and technical skills. If reorganization inevitably entailed a substantial increase in the level of salaries paid, at the time this rise was thought to be merely a belated recognition of the scale of local government activities and of the need to change assumptions about employment in the service. Concern about the quality of recruits to local government was not, however, directed solely towards the permanent employees of the service. By the 1960s it was also thought that it was becoming increasingly difficult to persuade talented and competent people to stand for election as councillors; and councillors, it appeared, were unrepresentative of the community in that there was generally among their number a much higher percentage of retired and middle-class people than the socio-economic characteristics of the society as a whole would warrant.

Detailed surveys of the characteristics of councillors, the hours devoted to council activities and the financial implications of their membership of a local authority have been undertaken since the 1960s. A study in 1976 by the Department of the Environment attempted to compare its findings with those of the surveys done for the Maud Committee on the Management of Local Government and in 1966 for the Royal Commission on Local Government in Scotland.[24] It is interesting to compare developments across the decade, partly because in the period between the two surveys the need to encourage people to stand for election to their local authorities had prompted the introduction of attendance allowances. Such payments, it was thought, would improve the representativeness of local councillors by ensuring that council service did not carry a financial disincentive in addition to the difficulties of combining council duties with normal employment.

The general impression given by the Department of the Environment survey was that, although the broad picture of the typical councillor had remained constant over the period 1964–76, there had been some slight changes. Women councillors had increased as a proportion of all councillors from 12 per cent in 1964 to 17 per cent in 1976, although this change was, as the report points out, still grossly out of line with the proportion of women in the population. It may be that women will continue to be under-represented despite a slight trend towards greater female participation in local elective politics; later figures showed that by 1982 the proportion of women councillors in England and Wales was 18.4 per cent, although that figure concealed variations between the London boroughs, where a higher proportion of women were serving councillors, and Wales and Scotland, where the proportion was considerably below that of the rest of the country.

Councillors remained older than the general population. However, by 1976 it seemed that the proportion of councillors in the younger age groups had increased; London boroughs had the highest proportion of young councillors; the English and Welsh counties tended to have slightly older councillors. The proportion of economically active councillors had also increased since 1964, and this trend was reflected in the corresponding decline in the proportion of councillors retired from their occupation and the change in the age distribution. However, with distribution between occupations, the Department's survey found that manual workers were still seriously under-represented in the ranks of local councillors: seven out of ten councillors either were, or had been, involved in non-manual occupations and councillors included more than twice the proportion of administrators, managers and technical workers found in the population as a whole.

One marked change in the characteristics of councillors as a group over the period 1964–76 was in their educational qualifications. Whereas only 23 per cent of all councillors in 1964 were graduates, by 1976 that figure had risen to 50 per cent. Perhaps this change reflected in part the increase in higher educational opportunities, but also perhaps a change in the kind of individual whom local selection committees were anxious to recruit for council membership.

The Department of the Environment's 1976 survey made a distinction between council members and 'leaders' – defined as councillors who held major jobs such as chairman or mayor, vice-chairman or deputy-mayor, majority party leader and committee chairman or convenor. The survey found women less represented among council 'leaders' than among councillors as a whole and it found that 'leaders' tended to be somewhat older than other members. It also found that the self-employed represented over one-third (35 per cent) of economically active councillors.

One interest of the survey was to ascertain how council members distributed their time and whether more hours were being spent by councillors on council activity in 1976 than in the past. It emerged that more time was indeed being spent by councillors on their duties in 1976 than in 1964 and that the increase had been around 50 per cent – from a level of fifty-two hours per month to seventy-nine hours per month. The vast majority of that extra time was spent on council and committee work and on electors' problems rather than on activities like serving on nominated authorities such as water boards, serving as school governors or attending semi-social functions related to the council.

It is difficult to attribute the increase in the amount of work associated with local government service to any single factor. Undoubtedly the size and complexity of local authority functions make it necessary to devote more time to their routine administration, while the expansion of competitive party politics has provided an impetus for additional contact between councillors and electors. On the other hand the trend – evident in the introduction of attendance allowances – has been to emphasize the need for councillors to approach their tasks in a professional manner so that the councillors elected in that period may expect to spend more time on council affairs. (It was noted that the average councillor claimed an attendance allowance for 42 per cent of the time spent on council work.) The rise in the proportion of councillors with higher educational qualifications suggests that local authority service is now attracting a fairer share of the best-educated sections of society – although the corresponding fall in the number of manual workers elected to councils might make some voters feel that their local authorities were remote from them and unresponsive to their needs.

The need to secure a greater proportion of economically active councillors was perhaps not the only reason for introducing attendance allowances for local councillors as part of local government reform in 1972. Another problem which had worried many observers of local authorities in the 1960s was that of corruption. The standards of probity at the national level of politics in the United Kingdom are high by comparison for example with those in the USA. In part this difference could be because British central government has limited direct commercial responsibilities, although the extent of governmental intervention in the economy obviously varies from administration to administration. At the national level, the alternation of parties in government is a disincentive to stray too far from an agreed code of ethics, although again with appointments and honours the situation may be changing. However, corruption has long been a feature of some local authorities, partly because the functions which local authorities perform – for example granting planning and building permissions – create opportunity for financial gain which do not exist at the national level. Another reason why opportunities for corruption are probably greater at the local level is that in many councils the overwhelming dominance of a single party makes opposition virtually non-existent, and business can then be dealt with conclusively in private party caucuses where there is no publicity control or accountability.

The Royal Commission on the Standards of Conduct in Public Life, reporting in the aftermath of the 'Poulson affair', which produced evidence of widespread corruption in the awarding of public contracts, was preceded by a special committee headed by Lord Redcliffe-Maud to examine local government law and practice where a conflict of interest existed between councillors' and officers' positions in local government and their private interests. The Redcliffe-Maud Committee recommended that a register of the interests of councillors should be kept, which should include information about such matters as paid directorships, consultancies, share-holding and the tenancies both of the councillor himself and his spouse. The Royal Commission, which made a much more far-reaching investigation of the topic, thought that the national code of local government conduct recommended by Redcliffe-Maud should be amended to emphasize the dangers inherent in attendance at any social function organized by outside bodies liable to undertake business with the local council; it suggested that a councillor's attendance at such a function should always require authorization.[25]

One important change in the system of local government in the United Kingdom – which was pointed out in an addendum to the Report of the Royal Commission – stems from the professionalization of local government service which has already been noted. The fact that local government service is now so time-consuming and that devotion to council activities can be financially damaging has meant that there is considerable interest in those appointments which may be affected by local authority decisions and which carry remuneration. Strictly speaking the ability of a local council to control a range of paid appointments to various local government positions and even the creation of new positions is not corruption but patronage; but it has led to concern about the extent to which such posts may be used to reward party political service. The National Code of Local Government Conduct which was published in 1975 after the Redcliffe-Maud Committee's Report and printed as an appendix to the Royal Commission report had included the warning that in making appointments the only question to be considered was which candidate would best serve the whole council and that neither party nor political preferences should be allowed to sway a councillor's judgement. But even if a transparent violation of the code occurred, it was hard to discover what sanction existed. The same was true of expenditure on party-related purposes, where such expedients as running a free newspaper could frequently be seen as subsidizing party propaganda out of public funds if the newspaper devoted attention to the council's services. It may be that the new Audit Commission will be able to deal more effectively with these kinds of issues than has been the case in the past, but they underline the existence of a blurred area in local politics.

Another important point to notice about the role which party politics may play in local government matters is that while councillors cannot by law be employed by the local authority on which they serve, they may be employees of an adjacent authority which could give them the necessary leave to play an important part in their own council's affairs. In this way, it could be argued that not merely can party political activities be seen as being doubly subsidized from the public purse – once through the leave granted and once through the attendance allowance; it could also be that a sharp conflict of interest could arise for example in decisions on housing or education.

The machinery through which individuals could challenge decisions made by a local authority was significantly improved by the Local Government Act of 1974, which provided for a network of local ombudsmen under the direction of a collegiate Commission for Local Administration in England and a Commission for Local Administration in Wales. (A separate Commission for Local Administration for Scotland was established a year later with a slightly different constitution, and quite different arrangements exist for Northern Ireland.) The Commissions' jurisdictions cover local authorities, water authorities and police authorities as well as any joint board of which local authorities are constituent parts; the Commission may examine any complaint made by or on behalf of a citizen who claims to have experienced 'injustice' in consequence of 'maladministration'. Thus the local ombudsmen, like their parliamentary counterpart, are restricted to examining procedural irregularities rather than the merits of decisions.[26] One significant development in the whole system occurred in 1978 when Parliament passed legislation amending the 1974 Local Government Act to empower local authorities to incur expenditure for the purpose of making a payment to an individual found to have suffered injustice at the hands of that authority.[27] Thus there is now not merely elaborate machinery for detecting maladministration at the local level but also the opportunity of providing compensation when such maladministration is discovered.

Relationships with Central Government

The relationship between central and local government is difficult to characterize because it varies considerably with the different priorities of successive governments and from one subject to another.[28] It is further complicated by the fact that whereas the Department of the Environment takes the lead in relations with local authorities many other departments – notably the Home Office, the DHSS, the DES and the Department of Transport – have interests of their own which have to be taken into account. In Scotland the relationship is simpler, since the Department of the Secretary of State covers most of the domestic functions of government and there is probably more centralism there than in financial control and policy determination in England and Wales. A final point is that while formal negotiations (especially on finance matters) are conducted with the bodies which represent local authorities – the AMA, the ADA, the ACC and the ALB – they in turn will be affected by the political complexion of the majority of authorities which they each represent. These bodies also conduct the national negotiations with the unions represented in the various categories of their employees, and the outcomes of these negotiations have a major effect on their collective expenditure. Thus to speak of a simple central-local government relationship is misleading, since both parties in the relationship are themselves fragmented. Nevertheless central government can set the policies and pattern of local government and the period since 1979 has seen a heated debate about the extent to which such central direction is desirable.

The formal position of local authorities is that they are entirely subordinate to Parliament. This subordination is reflected in the traditional *ultra vires* doctrine. The political subordination of local to national government is also apparent from the range of controls central departments can exercise over local authorities.[29] Moreover the importance of the Treasury's contribution to the revenue of local authorities means that in financial matters the relationship is one in which central government is increasingly the dominant partner. The trend has become more apparent since the 1975–6 grant settlement, which in many ways ushered in a period of prolonged controversy about the financial powers appropriate for local authorities.

Despite the overwhelming constitutional, political and financial domination of local by central government, the fact remains, however, that the normal mode of conducting central-local discussions is that of negotiation rather than coercion. And, although this has been much less true since 1979, the tone of most local authorities' discussions with central departments is one of cooperation and harmony rather than antagonism. The variation between the level of services offered by individual authorities has itself been taken as an indication of how little success has marked central government's attempts to impose its own priorities upon local government. Although the mechanisms for influencing local policy undoubtedly exist, they have not been systematically used to create uniformity of provision. Of course there will be topics – and the reorganization of secondary education on non-selective lines has been one – where central government's wish to force a controversial policy on re-calcitrant local authorities may lead to bitter conflicts between individual local authorities and a central department. Indeed in the case of secondary school reorganization the dispute led not merely to political arguments but also to court action, as at least one authority was determined to challenge the minister's interpretation of his statutory powers.[30]

A government commanding a parliamentary majority may of

course use it to legislate in pursuance of a particular policy which it wishes to see local authorities adopt. Thus the Conservative government elected in 1979 introduced legislation to make local authorities sell council houses to sitting tenants at favourable prices. Legislation was necessary because although the Conservative-controlled councils took immediate advantage of the general consent to such sales announced by the new government, most Labour-controlled councils refused to proceed with sales. Quite apart from the substantive merits or demerits of the policy, the issue was deeply divisive because of the general belief that home ownership had an impact on voting behaviour. The Conservative government's policy was enshrined in the Housing Act of 1980; but even after this legislation it was notable that local authorities were still able to impede a policy with which they disagreed, and their success may be demonstrated by the very uneven rate at which sales proceeded in different parts of the country. A bill further to extend the principle of council house sales was introduced in 1982 and, although this particular measure was lost when Parliament was dissolved in 1983, it was reintroduced and became the Housing Act 1984.

The degree of regard for local autonomy by the parties will thus to a large extent depend upon which party is in power in Whitehall, and in this respect there is some parallel with the typical federal situation. Since many local government votes seem often to be cast in ways which register popular discontent with the party in power nationally, it is always probable that large numbers of local authorities will be out of sympathy with the government of the day, though many local authorities – especially the smaller ones – seldom or never change hands.

Nevertheless the federal analogy should not be pressed too far, since the constitutional position of local authorities remains encapsulated in the *ultra vires* doctrine which would be anathema in a federal system. The doctrine means that local authorities may only lawfully engage in those activities for which they have express statutory authority or which are reasonably incidental to ones for which they do have statutory authority. Activities for which no statutory authority exists can be challenged in the courts and pronounced null and void if local authority action is found to conflict with the *ultra vires* rule. This restriction on local initiative was clarified by a 1921 case in which it was decided that statutory powers given to Fulham Corporation under the Baths and Washhouses Acts of 1846–7 did not give that body the power to operate a municipal laundry.[31]

Expenditure incurred in the pursuit of an activity which is *ultra vires* is illegal expenditure and the auditor responsible for the examination of local authority accounts may seek a declaration from the courts if he thinks any item of expenditure falls into that category. The legal control of unauthorized expenditure has in itself given rise to political controversy. Thus in 1925 the Poplar Borough Council, which had used its discretion to pay employees a minimum wage of £4 a week regardless of the work involved, was found to have incurred an illegal expenditure when the practice was challenged in the High Court. The financial loss occasioned to the authority had to be repaid by the councillors, a process known as 'surcharge'.[32]

Surcharge has been criticized as an unnecessarily savage penalty, for the scope of the concept of 'illegal expenditure' remains uncertain; doubts in this area can affect the whole style of local administration by acting as a brake on initiative and by making councillors extremely cautious in their conduct of public affairs. It is doubtful whether this argument still holds true, because councillors seem likely to reflect on the legality of expenditure before entering into it.

Perhaps the most controversial case of surcharge in recent times occurred in 1973 when the councillors of Clay Cross in Derbyshire refused to raise council house rents in accordance with the Housing Finance Act of 1972. The Secretary of State for the Environment ordered a special audit of the urban district council's revenue account and the district auditor found the council to be in default to the sum of £6,985, a sum which he ordered to be recovered by surcharge. The councillors appealed to the High Court under the Act which at that time governed this aspect of local authority finance – the Local Government Act of 1933. The Queen's Bench Division of the High Court held that the surcharge had been correctly imposed because the resolution of the council to refuse to implement the rent-rebate scheme contained in the Housing Finance Act constituted negligence or misconduct within the meaning of s. 228(1) of the 1933 Act.[33] As the Court put the position, 'no matter how sincerely they believed in the course they followed, no matter how strong were their feelings of moral obligation and no matter whether this was a matter of policy or politics, the inescapable fact is that they quite clearly broke the law'. Such was the political anger engendered by the case however that when a Labour government was returned to power in February 1974 it relieved the councillors of their obligation to make good the deficit by the Housing Finance (Special Provisons) Act of 1975.[34]

The scope for local initiative over expenditure was widened to some extent by s. 137 of the Local Government Act of 1972 which gives any local authority, including a parish council, the power to incur expenditure which is, in the authority's opinion, in the interests of some or all of its inhabitants; this spending can include purposes for which an authority is neither authorized nor required to make a payment by virtue of some other statutory provision. This discretionary power to spend money on the general interests of the area is controlled by the restriction of expenditure to the product of a rate of two pence in the pound, although the inflation rate persuaded the government to include in the Act a clause enabling the Secretary of State for the Environment to vary the rate upwards or downwards by statutory instrument. This section has been largely used to help with the finance of voluntary organizations.

Other extensions of the scope of local initiative, although they do not fundamentally affect the *ultra vires* principle, give local authorities the power to acquire land if in their opinion it is for the 'benefit, development, or improvement of their area', and the power to dispose of land held by them in any way that they wish. (This additional flexibility over land does not extend to compulsory purchase, which is still subject to strict procedures.) In addition certain statutory requirements concerning the committees which a local authority must appoint were also amended by the 1972 Act.

There are a variety of formal powers which central government can use if it wishes to influence the policy of local authorities in specific areas. The two most important are the powers to approve appointments and to hold inspections. The power to approve appointments is perhaps most important with the police: the home secretary has to approve the appointment or dismissal of a chief constable in the various police authorities.

Central intervention in local government is indeed extensive over the whole range of police functions, for the home secretary has a general responsibility for the level of pay and training in the police force. Since the passage of the Police Act in 1964 the involvement of the Home Office in the management of the country's police has increased, and such matters as police pay, the increase of crime and the eruption of terrorism have reinforced the national dimension of police administration. The home secretary also has substantial powers to issue detailed regulations on such topics as pay and service conditions, hears appeals from disciplinary proceedings inside local police authorities, and can ask for reports on the activities of the police within particular police authorities. These powers are rooted in the fact that the Home Office pays half the cost of the police services from money raised nationally from taxation; in the case of police efficiency the threat to withhold the percentage grant is a real one which has been used on a number of occasions. To a much lesser extent the Home Office also uses its powers to regulate pay and employment conditions to ensure that local authorities provide an efficient fire service.

The power to regulate senior appointments has recently been considerably extended. It became important over a new range of posts when the Local Government Act of 1972, s. 112(4)g made the appointment of directors of social services in the new authorities subject to the approval of the Secretary of State for Health and Social Security. This supervisory power was partly the result of the recommendations of the Seebohm Committee's Report on Local Authority and Allied Social Services; it was followed by legislation in 1970 – the Local Authority Social Services Act – which was a major attempt by central government to influence the long-term development of local provision in the field of social services and to introduce a more integrated approach to what had hitherto been a disparate group of services.

The power to inspect the manner in which local authority services are being conducted and to intervene in cases of inadequacy is as important as the power to approve appointments. The use of this power of inspection is especially relevant in the probation and after-care services and education: the DES maintains a corps of some four hundred inspectors who visit schools and institutions of further education financed by local authorities and report to the Department on their findings. Yet the educational service is a sector where devices such as circulars, consultations and discussions are used much more frequently than formal mechanisms to communicate government policy to local authorities. Departmental circulars are a good example of communications which can vary enormously in import and tone: some are merely for information, while others (and this is especially true of the DES) have almost the status of departmental fiats, although passive resistance is possible.[35]

A government that has a positive set of policies in a field such as education will seek as far as possible to take the local authorities along with it, using its financial resources to try to obtain compliance. However, as the experience of the Conservative government since 1979 demonstrates, where such incentives seem inadequate, legislation may be used to enforce central policy on local authorities. The 1979 Education Act of the newly elected Conservative government repealed the Act of 1976 which had made it compulsory for local authorities to reorganize schooling on comprehensive lines. A further Act in 1980 imposed upon local authorities the obligation to give greater scope for parental choice between schools. Both these pieces of legislation could be interpreted as diffusing power in the educational policy arena. More directly centralist in conception was the 'assisted places scheme' which provided for central government funds to support selected children taking up places in independent schools as a substitute for the former direct grant schools which had disappeared under the legislation of an earlier Labour government. In the implementation of the assisted places scheme, it proved possible for an unsympathetic local authority to make it difficult for parents to exercise their legal rights under the scheme.

Even more centralist in its implications was the evidence that the Department of Education and Science was directly concerning itself with the curriculum. While the document *The Schools Curriculum* (published by the DES in February 1981) was on the face of it merely for the guidance and encouragement of local authorities, it could be taken as denoting the assumption of new responsibilities by central government. And this was even more true of the technical education initiative in which the Manpower Services Commission used its financial resources to induce local authorities to take part with it in pilot schemes for introducing a greater technical element into the education of the 14–18 age group. Again the creation of a National Advisory Board for Higher and Further Education could be seen as a first step in creating a national system out of the network of polytechnics and colleges, hitherto very much the preserve of the individual local authorities. Finally, the decision that from the beginning of 1983, inspectors' reports on individual schools should become public documents was also a method by which central government could, by invoking parental pressure on local authorities, help to enforce the kinds of standards the national inspectorate thought appropriate.

The extent to which central government requires active collaboration from local authorities will depend upon the nature of the service. In 1982–5 considerable difficulty was experienced by the Home Office seeking to revive the somewhat dormant provisions for civil defence. Some local authorities refused to cooperate and used the government's efforts to stimulate action as material for propaganda in favour of unilateral disarmament.

However, it is over the various aspects of finance that central government control is felt most directly. Here, as has been mentioned, the period since the mid-1970s has seen an increasingly vigorous debate about the respective rights of central and local government. National concern with the overall level of public expenditure has meant that local autonomy in such areas as education has had to be severely curtailed, and many local education authorities have had to make sudden adjustments in their teaching ratios in order to comply with cuts imposed with some suddenness on local grants and budgets. Naturally what looks like a rational policy when viewed from a central government perspective occasions deep resentment when seen from the perspective of an individual school or local authority. Similarly an authority which has had to impose sudden and sharp rent increases on its tenants as a result of the change in central government policy will dispute the logic of the new policy even though, if viewed from the perspective of Whitehall, it should be acceptable. However the main problem is not that, in a period of financial stringency, cuts in public expenditure and the imposition of cash limits automatically mean a sudden reduction in local authority services, or even that at such a time medium-range planning becomes difficult; nor is it even that local authorities resent being used as instruments of financial planning and investment control. It is rather that, regardless of the level of local expenditure involved, central government is the major source of local authority revenue, and local authorities can control the distribution of this money only to a very limited extent; this enforces and sustains the feeling of dependence upon central government, and acts as a brake on the development of a truly autonomous structure of local democracy.

Local government expenditure is of two kinds: capital expenditure (which is expenditure on some asset of long-term benefit to the authority, such as a school) and revenue expenditure.[36] Capital expenditure is normally paid for by borrowing, and the major restrictions on capital expenditure are specific allocations by central government and the need for any loans necessary to finance it to be sanctioned by the relevant central government department, whether the money is raised on the market or from government funds through the Public Works Loan Board.[37]

Revenue expenditure is derived from three distinct sources, although the balance between them is extremely uneven. The first source is the rates, which are a tax levied on real estate. Rates may be levied on householders – when they are known as domestic rates – or on factories, shops, offices and public buildings – when they are known as non-domestic rates. (Agriculture has been exempt from rates since 1929.) The second, and less important, source is the income derived from charging for some of the services provided by local government: council house rents, school meals, public transport and other trading services as well as income from the sale of council houses. However, it is the third source of income – grants from central government – which has been the most important and which has raised questions about the whole role of local government in the British system of administration. Some of these grants may be specific contributions which represent a percentage cost of providing a particular service, such as the 50 per cent grant which central government pays towards police expenditure. Most of the money is however paid out to the local authorities each year in the form of a block general grant given to meet the shortfall between rates and total local authority expenditure.

The methods of calculating and distributing this general grant have varied over the years. From 1948 a general grant was given to rectify the disparity between local authorities in relation both to their needs and to what they could raise from the rates. In 1958, most grants for particular services were consolidated into a block grant which embodied the idea of equalization between authorities. After 1966 the main government grant to local authorities was known as the rate support grant; once the money had been distributed between authorities on the basis of a complex formula, an individual authority was free to determine its priorities as it saw fit, although inevitably that freedom was to some extent constrained by such factors as centrally determined minimum standards in some policy areas.

The balance between the different sources of revenue for local government shifted towards the centre through much of the postwar period as governments laid more obligations on local authorities and central government felt bound to finance a higher proportion of the cost of local authority services. By 1976 the proportion of local expenditure which came from national funds was 66.5 per cent – a figure which caused alarm for a variety of reasons. Thereafter the proportion declined, and was about 51.9 per cent in 1984–5.

The calculation of the total amount of money available to all local authorities was done in consultation with them through a committee established in 1975 – the Consultative Council on Local Government Finance. At this committee the major central departments concerned with local government services – the Department of the Environment, the Department of Health and Social Security, the Department of Education and Science, the Home Office and the Treasury – met with representatives of the local authorities to discuss the aggregate amount of assistance which the Exchequer can make available. This amount covered both specific grants, which are used primarily where national government insists upon a minimum level of provision and where costs are uniform and high (and which accounted for 10 per cent of the total grant), and the rate support grant.

Once the total level of the rate support grant had been determined it was then distributed between the various local authorities according to a formula which took into account the different social and economic characteristics of authorities. This formula had three elements known as 'domestic', 'needs' and 'resources'. The *domestic* element represented an attempt to compensate for the fact that rates are a regressive form of taxation and bore no relationship to the ability of a household to pay the sums demanded. National government therefore subsidized the rate directly through the rate support grant; in 1974–5 this subsidy represented the equivalent of a reduction of 10p in the £ for householders. The *needs* content was based on general demographic factors and the socio-economic profile of a particular neighbourhood. This enabled the basic allowance of each local authority to be weighted in proportion to such factors as population density and percentages of children of school age and of old persons; it could compensate authorities where there were particularly heavy calls on their services.

The *resources* element in the grant attempted to ensure that local authorities which were relatively poor in terms of the money which they could raise from the rates – often precisely those authorities which had the greatest demands made upon them for educational and social service provision – were brought up to the national average in *per capita* resources. Thus the overall formula for calculating the grant which each local authority would ultimately get had a strongly redistributive aspect; this contrasted markedly with the nature of the rating system itself, and represented an attempt by national government to iron out inequalities between areas. Unfortunately, the increasingly prominent role played by central government in funding local services blurred the distinction between local and central accountability. Not only was increased central government support used to justify additional central government intervention, but often local authorities felt unable to control their own policy areas and sought to shift responsibility for the conduct of local services onto central government.

The pressures on local government and the major explosion in the rates in the years immediately following reorganization in 1972 prompted the government to establish an inquiry into the funding of local government services. This committee, the Layfield Committee, started from the assumption that the overall level of local expenditure would need to be carefully controlled and suggested two broad ways of doing it. One method was further central intervention, although it should be noted that the Layfield Committee thought that the status quo itself involved centralization by stealth. The alternative method which Layfield seemed to advocate as a way of strengthening and clarifying local government accountability and responsibility was to reform local government finance by creating a local income tax as a source of revenue in addition to the rating system. Such a proposal would have gone a long way towards arresting the erosion of local government, but the then Labour government evidently thought that such an innovation was too radical, and in a green paper published in

1977 it denied the analysis on which Layfield had based its recommendations.[38] Instead the green paper chose what it called a 'middle way' between Layfield's supposed centralist and localist solutions, a middle way which seemed to be in effect a slightly centralized version of the existing arrangements.[39] The green paper did however make some recommendations for change. It recommended a change in the mechanism of central control over capital expenditure so that in future capital expenditure financed out of revenue and out of the proceeds of the sale of assets – as well as from loans – would need central government approval, although it would not be on a project-by-project basis. It also proposed an extension of the district auditor's role and an increase in the proportion of grants paid as specific grants or supplementary grants. Its major proposal – the substitution of a unitary grant for the rate support grant – seemed designed not so much to aid local accountability as to enable central government to exercise more direct control over local authority spending.

The advent of a Conservative government in 1979 shifted the argument about local authority resources and expenditure even further away from the terms in which Layfield had viewed the problem. The Conservatives in 1979 had three priorities. The first was to redress the balance in the calculation of the rate support grant and to redress it in favour of the counties. The background to this explicitly political and partisan concern arose from the fact that over the period 1974–9 when Labour was in office the calculations had been biased towards metropolitan areas at the expense of the Conservative-controlled shires.

The second Conservative priority in 1979 was to try to meet the complaints of domestic ratepayers about the heavy burden the rates were imposing upon them. This involved a search for alternatives to the rates rather than additional sources of local revenue as recommended by Layfield. The search did not look like providing any satisfactory policy initiatives, although ironically some minor concessions on business rates were made.[40]

The third and most important priority of Mrs Thatcher's new government was the highly controversial objective of bringing local government spending under tighter central control as a part of the general strategy of bringing down inflation. It was widely believed in government circles that not all the growth in the numbers of those employed in local government or in the general explosion of its expenditure could be justified, and the government held the view that greater economy could be achieved without any real hardship to the recipients of local government services. One possible economy which was much canvassed was for local government to contract traditional services out to private operators.[41]

But, while some of the local authorities did their best to comply with the government's wishes, others did not, and as long as the grant was the only financial weapon in the government's hands, they could not be prevented from making up for any shortfall from their point of view by increasing the amounts levied in the rates. The government thus found itself in a position where it was claiming the right to determine not only the level of grants but also the level of the rates. If this process were carried to its logical conclusion it could be argued that there was little point in pretending that local government was left with any financial autonomy.[42] Although the general trend after 1979 was even more towards central intervention in local government finance, there was some liberalization of certain central controls over capital expenditure in the Local Government Planning and Land Act of 1980 and in the scrapping of some other aspects of detailed control of specific activities.

The development of new financial controls went through several stages. The first step, important at a time of high inflation, was fixing the cash limit for the rate support grant for 1980–1. Of more lasting consequence was the establishment by the Local Government Planning and Land Act of 1980 of a new 'block grant' system to replace the rate support grant. Under the new system which came into effect for the year 1981–2, the determining element in the level of grant for each local authority would not be, as previously, its past expenditure but the central government's assessment of what amount of grant would be required to produce a standard level of services. If local councils exceeded the level considered appropriate by the central government, the grant would be progressively reduced, thus forcing local authorities which overspent in this way to make up the difference from their own ratepayers. For the first time the secretary of state was given powers to consider and deal with individual local authorities and their budgets.

Despite these new instruments of control and the new determination to curtail local expenditure, some local councils continued a pattern of expenditure which by central criteria constituted over-spending. Moreover it was evident that fear of retribution at the polls was no deterrent to such local authorities. Nor is this altogether surprising. Although Northern Ireland retained the ratepayers' franchise at local government elections – i.e. only those who paid the rates could vote – in the rest of the United Kingdom all those on the electoral register have been enfranchised for local elections since 1945. However only about 35 per cent of those eligible to vote in local elections pay full rates; about 30 of domestic ratepayers are eligible for rebates. Non-domestic ratepayers who contribute nearly three-fifths of the income have no vote, the 'business vote' having been abolished in 1948. There is also the problem of how the rates are levied. The counties, including the metropolitan counties and the GLC (as well as parish and community councils), do not levy rates themselves but precept the districts who are the rate-levying authorities. The demands received by an individual ratepayer thus represent the requirements of at least two authorities and make it harder for him to identify the source of any demand which might be considered excessive. For these reasons the government thought it had to intervene directly in the rating process itself.

In a Local Government Finance Bill published on 6 November 1981 it was proposed that any authority seeking to levy a supplementary rate during a year for which the rate level had already been fixed should have to seek the voters' approval through a referendum. But the strong hostility expressed in Parliament and elsewhere led to the withdrawal of this bill and its replacement by what became the Local Government Finance Act of 1982. This Act specifically abolished the power to levy supplementary rates and precepts and authorized the secretary of state to make adjustments in the block grant payable to individual authorities who ignored his expenditure guidelines. It also established a new Audit Commission for local government to take over the District Auditor Service from the Department of the Environment.

Although some impact had been made on the growth of local government expenditure and an actual reduction achieved in man-power, there were still high-spending authorities with budgets for 1983–4 some 25 per cent above what the grant allowed for and which had increased their rates by 8 per cent or more between 1982–3 and 1983–4. Further action was promised in the Conservative manifesto in 1983 by giving powers to the government to examine the budgets of high-spending authorities in advance of their fixing of the rates and to indicate to them the maximum acceptable level. (This resembled the system operating in Scotland.) In addition a general scheme for rate-limitation to apply to all authorities was envisaged. The reasons why this move was considered necessary and the scope of the proposed legislation were set out in a white paper published in August 1983.[43] It was made clear that while a selective scheme and a general scheme would be provided for in the same Act, the latter power would be a reserve one and would only be brought into effect by way of an Order under the affirmative resolution procedure for delegated legislation. Nevertheless such a major intrusion into local affairs as would be the result of maximum rates being centrally determined was a clear departure from what had until very recently been considered the normal relations between central and local government in Britain.

For these reasons the Rates Bill, which followed closely the lines of the white paper and which received the royal assent on 26 June 1984, had a very rough ride through Parliament. It was opposed not only by Labour councillors and the Labour Party in general but also by many Conservatives who, while aware that the original list of authorities to be rate-capped would include hardly any Conservative-controlled councils, felt that the general provisions implied a permanent change in central-local relations to the detriment of local government. The objections were forcefully expressed in the House of Lords, where the Conservative interests in local government were strongly represented.

Apart from the general points of principle involved there were continued arguments about the formulae to be adopted in setting the permissible limits of expenditure and about what was felt to be an alleged degree of arbitrariness in dealing with individual authorities. Two calculations were used – grant-related expenditure (GRE), which indicated the government's view of the level of expenditure required to meet a standard level of service for grant distribution; and 'targets', which expressed the government's view of what their expenditure ought to be.

During the passage of the Rates Bill through Parliament the issue became inevitably entangled with the proposed abolition of the metropolitan counties, since the GLC in particular was regarded as an authority which was spending money for political purposes of a general kind and giving extra employment in its service (and in that of the Inner London Education Authority) to its political sympathizers.[44] It was also caught up in the arguments about the new arrangements made for London Transport, which was taken away from the GLC in anticipation of the latter's abolition. The London Regional Transport Act of 1984 was followed by the removal by the minister from the board of London Transport of the GLC's political nominees to it.

The period was also marked by a long-running controversy with Liverpool City Council, which had since its capture by Labour in 1983 adopted a policy of refusing to make the economies demanded by the government, while at the same time refusing to raise the rates sufficiently to cover the council's financial commitments. This meant that Liverpool was in danger of passing an illegal budget, because local councils are legally obliged to balance their books year by year and are not permitted to run deficits. After talk of legal sanctions against the offending councillors and even of the possibility of an Act giving central government the power to replace the council with its own commissioners, an agreement was reached by which more government funding was made available to Liverpool and a legal budget was agreed. The arrangement allegedly constituted a climb-down by Whitehall, which however denied that concessions had been made, and it was suggested that the outcome there encouraged other Labour-controlled authorities to promise active resistance to rate-capping measures.

For its part the Labour manifesto of 1983 contained a series of pledges about a radical shift in relations between central and local government. The proclaimed intention was the abolition of the *ultra vires* rule which confines government expenditure to particular objects (with some small exceptions such as those contained in s. 137 of the 1972 Act) and to confer a general competence on local authorities to carry out any activities not expressly prohibited by statute. But this suggestion is so far from the centralizing tendencies of previous Labour governments that the depth of the commitment must be subject to some doubt, especially since any incoming Labour government might have to face councils controlled by local Labour parties far to the left of the government itself.

In spite of the Labour Party's strong defence of the GLC (which it is committed to restore) and the metropolitan counties (which it is not), one cannot be certain that they would be revived once abolished, although a central political authority for London might have some appeal for Labour. As has been mentioned, there had been pressure in the past from Labour-controlled districts in favour of greater powers for the metropolitan boroughs, and support might re-emerge for a generalized system of single-tier local government.

The Alliance manifesto of 1983 suggests that if it were ever elected to office even more radical change would take place in British local government. The Alliance committed itself to decentralization through the creation of regional institutions and the abolition of one existing tier of local government and the restoration of powers to some former county boroughs. The Alliance manifesto also promised to tackle what it saw as the problem of single-party domination of particular local authorities by the introduction of proportional representation.

While the reorganization of local government may occupy the attention of political parties and of those who – whether as councillors or officials – take part in its activities, it is unlikely that the general public will regard this topic as a matter of major concern. It regards the level of services and the burden of the rates as significant issues.

Yet the low turnouts for local elections remain an inescapable fact and there is a good deal of evidence that members of the public are unfamiliar with the institutions responsible for particular local matters. Certainly the two-tier system and the division of responsibilities between national, *ad hoc* and local government adds to the uncertainty about local government's role, and it is significant that while many members of the public have had contact with local government officials, their own elected councillors may well be unknown to them. Indeed when seeking assistance they are more likely to have recourse to the local MP than to a local councillor even when their problem falls within the sphere of local government.[45] Against this it could be argued that the evident electoral successes of the Liberal Party when they have preached 'community politics' suggest that there is an interest in genuinely local matters but that only occasionally can it find an outlet. Perhaps the truth is that no matter what changes or reforms are proposed for local government, the British political tradition with respect to local democracy remains ambivalent, and its defence will be undertaken by the major parties only spasmodically if at all.

I I Government on the Ground (II): The Diversity of the United Kingdom

The reassessment of the relationship between the component parts of the United Kingdom has been one of the most startling features of British politics since the 1960s. The most conspicuous aspect of this reassessment has of course been that posed by the political and security problems associated with Northern Ireland. But, in their separate ways, Scotland and Wales also presented challenges to existing assumptions about the character of the United Kingdom and about the pattern of administration in the various parts of the country. Until the late 1960s most commentators had assumed that the country's highly centralized and unitary state reflected an underlying cultural homogeneity and political integration such as was only to be expected in the world's first industrial nation. The earliest challenge to the unity of the United Kingdom in the twentieth century – the demand for Irish Home Rule – might have been recognized as an indication that nationalism could be a disruptive and disintegrative force even in these islands. Somehow, however, it had always proved possible to ignore the lessons of Ireland, and anyway it was for a long time confidently assumed – at least in the United Kingdom – that partition had settled the Irish question.[1] Developments since 1968 reawakened awareness of the diversity and variety within the United Kingdom and underlined the extent to which that diversity could form the basis for separatist political movements. Of course the cultural, ethnic and geographical divisions of the United Kingdom are not as multifarious as those that obtain for example in the United States; but nor are the sentiments of England – still less its political behaviour – identical to those of the rest of the United Kingdom.[2]

The rediscovery of cultural diversity and the emergence of a series of claims for political treatment on the basis of these cultural and national divisions generated an intense debate about the constitutional arrangements of the United Kingdom. In 1978, far-reaching proposals for changes in the distribution of power between the centre of the United Kingdom and the periphery reached the statute book in the form of the Scotland Act and the Wales Act. If those Acts had ever become operative not only would the government of the United Kingdom have been even more complex than at present; there would also have been considerable constitutional implications for the United Kingdom as a whole. For example it is difficult to believe that the relationship between central, regional and local governments embodied in the devolution Acts would not in due course have promoted at the very least a questioning of the existing relationship between central and local authorities in Britain – possibly in a way which would have been more sympathetic to localism than the questioning which has occurred since 1979. Similarly the devolution measures would probably have led to an enhanced role for the judiciary. As it happened the degree of support for the measures was not thought sufficient to warrant the implementation of the schemes, and the Acts were repealed. However, in the case of Scotland opinion was very divided about the desirability of devolution and the issue is likely to continue as a factor in Scottish politics, although it is unlikely that there will be any attempt in the immediate future to revive the devolution proposals of the late 1970s.

The emergence as serious influences on their countries' politics of nationalist movements in Scotland and Wales coincided with the resurgence of violence in Ulster.[3] That violence in turn reopened the question of the status of Northern Ireland and its form of government – questions which thereafter claimed an increasing amount of the British government's attention. Thus in a relatively short period of time the political arrangements prevailing in all three non-English parts of the United Kingdom were the matters of major national and international controversy. (Indeed the violence in Ulster was perhaps the main cause of many commentators' doubts that exclusively peaceful methods for the resolution of conflicts were still employed in the United Kingdom.)[4] Government policy did not, however, assume that developments in each part of the kingdom could be treated similarly; it accordingly worked out separate strategies to deal with each of them, although the schemes for Scotland and Wales had a common political origin and were much more alike than the series of policy initiatives attempted in Northern Ireland after 1972.

The impression given by successive governments' handling of the devolution issue and the problems associated with the peripheral areas of the United Kingdom is thus somewhat untidy, and many critics of the devolution proposals of the 1970s thought that a more comprehensive approach might have been preferable to the *ad hoc* construction of slightly different arrangements for Scotland, Wales and Northern Ireland. In retrospect, though, it seems fairly clear that however radical a government might have been prepared to be in relation to Scotland and Wales, it would have been impossible in the political circumstances of the late 1970s to have fitted Northern Ireland into a revised framework of devolved government. And, although the SDP-Liberal Party alliance took up the federalist option in relation to the component parts of the United Kingdom, both major parties were uncomfortable with the abstract arguments for devolution, let alone those for federalism.

In one way the refusal to apply similar forms of devolution to Scotland, to Wales and to Northern Ireland was soundly based: the separate regions and areas of the United Kingdom have very different histories and the political consciousness of each of them has been forged by specific historical experiences. To enable a fuller understanding of the politics of each area to be arrived at, it is necessary to underline the specific features of each area and to show how they have formed their particular subcultures.

Northern Ireland

Many of the issues which were raised in the devolution debates of the 1970s had been raised much earlier in relation to Northern Ireland. Indeed it was at the beginning of the twentieth century that the difficulties of governing Ireland and the solution of Home Rule prompted a general discussion of the merits of devolution for Scotland and Wales – 'Home Rule All Round' as the slogan had it. In addition the cause of devolution or Home Rule was taken up by a small all-party group of federalists who wanted to see a federal United Kingdom within the wider framework of the British Empire. The Irish question had bedevilled Westminster politics for much of the nineteenth and early twentieth centuries. Its return to the centre of the United Kingdom's political concerns – and the increasing international attention given to it – have had a number of repercussions for the whole country. The most obvious manifestation of the reopening of the Ulster issue has been terrorism, which has affected not merely the province of Northern Ireland but also the mainland of Britain. This has meant problems for police and security forces, the requirement for special anti-terrorist legislation and the need for revised arrangements for the direct government of the province. All of these problems have placed additional strains on the administrative and political system as a whole, as well as prompting special measures for law enforcement different from those obtaining elsewhere.

Within Ulster itself political life is polarized between those parties which wish to see the continuation of the constitutional link with

Britain – the Official Unionists, the Democratic Unionist Party and the much smaller Alliance Party – and those nationalist parties which wish to see the link terminated. Of the parties which wish to break the union with the rest of the United Kingdom, the most important are the SDLP (which is a constitutional party wedded to democratic methods of achieving its goals) and Sinn Fein, which is the political arm of the Irish Republican Army and which is willing to use both democratic methods and violence to advance its cause, to seek power through the Armalite and the ballot box. On the basis of the 1983 general election, some 65 per cent of Ulster's electors wanted to retain the union; 33 per cent wanted to end it.

The constitutional polarization is of course also a sectarian polarization between the province's Roman Catholic population and the Protestants. Thus the political life of the province is complicated both by religious divisions and by the extent to which some groups such as the Provisional IRA and the Ulster Defence Force (not to be confused with the Ulster Defence Regiment, which is part of the official security services in Northern Ireland) are willing to combine violent tactics with more orthodox electoral strategies. Thus, although the Official Unionists had direct ties to the Conservative Party until 1974 and retain some links, politics in Northern Ireland are unlike those in the rest of the United Kingdom. None of the major United Kingdom parties campaign or organize there, and the issues which are central to Ulster's political debate to some extent isolate it from the mainstream of British political life.

The Structure of Government in Ireland

Between the Act of Union of 1800 and the Irish Treaty of 1921 the whole of Ireland was an integral part of the United Kingdom, although the colonization of Ireland had begun long before 1800. By the Act of Union of 1800 Irish MPs sat in the House of Commons at Westminster and representatives of the Irish peerage sat in the House of Lords. The Act had been modelled in many ways on the earlier and much more successful Act of Union with Scotland. Yet the attitudes which marked relationships between England and Ireland, and the form of government employed across the Irish Channel, suggested that Ireland was hardly on the same footing as Scotland in the eyes of the English. Indeed the treatment accorded to Ireland was strikingly similar to that a colony would have received, and so were attitudes which supported that treatment. As formal head of the Irish administration there was a lord lieutenant who was responsible to the home secretary, the formal channel of communication with the Crown. The lord lieutenant had relatively little responsibility for the routine administration of the country; this role fell to the chief secretary for Ireland, who sat in the House of Commons and was answerable to Parliament for the details of Irish administration and policy.[5]

The difficulties of governing Ireland arose in part from the cultural conflicts which existed within the country. Hostility between the different communities was translated into political antagonisms which other divisions within the society could not transcend or mollify. Basically, the complexities of Irish politics can be traced to the three different communities, which differed in their customs, assumptions and values and which each regarded the values of other communities as a threat to their own survival.[6] First there was the native population, which was marked by an adherence to the Roman Catholic religion and its Gaelic cultural heritage (a heritage which the modern Fianna Fail party in the Republic in particular has sought to revive, preserve and strengthen); its attitude towards the other groups was that of a dispossessed peasantry, for it considered the settlers to be alien colonists, the machinery of rule from Westminster to be illegitimate, and the goal of true Irishmen to be independence. Needless to say it was this group which was to provide the backbone of the Irish nationalist movement, although not by any means all of its leaders.

The second group of significance was the Anglo-Irish component which had settled in Ireland and had taken over its estates. Although quite different in cultural heritage and manners from the native Irish – the group was for one thing Protestant – it was sufficiently distinct from the English on the mainland to make identification with London imperfect. Indeed the literature of the Irish renaissance (the great flowering of intellectual and creative activity in late nineteenth-century Ireland) and a great deal of the nineteenth-century agitation on Ireland's behalf owed as much to members of this section of the Irish population as to the native Irish.

The final cultural entity in the country's triangle of conflict was the group which settled primarily in Ulster and which, although Protestant by religion, had Scottish origins and adhered to the Presbyterian faith rather than to the Anglican Church in Ireland.[7] It was this group which settled and developed what became the industrialized parts of the country as the significance of shipbuilding and textiles grew. For this group Irish nationalism posed a threat to its economic status, political sentiments and cultural identity.

Between these groups there was little comprehension and still less social interaction. Religion was the badge of their distinct communities, but it also represented cultural divisions which went deeper than confessional differences alone. Also, just as the three communities were isolated from each other inside Ireland, so there was a comparable distance, both intellectual and social, between the inhabitants of Ireland and the rest of the United Kingdom. The spread of Irish nationalism in the late nineteenth century and the attempt from the 1880s to grant Ireland Home Rule stimulated the Protestants of Ulster to resist any settlement in which they might be left a small minority – no more than 27 per cent – in a political system dominated by the Roman Catholic Church. Indeed on the eve of the first world war it was apparent that Ulster's Protestant population would resist Home Rule if need be by force of arms.

As it became clear that only some form of partition offered any hope of a peaceful solution, Parliament in 1920 passed the Government of Ireland Act, providing for separate Parliaments for the northern and southern parts of the country. Although the border could have been drawn in a number of ways, six counties were brought within Northern Ireland and given a separate Parliament in Belfast; the remaining twenty-six counties were to have their own Parliament in Dublin. The subsequent strife in the south brought about the Irish Treaty of 1921 by which the south became a dominion, albeit a 'restless' one, until in 1949 it became an independent republic outside the Commonwealth.[8] Meanwhile Ulster continued to operate the devolved institutions conferred upon it by the 1920 Act. Unfortunately for the ultimate viability of this solution the division between north and south did not eradicate communal tensions: within Northern Ireland there was a substantial minority of Roman Catholics – about a third of the whole population – for whom the border was only a temporary solution and in whose eyes the institutions of the province enjoyed little or no legitimacy. This perception of the border as a temporary expedient led portions of the minority community in Northern Ireland to develop an unconstructive attitude to the institutions of the state.[9] Certainly the northern Protestants were determined to exploit their advantages within the system; but their domination of Northern Ireland's political institutions was reinforced by the negative attitudes of the minority community.

From 1921 until the suspension in 1972 of its separate Parliament, Ulster enjoyed a substantial measure of autonomy within the United Kingdom. The Ulster Parliament, which had both a House of Commons and a Senate, sat at Stormont; and there was a separate executive which dealt with a wide range of matters devolved to it under the 1920 Government of Ireland Act and was responsible to the Parliament of Northern Ireland. Westminster remained the superior legislature, responsible for the matters which had not been devolved – the most important of which were defence and foreign policy and the overall conduct of the economy. Although the broad guidelines of British legislation would be paralleled in Northern Ireland – including for example legislation relating to various forms of welfare benefits – on many subjects important differences were permitted. For example when the rest of the United Kingdom changed its laws to legalize homosexual conduct between consenting adults, Northern Ireland did not immediately follow suit.

The relationship between Northern Ireland and the rest of the United Kingdom was thus an extremely unusual one, both constitutionally and politically. For although there was theoretical subordination to Westminster and although there were twelve Northern Irish representatives at Westminster (increased to seventeen in 1983), the two political systems in many ways hardly interacted.[10] This was partly because London was unwilling to be drawn back into Irish politics and partly because the constitutional settlement of 1920 had been quasi-federal in character. It had recognized a division of powers on the basis of subject matter and had established – as did the abortive 1978 Scotland Act – a special procedure for determining disputes about the proper allocation of powers between the two authorities. The special procedure was designed to decide constitutional arguments with the minimum of political friction; disputes were referred to the Judicial Committee of the Privy Council, a court which was then the final court of appeal for Commonwealth countries.

The constitutional structure thus erected might have been expected to have reassured the Protestants of Ulster that the connection between the United Kingdom and their own way of life was safe. Indeed the Act which recognized the Republic of Ireland's final departure from the Commonwealth included a guarantee of Northern Ireland's position within the United Kingdom. However, the degree of autonomy accorded to Ulster was balanced by the retention of formal legislative powers which could be used to amend the settlement at any time – though it was not in fact until 1972 that Westminster used those powers to supersede the political wishes of the majority of the province's population. Because of the doctrine of parliamentary sovereignty, Stormont could not be entrenched. At the same time a differential birth rate between the Roman Catholic and Protestant populations provided another source of anxiety because it suggested that although the border had been drawn to maximize the

Protestant advantage, Protestants might not always be the majority in the province. Contemporary demographic predictions are ambiguous on this point; some authorities suggest that differential birth rates and emigration will produce a majority Roman Catholic population by the second decade of the next century, while others suggest that this prediction itself may encourage a growth in the number of Protestant births. Changing patterns in Roman Catholic families also cast doubts upon any predictions in the balance between Roman Catholics and Protestants. And even if a tiny Roman Catholic majority were to replace a tiny Protestant majority it is by no means clear that this would inevitably be accompanied by a demand for a new political settlement, much less by a demand for incorporation in the south.[11]

The formal guarantee of Northern Ireland's position within the United Kingdom is contained in the Ireland Act of 1949, which recognized the independence of the Irish Republic. That Act affirmed that the status of Northern Ireland would not be altered without the consent of its Parliament and a majority of its people, and the guarantee was repeated in the 1973 legislation which attempted to introduce new constitutional arrangements for Ulster.[12] However, despite the guarantee, Ulster's majority community has remained nervous that its wishes may be overridden by Westminster. For however clear the original commitment it is equally clear that no piece of legislation can forever bind Westminster constitutionally. Similarly opinion poll data and the pronouncements of policy-makers suggest that for many citizens in the rest of the United Kingdom the problems of Ulster are ones which might best be resolved within the framework of a united Ireland. The perception that their constitutional position lacks security largely explains the value attributed by Protestant militants, through such organizations as the Orange Order, to the symbolism of parades and marches, even where these are obviously inflammatory to the Catholic population. It also helps to explain why the apparently innocuous suggestion for a Council of Ireland which accompanied the short-lived power-sharing constitution of 1973 aroused Protestant suspicions that the Westminster Parliament was abnegating its commitment to the continuation of Ulster's link with the United Kingdom and trying to edge it towards a united Ireland. Thus the majority population in Ulster has been resistant to attempts to link them with their southern neighbours in any kind of joint organization however innocuous.[13]

It was not merely because of Ulster's constitutional status that its society and politics seemed anomalous to observers from the rest of the United Kingdom. Although Northern Ireland had been created because the majority of the province abhorred the idea of incorporation into a Roman Catholic Ireland, the majority of Protestants in the north initially made little attempt to conciliate those Catholics who remained within the province's boundaries and whose dissatisfaction might threaten Ulster's stability. The 1920 Act had recognized the dilemma of a political system in which a third of the population was likely to look across the border for a government which possessed legitimacy: there was thus an attempt to incorporate into the constitution guarantees of equal treatment before the law for both communities in the north. The Act of 1920 specifically prohibited Stormont from giving a 'preference, a privilege or an advantage' or imposing any 'disability or disadvantage on account of religious belief, or religious or ecclesiastical status'.[14]

Such a prohibition was however largely without force in the climate of mutual suspicion which prevailed between Ulster's religious communities. What has very aptly been called an 'institutionalized caste system' developed, and in that system the Protestant majority dominated the political institutions of Northern Ireland. Power was maintained through a variety of mechanisms such as the gerrymandering of local government boundaries. Such devices would have caused outrage had they been employed in the mainland of Britain; in Ulster they were accepted as part of the distorted political life of the country.

In addition to the political supremacy which they enjoyed through the Ulster Unionist Party, Protestants enjoyed a virtual monopoly of municipal jobs while segregation on religious lines was evident on municipal and private housing estates and in private employment. Indeed it was seen by many employers as a mark of loyalty to employ only Protestant workers and to give preference to members of one's own community.

As in all modern societies where religious issues retain political salience, the character and control of education has always been a controversial question. Education in Ulster remained firmly segregated, although it was seen increasingly as an important contributory factor in the lack of understanding between the communities of Ulster. The divisions caused by segregated education could be attributed to the Roman Catholic community's desire to send their children to schools which are both willing to provide instruction in the Roman Catholic faith and are sectarian in terms of teaching staff. But these divisions have also suited the more militant Protestants, and initially it was the Orange Order and the Protestant churches which took the lead in ensuring that Ulster's schools maintained a distinctive Protestant character.[15]

The virtual insulation of the internal political system of Northern Ireland from Westminster's scrutiny between 1921 and 1969 was perhaps the most eloquent testimony to London's weariness with Irish affairs. The Ulster MPs who came to Westminster were overwhelmingly Ulster Unionist in political complexion, and until 1974 they were formally allied with the Conservative Party. Yet few questions were ever asked about the nature of Ulster's domestic government between 1920 and 1966. Indeed, it was a convention that Northern Irish affairs were not proper subjects for Westminster's attention; from 1923 the Speaker refused to allow parliamentary questions dealing with matters devolved to Stormont. The other aspect of this convention was that Ulster's representatives in the Westminster Parliament tended to be docile, especially since most Ulster politicians with substantial ambitions would pursue them at Stormont rather than at Westminster.

Violence, which has marked so much of Irish history and which forcibly reminded the majority of the population about the complexities of the most remote part of the kingdom, terminated the ignorance in which Whitehall had chosen to live for so long. The 1960s however provided a series of historic anniversaries for all sides of the Irish question and for all parties in Ulster. There occurred in rapid succession the fiftieth anniversaries of the signing of the Ulster Covenant, of the Easter Uprising and of the Battle of the Somme (where an Ulster regiment was destroyed), and these events, as many commentators have noted, provided vivid reminders of the different symbols and allegiances of the various communities in Ulster.[16]

The revival of the cult of Irish nationalism inside and outside Ulster was complemented in the 1960s by a growing determination among the province's Catholic minority to combat the political economic and social discrimination to which it was subject. One dramatic form which this new political mobilization of the minority group took was direct action and mass protest. Through a civil rights campaign organized in 1967 the grievances of Ulster's Catholics were given prominence which they had not had before.[17] The use of demonstrations by the Northern Ireland Civil Rights Association and the experiments with the strategies used in the United States to combat discrimination against blacks proved a catalyst for change in the political structure of Northern Ireland. They also contributed to a cycle of events in which the ordinary political processes were subordinated to direct action and violence. Concessions to the Roman Catholic community were made in the wake of the civil rights campaign, but by so doing Ulster Unionist premier Captain Terence O'Neill alienated substantial sections of his own party. In a pattern which was to recur it was seen that by meeting the demands of the minority group he had lost his own constituency and was forced to resign. Ulster Unionism had been held together by the need to support Stormont and the status quo; as events began to shatter that stability the Unionist Party found itself increasingly divided over policy and tactics.

The activism of the civil rights movement had an impact on all sides of Ulster politics. It seemed to provide an alternative to the old-fashioned policies and attitudes of the Nationalist Party which had previously claimed the allegiance of the Roman Catholics in Ulster. The decline of support for the Nationalist Party, which had abdicated its role as a champion of Catholic grievances in the social and economic sphere because of its overriding concern with the issue of reunification, cleared the way for the formation of a new party based on the changing demands of the Catholic community inside Ulster. In the 1960s this community was less interested in romantic visions of an Ireland without a border than in economic opportunities and political rights. As the Northern Irish election of 1969 indicated splits in the ranks of Ulster Unionists there was an additional stimulus to opposition parties at Stormont to try for some kind of a realignment. The formation of the Social Democratic and Labour Party in 1970 was the first attempt to transcend the old and rather sterile pattern of Ulster politics in which all other issues were subordinated to nationalist concerns.[18] Initially the party claimed the loyalty of a large portion of the Catholic population. Since 1979 however there has been increasing electoral support for more extreme parties; and the decision by Sinn Fein in 1981 to contest all elections has meant that the Catholic vote is now divided.

It is possible that a political realignment could have emerged from the events of 1966–9. Unfortunately at the same time as the Catholic community was exploring political alternatives to nationalism the key question in Ulster's life was becoming how far Stormont could handle the growth of violence. The turning point here was perhaps the civil rights demonstration in Londonderry in October 1968, which led to a spiral of violence and ultimately to the prohibition of similar demonstrations. By August 1969 it was clear that the Ulster-controlled police force alone could not contain it, and the British army was sent in to restore order, especially in Belfast and Londonderry where inter-communal conflict had escalated during the season of marches and community demonstrations of solidarity and had prompted the erection of barricades in the cities. In addition it became clear that sections of the Roman Catholic and Protestant communities were arming themselves. Troops had been despatched

335

to Northern Ireland earlier in 1969; but with the heightened conflict in the summer the government in London felt that it was imperative to transfer responsibility for security to the GOC (NI) – a decision which thereby transferred a key aspect of Ulster's government back to London. Despite this move the containment of terrorism and the control of violence continued to elude the government, and it is this aspect of Northern Irish politics which more than any other separates Ulster from the mainland.

The record of violence in Ireland is a stark one, and the violence has had serious repercussions for the conduct of politics both in the Irish Republic and in the rest of the United Kingdom. In 1983 the New Ireland Forum estimated that some 2,300 people had been killed in the north since 1969 and that a further 24,000 had been injured or maimed. Altogether the same survey estimated that the north had seen some 43,000 separate incidents of shootings, bombings and arson, and it commented that there was hardly a family that had not been touched to some degree by death, injury or intimidation.[19]

Of the persons affected by the rise in violence in the north it seems clear that the Catholic population has suffered rather more than the Protestant community, with a total of 1,043 fatalities over the period 1969–83 as compared to a Protestant figure of 864 for the same period. However, if one takes the yearly trend it seems equally clear that from 1977 the number of Protestant fatalities has been greater than that of Catholics. Moreover an analysis of the agencies responsible for the killings shows that by far the most significant perpetrators of violence are the Republican paramilitary groups, who over the period 1969–83 were responsible for 1,264 deaths by comparison with 613 attributable to Loyalist paramilitary groups. The security forces were responsible for a further 264 deaths and another 163 deaths remained non-classified.

The spill-over of this violence into the Republic and into the mainland of Britain was also dramatic: since 1972 some forty-five people have been killed in terrorist explosions in the south and eight members of the *Garda Siochana* (the Irish police force) have been murdered. Three hundred and seventy members of the British army had been killed, and on the mainland of the United Kingdom seventy-two people had been killed since 1973.

Apart from the direct impact of this scale of violence – which is inevitably felt all the more keenly in a society the size of Ireland's – there are several indirect costs. It has been estimated that 60,000 people in Belfast have moved their place of residence as a result of the violence.[20] Emigration within the United Kingdom and from Northern Ireland to the Republic has accelerated and there has been a decline in the rate of growth of Ulster's population from 0.8 to 0.2 per cent. Several commentators have also pointed to the tendency of the more highly skilled and educated members of the Northern Irish population to leave the province, especially if they have been educated outside Northern Ireland.

The financial cost of attempting to contain the violence is also extremely heavy. Although precise figures for security services and the administration of justice in the north are difficult to calculate, it has been estimated that the sums devoted to law and order, protective services and the courts rose from £15 million in 1969–70 to £369 million
in 1982–3. To these figures must be added the costs of keeping the army in Northern Ireland, which rose from £2 million in 1969–70 to £143 million in 1982–3. Less obvious costs of the troubles include the loss of revenue to tourism which has occurred as a result of the image of violence that the whole of Ireland now projects; the loss of job opportunities in the north due to the unwillingness of investors to risk capital in an area where political instability threatens property; and the distortion of the economy which has occurred as a result of diverting so many resources into public sector activities, especially security.[21] Simple numbers alone cannot convey the manner in which violence has become a more central part of Ulster life. Initially the disorders involved relatively amateurish weapons – stones and home-made petrol bombs. However by 1971 guns became increasingly evident in the violence and it became apparent that the situation was viewed by many in Ulster and in the Republic as an opportunity to renew the struggle for a united Ireland. Indeed in 1970 the Irish Republic witnessed a spectacular political scandal as several ministers were put on trial for gun-running.[22]

The major force in escalating the violence was the Provisional IRA (PIRA), a splinter group from the old Irish Republican Army.[23] The splinter group had broken away from the official broadly Marxist IRA because it thought that more militant policies should be pursued, including a campaign of urban guerrilla warfare. As the number of bombings increased, the Ulster premier – by then Brian Faulkner – persuaded the British government to introduce internment without trial, which in turn exacerbated the situation. The viciousness of the IRA's reaction and the solidarity of its support among the Catholic population stunned both the Stormont government and Westminster and underlined the extent to which Stormont could no longer control the situation.[24]

The immediate reasons for the assumption of direct rule, as has been mentioned, related to the control of the security forces. British troops had originally been sent into Northern Ireland to separate the paramilitary forces on both sides; but as the violence escalated and the troops became the objects of attack from both sides it became anomalous for British soldiers to be seen implementing a security policy framed by Stormont. The British government's demand for sole responsibility for security matters was something which the Northern Irish government could not accept, and Brian Faulkner resigned. The Stormont Parliament was suspended and direct rule from London introduced. Under the Northern Ireland (Temporary Provisions) Act 1972 a secretary of state for Northern Ireland was appointed and a new Northern Ireland Office took over the functions previously exercised by Stormont and by the Northern Ireland Civil Service as well as the responsibilities previously discharged by the small Northern Ireland section of the Home Office.[25]

The Northern Ireland Office is separate from the functional Northern Ireland departments and now has four divisions in London and eleven in Belfast. The London divisions of the Office are responsible for liaison between other Whitehall departments (especially the Treasury) and the Northern Ireland departments. The Belfast Departments of the NIO deal with the administration of 'reserved and excepted matters' including the politically sensitive question of security.

At the level of routine administration there is now a dual structure of Civil Service control. With the imposition of direct rule the permanent secretary to the newly created Northern Ireland Office became the head of the Northern Ireland Civil Service. However there was of course an existing permanent secretary in Belfast who enjoyed that title. He became the second permanent secretary, retaining an interest, albeit a subordinate one, in such matters as recruitment and the machinery of government.

The suspension of Stormont was seen by many not as a temporary solution but as an admission that a form of government that had so patently failed to create a consensus behind it had to be replaced. Yet it seems clear in retrospect that a large number of the measures adopted in the wake of direct rule – including much of the legislation associated with the security situation – were adopted as short-term expedients. And it seems equally clear that many of the officials and politicians transferred to the Northern Ireland Office, frequently on secondment, also saw their task as one which would last only so long as it took to devise an acceptable way of reintroducing devolved government.

The prorogation of Stormont was infinitely easier than the search for a form of government to replace the devolved institutions of the north. It was perhaps ironic that it was the Conservative Party –

traditionally the Ulster Unionists' ally, and historically the party which had urged Ulster to resist incorporation into the south – which was faced with the arduous task of constructing a new system. The British government desired to return the responsibility for Northern Ireland's affairs to Ulster politicians without blatantly abnegating responsibility for events there – a responsibility which was by 1972 creating complications both with the Irish Republic and with other countries.

The solution suggested at first was a new Northern Irish assembly elected by proportional representation, with an executive which would exercise many domestic but no security responsibilities. This executive was to differ from the old one, however, in that its composition would be based on 'power-sharing'. In other words it had to include members of the minority Catholic population, so that devolved government could be seen to represent all groups in Northern Ireland. The use of the single transferable vote would it was hoped produce a majority for moderate parties. Perhaps the most controversial element in the proposals was the suggestion that a Council of Ireland should be formed to take account of the 'Irish dimension' of Ulster's affairs and to facilitate discussion between Dublin, Belfast and London. Provision for a Council of Ireland had been written into the legislation of 1920 as a way of transcending partition; but it had rapidly become a dead letter as partition assumed a permanent rather than a temporary status. Although it had always been clear that Irish governments had an intimate interest in what was happening across the border and were themselves divided about the proper response to the return of violence in the north, United Kingdom governments had hitherto resisted suggestions that Ulster's problems were anything other than a matter of internal British politics. And for their part the Protestants of Ulster looked with suspicion on any device designed to integrate them with the south, however innocent such a device might appear on the surface.

The proposals enacted in the Constitution Act of 1973 split the majority party in Northern Ireland.[26] Elections to the new Assembly showed that Brian Faulkner's moderate and pro-power-sharing Unionists had won a slightly smaller portion of the vote – 26.5 per cent – than had the hard-line coalition of Loyalists, who took 35.4 per cent of the vote. The latter group wanted a return to the old-style Stormont and would have nothing to do with power-sharing. However with the support of the constitutional nationalist and Roman Catholic oriented SDLP and the non-sectarian Alliance Party (and one Labour MP) a coalition government was formed with a majority of one in the Assembly.

Pressure on Faulkner from his own Unionist Party was nevertheless strong enough to cause him to resign the leadership of the Official Unionists only four days after the formation of the executive based on this fragile coalition, although Faulkner did not resign as leader of the executive. The refusal of the Unionists to support the power-sharing executive effectively doomed the whole constitutional edifice; although the executive lasted a full four months it was essentially without political roots in the majority community. The triumph of the extreme Loyalist faction at the February 1974 general election was taken as further evidence of the isolation of Faulkner's moderate position, and the return of Harold Wilson to Downing Street meant that there was no one in London committed to the scheme. The experiment was finally terminated when the Ulster Workers' Council, a hard-line Protestant organization, staged a general strike and forced Westminster to resume direct responsibility for Northern Irish affairs.

As a result of the strike it was recognized that no solution would work which could not elicit the consent of the major political forces in Northern Ireland. Thus the next initiative from London was to put the matter before the Northern Ireland Constitutional Convention of 1975–6; after long deliberation this merely revealed the political impasse in the province. No solution was likely to be acceptable to Westminster which did not provide adequate guarantees of equality for the Catholic community, including some form of participation in government; no settlement would enjoy Protestant support unless it allowed the majority community to control the government of the province.

The advent of another Conservative government in 1979 changed the situation once more. The first appointee as secretary of state under Mrs Thatcher – Humphrey Atkins – called a conference on future developments, but the Official Unionists did not attend it. In 1980 the prime minister had to announce that no agreement was forthcoming on the formation of a devolved executive. Atkin's successor, James Prior, after abandoning a scheme for a Northern Ireland Council, decided to have another attempt at securing agreement. Proposals for an Assembly which could take increasingly significant powers from Westminster were outlined in April 1982 in a white paper, *Northern Ireland: A Framework for Devolution*. Although the mood in the province had hardened and the attitude of the Irish Republic – which had earlier appeared conciliatory – was negative in relation to these proposals, Prior decided to press ahead with his scheme. The core of it was a new Northern Ireland Assembly elected by proportional representation. At first its powers were to be limited to scrutiny, but it was envisaged that if cross-party (or effectively cross-community) consent were achieved, the responsibilities and autonomy of the Assembly might be increased. This was the concept of so-called 'rolling devolution'.[27]

The idea found no favour with the SDLP – the constitutional nationalists. They boycotted the Assembly partly because their leader, John Hume, was sceptical of the mileage that could be made from further constitutional initiatives in the absence of any willingness on the part of the Unionist Party to share power with Roman Catholics. Increasingly that boycott was reinforced by the awareness that the SDLP had to compete with Sinn Fein for the Roman Catholic vote, and hence was fearful of any accusation that it had sold out to the British government. However, the DUP, the Alliance (a non-sectarian party) and a large section of the Official Unionists took their seats in the Assembly, which held its first meeting in November 1982.

The major work of the Assembly has been performed through six scrutiny committees each of which monitors specific areas of administration covered by the Northern Ireland Office. In addition there are some non-statutory committees which can discuss other areas of Northern Irish policy – most notably security.

In 1984 a different initiative was attempted when a body called the New Ireland Forum, which represented all the major constitutional and democratic parties of the Republic and the SDLP from Northern Ireland, came together to try to find new solutions to the problems of the north within the context of Ireland as a whole. Although their report (which examined a variety of constitutional mechanisms for achieving integration, including federalism and joint sovereignty) was hardly persuasive for the majority of Ulster Protestants, it was seen as indicative of a new mood in relation to the way the problems of Ulster were handled between the government of Ireland and the United Kingdom.[28]

The Forum initiative came at a time when many of the parties within Northern Ireland were considering their own proposals for change. Thus within a short period in 1984 the Official Unionists, the Democratic Unionist Party and the Alliance Party brought forward their own suggestions for achieving political progress in the province. Although these proposals seemed to indicate a change of mood it seemed that the British government was wary of attempting any new political initiatives, even though many thought that a policy of caution had its own dangers.

In the absence of any political solution or new political initiative, attention has to be given to the very real difficulties of administering a part of the United Kingdom which has a long tradition of self-government and a set of problems peculiar to itself. Of these by far the most important is security; but there are important differences in the more routine aspects of law and order as well as the different arrangements for handling local government matters. In addition the growth of the civil rights movement over the 1960s and the increasing concern to see equal and even-handed treatment for all citizens in Ulster has led to the establishment of new complaints institutions, including a Northern Ireland Complaints Commissioner and a Parliamentary Commissioner for Administration (whose jurisdiction is rather wider than that of his Westminster counterpart). A Housing Commission and a Fair Employment Agency were also established.

The problem of security in Northern Ireland is exacerbated by the fact that many nationalists find it difficult to identify with either the police or the security forces. The extent of the Roman Catholic community's alienation from the security forces is a matter of debate, and Protestants have tended to deny that attitudes towards law and order constitute what the New Ireland Forum called the 'symptoms of the crisis in Northern Ireland'.[29] Nevertheless the extraordinary measures taken to defend the population against terrorism are not merely unusual in a democratic society; they may be contributing factors to a climate of resentment and distrust. Mention has already been made of the Emergency Powers (Temporary Provisions) Act, which, like some other measures necessitated by the Ulster situation, has caused repercussions on the mainland. In Northern Ireland a number of crimes are heard in so-called Diplock Courts, which are courts distinguished by the absence of the normal safeguard of a jury. The logic of this is that in a divided society it is difficult to secure objective treatment of crimes, and in addition there is of course the problem of reprisals against jury members who convict terrorists.[30]

The key elements of the Ulster situation thus remain a continuing security problem, a stagnant economy and a political subsystem in which the major forces view the maintenance of direct rule as undesirable, but less undesirable than many other options. In the absence of any willingness by the parties to see movement which might threaten their own positions, it seems likely that direct rule will remain. Thus the social and political divisions of Northern Ireland seem calculated to deny Northern Ireland not merely any extensive form of devolved government but even some of the most rudimentary forms of local accountability which exist elsewhere in the United Kingdom.

Wales

It was somewhat ironic that just as events were leading to the suspension of devolved government in Northern Ireland, two other areas of the United Kingdom experienced a resurgence of nationalism and advanced claims for separate treatment from the rest of the United Kingdom. The different arrangements envisaged in the Scotland and Wales Act of 1978 could be justified to some extent by their different histories and cultural complexities, although to many observers the whole devolution episode exhibited a prime example of the politics of 'muddling through'. Wales, which is in many respects the part of the United Kingdom most assimilated to England in terms of administrative practice, was first annexed to England in 1282, when Edward I conquered the country. The formal consolidation of that conquest was the work of the early Tudors, Henry VII and Henry VIII. The integration of Wales into the Tudor state was achieved by two major acts of 1536 and 1542 – measures which also marked the beginnings of long conflict between the Welsh and the English cultures. The assertion of English superiority was enshrined in the provision in these Acts which forbade the use of the Welsh language in the administration.

Between the Tudor period and the onset of the Industrial Revolution the relationship between Wales and England was a relatively harmonious one. The subordination of the principality to the United Kingdom was accepted, and it was only with the changes engendered by industrial development that there emerged a new sense of a distinct Welsh identity. Yet the Industrial Revolution not only marked the beginning of the new period of Welsh consciousness but also caused new divisions within Welsh society. These internal divisions contributed at least as much to the tensions occasioned by the devolution proposals as any differences of sentiment, culture and politics between Wales and England.

The Industrial Revolution produced two distinct patterns of politics and two cultures in Wales. On the one hand there existed the rural and radical Nonconformist Wales which was for so long a bastion of the Liberal Party. Its exponents became increasingly conscious of the need to preserve a distinct Welsh identity as expressed above all in the survival of the Welsh language, which was still the mother tongue of a substantial portion of the inhabitants of the country. On the other hand the Industrial Revolution brought about a dilution of the Welsh identity by precipitating massive emigration from England into South Wales, where the coalmines and the steel industry needed workers. Here the bonds of class fortified the solidarity of common allegiances; and those sentiments ultimately found their expression not through nationalism but through the Labour Party. It is of course all too easy to oversimplify very complex patterns of interests and attitudes; however, the division between industrial and rural Wales (which broadly corresponds to the divisions between the south of Wales, where most mining and industry is concentrated, and the mid and north Welsh farming communities) does seem to correspond to a real division in political outlook.[31]

The industrialization of the southern part of Wales reinforced the fears of some Welshmen that their culture, especially their language, would be completely eradicated by the spread of English, which was the language of modernization. The Act of 1870 which introduced compulsory education exacerbated these fears, for though it was ironically the product of the Liberal Party, which was increasingly to be sensitive to Celtic interests, English was established as the medium for teaching in all state schools. Indeed it was only in 1889 that Welsh was allowed to be taught at all in grant-aided schools even as a foreign language, so detrimental to modern educational achievement was the use of the native language considered.

The challenge to the survival of Welsh stimulated its supporters to organize in its defence, and opinion began to change so that by the early years of the twentieth century, partly as a result of pressures from the Welsh Language Society (founded in 1885), there was a much stronger awareness of the need at all levels of the educational system for facilities for the study of Welsh language and literature. After the return of the Liberal government in 1906 a reorganization of the Board of Education recognized the cultural autonomy of Wales by the formation within it of a specialized Welsh Department whose secretary had direct access to the minister. Also in 1907, charters were granted to the National Library of Wales and the National Museum of Wales which, together with the University of Wales, were thereafter to play an important part in the preservation of Welsh traditions and cultural identity.

Today the Welsh language seems to have staged something of a comeback: in 1978 a survey of Welsh primary schools revealed that overall 12.8 per cent of all pupils in primary schools were fluent in Welsh, although there was great variation between the northern and western counties of Gwynedd and Dyfed – where 63 and 33 per cent of primary school pupils were fluent – and the southern counties of mid-Glamorgan, South Glamorgan and Gwent, where the proportions were 5, 3 and 0.3 per cent respectively. By 1984 one official source estimated that some 19 per cent of the population spoke Welsh.

In addition, since the Welsh Language Act of 1967 Welsh has enjoyed equality of status with English in such matters as legal proceedings and official documents.[32]

Resentment about the threats to Welsh cultural identity has fuelled political nationalism since the late nineteenth century, although its support has been uneven. The years between 1870 and 1920 saw substantial concessions to Welsh political sentiments: the Liberal Party which was for so long the vehicle of the United Kingdom's special sectional interests succeeded in disestablishing the Church of Wales – a minority Church in a country where the majority of the population subscribed to varieties of Nonconformity. Special legislation was also introduced to ban the sale of alcoholic drink on the sabbath. (Sunday opening of public houses in Wales is still immensely varied, for areas decide individually by periodic referendums whether they wish to be 'wet' or 'dry'. The number opting for prohibition has receded recently; the areas which favour closure on Sundays are the predominantly rural areas of the north and west.) However the decline of the Liberal Party after the first world war meant that Wales no longer had a champion at Westminster to advance its special concerns. The onset of the depression – whose impact was particularly heavy upon the areas of Wales dependent on basic industries – then ensured that for a long period the politics of Wales were the politics of the Labour Party and that they were directed towards securing special economic treatment for the distressed areas.

Plaid Cymru, which had been founded in 1925 primarily as an instrument of cultural promotion, became an explicitly political organization in 1932 when it adopted the policy of self-government for Wales. Yet self-government was still seen as a means to an end – the protection of the language and the culture which formed the basis of the nation. Because the numbers speaking Welsh were and still are a minority of the Welsh population as a whole, and because the cause was presented in a manner which reflected the perspectives of the movement's initial activists – teachers, lecturers and educationalists – the mass appeal of the party remained small and it excited suspicion among those who could not speak Welsh. In 1951 the Plaid put up only four candidates at the general election and obtained only 10,920 votes. Although its votes between 1951 and 1966 showed a steady increase this growth was more the result of the Plaid's contesting additional seats than of any substantial increase in popularity.

The by-election victory of Gwynfor Evans, the president of Plaid Cymru, at Carmarthen in July 1966 seemed to suggest that a breakthrough might be imminent. Personal factors played a part in the victory in what had been Lady Megan Lloyd George's seat as a Labour member; but the result was interpreted as more than a personal triumph for Evans. In subsequent by-elections in very different parts of the country – in Rhondda West and Caerphilly – Plaid Cymru's vote was quadrupled. As one commentator put it: 'the moral for the Labour Party in Wales was clear. Labour's hegemony in the Welsh valleys had ceased to be automatic. Commitments to socialism had become blurred in the face of pit closures, economic insecurity and high rates of unemployment under a Labour government.'[33] However at the general election of 1970 Plaid Cymru won no parliamentary seats at all. At the two general elections of 1974 the desertion of the major parties by a substantial portion of the electorate resulted in two seats being won in February and three in October, but Britain's electoral system allowed Plaid Cymru to retain only two seats in 1979 when Wales like the rest of the country swung heavily towards the Conservative Party. In 1983 of Wales's 38 MPs, twenty were Labour, fourteen were Conservatives and Plaid Cymru and the Welsh Liberal Party had two each.

It can thus be seen that the cultural element in Welsh nationalism is one factor which severely limits its appeal; those who cannot speak Welsh feel that they would become second-class citizens if Wales were given a great deal more governmental autonomy. This fear explains the massive rejection by the Welsh of the devolution proposals in 1979.

Although by comparison with Scotland and Northern Ireland the administrative arrangements for Wales exhibit less difference from those of England, two features should be noted. First, a Welsh Office was created in 1964 when Labour was returned to power. It took over responsibilities for local government, housing planning and a range of other functions which have been augmented from time to time. Richard Crossman at the time declared it an 'idiotic creation' but its staff, although few initially by comparison with the Scottish Office, have grown in number.[34]

Second, a forum for the discussion in Parliament of specialized Welsh measures and problems was established in 1960 as the Welsh Grand Committee. It considers bills relating exclusively to Wales and any other matters referred to it by the House of Commons. It consists of all MPs with Welsh constituencies together with no more than five other MPs nominated by the Committee of Selection for each topic to be considered. There is in addition a Welsh Select Committee which, like its Scottish counterpart, has a relatively high attendance rate and which might develop as a focus of activity relating to Wales, perhaps by operating – if this change is allowed – through subject sub-committees.

Scotland

Unlike Wales, which was first subdued by conquest in the thirteenth century, Scotland was never permanently incorporated into the United Kingdom by force of arms. In 1603 the succesion of James I to the throne of England united the Crowns of England and Scotland. However, the union was only a personal one and Scotland retained its own political and legal system and its own Church. The establishment of a common Parliament occurred as a result of the Treaty of Union of 1706, whereby the Scots gained political representation at Westminster but were guaranteed that certain features of their administrative systems would remain inviolate: the Church of Scotland, which is Presbyterian, would survive as the established Church, along with the Scottish legal system; in addition Scotland has maintained a distinct educational system, and a different system of local government from that obtaining in England and Wales.

The Scottish legal system is perhaps the single most important factor explaining why Scotland has been accorded separate governmental treatment since the Act of Union. Unlike the English legal system, the Scottish system has depended more on the principles of continental jurisprudence derived from Roman law than on indigenous common law. Consequently, whenever a piece of legislation has been intended to apply to Scotland as well as to England and Wales this has had to be achieved either by a separate appendix to the measure or by a distinct Act for Scotland. There is therefore some variation in the law between Scotland on the one hand and England and Wales on the other.

The growth of Welsh national sentiment and the sporadic success of Plaid Cymru have been fuelled by cultural factors, especially a fear of Anglicization; but this is much less true of Scotland. This is partly because certain Scottish institutions are already protected and recognized by London as deserving special consideration and partly because although a very tiny minority of the Scottish do have a distinctive language, the vast majority speak English.

The particular political and administrative arrangements in existence in the 1960s and 1970s were really of nineteenth-century origin, although inevitably the twentieth-century expansion of government had had its impact upon them, as it has upon so much else in the British administrative structure. Immediately after the Acts of Union, Scotland had a secretary of state to supervise and represent its interests in the British Parliament. But the abortive rebellion of 1745 put an end to that arrangement, and Scotland's special needs thereafter were largely the responsibility of the lord advocate, a law officer. The growth of governmental activity made the separation of administrative from legal functions necessary, and in 1885 it was decided that the lord advocate should concentrate primarily on his responsibilities for legal matters while administrative responsibilities in Scotland should be undertaken by a secretary for Scotland and a separate Scottish Office.

The revival of the office of Scottish secretary could perhaps be seen as one of the first steps along the road to administrative devolution. Already at the local level, as new functions were discharged by government in the course of the nineteenth century, a variety of specialized boards and *ad hoc* authorities had been created to meet Scotland's needs. Since 1892 the Scottish secretary had been a regular member of peacetime cabinets; and the status of the office was enhanced in 1926 when the secretary for Scotland was made a full secretary of state.

The Scottish Office was moved to St Andrew's House in Edinburgh in 1939. Although in many ways the structure of the Office remains what it was then – a loosely coordinated structure of functional departments – there have been certain changes since 1939. In 1960 as a result of a review of the distribution of functions among the existing departments, several changes were made. Fisheries for example was transferred from the Scottish Home Department to Agriculture, and responsibility for child care was transferred from the Health Department to Education. Then, following an inquiry by the Scottish Council into the economy, a Scottish Development Department was created in 1962 – an innovation that anticipated the creation of the Department of the Environment a decade earlier. (A separate Development Board for the Highlands and Islands was added in 1965).[35]

The task of a secretary of state with multiple functional responsibilities, as occurs in the Scottish, Welsh and Northern Ireland Offices, is administratively difficult. Such a secretary of state is also in a politically delicate position. The Scottish Office for example has responsibilities equivalent to those of nine English departments. Such responsibilities demand a range of expertise on the part of the secretary of state greater than that even of a minister in a super-department. In addition to his statutory responsibilities, the secretary of state has acquired the role of spokesman for Scottish interests, regardless of whether policy-making authority for the subjects in question has been devolved or not.

Such a role can create conflicts. If a secretary of state's brief is for his region as a whole – e.g. Scotland (or Northern Ireland or Wales) – and if he presses his case successfully in cabinet, regions of England may be unjustly treated. And there further arises the question of the extent to which a secretary of state for a particular region should see his primary responsibility as being in fact to promote sectional interests rather than the wider interests of the United Kingdom. Such questions may seem academic, but unlike a minister pushing the claims of a department such as Defence, a secretary of state for Scotland has a well defined electorate to whom he feels accountable.

In addition to the existence of separate administrative machinery for Scottish affairs, Westminster had even before the 1960s developed institutional arrangements to take account of the peculiarities of Scottish legislation. The Scottish Grand Committee – which is the oldest of the specialized committees dealing with Scottish affairs – was made permanent in 1907 and consists of all MPs sitting for Scottish constituencies together with enough English representatives to bring the balance of party strength into line with that of the House of Commons as a whole. In an experiment which has survived despite some criticism, the Scottish Grand Committee can hold meetings in Edinburgh, and when it does so it meets in the building refurnished for use by the projected Scottish Assembly under the devolution legislation. Also there have been experiments with smaller standing committees for the discussion of bills deemed insufficiently important for the Scottish Grand Committee, and in the post-1966 period a Select Committee on Scottish Affairs was established. However, this committee seems to have lost some of its clout and one commentator in 1982 described it as having slipped from 'its once proud position as a lethal weapon for the opposition and for backbenchers of both sides to the status of a rather ineffectual debating society'.[36]

The challenge of nationalism increased the amount of time which all Scottish MPs have felt obliged to devote to purely Scottish business within the House of Commons. Thus the period since 1964 has seen both the development of specialized parliamentary mechanisms for coping with Scottish matters and a growing tendency for Scottish MPs to concentrate in debate and in Question Time on advertising their concern for Scottish problems. Perhaps this *de facto* specialization has isolated them to some extent from the major business of the House of Commons as a whole; certainly Scottish MPs also bear a heavy burden in terms of commuting between their constituencies and London.

Local government in Scotland was reformed in 1973 and the new arrangements became fully operational in 1975 in accordance with the recommendations of the Wheatley Commission.[37] Scotland was divided into nine regions and fifty-three districts, including the cities of Edinburgh, Aberdeen, Dundee and Glasgow. The remote areas of the Orkneys and Shetlands and the Western Isles were given single-tier authorities for most purposes but, as between regions and districts, functions were divided. The regions were made responsible for major planning and related services including transport and water, as well as education and other local authority functions. The districts were made responsible for housing, local planning, building control and libraries except in the Highland, Dumfries, Galloway and Borders regions, where these functions were to be exercised by regional authorities. Certain adjustments were made to the distribution of responsibilities between the tiers in 1982 when the Local Government and Planning (Scotland) Act was passed.[38] It is also important to note that the spending plans of Lothian council provided an early test of the Conservative government's determination to bring local authority expenditure under control.[39]

One of the arguments which were used against the devolution proposals of the late 1970s was that if a Scottish Assembly had been added to the structure of local authorities, Scotland would have been over-governed, especially in those areas where population was sparse. (The population of the regions varies from 99,000 in the Borders region to 2.6 million in Strathclyde – a figure which constitutes half the total.) Yet although the government in 1978 intended to transfer local authority functions to the Assembly's overall control it did not envisage any immediate alteration of the local government structure but simply proposed to leave that for future consideration by a Scottish Assembly.

THE ROYAL COMMISSION ON THE CONSTITUTION AND THE DEVOLUTION DEBATE

The establishment of a Royal Commission on the Constitution was announced in 1968.[40] It was instructed to examine:

the present functions of the central legislature and government in relation to the several countries, nations and regions of the United Kingdom; to consider, having regard to the developments in local government organization and in the administrative and other relationships between the various parts of the United Kingdom and to the interests of prosperity and good government under the Crown, whether any changes are desirable in those functions or otherwise in present constitutional and economic relationships; to consider also whether any changes are desirable in the constitutional and economic relationships between the United Kingdom and the Channel Islands and the Isle of Man . . .

The Royal Commission sat for four years; when it reported it produced both a minority memorandum and a majority report, which reflected the disagreements about the nature of the problems before the Commission. The minority memorandum rejected the belief that there could be real divisions over policies between the centre of the United Kingdom and its peripheral areas. Instead of devising solutions to what it saw as the limited problems of Scottish and Welsh nationalism, the minority memorandum advocated reform of the regional or intermediate tier of government – a course which it was thought would be quite compatible with increased economic planning and the equal provision of services throughout the United Kingdom. As the authors of the minority memorandum pointed out, there was no need to create that intermediate tier of government, since it already existed in the plethora of authorities which had been created as local authority functions were transferred upwards and as central government functions were devolved. If there could be rationalization of what the memorandum called the 'jungle of boundaries', and if the intermediate tier could be made democratically accountable, the minority thought the whole British system of government would be brought closer to the people who were subject to it.

The essence of the minority scheme was therefore the creation of seven democratically elected regional assemblies and regional governments – five for England and one each for Wales and Scotland. If they were elected as recommended by proportional representation it was envisaged that such assemblies could exercise a wide range of powers then discharged by *ad hoc* authorities and by central government. Each regional government, it was suggested, should have its own civil service and its own ombudsman to deal with complaints against the administration. These changes in governmental structure were to be complemented by other reforms aimed at rejuvenating the democratic system as a whole, including the selection of parliamentary candidates through primaries. The memorandum of dissent thus saw its proposals as part of a broad process of adjusting the British constitution to new demands, although it recognized that this process would have to be implemented in stages.

The majority of the Commission took a different line. Instead of grappling with a host of interconnected constitutional issues they concentrated their attention on the governments of Scotland and Wales, where the Commission recognized that 'the added dimension of national feeling' had complemented general dissatisfaction with government in the United Kingdom during the 1960s. However dramatic the upsurge of nationalist sentiment might seem, the Commission nevertheless based its recommendations on the assumption that there was not a majority for independence in either Scotland or Wales and that their populations wanted to balance autonomy with the tangible economic benefits which London provided in the form of subsidies. The Commission therefore identified three possible approaches to the problem of Scottish and Welsh government. First, complete separation could be implemented. This the Commission roundly rejected, since it did not believe the political demand for independence existed. Second, the federal solution could be introduced. Third, some form of devolution could be attempted to try to reconcile the essential unity of the United Kingdom with the demands for greater self-government for specific parts of the country. Devolution – the preferred solution of the Commission – was defined as 'the delegation of central government powers which would leave over-riding control in the hands of Parliament' and which in 'its more advanced forms' would involve the 'exercise of powers by persons or bodies who, although acting on authority delegated by Parliament, would not be directly answerable to it or to central government for their actions'.

Unfortunately from the point of view of the authors of the majority report, although they were united on the merits of devolution as a halfway house between centralism and federalism, they could not agree on the form of devolution to be adopted, nor on whether the same form should be applied to Scotland, to Wales and to the English regions.

The Kilbrandon Commission's proposals were virtually ignored by the Heath government, but the general election of February 1974 gave a new urgency to the subject. With no single party getting an overall majority the seven SNP and two Plaid Cymru MPs could play a significant part in deciding what legislation would pass in the House of Commons. Yet the development of the minority Labour government's own legislative proposals on the issue of devolution was slow – partly because it wanted to see whether the number of SNP MPs and the 21.9 per cent of the Scottish vote obtained in February 1974 would be maintained, and whether it indicated a permanent shift away from the major parties rather than a freak protest vote. The different Kilbrandon schemes were accordingly published for general discussion, although as it turned out the response by the general public was 'disappointing' and the organizations which did respond were themselves deeply divided.[41]

The October 1974 general election did not produce the expected overall Labour majority which would have enabled the government to control the course of the devolution debate. Indeed the number of SNP MPs rose to eleven and the Plaid Cymru contingent rose to three, which at that time suggested a permanent challenge to the existing constitutional arrangements. The government accordingly published in November 1975 its white paper *Our Changing Democracy*, with an outline of the powers and responsibilities which would be exercised by the Assemblies for Scotland and for Wales.[42] Even here, however, the government had to concede a greater degree of autonomy than originally envisaged by reducing the reserve powers of the secretary of state on policy grounds; by transferring decisions about the legal power of any bill proposed by the Scottish Assembly to a neutral body, the Judicial Committee of the Privy Council; and by conceding that Acts of a Scottish legislature would of necessity be open to challenge in the courts once they had received the Royal Assent.[43] A Scotland and Wales Bill introduced into Parliament in 1976 met heavy opposition, and eventually had to be withdrawn in early 1977 when a cross-party alliance defeated a guillotine (i.e. timetabling) motion. The bill was thereafter divided into two.

THE SCOTLAND AND WALES ACTS OF 1978

After a difficult parliamentary passage, the Scotland and Wales Acts reached the statute book in July 1978. Concessions made to their opponents laid an obligation on the government not merely to hold referendums in both countries but to lay orders for the Acts' annulment before the House of Commons if the 'yes' vote reached less than 40 per cent of the total electorate.

In the Scotland Act provision was made for a directly elected fixed-term Assembly with wide legislative competence, although international affairs, taxation and economic policy were not to be devolved. The model on which the Scottish Assembly was to operate was that of Westminster. Thus provision was made for the appointment of an executive, one of whose members was to be known as the first secretary, but who in the period of debate about the legislation was inevitably spoken of as the Scottish prime minister. The first secretary's task was to be to advise the secretary of state for Scotland on the appointment of the other Scottish secretaries who would together in effect form a Scottish cabinet; no one except law officers was to be allowed to hold office without being elected to the Scottish Assembly. It was intended that the Scottish executive would exercise all executive powers concerning devolved matters and would have power to make subordinate legislation. The Assembly was not given power to levy its own taxation and its funds were to come from a block grant from the Exchequer, to be negotiated on a four-year basis. The absence of a general taxing power underlined the determination of London to keep overall responsibility for the management of the economy; but it raised the question of whether failures of policy or administration in Scotland might not be excused on the grounds of an inadequate grant, as well as the spectre of wranglings between London and Edinburgh over its level.

The Wales Act of 1978 was a much less far-reaching measure than the Scotland Act. The principal distinction between the proposed Welsh and Scottish Assemblies was that whereas the Scottish Assembly had full legislative competence the Welsh Assembly was only to be able to undertake functions hitherto exercised by ministers in the field of local government, housing, education, health, social services, planning and land use. The powers of the Assembly as envisaged in the Act would be exercised not by a single executive, as in Scotland, but by mandatory committees to deal with subjects devolved to it, although the Assembly might create other committees as well if it so desired. Each committee was to have a chairman and a leader – who would presumably also have been a member of the majority party in the Assembly – and the leader of the committee could be known as the executive member. The Assembly was also to appoint an executive committee consisting of all the leaders of the various subject committees. The secretary of state for Wales retained a great deal of control of devolved matters, both because of the absence of independent legislative powers for the Assembly and because he had general powers to revoke an instrument made by the Welsh Assembly if he thought it in the public interest to do so or if the instrument affected a reserved matter.

The manner in which these two devolution Acts would have operated would obviously have depended greatly on the political complexion of the elected assemblies and on the character of the government at Westminster. However when the referendums provided for in the Acts were held on 1 March 1979 it was clear that the necessary support for the legislation was not forthcoming. The figures for the total electorate were adjusted to allow for deaths, double registrations and other eventualities. The results with percentage figures for the adjusted electorate are shown in table 5.

Two things stood out from the results. In Wales turnout was very low and even the most Welsh-speaking counties did not return a 'yes' majority. In Scotland turnout was higher but the 'yes' majority was due entirely to the voters of the central industrial area; rural and small-town Scotland was largely hostile to the idea of devolution.

Conclusions

The very different histories and cultures of the three non-English

Table 5
The Devolution Referendum Results

Wales	Scotland	

Clwyd	Borders	Strathclyde
Yes 31,384 (11.1%)	Yes 20,746 (27%)	Yes 596,519 (34%)
No 114,119	No 30,780	No 508,599
Maj., No 82,735	Maj., No 10,034	Maj., Yes 87,920
Dyfed	Central	Tayside
Yes 44,849 (18.3%)	Yes 71,296 (36.4%)	Yes 91,482 (31.5%)
No 114,947	No 59,105	No 93,325
Maj., No 70,098	Maj., Yes 12,191	Maj., No 1,843
Gwent	Dumfries & Galloway	Western Isles
Yes 21,369 (6.7%)	Yes 27,162 (26.1%)	Yes 6,218 (28.1%)
No 155,389	No 40,239	No 4,933
Maj., No 134,020	Maj., No 13,077	Maj., Yes 1,285
Gwynedd	Fife	
Yes 37,363 (22.1%)	Yes 86,252 (35.4%)	
No 71,157	No 74,436	
Maj., No 33,794	Maj. Yes 11,816	
Mid-Glamorgan	Grampian	
Yes 46,747 (12%)	Yes 94,944 (27.9%)	
No 184,196	No 101,485	
Maj., No 137,449	Maj., No 6,541	
Powys	Highlands	
Yes 9,843 (12.3%)	Yes 44,973 (33.3%)	
No 43,502	No 43,274	
Maj., No 33,659	Maj., Yes 1,699	
South Glamorgan	Lothian	
Yes 21,830 (7.8%)	Yes 187,221 (33.3%)	
No 144,186	No 186,421	
Maj., No 122,356	Maj., Yes 800	
West Glamorgan	Orkney	
Yes 29,663 (10.8%)	Yes 2,104 (15.2%)	
No 128,834	No 5,439	
Maj., No 99,171	Maj., No 3,335	
TOTAL FOR WALES	Shetland	TOTAL FOR SCOTLAND
Yes 243,048 (11.9%)	Yes 2,020 (13.7%)	Yes 1,230,937 (32.85%)
No 956,330 (46.9%)	No 5,446	No 1,153,502 (30.78%)
Maj., No 713,282	Maj., No 3,446	Maj., Yes 77,435

parts of the United Kingdom have led to different administrative patterns and different political behaviour. The most striking divergence is clearly in Northern Ireland, where the structure of politics and of party competition is so different from that on the mainland as to isolate it from much of the political life of the United Kingdom as a whole. But Scotland continues to display a good deal of divergence in its politics from England. In 1983, for example, when the Conservatives won an overwhelming victory in England there was no majority for the Tories in Scotland, so that some Labour MPs from Scotland were quick to deny the government a mandate north of the border. Nevertheless the rough accommodations between the component parts of the United Kingdom have produced a system which can take some account of regional and national divergence without weakening the overall structure of government. Whether that rough accommodation will continue to prove satisfactory remains to be seen, but it is noteworthy that at the point when a radical recasting of the constitutional mould was a real prospect the populations of Scotland and Wales drew back from taking such a radical step.

The Citizen and the
Administration (I): The
Legal Order and Civil
Liberties

The Courts and the Administration of Justice

The British legal system is a complicated structure. Even today it
owes as much to the slow evolution of the political system between the
Norman Conquest and the Great Reform Act of 1832 as it does to the
attempts of nineteenth- and twentieth-century legislators to make the
country's legal arrangements respond to the needs of an expanding
and industrializing society. Thus, although an increasingly large part
of the network of courts and jurisdictions is governed by reference to
such recent statutes as the Courts Act of 1971, the historical
perspective is still extremely important for a proper understanding of
the role of law and its personnel in the British political system today.
For although the British legal system has its defenders and the
common law has been seen as one of England's finest intellectual
exports, the role of law and the role of the judiciary remain
controversial. It may be that recent constitutional developments –
most notably the entry of Britain into the European Communities –
will extend the role played by legal institutions in the British system of
government; however, the exercise of additional powers by the courts
will have to be delicately handled, for the attitude of politicians
towards legal intervention in government is frequently one of
suspicion and hostility.

The way in which a society views its legal machinery will frequently
reflect the style in which law and order is maintained there, and that
again will reflect the extent to which divisions within society present
threats to the public order. In the mainland of Britain, although not in
Northern Ireland, the police forces and other institutions responsible
for preventing crime for long enjoyed a high degree of public
confidence; Britain retained its ability to keep an unarmed police
force and maintained the tradition of a series of locally organized
forces which contrasted markedly with the centralized forces of
France and some other European countries. Serious crime by

comparison with other industrialized countries was relatively low.[1] However, by the late 1970s many of the old assumptions about Britain's manner of policing had been called into question. To some extent that questioning was the result of developments outside of the United Kingdom's control – for example the emergence of international terrorism, which demanded professional and specialized responses to incidents and which could not be handled simply by the regular police forces.[2] Advanced technology added its own dimension of apprehension. On one level, concern arose as the new technology was applied to different aspects of the policing process and seemed to change its familiar features; on another level civil libertarians became concerned about the extent to which computerized information about individuals could be made available to the police.[3] In addition there was also a sense in which new social tensions seemed likely to be reflected in attitudes towards the police and in a reduction of overall public confidence in them. In particular the degree of support accorded the police among ethnic minorities seemed very low, and in the aftermath of the riots which occurred in several cities in 1981 many police authorities started to establish special committees to try to repair the relationship between themselves and the minority communities.[4]

While the racial tension between the police and the ethnic minorities of the United Kingdom constituted one feature of a deteriorating relationship between the police and public, it was by no means the only one. The rise in unemployment was itself seen as a potential cause of an increase in the amount of crime, and in 1984 the miners' strike – in which there was violence as a result of the desire by some miners to return to work and in which some miners were accidentally killed – led to allegations of police brutality in the handling of pickets as well as to more general debate about the proper role of police in long-running industrial disputes.

The period of the late 1970s and early 1980s thus saw an intense and sustained debate about the role of the police in British society and about the more general questions connected with the functioning of the British legal system. The Labour Party at its 1981 conference adopted policies designed to secure greater police accountability, and the GLC played a vigorous role in the debate about policing London by such devices as the establishment of a Police Committee and a not altogether well-named Police Support Unit.[5] (London policing is the responsibility of two police forces, the small City Police Force and the very much larger Metropolitan Police Force. The Metropolitan Police Force is directly answerable to the home secretary, so that there is no additional police committee to supervise its operations.)

Together with the arguments put forward by such politicians as Tony Benn these developments served to give the discussion of police issues a more partisan tone than before. The Conservative Party which won the general election of 1979 had for its part become committed to a strengthening of the forces of law and order which it saw as one of the basic functions of the state. However in this sphere, as in others, the government was also aware of the limited resources which it had to spend on those functions. Pay rises for the police and additional expenditure on the prison building programme were combined with an attempt to legislate on some parts of the report of the 1981 Royal Commission on Criminal Procedure in a way which seemed calculated to strengthen the powers of the police.[6] However the original Police and Criminal Evidence Bill was extremely controversial, and when the general election of 1983 prevented it from becoming law the Conservative administration took the opportunity to make changes in the new bill which it brought back to Parliament in 1983. This bill finally became law in 1984, although not before the House of Lords had introduced further amendments.

Discussion of the police, of the legal system and of civil liberties has thus become highly charged in the period since 1979, although in a slightly different way from the concern expressed during the debates about bills of rights in the mid-1970s. In this chapter the analysis will cover the pattern of legal institutions to be found in England and Wales, since a separate legal system exists in Scotland and the machinery of justice in Northern Ireland has certain distinct features.

The English legal system has three peculiar characteristics which have been thought to distinguish its structure and style from most continental legal systems. First, there is the rigid division between barristers and solicitors. Solicitors are the lawyers who perform the routine non-litigious tasks and prepare the background material when litigation is necessary. They are the more numerous branch of the profession and may form partnerships which can vary in size from a large London specialist firm to a small firm of country solicitors. It is the solicitor with whom the general public normally comes into contact. The range of functions which a solicitor can perform is, however, limited. He may not argue cases in any of the higher courts; the senior and much smaller branch of the legal profession – the Bar – has the exclusive right of audience in those courts. Solicitors may become stipendiary magistrates and recorders and they are now eligible to become circuit judges, though very few have in fact done so. The most senior judges, that is judges of the High Court, are drawn exclusively from the Bar.

Whether this division of the profession is in the public interest is a fiercely debated question. Those who favour its retention argue primarily that this specialization – barristers are in effect specialists in the more difficult aspects of litigation and in advocacy – is beneficial to the client. Opponents say that this is but one of many restrictive features of the legal profession and that the cost of legal services would be greatly reduced if a solicitor could see a case through all its stages instead of having to hand it over to a barrister as soon as it involved litigation in the superior courts. (Following a report in 1976 by the Monopolies and Mergers Commission the expense of some litigation was reduced by the abolition of a rule which prevented senior counsel or 'silks' from appearing in court without the help of junior counsel. Even so, in the great majority of cases a silk still appears with a junior barrister rather than alone.)[7] A Royal Commission was set up in 1977 to consider whether the provision of legal services in the United Kingdom was in need of reform, and one of the issues which it examined was the organization of the legal profession.[8] However it rejected the idea of fusion and suggested only a number of minor amendments to the existing system and the acceleration of such trends as the development of a common professional examination for barristers and solicitors. Concern that the cost of legal services might effectively preclude resort to law has led not merely to schemes for publicly financed legal assistance but to a range of experiments with legal clinics and poor people's legal services. In March 1984 the Law Society launched a campaign for much wider rights of audience in British courts, but according to a parliamentary answer in May 1984 no such change was envisaged by the government.[9]

The second feature of the English legal system which distinguishes it from its continental counterparts – though not from the American one – is that it is adversarial. Legal proceedings are conducted by the presentation of arguments on behalf of the prosecution and of the accused in criminal cases and on behalf of the plaintiff and the defendant in civil suits. The function of the judge is to decide the case on the merits of the arguments put to him on behalf of each side. He is a passive umpire in the process of litigation and does not, as in an inquisitorial system, intervene to ascertain the facts of the case himself. The stark contrast between the inquisitorial and adversarial models is to some extent blurred by the fact that only a small proportion of cases reach the trial stage (the majority of civil cases being settled out of court or with criminal cases decided by the entry of a guilty plea by the accused) and by the existence in Britain of some courts – such as small claims courts – where the judge plays an altogether more active role in ascertaining the facts.[10]

The third distinguishing feature of the English legal system is the absence of a separate jurisdiction for public law cases – cases which involve the state (including local government) in some capacity, as opposed to cases where only private citizens are involved. Until the late 1960s it was generally assumed that the British system of public law was underdeveloped, and certainly there is nothing that compares to the system of *droit administratif* in France.[11] Public law issues are heard in the same courts as private law cases, and few special procedures apply when government is involved in a suit. Although it used to be the case that the monarch could not be sued in his or her own courts, much of this immunity was removed by the Crown

Table 6
The System of Courts Exercising Civil Jurisdiction

HOUSE OF LORDS
(Lord Chancellor, Lords of
Appeal in Ordinary (Law Lords)
and Peers who hold or have held
high judicial office)

Appeal (leave needed)

Leapfrogging appeal
(leave needed)

Civil Division of the
COURT OF APPEAL
(Master of the Rolls and Lords
Justices of Appeal)

Appeal

Appeal

| Queen's Bench Division includes Commercial Court, Admiralty Court (Lord Chief Justice and puisne judges) | Chancery Division (Vice-Chancellor and puisne judges) | Family Division (President and puisne judges) | Circuit courts at 24 provincial centres: High Court judges present continuously or for substantial periods |

COUNTY COURT
(Circuit judges)

HIGH COURT
(Justices of the High Court)

Source: R. M. Jackson, *The Machinery of Justice in England*, 7th ed. (C.U.P., 1977).

Table 7
The System of Courts Exercising Criminal Jurisdiction

HOUSE OF LORDS
|
Appeal
leave needed

DIVISIONAL COURT OF
QUEEN'S BENCH
DIVISION

CRIMINAL DIVISION OF
COURT OF APPEAL

Case stated,
law only

Appeal, not against acquittal.
Leave sometimes needed

CROWN COURT

As Court
of Appeal.
No jury

As court of
first instance.
Jury trial

Case stated,
law only

Appeal, on
fact and/or
law. (Generally
not against
acquittal.)

Commit for
trial to

MAGISTRATES' COURTS
(Courts of summary jurisdiction)

Summary jurisdiction.
(Trial of summary offences
and of indictable offences
triable summarily when
accused consents and the
court thinks it expedient.)
No jury

Preliminary inquiry into
indictable offences.
No jury

Source: R. M. Jackson, *The Machinery of Justice in England*, 7th ed. (C.U.P., 1977).

Proceedings Act of 1947.[12]

The structure of civil and criminal courts is set out in tables 6 and 7. At the bottom of the civil law hierarchy is the county court, which may hear only limited categories of cases which are assigned to it by statute. These are mainly disputes where small sums of money are at issue. The function of such courts is to effect a quick and relatively inexpensive determination of legal cases. The existing network of county courts can trace its origins back to the County Courts Act of 1846, although there have been several rearrangements of the districts covered by these courts as the population has shifted and the distribution of cases has changed.

The definition of a small dispute has had to be adjusted to take account of inflation, and this adjustment can now be done relatively quickly by Order in Council.[13] Prior to the Courts Act of 1971, which rationalized the whole system of courts in England and Wales, the county courts had been presided over by persons appointed as full-time county court judges. However the pressure of the number of cases and the difficulty of finding members of the Bar to act as county court judges prompted a change in the system of recruitment to the judiciary at this level. After the 1971 Courts Act a new category of judges known as circuit judges replaced the county court judges. However the Courts Act also opened the office of recorder – as has been seen, an office previously confined to barristers – to solicitors as well, and allowed additional circuit judges to be recruited from their ranks. Thus it is now possible for solicitors to reach the lower rungs of the judiciary.[14] Despite these efforts to broaden the pool of available judicial talent it still remains true that the English bench is understaffed. When the Beeching Commission reported on the system of Assizes and Quarter Sessions in 1969 it estimated that there would be a need for some 150 full-time circuit judges and 120 part-time recorders to deal with the case load in a reorganized system. However, as one authority has noted, this has proved to be something of an underestimate of the personnel required. By 1972 there were sixty-nine High Court judges, 205 circuit judges and 287 recorders. By the beginning of 1984 the pressure of work had made it necessary to increase the numbers to seventy-seven High Court judges, 349 circuit judges and 465 recorders. Even then the pressure on the system was intense, and there was a regular backlog of cases waiting to be heard, especially in the criminal courts.[15] The system is heavily dependent on the work done by the many recorders who are mainly barristers in ordinary practice devoting a few weeks a year to judicial duties.

Above the level of the county court there is the High Court, which is governed by the provisions of the Supreme Court Act of 1981. It has three specialized divisions – the Queen's Bench Division, which includes the Commercial Court and the Admiralty Court; the Chancery Division; and the Family Division. The Queen's Bench Division is headed by the lord chief justice. Cases are heard by him and by the forty-five puisne judges, as the High Court judges who are not heads of divisions are known. The Queen's Bench Division has original jurisdiction in civil matters. This means that a plaintiff must begin his action there if the amount of money in issue exceeds the county court limit. An action may be commenced in the High Court even if the amount in issue is small, and a plaintiff may choose to go to the High Court if the case involves some question of principle or is a test on which other claims may depend.

Another civil function of the Queen's Bench Division is that it exercises supervisory jurisdiction over the lower courts and the plethora of administrative tribunals which deal with such subjects as rent assessments, employment disputes and social security benefits. The High Court exercises this control over subordinate jurisdictions through its ability to issue *inter alia* prerogative writs and orders.

The third function of the High Court is to act as an appellate court, hearing appeals from magistrates' courts and tribunals on points of law. In criminal matters it may also hear appeals from the appellate jurisdictions of the Crown Courts. The appellate functions of the Queen's Bench Division are usually exercised by the Divisional Court, which consists of three (or exceptionally five) judges; but where a statute provides for an appeal to the Queen's Bench Division from a tribunal on a point of law, this appeal may come before a single judge.

The Chancery Division of the High Court had its origins in the development of a distinct set of legal processes and remedies known as equity, which was designed to supplement the inflexible common law procedures. The two aspects of English law, common law and equity, have now been almost entirely merged, so that the plaintiff no longer has to choose whether to bring his suit in the common law or equitable courts. The distinctive feature of the Chancery Court is still the type of case it deals with: trusts, land, taxation, company and bankruptcy matters are the special concern of this Division, as well as contentious probate and succession matters. The lord chancellor is the nominal head of the Division, but it is in practice presided over by a vice-chancellor and has twelve puisne judges. The Family Division of the High Court was created in 1971 when the old Probate, Divorce and Admiralty Division was abolished and its functions redistributed. The Family Division, headed by a president and having sixteen puisne judges, exercises jurisdiction in connection with the breakdown of marriage, the disposition of family property and the custody of children.

Above the level of the High Court is the Court of Appeal, which has two divisions – one for criminal and the other for civil matters. The Court of Appeal was established in the late nineteenth century to hear civil appeals under the Judicature Acts of 1873–5; it provides a tribunal which can hear appeals from both the county courts and the civil divisions of the High Court. The Civil Division is presided over by the Master of the Rolls and staffed by sixteen lords justices of appeal who sit together usually in courts of three. (The lord chancellor, ex-lord chancellors, lords of appeal in ordinary and the presidents of the various Divisions of the High Court are also *ex officio* members of this court and competent to hear appeals there.) Under Lord Denning, who held the office of Master of the Rolls for twenty years, the Court of Appeal acquired a reputation for being an innovatory force in English law; although its unorthodox approach to precedent occasioned criticism from the House of Lords from time to time (as well as criticism from politicians), on balance it may be said to have made a unique contribution to law reform in many areas. It remains to be seen whether the Court of Appeal under the new Master of the Rolls, Sir John Donaldson, will maintain this tradition.[16]

Above the Court of Appeal is the highest domestic court in the country – the House of Lords. Under the Administration of Justice (Appeals) Act of 1934 the right of appeal to this body is limited: leave from the House of Lords itself or from the Court of Appeal must be given, and this will generally happen only when there is a substantial point of law in dispute. The House of Lords' judicial functions originated when medieval monarchs delegated routine aspects of adjudication to members of the Great Council and, although it took time for the legislative and adjudicative processes to become distinct, it is clear that by the end of the sixteenth century the House of Lords was the pre-eminent court in Britain. Lay peers participated in judicial proceedings until the middle of the nineteenth century; however, this practice was effectively ended with *O'Connell's* case in 1844.[17]

Since that time the House of Lords has effectively reserved its judicial functions for specialists, although the appointment of professional judges to undertake them had to wait until the Appellate Jurisdiction Act of 1876. That Act provided for the appointment of paid lords of appeal in ordinary, and their number has been raised to cope with the additional judicial work so that it now stands at nine. As well as these specially created law lords – who are given life peerages – any peer who has held high judicial office may sit on appeals to the House of Lords. The lord chancellor himself does not normally participate in the routine judicial business of the House of Lords, although this very much depends on the personal preferences of individual lord chancellors and the work load of the House. Lord Hailsham, for example, who was Lord Chancellor in the Conservative administration of 1970–74 and again in the administration formed in 1979 and 1983, enjoyed this aspect of his duties and he, like his predecessor, Lord Elwyn-Jones, has regularly participated in appeals.

Two further points should be noted about the appeal structure in civil matters. First, it used to be the case that the House of Lords was bound by its own previous decisions, so that where the House had considered a legal point already – even if a long time previously – in theory it had to follow the earlier precedent.[18] Of course there were ways of getting round this rule, but in 1966 the House of Lords decided itself to modify the doctrine (formally known as the doctrine of *stare decisis*) and to give itself the freedom to depart from its own earlier decisions in the exceptional instances when it felt that such a change would be justified. In fact it has made relatively little use of the freedom thereby acquired.[19]

Second, the special role of the House of Lords in determining difficult points of law, especially in relation to statutory interpretation, has been recognized by a procedure introduced in 1969 which enables the appellant to bypass the normal route for appeals – i.e. via the Court of Appeal – and to go directly to the House of Lords from the High Court. To invoke this special procedure, which is known as 'leap-frogging', it is necessary for the trial judge to certify that a point of law of general public importance is involved and for the House of Lords to grant leave to appeal in this way. Although of theoretical importance it is a procedure which is not often used; in 1982 it seems that only seven appeals took advantage of it.[20]

A word should be said here about the Privy Council and its Judicial Committee. Until 1883 there was no specialized Judicial Committee and the Privy Council's jurisdiction was exercised by all its members including the lay majority. Now the Judicial Committee is composed of all those peers entitled to hear cases in the House of Lords, together with some members from the Commonwealth countries who have held high judicial office. (The lord president of the Council is formally a member also.) Its special jurisdictions include appeals from outside the United Kingdom, mainly from those Commonwealth countries which have deliberately chosen to retain this court and from the remaining colonies and protectorates. The Privy Council also hears domestic appeals from specialized tribunals, including the General Medical Council; and it hears appeals from ecclesiastical courts. It may also hear special references on matters which are not strictly appellate, such as the validity of legislation in Jersey or eligibility to take a seat in the House of Commons.

The criminal law is administered through a rather different system of courts, and the whole structure of criminal jurisdiction was subjected to radical overhaul in 1971. Perhaps the most peculiar feature of the criminal law in Britain is the role played by the 26,000 lay magistrates or justices of the peace who, as one commentator has written, see 97 per cent of all criminal cases through from start to finish.[21] The organization and operation of the magistracy and of magistrates' courts are now governed by two comprehensive statutes – the Justices of the Peace Act 1979 and the Magistrates' Courts Act of 1980. It would however be a mistake to neglect the long history of the lay magistracy – a history which has been interlinked with the history of local government.[22] Certainly by the end of the sixteenth century one finds a system in which minor offences could be tried by the appointed members of the gentry of an area, while more serious offences had to wait for visitations from the itinerant judges on assize. Administrative functions were also assigned to the magistracy, especially those concerned with the poor law. Appointed on a county basis, JPs would assemble four times a year in Quarter Sessions to perform their judicial duties. However, as the burden of work increased, magistrates developed the practice of dealing with trivial offences themselves at so-called 'petty sessions without a jury'. Magistrates' courts thus form the bottom rung in the judicial hierarchy and can perform a variety of minor judicial and administrative tasks. They also constitute the only point at which most citizens ever encounter the criminal justice system in the United Kingdom – for example in relation to traffic offences. It is therefore worth examining the characteristics of this aspect of the system a little further, since the lay magistracy is by no means an uncontroversial institution.

The powers of the lay magistrate today in criminal matters are broadly of three kinds. First, JPs can decide cases which are triable summarily. This they do by majority verdict sitting in benches or panels of at least three magistrates. There is no jury but there is always a legally trained clerk to inform the court on points of law. Second, with the consent of the accused and the prosecution, magistrates can try offences which are indictable but which may be decided summarily. Finally they can decide in the case of an indictable offence whether the prosecution has proved that there is a case to answer, so that the accused is committed for trial at the Crown Court. They will also decide whether bail should be granted if the accused is remanded for trial in the Crown Court. In addition to these judicial functions magistrates still perform such administrative duties as granting licences to sell alcohol, and they have retained significant civil law functions such as making affiliation orders. Juvenile courts are staffed by magistrates who hold separate sessions to deal with young offenders and to make orders whereby children in need of care and protection may be taken into local authority custody. In 1982 the Criminal Justice Act made radical changes to the sentencing procedure and treatment for young offenders in the hope that short sentences of up to four months in a detention centre, arrangements for longer custody known as 'youth custody sentences' and new powers to impose 'curfew' orders could be made to deter offenders under twenty-one from future crimes. Borstal sentences were abolished. These changes, together with such expedients as residential care orders and financial orders on parents, constituted both a rejection of earlier approaches to youth crime and a recognition that a more comprehensive approach was needed to deal with the problem.

The argument in favour of substantial lay participation in the administration of justice is a complex one. Some would argue that such participation reinforces the idea that the whole community, not just the specialized agencies of law enforcement, is responsible for the prevention and punishment of crime. Lay participation may also be justified on the grounds that, within limits, it enables the legal sanctions imposed to reflect the community's general values. By involving the public in the sentencing process the law can thus become rooted in the opinions of a wider section of society than would be the case if paid full-time lawyers were exclusively responsible for its enforcement. In addition it is customarily argued that a lay magistracy is cheaper than a professional system would be. The cost of training magistrates, it is thought, is much smaller than would be that of the salaries of professional magistrates – even if, which seems doubtful, the personnel were available for such a substitution. The routine expenses of the legal institutions of the country are not popular items in governmental budgets – and even when the 'law and order' issue is raised by a political party its enthusiasm for major extra expenditure is likely to be limited. Thus for example some observers have suggested that part of the interest in community policing derives not so much from a concern to adapt the styles of policing to a given neighbourhood but rather from the opportunities which it offers to make citizens more responsible for their own self-protection. In any event, whether justified or not, the argument that the lay magistracy is a cheap and flexible way of providing justice is likely to ensure the survival of amateurs in the British legal structure for some years to come.

Against the arguments for a continuing lay element in the administration of the criminal law, it could be maintained that the system is biased. Although it is undoubtedly true that magistrates as a whole are more representative of British society than are barristers and solicitors, the groups who become JPs can hardly be said to constitute a microcosm of modern Britain. Some sections of society, notably the young, the manual working classes and ethnic minorities, are under-represented on the bench – a fact which is doubly unfortunate when it is said the crimes involved are typically ones associated with these groups.

Equally, the manner of appointment to the bench has always attracted a good deal of criticism. Although efforts have been made to eliminate the cruder aspects of political patronage, the advisory committees which vet potential magistrates are carefully balanced to ensure that all parties are represented. And although it is argued that their anonymity is a protection against lobbying from would-be magistrates, the fact that a good deal of administrative secrecy surrounds their operation has given cause for criticism. Indeed one recent commentary wondered whether the Lord Chancellor's Department in this area was not so lacking in openness and accountability that it ought to be replaced with a proper Ministry of Justice.[23] In fact the work of scrutinizing the recommendations which come from the chairmen of the advisory committees and the lord lieutenants of the counties is done by the lord chancellor assisted by a secretary of commissions whose work is principally concerned with the appointment of stipendiary magistrates.[24]

Above all the lay magistracy may be critized on the grounds of competence. It is suggested for example that lay magistrates are prone to accept police evidence too easily and that they become too dependent on their professionally trained clerks.[25] In fact much of the sting of these criticisms has been removed by the greater emphasis on training which now underpins the system of lay magistrates, especially in relation to the more specialized aspects of the magistrates' work. Service on juvenile courts, for example, provides opportunities for further education covering such topics as sentencing and social welfare and for JPs to be given some training in psychology. However, it has to be admitted that the benefit from these opportunities is by no means universally apparent, and it could be argued that the justice which the JPs impose is still somewhat arbitrary. To some extent the remedy for the deficiencies of the lay magistracy lies in the comprehensive appeals mechanism which exists and in the variety of professional expertise and welfare services which is available to the bench. In large urban areas, including London, the work of lay magistrates is supplemented by stipendiary magistrates, that is full-time, salaried magistrates who have previously been barristers or solicitors.

The trial of more serious crimes takes place at a level above the magistrates' courts, in what are known now as Crown Courts. Crown Courts were established by the Courts Act of 1971. In order to understand their role it is necessary to remember that prior to that date there were two places at which indictable offences could be tried. The first was at Quarter Sessions, which until the local government reorganizations of 1972–4 were organized differently depending on whether they were county or borough courts.

In the boroughs, the court consisted of a recorder sitting alone; in the counties the Quarter Sessions were the lay magistrates – between two and nine in number – sitting with a legally qualified chairman. These courts had a wide jurisdiction, but usually they did not try offences carrying a maximum penalty of life imprisonment on first conviction; they could also hear appeals from magistrates' courts. More serious crimes therefore could not be tried at Quarter Sessions but had to be tried in the Assize courts.

Assize courts had been important since at least the reign of Henry II, when officials travelling around the country to dispense justice were also able to extend the administrative jurisdiction of the Crown. Despite the delays inherent in the system, the practice whereby High Court judges travelled to major towns at fixed times each year survived until 1971. Then, following a Royal Commission on Assizes and Quarter Sessions (the Beeching Commission), the system of Quarter Sessions and Assizes was abolished and a single court above the level of the magistrates' court – the Crown Court – took their place in a number of court centres.[26]

The Crown Courts are staffed by High Court judges, circuit judges and recorders. Criminal offences are divided into those which must come before a High Court judge – in other words very serious ones such as murder and treason; those which would normally be tried by a High Court judge but which may be released for trial by a circuit judge according to convenience; and those which would normally be tried by a circuit judge. The reform thus combined the merits of the old system, which meant that no area was in danger of continual subjection to the peculiarities of a single judge, with a new flexibility which had become increasingly necessary because the old Assize system took little account of the distribution of work between the different areas of the country.

Appeal from the Crown Courts in criminal matters is made to the Court of Appeal (Criminal Division) and, in very rare cases, to the House of Lords. A general right of appeal in criminal matters is actually a relatively recent innovation in the English legal structure; indeed the Court of Criminal Appeal itself was established only in 1907. It was merged with the Court of Appeal in 1966.[27] An appeal may be against conviction (i.e. on the ground that the conviction was wrong in law) or against sentence (i.e. on the ground that the sentence was too harsh.) In the latter case the Court of Appeal can reduce but not increase the sentence. Appeal from the Court of Appeal to the House of Lords requires the Court of Appeal to certify that a point of law of general public importance is involved; the House of Lords or the Court of Appeal must give leave to appeal on the grounds that there is a point which the House of Lords ought to consider. There is no appeal against acquittal in the Crown Court; but since 1972 the attorney-general may refer a point of law to the Court of Appeal.

Since British entry into the European Communities it should be noted that cases which have an element of Community law in them may be subject to a further examination: there is provision in the European Communities Act of 1972 for a reference on a point of law beyond the country's domestic courts to the Court of Justice of the European Communities. The European Communities Act and Article 177 of the EEC Treaty makes a reference to the Court of the Communities compulsory when a case with such a European element has exhausted all domestic remedies and has reached the House of Lords. However, a case may be referred to the European Court by any court in the judicial hierarchy if a matter of European Community law is at issue and the British court would like a ruling on it.[28] Strictly speaking the court and not the parties to a suit refer the matter to the European Court, whose jurisdiction is designed to produce harmony and uniformity of approach throughout the member states of the Communities rather than to provide simply another opportunity for appeal.[29]

Possibly also an appeal of sorts may lie beyond the domestic legal system if there is any question of the government having breached the European Convention on Human Rights.[30] Jurisdiction is exercised by the Commission on Human Rights, and cases where an allegation is *prima facie* substantial are heard by the Commission. Individuals were allowed to apply to the Commission directly from 1966, although it should be remembered that because Britain has not incorporated the Convention into British law (unlike most of the other signatories of the Convention) the Commission's decision is morally and politically persuasive rather than legally binding on the British government. Important and often embarrassing cases have been brought against the United Kingdom both by individual British citizens and by other European governments. Thus the Commission reached a different verdict from that of the British courts when it considered the *Sunday Times*'s right to publish an article alleging negligence on the part of the manufacturers of a drug – Thalidomide – which had caused grave birth defects in children whose mothers had taken it while pregnant.[31] The Commission defended the newspaper's right to discuss the issues involved even though they might be the subject of pending legal proceedings. The Commission also took a different line from the British courts on the question of whether individuals could be compelled to join a closed shop as a condition of employment.[32] And it has criticized the British government – after cases were referred to it by the Republic of Ireland – about internment and the treatment of prisoners in detention in Northern Ireland.[33] However in 1984 the Commission held that the use of plastic bullets by security forces in Northern Ireland was not in breach of the Convention.[34]

The network of institutions through which the law is administered obviously depends for its efficiency and fairness on the personnel who have to operate the system. In particular the respect of the community at large for the machinery of law enforcement will depend upon two groups – the judiciary and the police – which have been increasingly subjected to public criticism in recent years. Although judges are in theory politically neutral, they all owe their appointment to politicians. The prime minister appoints the lord chancellor, who is a senior member of the cabinet, presides over the House of Lords and is, in theory, the head of the Chancery Division of the High Court, although in practice he will perform his judicial duties in the Appellate Committee of the House of Lords. The lord chancellor is responsible for the vast majority of judicial appointments – High Court judges, circuit judges and recorders are appointed on his advice, as are the committees which recommend the appointment of magistrates. The prime minister, on the other hand, has a major voice in the appointment of judges to the Court of Appeal and to the House of Lords as well as to the office of lord chief justice. It is an important feature of British constitutional theory that High Court judges have security of tenure and cannot be removed from office except by an address from both Houses of Parliament. The retirement age is seventy-five.

Much criticism has been levelled at the social characteristics of the British judiciary.[35] Certainly the vast majority of judges come from middle-class backgrounds, and a high proportion have been educated at public schools and the traditional universities of Oxford and Cambridge. Yet the argument that, as a result, judges will be biased towards the interests of their class or against certain sections of society or display consistent political prejudices seems overstated. There is a range of opinion and outlook within the ranks of the judiciary on political matters and it is doubtful whether this overall situation would be much changed by the addition of persons with a different social background. However, it is obviously true that the world of the Bar, from whom senior judges are exclusively recruited, and that of the bench are atypical of British society as a whole, and that the kinds of problems which increasingly confront judges may be remote from their experience. Whether it is fair or not, many people in Britain do actually believe that the judiciary is biased against the working classes and in favour of established interests – a belief which largely explains the hostility of the trade union movement to any attempt at introducing legal procedures into the conduct of industrial relations.

Obviously one factor in shaping the public's perceptions of how fair the courts are is cost; here the British provisions have deteriorated recently. Legal aid first became widely available under the Legal Aid and Advice Act of 1949 and is now provided under the Legal Aid Act of 1974. Under this legislation different arrangements apply for civil and criminal cases. The system of legal aid in civil cases is administered by the Law Society (the governing body of solicitors) via its full-time officials and area and general practitioner committees. In criminal cases the provision of legal aid is governed by the Legal Aid Acts of 1974 and 1982. Until 1980 the administration of legal aid in criminal cases was the responsibility of the Home Office, but in 1980 this task was transferred to the Lord Chancellor's Department. Until 1982 it was not possible to appeal against a refusal to grant legal aid, but now general power of review has been given to the lord chancellor.

Legal aid is given on the basis of a combination of merits and need which is determined by a means test. Unfortunately the impact of inflation means that legal aid is available for a small part of the population only.[36] The recent development of law centres and legal clinics may help but the position is hardly satisfactory.

The second important component of law enforcement and administration is the British police force. The British experience of an organized police force dates from 1829, when Sir Robert Peel established the Metropolitan Police Force; in the succeeding decade both the counties and the boroughs established police forces of their own. Yet although the development of police forces occurred speedily in the nineteenth century, the notion of an organized police took root only slowly. Associations with continental despotism – for instance, Fouché's network of spies in France – served to make the British understanding of policing an inherently contradictory one. Indeed as late as 1929 the last Royal Commission on the Police before that of 1960 emphasized the extent to which the British conception of the police saw them as ordinary members of the public with no greater powers and responsibilities:

> The police in this country have never been recognised either in law or in tradition as a force distinct from the general body of citizens . . . the principle remains that a policeman, in the view of the common law, is only a person

paid to perform, as a matter of duty, acts which, if he were so minded, he might have done voluntarily.[37]

As many later commentators have noted, this idea about the police being no different from other citizens has become increasingly absurd: for example the police have developed *inter alia* powers to establish roadblocks, to amass large quantities of computerized data and to use sophisticated weaponry.[38] However, mythology dies hard, and it has at the very least precluded the rational consideration of both police efficiency and police accountability.

The original organization of police forces on the basis of local authority areas meant that for much of the nineteenth century there were over two hundred separate police forces in the United Kingdom. During the twentieth century this arrangement became increasingly anachronistic and inefficient, and in 1960 the Royal Commission on the Police urged the amalgamation of a number of forces, although it rejected in a rather cavalier fashion the arguments for a national police force.[39] (A national police force has traditionally been seen in Britain as a threat to democracy and a step towards authoritarian government, although it has become increasingly clear that such factors as the need for specialized services, Home Office attempts to influence policy on such matters as relations with the public, and the informal efforts of bodies like the Association of Chief Police Officers have all led to a convergence and centralization of policing which is more significant in many ways than the theoretical local structure of the forces.) The implementation of the Royal Commission's proposals in the Police Act of 1964 set in motion a process of amalgamation of police forces, so that by 1984 there were fifty-two forces only in the United Kingdom as a whole.

The responsibility for the day-to-day operations of the police force is traditionally that of the chief constable of each force. A chief constable outside the Metropolitan Area is answerable for the performance of his duties to a local police authority composed of county councillors and magistrates in a ratio of two to one. In London (outside the City of London, which has its own force) the chief commissioner of the Metropolitan Police is directly answerable to the home secretary for the conduct of his force's activities. The precise nature of the relationship between the chief constable and his local police authority is difficult to define. Although during the nineteenth century local authorities frequently gave their police forces instructions on prosecutions policy, this practice declined during the twentieth century. Then the general view developed that policing policies were not a proper subject for detailed supervision by local government, and this view was apparently reinforced by the common law doctrine that the relationship between a chief constable and the local authority was not one of servant and master, so that a local authority could not be sued for the wrongdoings of its local police force.[40]

The Police Act of 1964 gave local authorities the power to request reports about the policing of their local areas, but in practice these have been very little used. The home secretary's powers in relation to the police are diffuse but can be used effectively when there is a determination to influence policy. The home secretary is subject to parliamentary questioning on the general level of policing in the country, although not on the detailed administration of police forces and their operations except in relation to the Metropolitan Police. His most significant power may well be the requirement that he must approve the appointment of every chief constable – a fact which in 1984 caused some controversy among local government represent- atives who alleged that the home secretary had been using this power to influence policy to a much greater extent than in the past. The financing of the police is effected through a percentage grant, and as the home secretary has a variety of powers – including the power to issue circulars on such matters as the conditions of service – there is obviously a substantial, and perhaps an increasing, amount of central government influence in the administration of Britain's police forces.

The way in which that centralization could operate was shown in the wake of the Scarman Report, when the Home Office issued circulars to encourage police authorities to establish liaison com- mittees to facilitate police contact with their local communities.[41] Yet the same process also illustrated the wide variety of practice between police authorities, as some dragged their feet over the issue and others quickly established the requisite committees. Moreover there was very little uniformity in the way the liaison committees were constituted: some utilized the existing local community notables, while others advertised their meetings but let anyone who wished to participate do so.

Moreover over the late 1970s and early 1980s it became apparent that there was a considerable amount of variation in the way in which these police authorities exercised control over their local forces. For some the relationship was a purely formal one, with very little discussion of policy; for others – and there was increasing pressure to extend this development in the 1980s – police matters were as much a subject for political examination and discussion as education policy for example. The experience of unrest in a number of British cities in the early 1980s and the publication of such studies as the Policy Studies Institute's Report on the Metropolitan Police undoubtedly heightened the political salience of police-related issues and made many on the left in particular demand a greater degree of control over policing than had hitherto been tolerated.[42] For their part the police forces responded largely by emphasizing the extent to which it was necessary to expand police powers in the fight against crime and the view that police conduct at the day-to-day operational level was a matter of professional judgement rather than political concern. This dichotomy of approach to police affairs is likely to be exacerbated in the 1980s, and it is uncertain whether Britain is ever again likely to revert to a situation where police questions are outside the normal bounds of political controversy.

The 1960s and 1970s also witnessed a number of incidents of police corruption. In the Metropolitan Police this led to the establishment of a special unit – A 10 – to root out such practices as bribery and protection rings, especially in the CID. It also led to the establishment of a procedure for complaints against the police. Until 1976 the investigation of complaints against the police was largely undertaken by the police themselves, except where the offence was serious enough to warrant the institution of criminal proceedings. Thus an allegation by a member of the general public could lead to an inquiry headed by a senior member of another force. In 1976, however, a Police Complaints Board was established to provide an independent review of action taken as a result of complaints by the public against the police.[43] The inclusion of an independent element in the Complaints Board had been bitterly disputed, and some officers, such as the ex-Chief Commissioner of the Metropolitan Police, Sir Robert Mark, argued that it would undermine the morale of the police forces. In fact the operation of the Board seems to have given the police very little cause for concern. By contrast however the mounting concern about deteriorating relationships between the police and public led to demands for greater independence at all stages of the complaints processes – a demand which in 1982 received powerful endorsement from the House of Commons Select Committee on Home Affairs.[44] As a result the Police and Criminal Evidence Bill included moderate reforms in the system and an independent assessor who could direct that investigations be undertaken but would not himself undertake them. This was much less radical than the National Council for Civil Liberties, for example, wanted. [45] In their view the machinery for securing police accountability needed thorough overhaul, and they wished to see a regionalized series of investigators. Interestingly, the Police Federation, from a position of some hostility towards the independent element in the complaints procedure, had moved towards accepting and even welcoming the inevitable as the only way of improving the police's image. Under the Police and Criminal Evidence Act of 1984 a new Police Complaints Authority is established with somewhat broader powers than the old Police Complaints Board. Thus it can, for example, supervise the investigation by the police of the complaints against them. Although there are still informal procedures for the resolution of complaints, complaints which allege that the conduct complained of resulted in death or serious injury must be referred to the PCA. In addition the secretary of state for the Home Office may specify that a category of complaint must be referred to the PCA and both the police officer or the complainant may refer matters to it. In addition two 1983 cases have clarified the situation where allegations which might give rise to prosecution can still be referred to the Police Complaints Board even though the evidence on which the complaint is based is the same in both instances.[46]

One important change in relation to the role of the police which is likely to occur in the near future involves the decision to initiate prosecutions. The police themselves have a good deal of discretion as to whether to prosecute in criminal cases, subject in some cases to the need to secure the consent of the attorney-general or the DPP. If the government's proposals as announced in 1983 are actually made law, there will be an independent prosecution service headed by the DPP under the attorney-general. This change, it is thought, will make the prosecution process a more independent and fair one, although it is not intended that the decision to prosecute should be taken centrally.[47]

Public Order and Civil Liberties

The fact that it was only in 1976 that the British government felt it necessary to introduce machinery for securing an independent review of complaints against the police underlines the general complacency that had previously existed in the United Kingdom about the country's arrangements for protecting the citizen from administrative error or excess. Indeed, although national and international developments have focused attention on individual and human rights to a remarkable extent throughout the 1970s and early 1980s, it is surprising how slowly this new sensitivity towards issues of civil liberties and accountability has been translated into legislative and administrative action. For the British tradition of thought in the area of civil liberties is still very much shaped by a long-standing hostility to abstract formulations of rights and a reliance on common sense and common values to keep those in authority under control. Moreover, the preference for political rather than judicial protections for the citizen has meant that even in those areas where legal safeguards are most important, such as police powers, the judiciary has sometimes been far too deferential to executive claims of administrative necessity.

Satisfaction with the manner in which the British system of government provided for the protection of individual liberties and the more complex question of government accountability had a partly historical explanation: Britain developed a tradition of parliamentary democracy at a time when most European countries were still suffering the abuses of absolute monarchy. The early appreciation of the need to provide adequate and effective remedies against the executive can be indicated by a study of the range and depth of the constitutional debates of the seventeenth century – debates which left their imprint on American as well as English theories of constitutional government. Yet the sheer length of the British parliamentary tradition may have acted as a brake on the development of remedies to protect the individual in contemporary Britain. The peculiar concerns of the seventeenth century could not provide a set of constitutional principles appropriate to a period in which the balance between the state and the individual has been altered radically by a massive extension of governmental activity and by rapid changes in technology. Moreover the rhetoric of parliamentary supremacy, which is the historic achievement of the seventeenth-century struggles between the Crown and the House of Commons, has served to disguise the extent to which the legislature itself can threaten individual liberty, especially when, as is normal, the legislature is controlled by the executive through the discipline of the two-party system.

Protection of the interests of individuals in British political debate has thus invariably been associated with protection of majority interests expressed through political parties inside Parliament. The problem of how to balance minority interests against those of the majority has either been ignored entirely or resolved by appealing to the expectation that at least two political parties would alternate in government. Even one of the most prominent pressure groups in the field, the National Council for Civil Liberties, when it tried to articulate its policies in 1984 did not do so in a way that made its role that of defender of all minorities, but suggested that it had a natural constituency of groups associated with the political left.[48] The alternation of parties in government and the diffused, if diminishing, spirit of compromise in British political affairs have generally ensured that the absence of a clear statement of individual rights and a coherent body of principles to govern executive action has not led to tyranny. A British citizen may find it difficult to predict the limits which a court will impose on his freedom of speech, or to ascertain the circumstances in which he may challenge a government decision successfully; however, for the most part he may assume that governmental agencies in the United Kingdom will recognize fairness to individuals as an important value to be given weight in their decisions, even if they are not always consistent about applying it.

Discussions about formalizing the rights accorded to individuals formed part of a wider debate about the adequacy of British constitutional arrangements. In that debate which marked the latter part of the 1970s especially, lawyers played a prominent part. Both Lord Scarman in his 1974 Hamlyn Lectures and Lord Hailsham advocated introducing into the British system of government an entrenched bill of rights as part of a comprehensive revision of the constitutional system.[49] Despite ambiguities in both Labour and Conservative attitudes on the question, the 1970s saw internal working groups set up on the topic; and the Liberal Party was known to be sympathetic to the idea, as was the newly formed Social Democratic Party. And in 1977 the House of Lords, following the introduction of a bill on the subject by the Liberal peer, Lord Wade, established a Select Committee to examine the question of whether Britain should enact a bill of rights.[50] These developments – and especially the prominent role which Lord Hailsham played in the debates – might have been expected to lead to some concrete political action once the Conservative Party took office in 1979 and Lord Hailsham became Lord Chancellor. Yet such is the resistance to major constitutional change that no action was taken by the Conservative administrations of Mrs Thatcher – a point which was underlined by left-of-centre critics of the judiciary. Indeed over the period 1979–84 the character of the arguments about civil liberties changed so that the issues which dominated the agenda were very much focused on particular themes such as police powers, rather than on the more general issues of principle articulated over the 1970s.[51]

The fact that the House of Lords had debated the issue at all was, however, in itself an important indicator of a changing political reality as well as a contribution to the understanding of the issues associated with the topic. The House of Lords had considered two specific questions in relation to the desirability of such a step. First, was such a measure desirable in principle? Second, if it was desirable what form should such an enactment take? The second question, which had been raised in the government's discussion paper, really turned on whether Britain should acquire a bill of rights by incorporating the European Convention on Human Rights into United Kingdom law, or whether it would be better to enunciate a bill of rights which could take account of Britain's own political system and the difficulties that were thought to be associated with the doctrine of parliamentary sovereignty.[52]

The status of the European Convention for the Protection of Human Rights and Fundamental Freedoms is rather anomalous as far as the United Kingdom is concerned. While the United Kingdom was the first country to ratify the Convention, which she did in November 1950, the British government seems not to have taken its implications for enforcement very seriously, and is the only signatory of the Convention to have neither incorporated its provisions into its own law nor to have a bill of rights of its own.[53] The fact that the Convention does not form a part of British law was made clear in a case before the Court of Appeal in 1976, although the case also suggested that it was legitimate where possible to construe Acts of Parliament so that they do not conflict with the Convention.[54] Moreover, although Britain gave early moral support to the idea of guaranteeing individual freedoms against governments, it was not until 1966 that she was prepared to admit the right of individual British citizens to petition the Commission on Human Rights directly and take what the Select Committee called 'the long road to Strasbourg'. Even now there is no guarantee that a complaint which reaches the European Court of Human Rights and is upheld by it will be remedied. Although decisions of the Court of Human Rights are binding in international law, the enforcement of the Convention depends upon the assumption that countries which have ratified the document will want to harmonize their approach to civil liberties and that moral political criticism from other European countries will be more effective than sanctions against a state found to be in breach of the Convention. And even if not justiciable in British courts, the values of the Convention have an educative and persuasive force both in British courts and with the wider public.

Certain references to the Commission have moreover proved highly embarrassing for Britain. One especially sensitive area is the treatment of prisoners in Northern Ireland, which has generated a range of civil liberties-related issues.[55] After the introduction of internment in 1971 the government of the Irish Republic brought a number of charges against the United Kingdom. Although the Commission exonerated the United Kingdom on some of them and recognized the peculiar nature of the situation there, it also found against the United Kingdom on some charges. In particular some of the British security forces' 'deep interrogation techniques' were found to have violated Article III of the Convention, which states that 'no person shall be subjected to torture or to inhuman or degrading treatment or punishment'.[56] The same provision was also invoked successfully to condemn the practice of birching as a judicially enforceable punishment in the Isle of Man.[57] In addition to these cases the European Commission also deemed admissible a number of petitions which alleged that the legal remedies for mental patients within the United Kingdom were inadequate by the standards of the Convention.[58]

Although the House of Lords Select Committee reported in favour of introducing a bill of rights into British law by a narrow margin of six votes to five, the Committee was unanimous in its decision that if such a step were taken the bill should be based on the European Convention. One argument which was pressed in favour of the introduction of a bill of rights was that by joining the European Economic Community Britain had already taken a decision which would have a growing impact on her domestic law and give an extended role to the British judiciary. It is, of course, precisely this transfer of powers to the British judiciary which makes many on the left in Britain hostile to the idea of a bill of rights. In addition to the fear that an activist judiciary might emerge in Britain, the Select Committee also noted a number of arguments against the idea, including the view that there were really no more than a 'few marginal situations' where the introduction of a bill of rights would bestow a remedy not already available under existing law. Thus in the view of many of those opposed to a bill of rights for Britain the traditional British approach to civil liberties was entirely justifiable and unlikely to be improved by the device of a formal declaration.

The traditional British approach to civil liberties has been called a 'negative' approach in that it allows the citizen complete freedom to do anything which has not been specifically prohibited. Also in a number of identifiable spheres such as freedom of the person it gives the citizen specific remedies to be used in the case of an invasion of liberty. In order to see how this system operates it is necessary to look a little more closely at the spectrum of issues involving civil liberties in Britain and the contemporary position in relation to them.

The liberty which has traditionally been seen as the most important item in Britain's catalogue of civil liberties is freedom of the person. American and British lawyers have traced its origins back to Magna Carta; Dicey gave it a special pre-eminence when he cast scorn upon the idea that formal declarations of rights were necessary and pointed out that, had Voltaire been imprisoned in a country with

Britain's legal remedies, he would have been able to secure his release from the Bastille. The legal remedy most closely linked to freedom of the person is the prerogative writ of *habeas corpus ad subjiciendum*, which provides a procedure for effecting the immediate release of an individual from unlawful detention by either a public or a private authority. Initially the point of the writ was to prevent imprisonment without trial; it acquired an important status as a symbol of procedural fairness in the period of conflict between Crown and Commons in the seventeenth century. Today it is of relatively limited use, for its scope is restricted to circumstances where no legal process has been concluded and no alternative remedies are available. Thus it cannot be used to challenge imprisonment after a conviction. Moreover in Northern Ireland, where the writ might have been useful as a way of challenging internment, the government has in times of crisis suspended the Habeas Corpus Act. (The whole question of civil rights in Northern Ireland is now supervised by a standing committee on civil rights.) However, the remedy of *habeas corpus* has occasionally been used in connection with vulnerable categories of the population. Thus it has been used to challenge detention in a mental hospital, and it should be noted that until the coming into force of the Mental Health (Amendment) Act of 1982 – which amended the Mental Health Act of 1959, established a supervisory Mental Health Commission and improved the situation of mental patients in a number of areas, including *inter alia* treatment, appeals against detention and the exercise of voting rights – persons detained against their will in a mental hospital could not have access to legal aid.[59] Similarly it has been used to challenge detention by immigration authorities – an area where Britain's approach has frequently been criticized as being in contravention of the European Convention. But in general it is of very little use to the average citizen.

It should perhaps be noted that one area where there has been a very considerable change in recent times has been in relation to the ability of prisoners to make complaints against the prison authorities. The House of Lords in 1983 decided that prison authorities could not obstruct a prisoner's access to the court by interfering with his letters or by impeding his attempts to contact a solicitor.[60] This decision followed an earlier case which made it easier for prisoners to contact their legal advisers with a view to instituting civil proceedings.[61] And it was followed by a decision which effectively eliminated the practice of requiring prisoners to seek internal satisfaction of their grievance before they were allowed to turn to external authorities for help.[62]

In part the infrequency of applications for *habeas corpus* writs underlines the general conformity of British administrative practice to the principle that there should be no detention without trial. Yet in relation to other aspects of the administration of law and order, Britain cannot claim so unquestionably successful a record. In particular the police powers of arrest and the questioning of suspects – which were revised to give greater powers to the police in the Police and Criminal Evidence Act of 1984 – as well as such related matters as the invasion of privacy and the seizure of potential evidence vividly illustrate the weaknesses of the pragmatic British approach to civil liberties. (The first version of the Police and Criminal Evidence Bill, which was lost with the May 1983 general election, attempted to extend police powers to enter private property to search for evidence, but the criticism from professional groups especially likely to be affected, such as journalists and priests, was such that the government dropped the clause.) The problem is not that a citizen who finds himself in the situation of confrontation with the police is likely to be treated less fairly than his American counterpart, for example, even after the so-called 'due process revolution' in the United States. It is rather that the British reliance on the fair play of policemen, internal codes of discipline and the discretion of the courts places a tremendous premium on the consistent integrity of institutions which by their very nature are often subject to pressures and prejudices that may prove difficult to resist. Overworked policemen who suspect that someone is guilty are not perhaps the best protectors of the suspect's rights. The so-called Judges' Rules which govern police practice in relation to the gathering of evidence were codified in the Police and Criminal Evidence Act; but the clarification which that Act effected did not go so far as to exclude improperly obtained evidence from court, even if this recent step has removed some of the obscurity surrounding the code of conduct which must be adhered to.

The precise powers of the police in relation to arrest, interrogation, search and seizure are beyond the scope of this book, and they are in any event at the time of writing subject to revision as a result of the Police and Criminal Evidence Act. (That Act itself resulted from concern about a number of matters connected with police powers of arrest, detention and questioning which emerged as a result of the *Confait* case and the subsequent Committee of Inquiry and Royal Commission on Criminal Procedure.)[63] Only the outlines of the position will be attempted here, but it is perhaps important to bear in mind that because the situation with respect to arrest is complex – some critics would go so far as to say confused – one major problem with the law in this area is that it is very difficult for the ordinary citizen at the time of an arrest or attempted arrest to know his rights in the matter.

The tradition of the police as a body of men with powers similar to ordinary members of the public is maintained in relation to arrest. In England and Wales the citizen and the policeman both enjoy statutory powers of arrest, although if the arrest turns out to be unjustified they may be sued for assault or false imprisonment. Most arrests, however, are made by the police with warrants from a magistrate. It was established in the seventeenth century that a warrant must be a specific one, naming the individual and the offence. The police and private citizens also have powers under the Criminal Law Act of 1967 to arrest without warrant in connection with a range of serious offences known as arrestable offences. If the arrest is to be lawful the accused must be brought before a magistrate as soon as is practicable. The magistrate can then either remand the accused in custody or grant bail until full legal proceedings can occur. The conditions on which bail will be granted have traditionally concerned libertarians; the conditions under which it may be refused have been restrictively defined by the Bail Act of 1976.

This Act makes bail no longer dependent on the ability of the accused to provide recognizances and gives a general right to bail except where it is thought that the accused might escape, commit further offences or try to interfere with witnesses. It was seen as a liberalizing measure but, although popular in some quarters, it was much criticized by the police. Moreover it was restrictively interpreted by the courts, who upheld a controversial magistrates' court decision which refused to hear a second application for bail.[64]

One controversial aspect of the Police and Criminal Evidence Act of 1984 was that it extended the power of the police to arrest without a warrant anyone who failed to give his name and address. It also extended the period for which an accused person could be held without access to a lawyer.

The rules about police behaviour while a suspect is being questioned derive from the so-called Judges' Rules and a number of administrative directions to the police. The Police and Criminal Evidence Act of 1984 gave the secretary of state the power to issue codes of practice in connection with the treatment, questioning, identification and detention by police forces of persons suspected of committing criminal offences.[65] But − and this to a large extent weakens the effect of such a code − a failure to observe it does not by itself render the person who is in breach of the code liable to either criminal or civil proceedings, although it does render that person liable to disciplinary action. Thus the British system continued to rely on internal discipline and the availability of civil actions against the police for malpractice and, at the same time, to allow the judges considerable discretion as to the admissibility of improperly acquired evidence.

It should be noted that because of the unusual circumstances which exist in Northern Ireland it has been necessary to introduce different rules there in relation to the powers of the police and security forces – enabling the police, for example, to exercise powers of arrest where no specific offence is suspected.[66] There are also different rules governing the length of time a suspect may held for interrogation, although the rules regulating the interrogation process and the rights of suspects during questioning are embodied in the code of the Northern Ireland police force, the Royal Ulster Constabulary. Because of the dangers of suspects absconding or interfering with witnesses there are different and stricter rules governing the granting of bail in Northern Ireland. The courts also have adopted different methods of procedure in relation to what are known as 'scheduled' – i.e. largely terrorist – offences. The jury system has been dispensed with in such cases, and the decision is taken by a single judge who determines points of fact and law and pronounces on sentence. These courts – the so-called Diplock courts – are controversial, as is the modification of the standards of admissibility of evidence in such courts. The fact that the Diplock courts have relied heavily on the use of confessions obtained during interrogation, and on informants – the so-called 'super-grasses' – has made the operation of these courts subject to criticism from many quarters and has been thought to have undermined the confidence of the Roman Catholic community in the fairness of the judicial system. However it is difficult to see what alternatives there are in a situation where juries might be intimidated.

The additional powers given to the police and security forces in Northern Ireland derive from two pieces of legislation – the Northern Ireland (Emergency Provisions) Act 1978 and the Prevention of Terrorism Act 1984. Because of the unusual powers granted in these Acts they have been subject to review, so that the Prevention of Terorrism Act was the subject of a wide-ranging review by Lord Jellicoe in 1976 and the Northern Ireland (Emergency Provisions) Act was reviewed by a committee headed by Sir George Baker in 1984.[67]

The conflict between the need to have enforceable standards to govern police behaviour and the need to maintain flexibility for the police in the detection of crime recurs in a number of other aspects of the law relating to police behaviour. Indeed it is in this general area that many advocates of a bill of rights for Britain thought that such a formal statement of citizen's rights could be most useful. Although the National Council for Civil Liberties has displayed a somewhat ambiguous attitude towards such a bill – because it was seen as a way of handing power from politicians to the judiciary – the NCCL evidence to the House of Lords Select Committee on a Bill of Rights, to the Royal Commission on Criminal Procedure and to the public debate on the Police and Criminal Evidence bills has frequently reiterated the need to improve this aspect of British practice, including for example the need for greater care to see that access to lawyers is available at various stages of the criminal process.[68]

Holding the balance between the general interest in seeing that crime is detected and the equal interest in ensuring that individuals continue to enjoy a substantial degree of procedural protection is clearly difficult, especially when it is remembered that in most societies the majority of the population may be as likely to support authoritarian measures as libertarian ones. The difference of opinion among those who wish to maintain civil liberties even when a price has to be paid for them has become increasingly apparent in the field of freedom of speech and assembly. The freedom to hold peaceful meetings and to take part in demonstrations is acknowledged in most international and national statements of civil liberties. In Britain, however, the law guarantees no absolute right either to hold a political meeting or to demonstrate; both rights are subject to statutory and common law restrictions which in effect allow the police and the courts a good deal of discretion in their methods of maintaining public order, as well as a variety of powers to curtail and control public meetings if they decide that to be necessary.

Police discretion and the attitudes of the courts about public order became the subject of controversy during the 1970s as a variety of organizations and causes sought to advance their message by recourse to direct action. In particular the revived Campaign for Nuclear Disarmament adopted this tactic, which led in 1983–4 to a prolonged 'sit-in' at the site at Greenham Common where American nuclear weapons were installed. Moreover the experience of serious disturbances in British cities in the early 1980s and the findings of the Scarman Report underlined the extent to which public order might have to be maintained by police intervention, and the capacity which that intervention itself had to exacerbate disorder.

The law relating to public meetings and to processions is complex. In theory the only restriction on a public meeting is the absence of a suitable meeting place: a hall may for example prove difficult to find if the group involved has a history of violent meetings. Thus authorities have become increasingly unwilling to hire halls to the National Front. Indeed in 1979 there was a strong demand for a tightening of the law when riots, in which one man was killed, followed a National

Front meeting in Southall.[69] In addition there has been more general concern about the role of the police and the Special Patrol Group in such events. Open-air meetings require the consent of the local authority if its land is to be used, and for the special centres of public protest – Hyde Park and Trafalgar Square in London – the consent of the secretary of state for the Environment is required. As far as processions are concerned the police have additional statutory powers which are the product of the fascist marches of the 1930s which led to legislation. The Public Order Act of 1936 gave the home secretary additional power to regulate processions which seemed likely to produce serious disorder, and gave the chief police officer in each police authority the power to impose conditions on the organizers of marches and demonstrations. Thus if the circumstances of a proposed march warrant such intervention – if, for example, the National Front propose to march through an area of heavy ethnic minority residence – the police can prescribe the route which a procession must take. In addition the chief of police can, if he thinks the overall situation in an area sufficiently serious, ask for a general ban on all processions in the area for a period not exceeding three months. The application for such a ban has to be made to the appropriate local authority, which may then make an order imposing it, providing that the consent of the home secretary has been obtained. In London the Metropolitan Police commissioner himself makes the order if the consent of the home secretary is given.

Quite clearly these provisions give the police, the local authorities and the home secretary substantial power to control the arrangements governing processions, and in the last resort would enable the imposition of a blanket prohibition on certain kinds of marches. The problem from the point of view of the police is to know when to use their powers. Lord Scarman, who headed the inquiries into the causes of the Brixton disorders of 1981 and into the earlier demonstrations in Red Lion Square in which one death occurred, put the point succinctly in a lecture: 'A policeman is the servant of both sides in a street disorder.'[70] Although in the riots of the early 1980s this position became difficult to sustain, as frequently the disorders seemed to be directed against the police, it remains a difficult and delicate question as to when to sacrifice one party's right to demonstrate for another's right to try to interfere with its message. It is an equally difficult question as to when to sacrifice the right of peaceful protest to the general interest of the public in being free to carry on their business and use the streets without interruption.

The problem of restricting demonstrations is especially sensitive when it relates to groups – whether of the right or left – which claim they have only limited access to the normal channels of political communication such as Parliament and the mass media, and it is also made difficult by the obscurity of the law. As Lord Scarman emphasized, the law has not 'adjusted itself to the realities of an industrial society entitled to exercise freedom of speech, protest and assembly not only through representative institutions but directly – by assembly, march and protest in public places'.[71] The principle that any lawful use of the highway is permissible and that a procession is nothing more than a number of people passing along it will not really help either the courts or the police to cope with such phenomena as mass picketing and concerted demonstrations. Indeed, if Lord Scarman's assertion that 'there is no modern law governing the basic priorities in the use by society of streets and public places' is correct, then the traditional approach to civil liberties once more seems deficient. It is moreover deficient in a way which places, as Lord Scarman suggested, a heavy burden on the police – a burden which with the growing social tensions of the 1980s it seems unfair to ask them to bear.[72] At the time of writing the difficulties inherent in balancing concern for civil liberties with the need to maintain public order are being examined by the government in the context of a review of the Public Order Act of 1936, perhaps with a view to introducing some of the earlier recommendations of the Law Commission on public order.[73]

A large part of the controversy generated by the National Front's demonstrations of the 1970s stemmed from the fear that they would not merely cause civil disorder but would also stimulate racial antagonisms if given wider publicity as a result of their violence. By the time of the Brixton riots and the disturbances in the other British cities of 1981 it was clear that the position of the ethnic minorities constituted a special cause of concern as far as relationships between the police and the general public were concerned.

Concern for the promotion of racial harmony in an increasingly plural society had over the period since 1965 prompted successive British governments to provide specific protections for minority groups, and the exercises in attempting to repair relationships between police and minority communities in the aftermath of the disorders constituted another self-conscious attempt to improve understanding by legislative intervention.

Although the various Race Relations Acts which were passed between 1965 and 1976 have gained widespread acceptance, they do have implications for the exercise of civil liberties, for they constitute an additional inroad into the freedom of speech of society as a whole. The Race Relations Act of 1965 effectively extended the Public Order

Act of 1936 by making it an offence to use in a public place or meeting any threatening, abusive or insulting words or behaviour or to distribute or display any writing sign or visible representation with intent to provoke a breach of the peace or whereby a breach of the peace was likely to be occasioned. It created a new offence of incitement to racial hatred, which made it illegal to stir up hatred against any section of the public distinguished by colour, race, or ethnic or national origins, regardless of whether a breach of the peace was likely to be committed as a result. With this Act, the law began to move away from the prohibition of offences because of their contribution to civil disorder and instituted a category of offences which were to be prohibited on grounds of their inherent undesirability. When this category is added to the already formidable, if archaic, range of common law and statutory offences which bedevil the exercise of the liberty to march, demonstrate and to speak freely – riot, affray, rout, unlawful assembly, public nuisance, obstructing the highway and obstructing a police officer in the course of his duty – it would seem that public protest is likely to become an increasingly hazardous venture.[74]

Freedom of expression in Britain, like freedom of assembly, exists only in so far as it is not specifically restricted by legislation or common law. Thus the extent of that freedom in any period depends very much on the prevailing attitudes among legislators and the judiciary. Those attitudes are not always consistent; after a period of liberalization, the United Kingdom may now be experiencing something of a return to less permissive attitudes on such questions as censorship. Nor is the question of freedom of expression one which is affected by formal restraints only; the legal provisions do affect what newspapers and the media say and publish but also, alongside the formal restrictions, there is a range of informal ones which effectively constrain and control the free circulation of ideas. Thus – and this has caused the Monopolies Commission to seek to exert control over the ownership of newspapers – there is concern that control over the mass media may be concentrated in too few hands. In fact the range of television companies has expanded and looks likely to expand further with the advent of new opportunities in cable and satellite. However, newspaper ownership remains concentrated and, for some critics, the spread of opinion within British newspapers is not great enough. Even within an expanding television industry it may also be the case that internal censorship for whatever reason may also serve to exclude some points of view and to impose a certain uniformity of opinion.

Several branches of the law constrain the free expression of opinion in the United Kingdom. Statements likely to damage an individual's reputation may fall foul of the defamation laws, which in the United Kingdom, unlike the United States, protect persons in public life on the same basis as private citizens.[75] Certain categories of proceedings, such as verbatim reporting of parliamentary debates and legal proceedings, are protected; this privilege sometimes protects reporters who might be at risk from a libel suit by allowing them simply to repeat allegations made for example in the context of a court case. This was the way in which the highly sensational series of allegations surrounding the former Liberal leader Mr Jeremy Thorpe became public.[76] Journalists may invoke defences which mitigate the effects of the law – for example the defence of fair comment; but British newspapers are often forced to delay their discussion of political scandals either until their evidence is watertight or until foreign newspapers and the underground press have made an item common knowledge. Since not merely the author but also the publisher and vendor of a libel can be sued, journals such as *Private Eye*, although now perhaps more establishment than underground, are frequently sold only by small newsagents and not by big retail chains.

A second restriction on freedom of speech is the law of obscenity and blasphemy. The obscenity laws were liberalized by the Obscene Publications Act of 1959 as amended in 1964; although there were spectacular prosecutions against well-known works of literature to test the law in the early 1960s – both D. H. Lawrence's novel *Lady Chatterley's Lover* and Cleland's *Fanny Hill* were prosecuted – the general climate had so changed by the end of the 1960s that it was difficult to persuade the Director of Public Prosecutions to initiate prosecutions and to obtain convictions from juries. However, occasionally prosecutions do succeed, as happened in 1971 when the so-called 'School-Kids' Issue' of *Oz* produced one of the longest obscenity trials in British legal history and led to the conviction of the three editors, Richard Neville, Felix Dennis and Jim Anderson.[77] Not all prosecutions take place under the Obscene Publications Act, however. It is an offence to send obscene literature through the post, so that a conviction may be secured if the police wish to stamp out the distribution of pornography. Similarly Customs officers have the power to seize obscene material under the Customs and Excise Act of 1952 – although Britain's right to regulate such *European* imports occasioned legal controversy.

The courts have also from time to time revived archaic common law crimes, despite the important objection that a criminal conviction is such a serious matter as to be only acceptable in contemporary society where the offence is clearly defined in advance. Thus in 1961 the House of Lords created a storm of controversy when it used the crime of 'conspiracy to corrupt public morals' to secure the conviction of a man named Shaw who published and distributed a directory of prostitutes.[78] More recently the common law crime of blasphemous libel was used to secure the prosecution and conviction of the editor of *Gay News*, a magazine which later went out of business. This prosecution occasioned protest not merely because it seemed out of place in an increasingly secular and liberal society but because the law of blasphemous libel had not been invoked since 1921.[79] It was a judgement which if extended to other religions could have profound implications for freedom of expression in Britain.

Other legal restrictions on freedom of speech stem from the Race Relations Acts which make incitement to racial hatred an offence, from the Official Secrets Act of 1911 and from the developing law of confidentiality. The initial caution of the government in the sphere of race relations was evidenced by the fact that under the 1965 Act no prosecution could be brought without the consent of the attorney-general, and intention to stir up racial hatred had to be proved. While it is difficult to tell how many complaints have been referred to the attorney-general since 1965, there have been very few prosecutions. An early opportunity to test the law occurred in 1967 when Colin Jordan was prosecuted for distributing stickers and pamphlets on behalf of his National Socialist Party. In the same year Michael X, a black power leader, was prosecuted for using inflammatory language at a meeting of his group.

The problem of securing a conviction under s. 6(1) of the 1965 Race Relations Act and the development of opinion in favour of strengthening the legislation in this sphere encouraged the government to eliminate in the 1976 Race Relations Act the need to prove subjective intention to stir up racial hatred.[80] Section 70 of the Act therefore made it a criminal offence to use, publish or distribute threatening words or written matter in circumstances where it was likely that racial hatred would be stirred up. The maximum penalties for committing this offence are quite severe – six months' imprisonment or a fine of £400 on summary conviction, and a maximum of two years' imprisonment on indictment. However a prosecution still requires the consent of the attorney-general, and it may be assumed that this law will be used sparingly.[81] Indeed it may be that the advent of a Conservative government has made it unlikely that there will be major extensions in the use of the law to control racial discrimination and, although the Commission on Racial Equality is still actively pressing for further government initiatives, it seems that moves in the direction desired by the CRE (for example to some limited form of affirmative action, and to shift the burden of proof onto the respondent once a finding of unfavourable treatment has been established) will not find favour in Whitehall.[82]

The restrictions on freedom of speech inherent in the Official Secrets Act raise a number of difficult questions about the character and quality of British government. Over the 1960s and 1970s there developed a general feeling that much of British government was too secretive and that to shroud the ordinary processes of decision-making in mystery was not merely undemocratic but positively damaging to effective government. Accordingly a start was made on trying to redress the balance between the need for openness and information in government and the natural tendency of politicians and officials to try to conceal the activities of government from inspection. Thus consultative papers were increasingly published in advance of government's formulation of its own views and in 1977 permanent secretaries were encouraged to make such information available by Sir Douglas Allen, later Lord Croham. Although the so-called 'Croham directive' was restrictively interpreted, government departments were supposed to release a wide variety of background material of a factual nature, so that press and public could make their own judgements about the reasoning behind policy decisions.[83]

On one front however – reform of the Official Secrets Act – progress has been extremely slow. Indeed the various attempts to reform the Act which occurred over the 1970s underlined the difficulty of striking a balance which could satisfy concern for state security with concern for openness and civil liberties. Moreover the series of scandals with security implications which Britain experienced during the late 1970s and 1980s created a climate in which there was little enthusiasm for any reform which might be interpreted as reducing the government's arsenal against subversion.

The Official Secrets Act is unpopular in many quarters partly because of the uncertain way in which it operates and partly because it encapsulates a large number of assumptions about what should be the proper balance between public scrutiny and government confidentiality. The 1911 Act was passed in the wake of the Agadir incident, and Parliament, assuming that its purpose was to produce additional legislative powers to deal with German espionage, subjected its detailed provisions to very little detailed examination. Thus the broad terms of s. 2, which have occasioned the most hostility, were not commented upon despite the fact – and it is this which makes it so obnoxious to journalists – that it makes the unauthorized *receipt* as well as the unauthorized communication of information an offence. In practice governments have not used the Act in a consistently repressive manner; but it hangs over the media and the public as a weapon which could be used if government felt strongly enough that certain information should be not be published. The fact that it is not a dead letter was deliberately underlined in 1984 when Sarah Tisdall, a government employee who had revealed details of the planned deployment of Cruise missiles to the *Guardian*, was sent to prison for six months. Her appeal against sentence was dismissed.[84]

It is however the sheer unpredictability of the government's attitudes towards leaks and disclosures which has made the operation of the law in this area seem arbitrary; and on those occasions when it has been used against journalists it has inevitably made them seem martyrs in the cause of press freedom. Thus the Heath government of 1970–4, shortly after deciding to establish a committee to review the Official Secrets Act, used the legislation to prosecute two *Daily Telegraph* journalists who had published a secret assessment of the Nigerian civil war. Both journalists were acquitted and the judge's comments on the nature and scope of s. 2 were sufficiently hostile to add further strength to the demand for radical revision of its provisions.[85]

Above all, however, exception to the Official Secrets Act has arisen because it symbolizes the contrast between the British approach to governmental relations with the general public and the approach adopted by some other countries. In the United States and Sweden it is assumed that the public has a right of access to information unless there is some good reason, usually of compelling national security, why such information should not be disclosed. The burden of proof then falls on the government to justify withholding information. The goal of open government is embodied in Sweden's Freedom of the Press Act of 1949 and the United States' Freedom of Information Act of 1974. In Britain, on the other hand, no such right is acknowledged in principle and the timing and speed of government concessions on the release of information is entirely within the hands of the executive. Green papers, background material, greater publicity for civil servants and more frequent examination of departments by select committees and mechanisms such as the parliamentary commissioner – certainly all these have been gains for the proponents of a more democratic and accountable governmental system. Yet the British system resists acknowledging the elementary principle that the executive and its workings ought to be open to public scrutiny.

The committee which the Conservative government of 1970–4 established to review the workings of the Official Secrets Act admitted that s. 2 was 'a mess'. However it was not prepared to see the defence of disclosure in the public interest introduced, and indeed, for many people, the committee's proposals suggested a tightening up rather than a liberalization of the law. The Conservative government which set up the Franks Committee did not, it should be noted, introduce any legislation on the basis of the 1973 report – perhaps just because its proposals were too liberal for the government while too timid for the critics of the existing Act. The Labour government that succeeded Edward Heath's administration announced in 1976 that it intended to legislate to replace s. 2. of the Official Secrets Act with a law, usually referred to as an Official Information Act, which would restrict the operation of the criminal law to certain categories of information. Then in 1978 the government published a white paper which discussed the options available to it, although it stated that legislation would not be possible in that parliamentary session.[86] The Conservative government elected in 1979 had been committed to introducing reforming legislation, but its efforts to do so were stymied by the Blunt affair (in which it was revealed that an eminent scholar who held the office of keeper of the Queen's pictures had been an important member of the Soviet espionage network) and by the fact that it could find little agreement on which to base new legislation.

The question of the secrecy of cabinet papers was raised in two dramatic incidents in the 1970s – controversies which did much to extend openness in British administration. The first was the publication by Jonathan Cape and the *Sunday Times* of the diaries of the late Richard Crossman, who had been a cabinet minister from 1964 to 1970. The novelty of the diaries was their detailed recording of cabinet proceedings, sometimes with quotations from cabinet papers, and their frank, if not tactless, remarks about colleagues including civil servants. The convention of ministerial memoirs had been understood to require that all material intended for publication should be submitted for approval to the cabinet secretary first. However, for Richard Crossman the point of his diaries was to cut through the web of secrecy and hypocrisy which he saw permeating Whitehall. Therefore, although his executors submitted the manuscript to the cabinet secretary for comment, they were unwilling to allow his objections to publication to alter their determination to publish the diaries in full.[87] The attorney-general sought an injunction to prevent publication, but Lord Widgery – the Lord Chief Justice – refused to grant one. Two points of interest emerged from his judgement, which turned not on whether there was any statutory bar on publication – the attorney-general was not relying on the Official Secrets Act – but on whether the court had the legal power to restrain the publication of confidential information. Although the court allowed the publication of the diaries it asserted that it did indeed have such a power, by analogy with its power to protect confidences given in private relationships such as marriage.[88] However, whether court should restrain publication depended upon the circumstances, including for example the nature of the confidential information disclosed and the time which had elapsed between the events and the revelations. Thus the court in the Crossman case not merely expanded the law of confidentiality in a way which gave government potential new instruments for protecting its operations; it also transferred the question of disclosure in this area from the realm of convention and consensus to that of judicial control.

The establishment of a Committee of Privy Councillors to examine the whole question of the publication of ministerial memoirs, together with its recommendations, seemed to suggest that there is still substantial faith in the efficacy of informal guidelines rather than precise legal rules, and that the iconoclastic actions of Mr Crossman will prove the exception rather than the rule. (In fact only Barbara Castle's diaries approached Crossman's in details and frankness in the post-1976 period, and there have been few revelations by Conservative cabinet ministers which have illuminated the understanding of how government decisions are taken.[89] Since the publication of the Castle diaries much of the initiative in eliminating government secrecy and broadening understanding of the role of cabinet committees, for example, has been taken by journalists such as Peter Hennessy.)[90] The Committee of Privy Councillors recommended that the publication of material affecting national security, international relations and the relations between ministers and their official advisers should not occur for fifteen years after the events described. Only time will tell whether this recommendation leads to any further easing of the restrictions on access to papers for scholarly purposes.

The second incident which raised the question of the confidentiality of cabinet documents was the publication by *New Society* of papers relating to the withdrawal of a proposed child benefit. In this case it was clear that either a member of the government or someone with access to cabinet papers had leaked the documents to the journal. The disclosure sparked off an internal cabinet inquiry and a police investigation, both of which proved inconclusive but which raised again the logic of a system which could penalize publication of material of public interest. In the period after Mrs Thatcher took office in 1979 a large number of leaks occurred, and indeed some suggested that it was because of the leakiness of the CPRS or 'think-tank' that the latter institution was abolished in 1983.

One further source of legal restriction on the media ought to be mentioned, although it applies equally to private citizens, and that is the law of contempt. The attorney-general has power to prevent the publication of material which relates to pending legal proceedings, both civil and criminal. The justification for this power is that it prevents 'trial by newspaper' which, especially in a criminal trial, would mean that the jury would be exposed to discussions that might make an objective assessment of the legal evidence impossible. The reverse of the coin is that a number of cases have arisen in which the law of contempt has been used to restrict comment on matters of public controversy. The *cause célèbre* – which went to the European Court on Human Rights – was the Thalidomide tragedy, where the *Sunday Times* risked contempt proceedings by commenting on Distillers Ltd's responsibility for the effects of their drug. Following the report of the Phillimore Committee on the law of contempt a new Contempt of Court Act was passed in 1981. This makes it unlawful to publish anything which creates 'a substantial risk that the course of justice in the proceedings will be seriously impeded or prejudiced.'[91] This restriction takes effect from the time civil proceedings become active or, in criminal cases, from the point at which an arrest without warrant is made or a warrant issued. However for some critics the extension to the appellate courts of the contempt provisions was a retrograde step, since it had previously been assumed that senior judges, unlike juries, would not be affected by newspaper comment.

Despite the fact that the 1981 law did something to remove the abuse of so-called 'gagging writs' – i.e. writs which were issued or threatened in order to prevent publication of damaging material – the law of contempt is still controversial, and in criminal cases especially it cannot be said to be working well. Whenever spectacular cases occur, as in the case of the so-called Yorkshire Ripper, it is difficult to get the press to observe the rules of contempt, and indeed the courts seem to have acknowledged the difficulty of controlling newspapers in this way.

Apart from these restrictions on what can be said or published, the Theatre Act of 1968 subjects live performances to the same guidelines as those that govern books under the Obscene Publications Act of 1959. Although it was long assumed that prosecutions under the Act would be rare, Mrs Mary Whitehouse – a controversial campaigner for cleansing British public life – initiated a private prosecution of a play, *The Romans in Britain*, in 1981.[92] Films are handled by a slightly different system, and the British Board of Film Censors is an independent body which classifies all films to be shown publicly in the United Kingdom. Ultimately however it is the local authorities who must decide what may be shown in their jurisdiction, thereby allowing a certain degree of flexibility and adjustment to local tastes. Local authorities need not take account of certificates granted by the British Board of Film Censors and many exclude a film from their area altogether, although the system also allows liberal authorities to show films which have not been granted a certificate.

The spread of video recorders and video cassettes led to demands for an extension of control to these products. Although video films were shown privately, there developed a market for so-called video nasties – which were films of a violent and pornographic kind and which frequently were made available to adolescents and even very young children. In 1984 the government made time for a private member's bill which sought to extend the classification scheme applied by the British Board of Film Censors to videos.[93]

As far as radio and television are concerned both the British Broadcasting Corporation and the Independent Broadcasting Authority have elaborate arrangements for operating internal self-censorship. The British Broadcasting Corporation, although its connection with government is ostensibly greater than that of the IBA, paradoxically may exercise greater latitude in its interpretation of what needs to be censored. This is because the prestige of the BBC and its very public link with government – the original powers of the Corporation derive from a Royal Charter – make it less likely that political pressure will be exerted successfully to influence what the BBC shows. However, the delicacy of the BBC's position was underlined during the Falklands war when the BBC found itself subject to parliamentary criticism for its independent reporting of the situation. The IBA's position is very different. It is a government-appointed body and subcontracts programmes to a variety of independent television companies; while the possibility of using the power to grant franchises may be used to influence programme output, it seems that considerations of commercial viability are likely to weigh more heavily in the minds of the IBA. The recent expansion of television facilities – such as additional channels, cable and satellite – makes the opportunity for direct governmental pressure on television all the more remote.

The closeness which long marked the relationship between the broadcasting authorities and the state has not affected the press in the same way. Its problems in the post-1960 period stemmed from rather different sources. First there has been the problem of concentration of ownership, which in the view of many critics had serious implications for the diversity of opinion to be found at the national and provincial levels of the press. Labour in particular has frequently charged that the press has a pro-Conservative bias, although when the Social

Democratic party was formed in 1981 it was noted by many commentators that this event was treated in a way which suggested overwhelming media sympathy for that strand of political thinking. Second, there has been the problem of lack of commercial viability – a problem which accounted for the closure of two newspapers, the *Daily Herald* and the *News Chronicle*. Finally there has been the not unconnected problem of difficulties which have arisen from staffing problems. In Britain the print unions are strong, and they have frequently seemed to prefer to cripple their newspapers rather than moderate their stance on manning, pay or methods of work. This attitude was in large part responsible for conflicts which caused *The Times* to suspend publication for a large part of 1978. The refusal of the National Union of Journalists to allow journalists to be exempted from the closed-shop provisions of the Trade Union and Labour Relations Act suggests that those few newspapers which do survive will find it difficult to avoid the uniformity of outlook which stems from a concentration of ownership on the one hand and the homogeneity of practice in such matters as recruitment on the other. It may, alas, be that although Britain will continue to exhibit more diversity in terms of its population, its politics and its social life, the trend of journalism will be in the opposite direction.

13   The Citizen and the Administration (II): The Control of Government and the Redress of Grievances

As was seen in the last chapter, constitutional history and political expediency have combined to make the protection of civil liberties in the United Kingdom dependent upon the self-restraint of Parliament and on the ordinary processes of the common law. However, as the debate about the desirability of introducing a codified bill of rights into the British legal system suggests, opinion is now very much divided as to whether a more self-conscious and comprehensive approach to questions of individual rights and freedoms is required. The provisions made for the defence of the classic political freedoms such as freedom of speech and assembly will always be a sensitive matter, since those freedoms lie at the heart of the relationship between the individual and the state. Equally important, in the context of a society where the activities of government are extensive, where there is a wide area of discretionary decision-making and where the individual comes into frequent contact with public authorities, the quality of the administration itself will be a matter of major concern. The procedures employed by government in assessing a whole range of entitlements and obligations, from welfare benefits to income tax, must be able to command the respect of those who are likely to be affected. Since the 1960s there have been increased opportunities to subject administrative decisions to scrutiny and to demand an explanation of the policies on which those decisions are based. Thus the individual who finds himself in conflict with an agency of the state is in a better position to secure a fair resolution of any dispute with government than he was twenty years ago. And even if some critics have sensed a certain slowing of the process, there is now a greater awareness than in the past of the need to keep the administration responsive to the variety of demands upon it.[1]

The long-standing view that Parliament should be the primary channel for voicing complaints against government, and the emphasis placed on the MP's role as the champion of his constituents against executive error, meant that the process of devising remedies for maladministration lagged far behind the expansion of governmental functions. For their part, British lawyers frequently seemed unhappy with the legal implications of administrative developments and the problems associated with discretionary powers. Although new areas might have been expected to generate new approaches, both Parliament and the legal profession preferred to adhere to traditional doctrines and assumptions. Alternative procedures to parliamentary ones for reviewing the decisions of public authorities were for a long time weak and ill-developed; and the analysis of the problem of securing justice in the welfare state was frequently ill-informed or antediluvian. Rapid developments in the intellectual climate have now, however, had an impact on the political system; new techniques for obtaining governmental accountability and the redress of grievances (and indirectly for monitoring administrative performance) have been introduced and adapted to the existing pattern of institutions. And, as these experiments have proved successful, it has become apparent that devices adopted initially to supplement existing constitutional and administrative arrangements have themselves generated further pressures for reform.

Ministerial Responsibility and the Franks Report

Parliament's central position as the instrument whereby accountability could be secured in the United Kingdom was enshrined in the doctrine of ministerial responsibility. This doctrine has however been subjected to a great deal of pressure, and its operation is somewhat unpredictable. In essence it meant that Parliament would hold ministers responsible for all that occurred in their departments. Civil servants, while they might in extreme circumstances be the subject of public criticism, could normally expect to be shielded by their minister, who would therefore take the praise or blame for their conduct.[2] The distinction between errors made as a result of personal incompetence by civil servants and mistakes occasioned by faulty administrative practices was not significant in this doctrine; nor was it significant that the responsibility for an erroneous decision was made to lie with a minister who might not himself have taken it. In theory a minister was as responsible to Parliament for maladministration by his department as if he had himself carried out the action complained of. In practice the effect of this doctrine was uncertain. The kind of sanction which Parliament would impose on a minister responsible for a department in which mistakes were discovered naturally varied with the seriousness of the offence, the reasonableness of holding him accountable for it and the political position of the individual minister – all of which were factors more likely to be affected by party control of the House of Commons than by constitutional niceties.

However, in theory there was no doubt about Parliament's right to impose some sort of sanction, whether it took the form of a critical debate – which might result in a loss of esteem for the minister concerned and perhaps for the government as a whole – or of an enforced resignation. Parliamentary procedures reflected the importance attached to the theory of how the people's representatives might keep control of the executive: Question Time afforded regular opportunities for the quality of a minister's stewardship to be examined, and in the event of a serious allegation of malpractice or incompetence the device of an adjournment debate was always available.

Although weaknesses and inconsistencies had become apparent in this doctrine over the course of the twentieth century, it took a very long time before Parliament would admit to them. Instead, subtle shifts occurred in the interpretation of ministerial responsibility in order to take account of political reality. However, while these shifts were able to conceal the fictitious aspects of the doctrine, they did little to reassure critics that the vast apparatus of modern government was subject to effective political scrutiny or that an individual grievance would be thoroughly investigated. For example, although it was evident that sanctions were in fact rarely imposed on a minister and that cabinets would usually prefer to support one of their number rather than admit to an error which might reflect on the competence of the administration, this tendency could be accommodated by defenders of the traditional version of the doctrines associated with parliamentary control of the administration. It was the *potential* embarrassment of a pertinent parliamentary question which was the important factor in keeping the administration on its toes; and it was not important that Question Time had been increasingly transformed into an extension of the adversarial badinage between the parties which marked other aspects of the style of the Commons rather than a genuine forum for the redress of grievances or the probing of administrative failures. If necessary, it was confidently assumed, the occasion could still be employed for its theoretical purpose and the exposure of maladministration would not be obscured by the ritualistic character of Question Time.

Also, although by the early postwar period it had become increasingly apparent that ministers had little hope of understanding all the complexities of their departments' internal arrangements –

much less of controlling them – it was still thought possible that clear organization of responsibilities could produce a chain of command which would permit a minister to identify where and how individual decisions were taken. Few MPs were prepared to concede that, while such an aspiration might have been justified in a period when central government's activities were limited, it hardly corresponded to the situation of the vastly expanded personnel and functions of government that followed the second world war.

The deficiencies of the doctrine of ministerial responsibility and the need to reappraise the machinery for reviewing administrative actions were highlighted in 1954 by the Crichel Down affair, which jerked the British public, albeit temporarily, out of its complacency about the methods available for citizens to challenge executive actions. Debate continues about the significance of the Crichel Down case; but it focused attention on a range of issues connected with the quality of accountability in Britain and brought into the open the flaws in orthodox constitutional assumptions about the relationship between Parliament and the public on the one hand and between ministers and officials on the other.[3] In particular it underlined the extent to which a minister, far from being able to control his civil servants, was often their prisoner when it came to understanding an issue and explaining it to Parliament – a point which, while it may now have become exaggerated as a result of such television programmes as 'Yes Minister', was not generally appreciated in the 1950s.[4] And Crichel Down revealed the effort, resources and sheer luck required to extract a remedy for administrative injustice from the existing governmental machinery.

The facts of the Crichel Down case – which involved a compulsory purchase of land for use as a bombing site and a refusal to return it when it was no longer required for that purpose – were perhaps less important than the general questions which it raised.[5] How widespread was the arrogant and peremptory attitude which the civil servants engaged in the decision had displayed towards the general public? Were ministers regularly as ill-informed as Sir Thomas Dugdale had been? Were there large numbers of other citizens whose complaints had not been effective because they lacked the skills, persistence and resources of the complainant in that case? And to what extent could the resignation of a minister like Sir Thomas Dugdale really be taken as an effective method of compelling government to admit error, or even as a spur to improved administrative habits?

Between 1954 and 1982 Sir Thomas Dugdale's resignation – although itself representing no real threat to the government of the day – provided the last major instance of a resignation because of administrative failings within a department; individual ministers had resigned because of policy disagreements or personal indiscretions, but not because of criticism of departmental policy. In 1982, however, three Foreign Office ministers including the Foreign Secretary, Lord Carrington, resigned because of what proved to be over-optimistic assessments of the danger of an Argentinian invasion of the Falklands; and their resignations were widely held to be required by the doctrine of ministerial responsibility.[6] It has been pointed out by one authority however that no minister has resigned when the mistake has been shown to be that of the civil servants alone, and that both the Dugdale resignation and the Carrington departure were occasioned by decisions and errors of judgement in which the ministers were personally involved.[7] This would seem to be consistent with the line taken by the secretary of state for Northern Ireland after an inquiry into a major escape of prisoners in Northern Ireland revealed departmental errors. No minister at the Northern Ireland Office resigned – partly because the minister who had been responsible for prisons at the time of the escape, Lord Gowrie, was by then in another post.[8]

Perhaps the Crichel Down case had raised too many fundamental issues for the public criticism which followed it to produce an adequate response from the government. Because of general dissatisfaction with the protection afforded to the citizen against governmental decisions which materially affected his interests, in 1954 the government established the Franks Committee on Administrative Tribunals and Inquiries.[9] It was widely assumed that this Committee would be permitted to undertake the general examination of administrative decision-making processes which Crichel Down had shown to be necessary; but in fact the restriction of the Committee's terms of reference to formal tribunals and inquiries excluded the kind of discretionary decision which had aroused so much criticism in that instance.[10] In other words, the decisions outside the Franks Committee's deliberations were precisely those where the remedy could only be secured through parliamentary questioning, with all the defects exhibited during Crichel Down. It was not until the institution of a parliamentary commissioner for administration (popularly known as the Ombudsman) was created in 1967 that any reform occurred which involved this large area of decision-making.

Although the Franks Report was confined to the area where formal machinery for challenging governmental decisions already existed, the Committee's work did bring about significant improvements; and it stimulated discussion of the mechanisms of accountability in

Britain. Moreover, by defining the characteristics which ought to mark tribunals – the holy trinity of 'openness, fairness and impartiality' – it articulated values which could be applied by others to the administrative process as a whole. Thus, even if the range of the Franks Committee's work was a disappointment, it was able to make a not inconsiderable contribution of its own to the intellectual climate in which administrative procedures were discussed.

The Franks Committee recognized that a large part of the problem under its consideration was a result of the rapidly changing character of governmental activity and the sheer increase in the number of contentious decisions taken by government. The need was 'to consider afresh the procedures by which the rights of individual citizens' could be harmonized with 'wider public interests'. It also recognized that, while the administration should be efficient in the sense of being able to secure policy objectives speedily, care had to be taken to show that where an individual's interest was disturbed in order to promote the general interest, every consideration had been given to that affected individual's case. If this care was not thoroughly demonstrated, the administrative process would not be able to command the assent of the general public and would be unlikely to remain efficient in the long term. The specific recommendations of the Franks Committee were largely directed towards identifying the conditions which would produce that assent.

The major institutional innovation which occurred as a result of the Franks Committee was the establishment of two general review bodies – one for England and Wales (the Council on Tribunals) and a Committee for Scotland. Northern Ireland falls outside the scope of these review bodies, and there has been some concern that there is inadequate machinery for supervising the structure of tribunals there. The task of these bodies was to supervise generally the constitution and workings of all tribunals; they would keep the general principles enunciated by Franks under consideration and seek ways of applying them to the diversity of tribunal procedures and constitutions. The point that tribunals were part of the machinery of justice was emphasized by the suggestion that the Council on Tribunals for England and Wales should be appointed by and report to the lord chancellor, rather than – as had been suggested – to the prime minister. The 1958 Tribunals and Inquiries Act, which followed the Franks Report but by no means entirely adopted all its proposals, since Franks had proposed to give the review bodies executive as well as advisory and consultative powers, thus established two bodies which could both supervise the operations of tribunals and, albeit in a different manner, of inquiries, and by its reports contribute to the discussion of the role of these bodies in the wider political system. In 1971 the 1958 Act was superseded by a new Tribunals and Inquiries Act which for the most part simply consolidated the powers and functions acquired by the review bodies over the period 1958–70.

Although the Franks Committee was limited in its inquiries to the field where statutory appeal machinery already existed, there was even within this area a great diversity of institutional structures, as well as a wide variety of subject matter covered by the tribunals. Appeal against a tribunal's decision might, for example, be made to a court, to a specially constituted appeal tribunal or to a minister who was bound to follow a specific procedure if the matter related to compulsory purchase orders or planning appeals. As the Committee noted in 1957, the heterogeneity of tribunals made even this classification something of a simplification. But since Franks called attention to the amorphous area covered by tribunals, further legislation has extended their scope and number and has magnified the complexity of their jurisdiction.

By 1980 the most frequently used kind of tribunal was that which determined entitlement to welfare benefits. Indeed so frequent had the practice of appealing against decisions of the various authorities administering these benefits become, that in 1980 the recently elected Conservative government modified the structure of appeals so as to limit the number of challenges in this field.[11] Tribunals operate in a number of other contentious areas. Immigration has proved an especially sensitive topic both domestically and in terms of Britain's international obligations.[12] Since 1971 a tribunal structure has existed to hear appeals from those denied permission to stay in the United Kingdom. There are a range of tribunals to deal with industrial and employment disputes, and tribunals exist to hear appeals in relation to such matters as the granting of patents and the assessment of the reasonableness of rents required by private landlords. There is also an extremely important and elaborate series of tribunals to hear appeals against tax assessments. Whereas in the case of entitlement to welfare benefits the parties in the dispute will actually be the individual citizen (though perhaps supported by a pressure group such as the Child Poverty Action Group or a trade union) and a state agency, this is by no means true of all disputes which come before tribunals. Some (such as conflicts between landlord and tenant or employer and employee) are primarily between private individuals, although the conflict is regulated by principles laid down in public legislation.[13]

The reasons for using tribunals to decide appeals against administrative decisions, or to provide some protection to the citizen in the context of such special relationships as that of employer and employee, have been varied. Tribunals were established in connection with the initial legislation on welfare matters passed by the Liberal governments of 1905–15. The justification for using tribunals rather than the ordinary courts was a lingering suspicion that the judiciary would be hostile to the collectivist philosophy behind the legislation, and that it would be better administered by specialist bodies. Tribunals have also been thought to have advantages of speed, cheapness and informality, and to offer a degree of expertise which the ordinary courts may not be able to match. Like so much else in British government therefore they are a pragmatic response to the problems created by the need to administer new policies and to adjudicate disputes in areas where hitherto government and the formal processes of law have not intervened.

When it surveyed the burgeoning sphere of tribunal activity, the Franks Committee isolated one aspect of tribunals which seemed to distinguish them from other mechanisms of appeal. The point of Parliament's setting up a structure of tribunals to hear appeals, the Franks Committee thought, was that this guaranteed independence in the appeals mechanism. The very existence of a tribunal in a particular area of administration indicated that the issues involved were not so suffused with policy considerations as to render neutral determination impossible. Thus Franks drew a sharp distinction between areas of tribunal jurisdiction and fields where the policy element was so important that even individual cases had to remain subject to ministerial or departmental intervention. The conclusion which the Committee drew from this observation was that the procedure and the structure of tribunals ought to be treated as part of the machinery for adjudication rather than as an extension of the machinery of administration. In other words, the principles governing their operations ought to be similar to those applied in the courts, and they ought not to be approached as though they were simply appendages of government departments. By conceptualizing tribunals as instruments of adjudication Franks was able to elaborate the manner in which the characteristics of the judicial process – openness, fairness, and impartiality – could be applied to their operation.

Despite the succinct clarity of the Committee's approach, it proved more difficult in practice to apply these criteria than it had been to identify them. Improvements have been made since 1957 but the values of openness, fairness and impartiality do not fit the subject matter of every set of tribunals equally well. Openness, for example, might seem a straightforward ideal which could be attained simply by forcing all tribunals to sit in public. Not merely would this be reassuring to the general public, but it could have an educative role if proceedings were reported in the local press. However, the fact that many tribunals deal with such personal matters as tax assessments, social security and mental health precludes the imposition of a general requirement for open hearings. The Franks Committee could therefore only endorse the principle of making proceedings public in appropriate cases; it had to accept the continuation of a discretion on the part of a tribunal to exclude observers. Thus, although many tribunals do sit in public, many of the ones which are most used by the average citizen – for example the General Commissioners of Income Tax and the Social Security Appeal Tribunal – may sit in private.

The view of tribunals as fair and impartial bodies was enhanced by a number of the Franks Committee's recommendations. Some were admittedly symbolic rather than substantive, as for example the recommendation that tribunals should not hold their proceedings in the offices of government but should operate in some neutral building. This suggestion was designed to dispel any impression on the part of the public that tribunals were adjuncts of government rather than genuinely neutral bodies. A more significant recommendation was the requirement that all tribunals should give reasoned decisions to the appellant. However, there has been something of a shift away from this requirement which has alarmed the Council, although it is not clear how effective its concern has proved. In 1980 the Council recorded its vehement opposition to the proposal that Rent Assessment Tribunals should no longer be expected to give reasons for their decisions automatically but could do so on request. In 1982–3 the Council reiterated its concern and noted that the question of retreating from the requirement to give reasons had also been raised in connection with two other tribunals (dealing with the licensing of goods vehicles and agricultural holdings). The Council was then able to record 'negotiations with departments' to try to ameliorate the situation, but it seems that there is now something of a division between the Council on the one hand (which assumes the need to give reasons in all but the most exceptional cases) and the government, which is increasingly influenced by arguments which stress the need to save time and money.[14]

The form of reasoning employed by tribunals is not easy to categorize; and certainly they do not adopt the same approach to precedent and rule-following as that employed in the ordinary courts. Indeed it has been seen as a major advantage of tribunals that these bodies can decide cases on their individual facts and merits rather than rigidly following a corpus of rules or precedents. Nevertheless, because there are formulae which tribunals apply, it is important that parties to a case, even in the relatively informal circumstances of a tribunal, should know the grounds of a decision, and this practice is now regularly followed. In addition the Franks Committee was of the opinion that while appeals to the courts on points of fact should not be entertained, there ought usually to be an opportunity for such an appeal on points of law. It also thought that there should normally be some appellate tribunal to which general appeals on points of law, fact or merit could go, and that such appeals as a matter of principle should never be to a minister.

In 1980 the Council on Tribunals, which had had a committee working on the subject for some time, published a special report on its functions.[15] The background to this initiative was that the Council felt that no general survey of its field of work had been carried out since the Franks Committee reported in 1957 and that the time was then ripe for a general review of the constitution, powers, functions and practices of the Council. The Council believed that the case for a statutory advisory body with the kind of general oversight powers which would enable it to make a contribution to an effective and well planned system of tribunals was even stronger in 1980 than at the time of the Franks Committee. Since 1957, the Council argued, there had been a considerable growth in the number of tribunals, and they tended to operate increasingly in such difficult and politically sensitive areas as immigration, compulsory detention under the mental health legislation, misuse of drugs, registration of child care homes, equal pay, redundancy and unfair dismissal and supplementary benefits. And in 1980 another significant tribunal area was created when the Education Act established a system of appeal committees to deal with the allocation of school places by local authorities.

Moreover the Council thought that since it had been set up there had been a number of changes in the political and administrative climate, and it pointed in particular to the growing formalization of procedures for settling disputes. This, while perhaps inherent in the Franks recommendations for making tribunals more like courts, created greater complexity which might worry the complainant. Certainly, in the opinion of the Council, it required perpetual oversight to ensure that the right balance was struck.[16] And the Council was also aware that the introduction of the various ombudsmen and the more general concern for open government meant that it was operating in a very different environment from that of its early years.[17]

The Council made a number of specific recommendations about

how its position might be adjusted to enable it to cope with a developing constitutional and administrative climate. Some proposals needed legislation. For example one proposal related to the somewhat patchy practice of consultation between government and the Council whenever legislation affecting the Council's jurisdiction was contemplated. In some instances – as with the Education Act of 1980 – there was early consultation and the government had time to take account of the Council's views; in others – such as the Social Security Act of 1980 – the formal consultation occurred only a few days before the introduction of the legislation.

The Council suggested that it should be given 'a clear general power (in addition to the supervision of Tribunals named in Schedule 1 of the Act of 1971) to act as an advisory body over the whole area of administrative adjudication and the general pattern and organisation of tribunal structure'.[18] The Council also thought it should be given a clear right to be consulted and empowered to offer views in relation to matters arising on draft primary legislation affecting its area of jurisdiction; and its right to be consulted about procedural rules should be restated in clearer and more general terms. Moreover, when such legislation on which the Council had been consulted was brought forward, it was the Council's view that the minister should be obliged to disclose its advice to MPs.

Another proposal of the Council in its 1980 review was that it should be given a statutory power to investigate and issue findings on complaints which raised matters of principle in relation to tribunals and inquiries; and in that connection the Council wanted the power to call for relevant papers from departments and tribunals. The point of this proposal was that complaints against the way tribunals and inquiries operated had always formed a substantial part of the Council's work; yet it had no statutory power to deal with them. The creation of the parliamentary commissioner for administration in 1967 had aided the situation somewhat; since, although he may not consider the substance of a matter which has been referred to a tribunal or public inquiry, he can investigate a department's administrative handling of its own procedures before and after a tribunal or inquiry hearing; and the PCA can also investigate the way in which public local inquiries are conducted. The number of complaints about tribunal and inquiry proceedings had been reduced by the arrangement which referred complaints against the chairmen or members of a tribunal to the lord chancellor or other ministers who appoint such members. Nevertheless there remained a residual category of complaints and the Council, while it considered the alternatives of extending the jurisdiction of the PCA to cover them and of establishing a new ombudsman with jurisdiction over tribunals and inquiries, concluded that the best course was to clarify and extend the Council's own jurisdiction in this respect.

Proposals from the Council which did not require legislation included the creation of a code of practice to strengthen and improve the process of consultation with government departments on new primary and secondary legislation. In its 1981–2 Report the Council was able to record that such a code had been agreed with the lord chancellor and lord advocate and was being sent to appropriate ministers.[19]

One defect in the tribunals system has long been the ambiguity surrounding the role to be played by those with legal qualifications in the daily operations of these bodies. As has been seen, the rationale of many of the Committee's arguments was that the whole network of tribunals should be regarded as a part of the legal system, and it was therefore thought important that tribunals should have legally qualified chairmen who could follow legal arguments. In order to improve the quality of tribunal chairmanship the Council has advocated what is known as a 'presidential system' of organization. In this way a particular class of tribunal has a national president or chairman (and perhaps if the category is large enough regional chairmen also). The theory behind this form of organization is that in addition to providing a useful channel of communication, it 'facilitates the training of chairmen and members, fosters a desirable spirit of independence and properly emphasises a feeling of separation between tribunals and the administration of the responsible Government department'.[20]

However, there remains a general unwillingness to acknowledge the general right to legal representation before a tribunal in case this should interfere with the informality of the proceedings. Even where legal representation is permitted there is the additional problem of cost, for although Franks recommended that legal aid should be made available to parties in a tribunal hearing on the same basis as in a court case, the situation was not remedied until 1980. After the strong evidence given by the Council on Tribunals to the Royal Commission on Legal Services, the Legal Aid Act of 1979 introduced a scheme known as 'assistance by way of representation', which has especially benefited appellants before Mental Health Review Tribunals. Nevertheless, the Council remains critical of the non-availability of legal aid before tribunals and of the injustice which this may cause to some categories of appellant. The Council has frequently restated its view that legal aid should in principle be available at all tribunals where legal representation is permitted, subject to a procedure to ensure that legal aid is not granted in cases which do not really merit it. And it would like to see better coordination of the various agencies which exist to help those who appear before tribunals, whether the help be of a formal legal or informal kind.[21]

Considerations of cost and practicality tend to delay needed reforms. Thus while it may be admirable in theory to suggest that tribunals should have legally qualified chairmen, the number of such appointments places a heavy burden on the pool of talent available. Indeed when an increase in the jurisdiction of industrial tribunals was proposed in early 1970, the chairman of the Council on Tribunals wrote to the lord chancellor (whose office is responsible for the appointment of tribunal members with legal qualifications) warning him that it would be necessary to revise the qualification requirements for their chairmen. The number of people available with the very high qualifications previously demanded was not infinite; whereas it had previously been customary to select chairmen from the ranks of barristers with at least seven years' experience of practice – though solicitors were also eligible for appointment – it would in future, the chairman of the Council on Tribunals suggested, be necessary to rely more heavily on local solicitors to perform these tasks. At present the requirement of a legally qualified chairman is not applicable to all tribunals: for some, such as industrial tribunals, betting levy appeal tribunals and the new Social Security Appeal Tribunals, the qualification is a statutory requirement, while for others, such as rent tribunals, it is not.

The Franks Report also covered inquiries, although the legislation based on the Report gave the Council on Tribunals and Inquiries different powers in relation to the latter.[22] They are used in a number of situations, but they nearly always involve proposals for the use of land, whether on a large or a small scale. For example, an inquiry might be used in connection with an issue of national importance such as a projected siting of a nuclear waste plant; or it may be used in connection with a county council's structure plan or, at a lower level, an appeal from a refusal of planning permission. The Second Report of the Council on Tribunals drew a distinction between tribunals and inquiries by underlining the fact that whereas tribunals could be seen as part of the machinery for adjudication, inquiries were an integral part of the process of exercising ministerial discretion.[23] Since a minister would be answerable to Parliament for the resolution of any conflict between private and public interests he could not be entirely impartial, though he could – and this was the purpose of an inquiry – ensure that all the evidence relevant to a decision had been heard. Thus although it is important that the inquiry part of the procedure be entirely fair and that opportunites exist for objections to any scheme to be heard, there can be no guarantee that the evidence brought out by an inquiry will carry any weight with the minister concerned. As the Council on Tribunals put it: 'The inquiry is modelled on judicial procedure, but it cannot lead to an equally objective decision. In the last resort the Minister must do what he thinks most expedient.'[24]

Nevertheless, the Council on Tribunals took as its mandate the application to inquiries and hearings of standards which would satisfy the average citizen's sense of justice and the observation of the Franks values of openness, fairness and impartiality in this sphere also. Thus when an incident like the Saffron Walden Chalk Pit case came to light a change in the rules governing inquiries was secured. (In that case the minister had rejected the report of an inspector on the basis of fresh evidence which had come to light *after* the inquiry without offering the objectors any opportunity to challenge the new evidence.)[25] The greater political salience of inquiries, compared with tribunals, has entailed rather more controversy surrounding their operation in the past twenty years, especially with the increase in demand for participation in the planning process. Some inquiries, such as those into the siting of airports and nuclear fuel plants, therefore not only have to ensure that procedures are followed which are scrupulously fair to individuals; they also have to reckon with the range of pressure groups which may use inquiries as a means of influencing decisions about local amenities and the general environment.[26] And if the planned proposal is a highly controversial one – for example if it involves nuclear power – an inquiry may be turned into a full-scale battle between different political forces. The experience – some of it unhappy – with a number of major inquiries over the 1970s led to the drafting of a code of practice for major inquiries in 1980–1.[27]

The Skeffington Report of 1969 advocated a much greater association of individuals and pressure groups in the planning function but, as was the case with the Franks criteria, there are limits to the extent to which this ideal can be implemented.[28] Considerations of cost and delay inevitably restrict the processes of examining objections to a planning proposal as well as the amount of publicity which can be given beforehand to each proposal. Even where, as in the case of the Windscale inquiry, the proceedings are exhaustive, at the end of the day the objectors may still feel that the hearings were window-dressing for a decision which had already been taken by the minister concerned.[29] In 1980, as part of its general review of the function of the Council on Tribunals and Inquiries, the Council recommended that the differences between the wording of its own jurisdiction in connection with tribunals and inquiries should be eliminated. What the council wanted was a broad power to offer advice on general or particular matters, whether or not on request and without a matter having to be regarded as one of special importance.

One change occasioned by the altered climate of the 1960s and 1970s relates to structure plans which are concerned with general land use. Formal inquiries using the adversarial method of cross-examination of witnesses have been replaced when an area's structure plan is being prepared. Instead, a more informal seminar approach is used and public examinations of the plan take place without the delay and stiffness occasioned by rigid rules of procedure, a system which appears to be working relatively smoothly.[30] In addition the demand for greater openness at inquiries led to the passage of the Public Inquiries (Attendance of Public) Act of 1982 – originating in a private member's bill – which provides that all the evidence available at an inquiry shall be made public unless there is some overwhelming objection (such as national security) for its being kept confidential.[31]

The Council on Tribunals was in some ways the first institutional expression of the new demand for greater accountability in the British system of administration. Later critics have charged that its interpretation of its mandate has been too cautious and that it should have adopted a more flexible and expansive approach to the task of striking the balance between individuals and government in administrative decision-making.[32] Perhaps the Franks values do now seem unduly procedural and legalistic from the perspective of the 1980s, and certainly the very limited budget on which the Council has operated and its preference for cooperation with departments rather than outright confrontation suggest that its position is and was intended to be very much less than an ombudsman-type institution. Yet, although the Council's achievements may seem peripheral, it has established itself as a part of the British constitutional machinery; and its contributions to the climate of opinion about how best to control decisions have resulted in the development of other more radical ideas.

The Parliamentary Commissioner for Administration

If the episode of Crichel Down brought improvements to the procedures employed by tribunals and inquiries, progress was infinitely slower in the area where no formal machinery for review existed. The catalyst for change in this sphere was the British Section of the International Commission of Jurists, which in 1958 established a small study group to examine how ombudsmen operated in other countries as a protection against maladministration.[33] A further inquiry followed the initial one, and the result was a recommendation that Britain should establish a modified version of the ombudsman, to be called the parliamentary commissioner for administration. The idea was rejected by the then Conservative government, but was taken up by the Labour Party immediately prior to the general election of 1964. The ultimate result of that commitment was the Parliamentary Commissioner Act of 1967, which created the British version of an ombudsman.

Although the House of Commons returned in 1966 contained a large number of new recruits to politics who were sceptical about the relevance of traditional constitutional theories to the conditions of a complex welfare state, there remained some ambiguity about the parliamentary commissioner's functions. The introduction of such an institution threatened to erode one of the most cherished roles of the backbencher; and, even if the proliferation of governmental activities made the MP's role more difficult to perform, such a development was unlikely to be viewed with enthusiasm. Moreover, although MPs and civil servants were becoming increasingly aware of the difficulties of maintaining detailed control within the departmental structure, natural conservatism and inertia – not entirely absent from the British bureaucracy – produced hostility to an innovation which, like the experiment with select committees, threatened to lead to extra work and additional expenditure. The nature of the proposal, even in the diluted form brought forward by the Labour government, was indeed inherently radical, for it threatened the anonymity associated with the Civil Service and seemed likely to reveal the inner workings of the governmental machine in ways which could have numerous repercussions. It was thought that the development might seriously undermine the principle that advice given to ministers by officials is confidential, and that this in turn would transform the whole character of the relationship between the elected and the permanent elements in British government.

In practice, while the parliamentary commissioner has stimulated further movements in the direction of a more open style of government, his existence has not fundamentally undermined the morale of the Civil Service. Indeed it could be argued that the existence of the PCA has improved it by serving as a public witness to the generally high standards of British central government.

The initial fears about how well the parliamentary commissioner would fit into the British administrative process largely explain the restricted jurisdiction and powers given to the office, and the style adopted by the first PCA, Sir Edmund Compton. Sir Edmund had been Comptroller and Auditor-General, and the cautious approach to the office which he adopted reflected a conception of what the PCA's role should be which paralleled the internal auditing functions of the Comptroller's Office.[34] Since Sir Edmund Compton's time, however, the incumbents of the office of PCA have gradually modified many of the initial interpretations of the PCA's powers. In this development, successive parliamentary commissioners have been encouraged by the Select Committee on the Parliamentary Commissioner for Administration, which has over the years pushed for a more liberal interpretation of the PCA's powers and jurisdiction, taken up the comments made in his various reports, especially in connection with the workings of Whitehall, and been able to publicize in Parliament issues which the parliamentary commissioner has had to treat more discreetly.[35] The appointment for a five-year period of a non-civil servant, Mr (later Sir) Cecil Clothier, QC, in 1979 marked a further departure from the original conception of the office. For not merely was the office of the parliamentary commissioner seen initially as an instrument for aiding *parliamentary* control of the administration rather than as a wholly independent institution with its own direct relationship with the public; it was also felt that the investigation of complaints should be handled by civil servants, since they were best placed to understand the internal practices and norms of departments. Although the majority of the parliamentary commissioner's staff are civil servants on secondment (and it seems that a period in the PCA's Office is seen as a route to promotion) the fact that a lawyer rather than a retired civil servant has been appointed to the post indicates a greater willingness to conceive of the job in broader terms than was at first the case. Certainly, Sir Cecil Clothier displayed a great willingness to get publicity for his work. The small number of complaints received in his first year was interpreted as evidence that a different approach was needed, and after a concerted campaign he was able to record that there had been an increase of 36 per cent; the number of complaints received in 1980 was 1,031 – the fourth highest figure since the office was founded. However the number declined again in 1981 to 917.[36]

The assumption that the parliamentary commissioner for administration would operate in a manner analogous to the functioning of the comptroller and auditor-general, combined with the need to allay MPs' fears that they might be rendered redundant as far as constituency casework was concerned, was responsible for the most controversial feature of the British ombudsman. Unlike the majority of other ombudsmen, with the exception of the French *médiateur*, the parliamentary commissioner was precluded from receiving complaints from the public directly, and could only consider a case if it had been forwarded to him from an MP.[37] In theory this restriction was designed to locate the responsibility for the redress of grievances very firmly in the House of Commons; in practice it seems clear that it has limited the utility of the PCA and caused some confusion to the public – especially since slightly different rules apply to the commissioners for local government and to the PCA himself when acting in his capacity as commissioner for the National Health Service. The Health Service commissioner permits direct access; and the local commissioners can in extreme cases take complaints directly from the public, although complaints would normally be referred through a councillor. The drawbacks of indirect access can, its critics argue, be measured by the fact that the United Kingdom's parliamentary commissioner investigated only 252 cases in 1974, although Britain has a population of over 55 million. In Sweden in the same year 2,368 cases were investigated for a population of only 8 million.[38]

The criticisms directed at the restrictions on access to the PCA prompted Sir Idwal Pugh, the third parliamentary commissioner, to modify his practice when complaints were sent directly to him instead of through an MP. Rather than simply returning the complaints to the citizen, he would with the consent of the complainant write to the relevant MP asking whether the MP would prefer to deal with the matter himself or would like to send it back for investigation by the parliamentary commissioner. This device may seem rather awkward, but it at least prevents some complaints from going uninvestigated simply because the rules of access have discouraged the complainant at an early stage. In the long run it is possible that as MPs come to realize that the ombudsman is no threat to their relationship with their constituents, and perhaps as they acquire more satisfying roles through the development of the comprehensive select committee system, they will no longer cling to indirect access.

On the other hand, it has been argued that the nature of many complaints is such that they do not warrant the very thorough and costly investigation given by the parliamentary commissioner and that the so-called 'MP filter' improves the efficiency of the PCA.[39] And if, as some critics suspect, the economic climate is beginning to act as a restraint on the improvement of the institutions of accountability, such a filter may well be essential to prevent it becoming so overloaded that government feels justified in curtailing it. Certainly considerations of cost appear to have been important in the recent refusal of the government to contemplate major extensions of the local commissioners' jurisdiction to include parish councils and the New Towns Commission, although it is important also to remember that there are alternative channels for obtaining solutions to grievances and that in some cases ombudsman-type investigations are not the most appropriate.[40]

One of the most serious objections to indirect access is the fact that many people who might want to use the mechanism to challenge a government decision would probably not be familiar with the intricacies of government and might be easily put off pursuing their complaint by even the most simple of restrictions. In this respect also the early style of the parliamentary commissioner was perhaps damaging. The emphasis on the PCA's subordination to Parliament meant that initially there was some reluctance by the incumbents of the office to seek publicity or popularize their work. The lack of publicity was partly a reflection of the format of reports and of the process of indirect access, which also meant indirect communication to the press. But in part it was also the corollary of the rather cautious, low-key approach that was initially felt necessary in order to allow Whitehall to accommodate itself to the innovation. More recently, as has been seen, the parliamentary commissioner has been taking a more aggressive approach to the problem of publicity. Starting in 1977, when the Central Office of Information assisted in a concerted campaign to spread details about the operation of the PCA, the trend has been towards popularization and professionalization. Although the PCA now releases detailed reports only on selected cases, in 1984 the reports were issued in a new format designed to gain a more general audience than before.[41]

The 1967 legislation was viewed by many observers as inadequate for reasons other than the difficulties produced by indirect access. Those who hoped that the PCA might provide a remedy where no other machinery existed to challenge decisions obviously wanted the sphere of his potential investigations to be as broad as the sphere of governmental operations. Yet large areas of governmental activity were excluded from his jurisdiction. Moreover the jurisdiction of the parliamentary commissioner was further confined by limiting it to cases of maladministration; this was intended to put the emphasis firmly on procedural irregularities rather than substantive errors of judgement. However, the ambiguity surrounding the concept of maladministration has in some ways aided successive ombudsmen. As parliamentary commissioners have become bolder, they have found it possible to expand their jurisdiction by altering their interpretation of the concept of maladministration.

The early interpretation of maladministration relied on the so-called 'Crossman catalogue' of administrative disorders – instances where 'bias, neglect, inattention, delay, incompetence, ineptitude, perversity, turpitude, or arbitrariness' entered the decision-making process. Decisions which were simply unjust, unreasonable or oppressive *in substance* were apparently excluded from investigation so long as they had been made without maladministration, i.e. in a manner which was *procedurally* correct.

However, with encouragement from the Select Committee the PCA has moved towards finding maladministration in decisions which are 'thoroughly bad in quality'. Indeed in 1978 the PCA announced his belief that he already had powers to investigate 'unjust or oppressive' governmental actions, although he combined this with the reservation that it was no part of his function to reconsider decisions taken without maladministration, nor to substitute his decision for a minister's. However, it is perhaps a pity that an institution primarily designed to reassure the individual that bureaucracy and government can be subordinated to standards of fairness which the layman can understand should be saddled with such a restrictive conception as maladministration as its guiding principle. Even if the ingenuity of successive parliamentary commissioners in developing such notions as constructive maladministration – inferring procedural error from bad decisions so as to bring a case within the PCA's jurisdiction – has made the initial restriction less of an impediment in practice than was initially feared, it hardly makes the office more intelligible to the public.[42]

The subject areas which the parliamentary commissioner was empowered to investigate are approximately those for which a parliamentary question would be accepted – roughly the functions covered by the central government departments. The Select Committee and the PCA have frequently sought extensions of jurisdiction and, although they have succeeded in only a few small instances, the trend is towards an expanded area of coverage. The 1967 legislation excluded the parliamentary commissioner from local authority matters, from the decisions of health authorities, the nationalized industries, the police, and Civil Service and personnel matters. He was also excluded from matters of a commercial or contractual nature. Some of these exclusions reflected the government's intention to tie the office to central government; others indicated a conception of the parliamentary commissioner as a weapon for the individual citizen against government, not for public employees to use against their employer or for one citizen to use against another.

The subjects which fall within the parliamentary commissioner's jurisdiction have also been changed by subsequent legislation which has set up specialized institutions covering some of the fields initially excluded.

In 1969 a Northern Ireland Parliamentary Commissioner for Administration and a Commissioner for Complaints were established and the same individual (Mr T. H. Kernohan) has combined the two offices. The parliamentary commissioner handles complaints against Northern Ireland departments; the commissioner for complaints deals with matters of administration for which local government or other public bodies in Northern Ireland are responsible.[43] Complaints made to the Northern Ireland parliamentary commissioner may be made directly or through an MP, although if they are made directly an MP must be asked to sponsor the complaint. Because discrimination in employment has been a subject of controversy in the province, the Northern Ireland PCA's powers include the right to investigate personnel matters within the Northern Ireland Civil Service; and he may also investigate matters of a commercial and contractual nature. Indeed the fact that these powers have been exercised without any ill effect on the Civil Service has been used by advocates of an extension of jurisdiction to argue that they should be given to the PCA as well.[44] As was shown by the government's reply to the 1979–80 Report of the Select Committee, opposition to such a move remains strong, and any such extension of the parliamentary commissioner's jurisdiction is likely to be far off.[45]

A system of local government ombudsmen was established in 1974, and following the 1973 reorganization of the National Health Service a Health Service commissioner was established – an office which the parliamentary commissioner in practice occupies, although he issues separate reports in that capacity. Moreover since the 1967 legislation established the parliamentary commissioner, as has been seen, new arrangements have been made for complaints against the police and for including an independent element in the machinery which deals with them.[46]

Also, although initially complaints against consular officials were outside the parliamentary commissioner's jurisdiction, a change was made by Order in Council in 1979 to enable the PCA to deal with such complaints. A further extension occurred when legislation – the Parliamentary Commissioner (Consular Complaints) Act of 1981 – enabled those resident abroad to make complaints to the PCA about the quality of the assistance which they had received.

Each specialized jurisdiction has spawned its own problems, but there seems to be a common tendency for commissioners now to be more willing to contemplate extensions of their functions. Thus the Health Services commissioner has tried to ease the restriction on his jurisdiction in the 1977 Act which ostensibly prevented him from questioning a decision where a clinical judgement was involved. The Select Committee in 1980–1 called for changes in this respect. By using his discretion to seek a second opinion in some cases he has thus been able to expand the scope of his office and, although perhaps not extensively, he has ameliorated the worst effects of a distinction which is often difficult to draw in practice and certainly difficult for an aggrieved member of the public to understand.[47] Interestingly, the number of complaints handled by the Health Service commissioner has increased, partly perhaps because his office has become better known since 1973 and partly perhaps because of the effect of economic stringency on the quality of service provided in the National Health Service.[48]

The local commissioners by contrast have attempted to ensure that they do not waste time unnecessarily and have adopted a practice – which many would like to see the parliamentary commissioner adopt – of engaging in conciliation before a full investigation of a complaint is undertaken. In effect there is now at the local level a four-stage rolling process of dealing with complaints so that only at the final stage and in the smallest number of cases is a full investigation undertaken.[49] For some critics this move represents a sensible way to handle small errors which may well fall short of maladministration, and an opportunity for the commissioners to make suggestions about general administrative practice; for others it may represent a taming of a watchdog already rather toothless.[50] Certainly, the introduction of legislation to enable financial remedies to be offered where maladministration was found was generally welcomed. Yet it may be that, if there is a contraction of the ombudsman machinery because of cost, the local ombudsmen will be among the first to feel the restrictions. Any such move would be regrettable since, although central government has been found to display relatively few flaws, the same could not be said of local government. It should be noted that although the various commissioners issue separate reports they are very much aware of developments in each other's jurisdictions, and frequently use evidence from one to argue for changes in another. And there is a growing interchange of experience between ombudsmen in different countries, despite the obvious variety in powers and legal systems.[51]

The original intention of the 1967 legislation was to confine the PCA to the review of action taken in the exercise of *administrative* functions. This restriction is open to criticism as unnecessarily restrictive. Clearly the government could not allow individuals to use the new machinery to challenge its control of the legislative process, but the distinction between the legislative and administrative processes within a department are not always clear-cut. For example, the pre-legislative stages of policy-making are very much administrative functions. As one authority has pointed out, faults in the routine processes of consultation with affected interests could well lead to maladministration.[52] And the process of making secondary or delegated legislation by departments could also lead to administrative injustice.

The complaints which the PCA has investigated have ranged from the mundane to the politically contentious. By far the largest number seem to reflect general dissatisfaction with the Inland Revenue and the DHSS – both areas where the volume of work is likely to produce a corresponding number of errors.

The parliamentary commissioner himself has no authority to compel a government department to consider making recompense for cases in which maladministration has been found. He may however, under s. 10(3) of the 1967 legislation, make a 'special' report to Parliament where it seems that an injustice caused by maladministration has not been or is unlikely to be remedied. Normally, however, it will be logical for the appropriate department to make amends, whether it is a formal apology or an *ex gratia* payment,[53] and departments rarely resist making some form of amends when the PCA finds that a complaint is justified. Apart from the natural desire to close the matter, the opportunities for parliamentary follow-up are a powerful incentive for a department to comply with the PCA's verdict. (It has become a convention that where a department does reject a finding of maladministration which the parliamentary commissioner thinks warrants a remedy, its permanent secretary must appear before the Select Committee on the Parliamentary Commissioner for Administration to explain why – a convention which, it is thought, reduces the likelihood of such rejections occurring.)[54] Sometimes however there is a prolonged wrangle. Thus in 1977 the PCA was able to report that a taxpayer who was found by him in 1975–6 to have suffered an injustice was ultimately granted restitution from the Inland Revenue, although the department had initially declined to restore the money lost.

Departments seem fairly willing to make *ex gratia* payments where these seem appropriate. Thus in the third report for the 1976–7 session the PCA showed that such payments had been made in six cases, although the amounts ranged from £17.82, the cost of car hire while a licence was being issued, to £500, which represented the cost of treatment abroad undertaken by the complainant when he was misled by the DHSS into thinking that the department would finance it.[55] Some authorities argue that in many respects the negative aspects of the PCA's work – what he does *not* find – are as important as the positive ones. The existence of the office and the relatively small number of cases in which maladministration is discovered may serve to reassure the public that the general standards of administration are high and that the small proportion of errors will be swiftly corrected. Moreover suggestions for improvement in administrative practice have been effected by the PCA in instances where regular difficulties were likely to arise. Thus during the 1976–7 session the PCA investigated two cases in which immigration officers imposed restrictive conditions of entry on returning residents whose passports did not record the fact that they were entitled to unrestricted abode in the United Kingdom. The PCA suggested that the Home Office might therefore more widely publicize the need to carry adequate documentation when travelling abroad; he also proposed that when a passport expired it should be returned to the owner if it recorded the permission to reside in the United Kingdom. Indeed it seems that as a result of the PCA's strictures the Home Office decided to issue revised instructions to immigration officers for cases where it was necessary to determine residence qualifications at the port of entry.[56]

Most of the cases for consideration will be ones where a department's officials – not a minister – will have taken the decisions which are disputed. However in a few cases ministerial judgement is involved: here the association of the Select Committee with the work of the PCA as an impartial servant of the House of Commons is invaluable because the Select Committee can pursue politically contentious matters which he would find embarrassing. Indeed it was partly the recognition of the value of this follow-up which enabled that select committee to survive the 1979 reorganization as a single committee rather than allow, as the Procedure Committee had suggested, the individual select committees to pursue maladministration in their own subject areas.

Two examples of politically contentious cases which arose in 1975 proved the ability of the PCA to generate but survive political controversy. In one, the safety of invalid tricycles was questioned; in the other (the so-called Court Line affair) a major travel company went bankrupt, although the government had vouched for its financial viability after cabinet consideration of the matter.[57] In the case of the tricycles the PCA actually commented that DHSS ministers had been 'less frank than they should have been' in response to parliamentary questions on the subject – a comment on internal parliamentary proceedings which was unusual for an agent of Parliament. However, in the second case there seemed, as happened in the 1968 Sachsenhausen affair, to be a doubt in the government's mind: should it seek to return to the pre-1967 doctrines of ministerial responsibility and simply reject the PCA's conclusions and the Select Committee's probings? Or did the fact that the PCA had found maladministration mean that his authority had to be accepted and recompense be made to the aggrieved persons? The fact that a cabinet minister was involved in the Court Line case naturally made the government reluctant to accept the latter proposition; but equally any attempt to close the matter was much more difficult with the evidence of the PCA before the House of Commons. (However in Court Line the government pre-empted any support for the Select Committee by making its views known to the House first.) Thus in Court Line as in Sachsenhausen two approaches to accountability were in conflict.

In the Sachsenhausen affair in 1968 George Brown, then foreign secretary, attempted to protect civil servants after an investigation by the PCA had found maladministration in the execution of an Anglo-German compensation scheme for concentration camp victims.[58] His argument was that it was not appropriate for the Select Committee to attempt further debate on a matter once the PCA had achieved a reversal of the decision. In particular the Select Committee excited controversy by attempting to interview the civil servants who had made the initial error over the payment of compensation. Ultimately the attorney-general informed the Select Committee that it could interview only the principal officer of a department and not his subordinates. In other words the doctrine of ministerial responsibility, though flexible enough to accommodate the PCA's inquiries, would, it was thought, be undermined by routine investigations by select committees against the wishes of the permanent secretary and the minister. The Select Committee has not forced this issue any further, and it may be taken as a general rule that civil servants do not appear before the Committee unless the permanent secretary gives his permission, although as has been seen the permanent secretary will be called upon whenever a report finding maladministration is rejected by a department.

One aspect of the PCA's activities which has since been scrutinized by the Select Committee is the range of documents he can see. The 1967 Act precluded him from viewing cabinet papers, but the Select Committee later recommended that he should be able to see all cabinet papers relevant to an inquiry.[59] The effect of a change of this sort would be to bring the PCA much closer to the heart of the political process and to make his relationship with government potentially more inflammatory. Yet the logic of the way the institution has been developing suggests that the PCA should be allowed access to those documents in the few cases where it would be necessary to see cabinet papers in order fully to understand a complaint.

Overall the operations of the Select Committee and the inquiries conducted by the parliamentary commissioner himself have subjected the actions of civil servants at all stages of the policy process to more effective scrutiny, and have at the very least enabled a more informed understanding of British administration as well as concrete improvements in the machinery of accountability. And, as the traditional procedures of control have come under review for their efficiency and effectiveness, this in turn has caused effective criticism of other parts of the system.

The Courts and the Development of Administrative Law

The central importance of the theory of ministerial responsibility in the British constitution thus partly explains some of the peculiar features of the British ombudsman, features which can still raise difficulties in his relationship with the general public. The central role of Parliament as the primary institution for securing redress may also have been a factor in the relatively slow growth of judicial techniques for controlling and regulating administrative action. However, just as the frequency of individual grievances against discretionary decisions caused Parliament to reconsider its methods in this sphere, so the multiplication of individual encounters with administrative authority prompted an increased likelihood of judicial intervention in the administrative process and an elaboration of the principles on which that intervention is possible. Thus the past few years have seen the courts struggling to reconcile public and private claims and openly acknowledging the need to articulate more general principles of administrative justice irrespective of the opportunities for parliamentary control of government. Sometimes their attempts – involving as they have done pronouncements in areas which are often unfamiliar to traditional legal exegesis – have forced the courts to become more innovative than before, and they have on occasion incurred the criticism of politicans.

Part of the reason for the late development of British public law is historical; it has to be traced probably at least to the seventeenth-century alliance of the common lawyers with Parliament against the claims of the monarch, which included the claim that matters affecting the state (or more precisely the Crown) should be tried in special courts.[60] Dicey gave eloquent, if misguided, expression to this traditional hostility to special administrative jurisdictions; his attitude appears to have remained part of the British legal orthodoxy at least until the 1950s when academic authorities began pointing out that such specialized jurisdictions as prevailed in France and the Federal Republic of Germany were as much there to protect the citizen from the arbitrary exercise of governmental power as to support it.[61]

Yet it was not really until the early 1960s that English judges commenced the task of refining the rules and principles which should govern the relationships between public authorities and private persons in the modern welfare state. Obviously the development of the law in this area was somewhat piecemeal and not necessarily consistent, because individual judges took very different views as to the urgency of the task and action could only be taken when appropriate cases presented themselves. And because the courts have not been used by pressure groups, as in the United States, the way in which such cases came forward was rather haphazard, although this is now changing as groups such as Child Poverty Action Group adopt more of a test-case strategy.[62]

Some features of the last few years deserve specific mention. First, the doctrine of natural justice has been developed by the judges so that it can now be applied to decisions which are administrative as well as judicial or quasi-judicial. The distinction between administrative decisions and judicial or quasi-judicial decisions seems to have been injected into British administrative law in the 1930s when the Donoughmore Committee had considered the remedies necessary to cope with the enormous growth of ministerial powers. The principles of natural justice, the Committee asserted, had to be observed in decisions which were of a judicial or quasi-judicial character; but certain aspects of these principles – particularly the right to know the reasons for a decision – made them inappropriate for administrative decisions.[63] Although the Franks Committee, a quarter of a century later, also underlined the significance of the principles of natural justice in areas where tribunals operated, it was not until 1964 that they were applied to administrative decisions. In 1964 a police authority's decision to dismiss a chief constable was held to be a nullity because he was afforded no opportunity to make representations to the committee before the decision was taken.[64] Thus the decision-making body had failed to observe one of the fundamental principles of natural justice, i.e. that 'no party ought to be condemned unheard'. Lord Reid, one of the judges who decided the case when it reached the House of Lords, commented in his speech that the concept of natural justice was vague, but that it did not follow that because a thing could not be cut and dried or nicely measured it did not exist. Lord Reid and his fellow law lords emphasized that the principles of natural justice were inherent in all legal thinking, even if they now had to be applied to a host of new situations.

The new situations to which these principles of natural justice were to be applied were as varied and as complex as the welfare state in which they had to subsist. Nevertheless since 1964 the courts have applied these standards to a range of decision-making authorities which have the power to affect the lives of individuals. The duty to allow the affected party to make his case heard has been imposed on tax tribunals, on immigration officers, on such bodies as the Monopolies Commission and the Race Relations Board, and even on private bodies such as professional organizations and trade unions. And although, as has been seen, there is no general right to be represented by counsel, individuals do also in many cases have the right to legal representation and the right to know the basis on which a decision was taken.[65]

A second area in which a new determination to subordinate the exercise of public power to principles of law was seen was that where ministerial discretion was involved. One of Dicey's main arguments against a separate system of administrative law in Britain had been that the rule of law demanded the absolute equality of parties before the law and the determination of any dispute between them in the ordinary courts. However, as many commentators have pointed out, the idea that there was equality between public authority and private citizen was a fantasy: even in Dicey's day ministerial discretion, growing collectivism and Crown privilege were facts of life.

A third area in which the courts exerted their power to review the discretion of the executive concerned the discovery of documents which were needed in a legal suit. In 1942 the House of Lords had laid down that when a minister objected to the production of documents in legal proceedings because they were potentially damaging to the public interest, that objection was conclusive. It was not for the courts therafter to question the reasonableness of such an assertion.[66] However the particular case involved had been decided in the middle of the second world war, and related to the militarily sensitive matter of submarine plans. During the postwar years the extent of this doctrine – which meant that many litigants were deprived of documents germane to their case – aroused considerable distaste. Finally in 1968 the House of Lords modified its 1942 ruling and stated that refusal by a minister to produce documents on the grounds that their production would be contrary to the public interest was not necessarily conclusive.[67] The courts could review a decision, in camera if necessary, in order to weigh justice to litigants against claims of executive privilege and public interest as defined by the government.

One authority called this change the most striking example of judicial activism in administrative law since the war.[68] Certainly in broad terms it accorded well with the new mood of hostility towards sweeping claims of governmental discretion, and with the growing sensitivity to the need for more openness in the administrative process. Yet the extent of the effect of the change is still uncertain; the courts still seem willing to give full consideration to executive claims for secrecy where for example taxation matters are concerned or where, even more importantly, matters relating to national security are involved. (Such a case arose in 1977 over the decision to deport Mark Hosenball, a journalist who claimed that the Home Office should have disclosed the case against him on the grounds of natural justice; the Court of Appeal however found that there was no necessity for the Home Office to disclose any of the reasons for the decision.)

Unwillingness to tolerate broad claims of executive discretion had also been evident in another significant case of 1968, *Padfield* v. *The Minister of Agriculture, Fisheries and Food*.[69] Increasingly, the courts have proved willing to review statutory discretions to see whether discretionary powers have been exercised in accordance with the intentions of Parliament. (In the dispute over trade union rights at GCHQ Cheltenham they also seemed willing to review powers exercised by virtue of the prerogative.) *Padfield's* case spelled out the legal standards which controlled such powers; in particular it emphasized the importance attached by courts to ensuring that only legally relevant considerations are taken into account when reaching a discretionary decision. In the court's view the only legally permissible considerations were ones which did not frustrate the purpose of the parent Act. Thus judicial review sought its justification in the doctrine of parliamentary supremacy rather than in abstract notions of the public interest such as might apply in France for example. In this instance the minister had refused to establish an investigatory committee to review prices under a statutory milk-marketing scheme, and it emerged that his reason for refusing was that he might be politically embarrassed by the report of such a committee. Although the House of Lords acknowledged that the decision to establish a review committee was a discretionary one, it declared that discretionary powers were not unfettered. They had to be exercised reasonably, and they were not being so exercised if irrelevant considerations were allowed to enter into the decision-making process. The question of political embarrassment was not a relevant consideration and was unlawful because its intrusion tended to frustrate the purpose for which discretion had been given to the minister by Parliament. Moreover Lords Reid, Hodson, Upjohn and Pearce went even further and said that where there was even *prima facie* evidence of irregularity the courts could infer from a minister's refusal to justify his decision that he had acted unlawfully.

It would be a mistake to see the *Padfield* decision as one which entirely clarifies the law in this area. Administrative law has at its heart the notion that there are peculiar circumstances surrounding decisions in which public policy is involved. The more we move towards a system of administrative or public law, the more we may have to rely on particular courts to weigh the competing circumstances and special considerations. Individual judges and perhaps courts vary in their willingness to critize executive judgements directly – especially since, in the environment of modern Britain, there is a lingering suspicion that the individualistic approach of the legal system and the middle-class background of the legal profession combine to produce hostility to collectivism and working-class interests. Despite the natural tendency of the judiciary to avoid political controversy where possible, *Padfield* has been applied, and in circumstances where it might have been thought that the courts would be wary of a clash with central government. In 1976 a local authority was supported by the courts when it claimed that the Secretary of State for Education had no powers to compel the authority to introduce plans for comprehensive reorganization of its schools.[70] Also the Home Office incurred judicial criticism for its attitude in a case which was unusual because it had previously been considered by the PCA, who had criticized the Home Office's attempt to collect additional sums from persons who had pre-empted a rise in the cost of television licences by buying them early.[71]

The constraints on ministerial discretion and the role of the judiciary became the subject of intense political controversy in 1977 when Lord Denning in the Court of Appeal suggested that the attorney-general's discretion had to be exercised in conformity with the legal standards of reasonableness and that unlawfulness might be inferred from a refusal to furnish reasons for a decision.[72] The attorney-general claimed that the exercise of his discretion was subject to parliamentary control, not to control by the courts, and the House of Lords upheld his view of the law. Whether this decision will in fact serve as a warning to activist judges that in the field of administrative law they risk political censure if they go too far too fast remains to be seen. Certainly the controversy revealed that judicial intervention was no more acceptable in some political quarters in the 1970s and 1980s than it had been at the beginning of the twentieth century; it showed that the arguments in favour of a detailed code of administrative fair practice to which even government itself would be subject were still alien to parliamentarians.

Another example of a judicial review of a discretionary decision which caused political controversy – including an emergency debate under S.O. 9 on 22 December 1981 – was the so-called GLC fares case.[73] The Labour-controlled GLC, following an election manifesto pledge, attempted to cut the cost of public transport in London by 25 per cent. To do this it proposed to make a grant to the London Transport Executive to enable it to budget for a deficit, even though the terms of the 1969 legislation establishing the LTE seemed to preclude deficit budgeting (by demanding that transport be 'integrated, efficient and economic'), and despite the fact that the precept which would have to be imposed on the individual London boroughs to finance this grant had deleterious implications for central government funding under the provisions of the Local Government Planning and Land Act of 1980. (This Act identified local authorities which, in the government's view, were overspenders and reduced their central grant accordingly). One of the boroughs which stood to lose financially (and which did not benefit directly from the subsidy to London Transport because it was an outer London borough), the Conservative-controlled Borough of Bromley, applied for *certiorari* to quash the precept and, while the Divisional Court rejected the application, Bromley won in the Court of Appeal. It also won in the House of Lords against an appeal by the GLC.

Several features of the case excited interest. The House of Lords acknowledged that the courts should normally be cautious of interfering with the discretion given to a local authority by Parliament; but it said the council's actions might be examined by the courts to see whether the local authority had exercised its discretion reasonably. Several factors were introduced into the reasoning of the different judges to determine this question, including the intention of the various Acts. The interpretation of the term 'economic' meant at least cost-effective or on business principles in the opinion of the courts which held that the interests of the various categories of persons to whom the GLC owed an obligation ought to have been considered.

The problem about this kind of argument is, of course, that while judges may perceive their balancing of interests to be a neutral process, for those who lose the decision the judiciary is substituting its policy preferences for those of an elected body.[74] And the proposition that a mandate is but one factor to be taken into account in the exercise of discretion alongside others is clearly controversial. Yet if one of the purposes of administrative law and administrative legal systems is to ensure that balances between different interests are struck in the context of a complex political system then it is difficult to see how this kind of objection can be avoided. Any legally regulated state will seek to enforce principles which may at times constrain political judgements and majority preferences.

One reform in the field of administrative law which was conceded by the government in the late 1970s was a rationalization of the method whereby an individual could seek judicial review of an administrative decision. Until 1977 the procedures for doing this were exceedingly complex – and an application for the wrong remedy could mean that an action would fail altogether. (Review might be sought through the ordinary civil procedures for an injunction or a declaration, or through the prerogative orders of *certiorari*, which quashes a faulty decision; *prohibition*, which will restrain the performance of an unlawful action; *mandamus*, which is sought when an authority is failing to perform a legal duty.) The courts which granted review could not award damages for a defective decision and it was frequently found that an application for review, even if successful, was of little concrete benefit to the aggrieved citizen. The deficiencies in the procedures for seeking judicial review of administrative activity had been pointed out by the British Section of the International Commission of Jurists and by two Law Commission working parties. Indeed in 1969 the Law Commission recommended a Royal Commission with broad terms of reference, and in 1971 it proposed that a general procedure – an application for review – should replace all the distinct remedies. The 1977 changes, which have been effected not by legislation but by amendments to the Rules of the Supreme Court, replaced applications for existing prerogative orders by applications for judicial review; they also allowed applications for review to be combined with applications for other remedies, including the award of damages.

Although it was at first unclear what impact this change would have on the style of British administrative law, it seems that Order No. 53 – combined with other factors such as the reorganization of the work of the Divisional Court of the Queen's Bench Division – has had a substantial impact on the judicial review of administrative action. The Order, as further amended in 1981, is now very much more streamlined than before; and by effectively creating an 'administrative list' which will be heard by judges with expertise in administrative questions there has been produced the equivalent of an administrative division of the High Court with its own flexible procedure – a development urged by many reformers for some time.[75]

Moreover the decision in *O'Reilly* v. *Mackman* (which ruled that it was improper to attempt to use the ordinary processes of civil law when a public law remedy was available) suggests an attempt by the court to channel public lawsuits through the new procedure.[76]

The position of the individual who wishes to challenge an administrative decision is in many ways infinitely better in 1984 than it was in 1954. However the progress which has been made is uneven and the position is not one to justify complacency. British government is still reluctant to concede much to the principle of open government; and the pressure of economy and efficiency in government may make administrations impatient of those whose prime concern is with procedural fairness and administrative justice. Further progress is inevitably to a large extent dependent upon the incumbents of the various offices – ombudsmen at all levels, judges and members of tribunals – to keep the institutions and procedures of accountability supple, and capable of adaption to new circumstances. The slow but steady extension of the jurisdiction of the PCA, reinforced by the support of the Select Committee on the PCA, suggests an optimistic assessment of future trends in this field. If the progress made by the judiciary is neither as even nor as comprehensive, the fault perhaps lies not so much with the judges but with the politicians in their failure to articulate their interpretation of the role of law in the modern state.

14   The Limits of Independence

Much of the argument of the preceding chapters has tacitly assumed that the government of the United Kingdom is fully autonomous in the decisions that it makes. It is however clear that in reality the situation is a very different one and that the making of policy is powerfully affected by external constraints. In the contemporary world all countries are to some extent in this situation. In Britain's case there are three factors that bulk particularly large. First there is the legacy of Empire; second there is the country's continued dependence upon external trade; and finally there is the continuing ambiguous relationship within the European Communities of which Britain is a member. These three factors affect not only British policy but also the machinery through which it carries on its external relations.

To illustrate the importance of these constraints, two very different examples may be given. Because of Britain's position as a trading nation and the particularly important role assumed by invisible exports in compensating for a balance of payments which is often adverse where visible trade is concerned, much attention has to be paid to the views of the City of London and to the Bank of England as its spokesman. In the late 1970s and early 1980s the pressure on Britain's trade balance was less acute than previously because the exports of North Sea oil made an important positive contribution to the balance of payments. In due course however the problem is likely to recur.

Second, Britain's former reliance on overseas garrisons and on naval power to guard its trade routes meant that it developed a professional army rather than the mass conscript army that became normal among its continental neighbours. Furthermore, except for its duties in Northern Ireland the army's role since the seventeenth century has been overwhelmingly an external one. In consequence the army has played no significant role in domestic politics – in marked contrast to Britain's principal European partners, and to the other former island empire, Japan.

As for the imperial inheritance itself, the problem of determining the impact upon the British social structure and the British public mind of the rapid withdrawal from Empire over the past three and a half decades remains an intractable one. Quite apart from the demographic contribution of former imperial territories to the population of the United Kingdom, some of whose consequences have been referred to already, what other effects have there been on the British themselves? How far were enterprise and the exercise of rule overseas a cause of the frequently noted failure to recruit the best talents for industry itself? How far does the cessation of career opportunities abroad help to explain the current malaise referred to in the opening chapter? Where does the typecast district officer, or for that matter governor-general, find his niche today? Is there widespread resentment at the sense of the country's being diminished in stature and, if so, how does it manifest itself? Can one deduce, because the European cause has been predominantly a middle-class rather than a working-class enthusiasm, that there is some feeling – however obscure – that the creation of a new Europe may provide an alternative field of activity for frustrated imperialists? These are questions which must be answered by future historians.

Traditionally the different geographical areas covered by Britain's external relations were on the whole dealt with separately. The Foreign Office was responsible for the conduct of relations with foreign countries, and the Colonial Office and India Office for relations with areas which were outside the British Isles but inside the area over which the United Kingdom claimed sovereignty. As the original dominions came to exercise autonomy within the system, the Colonial Office seemed an improper vehicle for relations with their governments. The Dominions Office – later the Commonwealth Relations Office – was thus brought into being to handle these relations. With the increasing insubstantiality of the Commonwealth tie, and the granting of independence to the component parts of the Indian Empire and later in turn to all but a few colonies, the situation changed back again. The Foreign and Commonwealth Office, supported by a single Diplomatic Service, now conducts all of Britain's external affairs, and there are only small differences of nomenclature to betray the existence of the earlier situation – for instance while Britain maintains an ambassador at Washington DC it is represented by a high commissioner in Canada.

The Commonwealth today retains very few vestiges of a common institutional structure. The monarch remains the sovereign in Canada, Australia, New Zealand and a number of very small territories. And in all these countries the monarch, if present, acts upon the advice of responsible ministers according to the British doctrine of cabinet government. Otherwise the governor or governor-general exercises the royal authority without recourse to the

433

sovereign. When the governor-general of Australia intervened in that country's political crisis in November 1975 it was at once made plain that the Queen herself had not been consulted in any way.

More ambiguous is the significance of the title Head of the Commonwealth, which has been accepted as the symbolic link between all its members. This title became a matter of debate in relation to the Queen's Christmas broadcast in 1983, which was addressed to the Commonwealth at large rather than to the United Kingdom and included references to economic and social policy which were regarded in some conservative quarters as controversial, especially as the broadcast included an interview with the then prime minister of India, Mrs Gandhi, who was of course a politically partisan figure in her own country. It was made clear that since the Queen was speaking as head of the Commonwealth her remarks were not the result of advice from her United Kingdom ministers. But in that case there would seem to have been a departure from the normal constitutional principle that the monarch can 'do no wrong' because the responsibility is that of elected ministers. On the other hand the political and constitutional responsibility could not be that of all the governments of the Commonwealth. (The Commonwealth in fact only issues political statements when all its member states agree, which means in effect that it rarely does so.) Clearly if the title of Head of the Commonwealth is to be given some content – and the monarch is in that capacity to be able to make independent statements – new conventions will have to be worked out.

More important than these somewhat academic points are the practical results of the continued existence of the Commonwealth. It does involve some political constraints upon the actions of the United Kingdom government both in the field of external policy and even in some domestic matters. Some of these constraints are less powerfully felt with the virtual end of decolonization. Before the transformation of Rhodesia into the Republic of Zimbabwe, Commonwealth members insisted that Britain had special responsibilities to end the 'illegal' regime in Rhodesia. It is still assumed that in framing her economic policies Britain will pay particular attention to the needs of Commonwealth countries in respect of markets or of aid, and that Commonwealth citizens will be given a preferential status in respect of immigration, access to educational facilities and military training and so forth. Demands were also made by countries which gave priority to their antipathy towards apartheid in South Africa for action against that country, such as the 'Gleneagles Agreement' of 1977 which discouraged sporting ties with South Africa.

The forum for the expression of such grievances and claims is the

Conference of Commonwealth Prime Ministers, which is the successor to the former Imperial Conference. Because these conferences are meetings of the heads of independent states, members have no sanctions against a recalcitrant member other than those generally available in the international community; however successive British governments have obviously attached great importance to maintaining the Commonwealth in being, and have thus been susceptible to the threats of withdrawal from it. They have in the past gone to some lengths to try to prevent this happening. Yet as regional and other bloc politics have come to dominate the international scene more and more, and as the currents of world trade and investment increasingly follow channels quite different from those followed under the earlier British imperial system, the Commonwealth aspect of British policy has steadily declined in importance. Member governments are now readier to ignore the opinions of their Commonwealth partners and to give priority to relationships of more immediate concern to their own national interests.

It is not without relevance that Britain does not receive much assistance or even sympathy from many Commonwealth governments in international disputes to which the United Kingdom is a party. Such disputes have arisen over what would once have been considered Commonwealth issues – notably where the population of a dependency prefers British rule or protection to absorption in another sovereignty. Many Commonwealth countries take their cue from the group of 'non-aligned' countries, and as a result promote the view that British policy is more or less pursuing a colonialist goal. There was a partial exception in the case of the Argentinian invasion of the Falkland Islands in 1982, where Commonwealth countries felt bound to condemn open and armed aggression; but on the substance of the issue most 'New Commonwealth' countries did not endorse the British stance. On other occasions too the Commonwealth has split over foreign policy. Over the invasion of Grenada by the United States and the subsequent ousting of the Cuban-oriented dictatorship in 1983, some of the Commonwealth countries of the Caribbean supported the USA, and indeed participated in the military operation; others like the United Kingdom itself expressed reservations about the enterprise. An active role by the Commonwealth as such in any effort to bring about the restoration of normal government was precluded by the already mentioned requirement of unanimity.

Such differences of perspective and of ideology combine to diminish the impact of the legacy of the Westminster style of constitutional government in Commonwealth countries. The changes in the character of the Commonwealth make its perpetuation as an organization a matter of dwindling significance to most of the British electorate. Yet because all the ties that the member states have developed run through Britain, a Commonwealth without Britain (as is occasionally mooted when Britain is at odds with some of the newer African states) would be almost meaningless. The survival of the Commonwealth might thus in the long run appear most improbable. Instead it is likely that Britain will retain particularly close links with certain individual countries where economic ties are reinforced by those of history, race and culture – although postwar immigration has extended those links beyond the white Commonwealth dominions of Australia, New Zealand and Canada.

Even the ties with the latter group of countries have been affected by changes in circumstance such as the British decision to join the European Economic Community. Their internal development also calls into question some of the historic links between themselves and the United Kingdom. Thus for example changes in the make-up of the population of both Canada and Australia have diminished the weight of citizens of British descent, and so of attachment to such traditional symbols as the monarchy. By 1984 Australia seemed in the process of moving towards becoming a republic.

From the point of view of British domestic government the most important survival from the imperial past is the United Kingdom's anomalous relationship with the Irish Republic. The Irish Republic, although a completely independent country and by its own choice not a member of the Commonwealth, has been allowed to enjoy important privileges. Some, such as the freedom of travel with passports between the two countries, are reciprocal; others are not. For example, Irish citizens are free to settle at will in Britain, and enjoy equality of treatment with British citizens including, as has been seen, the right to vote – a right which British citizens will soon enjoy in the Republic. In addition the Irish Republic has been recognized by successive United Kingdom governments as having a valid claim to a consultative voice in making the political arrangements for Northern Ireland, although the territory is a component part of the United Kingdom.

Direct relations with other foreign countries, or indirect relations through international organizations of the United Nations type, impose upon British governments constraints which are no different from those experienced by many other states. In general the degree to which such constraints are felt by a particular state depends upon that state's own strength. As a permanent member of the United Nations Security Council – and therefore a country with a veto – Britain has some advantages over many other states, though it is bound by valid resolutions of that body in such matters as the imposition of sanctions.

The most serious limitation upon Britain's independence of action is its inevitable reliance upon its allies within the North Atlantic Treaty Organization, and in particular on the USA, for its own defence. It involves the presence in peacetime of American forces on British soil, including those armed with nuclear weapons, and a high degree of technical dependence on the USA even in respect of Britain's own armed forces. In general the size and direction of Britain's defence effort rest largely upon agreements reached in the forum of NATO – a fact which has affected Britain's machinery of government.

Another striking feature of the international scene since the second world war has been the regulation by treaty of economic relations between countries. The tariff policies of almost every major trading country, including Britain, are governed by the provisions of the General Agreement on Tariffs and Trade, commonly known as GATT. Even more important is the influence of international monetary institutions which can directly control the domestic policies of individual governments if they have severe balance of payments problems. During the economic crisis in the second half of 1976 the British government sought help from the International Monetary Fund. Before receiving help it was necessary to give officials of the IMF a good deal of information about the country's economic situation and to enter into formal undertakings about its policies on public expenditure and the money supply. The existence of such external constraints on British policy undermines the plausibility of assertions about the ability of the United Kingdom to cope with economic problems on its own.[1]

Even before Britain became a member of the European Communities – the most important single source of constraints on the United Kingdom's freedom of action – the machinery of British government was in all its aspects showing the impact of the growing international dimension in Britain's affairs. Departments that were previously considered wholly domestic now had to take into account many factors outside the national jurisdiction. The representation of British interests abroad and in international conferences cannot now be left entirely to professional diplomats, nor can the framing of policy be left wholly to the Foreign and Commonwealth Office. Delegations to the major international organizations and the staffs of embassies and high commissions have to include specialists on many topics who will work closely with their relevant home departments, from which the civil servants will probably have been seconded.

The British embassy in Washington is a particular problem in respect of representation, given the multiplicity of British interests that need to be negotiated with the United States government and the diffusion of power within that government. Negotiations have to be carried on not merely with the State Department but also with the White House, the Pentagon, the domestic departments and Congress itself, because of the important independent role which the legislature plays in the American system of government. The Washington embassy team thus contains a large number of non-diplomatic personnel, of whom the military form the largest contingent.

International conferences of a specialized kind – some of them meeting over very long periods of time – claim much of the energies of home-based civil servants.[2] The proposals of the Central Policy Review Staff mentioned earlier advocated replacing the Diplomatic Service itself with a 'foreign policy group' within a unified Civil Service. They also recommended downgrading the Foreign and Commonwealth Office from its role as the main coordinator of external policy.[3] These proposals were subject to severe criticism from a number of quarters.[4] And in all except comparatively minor respects they were ultimately rejected by the government.[5] It must be assumed therefore that although greater opportunities for inter-change between the home departments and the Diplomatic Service will be actively encouraged, the basic structure of overseas represent-ation will not be fundamentally altered in the near future.

The frequency with which ministerial meetings take place within a Commonwealth, a European or a United Nations context means that civil servants from these departments are increasingly drawn into international work of a kind where coordination cannot easily be supplied by the Foreign and Commonwealth Office. Questions of policy enter into the equation as well. In the case of negotiations with the European Communities, control is exercised by a unit in the Cabinet Office presided over by home civil servants. The Foreign and Commonwealth Office is thought of as having a distinct interest of its own – namely a successful and smooth relationship with the Community institutions and other member states. Sometimes as a result there is a suspicion that the FCO is not as committed as are the home departments to safeguarding particular British interests – for example in relation to agriculture or the budget.

Britain's international obligations are not confined to the military or economic sphere. As has been seen, by adherence to the European Convention on Human Rights, Britain laid itself open to the investigative and judicial functions of the European Commission on Human Rights and the European Court of Human Rights. This situation has enabled the Irish government to bring proceedings against the British government over the alleged ill-treatment of members of the IRA in prisons in Northern Ireland. It is true that the Convention cannot be directly applied by British courts, and that the decisions of the European Court of Human Rights are not binding in British courts, but it is difficult for a British government to ignore such decisions. Indeed Britain would be in breach of her international obligations if she were to do so. Because of the very different traditions of the English legal system – as well as differences of substantive law in relation to such fields as industrial relations – the chances of the European Court finding against Britain on a matter relating to the application of the Convention have turned out to be considerable.

British membership of the European Communities – the Coal and Steel Community, Euratom, and above all the Common Market or European Economic Community set up by the Treaty of Rome – raises a new and potentially more far-reaching set of issues. The problems posed by membership arise in part from the ambiguity inherent in the concept of the EEC itself. From one point of view it can be regarded as simply a further tier of inter-governmental activity not essentially different from what goes on in other international organizations. The countries concerned have agreed by treaty to certain derogations from their own autonomy, principally in the fields of commercial policy and the control of the market in agricultural products. They have also accepted, as part of the machinery for carrying through these common policies, a role for the executive of the Communities – the European Commission – which although more extensive than that customarily allocated to the secretariats of international organizations is not so distinct from them as to be unrecognizable. The main powers of decision have in fact come to rest with the national governments, who possess the ultimate right of veto. However, there is another point of view. For in addition to the powers about which the Treaties are explicit, there are aspects of the Communities which suggest a very different result from their creation – namely the establishment in some form of a United States of Europe. The unease that all member governments feel from time to time when confronted with the demands made upon them by the Communities is caused by an awareness of this fundamental duality of character. In the British case, where the issue of membership has been argued on pragmatic rather than ideological grounds and where attachment to the country's own constitutional arrangements, including the notion of parliamentary sovereignty, has remained very much alive, this ambiguity is particularly difficult to accept.

One can summarize the objections to membership of the Communities. Even with their present powers, which are very much limited by the existence of the national veto, there are still those who believe in the desirability of independent national action and who think that the Communities are an impediment to it. To begin with, the Communities have legislative powers in the spheres of economic activity that they regulate. As already noted, this means that whereas for British courts an Act of Parliament has hitherto been the supreme source of law on a particular topic, they now have to take into consideration another body of law. This law is derived from the Treaties themselves, or consists of legislation made under their provisions by the Communities. Some of it consists of regulations which have the immediate force of law in the countries concerned; the remainder consists of directives which oblige the member states to alter their domestic legislation to conform with them. Ultimate decisions about the interpretation of the Treaty and about any conflict between Community law and the domestic laws of the member states are made by the European Court. In other words we face for the first time the possibility of a British Act of Parliament being adjudged subordinate to other legislation, because Parliament's right to override earlier Acts does not hold good for the Treaties or for general Community legislation.

The question has arisen as to whether Parliament could repeal the European Communities Act itself. The Treaty of Rome itself contains no provision for member states to withdraw. But it was the policy of the Labour Party as proclaimed during the election of 1983 to withdraw from the Communities by repealing the relevant legislation and denouncing the Treaty. Labour assumed that Britain's interest in Europe could be preserved by negotiating a new external relationship with the EEC. Such a position presupposes that British sovereignty has not been abrogated irrevocably; but pending the test of such a course being pursued by any British government, one can only endorse what one of the main partisans of British entry said at the time the United Kingdom joined the EEC, namely that we have 'for the first time in part and covering a relatively narrow field, a written constitution in the shape of the treaties'.[6]

Also, the techniques of statutory interpretation would seem to require some revision. For instance in 1978 the very active House of Lords Select Committee on the European Communities devoted a report to the subject of the use by the EEC of Article 100 of the Treaty of Rome, under which directives can be issued to member governments to ensure that their laws on certain subjects are 'approximated', i.e. made as close in substance as possible. The Committee pointed out that this article should be interpreted under Article 2 of the Treaty, which sets out the objectives of the EEC in economic terms. Economic goals are accordingly to be attained by the establishment of a common market and the progressive approximation of the economic policies of the member states. The Committee proceeded to argue that therefore directives under Article 100 are not valid if the areas they affect lie outside this essential framework.[7] While this argument has some resemblance to the way in which delegated legislation may be challenged on *ultra vires* grounds, the broad scope of the matters involved makes the debate much more akin to that concerning the constitutional jurisdiction of the US Supreme Court. Thus aspects of British law are likely in the long run to be affected by European Community law. Lord Denning's prediction in 1974 that the effect of the change would be like that of an incoming tide, flowing into the estuaries and up the rivers, was held to be an exaggeration; four years later – and certainly by the mid-1980s – it was obviously an understatement.[8]

The House of Commons instrument for dealing with such questions is the Select Committee on European Legislation (formerly the Select Committee on European Secondary Legislation etc.). This Committee is entitled to receive draft legislation emanating from the Commission within two weeks of its arriving in Whitehall. Its main task is to decide which of the thirty or forty documents received weekly are so important that they should be given further consideration. Since time is limited, a considerable backlog builds up of documents recommended for consideration by the Committee but not yet debated by it.[9] The Committee has expressed disquiet about the limited time available for the consideration of these documents and about the refusal of ministers to accept the view that no action should be taken until the House has had its say.[10]

The House of Lords' scrutiny of Community proposals is much more intense. It accomplishes this scrutiny through its Select Committee on the European Communities, and this represents the most serious attempt at some form of monitoring of European legislation by any Parliament of the EEC member states. The actual work of scrutiny is performed through seven subject subcommittees, each of them empowered to employ special advisers and to hear evidence from British and Community civil servants, MEPs and bodies concerned with the matter under review. It does, of course, keep in touch with the House of Commons Committee, so that it is unlikely that anything of significance will slip through unobserved. The House of Lords does find time to debate the subcommittee reports, and thus in theory it alerts the general public as well as Parliament itself to matters of importance. It could be argued that Britain needs such machinery of scrutiny more than most other Community countries. On the one hand, the country's economic structure – especially the role of agriculture – often places it in a minority in matters of policy within a European framework; on the other hand Britain's common law traditions and the different role played by the judiciary in relation to the administration calls into question some regulatory procedures which other EEC member states find quite acceptable.

However the matter is not simply one of alerting Parliament; there is also the problem of what Parliament can do if it objects to a piece of Community legislation to which the government has already agreed. As has been seen there is no way in which Parliament can force a minister to alter his policy, except by withdrawing support from government as a whole. The unlikelihood of such an eventuality has already been made plain.

These institutional problems have not prevented Britain from playing an active part in all aspects of the work of the Communities.[11] But there have been important problems on the financial side which have rendered Britain a less than comfortable member of the Communities and have often put the United Kingdom in a minority of one within the EEC. The Communities have been financed primarily from two sources: levies on agricultural imports and a proportion of receipts from each country's notional receipts from VAT. Because Britain remains a major importer of food from outside the Community she finds herself paying a high proportion of the levies; thus, although Britain is one of the poorest members of the Communities, it has been the largest net contributor to the Community budget.[12] Britain's own relatively small agricultural sector does not get back in grants the equivalent of what Britain contributes nor, given the relatively small proportion of Community funds spent upon regional and social policies, can its receipts under these heads of expenditure make up for the difference.

Britain's pressure to have this imbalance remedied was met in the late 1970s and early 1980s by *ad hoc* adjustments without removing the differences of principle. For the enthusiast for the European ideal, the EEC differed from other international organizations in having its 'own resources'; there could thus be no question of individual countries being entitled to balance their contributions against their receipts. By the end of 1983 there was a deadlock on this issue. But it seemed likely that a solution would have to be found, since in order to maintain its planned levels of expenditure, the Community would need to have the proportion of VAT it could claim increased. And here Britain like other countries had a veto which it could exercise if its budgetary demands were not met. An agreement between heads of government was reached at a 'summit' at Fontainebleau in June 1984. A formula for reimbursement to Britain on a long-term basis was accepted, together with the need for budgetary discipline and a shift away from expenditure on agriculture, in return for Britain's agreement to a shift upwards in payments from VAT. But the ultimate ability of the Community to make the bargain stick would depend upon the actions of national governments and Parliaments.

In the period immediately after Britain joined the Communities much attention was paid to another aspect in which the Communities differed from other international organizations – the provision for a directly elected European Parliament instead of the previous Assembly of delegations nominated by the member states' Parliaments.

Although the British commitment to direct elections was implicit in its membership of the Communities, the issue played little part in the national referendum campaign and was indeed deliberately muted by the pro-Europeans to prevent alarm.[13] However, because new legislation to provide for direct elections was necessary it provided an issue for a last-ditch struggle by the anti-Europeans from 1975 to 1978. The issue was further highlighted by the argument over devolution which was going on at the same time, since it was clear that whatever the mode of election to the European Parliament, Scotland and Wales's share of the total UK representation would be settled by the size of their populations and would therefore be much less than England's share. It was provided that each country could use any system it chose for the first direct elections only, pending agreement on a common system which would have to be introduced before the second round of direct elections; nevertheless the choice of methods was a burning issue in Britain because of the parallel discussions over the Scottish and Welsh assemblies and the feeling that the introduction of proportional representation in a European context might create a precedent for electoral reform affecting the House of Commons itself.

In 1975 a Select Committee was appointed to look into the question; it reported that it would be possible to hold the elections in 1978, the EEC's target date, and suggested that a single-member constituency system of the ordinary first-past-the-post kind should be adopted. Only Jeremy Thorpe, the representative of the minor parties on the Committee, disagreed with this recommendation. The government was in no hurry to legislate, which was understandable because the Labour Party conference in September had opposed the whole idea of direct elections. The government's bill was published only in 1977. As part of the pact with the Liberals, the bill provided for a form of proportional representation but allowed the House of

Commons a free vote if it so chose. The bill got its second reading towards the end of the session. In the new session it was reintroduced and again received a second reading; but when it came to voting on the proposed electoral system, the choice was for the single-member constituency system in preference to proportional representation, by a majority of 321 votes to 224. The majority consisted of 115 Labour MPs, 198 Conservatives and 8 Ulster Unionists.

The time required to demarcate the eighty-one new European constituencies and to make other necessary arrangements made it impossible for elections to take place in 1978. They were in fact held in June 1979, a month after the British general election. Although the EEC member states had agreed to harmonize their methods of election before another round of elections, the government resisted pressure from the Alliance parties to change the British system, and the elections scheduled for June 1984 were again held in single-member constituencies.

British legislation had not specified whether individuals could be members of both the House of Commons and the European Parliament. The Labour Party, however, decided to bar the dual mandate for its own candidates, so that Labour nominations to the European Parliament could not be sought by those wishing to remain in or enter the House of Commons. The Conservative Party took no formal decision, although it was made clear that the Conservative leadership would not take kindly to the idea of a dual mandate, which might make the whips' task harder in assembling members for divisions, since there would be no Labour members with whom to 'pair' their own MPs.

In the event four Conservative MPs were elected to the European Parliament, as well as four Conservative peers. Six Euro-MPs were elected to the House of Commons in 1983, but it was not clear how long any of them would retain their membership of the Euro-Parliament, which had become a very demanding occupation; in fact only one stood again in 1984.

What was now in question was the nature of the future links between the European Parliament and the Parliament of the United Kingdom. Various methods of dealing with the problem were canvassed, including *ex officio* non-voting membership of the House of Lords for all Britain's European MPs, or the establishment of some new committee structure.[14] Formal links might however matter less than informal ones between ideologically sympathetic parties across national boundaries. For British parties, the non-elected European Assembly had already shown the difficulties. The Labour representatives, coming as they did from a party which was officially anti-

European, found it hard to discover common ground with the continental socialists who were essentially pro-European. The gap between British and continental European socialists was at its widest when Michael Foot was leader of the Labour Party; in 1983–4 there were signs that the new leader, Neil Kinnock, wished to do something to heal that breach. The Liberals, unrepresented in the first European Parliament, maintained links with continental Liberals, though they were far apart ideologically. The Social Democrats, who were close to some continental socialist parties, found it difficult to enter into a close relationship with those parties because the European socialists had already made a prior commitment to the British Labour Party.

The Conservatives found the going difficult also. The Christian Democrats seemed too close to their clerical origins for the Conservatives to feel wholly at home with them. The right in France was divided, and the Gaullists preferred to think of themselves as straddling the right-left divide. The Democratic Group in the European Parliament thus consisted of sixty British Conservatives, two Danish Conservatives and one Ulster Unionist. But the international links of the Conservative Party were strengthened by its leading role in creating the International Democratic Union of Conservative, Christian Democrat and other 'like-minded' parties, which extended outside Europe to include American Republicans, Canadian Progressive Conservatives and Japanese Liberal Democrats. Nevertheless it was in relation to the European Parliament that the most practical issues arose, since its work was divided between committees manned on the basis of party groupings, not nationality.

These considerations affected the parties' attitudes to the second European elections fought in June 1984. But, as on the previous occasion, the electorate seemed uninterested in the properly European aspects of the contest and, in so far as it took an interest at all, seemed to treat them as a form of public opinion poll on the national parties. As in 1979 the turnout – around 32 per cent – was the lowest in Europe, far behind the majority of the other members. The shift of votes away from the Conservatives involved the loss of fifteen seats, so that the membership of the European Democratic Group at Strasbourg was decreased, while British Labour gains to some extent compensated for socialist losses elsewhere. The choice of Labour candidates in winnable seats also suggested that the Labour representation in the second European Parliament would be even more strongly biased against British membership than after the first elections of 1979. Nevertheless, as some shift in the language of the Labour leadership had suggested, the difficulties involved in actually extracting Britain from the EEC commitment were becoming more widely appreciated.

Enough has been said to show that in Britain – as indeed elsewhere in Western Europe – the tasks of government and the manner in which they are performed can no longer be assessed solely by reference to the framework of national politics or domestic institutions. Much of the traditional language of political analysis is therefore difficult to use with conviction.[15] Moreover such a development does not result merely from Britain's membership of the EEC; rather it is changing circumstances that have brought about both the creation of the EEC and Britain's decision to join it. For many centuries it seemed that the way forward in European politics was towards the creation of self-contained nation states, organizing their affairs and making their decisions, guided only by their own conceptions of the national interest. A clear distinction was made between international relations and domestic matters. In the twentieth century this process has gone into reverse. At both the formal and the informal levels of government and politics, we have to take account of institutions and allegiances that transcend national frontiers. Despite the apparent continuities in the substance and form of British institutions there are now real differences from the situation of the nineteenth century from which we derive many of our classical definitions of British constitutional practices. Of these differences, by no means the least is the now very qualified sense in which Britain can be regarded as a wholly independent state.

Appendix I
General Election Results,
1918–83

	Total Votes	MPs Elected	Candidates	Un-opposed Returns	% Share of Total Vote	Average % Vote per Opposed Candidate	% Share of Seats
Coalition 1918. Sat., 14 Dec.							
Coalition Unionist	3,504,198	335	374	42	32.6		47.38
Coalition Liberal	1,455,640	133	158	27	13.5		18.81
Coalition Labour	161,521	10	18	—	1.5		1.41
(Coalition)	(5,121,359)	(478)	(550)	(69)	(47.6)		(67.61)
Conservative	370,375	23	37	—	3.4		3.25
Irish Unionist	292,722	25	38	—	2.7		3.54
Liberal	1,298,808	28	253	—	12.1		3.96
Labour	2,385,472	63	388	12	22.2		8.91
Irish Nationalist	238,477	7	60	1	2.2		.99
Sinn Fein	486,867	73	102	25	4.5		10.33
Others	572,503	10	197	—	5.3		1.41
Elec. 21,392,322 Turnout 58.9%	10,766,583	707	1,625	107	100.0		100.00
Conservative (Maj) 1922. Wed., 15 Nov.							
Conservative	5,500,382	345	483	42	38.2	48.6	56.10
National Liberal	1,673,240	62	162	5	11.6	39.3	10.08
Liberal	2,516,287	54	328	5	17.5	30.9	8.78
Labour	4,241,383	142	411	4	29.5	40.0	23.09
Others	462,340	12	59	1	3.2	28.3	1.95
Elec. 21,127,663 Turnout 71.3%	14,393,632	615	1,443	57	100.0	—	100.00

	Total Votes	MPs Elected	Candi- dates	Un- opposed Returns	% Share of Total Vote	Average % Vote per Opposed Candidate	% Share of Seats
Labour (Min) 1923. Thu., 6 Dec.							
Conservative	5,538,824	258	540	35	38.1	42.6	41.95
Liberal	4,311,147	159	453	11	29.6	37.8	25.85
Labour	4,438,508	191	422	3	30.5	41.0	31.06
Others	260,042	7	31	1	1.8	27.6	1.14
Elec. 21,281,232 Turnout 70.8%	14,548,521	615	1,446	50	100.0	—	100.00
Conservative (Maj) 1924. Wed., 29 Oct.							
Conservative	8,039,598	419	552	16	48.3	51.9	68.13
Liberal	2,928,747	40	340	6	17.6	30.9	6.50
Labour	5,489,077	151	512	9	33.0	38.2	24.56
Communist	55,346	1	8	—	0.3	25.0	.16
Others	126,511	4	16	1	0.8	29.1	.65
Elec. 21,731,320 Turnout 76.6%	16,639,279	615	1,428	32	100.0	—	100.00
Labour (Min) 1929. Thu., 30 May							
Conservative	8,656,473	260	590	4	38.2	39.4	42.28
Liberal	5,308,510	59	513	—	23.4	27.7	9.59
Labour	8,389,512	288	571	—	37.1	39.3	46.83
Communist	50,614	—	25	—	0.3	5.3	—
Others	243,266	8	31	3	1.0	21.2	1.30
Elec. 28,850,870 Turnout 76.1%	22,648,375	615	1,730	7	100.0	—	100.00

	Total Votes	MPs Elected	Candidates	Un-opposed Returns	% Share of Total Vote	Average % Vote per Opposed Candidate	% Share of Seats
Coalition 1931. Tue., 27 Oct.							
Conservative	11,987,745	473	523	56	55.2 ⎱		76.91
National Labour	341,370	13	20	—	1.6 ⎰	62.9	2.11
National Liberal	809,302	35	41	—	3.7 ⎰		5.69
Liberal	1,403,102	33	112	5	6.5	28.8	5.37
(National Government)	(14,532,519)	(554)	(696)	(61)	(67.0)	—	(90.08)
Independent Liberal	106,106	4	7	—	0.5	35.8	6.5
Labour	6,649,630	52	515	6	30.6	33.0	8.46
Communist	74,824	—	26	—	0.3	7.5	—
New Party	36,377	—	24	—	0.2	3.9	—
Others	256,917	5	24	—	1.2	21.9	.81
Elec. 29,960,071 Turnout 76.3%	21,656,373	615	1,292	67	100.0	—	100.00
Nat. Govt. (Con) 1935. Thu., 14 Nov.							
Conservative	11,810,158	437	585	26	53.7	54.8	70.09
Liberal	1,422,116	21	161	—	6.4	23.9	3.41
Labour	8,325,491	154	552	13	37.9	40.3	25.04
Independent Labour Party	139,577	4	17	—	0.7	22.2	0.65
Communist	27,117	1	2	—	0.1	38.0	8.16
Others	272,595	4	31	1	1.2	21.3	0.65
Elec. 31,379,050 Turnout 71.2%	21,997,054	615	1,348	40	100.0	—	100.00
Labour (Maj) 1945. Thu., 5 July							
Conservative	9,988,306	213	624	1	39.8	40.1	33.28
Liberal	2,248,226	12	306	—	9.0	18.6	1.88
Labour	11,995,152	393	604	2	47.8	50.4	61.41
Communist	102,780	2	21	—	0.4	12.7	0.31
Common Wealth	110,634	1	23	—	0.4	12.6	0.15
Others	640,880	19	104	—	2.0	15.4	2.97
Elec. 33,240,391 Turnout 72.7%	26,085,978	640	1,682	3	100.0	—	100.00

	Total Votes	MPs Elected	Candi- dates	Un- opposed Returns	% Share of Total Vote	Average % Vote per Opposed Candidate	% Share of Seats
	Labour (Maj) 1950. Thu., 23 Feb.						
Conservative	12,502,567	298	620	2	43.5	43.7	47.68
Liberal	2,621,548	9	475	—	9.1	11.8	1.44
Labour	13,266,592	315	617	—	46.1	46.7	50.40
Communist	91,746	—	100	—	0.3	2.0	—
Others	290,218	3	56	—	1.0	12.6	0.48
Elec. 33,269,770 Turnout 84.0%	28,772,671	625	1,868	2	100.0	—	100.00
	Conservative (Maj) 1951. Thu., 25 Oct.						
Conservative	13,717,538	321	617	4	48.0	48.6	51.36
Liberal	730,556	6	109	—	2.5	14.7	0.96
Labour	13,948,605	295	617	—	48.8	49.2	47.20
Communist	21,640	—	10	—	0.1	4.4	—
Others	177,329	3	23	—	0.6	16.8	0.48
Elec. 34,645,573 Turnout 82.5%	28,595,668	625	1,376	4	100.0	—	100.00
	Conservative (Maj) 1955. Thus., 26 May						
Conservative	13,286,569	344	623	—	49.7	50.2	54.60
Liberal	722,405	6	110	—	2.7	15.1	0.95
Labour	12,404,970	277	620	—	46.4	47.3	43.97
Communist	33,144	—	17	—	0.1	4.2	—
Others	313,410	3	39	—	1.1	20.8	0.48
Elec. 34,858,263 Turnout 76.7%	26,760,498	630	1,409	—	100.0	—	100.00
	Conservative (Maj) 1959. Thu., 8 Oct.						
Conservative	13,749,830	365	625	—	49.4	49.6	57.94
Liberal	1,638,571	6	216	—	5.9	16.9	0.95
Labour	12,215,538	258	621	—	43.8	44.5	40.95
Communist	30,897	—	18	—	0.1	4.1	—
Plaid Cymru	77,571	—	20	—	0.3	9.0	—
Scottish Nat. P.	21,738	—	5	—	0.1	11.4	—
Others	12,464	1	31	—	0.4	11.0	0.16
Elec. 35,397,080 Turnout 78.8%	27,859,241	630	1,536	—	100.0	—	100.00

	Total Votes	MPs Elected	Candi- dates	Un- opposed Returns	% Share of Total Vote	Average % Vote per Opposed Candidate	% Share of Seats
Labour (Maj) 1964. Thu., 15 Oct.							
Conservative	12,001,3396	304	630	—	43.4	43.4	48.25
Liberal	3,092,878	9	365	—	11.2	18.5	1.43
Labour	12,205,814	317	628	—	44.1	44.1	50.32
Communist	45,932	—	36	—	0.2	3.4	—
Plaid Cymru	69,507	—	23	—	0.3	8.4	—
Scottish Nat. P.	64,044	—	15	—	0.2	10.7	—
Others	168,422	—	60	—	0.6	6.4	—
Elec. 35,892,572 Turnout 77.1%	27,655,374	630	1,757	—	100.0	—	100.00
Labour (Maj) 1966. Thu., 31 Mar.							
Conservative	11,418,433	253	629	—	41.9	41.8	40.16
Liberal	2,327,533	12	311	—	8.5	16.1	1.90
Labour	13,064,951	363	621	—	47.9	48.7	57.62
Communist	62,112	—	57	—	0.2	3.0	—
Plaid Cymru	61,071	—	20	—	0.2	8.7	—
Scottish Nat. P.	128,474	—	20	—	0.2	14.1	—
Others	170,569	2	31	—	0.6	8.6	0.32
Elec. 35,964,684 Turnout 75.8%	27,263,606	630	1,707	—	100.0	—	100.00
Conservative (Maj) 1970. Thu., 18 June							
Conservative	13,145,123	330	628	—	46.4	46.5	52.38
Liberal	2,117,035	6	332	—	7.5	13.5	0.95
Labour	12,179,341	287	624	—	43.0	43.5	45.56
Communist	37,970	—	58	—	0.1	1.1	—
Plaid Cymru	175,016	—	36	—	0.6	11.5	—
Scottish Nat. P.	306,802	1	65	—	1.1	12.2	0.16
Others	383,511	6	94	—	1.4	9.1	0.95
Elec. 39,342,013 Turnout 72.0%	28,344,798	630	1,837	—	100.0	—	100.00

	Total Votes	MPs Elected	Candi-dates	Un-opposed Returns	% Share of Total Vote	Average % Vote per Opposed Candidate	% Share of Seats
Labour (Min) 1974. Thu., 28 Feb.							
Conservative	11,868,906	297	623	—	37.9	38.8	46.77
Liberal	6,063,470	14	517	—	19.3	23.6	2.20
Labour	11,639,243	301	623	—	37.1	38.0	47.40
Communist	32,741	—	44	—	0.1	1.7	—
Plaid Cymru	171,364	2	36	—	0.6	10.7	0.32
Scottish Nat. P.	632,032	7	70	—	2.0	21.9	1.10
National Front	76,865	—	54	—	0.3	3.2	—
Others (G.B.)	131,059	2	120	—	0.4	2.2	0.32
Others (N.I.)[1]	717,986	12	48	—	2.3	25.0	1.89
Elec. 39,798,899	31,333,226	635	2,135	—	100.0	—	100.00
Turnout 78.7%							
Labour (Maj) 1974. Thu., 10 Oct.							
Conservative	10,464,817	277	623	—	35.8	36.7	43.62
Liberal	5,346,754	13	619	—	18.3	18.9	2.05
Labour	11,457,079	319	623	—	39.2	40.2	50.24
Communist	17,426	—	29	—	0.1	1.5	—
Plaid Cymru	166,321	3	36	—	0.6	10.8	0.47
Scottish Nat. P.	839,617	11	71	—	2.9	30.4	1.73
National Front	113,843	—	90	—	0.4	2.9	—
Others (G.B.)	81,227	—	118	—	0.3	1.5	—
Others (N.I.)[1]	702,094	12	43	—	2.4	27.9	1.89
Elec. 40,072,971	29,189,178	635	2,252	—	100.0	100.00	
Turnout 72.8%							

	Total Votes	MPs Elected	Candidates	Un-opposed Returns	% Share of Total Vote	Average % Vote per Opposed Candidate	% Share of Seats
Conservative (Maj) 1979. Thu., 3 May							
Conservative	13,697,690	339	622	—	43.9	44.9	53.38
Liberal	4,313,811	11	577	—	13.8	14.9	1.73
Labour	11,532,148	269	623	—	36.9	37.8	42.36
Communist	15,938	—	38	—	0.1	0.9	—
Plaid Cymru	132,544	2	36	—	0.4	8.1	0.31
Scottish Nat. P.	504,259	2	71	—	1.6	17.3	0.31
National Front	190,747	—	303	—	0.6	1.6	—
Ecology	38,116	—	53	—	0.1	2.0	—
Workers Rev. P.	13,535	—	60	—	0.1	0.5	—
Others (G.B.)	85,338	—	129	—	0.3	1.3	—
Others (N.I.)[1]	695,889	12	64	—	2.2	18.8	1.88
Elec. 41,093,264 Turnout 76.0%	31,220,010	635	2,576	—	100.0		100.00
Conservative (Maj.) 1983. Thu., 9 June							
Conservative	13,012,315	397	633	—	42.4	43.5	61.07
Liberal	4,210,715	17	322	—	13.7	27.7	2.61
Social Democrat	3,570,834	6	311	—	11.6	24.3	0.92
(Alliance)	(7,780,949)	(23)	(633)	—	(25.4)	(26.0)	(3.53)
Labour	8,456,934	209	633	—	27.6	28.3	32.15
Communist	11,606	—	35	—	0.04	0.8	—
Plaid Cymru	125,309	2	36	—	0.4	7.8	0.3
Scottish Nat. P.	331,975	2	72	—	1.1	11.8	0.3
National Front	27,065	—	60	—	0.1	1.0	—
Others (G.B.)	193,383	—	282	—	0.6	1.4	—
Others (N.I.)[1]	764,925	17	95	—	3.1	17.9	2.61
Elec. 42,197,344 Turnout 72.7%	30,705,061	650	2,579	—	100.0	—	100.00

[1]From 1974 onwards, no candidates in Northern Ireland are included in the major party totals although it might be argued that some independent Unionists should be classed with the Conservatives and that Northern Ireland Labour candidates should be classed with Labour.

Sources: Butler & Sloman, *British Political Facts 1900–79*.
   Butler & Butler, *British Political Facts 1900–1985*.

NB: Percentage figures in each column may not add up precisely to 100.

Appendix II
European Election Results, 1979 and 1984

The first direct elections to the European Assembly (Parliament) were held on 7 June 1979. In Great Britain itself the elections were run on the customary first-past-the-post system with the country divided into 78 constituencies. The turnout was barely 31% compared with 76% in the general election a month earlier and 65% in the referendum on Europe in 1975.

The results were as follows:

	Votes Cast	Percentage of those Voting	Seats
Conservatives	6,504,481	50.6	60
Labour	4,253,210	33.0	17
Liberals	1,690,600	13.1	0
Others	421,533	3.3	1 (Scottish Nat. P.)

In Northern Ireland the whole province was treated as a single constituency electing three members by the single transferable vote system. This produced one Democratic Unionist (Rev. Ian Paisley), one SDLP member and one Official Unionist.

Of the Conservatives elected, four had been elected to the new House of Commons. In the European Parliament with a handful of continental colleagues they formed the European Democratic Group.

In the 1984 European elections the turnout was 32%. The votes cast were as follows:

	Votes Cast	Percentage of those Voting	Seats
Conservatives	5,426,752	40.8	45
Labour	4,865,297	36.5	32
Alliance	2,593,628	19.5	0
Others	429,149	3.2	1 (Scottish Nat. P.)

In Northern Ireland the vote repeated the outcome of the 1979 elections. However, the threat to the SDLP from Sinn Fein caused a turnout of 65% – i.e. twice as high as in the rest of the United Kingdom.

Appendix III
Prime Ministers in the Twentieth Century

Arthur Balfour	(*Conservative*)	12 July 1902
Sir Henry Campbell Bannerman	(*Liberal*)	5 December 1905
Herbert Henry Asquith	(*Liberal*)	7 April 1908
	(*Coalition*)	25 May 1915
David Lloyd George	(*Coalition*)	7 December 1916
Andrew Bonar Law	(*Conservative*)	23 October 1922
Stanley Baldwin	(*Conservative*)	22 May 1923
J. Ramsay MacDonald	(*Labour*)	22 January 1924
Stanley Baldwin	(*Conservative*)	4 November 1924
J. Ramsay MacDonald	(*Labour*)	5 June 1929
	(*National*)	24 August 1931
Stanley Baldwin	(*National*)	21 January 1936
Neville Chamberlain	(*National*)	28 May 1937
Winston Churchill	(*Coalition*)	10 May 1940
	(*Conservative*)	23 May 1945
Clement Attlee	(*Labour*)	26 July 1945
Winston Churchill	(*Conservative*)	26 October 1951
Sir Anthony Eden	(*Conservative*)	6 April 1955
Harold Macmillan	(*Conservative*)	10 January 1957
Sir Alec Douglas-Home	(*Conservative*)	19 October 1963
Harold Wilson	(*Labour*)	16 October 1964
Edward Heath	(*Conservative*)	19 June 1970
Harold Wilson	(*Labour*)	4 March 1974
James Callaghan	(*Labour*)	5 April 1976
Margaret Thatcher	(*Conservative*)	4 May 1979

Notes

Introduction

1 For an overview of the race and immigration issues in British politics see Z. Layton Henry, *The Politics of Race in Britain* (London, 1984).

2 The figures are those given by the Runnymede Trust. On a mid-year estimate of the situation they reckoned the proportion represented by those of new Commonwealth or Pakistani descent to be 3.4%. We have taken their mid-year figures and compared them with official population figures for 1977.

3 David Butler and Robert Waller, *The Times Guide to the House of Commons. June 1983* (June 1983), p. 256.

4 The term 'EEC' is used in this book to connote the European Communities, although this usage is not altogether accurate. The first of the European Communities to be established was the Coal and Steel Community set up by the Treaty of Paris of 18 April 1951. The Treaties of Rome of 25 March 1957 established the European Economic Community (the 'Common Market' or EEC) and the European Atomic Energy Community. At the same time it was agreed that the institutions of the Coal and Steel Community, the High Authority (its executive), the Council of Ministers, the Assembly and the Court would be fused with those of the two new Communities – the Commissions, the Council of Ministers, Assembly and Court. The United Kingdom's entry into the 'Common Market' involved participation in all three Communities and their common institutions. For this reason the term 'EEC' is conveniently used for all three Communities. When the Assembly, which had been a nominated body, became one subject to direct election (in 1979) it assumed the title of European Parliament by which it is now usually known.

5 See *The Brixton Disorders 10–12 April 1981*, Report of an Inquiry by Lord Scarman (Cmnd 8427, 1981).

6 *Handbook to Britain*, 1984 (London, 1984).

7 For the salience of moral questions in current American politics see Gillian Peele, *Revival and Reaction: The Right in Contemporary America* (Oxford, 1984).

8 *Criminal Statistics. England and Wales. 1982* (Cmnd 9048, 1983).

9 These opinion polls were conducted by Marplan for New International Ltd and originally published in the *Sun*. We have taken the surveys here referred to from a collection of such polls published under the title *The Public View* (London 1977).

10 R. Jowell and C. Airey (eds), *British Social Attitudes: the 1984 Report* (Aldershot, 1984).

Chapter 1

1 For a general discussion see Sir Douglas Wass, *Government and the Governed* (London, 1984).
2 *Attorney-General* v. *Jonathan Cape Ltd* and *Attorney-General* v. *Times Newspapers* 3 AER (1975), 484.
3 See for example Sir Leo Pliatzky, *Getting and Spending* (London, 1982). It was noted that Sir Robert Armstrong in participating in a Channel Four discussion was one of the first serving civil servants to make his views public: see *The Times* 2 July 1984.
4 *Dr. Bonham's Case* (1610), 8 Co. Rep.
5 *Edinburgh & Dalkeith Railway* v. *Wauchope* (1842), 8 Cl. & F. 70.
6 *Marbury* v. *Madison*. 1 Cranch 103.
7 See *R.* v. *Secretary of State for the FCO and Another ex parte Council of Civil Service Unions and others. The Times* 17 July 1984. Overturned in the Court of Appeal, 7 August 1984. The House of Lords' judgement may be found in 3 WLR 1174 HL (1974).
8 See for example the writings and speeches of Lord Hailsham, especially *Dilemma of Democracy* (London, 1978). Also Lord Scarman, *English Law – the New Dimension* (London, 1974).
9 B. Särlvik and I. Crewe, *Decade of Dealignment: The Conservative Victory of 1979 and Electoral Trends in the 1970s* (Cambridge, 1983).
10 V. Bogdanor, *Multi-party Politics and the Constitution* (Cambridge, 1983).
11 A. V. Dicey, *Introduction to the Study of the Law of the Constitution* (10th ed., London, 1959).
12 Useful general discussions are to be found in G. Marshall, *Constitutional Theory* (Oxford, 1971), and the same author's *Constitutional Conventions* (Oxford, 1984); also P. Bobbitt, *Constitutional Fate: Theory of the Constitution* (Oxford and New York, 1983).
13 *Vauxhall Estates Ltd.* v. *Liverpool Corporation* (1932), 1 KB 733; *Ellen Street Estates* v. *Minister of Health* (1934), 1 KB 590.
14 *MacCormick* v. *The Lord Advocate* (1935), SLT 255; *Gibson* v. *The Lord Advocate* (1975), SLT 134.
15 See *Bulmer* v. *Bollinger* (1973), 2 CMLR 114 (CA) (1974) Ch. 40.
16 For Lord Denning's view see his own writings and especially *Freedom Under the Law* (London, 1959), *The Discipline of Law* (London, 1979) and *The Due Process of Law* (London, 1980).
17 See *Pigs Marketing Board* v. *Redmond* (1978), ECR 2347; also *Macmahon* v. *Secretary of State for Education and Science* (1982), 3 CMLR.
18 This point was made forcibly by Denning M.R. in *Macarthy's Ltd* v. *Smith* (1979), 3 AER 325.
19 See *Garland* v. *British Rail Engineering Ltd* (1982), 2 AER 415.
20 On the Brixton riots see *The Brixton Disorders 10–12 April 1981*, Report of an Inquiry by Lord Scarman (Cmnd 8427, 1981). For a more general account see M. Kettle and L. Hodges, *Uprising: The Police, The People and The Riots in Britain's Cities* (London, 1982).
21 On this see J. Benyon (ed.,), *Scarman and After: Essays Reflecting on Lord Scarman's Report, the Riots and their Aftermath* (Oxford, 1984). Also

R. Clutterbuck, *Britain in Agony* (London, 1978, rev. ed. 1980); and the same author's *The Media and Political Violence* (London, 1981, rev. ed. 1983).

22 The figures are taken from New Ireland Forum, *The Costs of Violence in Northern Ireland* (Dublin, 1983).

23 Quoted in M. Hatfield, *The House the Left Built* (London, 1975).

24 H. Wilson, *The Governance of Britain* (London, 1975).

25 See M. Holmes, *The First Thatcher Government: Contemporary Conservatism and Economic Change 1979–83* (Brighton, 1985).

26 For a recent overview see D. Wilson (ed.), *The Secrets File* (London, 1984).

27 HC Deb. 24 May 1979. Quoted in M. Cockerell, P. Hennessy & D. Walker, *Sources Close to the Prime Minister: Inside the Hidden World of News Manipulators* (London, 1984), p. 83.

28 The list is printed in *The Times*, 30 April 1984.

29 See for example P. Norton, *Conservative Dissidents 1970–1974* (London, 1978).

30 The phrase 'adversary politics' is explained in S. E. Finer (ed.,), *Adversary Politics and Electoral Reform* (London, 1975).

Chapter 2

1 *The Reorganization of Central Government* (Cmnd 4506, 1970).

2 *The Government's Expenditure Plans 1984–85 to 1986–87* (Cmnd 9143, 1984), I, p. 9.

3 Ibid. p. 10.

4 See *Report on Non-Departmental Public Bodies* (Pliatzky) (Cmnd 7797, 1980).

5 At the end of 1981 there were (including Scotland and Northern Ireland) 52 bodies classified as public corporations; there was a great variety in their origins, scope and size. See the list in Central Statistical Office, *National Income and Expenditure* (1982 edition), pp. 111–12.

6 See *The Next Ten Years: Public Expenditure and Taxation into the 1980's* (Cmnd 9189, 1984), Annex 2.

7 HC Deb. 12 March 1984; Ministry of Defence: *MINIS and the Development of the Organization for Defence*, Defence Open Government Document 84/03 (March 1984); *Statement on the Defence Estimates 1984* (Cmnd 9227, 1984); *The Central Organization for Defence* (Cmnd 931, 1984).

8 See the letter to *The Times* from Admiral of the Fleet Lord Lewin, 20 March 1984, and HL Deb. 14 June 1984.

9 See A. H. Hanson (ed.), *Planning and the Politicians* (London, 1969); J. Hayward and M. Watson (eds), *Planning, Politics and Public Policy* (Cambridge, 1975); M. Shanks, *Planning and Politics* (London, 1977).

10 See House of Lords Select Committee on Science and Technology, Session 1981–82; 1st Report, Science and Government (HL 201, 1981). For earlier developments see Philip Gummett, *Scientists in Whitehall* (Manchester, 1980).

11 Ministry of Defence Open Government Doc. 84/03, Para 25.

Chapter 3

1 The best descriptions of the system of cabinet committees in existence at the moment have come from journalists specializing in Whitehall questions. See the list of committees and their chairmen in *The Times*, 30 April 1984. Also the list printed in Michael Cockerell, Peter Hennessy and David Walker, *Sources Close to the Prime Minister* (London, 1984).

2 See Norman St John Stevas, Introduction to Walter Bagehot, *The English Constitution*, in *The Collected Works of Walter Bagehot* (ed. N. St John Stevas), vol. V (London, 1974), p. 138.

3 Ministry of Reconstruction, *Report of the Committee on the Machinery of Government* (Cd 9320, 1918).

4 L. S. Amery, *Thoughts on the Constitution* (London, 1946).

5 See F. M. G. Willson, 'Coping with Administrative Growth: Super-departments and the Ministerial Cadre', in D. E. Butler and A. H. Halsey (eds), *Policy and Politics* (London, 1978).

6 *First Report from the Select Committee on Procedure*, Session 1977–8 (HC 588. I. 1978), ch. 7, para. 6.

7 For the background to this see *Falkland Islands Review: Report of a Committee of Privy Councillors* (Franks) (Cmnd 8787, 1983). It does not deal with the issue of the resignations.

8 *Fourth Report from the Select Committee on the Parliamentary Commissioner for Administration*, Session 1977–78 (HC 615, 1978), para. 34.

9 For a prewar example see A. E. Booth, 'Administrative Experiment in Unemployment Policy in the Thirties', *Public Administration* 56 (1978).

10 On the patronage aspect see R. S. Goldston, 'Patronage in British Government', *Parliamentary Affairs* XXX (1977); Alan Doig, 'Public Bodies and Ministerial Patronage', ibid. XXXI (1978); P. Holland and M. Fallon, *The Quango Explosion: Public Bodies and Ministerial Patronage* (London, 1978).

11 *Report on Non-Departmental Public Bodies* (Pliatzky) (Cmnd 7797, 1980).

12 For a personal view from someone who was very conscious of the nuances of ministerial relationships with civil servants see R. H. S. Crossman, *The Diaries of a Cabinet Minister* (vol. 1, London, 1975).

13 M. Beloff, *The State and Its Servants: Reflections on the Machinery of Government* (London, 1979). An important point not made clear in this pamphlet is that the officials of the trade unions who negotiate on behalf of civil servants are not themselves civil servants.

14 See Christopher Pollitt, 'The Central Policy Review Staff 1970–4', *Public Administration* 52 (1974); Lord Rothschild, 'The Government's Think Tank and the Nation's Business', in *Meditations of a Broomstick* (London, 1974).

15 *The Reorganization of Central Government* (Cmnd 4506, 1970).

16 On the general subject of scientific advice to government see House of Lords First Report from the Select Committee on Science and Technology, Session 1981–82, *Science and Government* (HL 20. I. 1981).

Chapter 4

1 HC Deb. 28 October 1983.

2 The history and development of the new methods of selection are dealt with in R. A. Chapman, *Leadership in the British Civil Service: a study of Sir Percival Waterfield and the Creation of the Civil Service Selection Board* (London, 1984).

3 H. Roseveare, *The Treasury* (London, 1969), pp. 246ff.

4 *Report of the Committee on the Civil Service* (Fulton) (Cmnd 3638, 1968).

5 M. Beloff, 'Examining the Working of Whitehall', *The Times*, 19 June 1968, reprinted in M. Beloff, *The Intellectual in Politics and Other Essays* (London, 1970). See also Arthur (later Lord) Salter, *The Slave of the Lamp* (London, 1967).

6 *Eleventh Report from the House of Commons Expenditure Committee* (HC 535, 1976–7).

7 Sir James Dunnett, 'The Civil Service after Fulton', *Public Administration* 54 (1976).

8 R. H. Heaton and Sir Leslie Williams, *Civil Service Training* (London, 1974).

9 Dunnett, loc. cit.

10 For a discussion of the French civil service see J. E. S. Hayward, *Governing France: the One and Indivisible French Republic* (London, 1983).

11 *Eleventh Report from the House of Commons Expenditure Committee* (HC 535, 1976–7).

12 J. E. Mitchell, 'Special Advisers: A Personal View', *Public Administration* 56 (1978).

13 *Report of the Committee of Inquiry on Industrial Democracy* (Cmnd 6706, 1977).

14 *Eleventh Report from the House of Commons Expenditure Committee* (HC 535, 1976–7), pp. xxviii–lxxxiii.

15 Fourth Report from the Treasury and Civil Service Select Committee, Session 1980–1, *Acceptance of Outside Appointments by Crown Servants* (HC 216), Appendix 2. Memorandum by the Civil Service Department.

16 HC Debs 28 & 29 June 1978.

17 A list of all special advisers appointed since May 1979 is given in HC Deb. 12 April 1984, cols 155–6.

18 P. Holland and M. Fallon, *The Quango Explosion: Public Bodies and Ministerial Patronage* (London, 1978) and P. Holland, *Quelling the Quango* (London, 1982).

19 *Report on Non-Departmental Public Bodies* (Pliatzky) (Cmnd 7797, 1980).

20 Civil Service Department, *Non-Departmental Public Bodies: A Guide for Departments* (London, 1984).

21 See Peat, Marwick, Mitchell and Co., *Financial Management in the Public Sector: A Review 1979–1984* (London, 1984).

22 HC Deb. 8 November 1983; *The Government's Expenditure Plans 1984–1985 to 1986–1987* (Cmnd 9143, 1984), table 1.15. A detailed breakdown of the employment of civil servants is given by departments and region for the period Jan. 1979 to Jan. 1983 and will be found in *Civil Service Statistics*

(HMSO 1983).

23 HC Deb. 28 October 1983, col. 554.

24 HC Deb. 12 April 1984, col. 156.

25 See Ministry of Defence, *MINIS and The Development of the Organization for Defence*, Open Government Document 84/03 (March 1984).

26 *Third Report from the Treasury and Civil Service Select Committee*, Session 1981–1982 (HC 236. I–III, 1982).

27 *Efficiency in the Civil Service* (Cmnd 8293, 1981).

28 *Transfer of Functions (Minister for Civil Service and Treasury) Order*, 1981 (No. 1670).

29 Lord Bancroft, 'Whitehall and Management: A Retrospect', *Royal Society of Arts Journal* (May 1984).

30 HC 236. II. (1982), pp. 434–6.

31 *Efficiency and Effectiveness in the Civil Service* (Cmnd 8616, 1982).

32 *Report by the MPO/Treasury Financial Management Unit* (September 1983).

33 MPO, *Qualifications: the Role of Qualifications in the Post-Recruitment Development of Civil Servants for Administrative Work: a discussion document* (1983).

34 MPO, *Selection of Fast-Stream Graduate Entrants: Report by Sir Alec Atkinson* (April 1983). See also HL Deb. 1 Dec. 1983. In 1981 there were 53 recruits for 54 vacancies; in 1982, 24 for 44 vacancies; in 1983, 45 recruits for 60 vacancies.

35 MPO *Review of Personnel Work in the Civil Service* (July 1983). See also *Civil Service Management and Development in the 1980s* (July 1983).

36 *Equal Opportunities for Women in the Civil Service* (1982).

37 *Inquiry into Civil Service Pay* (Megaw) (Cmnd 8590, 1982).

38 *Select Committees: Memorandum of Guidance for Officials* (May 1980).

39 *First Report from the House of Commons Liaison Committee*, Session 1982–1983 (HC 92, 1982), para. 46.

40 Joel Barnett, *Inside the Treasury* (London, 1982), p. 188.

41 Central Policy Review Staff, *Review of Overseas Representation* (1977); M. Beloff, 'The Think-Tank and Foreign Affairs', *Public Administration* 55 (1977).

42 For a more recent discussion of this topic, see *Second Report from the Select Committee on Foreign Affairs*, Session 1983–1984 (HC 226); *Observations on the Report by the Secretary of State for Foreign and Commonwealth Affairs* (Cmnd 9627, 1984).

Chapter 5

1 See the views expressed in cabinet on 17 November 1966 by Michael Stewart (later Lord Stewart), then First Secretary of the Treasury, as recorded in R. H. S. Crossman, *Diaries of a Cabinet Minister* (London, 1976), p. 130.

2 See Ivor Burton and Gavin Drewry, 'Public Legislation: a survey of the sessions 1975–76; 1976–77', *Parliamentary Affairs* XXX (1978).

3 Philip Norton, *Dissension in the House of Commons 1945–74* (London, 1975). Also Philip Norton, 'Parliament and Policy in Great Britain', unpublished paper presented to the American Political Science Association, September 1983.

4 On this see Vernon Bogdanor, *Multi-Party Politics and the Constitution* (Cambridge, 1983).

5 S. E. Finer (ed.), *Adversary Politics and Electoral Reform* (London, 1975).

6 Review Body on Top Salaries, Report No. 20, *Review of Parliamentary Pay and Allowances* (Cmnd 8881. I–III, 1983).

7 HC Deb. 19 July 1983; 26 July 1983.

8 For a full analysis of the work of the MP in all its aspects see *Review of Parliamentary Pay and Allowances*, II, pp. 149–53. For the constituency welfare aspect of the MP's role see James W. Marsh, 'The Value of the Constituency Member of Parliament', *Hull Papers in Politics* (Hull, 1983).

9 See J. P. Morgan, *The House of Lords and the Labour Government 1964–70* (Oxford, 1975).

10 See Nicholas Baldwin, 'The House of Lords: a study in evolutionary adaptability', *Hull Papers in Politics* (Hull, 1983).

11 See Nora Beloff, *Freedom under Foot* (London, 1976).

12 See *Report of the Committee on the Preparation of Legislation* (Renton) (Cmnd 6053, 1975).

13 J. A. G. Griffith, *Parliamentary Scrutiny of Government Bills* (London, 1974).

14 See S. A. Walkland, 'Government Legislation in the House of Commons', in S. A. Walkland (ed.), *The House of Commons in the Twentieth Century* (Oxford, 1979). For statistics on the membership and work of the standing committees, see *Standing Committees: Return for the Session 1983–84* (HC 107, 1983–4). In all 584 members took part in this work during the session.

15 See the speech by the Lord Chancellor (Lord Hailsham of St Marylebone), HL Deb. 15 Dec. 1982.

16 See Michael Ryle, 'Supply and Other Financial Procedures', in Walkland (ed.), op. cit.

17 The National Audit Act 1983. See also J. Redwood and J. Hatch, *Controlling Public Expenditure* (Oxford 1982), ch. 2, 'The Function of Parliament'.

18 See Sixth Report from the Treasury and Civil Service Select Committee, *Budgetary Reform in the United Kingdom* (HC 137, 1981–2). *First Report from the Select Committee on Procedure (Finance)* (HC 24, 1982–3).

19 See Nevil Johnson, 'Select Committees and Administration', in Walkland, op. cit.

20 See D. N. Chester and N. Bowring, *Questions in Parliament* (Oxford, 1962), and R. Borthwick, 'Questions and Debates', in Walkland, op. cit.

21 For a statistical analysis of the activity of all select committees for the 1982–3 session, see *Select Committees: Return for the Session 1982–83* (HC 50, 1982–3). Statistics about the select committees in the whole of the 1979–83 Parliament including membership, attendance and turnover can be found in House of Commons written answers for 19 July 1983 (HC Deb. cols 628–48). For a discussion of the central themes see also Dermot Englefield (ed.), *Commons Select Committees: Catalysts for Progress?* (London, 1984).

22 See *The Times*, 7 January 1985.

23 See P. Laundy, 'The Speaker and His Office in the Twentieth Century', in Walkland, op. cit.

Chapter 6

1 See Walter Bagehot, 'Why has the "Settlement" of 1832 so easily melted away?', in N. St John Stevas (ed.), *The Collected Works of Walter Bagehot* Vol. VI (London, 1974).
2 A general history of the British electoral system is given by D. E. Butler, *The British Electoral System Since 1918* (2nd ed., Oxford, 1963).
3 *Report of the Committee on the Age of Majority* (Latey) (Cmnd 3342, 1967).
4 See D. E. Butler, 'Modifying Electoral Arrangements', in D. E. Butler and A. H. Halsey (eds), *Policy and Politics: Essays in Honour of Norman Chester* (London, 1978).
5 See Daniel Lawrence, 'Race, Elections and Politics', in Ivor Crewe (ed.), *British Political Sociology Yearbook*, vol 2, *The Politics of Race* (London, 1975).
6 First Report from the House of Commons Home Affairs Committee, Session 1982–3, *Representation of the People Acts*, vol. II, 'Memorandum submitted by the Home Office' (HC 32–II (1982—3), p. 19).
7 *Report of the Committee on Financial Aid to Political Parties* (Houghton) (Cmnd 6601, 1976).
8 HC 32–II (1982–3), p. 237.
9 See L. Gostin, 'A Mental Patient's Right to Vote', *Poly Law Review* 2, no. 1 (1976).
10 Mental Health (Amendment) Act 1982, c. 51, s. 62 and Schedule 2.
11 HC 32–II (1982–3), pp. 3 and 264.
12 Ibid., pp. 312–15 (memorandum submitted by Sir John Biggs-Davidson, MP).
13 On the elimination of corruption see C. O'Leary, *The Elimination of Corrupt Practices in British Elections 1868–1911* (Oxford, 1962).
14 For Salisbury's attitude on the extension of the franchise see M. Pinto-Duschinsky, *The Political Thought of Lord Salisbury* (London, 1967).
15 House of Commons Home Affairs Committee, Session 1982–83, *Representation of the People Acts* (HC 32). Government reply to the Report, *Representation of the People Acts* (Cmnd 9140, 1984).
16 *Grieve* v. *Home Office* (1965) Scotland 251.
17 See *The Sunday Times*, 20 August 1978.
18 See D. E. Butler and D. Kavanagh, *The British General Election of October 1974*. Also J. Whale, *The Politics of the Mass Media* (London, 1977). For a comparative perspective see A. Smith (ed.), *Television and Political Life: Studies in Six European Countries* (London, 1979).
19 On the background to the first direct elections see C. Cook and M. Francis (eds), *The First European Elections: A Handbook and Guide* (London, 1979).
20 See *Draft Regulations for the Conduct of European Assembly Elections in Great Britain* (London, 1978).

21 See for example S. E. Finer (ed.), *Adversary Politics and Electoral Reform* (London, 1975). Also N. Johnson, *In Search of the Constitution* (Oxford, 1977). For a discussion of the impact of the party and electoral systems on economic policy see M. Stewart, *The Jekyll and Hyde Years* (London, 1977).

Chapter 7

1 See N. Gash, 'From the Origins to Sir Robert Peel', in Lord Butler (ed.), *The Conservatives* (London, 1977).
2 See John Ramsden, *The Age of Balfour and Baldwin* (London, 1978).
3 For a critical review of the first Thatcher administration see P. Riddell, *The Thatcher Government* (London, 1983). Also M. Holmes, *The First Thatcher Government 1979–83* (Brighton, 1985).
4 T. Forrester, *Labour and the Working Class* (London, 1976).
5 J. D. Lees and R. Kimber, *Political Parties in Modern Britain: An Organizational and Functional Guide* (London, 1972), p. 15.
6 See D. Steel, 'Nationalization and Public Ownership', in J. Ramsden and C. Cook (eds), *Trends in British Politics Since 1945* (London, 1978).
7 The manifestos of the parties are reprinted in *The Times Guide to the House of Commons* (London, 1983).
8 See F. W. S. Craig (ed.), *British General Election Manifestos* (London, 1975).
9 See I. McLean, 'Labour Since 1945', in Ramsden and Cook (eds), op. cit.
10 See Max Beloff, *Wars and Welfare: Britain 1914–1945* (London, 1984), pp. 103, 126–9.
11 John Vincent, *The Formation of the Liberal Party* (London, 1966).
12 See J. Rasmussen, *The Liberal Party* (London, 1966); C. Cook, *A Short History of the Liberal Party* (London, 1976).
13 See I. Crewe, J. Alt and B. Särlvik, 'Angels in Plastic: The Liberal Surge in 1974', *Political Studies* XXV (1977); P. H. Lemieux, 'Political Issues and Liberal Support in the February 1974 General Election', ibid.
14 D. E. Butler, *Coalitions in British Politics* (London, 1978).
15 See A. Michie and S. Hoggart, *The Pact: The Inside Story of the Lib-Lab Government, 1977–1978* (London, 1978).
16 See J. Grimond (Lord Grimond), *A Personal Manifesto* (London, 1983).
17 See Ian Bradley, *Breaking the Mould* (London, 1981); Hugh Stephenson, *Claret and Chips: The Rise of the SDP* (London, 1982); Jeremy Josephs, *Inside the Alliance* (London, 1983).
18 David Marquand, 'Inquest on a Movement', *Encounter*, July 1979.
19 The 'Limehouse Declaration' and the 'Statement of Principles' are printed as appendices to Stephenson, op. cit.
20 See H. Pelling, *The British Communist Party: A Historical Profile* (London, 1975).
21 See R. Taylor, *The Fifth Estate* (London, 1977).
22 See John Callaghan, *British Trotskyism: Theory and Practice* (Oxford, 1984).
23 See M. Walker, *The National Front* (London, 1977).
24 See Z. Layton-Henry, 'Race, Electoral Strategy and the Major Parties',

Parliamentary Affairs XXXI (1978); and Z. Layton-Henry, *The Politics of Race in Britain* (London, 1984).
25 See M. Steed, 'The National Front Vote', ibid.
26 See I. McAllister, *The Northern Ireland Social and Democratic Labour Party: Political Opposition in a Divided Society* (London, 1977).
27 See I. McAllister and S. Nelson, 'Developments in the Northern Ireland Party System', *Parliamentary Affairs* XXXII (1979).
28 See Patrick Dunleavy, 'Voting and the Electorate' in H. Drucker, P. Dunleavy, A. Gamble and G. Peele (eds), *Developments in British Politics* (revised ed., Basingstoke, 1984); B. Särlvik and I. Crewe, *Decade of Dealignment: The Conservative Victory of 1979 and Electoral Trends in the 1970's* (Cambridge, 1983).

Chapter 8

1 R. T. McKenzie, *British Political Parties* (London, 1964).
2 See for example S. E. Finer (ed.), *Adversary Politics and Electoral Reform* (London, 1975). Also S. E. Finer, *The Changing British Party System 1945–1979* (Washington, 1980).
3 See N. Fisher, *The Tory Leaders* (London, 1977).
4 See J. Ramsden, *The Making of Conservative Policy: The Conservative Research Department Since 1929* (London, 1980).
5 See P. Norton, *Dissension in the House of Commons 1945–1974* (London, 1975).
6 See C. Mellors, *The British M.P.* (London, 1978).
7 See R. Rose, 'Parties, Factions and Tendencies in Britain', *Political Studies* XII (1964).
8 See P. Norton, *Conservative Dissidents* (London, 1978).
9 See T. Russell, *The Tory Party* (London 1978). Also P. Norton and A. Aughey, *Conservatives and Conservatism* (London, 1981).
10 See Norton, op. cit.
11 See P. Goodhart, *The 1922: the Story of the Commons Backbenchers' Parliamentary Committee* (London, 1973).
12 The programme for each annual conference, usually available in September each year, is the principal source for the current organization of the Party and the names of the office-holders.
13 National Union of Conservative and Unionist Associations, *The Selection of Parliamentary Candidates* (London, 1971).
14 See D. E. Butler and D. Kavanagh, *The British General Election of October 1974* (London, 1975).
15 For an account of developments between 1979 and 1981 see D. Kogan and M. Kogan, *The Battle for the Labour Party* (London, 1981). For a more general overview of Labour politics see D. Kavanagh (ed.), *The Politics of the Labour Party* (London, 1982).
16 See R. Punnett, *Front Bench Opposition* (London, 1973).
17 See Max Morris, 'The Other Way That Labour Isn't Working', *The Guardian*, 28 February 1983.

18 D. E. Butler and D. Kavanagh, *The British General Election of 1983* (London, 1985).

19 See Lewis Minkin, *The Labour Party Conference* (London, 1978).

20 The problem is put in historical and comparative perspective by Michael Pinto-Duschinsky, *British Political Finance* (Washington and London, 1981), and V. Bogdanor (ed.), *Parties and Democracy in Britain and America* (New York, 1984).

21 *Report of the Committee of Inquiry on Financial Aid to Political Parties* (Houghton) (Cmnd 6601, 1976).

22 See D. E. Butler and D. Stokes, *Political Change in Britain* (2nd ed., London, 1974).

23 *Labour Party Annual Conference Report, 1977.*

24 D. E. Butler and D. Kavanagh, *The British General Election of 1983,* (London, 1985), pp. 276–7.

25 Pinto-Duschinsky, op. cit., p. 280.

26 *The Guardian*, 4 October 1983.

27 *Report of the National Executive Committee of the Labour Party 1982–3.*

28 'The Alliance Parties after the General Election', *Politics Today*, 7 October 1983.

29 HC Deb. 22 November 1983, cols 181–3.

30 *Government Reply to the First Report from the Home Affairs Committee*, Session 1982–3 (HC 32–1); *Representation of the People Acts* (Cmnd 9140, 1983).

Chapter 9

1 The basic literature on pressure groups is vast; but especially helpful is S. E. Finer, *Anonymous Empire: A Study of the Lobby in Britain* (London, 1966). Also B. Frost (ed.), *The Tactics of Pressure* (London, 1975); R. Kimber and J. J. Richardson, *Pressure Groups in Britain* (London, 1974). A short but helpful recent study is G. Alderman, *Pressure Groups and Government in Great Britain* (London, 1984). A more theoretical perspective can be found in M. Olson, *The Logic of Collective Action* (Cambridge, Mass., 1965).

2 See D. Marsh's introduction to *Pressure Politics: Interest Groups in Modern Britain* (London, 1983), p. 4, quoting *The Guardian Directory of Pressure Groups* (London, Wilton House, 1976), p. 21.

3 On the Howard League see M. Ryan, 'The Acceptable Pressure Group: Inequality in the Penal Lobby, a Case Study', in Marsh (ed.), op. cit.

4 The term ideological is used in Marsh (ed.), op. cit. For another discussion of terminology see Kimber and Richardson, op. cit., pp. 1–19.

5 The example of the conflict over the control of the water supply is used frequently in J. J. Richardson and A. G. Jordan, *Governing Under Pressure: The Policy Process in a Post-parliamentary Democracy* (Oxford, 1979); on the role of local authority associations see K. Isaac-Henry, 'Local Authority Associations', *Public Administration* 62 (1984). Also K. Isaac-Henry, 'The English Local Authority Associations', in G. W. Jones (ed.), *New Approaches to Central-Local Relations* (Farnborough, 1981).

6 On farmers see P. Self and H. Storing, 'The Farmers and the State', in Kimber and Richardson, op. cit. A more radical perspective can be found in R. Body, *Farming in the Clouds* (London, 1984), where *inter alia* it is suggested that the close relationship between the NFU and the MAFF extends to the chemical industry.

7 For a discussion that focuses specifically on policy making, see Richardson and Jordan, op. cit.

8 The phrase 'gold-plated six' is taken from Anthony Sampson, *The New Anatomy of Britain* (London, 1983), p. 64.

9 On the Heath government see M. Holmes, *Political Pressure and Economic Policy* (London, 1982). More theoretical approaches are to be found in T. Smith, *The Politics of the Corporate Economy* (Oxford, 1976) and R. Harrison, *Pluralism and Corporatism: The Political Evolution of Modern Democracies* (London, 1980).

10 CBI *Annual Report*, 1983.

11 On the role of the BMA see P. Jones, 'The B.M.A.: Public Good or Private Interest?', in Marsh (ed.), op. cit. A longer account can be found in H. H. Eckstein, *Pressure Group Politics: The Case of the B.M.A.* (London, 1960).

12 The notion of 'corporatist bias' is taken from K. Middlemas, *Politics in Industrial Society* (London, 1979).

13 This point is made in Richardson and Jordan, op. cit.

14 On capital punishment see J. B. Christoph, 'Capital Punishment and British Politics: The Role of Pressure Groups', in Kimber and Richardson, op. cit., pp. 143–9.

15 On CND see R. Taylor and C. Pritchard, *Politics of Protest: The British Nuclear Disarmament Movement 1958–65 Twenty Years On* (Oxford, 1980); also the essay by Paul Byrne and Joni Lovenduski in H. Drucker, P. Dunleavy, A. Gamble and G. Peele (eds), *Developments in British Politics* (revised ed., Basingstoke, 1984) pp. 222–37.

16 On Labour policy see D. E. Butler and D. Kavanagh, *The British General Election of 1983* (Basingstoke, 1984).

17 On the role of Child Poverty Action Group see F. Field, *Poverty and Politics* (London, 1982).

18 PROP and RAP are discussed in Ryan, loc. cit.

19 A useful introduction to American pressure groups is R. Scott and R. Hrebenar, *Interest Groups in American Politics* (Englewood Cliffs, 1982).

20 K. Newton, *Second City Politics* (Oxford, 1976).

21 On pressure groups active in relation to British entry into the EEC, see R. Lieber, *British Politics and European Unity* (Berkeley, 1970). The point about agricultural interests and the MAFF becoming even closer since 1973 is made in Richardson and Jordan, op. cit. See also G. K. Wilson, *Special Interests and Policy Making* (London, 1977).

22 On this see J. Bruce-Gardyne, *Mrs Thatcher's First Administration: The Prophets Confounded* (London, 1984), especially ch. 4.

23 See W. Grant and D. Marsh, *The C.B.I.* (London, 1977), especially ch. 2.

24 On this see Middlemas, op. cit.

25 *Report of the Committee of Inquiry on Industrial Democracy* (Bullock) (Cmnd 6706, 1977).

26 For general background see Hugh Stephenson, *Mrs Thatcher's First Year* (London, 1980); P. Riddell, *The Thatcher Government* (London, 1983), and J. Bruce-Gardyne, op. cit.

27 This point is made forcefully by D. Marsh and G. Locksley, 'Capital: the Negative Face of Power', in Marsh (ed.), op. cit., pp. 21–52.

28 R. Jowell and C. Airey, *British Social Attitudes: The 1984 Report* (Aldershot, 1984), p. 57.

29 Ibid.

30 For a general assessment of the unions see Robert Taylor, *The Fifth Estate: British Unions in the 1970's* (London, 1978).

31 R. Undy, V. Ellis, W. E. J. McCarthy and A. M. Halmos, *Change in Trade Unions: the Development of U.K. Unions Since the 1960's* (London, 1981).

32 TUC, *Annual Statistical Report*, 1983.

33 Ibid.

34 C. Crouch, 'The Peculiar Relationship: the Party and the Unions', in D. Kavanagh (ed.), *The Politics of the Labour Party* (London, 1982).

35 See the discussion in Alderman, op. cit.

36 P. Stanworth and A. Gittens, *Elites in British Society* (Cambridge, 1974).

37 F. Chapple, *The Sparks Fly* (London, 1984).

38 On the use of the ballot in trade union affairs, see R. Martin and R. Undy, *Ballots and Trade Union Democracy* (Oxford, 1984).

39 P. Lowe and J. Goyder, *Environmental Groups in Politics* (London, 1983).

40 For a discussion of planning procedures and participation see C. Harlow and R. Rawlings, *Law and Administration* (London, 1984), especially Chs. 14 and 15.

41 For a recent discussion see G. Almond and S. Verba, *The Civic Culture Revisited* (Boston, 1980).

42 For a discussion of Jewish groups see G. A. Alderman, *The Jewish Community in British Politics* (Oxford, 1983).

43 Z. Layton Henry, *The Politics of Race* (London, 1984).

44 For a discussion see S. Beer, *Britain Against Itself: The Political Contradictions of Collectivism* (London, 1982).

Chapter 10

1 There is an important school of thought which would argue that central government should have no interest in what local government spends unless it is itself providing the money through central grants. This position – which rejects the significance attached to public expenditure as a whole by the Thatcher administrations – is frequently combined with support for a high degree of local autonomy in other aspects of central-local relationships. For an important statement of some of these views see G. W. Jones and J. Stewart, *The Case for Local Government* (London, 1983).

2 The reform was achieved by the London Government Act 1963.

3 *Streamlining the Cities: Government Proposals for Reorganizing Local Government in Greater London and the Metropolitan Counties* (Cmnd 9063, 1983).

4 See J. Garner, 'The Ultra Vires Rule', *Local Government Studies* vol. I no. 2 (1973).

5 See L. J. Sharpe, 'Theories and Values of Local Government', *Political Studies* XVIII, no. 2, 1970; A. Alexander, *Local Government in Britain Since Reorganization* (London, 1982).There are however some who would emphasize the extent to which the activity of pressure groups at the local level constitutes something of a reversal of the trend towards centralism in Britain. This theme is further explored in Jones and Stevens, op. cit.

6 See J. G. Griffith, *Central Departments and Local Authorities* (London, 1966).

7 *Report of the Committee of Enquiry into Local Government Finance* (Cmnd 6543, 1966).

8 See G. W. Jones, 'Central-Local Relations', in D. E. Butler and A. H. Halsey (eds), *Policy and Politics* (London, 1978).

9 See B. Keith-Lucas and P. Richards, *A History of Local Government in the Twentieth Century* (London, 1977).

10 On this see Ken Young, *Local Politics and the Rise of Party: The London Municipal Society and Conservative Intervention in Local Elections 1894–1963* (Leicester, 1975).

11 S. E. Finer, *Edwin Chadwick* (London, 1954), p. 17.

12 W. A. Robson, *The Development of Local Government* (London, 1931).

13 On local government in London see G. Rhodes and S. K. Ruck, *The Government of Greater London* (London, 1970).

14 See R. H. S. Crossman, *The Diaries of a Cabinet Minister*, vol. I, *1964–66* (London, 1975).

15 *Report of the Royal Commission on Local Government in England* (Redcliffe-Maud) (Cmnd 4040, 1969), *Report of the Royal Commission on Local Government in Scotland* (Wheatley) (Cmnd 4150, 1969). For Scotland since reorganization see Alexander, op. cit., ch. 6.

16 See C. Jones, *Immigration and Social Policy in Britain* (London, 1977).

17 See *Report of the Committee on Local Authority and Allied Social Services* (Cmnd 3703, 1968).

18 *Local Government Boundary Commission for England: Reports Nos 3, 5 & 6* deal with the question of successor parish status.

19 *Local Government Boundary Commission for England: Report No. 6* covers the Commission's review programme up to 1978; the intended programme up to 1983 was set out in Department of the Environment circulars 121/77 and 33/78.

20 *Report of the Committee on the Management of Local Government* (Maud) (1967); *Report of the Committee on Staffing in Local Government* (Mallaby) (1967); Department of the Environment, *New Local Authorities: Management and Structure* (Bains) (1972).

21 See J. Gyford and M. James, *National Parties and Local Politics* (London, 1983).

22 See Wyn Grant, *Independent Local Politics in England and Wales* (London, 1977).

23 See C. Mellors, *The British M.P.* (London, 1978).

24 Department of the Environment, *Report of the Committee of Enquiry into the*

System of Remuneration of Members of Local Authorities (Robinson) (Cmnd 7010, 1977). For a discussion of the characteristics of local councillors see especially vol. II, *Survey of Councillors and Local Authorities*.

25 *Report of the Committee on Local Government Rules of Conduct* (Redcliffe-Maud) (Cmnd 5636, 1974); *Report of the Royal Commission on Standards of Conduct in Public Life* (Salmon) (Cmnd 6525, 1976).

26 See N. Lewis and B. Gateshill, *The Commission for Local Administration: A Preliminary Appraisal* (London, 1978). The role of the Commission is further discussed in chapter 13.

27 Local Government Act 1978.

28 On the general question of central-local relationships see Central Policy Review Staff, *Relations between Central and Local Authorities* (London, 1977).

29 It could however be argued that the form which Acts of Parliament use to grant powers to local authorities underlines the extent to which local government is intended to be autonomous.

30 See *Secretary of State for Education and Science* v. *Tameside Metropolitan Borough Council* (1976), 3 AER 665.

31 See *Attorney General* v. *Fulham Corporation* (1921), 1 Ch. 440.

32 See *Roberts* v. *Hopwood* (1925), AC 578.

33 See *Asher* v. *Lacey* (1973), 1 WLR 1412.

34 The legislation did not remove the disqualification to serve as councillors imposed by the court.

35 See M. Kogan, *The Politics of Educational Change* (London, 1978).

36 For an introduction to local government finance see N. Hepworth, *The Finance of Local Government* (4th ed., London, 1978).

37 See W. B. Taylor, 'Borrowing by Local Authorities in the United Kingdom', *National Westminster Bank Quarterly Review*, August 1983.

38 See *Local Government Finance* (Cmnd 6813, 1977).

39 See for example G. W. Jones's comments in D. E. Butler and A. H. Halsey (eds), *Politics and Policy* (London, 1978).

40 See the green paper *Alternatives to Domestic Rates* (Cmnd 8449, 1981); House of Commons Environment Committee Session 1981–82. Second report: *Enquiry into methods of financing local government in the context of the Government's green paper* (Cmnd 8449) (HC 217–I–III).

41 For a summary of the arguments for privatizing local government services see M. B. Forsyth, *Down with the Rates* (London, 1983).

42 See David N. King *et al.*, *Town Hall Power or Whitehall Pawn* (London, 1980).

43 *Rates: Proposals for Rate Limitation and Reform of the Rating System* (Cmnd 9008, 1983).

44 David Walker, *Municipal Empire* (London, 1983); M. Forsyth, *Politics on the Rates* (London, 1984).

45 See J. W. Marsh, 'The Value of the Constituency Member of Parliament', *Hull Papers in Politics* No. 30 (1983). But for a contrasting perspective on local politics see G. W. Jones and J. Stewart, *The Case for Local Government* (London, 1983).

Chapter 11

1 For a recent discussion of the role of the Ulster issue in the politics of the Irish Republic see John Bowman, *De Valera and the Ulster Question* (Oxford, 1982).

2 For a recent general study of Ireland's several divisions see Padraig O'Malley, *The Uncivil Wars* (Belfast, 1983); on the diversity of voting behaviour within the United Kingdom see R. Rose and I. McAllister, *The Nationwide Competition for Votes: The 1983 Election* (London, 1984).

3 For an account of the development of violence see P. Arthur, 'Northern Ireland', in H. Drucker, P. Dunleavy, A. Gamble and G. Peele, *Developments in British Politics* (revised ed., Basingstoke, 1984); also P. Arthur, *The Government and Politics of Northern Ireland* (2nd ed., Harlow, 1984).

4 See for example R. Clutterbuck, *Britain in Agony: The Growth of Political Violence* (London, 1978).

5 The general history of Ireland can be traced in F. S. L. Lyons' magisterial book, *Ireland Since the Famine* (London, 1971). For a shorter history see David Harkness, *Northern Ireland Since 1920* (Dublin, 1983).

6 On the cultural divisions see the succinct account offered by F. S. L. Lyons, *Culture and Anarchy in Ireland. 1890–1939* (Oxford, 1979).

7 On the attitudes of Ulster Protestants see A. T. Q. Stewart, *The Narrow Ground* (London, 1977). Also S. Nelson, *Ulster's Uncertain Defenders: Loyalists and the Northern Ireland Conflict* (Belfast, 1984). A history of the Ulster Unionist Party is provided in P. Gibbon, *The Origins of Ulster Unionism* (Manchester, 1974).

8 See D. Harkness, *The Restless Dominion* (London, 1972).

9 See O'Malley, op. cit.

10 On this see David Harkness, 'England's Irish Question', in G. Peele and C. Cook (eds), *The Politics of Reappraisal* (Basingstoke, 1975).

11 For a general discussion see P. Compton, 'The Demographic Background' in D. Watt (ed), *The Constitution of Northern Ireland* (London, 1981).

12 David Harkness, *Northern Ireland Since 1920* (Dublin, 1983).

13 O'Malley, op. cit., especially Chs. 3 and 4.

14 Conor Cruise O'Brien, *States of Ireland* (London, 1972).

15 The point is made in O'Malley, op. cit., p. 144. For a general discussion of the role of religion in Ireland see J. Whyte, *Church and State in Modern Ireland 1923–79* (2nd ed., Dublin, 1980).

16 See for example the comments of Conor Cruise O'Brien, op. cit., pp. 143–144; also Arthur, op. cit., p. 92.

17 A chronology of the troubles can be traced in V. Magowan and R. Deutsch, *Chronology of Events in Northern Ireland* (Belfast, 1973–5). Also R. Rose, *Governing Without Consensus* (Basingstoke, 1971).

18 The emergence of the SDLP has been well covered by Ian McAllister, *The Northern Ireland Social and Democratic Labour Party* (Basingstoke, 1977).

19 New Ireland Forum, *The Cost of Violence* (Dublin, 1983).

20 Ibid.

21 Ibid.

22 Bruce Arnold, *What Kind of Country: Modern Irish Politics 1968–83* (London, 1984).

23 On the IRA see J. Bowyer Bell, *The Secret Army: The I.R.A. 1916–1979* (Dublin, 1979).

24 For personal memoirs of this period see T. O'Neill *Autobiography* (London, 1972) and B. Faulkner, *Memoirs of a Statesman* (London, 1978).

25 Christopher Pollitt, *Manipulating the Machine: Changing the Pattern of Ministerial Departments 1960–83* (London, 1984); also HMSO, *Ulster Yearbook*.

26 *The Northern Ireland Constitution* (Cmnd 5675, 1973).

27 *Northern Ireland: A Framework for Devolution* (Cmnd 8541, 1982).

28 *Report of the New Ireland Forum* (Dublin, 1984) and *Report of the Independent Inquiry* (London, 1984).

29 *Report of the New Ireland Forum.*

30 On the security situation see D. Walsh, *The Use and Abuse of Emergency Legislation in Northern Ireland* (Nottingham, 1983).

31 On this see K. Morgan, *Rebirth of a Nation 1880–1980* (Oxford, 1981).

32 *Statistics of Education in Wales* no. 3, quoted in *The Economist* 7 October 1978; the 1984 figure is drawn from the 1981 census and quoted in HMSO, *Handbook to Britain 1984.*

33 See A. Butt Philip, *The Welsh Question* (London, 1975).

34 R. H. S. Crossman, *Diaries of a Cabinet Minister* (London, 1975); also C. Pollitt, op. cit.

35 See Pollitt, op. cit.

36 H. Drucker in *Yearbook of Scottish Government 1983* (Edinburgh, 1983).

37 *Report of the Royal Commission on Local Government in Scotland* (Wheatley) (Cmnd 4150, 1966–9).

38 See *Yearbook of Scottish Government 1983.*

39 Ibid.

40 *Report of the Royal Commission on the Constitution* (Kilbrandon) Cmnd 5460, 1972).

41 *Democracy and Devolution: Proposals for Scotland and Wales* (Cmnd 5732, 1974).

42 *Our Changing Democracy* (Cmnd 6348, 1975).

43 *Devolution to Scotland and Wales: Supplementary Statement* (Cmnd 6585, 1976).

Chapter 12

1 Crime statistics are of course notoriously unreliable and can be interpreted in a number of ways. However a broad picture can be gleaned from *Handbook to Britain 1984*, p. 97. For more detailed information see *Criminal Statistics England and Wales 1983* (Cmnd 9349).

2 For an overview of the phenomenon of terrorism, see Grant Wardlaw, *Terrorism: Theory, Tactics and Counter Measures* (Cambridge, 1982).

3 On the general theme of public accountability, see T. Jefferson and R. Grimshaw, *Controlling the Constable* (London, 1984); on police technology see S. Manwaring White, *The Policing Revolution: Police Technology, Democracy and Liberty in Britain* (Brighton, 1983).

4 On the riots, see *Report of a Committee of Inquiry into the Brixton Disorders 10–12 April 1981* (Scarman) (Cmnd 8427, 1981); on the Report and its impact see J. Benyon (ed.), *Scarman and After: Essays Reflecting on Lord Scarman's Report, the Riots and their Aftermath* (Oxford, 1984).

5 On this see S. Bundred, 'Accountability and the Metropolitan Police', in D. Cowell, T. Jones, and J. Young, *Policing the Riots* (London, 1982).

6 *Report of the Royal Commission on Criminal Procedure* (Phillips) (Cmnd 8092, 1981).

7 *Report of the Monopolies and Mergers Commission 1976*; see also M. Zander, *Cases and Materials on the English Legal System* (4th ed., London, 1984), p. 571.

8 See *Report of the Royal Commission on Legal Services* (Benson) (Cmnd 7468, 1979).

9 See *The Times*, 27 March and 4 May 1984.

10 On this see Zander, op. cit., especially ch. 4.

11 For a short introduction to the system of administrative law in France see L. Neville Brown and J. F. Garner, *French Administrative Law* (3rd ed., London, 1983).

12 More general discussion of the state of administrative law in Britain may be found in chapter 13.

13 Administration of Justice Act 1969.

14 Courts Act 1971.

15 On this general point see Zander, op. cit., ch. 1.

16 For a discussion of Lord Denning's work see his own writings, *The Discipline of Law* (London, 1979); *The Due Process of Law* (London, 1980); and *What's Next in the Law?* (London, 1982). A radical discussion of his approach to the legal function can be found in P. Robson and P. Watchman, *Justice, Lord Denning and the Constitution* (Farnborough, 1981).

17 *O'Connell's Case* (1844), 11 CL & F 155. For a discussion see L. Blom Cooper and G. Drewry, *Final Appeal* (Oxford, 1972).

18 The rule was formalized in *London Tramways* v. *London County Council* (1898), AC 375.

19 See the Practice Statement, 26 July 1966, 1 WLR 1234.

20 See Zander, op. cit., p. 521.

21 Tim Tate, 'Magistrates on Trial', *The Listener*, 15 September 1983.

22 For a brief history of the magistracy see Esther Moir, *The Justice of the Peace* (Harmondsworth, 1969).

23 Tate, loc. cit.

24 T. Skyrne, *The Changing Image of the Magistrate* (2nd ed., London, 1983).

25 Ibid., p. 7.

26 *Report of the Royal Commission on Assizes and Quarter Sessions* (Beeching) (Cmnd 4153, 1969).

27 For the background to this merger see *Report of the Interdepartmental Committee on the Court of Criminal Appeal* (Donovan) (Cmnd 2755, 1965).

28 On references to the European Court see *Bulmer* v. *Bollinger* (1973), 2 CMLR 114 (CA) (1974) Ch. 40 and *McCarthy's Ltd* v. *Smith* (1979), 3 CMLR 44 (CA).

29 For a general overview of the relationship between national and European law see J. Usher, *European Community Law and National Law – the*

Irreversible Transfer? (London, 1981).

30 For a general overview of the impact of the European Convention see R. Beddard, *Human Rights and Europe* (2nd ed., London, 1980).

31 *The Sunday Times Case (Times Newspapers Ltd* v. *U.K.*, 1979), 2 EHRR p. 245.

32 *Young, James and Webster* v. *U.K.* (1981), 4 EHRR p. 38.

33 *Ireland* v. *U.K.* (1978), 2 EHRR p. 25.

34 See *The Times*, 9 July and 23 October 1984.

35 A good starting point for an appreciation of the merits of this approach is J. G. Griffith, *The Politics of the Judiciary* (2nd ed., London, 1981).

36 For a general discussion of legal aid and costs see Zander, op. cit., pp. 419–76.

37 *Report of Royal Commission on Police Powers and Procedure* (Cmnd 3297, 1929).

38 Geoffrey Marshall, *Constitutional Conventions* (Oxford, 1984).

39 *Report of Royal Commission on the Police* (Cmd 1728, 1962).

40 See *Fisher* v. *Oldham Corporation* (1930), 2 KB 364, and the discussion in G. Marshall, *Police and Government* (London, 1965) and G. Marshall, 'Police Accountability Revisited', in D. E. Butler and A. H. Halsey, *Policy and Politics* (Basingstoke, 1978). For a discussion of police accountability in a more general constitutional context see G. Marshall, *Constitutional Conventions* (Oxford, 1984).

41 On the impact of Scarman, see Benyon, op. cit.

42 David Smith *et al.* for the Policy Studies Institute, *Police and People in London* (4 vols, London, 1983).

43 Police Act 1976.

44 Report of the Select Committee on Home Affairs, *Police Complaints Procedures* (HC 98, 1981–2).

45 See for example Peter Wallington (ed.), *Civil Liberties 1984* (London, 1984).

46 *R.* v. *Police Complaints Board ex parte Rhone; R.* v. *Police Complaints Board ex parte Madden* (1983), 2 AER 353; (1983), 1 WLR 447.

47 See Cmnd 9074, 1983.

48 On the politics of the NCCL see Patricia Hewitt, 'The N.C.C.L. Fifty Years On', in Peter Wallington (ed.), *Civil Liberties 1984* (London, 1984).

49 See Lord Scarman, *English Law: The New Dimension* (London, 1974), and Lord Hailsham, *The Dilemma of Democracy* (London, 1978).

50 *Report of the Select Committee on a Bill of Rights* (HL 176, 1978). See also Minutes of Evidence HL Sessions 1976–7 and 1977–8.

51 See for example the points made by J. G. Griffith in 'The Democratic Process' in Wallington (ed.), op. cit.

52 On the general question of enactment see J. Jaconelli, *Enacting a Bill of Rights: The Legal Problems* (Oxford, 1980).

53 For a general discussion see A. Lester, 'Fundamental Rights: The United Kingdom Isolated', in *Public Law* (Spring 1984), pp. 46–72.

54 *R.* v. *Chief Immigration Officer ex parte Salamat Bibi* (1976), 3 AER 843. Two earlier cases had seen Lord Scarman and Lord Denning attempting to construe immigration cases more liberally to meet the standards of the

Convention: *R.* v. *Secretary of State for the Home Department ex parte Bhajan Singh* (1976), 2 QB; *R.* v. *Secretary of State for the Home Department ex parte Phansopkar* (1976), 2 QB. For a more recent case which asserted that the home secretary need take no account of the European Convention when framing immigration rules see *Fernandes* v. *Secretary of State for Home Department* (1981), Immigration ARI (CA).

55 On this see K. Boyle, T. Hadden and P. Hillyard, *Ten Years on in Northern Ireland: The Legal Control of Political Violence* (Nottingham, 1980).

56 See *Ireland* v. *United Kingdom* (judgement delivered 18 January 1978).

57 *Tyrer* v. *U.K.* (1978), 2 EHRR p. 1.

58 See *X* v. *UK.* Series A. No. 46. 4 ECHR (1981).

59 On this see A. C. Evans, 'United Kingdom Immigration Policy and the European Convention on Human Rights', *Public Law* (Spring 1983), pp. 91–107.

60 *Raymond* v. *Honey* HL (1983), 1 AC 1.

61 *Knechtl and Golder* v. *U.K.* (1975), 1 HRR.

62 *Secretary of State for the Home Department ex parte Anderson* (1984), 1 AER.

63 The Confait case was the subject of a special inquiry by Sir Henry Fisher (HCP 90 1977–78). See also *Modern Law Review* (1978), 455.

64 *R.* v. *Nottingham Justices ex parte Davies* (1980), 3 WLR p. 15.

65 *Police and Criminal Evidence Act* (1984).

66 For a general discussion see Boyle, Hadden and Hillyard, op. cit.; also D. Walsh, 'Civil Liberties in Northern Ireland', in Wallington (ed.), op. cit.

67 *Review of the Prevention of Terrorism Act 1976* (Jellicoe) (Cmnd 8803, 1983); *Review of the Operation of the Northern Ireland (Emergency Provisions) Act 1978* (Baker) (Cmnd 9222, 1984).

68 On the general question of access to the law see Walter Merricks, 'Access to the Law', in Wallington (ed.), op. cit.

69 On the Southall incident see the two NCCL publications, *Southall 23 April 1979* and *The Death of Blair Peach* (London, 1980).

70 Lord Scarman's Frank Newsom Memorial Lecture, delivered at the Police College, Bramshill, July 1978.

71 Ibid.

72 Ibid.

73 See Law Commission, *Report No 123: Offences Relating to Public Order* (October 1983). Also Law Commission, *Working Paper No. 82.*

74 For a general discussion of the law of public order, see M. Supperstone (ed.), *Brownlie's Law Relating to Public Order and Security* (2nd ed., London, 1981).

75 For the general position see Gatley, *On Libel and Slander* (8th ed., London, 1981).

76 The Thorpe affair is covered in B. Penrose and R. Courtiour, *The Pencourt File* (London, 1978).

77 On the *Oz* trial see T. Palmer, *The Trials of Oz* (London, 1971). For a general survey of the law in this area see G. Robertson, *Obscenity* (London, 1979).

78 *Shaw* v. *D.P.P.* (1961), AC 220 and *Knuller* v. *D.P.P.* (1973), AC 435.

79 *R.* v. *Lemon* (1979), AC 617.

80 On the development of the offence of incitement to stir up racial hatred see P. Leopold, 'Incitement to Hatred – the History of a Controversial Criminal Offence', *Public Law* (Winter 1977).

81 See *New Society, Guide to the Race Act* (London, 1976).

82 See for example the discussion document published by the Commission for Racial Equality, *Time For a Change* (July 1983). See also L. Lustgarten, 'The Commission for Racial Equality Under Attack', *Public Law* (Spring 1982).

83 On the role of open government and the campaign for freedom of information see Des Wilson, *The Secrets File: The Case for Freedom of Information in Britain Today* (Guildford, 1984). For a more neutral approach see R. Wraith, *Open Government* (London, 1977).

84 See *Secretary of State for Defence* v. *Guardian Newspapers Ltd* (1984), 2 WLR 268 CA.

85 On this incident see J. Aitken, *Officially Secret* (London, 1971).

86 *Reform of the Official Secrets Act* (Cmnd 7285, 1978).

87 See Hugo Young, *The Crossman Affair* (London, 1976).

88 *Attorney General* v. *Times Newspapers Ltd* (1975), 1 AER.

89 Barbara Castle, *The Castle Diaries 1964–70* (London, 1984) and *The Castle Diaries 1974–76* (London, 1980).

90 Peter Hennessy, M. Cockerell and D. Walker, *Sources Close to the Prime Minister* (Basingstoke, 1984).

91 Contempt of Court Act 1981.

92 The charge was eventually dropped.

93 The bill was introduced by Graham Page and became the Video Recordings Act 1984.

Chapter 13

1 For a stimulating overview of the general relationship between law and administration see Carol Harlow and Richard Rawlings, *Law and Administration* (London, 1984).

2 Under the Tribunals Act of 1921 a tribunal of inquiry can be established to inquire into any allegation of misconduct by officials. Public condemnation of civil servants may also occur when there has been a ministerial resignation, as it did in the aftermath of Crichel Down.

3 For a general discussion see K. C. Wheare, 'Crichel Down Revisited', *Political Studies* XXXIII nos 2 & 3 (1975).

4 See J. Lynn and A. Jay, *Yes Minister: The Diaries of a Cabinet Minister by the Right Honourable James Hacker M.P.* (2 vols, London, 1981).

5 K. C. Wheare, loc. cit., has a succinct statement of the facts of Crichel Down. See also R. Douglas Brown, *The Battle of Crichel Down* (London, 1955).

6 See *Falkland Islands Review* (Franks) (Cmnd 8787, 1983); also Lord Hunt, 'Access to Previous Governments' Papers', *Public Law* (1982) 514–18.

7 G. Marshall, *Constitutional Conventions: The Rules and Forms of Political Accountability* (Oxford University Press, 1984), pp. 54–77.

8 See *The Times*, 13 January and 2 February 1984.

9 *Report of the Franks Committee on Administrative Tribunals and Inquiries* (Cmnd 218, 1957).

10 See Wheare, loc. cit.

11 See *Annual Report of the Council on Tribunals 1979–80*, paras 3.21–3.23. (The Social Security Act of 1980 restricted the right of appeal on fact and on law to the National Insurance Commissioners – renamed Social Security Commissioners – so that where the initial decision is unanimous leave to appeal must be granted by either the Social Security Appeal Tribunal or the Commissioners.)

12 On this see Anthony Lester, 'Fundamental Rights: The United Kingdom Isolated', *Public Law* (Spring 1984), pp. 46–72.

13 For a general survey of the range of tribunals in Britain see R. E. Wraith and P. G. Hutchesson, *Administrative Tribunals* (London, 1973), and J. A. Farmer, *Tribunals and Government* (London, 1974); also the discussion in Harlow and Rawlings, op. cit., especially ch. 6.

14 *Annual Report of the Council on Tribunals 1981–2*; also *Annual Report of the Council on Tribunals 1982–3*, para. 2.6.

15 See *The Functions of the Council on Tribunals* (Cmnd 7805, 1980).

16 Ibid., para. 9.5.

17 Ibid., para. 9.9.

18 Ibid., ch. 10.

19 *Annual Report of the Council on Tribunals 1981–2*, para. 2.1.

20 See the special report *The Function of the Council on Tribunals* (Cmnd 7805, 1980), paras 6.8, 6.10, and 6.13; also *Annual Report of the Council on Tribunals 1981–2*, para 3.54; *1982–3*, paras 3.32–3.38.

21 See especially the *Annual Report of the Council on Tribunals 1978–9*, paras 2.12–2.13, 2.15 & 2.16. The Council felt that it was especially important to give priority in this respect to industrial tribunals, mental health review tribunals, medical appeal tribunals, the Immigration Appeal Tribunal and the National Insurance Commissioners.

22 On the topic of inquiries see R. E. Wraith and G. B. Lamb, *Public Inquiries as Instruments of Government* (London, 1971).

23 *Second Report of the Council on Tribunals* (1961).

24 Ibid.

25 On this see *Buxton* v. *Minister of Housing and Local Government* (1961), 1 QB 278, and the white paper on inquiries (Cmnd 3333, 1967).

26 See for example the discussion in Harlow and Rawlings, op. cit., chs 14 & 15, and the discussion in P. Lowe and J. Goyder, *Environmental Groups in British Politics* (London, 1983).

27 On this see *Annual Report of the Council on Tribunals 1981–2*, para. 4.10.

28 *Report of the Committee on Participation and Planning* (Skeffington) (1969). See also the Benson Report (Cmnd 7468, 1979).

29 On the Windscale issue see I. Breach, *Windscale Fallout* (London, 1978).

30 Town and Country Planning Act 1971.

31 Public Inquiries (Attendance of Public) Act 1982.

32 See for example the comments of Harlow and Rawlings, op. cit.

33 The history of the parliamentary commissioner for administration can be found in F. Stacey, *The British Ombudsman* (Oxford, 1971), and in R. Gregory and P. Hutchesson, *The Parliamentary Ombudsman: A Study in the Control of Administrative Action* (London, 1975). An excellent comparative perspective is provided in F. Stacey, *Ombudsmen Compared* (Oxford, 1978).

34 On this point see Stacey, op. cit.

35 For the role of the Select Committee on the Parliamentary Commissioner for Administration see R. Gregory, 'The Select Committee on the Parliamentary Commissioner for Administration 1967–80', *Public Law* (Spring 1982), pp. 49–88.

36 *Annual Report of the Parliamentary Commissioner for Administration 1981–2* (HC 258).

37 Parliamentary Commissioner Act 1967. The French *médiateur* is of course in a slightly different position because of the highly developed French system of administrative law.

38 These figures are taken from Justice, *Our Fettered Ombudsman* (London, 1977).

39 See especially the article by Carol Harlow, 'Ombudsmen in Search of A Role', *Modern Law Review* 41 (1978), 446.

40 See for example F. F. Ridley, 'The Citizen Against Authority: British Approaches to the Redress of Grievances', *Parliamentary Affairs* vol. 37 no. 1 (Winter 1984).

41 *Annual Report of the Parliamentary Commissioner for Administration 1984.*

42 An excellent discussion of the difficulties associated with the concept of maladministration is to be found in G. Marshall, 'Maladministration', *Public Law* (Spring 1973) and 'Parliament and the Redress of Grievances' in S. Walkland and M. Ryle, *The Commons in the 1970s* (London, 1977).

43 Parliamentary Commissioner (Northern Ireland) Act 1969; Commissioner for Complaints (Northern Ireland) Act 1969.

44 See *Fourth Report from the Select Committee on the Parliamentary Commissioner for Administration*, 1979–80 (HC 593).

45 See *Observations by the Government* (Cmnd 8274, 1981).

46 See National Health Service Act 1969; also Local Government Act 1974; the Police Act 1976; and the Police and Criminal Evidence Act 1984.

47 See *Report of the Select Committee on the Parliamentary Commissioner for Administration*, 1980–81 (HC 650).

48 See *Annual Report of the National Health Service Commissioner 1983–4* (HC 537), para. 14.

49 See for example the comments by Harlow and Rawlings, op. cit.

50 For a critical appraisal see the review by Justice, *The Local Ombudsman: A Review of the First Five Years* (London, 1980). Also N. Lewis and B. Gateshill, *The Commission for Local Administration: A Preliminary Appraisal* (London, 1978).

51 For a comparative perspective see Stacey, *Ombudsmen Compared.*

52 See the comments by Geoffrey Marshall, 'Parliament and the Redress of Grievances', in S. Walkland and M. Ryle (eds), *The Commons in the 70's* (London, 1977).

53 There are no statutory provisions governing *ex gratia* payments, although inevitably the departments will be mindful of Treasury policy. See Harlow and Rawlings, op. cit., p. 386. A fuller discussion is to be found in C. Harlow, *Compensation and Government Torts* (London, 1982).

54 Hutchesson, op. cit.

55 *Annual Report of the Parliamentary Commissioner for Administration 1976–77.*

56 Ibid.

57 For a discussion see R. Gregory, 'Court Line, Mr. Benn and the Ombudsman', *Parliamentary Affairs* XXX (1977), p. 269.

58 A good account of Sachsenhausen is given in Gregory and Hutchesson, op. cit.

59 The whole question of access to cabinet papers is reviewed in Lord Hunt, loc. cit.

60 For a stimulating general discussion of the conception of the state in different countries see K. Dyson, *The State Tradition in Western Europe* (Oxford, 1980).

61 On the general topic of judicial scrutiny of the administration see the classic work by S. A. de Smith, *Judicial Review of Administrative Action* (London, 1973); also H. Street and R. Brazier (eds), *De Smith's Constitutional and Administrative Law* (4th ed., Harmondsworth, 1981).

62 This point is made in Harlow and Rawlings, op. cit.

63 *Report of the Committee on Ministers' Powers* (Donoughmore) (Cmd 4060, 1932).

64 *Ridge* v. *Baldwin* (1964), AC 40.

65 See Michael Beloff, 'The Silkin Squeeze', *New Society*, 10 February 1977, for a crisp summary of developments up to that date.

66 See *Duncan* v. *Cammell Laird* (1942), AC 624.

67 *Conway* v. *Rimmer* (1968), AC 910.

68 See Street and Brazier (eds), op. cit., p. 620.

69 *Padfield* v. *The Minister of Agriculture Fisheries and Food* (1968), AC 997.

70 *The Secretary of State for Education and Science* v. *The Tameside Metropolitan Borough Council* (1976), 3 WLR.

71 *Congreve* v. *The Home Office* (1976), QB 629. See also *Special Report of the Parliamentary Commissioner for Administration* (1975), HC 680.

72 *Gouriet* v. *Union of Post Office Workers* (1977), 2 WLR. See also 3 WLR 300. For Lord Denning's view see his book, *The Discipline of Law* (London, 1979).

73 *Bromley L.B.C.* v. *Greater London Council* (1982), 2 WLR 62.

74 See also 'The G.L.C. Fares Case', *Law Quarterly Review* 99 (1983), 605, and 'Taking a Rise Out of the G.L.C.', *Public Law* (Spring 1982), pp. 171–8.

75 See Rules of the Supreme Court Amendment No. 53 Order 1977. The Order was reenacted in statutory form in the Supreme Court Act 1981, s. 31. For comment see editorial in *Public Law* (Spring 1978) and L. Blom-Cooper, 'The New Face of Judicial Review: Administrative Changes in Order 53', *Public Law* (Summer 1982), pp. 250–61.

76 *O'Reilly* v. *Mackman* (1982), 3 AER 1124.

Chapter 14

1 On the 1976 crisis and its sequel see Samuel Brittan, *The Economic Consequences of Democracy* (London, 1977), ch. 12.

2 On the earlier phases in this process see M. Beloff, *New Dimensions in Foreign Policy: A Study of the British Administrative Experience* (London, 1961). See also *Report of the Committee on Representational Services Overseas* (Plowden) (Cmnd 2276, 1964); *Report of the Review Committee on Overseas Representation* (Dunlop) (Cmnd 4107, 1969); R. Boardman and A. J. Groom, *The Management of Britain's External Relations* (London, 1973); and W. Wallace, *The Foreign Policy Process in Britain* (London, 1975).

3 Central Policy Review Staff, *Review of Overseas Representation* (1977).

4 See J. Mackintosh, 'The Think-Tank should have remembered what foreign policy is for', *The Times*, 22 August 1977; M. Beloff, 'The Think-Tank and Foreign Affairs', *Public Administration* 55 (1977); and *Fourth Report from the Expenditure Committee*, 1977–78 (HC 286. 1978).

5 See *The United Kingdom's Overseas Representation* (Cmnd 7308, 1978), and *Interchange Between the Home Civil Service and the Diplomatic Service: Report of a Working Group* (London, 1978).

6 Sir Con O'Neill, *Our European Future* (London, 1972).

7 *Twenty-Second Report from the Select Committee on the European Communities*, 1977–8 (HL 131, 1978).

8 See Marcel Berlins, 'Britain in Europe: Impact of Community Law', *The Times*, 2 February 1977. On the European impact on one branch of British law see A. I. Ogus and E. M. Barendt, *The Law of Social Security* (London, 1978), pp. 663–5, and 668–83.

9 *Twenty-second Report from the House of Commons Select Committee on European Legislation*, Session 1983–1984 (HC 78–xxii).

10 *First Report from the Select Committee on Procedure*, Session 1977–1978 (HC 588 I–IV, ch. 4).

11 For a useful general survey of Britain and the Communities for the period 1979–84, see Conservative Research Department and European Group Secretariat, *Handbook for Europe 1984* (London, 1984).

12 See Robert Jackson, *From Boom to Bust: British Farming and C.A.P. Reform* (London, 1983).

13 D. E. Butler and Uwe Kitzinger, *The 1975 Referendum* (London, 1975), p. 172.

14 House of Lords Select Committee on the European Communities, *Relations Between the United Kingdom Parliament and the European Parliament After Direct Elections* (HL 256–I, 1978).

15 For an early expression of this point of view see M. Beloff, 'The Frontiers of Political Analysis', *The Cambridge Journal* IV (1951), reprinted in M. Beloff, *The Great Powers* (London, 1959).

Further Reading

The literature on British government is vast, and what follows is a select bibliography of some of the most important works of recent years together with a few classic treatments of British government where they may still be relevant. Government papers are referred to in the chapter notes but not listed here. For basic statistics reference should be made to the current editions of *Britain: An Official Handbook* (London, HMSO) and the *Ulster Yearbook* (Belfast, HMSO).

R. Jowell and C. Airey, *British Social Attitudes: the 1984 Report* (Aldershot, 1984), provides a useful snapshot of British opinion on a variety of political and social themes.

General

Walter Bagehot's *The English Constitution* gives useful insight into the operation of British government on the eve of the Second Reform Act of 1867. It could be compared with J. S. Mill's *Representative Government* (1861). Bagehot's work inspired R. H. S. Crossman to develop the thesis of prime-ministerial government in his introduction to the Fontana edition of *The English Constitution* (London, 1963); the whole debate is summarized with a judicious commentary by Norman St John Stevas in the *Collected Works of Walter Bagehot*, vol. V (London, *The Economist*, 1974).

The classic doctrines of the rule of law and parliamentary sovereignty are to be found in A. V. Dicey, *An Introduction to the Law of the Constitution* (10th ed., London, Macmillan, 1959).

For some different perspectives on the constitution and British government as they appeared to writers in the 1950s see Harold Laski, *Reflections on the Constitution* (Manchester University Press, 1951), and L. S. Amery, *Thoughts on the Constitution* (London, OUP, 1953). Herbert Morrison's *Government and Parliament* (3rd ed., London, OUP, 1964) is still of use; and the works of Sir Ivor Jennings contain a standard treatment of several major themes in British politics, as well as some interesting criticisms of other writers. Of particular interest are his *Cabinet Government* (3rd ed., Cambridge University Press, 1969), and *Parliament* (Cambridge University Press, 1957). The three-volume work *Party Politics* (Cambridge University Press, 1960–2) is useful as a guide to thinking in the 1950s about the role of parties in the British system. *The Law and the Constitution* offers a succinct essay on the British constitution which diverges from Dicey's theory.

A number of stimulating interpretations of British politics have appeared since the 1960s. One, by an American author, is S. H. Beer, *Modern British Politics* (London, Faber, 1965; revised ed. 1982), but this should now be supplemented with the same author's *Britain Against Itself: The Contradictions of Collectivism* (London, 1982). More recently reference should be made to Douglas Ashford, *Policy and Politics in Britain: The Limits of Consensus* (Oxford, Basil Blackwell, 1981).

Recent Periodicals and Collections

Parliamentary Affairs, Public Law and *Public Administration* are the most useful periodicals for following British constitutional and political developments; a certain amount of relevant material is also to be found in *Political Studies, Political Quarterly* and the *British Journal of Electoral Studies*. The *British Journal of Political Science* is a useful guide to debates within the discipline.

Newspaper sources provide additional contemporary information and reference should be made to *The Economist* and *New Society*. K. Macdonald's *Essex Reference Index* (London, Macmillan, 1975) is an invaluable guide to articles in the political science and sociological literature up to that date.

Recent collections of essays are a useful corrective to the standard treatments of British government. H. Drucker, P. Dunleavy, A. Gamble and G. Peele, *Developments in British Politics* (Basingstoke, Macmillan, 1983), aims to provide at frequent intervals articles covering the major topics in British politics. Also of relevance are the essays contained in *The Political Sociology Yearbook*.

The Constitution

The best theoretical introduction to the issues and problems of the British constitution is Geoffrey Marshall's *Constitutional Theory* (Oxford, The Clarendon Press, 1971), which contains helpful American and Commonwealth comparisons. It should be read together with the same author's *Constitutional Conventions* (Oxford: The Clarendon Press, 1984), which is a succinct and scholarly examination of the forms of accountability in Britain.

Nevil Johnson's *In Search of the Constitution* (Oxford, Pergamon, 1977) is a stimulating personal critique of British government. The best legal survey from the point of view of non-lawyers is H. Street and R. Brazier, *De Smith's Constitutional and Administrative Law* (4th ed., Harmondsworth, The Penguin Press, 1981). Also of use is Wade and Phillips *Constitutional and Administrative Law* (9th ed., London, 1977) and O. Hood Phillips and P. Jackson, *Constitutional and Administrative Law* (London, Sweet & Maxwell, 1978). Philip Norton, *The Constitution in Flux* (Oxford, Martin Robertson, 1982), is a useful summary of constitutional developments.

The Functions of Government in the British Welfare State

The intellectual development of the British state has been traced in W. H. Greenleaf's magisterial *The British Political Tradition* (2 vols, London, Methuen, 1983). Useful historical introductions are also to be found in B. B. Gilbert, *British Social Policy 1914–1939* (London, Batsford, 1970), and D. Fraser, *The Evolution of the British Welfare State* (London, Macmillan, 1963). T. Marshall, *Social Policy* (4th ed., London, Hutchinson, 1975), provides a useful historical review. Richard Titmuss's work provides an interesting perspective on the goals of the welfare state. *Essays on the Welfare State* (3rd ed., London, Allen and Unwin, 1976), *Commitment to Welfare* (2nd ed., London, Allen and Unwin, 1976) and *Social Policy* (London, Allen and Unwin, 1974) are all worth reading.

P. Dunleavy, *The Politics of Mass Housing* (Oxford University Press, 1982), is important not merely as a study with policy relevance but because of the implications for voting patterns.

Catherine Jones, *Immigration and Social Policy in Britain* (London, Tavistock Publications, 1977), is an excellent introduction to the impact which immigrants have had on the social services and the deficiencies which have been revealed in the structure of social administration.

On planning see A. H. Hanson (ed.), *Planning and the Politicians* (London, 1969), and J. Hayward and M. Watson (eds), *Planning, Politics and Public Policy* (Cambridge, 1975). Also of interest is M. Shanks, *Planning and Politics* (London, 1977). On the role of science in government see P. Gummett, *Scientists in Whitehall* (Manchester, 1980).

Defence policy in J. Baylis (ed.), *British Defence Policy in a Changing World* (Croom Helm, 1979), and foreign policy in J. Barber, *Who Makes British Foreign Policy?* (Milton Keynes, The Open University Press, 1977). The two Conservative administrations since 1979 were both influenced by and stimulated new ideas on the welfare state and the provision of services. On this see N. Bosanquet, *Future for Old Age* (London, Temple Smith, 1978); *Industrial Relations in the National Health Service* (Oxford, University Press, 1982). More generally J. Bruce-Gardyne, *Mrs Thatcher's First Administration: The Prophets Confounded* (London, Macmillan, 1984), and P. Riddell, *The Thatcher Government* (Oxford, Martin Robertson, 1983). Also of relevance is M. Holmes, *The First Thatcher Government 1979–83* (Brighton, Wheatsheaf, 1985).

The Executive

The role of the British cabinet is covered in J. Mackintosh, *The British Cabinet* (3rd ed., London, Stevens, 1977), and in Patrick Gordon Walker's much shorter work, *The Cabinet* (rev. ed., London, Collins, 1972). Hans Daalder, *Cabinet Reform in Britain* (London, Stanford University Press, 1964), is a more specialized study and B. Headey, *British Cabinet Ministers* (London, Allen and Unwin, 1974), is helpful.

Personal insights are provided by R. H. S. Crossman, *Diaries of a Cabinet Minister* (3 vols, London, Hamish Hamilton, 1975–7), and by B. Castle, *Diaries* (2 vols, London, Weidenfeld and Nicolson, 1980, 1984). Harold Wilson, *The Labour Government: A Personal Record* (London, Michael Joseph/Weidenfeld and Nicolson, 1971), and *The Governance of Britain* (London, Michael Joseph, 1976) has interesting information on the problem of collective responsibility. D. N. Chester and F. Willson, *The Organization of British Central Government 1914–1964* (2nd ed., London, Allen and Unwin, 1968), should now be supplemented with C. Pollitt, *Manipulating the Machine* (London, Allen and Unwin, 1984).

N. Lawson and J. Bruce-Gardyne, *The Power-Game* (London, Macmillan, 1976), has revealing studies of the decision-making process viewed through several case studies. A. King (ed.), *The Prime Minister* (London, Macmillan, 1969), is still very relevant to discussions of the office, as is the two-volume *British Prime Ministers* edited by John Mackintosh (London, Weidenfeld and Nicolson, 1977–8).

The Civil Service

An excellent general introduction to the British Civil Service is G. K. Fry, *Statesmen in Disguise* (London, Macmillan, 1969). More polemical but essential is Lord Crowther Hunt and P. Kellner, *The Civil Servants: An Inquiry into Britain's Ruling Class* (London, Macdonald and Jane's, 1980).

The Treasury has always attracted a good deal of scholarly attention. Particularly useful are H. Roseveare, *The Treasury* (London, Allen Lane, 1969) and A. Wildavsky and H. Heclo, *The Private Government of Public Money* (London, Macmillan, 1974). Joel Barnett, *Inside the Treasury* (London, Deutsch, 1982) is also useful, as is L. Pliatzky, *Getting and Spending* (Oxford, Blackwell, 1982).

More specialized is R. A. Chapman, *Leadership in the British Civil Service: A Study of Sir Peter Waterfield and the Creation of the Civil Service Selection Board* (London, 1969), and R. Heaton and Sir Leslie Williams, *Civil Service Training* (London, 1974).

Lord Salter, *The Slave of the Lamp* (London, 1967), offers an insight into the Civil Service by someone who held both senior administrative and ministerial posts.

Parliament

The development of opinion on parliamentary reform can be traced by comparing the successive volumes published under the aegis of the Study of Parliament group – A. H. Hanson and B. Crick, *The Commons in Transition* (London, Fontana, 1970), S. Walkland and M. Ryle, *The Commons in The Seventies* (London, Fontana, 1977). B. Crick, *The Reform of Parliament* (London, Weidenfeld and Nicolson, 1964) is still of interest. For a detailed overview see P. Norton, *The Commons in Perspective* (Oxford,

Martin Robertson, 1981); Also S. Walkland (ed.), *The House of Commons in the Twentieth Century* (Oxford University Press, 1979). Also relevant to the whole reform theme is D. Judge, *The Politics of Parliamentary Reform* (London, Heinemann, 1982).

A detailed study of the legislative process is provided by J. A. G. Griffith, *Parliamentary Scrutiny of Government Bills* (London, Allen and Unwin, 1974). On financial procedure see D. Coombes (ed.), *The Power of the Purse* (London, Allen and Unwin, 1976), which has the merit of putting British practice in some comparative perspective. Ann Robinson provides a useful discussion of the work of the Expenditure Committee between 1970 and 1976 in *Parliament and Public Spending* (London, Heinemann, 1978).

D. Coombes, *The Member of Parliament and the Administration* (London, Allen and Unwin, 1966), though dated is still useful. On parliamentary questions the standard work is still D. N. Chester and N. Bowring, *Questions in Parliament* (Oxford University Press, 1962), though this should be supplemented with D. N. Chester, 'Questions in the House', in Walkland and Ryle, op. cit.

On the role of backbenchers see P. G. Richards' study *The Backbenchers* (London, Faber and Faber, 1972). Also R. Barker and M. Rush, *The Member of Parliament and His Information* (London, Allen and Unwin 1970), which is invaluable, as is M. Rush (ed.), *The House of Commons: Services and Facilities 1972–1982* (London, Policy Studies Institute, 1983).

R. Punnett, *Front Bench Opposition* (London, Heinemann, 1973), gives an excellent comprehensive coverage of opposition in Britain.

A. Morris (ed.), *The Growth of Parliamentary Scrutiny by Committee* (Oxford, Pergamon, 1970), contains some excellent individual essays, but this should now be seen as superseded by D. Englefield (ed.), *Commons Select Committees: Catalysts for Progress?* (London, 1984).

On the legislative process itself see J. A. G. Griffith, *Parliamentary Scrutiny of Government Bills* (London, 1974).

Philip Norton's work on dissension in the House of Commons has become an important part of the literature on Parliament. See P. Norton, *Dissension in the House of Commons 1945–1974* (London, 1975).

There is surprisingly little of quality written on the modern role of the House of Lords. J. P. Morgan, *The House of Lords and the Labour Government 1964–1970* (Oxford, Clarendon Press, 1975), does however shed light on the workings of the Lords at that time.

There are some useful compendia and bibliographies on Parliament. One is R. V. Goehlert and F. S. Martin, *The Parliament of Great Britain: A Bibliography* (Lexington: Lexington Books, 1983).

The Electoral System

The authoritative introduction to the history of the British electoral system is D. E. Butler, *The Electoral System in Britain Since 1918* (2nd ed. Oxford,

Clarendon Press, 1963). Other works of relevance to the development of the electoral system include C. O'Leary, *The Elimination of Corrupt and Illegal Practices in British Elections* (Oxford, 1967). David Butler has also produced (with Dennis Kavanagh) studies of the 1974, 1979 and 1983 general elections. A wealth of information about the new revised electoral system is to be found in R. Waller, *The Almanac of British Politics* (Beckenham, Croom Helm, 1983).

Although now somewhat dated, Peter Pulzer, *Political Representation and Elections in Britain* (3rd ed., London, Allen and Unwin, 1975), is useful as a guide to the way the electoral system was viewed in the 1950s and 1960s. It should however be supplemented by more recent critical works both on electoral behaviour and electoral reform. On electoral reform a starting point for the modern debate is S. E. Finer, *Adversary Politics and Electoral Reform* (London, Anthony Wigram, 1975), and the various works by Vernon Bogdanor. The impact of the electoral and party systems on the policy process is explored in M. Stewart, *The Jekyll and Hyde Years* (London, 1977).

On voting behaviour see B. Särlvik and I. Crewe, *Decade of Dealignment* (Cambridge University Press, 1983). Also I. McAllister and R. Rose, *The Nationwide Competition for Votes: The 1983 British Election* (Frances Pinter, 1984).

The European electoral systems are covered in G. Hand, J. Georgel and C. Sasse (eds), *European Electoral Systems* (London, Butterworths, 1979).

The Political Parties

There are a number of general works on British political parties and their role in the British political system. Robert McKenzie, *British Political Parties* (London, Heinemann, 1st ed. 1955, 2nd ed. 1963), though dated is a useful starting point for those anxious to trace the changes in the character of British parties. R. Rose, *The Problem of Party Government* (London, Macmillan, 1974), is helpful, as is the same author's *Do Parties Make a Difference?* (2nd ed., London, Macmillan, 1984).

On the history and politics of the individual parties see R. Blake, *The Conservative Party from Peel to Thatcher* (London, Fontana, 1985). Lord Butler (ed.), *The Conservatives* (London, Allen & Unwin, 1977) is also worthwhile, although it concentrates very much on 'high politics' rather than the history of the Party as such. A major history of the Conservative Party is being written but the volume most relevant to the contemporary Conservative Party has yet to appear; however J. Ramsden, *The Age of Balfour and Baldwin* (London, Longman, 1978), is excellent on the interwar period.

P. Norton and A. Aughey, *Conservatives and Conservatism* (London, Temple Smith, 1981), examines the subject from a number of views. Reference should also be made to Z. Layton-Henry (ed.), *Conservative Party Politics* (London, Macmillan, 1980).

On the Labour Party, Henry Pelling has produced two excellent studies,

A Short History of the Labour Party (6th ed. London, Macmillan, 1978), and *The Origins of the Labour Party* (2nd ed., Oxford University Press, 1965). On the ideology see F. Bealey (ed.), *The Social and Political Thought of the Labour Party* (London, Weidenfeld and Nicolson, 1970). On the role of trade unions a useful starting point is M. Harrison, *Trade Unions and the Labour Party since 1945* (London, Allen and Unwin, 1960), though this should now be supplemented by R. Taylor, *The Fifth Estate* (London, Routledge, 1978), and the useful collection edited by B. Pimlott and C. Cook, *Trade Unions in British Politics* (Longman, 1982). A helpful general collection is D. Kavanagh, *Labour Party Politics* (London, Allen and Unwin, 1982).

Detailed examination of the policy process in the aftermath of the 1970 election can be found in M. Hatfield *The House the Left Built* (London, Gollancz, 1978). The constitutional debate since then can be followed in M. Kogan and D. Kogan, *The Battle for the Labour Party* (London, Fontana, 1982).

On the Liberal Party, C. Cook, *A Short History of the Liberal Party* (London, Macmillan, 1976), is reliable. Different aspects of Liberal Party history can be gleaned from J. Vincent, *The Formation of the Liberal Party 1857–1868* (London, Hutchinson, 1966), T. Wilson, *The Downfall of the Liberal Party 1914–1935* (London, Collins/Fontana, 1968) and A. Cyr, *Liberal Party Politics in Britain* (London, Calder, 1977).

On the Alliance see H. Stephenson, *Claret and Chips: The Rise of the Social Democratic Party* (London, Michael Joseph, 1982).

On the National Front and other parties of the extreme right see M. Walker, *The National Front* (London, Fontana, 1977). More extensive is S. Taylor, *The National Front in English Politics* (London, Macmillan, 1982). Also of interest is N. Fielding, *The National Front* (London, Routledge and Kegan Paul, 1981).

The Communist Party is covered in H. Pelling, *The British Communist Party* (London, A. & C. Black, 1975) and in K. Newton, *The Sociology of British Communism* (London, Allen Lane, 1969).

There are as yet no full-scale histories of either the Scottish National Party or Plaid Cymru, but much material on these parties can be found in general works on Scottish and Welsh political life. Northern Irish parties are better served. The Ulster Unionists are covered in J. F. Harbinson, *The Ulster Unionist Party 1872–1973* (Belfast, Blackstaff, 1974), and Ian McAllister, *The Northern Ireland Social Democratic and Labour Party* (London, Macmillan, 1977) provides a useful, though dated, study of the province's major Roman Catholic party.

On voting behaviour and party choice there is now an enormous literature. D. E. Butler and Donald Stokes, *Political Change in Britain* (London, Macmillan, 1st ed., 1969, 2nd ed., 1974), has become a classic, although readers should be careful to compare the first and second editions. *Decade of Dealignment* and P. Dunleavy and C. Husbands, *British Democracy at The Crossroads* (London, Allen and Unwin, 1985) offer newer approaches.

On finance see M. Pinto-Duschinsky, *British Political Finance 1830–1980* (Washington, AEI, 1982).

Pressure Groups

A useful compendium is P. Shipley (ed.), *The Guardian Directory of Pressure Groups and Organizations* (London, Wilson House, 1976).
General works on pressure groups include S. E. Finer, *Anonymous Empire* (London, 1966). J. J. Richardson and A. G. Jordan, *Governing Under Pressure* (Oxford, Martin Robertson, 1979), is strong on the policy process. B. Frost (ed.), *The Tactics of Pressure* (London, 1975), and D. Marsh (ed.), *Pressure Politics: Pressure Groups in Modern Britain* (London, Junction Books, 1983), are both useful collections of essays. G. Alderman's short but sensible book *Pressure Groups in Great Britain* (London, 1984) is quite helpful, as is R. Kimber and J. J. Richardson, *Pressure Groups in Britain* (London, 1974). Reference should also be made to C. Crouch (ed.), *British Political Sociology Yearbook III: Participation in Politics* (Croom Helm, 1977).
On agriculture see G. K. Wilson, *Special Interests and Policy-Making: Agricultural Politics in Britain and America 1956–1970* (John Wiley, 1978).
On the poverty lobby reference should be made to F. Field, *Poverty and Politics* (London, Heinemann, 1982) and K. Hudson, *Help the Aged* (London, Bodley Head, 1982). K. Banting, *Poverty, Politics and Policy* (London, Macmillan, 1979), is more general.
On the economy and the debate about corporatism see K. Middlemas, *Politics in Industrial Society* (London, Deutsch, 1980); W. Grant and D. Marsh, *The C.B.I.*, (Hodder and Stoughton, 1977) offers the only full-length account of this important pressure group. See also M. T. S. Holmes, *Political Pressure and Economic Policy* (London, Butterworths, 1982), T. Smith, *The Politics of the Corporate Economy* (Oxford, Martin Robertson, 1979), R. Harrison, *Pluralism and Corporatism: The Political Evolution of Modern Democracies* (London, Allen and Unwin, 1980).
There is a large literature on trade unions. Especially helpful are R. Taylor, *The Fifth Estate* (London, Routledge, 1978), and R. Undy *et al.*, *Change in Trade Unions* (London, Hutchinson, 1981). The role of trade unionists in Parliament can be traced in W. D. Muller, *The Kept Men? The First Century of Trade Union Representation in the House of Commons 1874–1975* (Hassocks, Harvester Press, 1977).
On protest movements see R. Taylor and C. Pritchard, *The Politics of Protest: British Nuclear Disarmament Movement 1958–65 Twenty Years On* (Oxford, Pergamon, 1980). Also R. King and N. Nugent (eds), *Respectable Rebels: Middle Class Campaigns in Britain in the 1970's* (London, Hodder and Stoughton, 1979).
On the role of pressure groups in local politics see K. Newton, *Second City Politics* (Oxford University Press, 1976). On the important environmental lobby see P. Lowe and J. Goyder, *Environmental Groups in Politics* (London, Allen and Unwin, 1983).
Ethnic groups have so far not been extensively covered but one recent study of interest is G. Alderman, *The Jewish Community in British Politics* (Oxford University Press, 1983).

The Legal Order and Civil Liberties

The structure of the English legal system is described in R. M. Jackson, *The Machinery of Justice in England* (7th ed., Cambridge University Press, 1977). Also of use as a competent and straightforward introduction is R. J. Walker and M. G. Walker, *The English Legal System* (4th ed., London, Butterworths, 1976). B. Abel Smith and R. Stevens, *Lawyers and the Courts* (London, Heinemann, 1970), puts the law in social and historical perspective. Studies of the House of Lords can be found in L. Blom Cooper and G. Drewry, *Final Appeal* (Oxford University Press, 1972), and Alan Paterson, *The Law Lords* (London, Macmillan, 1982). Also of interest is R. Stevens, *Law and Politics: The House of Lords as a Judicial Body* (London, 1979).

A critical appraisal of the current organization of legal services can be found in M. Zander, *Lawyers and the Public Interest* (London, Weidenfeld and Nicolson, 1968). The same author's *The Lawmaking Process* (London, Weidenfeld and Nicolson, 1980), and *Cases and Materials on the English Legal System* (London, Weidenfeld and Nicolson, 1980), are also useful.

The machinery of law enforcement and the penal system is covered in R. M. Jackson, *Enforcing the Law* (London, Penguin, 1972). G. Marshall, *Police and Government* (London, Methuen, 1965) raises some interesting questions of police accountability which have been carried further by the same author in his various articles. A later general work on police accountability is T. Jefferson and R. Grimshaw, *Controlling the Constable: Police Accountability in England and Wales* (London, Muller/the Cobden Trust, 1984).

The impact of immigration can be found in J. Lambert, *Crime, Police and Race Relations* (Oxford University Press, 1970), and in a rather different vein in D. Humphrey, *Police Power and Black People* (London, Panther, 1972). Also of interest are M. E. Cain, *Society and the Policeman's Role* (London, Routledge and Kegan Paul, 1973), and T. Bunyan, *The History and Practice of the Political Police in Britain* (London, Friedmann, 1976).

Two works dealing with violence in Britain from different perspectives are R. Clutterbuck, *Britain in Agony* (London, Faber, 1978), and S. Hall *et al.*, *Policing the Crisis* (London, Macmillan, 1978).

Civil liberties are discussed in H. Street, *Freedom, the Individual and the Law* (Penguin, 1977), and Peter Wallington (ed.), *Civil Liberties 1984* (Oxford, Martin Robertson/The Cobden Trust, 1984).

The interconnection between legal and political processes is explored in G. Drewry, *Law, Justice and Politics* (London, Longman, 1975), and in T. C. Hartley and J. G. Griffith, *Government and Law* (London, Weidenfeld and Nicolson, 1975). J. G. Griffith, *The Politics of the Judiciary* (1st ed., Manchester University Press, 1977; 2nd ed., London, Fontana, 1981) is a controversial account of the politics of the bench.

Local Government

The excellent New Local Government Series of which Peter Richards is editor and Allen and Unwin the publisher has a number of important studies. There have also been published a number of studies of local government which employ new approaches to the subject, so that the whole field has begun in some ways to flourish again academically. Thus in addition to some of the more familiar treatments, reference should be made to some of the newer studies of urban politics. A good introduction is provided by P. Dunleavy, *Urban Political Analysis* (London, Macmillan, 1980). A theoretical perspective is also to be found in R. J. Haynes, *Organization Theory and Local Government* (London, Allen and Unwin, 1980). A fresh approach to the whole subject can be found in J. Dearlove, *The Reorganization of Local Government: Old Orthodoxies and a Political Perspective* (Cambridge, 1979).

General themes are raised in L. G. Bayley, *Local Government: Is It Manageable?* (Oxford, Pergamon, 1980). Also important is G. Jones and J. Stewart, *The Case for Local Government* (Allen and Unwin, 1983).

Bryan Keith Lucas and P. G. Richards, *A History of Local Government in the Twentieth Century* (London, Allen and Unwin 1978), and Noel Hepworth *The Finance of Local Government* (rev. 4th ed., London, Allen and Unwin, 1978), are good basic introductions to their themes. A. Alexander, *Local Government in Britain since Reorganization* (London, Allen and Unwin, 1982) offers a succinct summary.

K. P. Poole, *The Local Government Service* (London, Allen and Unwin, 1978) is a useful study.

On central-local relations J. A. G. Griffith, *Central Departments and Local Authorities* (London, Allen and Unwin, 1966), though somewhat dated is still worth reading. More recent interpretations can however be found in R. A. W. Rhodes, *Control and Power in Central-Local Relations* (London, Gower, 1981) and G. W. Jones (ed.), *New Approaches to the Study of Central-Local Government Relationships* (London, Gower, 1980).

G. Rhodes, *Inspectorates in British Local Government: Law Enforcement and Standards of Efficiency* (London, Royal Institute of Public Administration, 1981) is also highly relevant to the theme of central control.

Studies of particular themes include D. E. Regan, *Local Government and Education* (London, Allen and Unwin, 1978).

There are also a number of case studies of individual local authorities. One worth reading because it deals with Newcastle-on-Tyne is D. C. Green, *Power and Party in an English City: An Account of Single Party Rule* (London, Allen and Unwin, 1981). There are also a number of semi-popular books on local government. See for example T. Byrne, *Local Government in Britain: Everyone's Guide to How It All Works* (Harmondsworth, Penguin, 1981).

There are also some more polemical works such as A. Seldon, *Town Hall Power or Whitehall Pawn?* (London, IEA, 1981).

The Diversity of the United Kingdom

A short introduction to the question of devolution is A. H. Birch, *Political Integration and Disintegration in the British Isles* (London, Allen and Unwin, 1977). Tam Dalyell, *Devolution – The End of Britain?* (London, Cape, 1977), conveys the flavour of those who opposed the idea. A succinct general discussion is V. Bogdanor, *Devolution* (Oxford University Press, 1979).

Ireland

The historical background to the present situation in Northern Ireland can be gleaned from F. S. L. Lyons' magisterial *Ireland Since the Famine* (2nd ed., London, Collins, Fontana, 1973) and the same author's *Culture and Anarchy in Ireland 1840–1939* (Oxford, Clarendon Press, 1979).

Richard Rose, *Governing Without Consensus* (London, Faber and Faber, 1971), remains useful. P. O'Malley, *The Uncivil Wars* (Belfast, Blackstaff, 1983) examines the whole Irish issue from a number of different perspectives.

Paul Arthur, *The Government and Politics of Northern Ireland* (2nd ed., London, Longman, 1984) is a short but useful account of Northern Irish politics. P. Bew, P. Gibbon and H. Patterson, *The State in Northern Ireland* (Manchester University Press, 1980) offers a more theoretical perspective.

H. Calvert, *Constitutional Law in Northern Ireland* (London, Stevens, 1968) provides a useful account of the constitution of Northern Ireland prior to the suspension of Stormont.

Relations between Church and state are covered in J. Whyte, *Church and State in Modern Ireland 1923–1970* (London, Macmillan, 1970).

Scotland

J. Kellas, *The Scottish Political System* (2nd ed., Cambridge University Press, 1975) is a stimulating introduction to Scottish government and politics. Also important is M. Keating and A. Midwinter, *The Government of Scotland* (Edinburgh, Mainstream Publishing, 1983).

D. Walker, *The Scottish Legal System* (4th ed., Edinburgh, Green, 1976), is useful.

A useful source of information about Scottish politics is to be found in the *Yearbook of Scottish Government* (Paul Harris Publishing, Edinburgh).

J. M. Bochel *et al.*, *The Referendum Experience in Scotland 1979* (Aberdeen University Press, 1981) provides a detailed summary of attitudes at that time.

Wales

There are now a number of excellent historical studies of the Welsh polity. Especially good are K. Morgan, *Rebirth of a Nation: Wales 1880–1980* (Cardiff, University of Wales Press, 1981), and *Wales in British Politics* (rev. ed., Cardiff, University of Wales Press, 1970). D. Williams, *A History of Modern Wales* (2nd ed., London, John Murray, 1977) is also useful.

A. Butt Phillip, *The Welsh Question* (Cardiff, University of Wales Press,

1975), provides a comprehensive examination of Welsh nationalism.

The Control of Government and the Redress of Grievances

On the ombudsman or Parliamentary Commissioner for Administration the most comprehensive work is R. Gregory and P. G. Hutchesson, *The Parliamentary Ombudsman: A Study in the Control of Administration* (London, Allen and Unwin, 1975). This should be supplemented with F. Stacey, *Ombudsmen Compared* (Oxford University Press, 1978). Carol Harlow and Richard Rawlings, *Law and Administration* (London, Weidenfeld and Nicolson, 1984) brings a number of the themes covered in this chapter up to date. Geoffrey Marshall, *Constitutional Conventions: The Rules and Forms of Political Accountability* (Oxford University Press, 1984) is essential reading. B. Schwartz and H. W. R. Wade, *Legal Control of Government* (Oxford University Press, 1972) puts the subject in Anglo-American perspective. The most detailed work on judicial review is S. A. de Smith, *Judicial Review of Administrative Action* (3rd ed., London, Stevens, 1973). The latest edition of the author's discussion of constitutional and administrative law is also highly relevant: see H. Street and R. Brazier, *De Smith's Constitutional and Administrative Law* (4th ed., Harmondsworth, 1981).

Tribunals and inquiries are covered in two useful publications by the Royal Institute of Public Administration: R. E. Wraith and P. G. Hutchesson, *Administrative Tribunals* (London, Allen and Unwin, 1973), and R. E. Wraith and G. B. Lamb, *Public Inquiries as Instruments of Government* (London, Allen and Unwin, 1971). Also of interest is J. Farmer, *Tribunals and Government* (London, Weidenfeld and Nicolson, 1974).

A general survey of the various methods of redress is to be found in K. C. Wheare, *Maladministration and Its Remedies* (London, Stevens, 1973).

The Limits of Independence

There is still relatively little on the management of Britain's foreign policy. But see William Wallace, *The Foreign Policy Process in Britain* (London, 1975).

Index